Women and the Criminal Justice System
A Canadian Perspective

Jane Barker, Nipissing University

2009
EMOND MONTGOMERY PUBLICATIONS LIMITED
TORONTO, CANADA

Emond Montgomery Publications Limited
60 Shaftesbury Avenue
Toronto ON M4T 1A3
http://www.emp.ca/highered

Printed in Canada.
Reprinted June 2014.

We acknowledge the financial support of the Government of Canada through the Canada Book Fund for our publishing activities.

Acquisitions and developmental editor: Mike Thompson
Marketing manager: Christine Davidson
Supervising editor: Jim Lyons
Copy editor: Mariko Obokata
Proofreader: David Handelsman
Production editor: Cindy Fujimoto
Text designer and typesetter: Tara Wells
Indexer: Paula Pike
Cover designers: Stephen Cribbin & Simon Evers

Library and Archives Canada Cataloguing in Publication

Women and the criminal justice system : a Canadian perspective / [edited by] Jane Barker.

Includes index.
ISBN 978-1-55239-240-9

1. Female offenders—Canada.   2. Women prisoners—Canada.
3. Women criminal justice personnel—Canada.
4. Women—Crimes against—Canada.   I. Barker, Jane, 1965-

HV9960.C2W64 2008   364.082'0971   C2008-901530-4

Brief Contents

Contents

PART I   Overview of Women and the Canadian Criminal Justice System

Chapter 1   *The Canadian Criminal Justice System and Women Offenders*

Jane Barker

Chapter 2   *Female Crime: Theoretical Perspectives*
Walter DeKeseredy

Part II   Canadian Women Offenders
Chapter 3   *A "Typical" Female Offender*
Jane Barker

Chapter 4   *Background Experiences of Women Offenders*

Jane Barker

Chapter 5   *Coping Strategies of Women Offenders*

Jane Barker

Chapter 6   *Correctional Assessment and Treatment:*
Toward Community Reintegration

Jill L. Atkinson and Jean Folsom

Part III   Topics of Special Interest

Chapter 7   *Violence and Women Offenders*

Franca Cortoni

Chapter 8   *Women Offenders and Mental Health*

Jean Folsom

Chapter 9   *Female Youth in Conflict with the Law*
Shahid Alvi

Chapter 10   *Aboriginal Women and the Criminal Justice System*
Brenda M. Restoule

Chapter 11   *Visible Minority Women as Offenders and Victims*
Shahid Alvi

Chapter 12   Girls and Women as Victims of Crime

Walter DeKeseredy

Part IV   Women Working in the Canadian Criminal Justice System

Chapter 13   *Women's Work? Feminization and the Future of Police Work in Canada*

Kellie Woodbury and Gregory P. Brown

Chapter 14   *Women Working in the Courts*

Shelley Lechlitner and Jane Barker

Chapter 15   *Women Working in Corrections*
Jane Barker

Preface

The impetus for this volume was selfish. I was teaching a course on women and the criminal justice system in Canada, and I needed a textbook. I tried using a few American textbooks, but I constantly had to explain the differences between what the US books described and the experiences of women in the Canadian system. Although some excellent books recently published in Canada delved into many of the issues facing women who have come into conflict with the law, none fit what I was looking for. To solve the problem, I embarked on this project.

The main objective of this textbook is to provide the reader with a thorough picture of women and the criminal justice system in Canada. This book is divided into four sections. The first portion is devoted to an overview of women and the criminal justice system. Using a historical perspective, we explore the Canadian criminal justice system as experienced by women who have come into conflict with the law. Included in this section is an examination of various theories that explain why some women become entangled in the legal system. The second section of this volume looks specifically at Canadian women offenders—who they are and how the correctional system attempts to address their needs. Readers are first introduced to the offenders, their background experiences, and the relevance of their past experiences to their conflicts with the law. Next, readers are led through an in-depth examination of the current state of women's corrections in Canada. The third section of this book explores some specific areas in greater depth: the experiences of Aboriginal and visible minority women offenders, women offenders and mental health issues, female youth crime, and women who engage in violent behaviour. These chapters provide the reader with the most up-to-date knowledge of the field from a Canadian perspective. The fourth and final section of this book provides a brief description of women's roles in the various agencies (police, courts, and corrections) of the criminal justice system in Canada. We hope that through reading each successive chapter, readers will develop a solid base of knowledge regarding women and the Canadian criminal justice system.

Acknowledgments

This book could not have been completed without the contributions of many talented academics, applied researchers, and practitioners in the field of criminal justice. Walter DeKeseredy and Shahid Alvi, both from the University of Ontario Institute of Technology, each contributed their expertise to two chapters. Walter DeKeseredy, a respected researcher and prolific author of many books, including a textbook on women in conflict with the law, provided a comprehensive theory chapter and a chapter on women and girls as victims of crime. Thanks also to Shahid Alvi, a well-known and respected researcher and author, whose expertise was greatly appreciated in his two contributed chapters: on female youth crime and on the experiences of visible minority women as offenders and victims. Jill Atkinson, from Queen's University, and Jean Folsom, who has decades of experience working in the federal correctional system, provided a thorough and comprehensive examination of the current state of correctional assessment, treatment, and reintegration needs of criminalized women. Jean Folsom also contributed her experience and knowledge to the chapter on the mental health needs of women offenders. Franca Cortoni, from the University of Montreal, an expert in the area of sex offenders, provided an up-to-date and empirically rich chapter on violent women. The unique expertise of psychologist Brenda Restoule (the first Aboriginal counsellor in the psychology department at the Prison for Women) was very much appreciated in her chapter on Aboriginal offenders. In addition, the contributions of Constable Kellie Woodbury added a real-world element to the chapter on policing. And lastly, my esteemed colleagues in the Criminal Justice department at Nipissing University, Greg Brown and Shelley Lechlitner, completed the picture of women in Canada's criminal justice system in their chapters describing the challenges and issues facing women who work in policing and the law. In addition to the contributing authors, I would like to thank Randall Tilander for his assistance with the completion of the glossary. This book would not have been complete without the valued contributions of all of these outstanding individuals.

In addition to those who wrote individual chapters in this book, Mike Thompson at Emond Montgomery deserves considerable recognition. It was Mike who first took an interest in my book proposal, offered his expertise, and continued to be a source of support throughout this project. He ensured that the whole process ran smoothly from start to finish. Mike, I cannot thank you enough for all of your assistance and guidance on this project. To Mariko Obokata, the copy editor for this textbook, words cannot express my appreciation. Mariko was absolutely amazing in her ability to transform an awkward sentence into a thing of beauty. I know my gratitude to Mariko is also shared by the other chapter authors. Thanks also to Jim Lyons at WordsWorth Communications, whose experience in the industry was of significant benefit, especially in the final stages of the book. To all of those at Emond Montgomery and WordsWorth Communications who had a hand in making this book a reality, I offer my heartfelt thanks.

This kind of book is like a pot-luck dinner—you gather the experience and expertise of a group of people who work in related areas, and you look forward to tasting their signature dishes, while hoping they don't all bring a Caesar salad. Please forgive any repetition that might exist; many of us note how women offenders have been overlooked by the criminal justice system but only because we each want to emphasize this point. The following chapters provide much food for thought, and we hope all readers will benefit from reading this volume.

The author and the publisher wish to thank the following people who provided feedback and suggestions during the development of this project: Jacqueline Faubert, Simon Fraser University; Kelly Hannah-Moffat, University of Toronto; Alice Propper, York University; and Anne-Marie Singh, Ryerson University.

About the Authors

Jane Barker (lead author and editor) is Assistant Professor of Criminal Justice at Nipissing University.

Shahid Alvi is Professor in the Faculty of Criminology, Justice and Policy Studies at the University of Ontario Institute of Technology.

Jill Atkinson is Associate Professor and Chair of Undergraduate Studies in the Department of Psychology at Queen's University.

Greg Brown is Associate Professor of Criminal Justice and Sociology at Nipissing University.

Franca Cortoni is Assistant Professor in the School of Criminology at the University of Montreal.

Walter S. DeKeseredy is Professor in the Faculty of Criminology, Justice and Policy Studies at the University of Ontario Institute of Technology.

Jean Folsom is Director of Psychology and Rehabilitation Services at the Regional Treatment Centre, Correctional Service of Canada, in Kingston.

Shelley Lechlitner is Assistant Professor of Criminal Justice at Nipissing University.

Brenda Restoule is a registered psychologist with the Northeast Mental Health Centre in Sudbury, specializing in First Nation mental health issues.

Kellie Woodbury is a police officer with the Ontario Provincial Police.

PART I

Overview of Women and the Canadian Criminal Justice System

CHAPTER 1

The Canadian Criminal Justice System and Women Offenders

Jane Barker

Introduction: The Canadian Criminal Justice System

The criminal justice system in Canada comprises three interconnected agencies: the police, the courts, and the correctional system. A woman who comes into conflict with the law will likely interact with many individuals from each of these agencies, not all of whom will treat her with respect and dignity. Unfortunately, in the criminal justice system, as in our society as a whole, girls and women are sometimes the targets of abuses of power.

The following brief description of the criminal justice system in Canada provides a very basic understanding of the structure and organization of the various agencies. A fairly cursory overview of the types of police agencies is followed by a brief introduction to the court system. A detailed account of the history of the correctional system's treatment of women illustrates how the needs of female offenders have historically taken a back seat to the needs of male offenders.

Policing

In Canada, policing occurs at three levels of government: federal, provincial or territorial, and municipal. In addition, numerous First Nations communities have their own police services.

In 2006, expenditures related to all levels of policing in Canada totalled $9.3 billion (Reitano, 2006). After adjusting for inflation, this figure represents a 4 percent increase over the preceding year. According to a Statistics Canada report, 2006 was the ninth consecutive year that policing costs increased (in terms of constant dollars) (Reitano, 2006). In total, more than 62,400 police officers were employed across Canada in 2006, an increase of 1,400 officers over 2005. Prince Edward Island and Newfoundland and Labrador had the lowest per capita costs for policing, whereas Quebec and Ontario had the highest per capita costs.

Federal Policing

Canada's federal police service is the Royal Canadian Mounted Police (RCMP). According to the RCMP website, this service is unique worldwide because the RCMP "is a national, federal, provincial and municipal policing body" (Royal Canadian Mounted Police [RCMP], n.d., "About the RCMP," ¶ 2). The RCMP is responsible not only for enforcing federal statutes but also for providing a variety of resources to police, including forensic analysis, identification services, the Canadian Police College, and the Canadian Police Information Centre (CPIC). The *Royal Canadian Mounted Police Act* governs the organization of the RCMP. As such, the RCMP is headed by a commissioner who reports to the Minister of Public Safety Canada. The RCMP is organized into four regions (Atlantic, Central, Northwestern, and Pacific), each operating under the direction of a deputy commissioner. Other deputy commissioners are assigned to head up operations and integration, national police services, and corporate management and comptrollership (RCMP, n.d., "Organization of the RCMP"). In addition to the headquarters located in Ottawa, the RCMP is further organized into 15 divisions, most of which correspond to provincial or territorial boundaries. As of January 1, 2007, a total of 25,417 people worked in the RCMP. More than 5,000 people were employed as civil servants, and more than 3,000 as civilian members. The bulk of the employees were constables (10,954 people) (RCMP, n.d., "Organization of the RCMP").

Provincial and Territorial Policing

Canada has three provincial police services: the Ontario Provincial Police (OPP), Sûreté du Québec, and the Royal Newfoundland Constabulary. Provincial police services are concerned with the enforcement of the *Criminal Code* and provincial statutes in areas where no municipal force exists. It is not unusual to find an overlapping of police boundaries. For example, in the city of North Bay, Ontario, a municipal police force (North Bay Police Services) is responsible for policing in the city of North Bay, while the OPP patrols the highways that pass through the city. In areas of Canada without a provincial or territorial police service, the RCMP is contracted to provide this service.

Municipal Policing

Officers who are employed to conduct policing at the municipal level enforce the *Criminal Code*, various provincial statutes, and municipal bylaws. Some municipalities operate their own policing force; others combine with a neighbouring municipality to provide police services to both areas or contract the work to either a provincial police service or the RCMP (Reitano, 2006).

Areas of Canada that do not have municipal policing include Nunavut, Yukon, the Northwest Territories, and Newfoundland and Labrador. The provincial police force in Newfoundland and Labrador provides municipal police services to four municipalities (St. John's, Corner Brook, Labrador City, and Churchill Falls), while the rest of the province contracts the RCMP to provide municipal and rural policing services (Reitano, 2006).

First Nations Policing

In June 1991, the First Nations Policing Policy (FNPP) was introduced by the federal government (Public Safety Canada [PSC], n.d.). The purpose of the FNPP is to "provide First Nations across Canada with access to police services that are professional, effective, culturally appropriate and accountable to the communities they serve" (PSC, n.d., ¶ 1). Under the direction of Canada's lead department for public safety, Public Safety Canada, the First Nations work with provincial, territorial, and federal governments to establish tripartite policing agreements that meet the needs of the communities they serve.

The Courts

The system of Canadian courts has been described as complex (Canada, Department of Justice, n.d.). This complexity stems from the four levels of court and various types of courts that exist in Canada. Very briefly, provincial and territorial courts deal with the majority of cases. These are the "lowest" courts in the system. Next up the ladder are the provincial and territorial superior courts, where appeals from the provincial and territorial courts are heard, as are cases involving the most serious crimes. At the same level as the provincial and territorial superior courts is the Federal Court. This court has jurisdiction over matters in the federal domain. At the third level are the provincial and territorial courts of appeal and the Federal Court of Appeal. And lastly, the highest court in Canada is the Supreme Court of Canada (Canada, Department of Justice, n.d.).

Provincial and Territorial Courts

Apart from Nunavut, every province and territory has a provincial or territorial court. Although their names may differ, the role and function of these courts are the same: they hear cases that involve provincial, territorial, or federal laws, the majority of criminal cases that come before the courts. These courts deal with criminal offences, crimes committed by young offenders, matters of family law (but not divorce), regulatory offences, traffic violations, and claims involving money. Also, all preliminary inquiries are held in provincial or territorial courts to determine whether a serious criminal case has sufficient evidence to warrant a full trial. Specialty courts also exist at this level. For example, some courts are mandated to hear specific types of cases, such as Toronto's Drug Treatment Court (DTC), which was established in 1998 to hear cases involving non-violent offenders who have come into conflict with the law as a result of their drug addiction (Canada, Department of Justice, n.d.). For non-violent offenders who qualify, their drug addiction can be addressed through the option of treatment combined with judicial supervision. Other specialty courts include youth courts and domestic violence courts (Canada, Department of Justice, n.d.).

Provincial and Territorial Superior Courts

All provinces and territories have their own superior court, and although their names may differ, their role is generally the same (except for Nunavut, where the Nunavut Court of Justice is concerned with both superior court and territorial court matters). These superior courts have "inherent jurisdiction" at the superior court level, which means they can hear any cases in any area unless the case is specifically limited to a different level of court (Canada, Department of Justice, n.d.). These courts try the most serious civil and criminal cases, including those that involve large sums of money and cases of divorce. Provincial and territorial superior courts can have special divisions, such as the family division. The provincial and territorial superior courts are also the court of first appeal (Canada, Department of Justice, n.d.).

Courts of Appeal

Appeals from decisions rendered at the provincial, territorial, or superior courts are heard at the court of appeal, where a number of judges (usually three) hear the cases as a panel. The court of appeal also addresses constitutional questions raised in relation to individuals, government agencies, or the government (Canada, Department of Justice, n.d.).

Federal Courts

The Federal Court of Appeal and the Federal Court are basically superior courts that have civil jurisdiction (Canada, Department of Justice, n.d.). However, the jurisdiction of these courts is limited because the courts (created by an act of Parliament) are permitted to deal only with matters specified in federal statutes. This authority differs from the provincial and territorial superior courts where the court has jurisdiction in all areas except where excluded by statute. Specialized federal courts have been established by the federal government to assist the courts in operating in an efficient and effective manner. For example, the Tax Court of Canada deals with matters pertaining to federal tax and revenue legislation. If a taxpayer exhausts all options under the *Income Tax Act*, then any dispute between the taxpayer (that is, an individual or a company) and the federal government will be dealt with at the Tax Court of Canada (Canada, Department of Justice, n.d.).

The Supreme Court of Canada

The final court of appeal is the Supreme Court of Canada, which has authority over all private and public law in Canada. This court has jurisdiction over matters in all areas of the law, including criminal and civil law, constitutional law, and administrative law. The Supreme Court of Canada comprises a chief justice and eight judges. The judges, three of whom must be from Quebec (as specified in the *Supreme Court Act*), are appointed by the federal government. In addition to the Quebec judges, traditionally one judge is appointed from the Maritimes, two from the West, and three from Ontario (Canada, Department of Justice, n.d.). The Supreme Court of Canada hears "as of right" appeals when a provincial or territorial appeal court has overturned an acquittal from a trial court, or when dissent about a question of law occurs at a provincial or territorial court of appeal. In addition, subcommittees of the Supreme Court can refer to the highest court in Canada cases involving legal issues that hold a particular relevance and cases of public importance (Goff, 2008).

The Correctional System

The correctional system in Canada is divided into one federal service, the Correctional Service of Canada (CSC), and 12 provincial or territorial services. In Ontario, correctional services are subsumed under the Ministry of Community Safety and Correctional Services.

Pre-Confederation Corrections

In 1849, member of provincial Parliament (MPP) George Brown submitted the *First Report of the Commissioners Appointed to Inquire into and Report upon the Conduct, Economy, Discipline, and Management of the Provincial Penitentiary*, later known as the Brown commission report. This report was primarily a scathing condemnation of the warden of Kingston Penitentiary, Henry Smith, and of the abusive practices that were all too common at the penitentiary. The Brown commission report (Canada, Commission Appointed to Inquire, 1849) details the horrific living conditions endured by both male and female inmates. The prison food was abominable, the cells were reported to be overrun with bugs, and the inmates suffered from brutalities inflicted by staff. The women's area, located in the basement, was described in the following manner:

> The cells of the female Convicts are built of pine; have been many years in use, and are small apartments, with little ventilation. There seems no doubt that the cells have been overrun with vermin, and that the women suffered frightfully from them for years. (Canada, Commission Appointed to Inquire, 1849, p. 136)

The Brown commission report included descriptions of all manner of punishments inflicted upon the women at the Kingston Penitentiary. A detailed account of what happened to inmate Charlotte Reveille serves as a disturbing reminder of the atrocities that can occur in a civilized society. The length of her sentence is not entirely clear, but it was noted that although her sentence expired on February 14, 1849, she was kept incarcerated for longer because the warden and inspectors did not want to discharge her during "this inclement season." Charlotte Reveille was imprisoned longer than her sentence because of the weather!

According to the warden's punishment ledger, during Reveille's stay at the Kingston Penitentiary, between July 11, 1846 and October 7, 1847, she was punished on no fewer than 50 occasions for a range of behaviours, including but not limited to using bad language, refusing to walk, refusing to wear shoes, tearing blankets, "great violence," abuse, and cursing the matron. Her punishments, as listed in the warden's ledger, included being confined to her cell for 48 hours, being placed in a dark cell for 24 hours, being placed in a box on bread and water, and being given six lashes with rawhide. Reportedly not included in the ledger was the order by inspectors on April 5, 1847 for "Charlotte Reveille to be gagged, whenever it might be necessary to reduce her to silence" (Canada, Commission Appointed to Inquire, 1849, p. 206). Charlotte Reveille's case was thoroughly investigated by the Brown commission, which concluded that although Reveille likely arrived at the penitentiary in poor health and with a "predisposition to insanity," her condition was very likely worsened by the extreme punishments that she received (Canada, Commission Appointed to Inquire, 1849, p. 208). The Brown commission believed that the flogging of women was not an isolated incident at the penitentiary: the flogging of female inmates as young as 12 years of age had also been reported. The Brown commission report viewed punishing women in this manner as "utterly indefensible" (p. 190).

The Brown commission found Warden Smith guilty of all charges levelled against him, including cruelty, financial impropriety, neglect of duty, falsifying records, and general mismanagement of the institution. As a result, the commission recommended Smith's immediate and permanent removal from the position of warden at the Kingston Penitentiary. With respect to the Prison for Females, the Brown commission reported that the construction of the cells was problematic: they were made of wood, and thus bred vermin, and the ventilation was very poor. Another recommendation was specific to the future needs of the women to be incarcerated at the penitentiary. The Brown commission noted that "a suitable building must, however, be erected before any reform can be attempted with success" (Canada, Commission Appointed to Inquire, p. 296).

Of interest, after the Brown commission report was presented, charges against George Brown were made by John A. Macdonald, then attorney general for Upper Canada. Macdonald alleged that Brown and his commission had falsely recorded witness testimony, altered witness testimony, convinced inmates to commit perjury, and implied that pardons would be forthcoming in order to gain false evidence from murderers (O'Brien, 1856). The committee decided that "the testimony so reported by the said Commissioners is not the true testimony given before them. … [I]t would appear that … there was a falsification of the original testimony" (O'Brien, 1856, p. 291). Of particular interest is the committee's statement that it expressed no opinion regarding the blameworthiness of George Brown with respect to the findings of their investigation. Nevertheless, the results of the Brown commission report are critical in the history of women's incarceration in Canada.

Provincial Corrections

An examination of the history of women's prisons in Canada suggests that public recognition of the plight of women prisoners has waxed and waned over the years. A pattern of collective ignorance about the state of women's incarceration has often been followed by a surge of interest expressed as outrage over the conditions of women's imprisonment. Despite considerable improvements over the last century to the physical conditions of women's prisons, criticisms are still being levelled against the provincial and federal governments responsible for the care of incarcerated women. To fully appreciate the current state of women's corrections in Canada, the history of its development is needed.

Prior to the opening of Toronto's Andrew Mercer Ontario Reformatory for Females in 1880, women who were sentenced to incarceration in Ontario were housed in local jails alongside male prisoners (Strange, 1985). Their accommodations in these facilities were abusive at their worst and mediocre at their best. In small facilities, women were sometimes locked up with men. In larger jails, separate cells were sometimes reserved for women; however, these cells were reported to be overcrowded (Strange, 1985). In a review of women's prisons from 1874 to 1901, Strange noted that an increase of approximately 6 percent over the previous year in the number of females sent to jail in 1878 was seen as evidence by then Ontario Prison Inspector J.W. Langmuir that a separate women's prison was needed.

The Mercer reformatory was designed and built at a time when Canadian society was willing to entertain two ideological viewpoints: (1) that prisons should focus on reformation not punishment; and (2) that men and women were so distinct in nature that their correctional experiences should also reflect this "differentness" (Strange, 1985). Langmuir, in his lobbying of Ontario legislators, looked to the United States for examples of how a separate women's reformatory could be instituted in the social climate of the day. Central to this proposal was the assertion that an all-female staff at such a facility could provide the "maternal reform" that would enable those incarcerated to become respectable women. In both the United States and Canada, some members of the moralistic middle class believed that "fallen" women could be reformed by the maternal qualities of these middle-class moral guardians (Strange, 1985). Langmuir's vision was never fully realized, as the history of the Mercer reformatory can attest (Strange, 1985). The ideological axiom of reform over punishment received only weak support from Ontarians, and the obstacles to the application of such a "maternal reform" in a prison setting were considered insurmountable (Strange, 1985).

Strange (1985) points out that around the time the Mercer facility was being planned, a number of economic benefits were associated with a separate reformatory for women. Among these benefits was an expectation that a women's facility would be far less expensive to operate than a men's jail because women were seen as being less dangerous and the associated security costs would therefore be lower. In addition, the women's reformatory was expected to contribute in kind to the government coffers through the inmates' work activities (laundry and sewing, for example). Another cost saving associated with a women's reformatory would come in the form of staff wages. An all-female staff could be paid less than a staff of men, which was customary at the time (Strange, 1985).

It should be noted that ultimately the establishment of the Andrew Mercer Ontario Reformatory for Females was not based on any type of intense public pressure for reform but instead resulted from some effective lobbying by Langmuir. He was able to convince the provincial government to earmark $90,000 from the estate of Andrew Mercer to build the reformatory (Strange, 1985). Some speculate that the failure of the prison to attain the idealistic rehabilitative goals set by its founder was the result of the sometimes blasé attitude of the legislators of the day, the public, and indeed the vast majority of those working in the criminal justice field toward the prison itself and the ideals upon which the prison was founded. Given this attitude, coupled with the pragmatic difficulties inherent in applying a maternal reformative approach to a prison atmosphere, it is not surprising that the Mercer reformatory failed to live up to Langmuir's expectations (Strange, 1985).

Today, provincial and territorial facilities across Canada house female offenders. For the most part, offenders in these institutions serve sentences of two years less a day, although some federally sentenced women, who serve longer sentences, are incarcerated in provincial facilities. Since 1973, **exchange of service agreements** (ESAs) have been in place between federal corrections and some provincial corrections to enable federally sentenced women to serve their time closer to home (Correctional Service of Canada [CSC], 1990). For example, in Quebec, prior to the building of a regional federal facility in Joliette, the Tanguay Agreement allowed federally sentenced Francophone women to remain in Quebec. The 1982 Tanguay Agreement marked the first time the Correctional Service of Canada purchased guaranteed accommodation from a province (at the approximate cost of a $1 million capital contribution for five years with an option to purchase an additional five years) (CSC, 1990). ESAs have also been in place between the CSC and various psychiatric institutions across

Canada to meet the needs of offenders with specific mental health issues. For example, the Institut Philippe-Pinel provides federal offenders with psychiatric care if the offender is referred by a federal institution (CSC, 1990).

Federal Corrections: The Early Years

Historically, the federal correctional system has been at a loss for how to deal with female offenders. With the passing of the *British North America Act* (the *BNA Act*) in 1867 and the creation of a federal dominion, the "establishment, maintenance, and management of penitentiaries" came under federal jurisdiction as outlined in section 91, item 28 (*Constitution Act, 1867*, 1867). Kingston Penitentiary and a number of existing penitentiaries in the Maritimes came under this new federal jurisdiction (*Constitution Act, 1867*, 1867; Hayman, 2006).

As is the case today, at the time of Confederation, Canada incarcerated significantly fewer female inmates than male inmates. The *First Annual Report of the Directors of Penitentiaries for the Year 1868* indicated 67 women incarcerated as of December 31, 1867: 3 women were incarcerated in the Halifax Penitentiary, 1 in Saint John, and 63 in Kingston Penitentiary (Canada, Directors of the Penitentiaries, 1870). Although 29 women were being held at the Rockwood Asylum on January 1, 1868, none appears to have been a "convict lunatic." According to the warden's report for Kingston Penitentiary, only 20 male "convict lunatics" housed at Rockwood were on the penitentiary's register (Canada, Directors of the Penitentiaries, 1870). Interestingly, at that time, proportionately more women were incarcerated in the federal penitentiaries than today. At the end of 1867, women accounted for approximately 6.75 percent of federal incarcerates (that is 67 women versus 925 men). In contrast, as of April 9, 2006, a total of 408 women and more than 12,000 men were federally incarcerated. Based on these data, women made up approximately 3.3 percent of all federally incarcerated persons in Canada on April 9, 2006 (Canada, Public Safety and Emergency Preparedness, 2006). In terms of admissions from the courts to federal jurisdiction, however, women represented about 5.8 percent of the total of all new federal admissions in 2005–6.

In the *First Annual Report of the Directors of Penitentiaries for the Year 1868*, the directors of the three federal penitentiaries in Kingston, Saint John, and Halifax and the Rockwood Lunatic Asylum in Kingston made brief mention of the women under their control (Canada, Directors of the Penitentiaries, 1870). The medical superintendent of the Rockwood Asylum, Dr. John R. Dickson, afforded more detail in his report to the analysis of expenditures for the year 1868 than to the state of its inhabitants (Canada, Directors of the Penitentiaries, 1870). According to his report, a total of 65 women were housed in the asylum as of December 31, 1868. Over the course of that year, 29 women were in the asylum at the beginning of 1868, 39 women were admitted, 1 was discharged, and 2 died. Of those women who were admitted to the Rockwood Asylum in 1868, the majority (71 percent) were diagnosed as suffering from **mania** (acute or chronic), while the remainder were classified as having either **melancholia** (12 percent) or epilepsy (17 percent).

It is worth noting that although the majority of the inhabitants of Rockwood were not considered "criminal lunatics" (that is, convicts with mental aberrations that made them too difficult to manage in the penitentiary), the "patients" of Rockwood were considered in the same report as the inmates from the penitentiary system. This perspective is a stark reminder of the negative way in which mental illness was viewed in the latter half of the 19th century.

Similarly scarce reporting of the condition or state of women inmates was reported by the directors of the Halifax and Saint John penitentiaries. The matron at the Halifax Penitentiary, Mary McGregor, noted that she was "happy to report that everything, in connection with the female department of this institution, is going on quietly and satisfactorily" (Canada, Directors of the Penitentiaries, 1870, p. 47). McGregor also expressed her exuberance concerning the behaviour of the women incarcerated in the Halifax Penitentiary when she stated, "I am happy to say that none of the women have needed, or received, punishment" (Canada, Directors of the Penitentiaries, 1870, p. 47). The language of the day is indicative of the attitude held toward the rights—or lack thereof—of offenders incarcerated in Canada around the time of Confederation.

In comparison with the other directors who filed reports for 1868, the director of the Kingston Penitentiary wrote the most detailed account of the state of the women's conditions of incarceration. The author of the report, Director Donald MacDonell, devoted a separate one-page section, "Remarks on the State of the Female Prison," to the situation of the incarcerated women. He included comments on the cleanliness and neatness of the facility, which was located in the basement. Although he noted that the basement was "very extensive," he did report that "a proper and convenient prison, for the female convicts, is much required" (Canada, Directors of the Penitentiaries, 1870, p. 22). This statement can be interpreted as one of the earliest recommendations at a federal level for the need to establish a women's federal prison. The matron of the female prison at Kingston Penitentiary, Belinda Plees, provided more detail concerning the makeup of the female inmate population, the one death, and the one birth that occurred at the prison that year, and the increase in the number of incident reports over the previous year. The matron concluded that the slight increase in the number of reports was "due to there being two or three exceedingly bad and turbulent women, who take delight in disturbing the prison" (Canada, Directors of the Penitentiaries, 1870, p. 22).

Unfortunately, this kind of sentiment was echoed more than a century later, in 1994, when a National Board of Investigation reported on the April 22nd incident that had occurred at the Prison for Women (P4W) earlier that year. According to the Commission of Inquiry into Certain Events at the Prison for Women (also known as the Arbour inquiry), the Board of Investigation report was deficient from a factual point of view because it downplayed the inadequate correctional response to the incident by overemphasizing the dangerousness of the offenders involved. The "April 22nd incident," as it became known, and the commission of inquiry that followed will be discussed in further detail in this chapter.

With respect to the *First Annual Report of the Directors of Penitentiaries for the Year 1868*, the comment that can perhaps best provide a glimpse of how women offenders were viewed in the latter half of the 19th century comes from the director of Kingston Penitentiary, Donald MacDonell:

> The poor creatures, who are sent here, are generally of the unfortunate classes and of the worst temperaments. They are, here, taught the usefulness of labor, and those, well disposed, are allowed to learn the working of the sewing machine, so that, on their release, they may be enabled to obtain a livelihood. (Canada, Directors of the Penitentiaries, 1870, p. 22)

Clearly, women were employed in stereotypical female roles within the prison. Most (72 percent) of the women at Kingston Penitentiary in 1868 were employed as knitters and sewers. The remaining women were employed in various domestic jobs, such as washing and ironing, cooking, cleaning, nursing the sick, and drying and folding clothes (Canada, Directors of the Penitentiaries, 1870).

By 1914, the women at Kingston Penitentiary were being housed in a building separate from the rest of the population of the penitentiary. In their report (known familiarly as the MacDonell report), the Royal Commission on Penitentiaries noted that although the women at Kingston Penitentiary were being kept in a "new and suitable" building, the establishment of a separate prison would be desirable in that "the interests of all concerned would be best served if these few inmates were transferred to an institution for women" (Canada, Royal Commission on Penitentiaries, 1914, p. 9). The MacDonell report also mentioned the possibility that arrangements could be established with the provinces for the custody of the federally incarcerated women.

A Separate Federal Prison for Women

In 1921, the *Report of the Committee Appointed by the Rt. Hon. C.J. Doherty, Minister of Justice, to Advise upon the Revision of the Penitentiary Regulations and the Amendment of the Penitentiary Act* recommended that section 63 of the *Penitentiary Act* be amended to include a provision for women to be incarcerated in facilities separate from men's institutions. The Biggar report, as it became known, noted that the *Penitentiary Act* as it was written did not allow for women to be housed in a separate penitentiary, but permitted them to be kept only in a separate ward of a men's penitentiary (Canada, Committee Appointed to Advise, 1921). The Biggar report also noted that "one of the recognized elements of imprisonment is the deprivation of the convict of opportunities for association with the opposite sex" and that housing men and women within the same penitentiary would bring "this deprivation constantly to the minds of both male and female convicts" (Canada, Committee Appointed to Advise, 1921, p. 19). For this reason, the committee recommended that section 63 of the *Penitentiary Act* be amended to allow the possibility for women to be incarcerated in a separate institution.

In 1921, the Nickle commission report was the first to specifically address the needs of federally incarcerated women (Canada, Commission on the State and Management of the Female Prison, 1921). In the report, Nickle described the accommodations and daily lives of the women incarcerated at the Kingston Penitentiary and commented on the behaviour of some women. One of the major concerns of the commission was that housing women within a male prison contributed to inappropriate behaviour that could be avoided if women were held in a separate locale. Nickle painted the picture of a hapless female, a victim of her own pathological biochemistry, unable to control her insatiable urges:

> Without doubt some of the women, more particularly at certain periods, are thrown into a violent state of sexual excitement by the mere sight of the men, more often by their being or working contiguously to the female quarters and my attention was called to one instance of this group of cases where a sedative had to be given to soothe desire. (Canada, Commission on the State and Management of the Female Prison, 1921, p. 3)

Concern was also voiced that by housing the women in a male facility, the women were being placed at risk and their vulnerabilities could be exploited by both male inmates and staff. In addition, it was noted that some male staff were fearful of accusations by the women, which could have dire consequences:

> As a matter of fact to-day the male staff, from the warden down, view with apprehension the administration of the Female Prison. While the disclosures of the past year have shown how unscrupulous officers have taken unfair advantage of opportunities for flirtations, improprieties and indecencies that presented themselves, yet it can be truthfully contradicted that many decent officers are fearful, knowing that a few designing and crafty women might ruin a well-earned reputation. (Canada, Commission on the State and Management of the Female Prison, 1921, p. 5)

As a result of the Nickle commission report, construction was begun on the new Prison for Women in Kingston, Ontario (Hayman, 2006).

The Prison for Women

Construction of the Prison for Women began in May 1925 and was completed in 1932. At that time, considerable rioting had taken place at Kingston Penitentiary, damaging an area that housed some male inmates (Hayman, 2006). As a result, some men were transferred temporarily to the new Prison for Women building in 1932 (Hayman, 2006). Finally, in January 1934, after the men had been removed, all the women who had been housed in Kingston Penitentiary were transferred to the newly built, separate prison (Canada, Royal Commission to Investigate the Penal System, 1938). Four years after the Prison for Women in Kingston opened its doors, a royal commission recommended that it be closed (Canada, Royal Commission to Investigate the Penal System, 1938).

EARLY REPORTS AND COMMISSIONS ON THE PRISON FOR WOMEN (1938–1956)

The *Report of the Royal Commission to Investigate the Penal System of Canada*, chaired by Justice Joseph Archambault, included recommendations specific to female inmates in Canada (Canada, Royal Commission to Investigate the Penal System, 1938). The Archambault report, as it was known familiarly, highlighted the relatively small number of female inmates compared with male inmates in the federal correctional system. The new women's prison was designed to hold a maximum of 100 inmates, but in the decade prior to the Archambault report, the average daily population of female federal offenders was approximately 37 inmates (Canada, Royal Commission to Investigate the Penal System, 1938). During that 10-year period (1928 to 1937), the highest population of female offenders (51 women) occurred in 1932, and the lowest population (26 women) was seen in 1936.

The Archambault report, in the chapter entitled "Women Prisoners," noted that women made up only 1 percent of all federal inmates (Canada, Royal Commission to Investigate the Penal System, 1938). Furthermore, the authors asserted that most women were "of the occasional or accidental offender class" and were "not a custodial problem" (p. 147). As such, the authors recommended the women could be as effectively housed in reformatories as they could in a penitentiary. According to the Archambault report:

There is no justification for the erection and maintenance of a costly penitentiary for women alone, nor is it desirable that they should be confined, either in the same institution as men, or in one central institution far from their place of residence and their friends and relations. (Canada, Royal Commission to Investigate the Penal System, 1938, p. 148)

According to the Archambault commission's conclusions and recommendations, the authors clearly did not perceive a need to build a separate women's prison in Kingston, Ontario. The commission report stressed the pecuniary savings from no longer incurring the operating expenses associated with the Prison for Women or having to transport women from the eastern and western provinces to Kingston. The commission recommended the Prison for Women be closed and arrangements be made with provincial authorities to provide custody for those federally sentenced women (Canada, Royal Commission to Investigate the Penal System, 1938). In 1947, the Gibson report later echoed this sentiment with recommendations that the Prison for Women be converted from a women's institution to a male facility for classification and segregation of offenders (Canada, Department of Justice, 1947).

Most reports written on P4W recommended that it be closed and other arrangements made to meet the needs of women sentenced to federal terms of incarceration. One of the few reports that did not recommend the closure of P4W was the Fauteux report of 1956, which acknowledged that the geographic isolation of women from the east and west coasts was unfortunate and the consequent lack of support from family and friends in their home communities was also undesirable. However, the authors of the Fauteux report concluded that the existence of one central institution for women was preferable for treatment delivery. Because of their small numbers, keeping the women in one facility would allow for economical service delivery that could take the form of an intensified treatment program (Canada, Committee Appointed to Inquire, 1956). This sentiment was not echoed in future reports.

REPORTS AND COMMISSIONS RECOMMENDING THE CLOSURE OF THE PRISON FOR WOMEN (1968–1996)

In 1968, the Canadian Corrections Association published its "Brief on the Woman Offender," a report prepared for the Royal Commission on the Status of Women, which addressed three key items specific to women offenders. The first item dealt with the criminal acts most often committed by women. The second focus was the problems experienced by women in conflict with the law at various stages of the justice process. The final concern was the detention facilities that existed for women. The authors of the brief sought recommendations specific to the needs of women in conflict with the law. Of particular interest is their recommendation that staff working with women receive training specific to working with women in prison. Additionally, the authors recommended that women's prisons be designed with the special needs of women offenders in mind and a variety of women's prisons be built to accommodate different kinds of female offenders. According to the brief, "prisons for women should not be patterned on male institutions but rather be planned on the basis of the special needs of women" (Canadian Criminology and Corrections Association, 1968, p. 42).

In 1969, the report of the Canadian Committee on Corrections (also known as the Ouimet report) identified a host of problems associated with having most federal female offenders serving their sentences at one prison. At the time of the Ouimet report, some women from the West (described as being drug addicted) had been incarcerated at Matsqui Institution in British Columbia. However, women from the rest of Canada were being sent to the Kingston Prison for Women. The Ouimet report identified issues related to geographic separation, lack of French-language programming, and the incarceration in one facility of women who differed with respect to "age, degree of criminal sophistication and emotional stability" (Canadian Committee on Corrections, 1969, p. 400). The report's recommendations specific to women offenders included the suggestion that the federal government consider purchasing the services of provincial government facilities in the larger provinces and the establishment of regional services that could serve the needs of both the federal and provincial regional governments. Clearly, the continued use of one central federal prison in Kingston was not fully supported by the report. An additional recommendation in the Ouimet report was that the federal government "appoint a suitably qualified woman to a position of senior responsibility and leadership in relation to correctional treatment of the woman offender in Canada" (Canadian Committee on Corrections, 1969, p. 403). Interestingly, the establishment of the position Deputy Commissioner for Women did not occur until recommended by the Arbour inquiry (Canada, Commission of Inquiry, 1996), after which Nancy Stableforth, in 1996, became the first person to hold this position (Correctional Service of Canada, n.d., "The Closing of the Prison for Women").

In 1974, seven individuals were appointed to the National Advisory Committee on the Female Offender; in 1977, they produced a report on their findings (known as the Clark report). The committee, which included representatives from stakeholder groups, such as the Elizabeth Fry Society and the National Parole Board, was tasked to:

> study the needs of federal female offenders and to make specific recommendations to the Commissioner of Penitentiaries and the Executive Director of the National Parole Service regarding the development of a comprehensive plan to provide adequate institutional and community services appropriate to her unique program and security needs. (Canada, National Advisory Committee on the Female Offender, 1977, p. 9)

The committee members chose not to limit themselves to only *federal* female offenders but also concerned themselves with the realities faced by *all* female offenders in Canada. At the time the Clark report was written, women comprised just less than 2 percent of all federal incarcerates in Canada. The percentage of provincially incarcerated women was higher, at about 7 percent (Canada, National Advisory Committee on the Female Offender, 1977). Not unlike the previous reports, the National Advisory Committee recommended that the Prison for Women be closed. The committee members even went so far as to state their opinion that P4W should be closed "within three years from publication of this report" (Canada, National Advisory Committee on the Female Offender, 1977, p. 30). Clearly this did not happen.

The National Advisory Committee identified many of the same concerns regarding the Prison for Women that had been identified in previous reports: women were housed too far from their homes, release planning was problematic, the physical building was unsuitable, the needs of French-speaking women were not being met, and protection was inadequate for those who were viewed as being "less criminally sophisticated" than other inhabitants of the prison (Canada, National Advisory Committee on the Female Offender, 1977, p. 19). The Clark report outlined two approaches that could be followed to "decentralize" the incarceration of federally sentenced women. The first plan was similar to the one proposed by the Ouimet report (Canadian Committee on Corrections, 1969) in which the federal government would remain jurisdictionally responsible for the women who had been sentenced to federal time, but women who did not require a high-security setting could be incarcerated in provincial institutions through the purchase of services from provincial facilities. This plan also recommended the establishment of regional secure facilities for women who required a more secure setting. Conversely, provincial governments could purchase services from the federal government for those provincially sentenced women who required a more secure facility. The second plan involved the provincial governments assuming responsibility for all women incarcerated in their respective areas, irrespective of the length of incarceration. The National Advisory Committee Report (Canada, National Advisory Committee on the Female Offender, 1977) outlined the pros and cons associated with both plans. Of particular note, yet again, a report was recommending the closure of the Prison for Women, a step that would not occur for decades.

The Clark report was evaluated by the Advisory Council on the Status of Women in the fall of 1977 (Rosen, 1977). In this evaluation, the Clark report was criticized for taking a "soft-line approach" and not presenting much original content (Rosen, 1977, p. 41). According to Rosen, the Clark report did "more harm than good" because by recommending the closure of P4W, the future of the facility remained uncertain, making it more difficult to attract both new staff and the funding needed for capital projects (p. 42). As a result of the recommendation to close, the prison would, in effect, be placed in a state of inertia with respect to future development (Rosen, 1977).

That same year, a report to Parliament was made by the Subcommittee on the Penitentiary System in Canada (Canada, Subcommittee on the Penitentiary System in Canada, 1977). In the report's section on female inmates, the authors noted that female inmates experienced "outright discrimination" in the lack of "recreation, programs, basic facilities and space" available to them (p. 134). The authors further pointed out that from their examination of the kinds of offences most often committed by women and women's institutional behaviour, women clearly did not need to be incarcerated in what amounted to an "1835-style of maximum security institution" (p. 134). It is in this report that we find the much referenced description of the Prison for Women as "unfit for bears, much less women" (p. 135). The report to Parliament summed up the Prison for Women in Kingston as being "obsolete in every respect—in design, in programs and in the handling of the people sent there" (p. 135). Obviously, the subcommittee was not in favour of the Prison for Women remaining in operation.

In 1978, a joint committee was struck to study the various alternatives for housing women who had been sentenced to federal time (Canada, Joint Committee to Study Alternatives, 1978). The committee consisted of representatives from the Elizabeth Fry Society, both federal and provincial corrections, and the Prison for Women Citizen's Advisory Committee. The joint committee considered options identified in previous reports and options they saw as potentially feasible. Two options dismissed were the takeover of federal female offenders by provincial corrections (because of the expected lack of consensus from all provinces) and the placement of all female offenders into community-based facilities (because of security concerns). Some options considered acceptable were various combinations and permutations of the following: purchasing the Vanier Institution from the Ontario government, rebuilding the Prison for Women in Kingston, building an entirely new prison for women in Kingston, and revisiting the concept of "co-corrections," in which men and women are jointly housed in one institution (Canada, Joint Committee to Study Alternatives, 1978).

Interestingly, the joint committee was in favour of at least one secure, centrally located facility for women. Although the committee referenced the importance of maximizing exchange of service agreements with provincial corrections and making optimal use of community-based facilities, the support for continuing to have a central facility was counter to the recommendations of previous reports (the Archambault, Ouimet, and Clark reports, for example).

In 1978, the Needham report further evaluated the plans that had been proposed in the Clark report (Canada, National Planning Committee, 1978). The Clark report's plan 2 (the provincial takeover of federally incarcerated women) was not supported by Needham because of the lack of unanimity from the provinces (Canada, National Planning Committee, 1978). If one province did not agree with being responsible for housing federally sentenced women, then the plan could not work. The Clark report's plan 1 involved building regional facilities for those women who required a secure setting and transferring (to provincial facilities) those women who did not require a secure setting. However, the recommendations of the Needham report included the need for, at minimum, one regional facility in the East and one in the West. In addition, an emphasis was placed on using community-based residences for the women (Canada, National Planning Committee, 1978). Although the Needham report did support regionalization, it did not comment on the feasibility of establishing secure facilities in all regions across Canada. The authors of the report clearly stated that evaluation of financial considerations needed further study. As in previous reports, and echoed in the Needham report, was the recommendation that P4W be closed (Canada, National Planning Committee, 1978).

CREATING CHOICES

The mandate of the Task Force on Federally Sentenced Women (TFFSW) was to assess the correctional management of women sentenced to federal prison in Canada, from the beginning of their sentences to the date of their warrants' expiry. Included in the mandate was the need to develop a strategic plan to guide and direct this process while respecting the needs specific to this group of women (Canada, Task Force on Federally Sentenced Women [TFFSW], 1990). In an innovative fashion, the TFFSW was actually co-chaired by the Correctional Service of Canada and the Canadian Association of Elizabeth Fry Societies, who took a women-centred approach to their work. The members of the TFFSW were thus able to gain considerable insight because the experience of women was valued throughout the process of the investigation.

As was the case in numerous previous reports, the TFFSW, in its report *Creating Choices*, found that the needs of federally sentenced women were not being met. The report noted that the building itself was inadequate, the women were being incarcerated in an over-secure setting, the available programming was poor, the women were geographically isolated from their families, and the needs of Francophone and Aboriginal women were not being met (Canada, TFFSW, 1990). The TFFSW recommended the Prison for Women be closed and the women be moved to five regional facilities to be operated across Canada. In addition, the report recommended an Aboriginal **healing lodge** be built in the Prairies to address the unique needs of Aboriginal women who were sentenced federally.

Five principles were emphasized to guide the CSC in implementing change: empowerment, meaningful and responsible choices, respect and dignity, supportive environment, and shared responsibility (Canada, TFFSW, 1990). Hannah-Moffat (2001) was critical of the manner in which the "CSC's cooption of the feminist politics of difference and empowerment" occurred in relation to the implementation of the TFFSW report (p. 161).[1] By embracing these five principles, the CSC hoped to move closer to what had been described as a community-based ideal able to recognize the importance of, and be sensitive to, the diversity in Canadian communities. The Arbour inquiry (Canada, Commission of Inquiry, 1996) noted that on the heels of *Creating Choices* (Canada, TFFSW, 1990), and while the plans for the new regional facilities (including the hiring of staff) were under way, the CSC, and particularly the Prison for Women, came under public scrutiny for the regressive manner with which some women were treated as a result of what was to become known as the April 22nd incident.

THE APRIL 22ND INCIDENT AT THE PRISON FOR WOMEN

In the early evening of April 22, 1994, an incident occurred outside the hospital area at the Prison for Women while some of the B range inmates were waiting for their medication. This area was controlled by four correctional officers. According to official accounts, two inmates approached the barrier, and one demanded her medication in an aggressive and loud manner. After what appeared to be a signal from one of the inmates, the group of six inmates jumped the officers. Threatening statements were reportedly made by inmates toward the correctional staff: "Give me the scissors so I can stick her" and "Grab the telephone cord. We'll string the bitch up, right here" (Canada, Commission of Inquiry, 1996, p. 33). The incident lasted only a few minutes.

As part of the correctional response to control the situation, a number of the inmates were maced by the correctional supervisor. All inmates involved were placed in the **segregation unit**. Five of the six inmates eventually plead guilty to various charges, including attempted prison breach, assault, threat to cause bodily harm, and possession of a weapon for a purpose dangerous to the public peace. The correctional officers directly involved in the incident were negatively affected in a variety of ways. One officer was off work for a year and eventually left P4W. Another was off for three months and later left the prison. One did return to work immediately following the incident, but transferred to another institution when it became too difficult to continue working at P4W. A fourth officer attempted to return to work, but could not. She eventually left the Correctional Service of Canada. Interestingly, this officer had a bachelor's degree in criminology and women's studies, had previous correctional work experience, and had sought out employment with the Correctional Service of Canada so that she could work at P4W (Canada, Commission of Inquiry, 1996). Additional officers and staff and inmates who were not directly involved in the incident were also negatively affected by a heightened sense of fear and distrust that was a direct result of the unpredictable nature of the incident.

Over the course of four days (April 22 to April 26) in the segregation unit, times of unrest were interspersed between periods of calm. The inmates were reportedly verbally abusive to staff, and their instances of "acting out" included the throwing of such items as food, water, juice, and urine. The unrest in the segregation unit was not limited to the women who had been directly involved in the incident. Inmates already in segregation also engaged in problematic behaviour, and inmates not directly involved in the incident were reportedly involved in a slashing, a suicide attempt, and an attempted hostage taking (Canada, Commission of Inquiry, 1996).

On the evening of April 26, Mary Cassidy, the warden of P4W, called in a male Institutional Emergency Response Team (IERT) from Kingston Penitentiary to perform cell extractions in the segregation unit. The warden wanted the women to be "restrained, stripped, gowned, the cells stripped and the women returned to their cells" (Canada, Commission of Inquiry, 1996, p. 74). The IERT entered the segregation area and proceeded to remove the women from the cells. The procedure was videotaped by a member of the IERT (see box 1.1).

On April 27, most of the women consented to a body cavity search. It was their understanding that after giving their consent for this intrusive procedure, they would receive a cigarette and a shower. As Madame Justice Arbour noted, "the absence of a culture respectful of individual rights is perhaps nowhere more disturbing than on this issue" (Canada, Commission of Inquiry, 1996, p. 96).

Box 1.1   Cell Extraction by the Institutional Emergency Response Team

The following is a description from the Arbour inquiry (Canada, Commission of Inquiry, 1996) of the all-male Institutional Emergency Response Team performing the first cell extraction in the segregation unit at the Prison for Women:

Prior to the video being turned on, the IERT marched into the Segregation Unit in standard formation, approached Joey Twins' cell and banged on the bars of her cell with the shield. She immediately did as she was ordered, and when the video begins she is lying face down in her cell surrounded by IERT members who are holding her down. An officer now identified as a female member of the Prison for Women staff, cuts off Ms. Twins' clothing ... while IERT members hold her down ... Ms. Twins' hands are cuffed behind her back and her legs shackled. She is marched backwards out of her cell naked, and led to the corner of the range. There she is held against the wall with the clear plastic shield, with her back against the wall ... Some IERT members stand around her while the IPSO [institutional preventive security officer], Mr. Waller, and maintenance men from the prison enter the Segregation Unit to begin stripping Ms. Twins' cell. The corner where Ms. Twins is standing is visible to anyone in the unit or standing in the doorway ... While she is still being held in the corner, a paper gown is brought to Ms. Twins and tied around her neck. The effect is something like that of a bib. The paper gown neither covers her, nor provides warmth. Upon her return to the cell, an IERT member begins the extremely lengthy process of attempting to apply a body belt in substitution of her handcuffs, during which procedure her gown comes off. A body belt is a form of restraint equipment which, as the name implies, consists of a locked chain around the inmate's waist to which are attached locked cuffs attaching wrists to the locked belt, more of less at the side of the body ... Finally, this lengthy procedure is completed and she is left lying on the floor of her cell in restraints (body belt and leg irons) and with a small paper gown.

Source: Canada, Commission of Inquiry into Certain Events at the Prison for Women in Kingston. (1996). *Commission of inquiry into certain events at the Prison for Women in Kingston* (The Arbour inquiry). Ottawa: Public Works and Government Services of Canada, p. 76.

The days following the cell extractions have been described as a time during which the women in the segregation unit were being denied so-called privileges that many of us would consider necessities. The women went without wearing anything but a paper gown until halfway through the day on April 27. They were without mattresses until May 10. They were not given the opportunity to shower regularly, their phone calls were restricted, and their initial requests for reading and writing materials were denied (Canada, Commission of Inquiry, 1996). The confinement of the women in segregation continued for many months (between seven-and-a-half and nine months). During this period, some women were transferred to the Regional Treatment Centre in the Kingston Penitentiary. Two of the women who had been transferred launched **habeas corpus**[2] applications, and eventually all of the women were returned to the Prison for Women (Canada, Commission of Inquiry, 1996).

If it were not for the airing of sections of the IERT videotape on CBC's *the fifth estate* on February 21, 1995, the Canadian public likely would not have heard about the April 22nd incident and its aftermath to the extent that it did. Interestingly, the Solicitor General of Canada announced the call for an independent inquiry into the matter on the same day that *the fifth estate* aired its program, after he tabled the special report from the correctional investigator in the House of Commons. The commission of inquiry was appointed on April 10, 1995 by the governor general in council.

COMMISSION OF INQUIRY INTO CERTAIN EVENTS AT THE PRISON FOR WOMEN IN KINGSTON (THE ARBOUR INQUIRY)

Late in the spring of 1995, a commission of inquiry was undertaken to "investigate and report on the state and management of that part of the business of the Correctional Service of Canada that pertains to the incidents that occurred at the Prison for Women in Kingston, Ontario" (Canada, Commission of Inquiry, 1996, p. ii). The purpose of the Arbour inquiry was to investigate not the details of the incident that occurred outside the hospital on the evening on April 22 but the correctional response to that incident during the days, weeks, and months that followed.

Eight groups were granted standing for the first phase of the commission of inquiry: (1) the Canadian Association of Elizabeth Fry Societies; (2) the Citizens' Advisory Committee; (3) the correctional investigator; (4) the Correctional Service of Canada and the commissioner of corrections; (5) some members of the IERT; (6) the Inmate Committee; (7) some of the inmates involved in the incidents; and (8) the Public Service Alliance of Canada and the Union of Solicitor General Employees. More than 100 people were interviewed by the staff of investigators. The hearings began in Kingston, Ontario, on August 9, 1995. During the second phase of the inquiry, roundtable discussions were held on topics of particular importance to federally sentenced women, such as cross-gender staffing, Aboriginal federally sentenced women, managing violence, and programming and treatment needs. Prior to the roundtable discussions, various women's prisons were visited, and policy consultations were carried out with established academics and researchers who specialized in the area of women's imprisonment (Canada, Commission of Inquiry, 1996).

The Arbour inquiry report was clear in its criticism of the Correctional Service of Canada, which was described as adhering to a "deplorable defensive culture" (Canada, Commission of Inquiry, 1996, p. 176). The CSC approach was "to deny error, defend against criticism, and to react without a proper investigation of the truth" (p. 175). In conclusion, the commission of inquiry found a "disturbing lack of commitment to the ideals of justice on the part of the Correctional Service" and the need for increased judicial supervision with respect to how the CSC managed segregation and the grievance process (p. 197). In an overall sense, the Arbour inquiry report can be viewed as critical in the history of women's corrections. It serves as a scathing reminder of the injustices that are possible and of the importance for all of those employed in the criminal justice system to follow the rule of law when carrying out their duties.

Regional Facilities

As a result of the Arbour inquiry's strong criticism of the CSC for some of its operations that did not respect the rule of law (Canada, Commission of Inquiry, 1996), the CSC mission statement was amended to include the rule of law:

> The Correctional Service of Canada (CSC), as part of the criminal justice system and respecting the rule of law, contributes to public safety by actively encouraging and assisting offenders to become law-abiding citizens, while exercising reasonable, safe, secure and humane control. (CSC, n.d., "Our Mission," ¶ 1)

By the early to mid-1990s, planning was under way to build the regional facilities and the healing lodge. The final locations of the regional facilities differed from the original recommendations of the TFFSW working group (Hayman, 2006). The new regional facilities[3] eventually included Grand Valley Institution for Women in Kitchener, Ontario; Nova Institution for Women in Truro, Nova Scotia; Joliette Institution in Joliette, Quebec; Edmonton Institution for Women in Edmonton, Alberta; and the Okimaw Ohci Healing Lodge in Maple Creek, Saskatchewan.

All the new regional facilities included cottage-style accommodations for the women, where each woman could have her own room. Communal kitchens, laundry areas, bathrooms, living rooms, and dining rooms were included in the plans for the cottages. The idea was to make the new prisons seem closer to the norms of community living (Hayman, 2006). An important feature of the new regional facilities was no permanent guard post in the living units. The guards, now called primary workers, patrolled the living units periodically throughout their shifts. Now, however, all multi-level facilities that accommodate maximum security offenders have a secure unit that does not operate like the cottages and has security personnel present at all times.

Federally sentenced women from the west coast of Canada were able to remain in British Columbia under an exchange of service agreement between the CSC and the province of British Columbia. The women were able to serve their sentences at the provincially run facility for women, the Burnaby Correctional Centre for Women (BCCW). Early in 2002, the BCCW was planned for closure, and the federal government was forced to investigate alternative locations to incarcerate federally sentenced women in British Columbia (Correctional Service of Canada, n.d., "Institutional Profiles"). The government decided to redesign the Sumas Community Correctional Centre and rename it the Fraser Valley Institution (FVI). Like other federal facilities for women, FVI consists of cottage-style living units and a secure unit for women classified as requiring maximum security needs.

Institutional profiles for the federally sentenced women's facilities across Canada are available on the website for the Correctional Service of Canada (n.d., "Institutional Profiles"). According to the website, all facilities, with the exception of the Isabel McNeil House and the healing lodge, are considered multi-level facilities that accommodate women classified as minimum, medium, or maximum security offenders. The Isabel McNeil House is a small minimum security facility located in Kingston. The Okimaw Ohci Healing Lodge (OOHL) is classified as a minimum/medium security facility with a capacity of 28 beds. As of March 31, 2005, the inmate population at most multi-level facilities was near capacity. See figure 1.1 for statistics of the inmate populations and a brief overview of these facilities.

The *Creating Choices* report was vague regarding how the principles of change could actually be implemented in the new regional facilities (Hayden, 2006). The report stressed the need for **"dynamic"** security, as opposed to **"static"** security. That is, the preferable mode of security should not rely on enhanced security features (cameras, fences, alarms, for example) but instead should be more interactive and driven through the relationships established between staff and the incarcerated women. The *Creating Choices* report also noted a discernible tendency to avoid acknowledging that women could be violent. Although the report suggested that approximately 5 percent of women might need a more secure setting, the report was not forthright in suggesting how a more secure setting could be implemented. The authors of the *Creating Choices* report characterized the majority of federal female offenders as "high needs" in terms of the interventions they would require and "low risk" in terms of their security status.

The CSC sought to address some of the recommendations of the *Creating Choices* report though various interventions, including those considered core programs. The primary thrust of these programs is usually for offenders to address their perceived inadequacies through the acquisition of a skill set. The treatment or intervention is more often than not cognitive-behavioural in nature. In this way, the woman is seen to be making "responsible choices" in an effort to take part in her own rehabilitation.

The various strategies employed by the CSC in the treatment of women offenders have been subjected to numerous criticisms (Hannah-Moffat & Shaw, 2000; Maidment, 2006; Pollack & Kendall, 2005). Others have pointed out that although the 2004 Program Strategy for Women Offenders clings to the notion of the voluntary aspect of the interventions and the need for informed consent, in reality, neither is likely (Hayman, 2006). A core program is identified as an area that a woman "should" address while incarcerated, even if she does not agree. In practice, an incarcerated woman is faced with only the appearance of choice. She can choose not to participate in a core program that has been included (possibly against her wishes) in her correctional plan; however, the parole board might take great interest in her decision not to participate and interpret the woman's rejection negatively.

Some have pointed out how the TFFSW report effectively "glossed over the difficult issues" (Hayman, 2006, p. 241). The language used in the *Creating Choices* report was such that the fact that they were actually talking about imprisonment was almost lost to the rhetoric (Hayman, 2006). By focusing on the language of victimization, the TFFSW essentially constructed an "image of the homogeneous federally sentenced woman" (Hayman, 2006, p. 241). As such, the federally incarcerated female became "idealized" so that all future plans, as put forth in *Creating Choices*, would "fit" this idealized fiction. For this reason, the new regional facilities were destined to be designed to accommodate the low-risk offender, in a cottage-

Figure 1.1   Comparison of Canadian Facilities for Federally Sentenced Women

Institution	Year opened	Security level			Population as of March 31, 2005	Maximum capacity
		Minimum	Medium	Maximum		
Fraser Valley Institution	2004	✓	✓	✓	46	52
Edmonton Institution for Women	1995	✓	✓	✓	92	110
Okimaw Ohci Healing Lodge	1995	✓	✓		12	28
Grand Valley Institution for Women	1997	✓	✓	✓	94	103
Isabel McNeil House	1990	✓			6	10
Joliette Institution for Women	1997	✓	✓	✓	69	99
Nova Institution for Women	1995	✓	✓	✓	34	70

Source: Correctional Service of Canada. (n.d.). Institutional profiles. Retrieved from www.csc-scc.gc.ca/text/region/inst-profil-eng.shtml.

style environment where correctional staff patrolled the living units, but were not stationed there. As Hayman (2006) pointed out, the approach taken by the TFFSW "inadvertently set federally sentenced women up for failure once they transferred to the new prisons" (p. 242). Because the women were diverse and did not fit the ideal image set up for them in the *Creating Choices* report, they, not surprisingly, did not fit into the new prisons.

Both the Edmonton and Nova institutions experienced incidents soon after they were opened; in both cases, the finger of blame was squarely pointed at the inmates. Hayman (2006) questioned this blame because to appreciate the reactions of the women to the new institutions, one must fully understand how the language used in the TFFSW report failed to identify the women as "prisoners," which had an effect on the women. Hayman (2006) contended that it was this "linguistic obfuscation" that "obscured the reality of their situation" (p. 242). In addition, Hayman holds the CSC to blame because the authorities allowed the Edmonton prison to be opened prior to its physical completion and transferred a disproportionately large number of maximum security women to an enhanced unit that could not adequately house them.

Watchdog Groups
The Office of the Correctional Investigator

The Office of the Correctional Investigator (OCI) serves as an ombudsperson for federal offenders. The mandate of the OCI is specified in part III of the *Corrections and Conditional Release Act*, which outlines the main function of the OCI to investigate and bring resolution to complaints from individual offenders (Canada, Office of the Correctional Investigator [OCI], n.d.). In addition, the OCI has a responsibility to review the policies and procedures of the CSC that relate to individual complaints of offenders, in the hopes that specific areas of concern are identified in a timely manner and subsequently addressed (Canada, OCI, n.d.). Recommendations from the OCI are directed to the commissioner of CSC and the Solicitor General (Canada, OCI, n.d.). As well, the OCI is responsible for generating an annual report that is presented to the Solicitor General (Canada, Commission of Inquiry, 1996). In addition, special reports may be submitted to the Solicitor General between annual reports, should any situation warrant immediate attention. For example, the Arbour inquiry was precipitated by a submission to the Solicitor General of a special OCI report regarding issues related to the April 22nd incident at P4W (Canada, Commission of Inquiry, 1996).

Female offenders who wish to file a complaint can call a toll-free number to speak with a representative from the OCI during business hours, or a message can be left if the woman is calling outside of business hours. The OCI encourages inmates to submit their concerns in writing. The coordinator for federally sentenced women's issues visits the prisons regularly.

In the OCI annual report for 2005–6, the correctional investigator addressed six key issues: (1) health services; (2) women offenders; (3) Aboriginal offenders; (4) institutional violence and investigation of inmate injury; (5) inmate grievances, allegations of harassment, and staff misconduct; and (6) case preparation and access to programs. In the section concerning women offenders, the correctional investigator noted some troubling statistics over the past two years. Specifically, a significant increase had occurred in cases of women being returned to the community not on day parole or full parole but on statutory release (Correctional Investigator of Canada, 2006). The number of postponements and waivers of National Parole Board (NPB) hearings had also increased, which was especially evident among cases involving Aboriginal women. A small increase was noted in the number of women on work release programs, but those participating in escorted temporary absences (ETAs) had decreased. The OCI also reported an increase in use of force incidents compared with the previous year (Correctional Investigator of Canada, 2006). The OCI recommended that its concerns be addressed, particularly a push to increase the number of women who, at their earliest eligibility date, are brought before the NPB.

Citizens' Advisory Committees

First established in the mid-1960s, the Citizens' Advisory Committees (CACs) were formed to allow members of the public to contribute to the quality of the various programs and services offered to federally incarcerated people (Correctional Service of Canada, n.d., "Citizens' Advisory Committee Portal"). CACs are now mandatory for all federal penitentiaries. Their mission is the protection of society through their interaction with CSC staff, the public, and offenders themselves. The CACs provide the CSC with both advice and recommendations concerning issues that pertain to correctional institutions. Each CAC functions as liaison with the community in which a particular prison resides.

Recent statistics indicate 106 CACs in Canada, composed of nearly 600 people of varying demographic backgrounds. CAC members are appointed (by a representative of the CSC) and serve a two-year term on the committee (Correctional Service of Canada, n.d., "Citizens' Advisory Committee Portal").

Canadian Association of Elizabeth Fry Societies (CAEFS)

The namesake of the Canadian Association of Elizabeth Fry Societies (CAEFS), Elizabeth Fry, was a Quaker prison reformer from England who sought to improve the conditions of people who were incarcerated in the early 19th century. Her tireless campaign to improve the lot of women and children incarcerated in London's Newgate Prison led to far-reaching prison reforms (Canadian Association of Elizabeth Fry Societies [CAEFS], n.d., "Origins of the Elizabeth Fry Societies"). According to the CAEFS website (www.elizabethfry.ca), Canada's first Elizabeth Fry Society was established in 1939 in Vancouver, but CAEFS was not incorporated as a non-profit voluntary organization until 1978. Currently, 25 Elizabeth Fry member societies operate across Canada: 5 in the Atlantic region, 1 in Quebec, 10 in Ontario, 4 in the Prairie provinces, and 5 in the Pacific region.

According to the CAEFS mission statement:

> CAEFS is an association of self-governing, community-based Elizabeth Fry Societies that work with and for women and girls in the justice system, particularly those who are, or may be, criminalized. Together, Elizabeth Fry Societies develop and advocate the beliefs, principles and positions that guide CAEFS. The association exists to ensure substantive equality in the delivery and development of services and programs through public education, research, legislative and administrative reform, regionally, nationally and internationally. (CAEFS, n.d., "Mission Statement," ¶ 1)

All member societies must follow three guiding principles in their day-to-day operations. The first principle highlights the role that the CAEFS holds with respect to the development of policies and positions that affect women and the importance to act on those issues that are common to women. The second principle emphasizes the rights of women to have access equal to that of men to participate in programs and opportunities within the Canadian justice system "without fear of prejudice or discrimination on the basis of such factors as sex, race, disability, sexual orientation, age, religion and freedom of conscience, social or economic condition" (CAEFS, n.d., "Principles," ¶ 2), The third principle espouses that "women who are criminalized should not be imprisoned" and that CAEFS will make every effort to prevent women from being incarcerated; in cases in which women are incarcerated, CAEFS will work to enable their earliest possible reintegration into the community (CAEFS, n.d., "Principles," ¶ 3).

The goals of CAEFS include the desire to promote and increase the public's awareness of what is referred to as the "**decarceration**" of women. A second, related goal is to decrease the number of women who are criminalized and incarcerated across Canada. A third goal involves improving criminalized and incarcerated women's access to community-based, publicly funded health, social service, and educational resources. Lastly, CAEFS wants to encourage the Elizabeth Fry Societies and other women's organizations to work together to tackle issues of oppression, such as racism and poverty (CAEFS, n.d., "Our Goals").

In Canada, the different member groups of CAEFS offer a variety of services, ranging from public education to pre-release planning and one-to-one support and counselling (CAEFS, n.d., "Programs and Services Directory"). The operation of CAEFS and the member groups is supported through the work of volunteers and by various governmental, public, and private funding sources (Elizabeth Fry Society of Edmonton, n.d.). In Canada, National Elizabeth Fry Week is observed in May in the week prior to Mother's Day. CAEFS chose this week because of the large percentage of incarcerated women who are mothers and whose children are "sentenced to separation" when their mothers are behind bars (CAEFS, n.d., "National Elizabeth Fry Week," ¶ 5).

Summary

The Canadian criminal justice system consists of three broad agencies: the police, the courts, and the correctional system. A person who comes into conflict with the law will likely interact with individuals from each of these interconnected bodies. Historically, criminalized women (and men for that matter) have not always been treated with respect by the justice system in Canada. The early history of corrections in Canada is replete with examples of abuses endured by those deemed to be criminal. The plight of criminalized women in Canada has been compounded by the tendency of correctional services (both federal and provincial) to treat women as an afterthought. Not until recently have attention and resources been directed toward correctional services for women.

Over the years, the majority of commissions studying the state of women's corrections have recommended the closure of Canada's infamous P4W. Key events have occurred in the last 20 years to shape the development of the federal correctional response to women. The TFFSW's report, *Creating Choices,* was the latest in a long line of reports to recommend the closure of P4W. The closing of P4W and the completion of the regional facilities for women (as suggested in *Creating Choices*) was no doubt hastened by the scathing condemnations of the CSC made in the Arbour inquiry report. Although the new prisons may be aesthetically more pleasing than P4W, they are not without their critics (Hannah-Moffat & Shaw, 2000; Hayman, 2006; Pollack & Kendall, 2005). In addition to academics who question the way in which criminalized women are processed through the federal correctional system, community organizations, such as the Elizabeth Fry Societies, advocate for respectful treatment of criminalized women by Canadian correctional systems.

Notes

1. For a comprehensive history of women's penal governance in Canada, see *Punishment in Disguise: Penal Governance and Federal Imprisonment of Women in Canada* (Hannah-Moffat, 2001).

2. "The writ of *habeas corpus* is available to any subject detained or imprisoned, not to hear and determine the case upon the evidence, but to immediately and in a summary way test the validity of his detention or imprisonment." The rules pertaining to said applications can be found in the *Criminal Code* of Canada (Dukelow, 2002, p. 195).

3. In March 2004, the Fraser Valley Institution for Women became the sixth regional federal institution for women to be opened in Canada.

Discussion Questions

1. Outline the three broad agencies in the criminal justice system in Canada. What is the function of each, and how do they relate to one another?
2. What are the advantages of having a number of regional federal correctional institutions for women? What are the disadvantages? Are there any advantages to having just one federal correctional facility for women in Canada?
3. Why did it take so long to close the Prison for Women?
4. Why is there a need for organizations such as the Canadian Association of Elizabeth Fry Societies (CAEFS), the Office of the Correctional Investigator (OCI), and Citizens' Advisory Committees (CACs)?

Suggested Readings

Canada, Commission of Inquiry into Certain Events at the Prison for Women in Kingston. (1996). *Commission of inquiry into certain events at the Prison for Women in Kingston* (the Arbour inquiry). Ottawa: Public Works and Government Services Canada.

Canada, Task Force on Federally Sentenced Women. (1990). *Creating choices: Report of the Task Force on Federally Sentenced Women.* Ottawa: Department of the Solicitor General.

Hannah-Moffat, K., & Shaw, M. (2000). *An ideal prison? Critical essays on women's imprisonment in Canada.* Halifax: Fernwood Publishing.

Hayman, S. (2006). *Imprisoning our sisters: The new federal women's prisons in Canada.* Montreal & Kingston: McGill-Queen's University Press.

Online Resources

1. Canadian Association of Elizabeth Fry Societies: www.elizabethfry.ca
2. Correctional Service of Canada: www.csc-scc.gc.ca
3. Canada, Department of Justice: www.justice.gc.ca

References

Canada, Commission Appointed to Inquire into and Report upon the Conduct, Economy, Discipline, and Management of the Provincial Penitentiary. (1849). *First report of the commissioners appointed to inquire into and report upon the conduct, economy, discipline, and management of the provincial penitentiary* (the Brown commission report). Montreal: Rollo Campbell.

Canada, Commission of Inquiry into Certain Events at the Prison for Women in Kingston. (1996). *Commission of Inquiry into Certain Events at the Prison for Women in Kingston* (the Arbour inquiry). Ottawa: Public Works and Government Services Canada.

Canada, Commission on the State and Management of the Female Prison at the Kingston Penitentiary. (1921). *Report on the state and management of the female prison at the Kingston Penitentiary* (the Nickle report). Ottawa: King's Printer.

Canada, Committee Appointed to Advise upon the Revision of the Penitentiary Regulations and the Amendment of the Penitentiary Act. (1921). *Report of the committee appointed by the Rt. Hon. C.J. Doherty, Minister of Justice, to advise upon the revision of the penitentiary regulations and the amendment of the Penitentiary Act* (the Biggar report). Ottawa: King's Printer.

Canada, Committee Appointed to Inquire into the Principles and Procedures Followed in the Remission Service of the Department of Justice of Canada. (1956). *Report of a committee appointed to inquire into the principles and procedures followed in the remission service of the Department of Justice of Canada* (the Fauteux report). Ottawa: Queen's Printer.

Canada, Department of Justice. (n.d.). Canada's court system. Retrieved from www.justice.gc.ca/eng/jl/index.html#court.

Canada, Department of Justice. (1947). *Report of General R.B. Gibson: A commissioner appointed under Order in Council P/C/ 1313, regarding the penitentiary system of Canada.* Ottawa: King's Printer.

Canada, Directors of the Penitentiaries. (1870). *First annual report of the directors of penitentiaries for the year 1868.* Ottawa: King's Printer.

Canada, Joint Committee to Study Alternatives for the Housing of the Federal Female Offender. (1978). *Report of the Joint Committee to Study Alternatives for the Housing of the Federal Female Offender* (the Chinnery report). Ottawa: Ministry of the Solicitor General.

Canada, National Advisory Committee on the Female Offender. (1977). *Report of the National Advisory Committee on the Female Offender* (the Clark report). Ottawa: Ministry of the Solicitor General.

Canada, National Planning Committee on the Female Offender. (1978). *Report of the National Planning Committee on the Female Offender* (the Needham report). Ottawa: Solicitor General Canada.

Canada, Office of the Correctional Investigator. (n.d.). Office of the correctional investigator. Retrieved from www.oci-bec.gc.ca/index_e.asp.

Canada, Public Safety and Emergency Preparedness Portfolio Corrections Statistics Committee. (2006). *Corrections and conditional release statistical overview: Annual report 2006.* Ottawa: Public Works and Government Services Canada.

Canada, Royal Commission on Penitentiaries. (1914). *Report of the Royal Commission on Penitentiaries* (the MacDonell report). Ottawa: King's Printer.

Canada, Royal Commission to Investigate the Penal System in Canada. (1938). *Report of the Royal Commission to Investigate the Penal System of Canada* (the Archambault report). Ottawa: King's Printer.

Canada, Subcommittee on the Penitentiary System in Canada. (1977). *Report to Parliament by the subcommittee on the penitentiary system in Canada* (the MacGuigan report). Ottawa: Minister of Supply and Services Canada.

Canada, Task Force on Federally Sentenced Women. (1990). *Creating choices: Report of the Task Force on Federally Sentenced Women.* Ottawa: Department of the Solicitor General.

Canadian Association of Elizabeth Fry Societies. (n.d.). Our goals. Retrieved from
www.elizabethfry.ca/egoals.html.

Canadian Association of Elizabeth Fry Societies. (n.d.). Mission statement. Retrieved
from www.elizabethfry.ca.

Canadian Association of Elizabeth Fry Societies. (n.d.). National Elizabeth Fry week.
Retrieved from www.elizabethfry.ca/eweek.html.

Canadian Association of Elizabeth Fry Societies. (n.d.). Origins: A short history of
Elizabeth Fry. Retrieved from www.elizabethfry.ca/ehistory.html.

Canadian Association of Elizabeth Fry Societies. (n.d.). Principles. Retrieved from
www.elizabethfry.ca/eprinciples.html.

Canadian Association of Elizabeth Fry Societies. (n.d.). Programs and services directory.
Retrieved from www.elizabethfry.ca/directory/cover.htm.

Canadian Committee on Corrections. (1969). *Report of the Canadian Committee on
Corrections* (the Ouimet report). Ottawa: Queen's Printer.

Canadian Criminology and Corrections Association. (1968). *Brief on the woman offender:
An official statement of policy.* Ottawa: Canadian Corrections Association.

Constitution Act, 1867. (1867). Retrieved from http://lois.justice.gc.ca/en/const/c1867_e
.html#legislative.

Correctional Investigator of Canada. (2006). *Annual report of the office of the correctional
investigator 2005–2006.* Ottawa: Minister of Public Works and Government Services
Canada.

Correctional Service of Canada. (n.d.). Citizens' advisory committee portal. Retrieved
from www.csc-scc.gc.ca/text/cac/index-eng.shtml.

Correctional Service of Canada. (n.d.). The closing of the Prison for Women in Kingston
July 6, 2000: Message from the Deputy Commissioner for Women, Correctional
Service of Canada. Retrieved from www.csc-scc.gc.ca/text/pblct/brochurep4w/
pre3-eng.shtml.

Correctional Service of Canada. (n.d.). Institutional profiles. Retrieved from www.csc-scc
.gc.ca/text/region/inst-profil-eng.shtml.

Correctional Service of Canada (n.d.). Our mission. Retrieved from www.csc-scc.gc.ca/
text/organi-eng.shtml.

Correctional Service of Canada. (1990). *The history of federal-provincial exchange of
service agreements.* Ottawa: Eden Communications.

Dukelow, D. (2002). *Dictionary of Canadian law* (3rd ed.). Toronto: Carswell.

Elizabeth Fry Society of Edmonton. (n.d.). Funders/donations. Retrieved from
www.elizabethfry.ab.ca/edmonton/edwhofr.htm.

Goff, C. (2008). *Criminal justice in Canada.* Toronto: Nelson Canada.

Hannah-Moffat, K. (2001). *Punishment in disguise: Penal governance and federal imprisonment of women in Canada.* Toronto: University of Toronto Press.

Hannah-Moffat, K., & Shaw, M. (2000). *An ideal prison? Critical essays on women's
imprisonment in Canada.* Halifax: Fernwood Publishing.

Hayman, S. (2006). *Imprisoning our sisters: The new federal women's prisons in Canada.* Montreal & Kingston: McGill-Queen's University Press.

Maidment, M. (2006). "We're not all that criminal": Getting beyond the pathologizing and individualizing of women's crime. *Women and Therapy, 29*(3/4), 35–56.

O'Brien, W.E. (1856). *Proceedings of the committee of the House of Assembly, appointed to investigate the charges made by the Hon. John A. Macdonald, against George Brown, Esq., M.P.P. with regard to his conduct as penitentiary commissioner.* Toronto: Lovell & Gibson.

Pollack, S., & Kendall, K. (2005). Taming the shrew: Regulating prisoners through women-centred mental health programming. *Critical Criminology, 13,* 71–87.

Public Safety Canada. (n.d.). First Nations policing policy. Retrieved from www.publicsafety.gc.ca/pol/le/fnpp-en.asp.

Reitano, J. (2006). *Police resources in Canada.* Ottawa: Canadian Centre for Justice Statistics.

Rosen, E. (1977). *An evaluation of the report of the national advisory committee on the female offender.* Ottawa: Advisory Council on the Status of Women.

Royal Canadian Mounted Police. (n.d.). About the RCMP. Retrieved from www.rcmp-grc .gc.ca/about/index_e.htm.

Royal Canadian Mounted Police. (n.d.). Organization of the RCMP. Retrieved from www.rcmp-grc.gc.ca/about/organi_e.htm.

Strange, C. (1985). The criminal and fallen of their sex: The establishment of Canada's first women's prison, 1874–1901. *Canadian Journal of Women and the Law, 1,* 79–92.

CHAPTER 2

Female Crime: Theoretical Perspectives

Walter DeKeseredy*

Introduction

Every day in Canada and elsewhere, men improve people's health and well-being, including through their work with women to seek cures for diseases such as AIDS and breast cancer. Further, many Canadian men are involved in the **White Ribbon Campaign**[1] and other efforts aimed at reducing the alarming rates of male-to-female victimization described in chapter 12. A much longer list of good things men do to benefit Canada and other countries could easily be provided. Still, despite all their good deeds, much of what is bad in the world, from genocide to terrorism, and including crimes committed behind closed doors and on the streets, is essentially the product of men (DeKeseredy & Schwartz, 2005). Similarly, men "have a virtual monopoly" on the commission of crimes of the powerful (Messerschmidt, 1997), such as those committed by newspaper mogul Conrad Black.

How often do we hear about women participating in massacres like the one at Virginia Polytechnic Institute and State University on April 16, 2007? That day, undergraduate student Seung-Hui Cho killed 32 people and wounded 25 others in the deadliest shooting in US history. Similarly, here in Canada, how many women have committed violent crimes, such as those that occurred at Montreal's Dawson College on Wednesday, September 13, 2006? Described in box 2.1, this terrifying event led many Canadians to question whether their country is actually a "kinder, gentler nation." And how many women flew planes into the World Trade Center and the Pentagon on September 11, 2001? At the risk of belabouring

---

* The author thanks Jane Barker and Mike Thompson for their advice and guidance.

Box 2.1   Montreal Gunman Called Himself "Angel of Death"

The gunman who went on a shooting rampage at a Montreal college Wednesday apparently left an online journal with chilling comments and photos of himself brandishing a rifle.

Kimveer Gill was the author of an online diary posted at the website vampirefreaks .com.

Gill, 25, was dressed entirely in black, wearing a trench coat and armed with a rifle when he arrived at Dawson College on Wednesday afternoon.

One woman was shot to death and 19 people were injured, at least six of them critically, in the rampage that followed. Montreal police said the victims ranged in age from 17 to 48.

On Thursday, police identified the dead student as Anastasia DeSousa, an 18-year-old from the greater Montreal area, who was a business student at Dawson College.

DeSousa was shot dead inside the building, said Montreal's ambulance agency.

"The environment was still very hostile when we got there," said André Champagne, a spokesperson for Urgences Santé.

Paramedics realized very quickly that there was nothing they could do to resuscitate or revive the young woman. "Her wounds were fatal, and the death was declared on site," he said.

DeSousa's body was removed from the college early Thursday morning.

Investigators with the Montreal police major crimes unit and the Sûreté du Québec, the provincial police force, spent the night picking through the crime scene to collect forensic evidence.

Eyewitnesses say they saw a tall, Goth-looking man in a long black coat drive up near the college on Maisonneuve Street in a black Pontiac Sunfire at around 12:30 p.m. He got out of his car, opened the trunk and removed a rifle.

The gunman then walked toward the college's southwest entrance. Witnesses said they saw him shoot at least one person outside before entering the building. Police said the first gunshots were heard at 12:41 p.m.

It was lunchtime and the school was packed when the gunman entered through the main doors and headed to the cafeteria. "He was shooting randomly," said Dawson student Michel Boyer, who witnessed the gunfire. "I'm not sure who he was shooting at, but the [cafeteria] atrium was completely cleared."

Chaos ensued, said Boyer. "The adrenaline was rushing. It was like something from a movie. It was completely unbelievable and incredible."

Source: Montreal gunman called himself "angel of death." (2006, September 14). *CBC News*. Retrieved from www.cbc.ca. CBC News with files from Canadian Press.

the issue, keep in mind that data sets generated by a variety of scientific projects show that men's involvement in most types of crime, especially violent offences, greatly exceeds that of women (DeKeseredy & Schwartz, 2005; Kimmel, 2000).

Some readers have been reading this chapter thinking, "But women do it too." Consider what happened to British Columbia resident Reena Virk on Friday, November 14, 1997. Described in box 2.2, her vicious murder led many Canadians to conclude that Canada was riddled with a new wave of "violent, unruly women ... running amok" (Faith, 1993, pp. 65–66) and of "girls gone wild" (Chesney-Lind & Irwin, 2008). Similarly, the case of female killer Karla Homolka and journalists' sensational reporting of her trial led many Canadians to believe that violence among Canadian women and girls was "sharply on the rise" (Chisholm, 1997). In the early 1990s, Homolka and her then husband, Paul Bernardo, sexually assaulted and murdered three young women from southern Ontario, one of whom was her sister.[2] Like the Reena Virk case, this case shocked and angered many Canadians and generated an unprecedented amount of media coverage (Boritch, 1997; DeKeseredy, 2000).

As described by Jane Barker in chapter 3, contrary to what the media may say, the girls who contributed to Reena Virk's death are not typical Canadian female offenders. Nor do we see a major surge in female youth violence such as that described in James Garbarino's (2006) controversial book, *See Jane Hit*, and on the cover of the *Boston Globe Magazine*:

Box 2.2   The Murder of Reena Virk

On 14 November 1997, fourteen-year-old Reena Virk, a girl of South Asian origin, was brutally murdered in a suburb of Victoria, British Columbia. Reena was first beaten by a group of seven girls and one boy, all aged between fourteen and seventeen. She was accused of stealing one of the girls' boyfriends and spreading rumours. Her beating was framed as retaliation against these alleged actions. According to journalistic accounts, the attack began when one of the girls stubbed out a cigarette on her forehead. As Reena tried to flee, the group swarmed her, kicked her in the head and body numerous times, attempted to set her hair on fire, and brutalized her to the point where she was severely injured and bruised. During the beating, Reena reportedly cried out, "I'm sorry" (Hall, 1999).

Battered, Reena staggered across a bridge, trying to flee her abusers, but was followed by two of them—Warren Glowatski and Kelly Ellard. The two then continued to beat her, smashing her head against a tree and kicking her to the point where she became unconscious. They then allegedly dragged her body into the water and forcibly drowned her. Reena's body was found eight days later, on 22 November 1997, with very little clothing on it. The pathologist who conducted the autopsy noted that Virk had been kicked eighteen times in the head and her internal injuries were so severe that tissue was crushed between the abdomen and backbone. She also noted that the injuries were similar to those that would result from a car being driven over a body. The pathologist concluded that Reena would probably have died even if she had not been drowned.

Source: Jiwani, Y. (2006). *Discourses of denial: Mediations of race, gender, and violence.* Vancouver: University of British Columbia Press, p. 68.

"Bad Girls: Girls Are Moving into the World of Violence That Once Belonged to Boys" (Ford, 1998).[3] Note, too, that the Homolka murder case is not a typical example of female violence. For example, in the United States, females account for only 12 percent of all serial killers (Hickey, 2005). Furthermore, no reliable study has found that men and women are equally likely to sexually abuse members of the opposite sex. However, the words of Holly Johnson (1987), 20 years ago, still hold true in Canada today: "The number of women who are charged with *Criminal Code* offences amounts to thousands each year" (p. 23).

Because other contributors to this book address the extent and distribution of crimes committed by Canadian women and girls, this chapter will not repeat these data. Instead, this chapter's main objective is to review the most widely read and cited theories of female crime. Most criminological theories are constructed and tested by men and focus primarily on men and boys in conflict with the law and on the societal reactions to their offences (Belknap, 2007). In other words, most criminological theories are "alarmingly gender-blind" (Gelsthorpe & Morris, 1988; Messerschmidt, 1993). Nevertheless, some criminologists deviate from this common trend. Prior to describing and evaluating their offerings, it is first necessary to answer the question "What is a theory?"

What Is a Theory?[4]

Social scientific theories of crime are like opinions: most people have them (Lilly, Cullen, & Ball, 2006). For example, of the 84 people murdered in Toronto in 2007, 42 of the victims had been shot ("Toronto Homicides in 2007," 2008). Because most of the shooting victims were people of colour, many people of different backgrounds, including journalists, have offered their own accounts of the high rate of homicide in Toronto's black community. Consider the controversial theory proposed by conservative *Toronto Sun* columnist Michael Coren (2007) in box 2.3. Of course, other reasons for such gun-related deaths were and continue to be offered. Nevertheless, most of these theories are grounded in personal experiences or what people see, hear, or read in the media (Cote, 2002; DeKeseredy et al., 2005). On the other hand, for people like me who make a living from studying crime and its control, theory construction is a much more complex process and is heavily grounded in scientific research. More specifically, following Curran and Renzetti's (2001) thinking, a theory is defined here as "a set of interconnected statements or propositions that explain how two or more events or factors are related to one another" (p. 2).

Box 2.3   One Journalist's Theory of Crime

Another murder in a Canadian black community, this time the victim being 11 years old. And it took only moments for white liberal politicians to blame law-abiding handgun owners and, yes, the United States of America.

Handguns have to be banned, they cried, and American gun laws are too soft. This has to be a first. Canadian leftists blaming a murder in Toronto on President George W. Bush. Orders of Canada and CBC T-shirts all round.

Such drivel does not, however, explain how Norway, with one of the highest rates of gun ownership in the world, manages to have one of the lowest crime rates.

Or how Israel, a society where guns are extraordinarily common, has so few criminal shootings.

Or how Britain with some of the most stringent gun control laws in the world has a violent crime rate that is virtually out of control.

It's too late to play silly games any more. If handguns are the cause of all this we have to ask why there are so few shootings in, for example, the Dutch, Ukrainian, Irish, Portuguese, Korean, Hindu or African communities. Why, in fact, there are so few shootings in any community outside of the West Indian and specifically Jamaican.

Oh Lord, the man must be mad. Silence him, stop him, call in a Human Rights Commission before it's too late!

Yet there is nothing racist about seeking answers that might save the lives of young black men and much that is racist about refusing to ask basic questions for fear that politically correct credentials be damaged.

If our leaders were braver they might admit that **matriarchy** is a fundamental theme of Jamaican society and the levels of fatherless families in the country's urban centres are staggering. This culture has been transferred to Canada. Just as it has to other Jamaican diaspora communities, which experience similar rates of violent crime.

It might be comforting to see every young single mom as a saint who works three jobs and is devoted to her children, but positive caricatures are just as unhelpful as are negative ones.

There are such mothers of course, but also young women who party late and work little. Who find themselves pregnant as teenagers and mothers of several children, perhaps from different fathers, by the time they are adults.

Such problems occur to various extents in all communities, but when the only male role model is the gangster on the street corner with the loud car, loud clothes and loud gun, the chances of leading a law-abiding life are minimal.

Made even harder by a dysfunctional obsession with disrespect.

A gesture or a harmless comment can indicate lack of respect and the need to shoot. Just last week in London, England, three young black men shot a doorman point blank in the face three times because he politely asked them not to smoke. Hard to believe that this was the result of oppression, racism and lack of government programs. Especially as the victim was himself black.

Poverty? Spare me. It is deeply insulting to assume that the poor are criminals.

Also ridiculous to assume that there is genuine, crippling poverty in a country with free education, health care and subsidized housing.

If we care we will halt the platitudes and try to help. No more patronizing blather, no more false scapegoats. If we care we will risk being called names. If we care.

Source: Coren, M. (2007, July 28). End the blather. *Toronto Sun*. Available at: www.torontosun .com. Reprinted by permission of Sun Media Corporation.

Many people view social scientific theories as academic products of "impractical mental gymnastics" (Akers, 1997, p. 1), "philosophy or logic that has little relevance for real-world situations" (Miller, Schreck, & Tewksbury, 2006, p. 5), or as "fanciful ideas that have little to do with what truly motivates people" (Akers, 1997, p. 1). As a student at Ohio University repeatedly told me, people "just want the facts."[5] Whether we like it or not, facts and data do not speak for themselves; they must be interpreted (Curran & Renzetti, 2001). For example, if I ask how many glasses of water you consume in a typical day, and you report drinking at least 12 glasses, this fact can be interpreted several ways. One explanation is that you believe that drinking that much water is good for your skin. Another person might interpret your water consumption pattern as indicative of having diabetes, whereas someone else may posit that you need to hydrate because you drink large amounts of alcohol each night.

Which of the above is the best explanation? Well, the answer depends on data uncovered through empirical testing. If you don't test a theory, then it is just an opinion (Miller et al., 2006). Certainly, evaluating the strength of a theory entails a more complex process than what has been briefly described here. Still, as you will discover from reading this chapter and other relevant materials, some theories are better than others. Moreover, every theory described in this book and other criminology texts has limitations. Crime has no "pat explanation"; what we have, then, are "bad, good, and better theories" (Curran & Renzetti, 2001, p. 5).

In addition to serving as conceptual tools that help us make sense of data, theories are practical. For example, if you want solutions to problems, such as those examined in this text, you must first identify their causes. In fact, almost every policy or strategy developed to prevent or control crime is derived from some theory or theories (Akers, 1997; DeKeseredy et al., 2005). Nevertheless, some, if not many, policies currently in place have been derived from what hundreds of international criminologists have viewed as bad theories of crime. It is two such examples that I turn to first. These perspectives are generally referred to as early theories of female crime (Chesney-Lind & Shelden, 2003).

Early Theories[6]

Lombroso and the Born Criminal

Cesare Lombroso (1835–1909) was a **positivist criminologist**. Positivism assumes that human behaviour is determined and can be measured (Curran & Renzetti, 2001). As John Hagan (1985), among others, correctly points out, within the discipline of criminology today is "an enduring commitment to measurement" (p. 78). Further, regardless of how many important progressive changes have occurred in contemporary North American society (the *Canadian Charter of Rights and Freedoms*, for example), racist, sexist, and classist visions of females in conflict with the law persist. Lombroso played a major role in setting the stage for such views (Belknap, 2007).

Lombroso and William Ferrero (1895) published one of the first attempts to explain female crime in *The Female Offender*, a book that continues to be influential today (Hahn Rafter & Gibson, 2004). For example, as widely read and cited feminist criminologist Meda Chesney-Lind (1999) points out in box 2.4, this book heavily informs Canadian journalist Patricia Pearson's (1997) controversial analysis of violent women. Positivists such as Lombroso were (and in many ways still are) concerned with drawing our attention to the characteristics of criminals rather than their behaviours (Steffensmeier & Broidy, 2001).

Box 2.4   Lombroso's Influence in the Late 1990s

Much of what Pearson's work serves up … is old hat. Consider that Lombroso spent a good part of his book, *The Female Offender*, combing through the sensationalistic crimes of violent women. Lombroso, though, spared no thought for the equity approach in violence; instead, he felt that "the female criminal is doubly exceptional, as a woman and as a criminal." Normal women, he argued, are kept on the path of virtue by "maternity, piety, weakness," which means that the "wickedness" of the female offender "must be enormous before it could triumph over so many obstacles" (Lombroso, 1958, pp. 151–152). Lombroso then presents a series of historic [*sic*] and contemporary vignettes of violent women engaged in chilling and brutal crimes. His examples include mothers who killed their children, women who killed spouses and lovers, women who killed their rivals, women who killed other family members, women who instigated and enticed others to kill, and women who killed for material gain.

Now consider Pearson's chapters which include discussions of women who abuse and kill children, women who assault their spouses and lovers, and women who kill with others and women who kill alone (including women serial killers). Pretty similar in my estimation. Also similar is the reliance on details (usually gruesome) of specific women's crimes.

Source: Chesney-Lind, M. (1999). [Review of the book *When she was bad: Violent women and the myth of innocence.*] *Women and Criminal Justice, 10*(4), 114–118.

Deemed the "father of positivist criminology," Lombroso was heavily influenced by Charles Darwin's evolutionary studies. Like Darwin, Lombroso believed the best way to study a scientific issue was to develop a research hypothesis, then go directly to the relevant subject to measure or observe.

Lombroso, an Italian physician who specialized in psychiatry, was performing an autopsy on a violent criminal whose skull, he thought, was more suited to an animal than to a human. From there, he developed a perspective that criminals were "biological throwbacks" or *atavistic*. In other words, he saw criminals as not as far along the evolutionary ladder as law-abiding human beings. For Lombroso, atavistic people shared a number of characteristics, such as chimpanzee-like ears, bumps on their heads, large jaws, and so on.

Lombroso and Ferrero argued that because many female offenders were very young, they showed fewer atavistic characteristics than male criminals. According to these theorists:

Very often, too, in women, the [degenerate] type is disguised by youth with its absence of wrinkles and the plumpness which conceals the size of the jaw and cheek-bones, thus softening the masculine and savage features. Then when the hair is black and plentiful … and the eyes are bright, a not unpleasing appearance is presented. In short, let a female delinquent be young and we can overlook her degenerate type, and even regard her as beautiful; the sexual instinct misleading us here as it does in making us attribute to women more of the sensitiveness and passion than they really possess. And in the same way, when she is being tried on a criminal charge, we are inclined to excuse, as noble impulses of passion, an act arises from the most cynical calculations. (Lombroso & Ferrero, 1895, p. 97)

Lombroso and Ferrero (1895) maintained that women were much less likely to commit crimes than men because of their special biological traits, such as their "piety, maternity, want of passion, sexual coldness, weakness and undeveloped intelligence" (p. 151). When a woman did commit a crime, however, she was viewed as a "monster," one whose "wickedness must have been enormous before it could triumph over so many obstacles" (p. 152). Interestingly, *Monster* is the title of a popular 2003 Hollywood movie based loosely on the life of female serial killer Aileen Wuornos. Charlize Theron won the Academy Award for Best Actress for her portrayal of Wuornos as a "masculine premeditating killer" of seven men in the late 1980s and early 1990s (Chesney-Lind & Eliason, 2006).

Many social scientists, especially feminists, agree with Gavigan's (1983) assertion that it "seems almost beyond absurd" that Lombroso's theory "should have ever been given credence" (p. 77). However, Lombroso was a "man of his times," and his perspective is a reflection of "malestream resistances to the suffragist movement and 19th century feminism" (Faith, 1993, p. 44). In addition to being denounced for propounding misogynistic views, Lombroso and Ferrero's work is attacked on methodological grounds. Certainly, they made extravagant claims without providing strong empirical support (Boritch, 1997). Their analysis also dismisses the influence of broader social, political, economic, and cultural determinants of crime (Smart, 1976). Despite these flaws, as Chesney-Lind and Shelden (1992) point out, Lombroso's work "actually set the tone for much of the later work on female delinquency and crime" (p. 56), including work done in Canada. For example, Patricia Pearson's (1997) focus on Aileen Wuornos in *When She Was Bad: Violent Women and the Myth of Innocence* perpetuates "homophobic, racist, and sexist notions of women's offending" (Chesney-Lind & Eliason, 2006, p. 39).

Contemporary academics such as Belinda Morrissey (2003) and journalists such as Pearson (1997) are not the only people influenced by Lombroso and Ferrero's (1895) perspective on female offenders. For example, if your knowledge of female crime is based only on watching US movies, you would probably conclude that women in conflict with the law are masculinized monsters, lesbian villains, incarcerated teenage predators, or pathological killer beauties (DeKeseredy, 2000; DeKeseredy & Schwartz, 1996; Faith, 1993; Holmlund, 1994). Think about the portrayal of female criminals in such popular movies as *Single White Female, Basic Instinct, Fatal Attraction, The Hunger,* and *The Hand That Rocks the Cradle.* Regarding the movie *Monster,* Chesney-Lind and Eliason observe:

> The film used several strategies to masculinize the character of Lee Wuornos. She is dressed in men's clothing, she is depicted as physically larger and dominates her petite, more feminine partner … Christina Ricci, who in no way physically resembles her real-life partner, Tyria Moore. Wuornos is depicted as the sole provider and the one who controls physical contact in the relationship. Placing the film's killing spree entirely within a nine-month time frame beginning with the initiation of her intimate relationship with a woman implies that her lesbian relationship, rather than her appalling life circumstances up to that point in her life, were to blame for her murders. Even the title suggests that to be lesbian and to be violent casts one into a non-human role. For a movie that is supposedly sympathetic to the horribly abused Wuornos, to name the film *Monster* is to perpetuate myths about the woman.[7] (Chesney-Lind and Eliason, 2006, p. 37)

Pollak and the Masked Nature of Female Crime

Otto Pollak's *The Criminality of Women* (1950) and his co-edited collection of readings, *Family Dynamics and Female Sexual Delinquency* (Pollak & Friedman, 1969), were heavily influenced by the positivistic approach of Lombroso and Ferrero's *The Female Offender* (1895), despite being published more than 50 years later. Pollak developed in *The Criminality of Women* (1950) what Ellis and DeKeseredy (1996) refer to as a *dual-focus theory* of female crime, in which he focuses on both the biological causes of female crime and causes of the reactions to female offences.

Pollak (1950) asserts that biological factors cause females to commit crimes as frequently as males; however, female crimes are more likely to involve sex, or cunning and deceit, or both. At the same time, official crime statistics (police arrest data, for example) show that much female crime is masked by the greater leniency with which female criminals are treated by chivalrous criminal justice personnel, such as police officers, judges, and prosecutors. Their chivalry is rooted in the social construction of women as passive, dependent, and requiring the protection of men. Pollak's key point is that women are better than men at hiding their offences (Belknap, 2007), which explains why many of their crimes have never attracted the agents of social control. Pollak associated women's ability to deceive criminal justice officials with the passive role they traditionally play during sexual intercourse:

> Not enough attention has been paid to the physiological fact that man must achieve an erection in order to perform the sex act and will not be able to hide his failure. His lack of positive emotion in the sexual sphere must become overt to the partner and pretence of sexual response is impossible for him, if it is lacking. Woman's body, however, permits such a pretense to a certain degree and lack of orgasm does not prevent her ability to participate in the sex act. (Pollak, 1950, p. 138)

According to Pollak (1950), "It cannot be denied that this basic physiological difference may well have a great influence on the degree of confidence which the two sexes have in the possible concealment and thus on their character pattern in this respect" (p. 10). Concealment and deceit are learned during childhood, at a time when "natural aggressions are inhibited and forced into concealed channels" (p. 11).

By now, many readers, especially the women, are either laughing or saying to themselves, "Unbelievable!" Well, not surprisingly, like Lombroso and Ferraro's (1895) offering, Pollak's theory lacks empirical support (Ellis & DeKeseredy, 1996). Further, his account does not recognize that women's traditionally passive role during sexual relations may be culturally, not biologically, determined. Another point to consider is that instead of hiding orgasms, women may not be experiencing them due to their partners' insensitivity to certain sexual acts that give the women pleasure (Belknap, 2007). Pollak's work is also criticized for ignoring the structural (that is, gender hierarchy) source of male–female differences in crime and its control. This theory assumes that the inferior status of women is biologically determined and ignores the so-called dark side of chivalry; that is, women are often treated more harshly by the police, especially women of colour (Barak, Leighton, & Flavin, 2007; DeKeseredy, 2000).

Contemporary Theories

If you continue taking courses in criminology and criminal justice, you will be exposed to many theories that ignore or trivialize female crime. Many criminologists once thought women were naturally inhibited from committing crime. Consider the words of Cohen (1955) in his widely read and cited book, *Delinquent Boys*:

> My skin has nothing of the quality of down or silk, there is nothing limpid or flute-like about my voice. I am a total loss with needle and thread, my posture and carriage are wholly lacking in grace. These imperfections cause me no distress—if anything, they are gratifying—because I conceive myself to be a man and want people to recognize me as a full-fledged, unequivocal representative of my sex. My wife, on the other hand, is not greatly embarrassed by her inability to tinker with or talk about the internal organs of a car, by her modest attainments in arithmetic or by her inability to lift heavy objects. Indeed, I am reliably informed that many women—I do not suggest that my wife is among them—often affect ignorance, frailty and emotional sustainability because to do so otherwise would be out of keeping with a reputation for indubitable femininity. In short, people do not simply want to excel; they want to excel as a man or as a woman ... Even when they adopt behaviour which is considered disreputable by conventional standards, the tendency is to be disreputable in ways that are characteristically masculine and feminine. (pp. 137–138)

Cohen's perspective exemplifies what is commonly labelled a **strain theory**, a variation of Robert K. Merton's (1938) **anomie theory**. As Hackler (1994) notes, "A long-standing deficiency of most strain theories is their neglect of the gender issue" (p. 198). To address this problem, Freda Adler (1975) and Rita Simon (1975) published important books that are outgrowths of strain perspectives. Here, and in many other sources, their theoretical contributions are referred to as women's liberation/emancipation theories of female crime.

Women's Liberation/Emancipation Theories

For Adler and Simon, the female nature does not inhibit crime. Instead, women lack opportunities to break the law; if given such opportunities, they would act just like men. Adler (1975) and Simon (1975) are among the "first wave of women" of their generation to conduct criminological research and to help legitimize serious research on female crime and punishment (Faith, 1993).

Adler (1975, p. 16) analyzed US Federal Bureau of Investigation (FBI) arrest statistics and found that between 1960 and 1972:

- the number of women arrested for robbery increased by 277 percent, whereas the male rate rose 169 percent;
- the female embezzlement arrest rate increased 280 percent compared with a 50 percent increase for men;
- the female larceny arrest rate rose by 303 percent compared with an 82 percent increase for men; and
- the number of women arrested for burglary increased by 168 percent, whereas the male rate rose by 63 percent.

What caused the increases in female arrest rates? Adler argued that although the women's liberation movement had opened up new roles for women in the military, education, business, and politics, it also opened up new roles for women in crime, which had historically been dominated by men. According to Adler (1975):

> But women, like men, do not live by bread alone. Almost every other aspect of their life has been similarly altered. The changing status of women as it affects family, marriage, employment and social position has been well documented by all types of sociologists. But there is a curious hiatus: the movement for full equity has a darker side which has been slighted even by the scientific community ...
>
> In the same way that women are demanding equal opportunity in the fields of legitimate endeavor, a similar number of determined women are forcing their way into the world of major crimes. (p. 13)

Girls are not exempt from Adler's liberation/emancipation thesis. She argued that the women's movement seems to be "having a twofold influence on juvenile crimes" (1975, p. 95). As she put it:

> Girls are involved in more drinking, stealing, gang activity, and fighting—behavior in keeping with their adoption of male roles. We also find increases in the total number of female deviancies. The departure from the safety of traditional female roles and the testing of uncertain alternative roles coincide with turmoil of adolescence creating criminogenic risk factors, which are bound to create this increase. These considerations help explain the fact that between 1960 and 1972 national arrests for major crimes show a jump for boys of 82 percent—for girls, 306 percent. (Adler, 1975, p. 95)

What Adler (1975) refers to as the "shady aspect of liberation" (p. 13) is also a major part of Simon's (1975) theory. However, Simon departs from Adler by arguing that the increase in female crime is limited mainly to property offences and that violent female crime has decreased. Moreover, Simon attributes the decrease in female violence to feminism, which makes women "feel more liberated physically, emotionally, and legally" and decreases their frustration and anger. Consequently, women's desire to kill the male objects of their anger or frustration on whom they are dependent (lovers, husbands, and cohabiting partners, for example) declines (p. 40). Simon also predicted that female emancipation would contribute to an increase in female white-collar crime for the following reasons:

> As women become more liberated from hearth and home and become involved in full-time jobs, they are more likely to engage in the types of crime for which their occupations provide them with the greatest opportunities. Furthermore ... as a function of both expanded consciousness, as well as occupational opportunities, women's participation role and involvement in crime are expected to *change* and *increase*. (Simon, 1975, p. 1, emphasis in original)

Simon's opportunities theory of female crime is described in figure 2.1.

As Curran and Renzetti (2001) remind us, the liberation or emancipation theories described here should be commended for forcing "a contemporary reassessment of the relationship between sex and participation in criminal activity" (p. 126). However, these perspectives remain problematic. First, they are based on police statistics, which are not

Figure 2.1   Simon's Opportunities Model of Female Crime

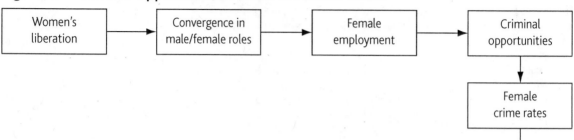

Source: DeKeseredy, W.S., Ellis, D., & Alvi, S. (2005). *Deviance and crime: Theory, research and policy.* Cincinnati: LexisNexis, p. 45.

accurate indicators of the extent of crimes committed by men and women. Police statistics tell us only the number of offences that police officers officially deem to be criminal; many illicit activities either never come to their attention or are ignored. Second, the number of females arrested in Adler's (1975) sample was so low that a small rise translated into major changes in percentage terms (Chesney-Lind & Shelden, 2003). When comparing male and female arrest rates, Adler (1975) did not control for the absolute base numbers from which the rates of increase were calculated. Thus, the rate changes she reports in her book, *Sisters in Crime,* are exaggerated (Curran & Renzetti, 2001).

Another example is warranted here. If, hypothetically, the absolute base number of Canadian women who committed homicide was two in 2007 and rose to four in 2008, one could argue that the female homicide rate rose by an alarming 100 percent. On the other hand, if the absolute number of males who committed homicide in 2007 was 750 and rose to 1,000 in 2008, the male rate would appear to be markedly lower than the female rate change. As Curran and Renzetti (2001) point out, "if we look only at percent changes without taking into account these major absolute base differences, we end up with a very distorted picture of men's and women's involvement in crime" (p. 126).

Several other problems are widely cited with the theories of Adler and Simon;[8] however, their popularity, at least in the minds of the general public, conservative politicians, and many journalists is undiminished (Chesney-Lind & Eliason, 2006; Chesney-Lind & Pasko, 2004; DeKeseredy, 2000). Indeed, today, it is not unusual to read newspaper stories similar to the one that appeared on December 23, 1992, in the *Washington Post*: "Delinquent Girls Achieving a Violent Equality in DC" (Lewis, 1992). Here in Canada, the *Alberta Report* ("You've Come a Long Way," 1995) similarly argued, "Girls, it used to be said, were made of sugar and spice. Not anymore. The latest crop of teenage girls can be as violent, malicious and downright evil as the boys. In fact, they're leading the explosion in youth crime. It's an unexpected byproduct of the feminist push for equality" (p. 1).

Several academics have also recently recycled the work of Adler and Simon (Chesney-Lind & Pasko, 2004). For example, based on their analysis of New York City arrest data, Baskin, Sommers, and Fagan (1993) argue that "the growing drug markets and a marked disappearance of males" interact with other factors in poor inner-city communities "to create social and economic opportunity structures open to women's increasing participation in violent crime" (p. 406). Next, we review another widely read and cited recent example of what Chesney-Lind and Pasko (2004, p. 22) refer to as "essentially a not-too-subtle variation of the ... 'liberation hypothesis' ": power-control theory.

Power-Control Theory

Described in figure 2.2 and often referred to as either a feminist or a social control perspective, the power-control theory developed by Hagan, Gillis, and Simpson (1987) and Hagan (1989) attempts to answer the question, "What differences do the relative class positions of husbands and wives in the workplace make for gender variations in parental control and delinquent behavior of adolescents?" (Hagan et al., 1987, p. 789). They argue that lower rates of female delinquency are present in a family where the father is controlling, and that more equal male and female rates of delinquency are indicated when parental power is equalized.

Figure 2.2   Power-Control Theory

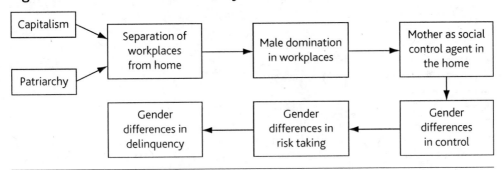

Source: DeKeseredy, W.S., Ellis, D., & Alvi, S. (2005). *Deviance and crime: Theory, research and policy*. Cincinnati: LexisNexis, p. 46.

Delinquency is, according to Hagan (1989), a type of risk-taking behaviour. It is fun, liberating, and gives youths the "chance to pursue publicly some of the pleasures that are symbolic of adult male status outside the family" (pp. 152–153). However, boys are more willing to take such risks than are girls, because they are supervised less closely and punished less severely by their parents. Thus, the "taste for such risk-taking is channelled along sexually stratified lines" (p. 154). Hence, Hagan asserts that we need to focus on the relationship between the family and the workforce.

Hagan et al. (1987) contend that parents' positions of power in the workplace are reproduced at home and affect the probability of their children committing delinquent acts. These theorists identify two general types of family structure based on parents' power in the workplace. The first type is **patriarchal**. It consists of a husband who works outside the home in a position of authority and a wife who is delegated responsibility for socializing and controlling the children. Such families are typically working-class and "socially reproduce daughters who focus their futures around domestic labor and consumption as contrasted with sons who are prepared for participation in direct production" (p. 791). In these families, male children are encouraged to take risks to prepare them for participation in the labour force, whereas females are closely supervised and are expected to grow up to be like their mothers and to avoid risk-taking behaviour.

The second type of family structure identified by Hagan et al. (1987) is *egalitarian.* In egalitarian families, husbands and wives work outside the home in positions of authority. An egalitarian family "socially reproduces daughters who are prepared along with sons to join the production sphere" (p. 792). Further, both sons and daughters are inclined to engage in risk-taking activities, such as delinquency.

Although some empirical evidence supports the power-control theory and its elaborated version (see McCarthy, Hagan, & Woodward, 1999), this perspective has several key problems. For example, having a job does not necessarily mean that a woman has equal power at home. Although a growing number of men help around the house, most married working women do all of the cooking, cleaning, and childcare, and most of them lack equal decision-making power (Alvi, DeKeseredy, & Ellis, 2000). Moreover, many middle- and upper-class women are beaten, psychologically abused, and sexually assaulted by their husbands or cohabiting partners (DeKeseredy et al., 2005; DeKeseredy & MacLeod, 1997; Finkelhor & Yllo, 1985).

In addition to neglecting the fact that a place in the paid marketplace does not automatically translate into power at home, Hagan and his colleagues ignore the influence of the following important variables: social class, negative parental sanctions, peer group influence, and the role of the school (Chesney-Lind & Shelden, 2003). However, from a feminist standpoint, "the worst problem of all" is that the power-control theory is a variation of the "women's liberation/emancipation-leads-to-crime" theories previously reviewed in this chapter (DeKeseredy & Schwartz, 1996). Of course, Hagan (1989) and Hagan et al. (1987) do not explicitly state that women's liberation causes female crime. Still, they strongly suggest that "mother's liberation" in joining the paid labour force causes daughters to commit crimes, which leads to an obvious discrepancy: despite a major increase of women in the paid workforce over the past several decades, female delinquency has shown no corresponding increase (Chesney-Lind & Pasko, 2004). In contrast, major *decreases* in self-reports of serious female delinquency are evident during this time period (Chesney-Lind, 2004; Chesney-Lind & Belknap, 2002).

Power-control theory, like the perspectives developed by Adler (1975), Simon (1975), and other mainstream criminological theorists (for example, Cohen, 1955), is referred to by Beirne and Messerschmidt (1995) as an example of the "disregard and misrepresentation of gender and women in a criminological theory" (p. 549). Feminist theories, on the other hand, are specifically designed to overcome this problem, and they warrant considerable attention here.

Feminist Theories[9]

Historically and in the current political atmosphere termed by journalist Susan Faludi (1991) as "the backlash," a substantial number of people mock feminist researchers, practitioners, and activists (DeKeseredy & Dragiewicz, 2007). Heavily influenced by the media and by some religious groups and conservative politicians, these critics equate feminism with hating men, not shaving one's legs, going braless, being gay or lesbian, and advocating pro-choice. Of course, some feminists fit into one or more of these categories; however, many men and women are feminists. In fact, I am a feminist man.[10] I and other feminists are united by a deep desire to eliminate all forms of gender inequality, several of which are described in other parts of this book. Moreover, as Claire Renzetti (1993) correctly points out, the goal of feminist scholars is "not to push men out so as to pull women in, but rather to gender the study of crime and criminal justice" (p. 234). Like Kathleen Daly and Meda Chesney-Lind (1988, p. 502) and other feminist scholars (for example, Maidment, 2006), I do not equate gender with sex. Instead, following Edwin Schur (1984), I refer to gender as "the sociocultural and psychological shaping, patterning, and evaluating of male and female behavior" (p. 10).

Because feminism takes many forms, painting all feminists with the same brush can be misleading. MaDonna Maidment (2006), for example, contends that at least 12 variations of feminist criminological theory exist, with major debates within each. For the purpose of this chapter, I offer Kathleen Daly and Meda Chesney-Lind's (1988) definition, which refers to feminism as a "set of theories about women's oppression and a set of strategies for change" (p. 502). Their elements of feminism make it distinct from other perspectives occasionally referred to as "male stream," because the latter theories omit and/or misrepresent both gender and women's experiences (Messerschmidt, 1993):

- Gender is not a natural fact but a complex social, historical, and cultural product; it is related to, but not simply derived from, biological sex difference and reproductive capacities.
- Gender and gender relations order social life and social institutions in fundamental ways.
- Gender relations and constructs of masculinity and femininity are not symmetrical but are based on an organizing principle of men's superiority to and social and political dominance over women.
- Systems of knowledge reflect men's view of the natural and social world; the production of knowledge is gendered.
- Women should be at the centre of intellectual inquiry, not peripheral, invisible, or appendages to men (Daly & Chesney-Lind, 1988, p. 504).

Further, feminist scholars attempt to address how the intersection of race, class, and gender shape both women's involvement in rule-breaking activities and societal reactions to their appearance or behaviour (DeKeseredy et al., 2005; Miller, 2003; Schwartz & Milovanovic, 1996).

Before reviewing several feminist theories of crime and its control, I should note the contention of some scholars that a feminist criminology does not exist because neither feminism nor criminology is a monolithic enterprise (Daly & Chesney-Lind, 1988; Morris, 1987). In other words, scholars use different feminist perspectives to explain a variety of criminological problems (Maidment, 2006), such as those discussed throughout this text.

Again, at least one dozen feminist criminological theories exist, each of which takes a distinct approach to understanding gender issues, asks different questions, and offers different theories of crime and the control of crime. In the sections that follow, I will limit my description of feminist contributions to the four major perspectives most frequently outlined in the feminist literature on criminology. Neither reality nor scholars fit neatly into slots. Writings by most feminist authors may easily bridge two or three perspectives, or may not easily fit any of them at all. Still, these categories are the ones most frequently identified by leading experts in the field. I begin by describing elements of liberal feminism.

LIBERAL FEMINISM

Arguably, of all the feminist theories developed, liberal feminism is the most widely recognized in North America. Liberal feminists contend that women are discriminated against based on their sex; consequently, they are denied access to the same political, financial, career, and personal opportunities as men (Messerschmidt, 1993). For example, as of August 15, 2007, only 22 percent of Prime Minister Stephen Harper's 32-member Cabinet were women. Moreover, none of the female Cabinet ministers was in charge of Harper's top priorities: Arctic sovereignty, the environment, and the fight against crime (Delacourt, 2007). Liberal feminists argue that such problems can be eliminated by:

* removing all obstacles to women's access to education, paid employment, political activity, and other public institutions;
* enabling women to participate equally with men in the public sphere; and
* enacting legal changes (Daly & Chesney-Lind, 1988, p. 537).

The problem of gender inequality can be solved by clearing the way for "women's rapid integration into what has been the world of men" (Ehrenreich & English, 1978, p. 19) and by eliminating sexist stereotypes promoted by gender-role socialization in domestic settings, educational contexts, the media, and the government (Messerschmidt, 1993).

Among the several criminologists who have used liberal feminist theory to explain crime, perhaps the most famous are Freda Adler (1975) and Rita Simon (1975). Although the women's crime wave they described has never happened (Chesney-Lind & Pasko, 2004; Gora, 1982; Steffensmeier & Steffensmeier, 1980), their perspectives are very popular among journalists. Further, although women are not becoming more violent, societal reactions to their behaviours have become more punitive, especially in the United States. For example, the public is now more likely to report violent females, the police are more likely to arrest them, the criminal justice system is more likely to prosecute them, and judges and juries are more likely to convict them (Davis, 2003; Maidment, 2006; Sudbury, 2005). Women who challenge the traditional patriarchal gender-role structure are viewed by some as "unruly women" worthy of punishment (Faith, 1993; Messerschmidt, 1986).

SOCIALIST FEMINISM

Socialist feminism is informed by some elements of Marxist and radical feminism. Marxist feminists view capitalism as the primary cause of both crime and male dominance over women, whereas radical feminists see male power and privilege as the root cause of all social relations, inequality, and crime (DeKeseredy & Schwartz, 1996). However, in socialist feminist analyses of crime and other social problems, neither class nor patriarchy is presumed to be dominant. Instead, class and gender relations are viewed as equally important, "inextricably intertwined," and "inseparable," interacting to determine the social order at any particular time in history (Jaggar, 1983; Maidment, 2006; Messerschmidt, 1986). Socialist feminists, such as Beirne and Messerschmidt (1991), argue that "to understand class ... we must recognize how it is structured by gender, conversely, to understand gender requires an examination of how it is structured by class." Thus, socialist feminists assert that we are influenced by both class and gender relations.

One of the most important contributions to the development of a social feminist theory of crime was the publication of Messerschmidt's *Capitalism, Patriarchy, and Crime* (1986). Like other socialist feminist accounts, Messerschmidt's perspective treats class and gender as equally important, interacting factors that shape the types and seriousness of crime. He contends:

> It is the powerful (in both the gender and class spheres) who do most of the damage to society, not as is commonly supposed, the disadvantaged, poor, and subordinate. The interaction of gender and class creates positions of power and powerlessness in the gender/class hierarchy, resulting in different types and degrees of criminality and varying opportunities for engaging in them. Just as the powerful have more legitimate opportunities, so they have more illegitimate opportunities. (Messerschmidt, 1986, p. 42)

Women and girls are not major criminal threats to Canadian society. Thus, according to Messerschmidt's social feminist perspective on social control:

> The criminal justice system deals with females as it does with marginalized males: its task is to control nontraditional behavior. Publicizing and exaggerating women's involvement in serious crime and linking it to the women's movement serves to delegitimize the general expansion of women into nontraditional roles in several ways. First, since criminal justice personnel are more likely today to label a female engaged in violence as criminal, female involvement in serious crime is exaggerated. Second, just as the state publicizes female involvement in criminality, it hides the criminality of *powerful males*. The overall contribution of women to serious crime is thereby magnified. Third, black and poor females in particular are publicized as increasingly dangerous. As with male offenders, racism and class bias in the criminal justice system results in more black and poor females being imprisoned than their white counterparts who have committed similar crimes. (Messerschmidt, 1986, p. 80, emphasis in original)

Messerschmidt's (1986) theory is directly relevant to the Canadian context. For example, as noted in subsequent chapters of this book and in other sources, First Nations women are more likely than female members of the dominant culture (those of European descent, for example) to be arrested and spend time in penal institutions for not paying fines. Further, although First Nations people officially comprise only 3.3 percent of Canada's population, nearly 30 percent of the women in federal prisons are First Nations (Griffiths, 2007). Unsurprisingly, most Aboriginal women view the Canadian criminal justice system as racist (DeKeseredy, 2000).

Messerschmidt's theory attempted to improve on radical and Marxist feminism by simultaneously explaining class and gender differences in crime; however, his perspective has several limitations. Messerschmidt agrees that two views in particular are problematic and need to be corrected in future theoretical work. First, although Messerschmidt tried to develop a perspective in which class and gender were equally important, some reviewers, including Carol Smart (1987), argue that his theory did not achieve this goal because it "retained basic Marxist formulations" onto which he simply added gender (p. 328). This is a difficult hurdle to overcome. Marxist formulations, as we have seen, are primarily interested in finding the "underlying cause" of current social arrangements. Although **Marxism** has several variations, all believe that the ultimate causative factor is economic interests. That is, social institutions, such as law, education, political structures, or our general beliefs, are in place because they essentially serve the interests of the dominant economic class. Feminist theory, on the other hand, has been mainly interested in our society's patriarchal nature, in which men have attained political and economic power over women. A feminist theorist "is more likely to see patriarchy as the cause of the problem being examined, and to leave aside the question of the cause of patriarchy itself" (Schwartz & Slatin, 1984, p. 246). Merging these two theories is particularly difficult.

In Messerschmidt's theory, crime was mainly seen as the product of patriarchal capitalism. In other words, those who committed crime were seen as having no creativity, perhaps unable to exercise free will or free choice, or even incapable of seeing crime as a meaningful social construct in itself (Maidment, 2006). The difficulty, as Messerschmidt agrees, is finding the middle ground where we allow for individual creativity without losing sight of the tremendous influence of social structures. After all, residents of remote northern Canadian communities act differently from residents of urban capitalist enclaves, such as Toronto.

Messerschmidt (1993) used these and other criticisms to develop a relatively new feminist theory of crime that emphasizes the relationship between masculinities and crime. It is to his *structured action theory* of corporate crime that I now turn, an account that builds on his earlier socialist feminist work.

STRUCTURED ACTION THEORY

Few women commit corporate crimes[11] in Canada and elsewhere (DeKeseredy, 2000; Friedrichs, 2007). For Messerschmidt (1993), to understand why men monopolize these "crimes of the powerful" (Pearce, 1976), we must examine the gender and racial division of labour within corporations. Men, especially white males, have the major decision-making power in corporations. Although women occupy about 40 percent of all corporate management, executive, and administrative positions in the United States, they are generally restricted to lower-level positions, such as personnel and affirmative action (DeKeseredy et al., 2005; Mooney, Knox, & Schacht, 2005). Because these management positions generally do not lead to more powerful positions within corporations, women have relatively few opportunities to commit criminal acts that further the goals of the corporation.

Messerschmidt further argues that "old-boy networks" play a key role in maintaining the gender division of labour and perpetuating corporate crime. Such networks achieve this goal by selectively recruiting junior men who share members' norms, attitudes, values, and standards of conduct. If these young executives meet their senior counterparts' expectations, they are rewarded with money, authority, corporate control, and power over women. Senior executives also teach their recruits to act according to executive conceptions of masculinity. One of the most important practices that exemplifies these conceptions of the sacrifice of personal principles to meet corporate goals is the accumulation of profit through illegitimate means.

If young executives have "nondemanding moral codes," they are more likely to be promoted to senior positions that free them to, if necessary, commit corporate crimes. Such behaviour benefits them and the corporation. According to Messerschmidt (1993):

Corporate crime simply assists the corporation and young upwardly mobile men to reach their goals. In other words, corporate crime is a practice with which men gain corporate power through maintaining profit margins. Moreover, as corporate executives do corporate crime, they simultaneously do masculinity—construct a masculinity specific to their position in the gender, race, and occupational divisions of labor and power. (p. 135)

Corporate masculinity is distinct from those masculinities found on the street, on assembly lines, in the family, and elsewhere. For example, being a corporate "real man" entails "calculation, rationality as well as struggle for success, reward, and corporate recognition" (Messerschmidt, 1993, p. 136). Male executives compete with each other and measure masculinity according to their success in the business community. Corporate crime, then, is one technique of advancing the "gendered strategy of action."

Corporations face many obstacles in their attempts to increase profits legitimately, such as uncertain and competitive markets, fluctuating sales, government regulations, and relations with unions (DeKeseredy et al., 2005). Messerschmidt asserts that these obstacles also threaten white corporate executive masculinity. Corporate crime, then, is a solution to both of these problems. That is, illegal and unethical practices are techniques of re-establishing or maintaining both a particular type of masculinity and profit margins.

As Curran and Renzetti (2001) put it, "What about women?" (p. 224). Indeed, some readers may now ask, "How is structured action theory different from mainstream theories that focus only on women? This is a theory about men!" Although Messerschmidt's account is about men, it is a feminist perspective. To explain why so few women commit corporate crime, Messerschmidt seeks to understand the ways in which patriarchal forces shape crime, which is difficult by focusing only on women. Messerschmidt's account of corporate crime is one of the first to theorize the relationship between gender, class, and race/ethnicity.

So far, hypotheses based on Messerschmidt's structured action theory have not been tested. Ideally, other scholars will do so by conducting interviews with junior and senior corporate executives.

POVERTY, UNEMPLOYMENT, FAMILY VIOLENCE, AND FEMALE CRIME

Another group of feminists focuses on three key factors that propel women into property crimes, prostitution, and drugs: poverty, unemployment, and family violence.[12] The relationship between these variables, the role of law, and girls' crime are described by Chesney-Lind and Pasko (2004):

> Young women, a large number of whom are on the run from sexual abuse and parental neglects, are forced by the very statutes designed to protect them into the lives of escaped convicts. Unable to enroll in school or to take a job to support themselves because they fear detection, young female runaways are forced into the streets. Here they engage in panhandling, petty theft, and occasional prostitution to survive. Young women in conflict with their parents (often for legitimate reasons) may actually be forced by present laws into petty criminal activity, prostitution and drug use. (p. 28)

Again, other feminist theories address female involvement in crime and societal reactions to these offences. Moreover, theories offered by Adler (1975), Simon (1975), and by Hagan and his colleagues (1987) are considered by several criminologists (for example, Curran & Renzetti, 2001) to be liberal feminist perspectives.

EVALUATION OF FEMINIST THEORIES

Feminist criminology is no longer in its infancy, and feminist theories have made many important contributions to the study of problems and issues discussed throughout this book. Moreover, feminist theorists and researchers have had a major impact on criminal justice policy (DeKeseredy et al., 2005; Lilly et al., 2006). Consider that, due in large part to the efforts of feminist scholars, Canadian men are no longer exempt from the purview of the law for raping their wives.[13] Still, because feminist work calls into question conservative "male-centred" ways of understanding crime and social control, it is constantly challenged and often ridiculed by conservative students, practitioners, and academics "who incorrectly" reduce feminist criticisms of gender-blind theories and research to "an attack on the sex of the researcher" (Flavin, 2004, p. 36).

Another common conservative attack on feminist scholarship is that it offers little more than single-factor explanations driven by a political agenda instead of "value-free" scientific thought (Dutton, 2006; Fekete, 1994). By now, you are aware that there is more than one feminist perspective on crime and more are being constructed to combine both macro- and micro-level factors, such as unemployment, globalization, deindustrialization, life events, stress, familial and societal patriarchy, and other factors. Note, too, that feminists have no problem being labelled as political. After all, as Sartre (1964, p. 29) states, "all writing is political," and feminists hope that their work will help end much pain and suffering. Moreover, feminists, like many other contemporary social scientists, contend that no scientific method, theory, or policy proposal is value-free, nor are the theories, methods, and policies advanced by conservative critics of feminism, such as Canadian psychologist Donald Dutton (2006).

In what remains one of the most widely read and cited social scientific articles in the world, Howard Becker (1967) asks scholars, "Whose side are we on?" Although some paint feminists as ideologues and portray themselves as objective scientists (Dutton, 2006, for example), in reality they are advancing a political agenda that supports the goals and claims of conservative political movements determined to oppose all attempts to achieve total gender equality (DeKeseredy & Dragiewicz, 2007). Most feminist scholars, on the other hand, put their politics up front for all to scrutinize and are committed to putting gender at the forefront of research, theory construction, and policy development.

Feminist theoretical work has also been critiqued by feminists and other progressive scholars. In fact, as Miller (2003) reminds us, "some of the most important critiques of feminist criminology have come from debates *among* feminists" (p. 22, emphasis in original). For example, the influence of class and race or ethnicity requires more attention, given that the experiences of poor females and women of colour are often distinct from the experiences of women who are economically privileged or of European descent. Consider women living in Canadian public housing, who report much higher rates of male violence than women in the general population (DeKeseredy, Alvi, Schwartz, & Perry, 1999; DeKeseredy, Alvi, Schwartz, & Tomaszewski, 2003).

Feminist theorists have also not paid much attention to white-collar and corporate crime. Some feminists, such as Messerschmidt, are addressing this concern; however, much more work is required. Feminists also need to develop a sophisticated theory of women's aggression and violence that situates these behaviours in the context of patriarchy (Chesney-Lind & Eliason, 2006).

Some criminologists (not surprisingly, male mainstream or conventional scholars) contend that it is "difficult to find direct empirical tests of feminist hypotheses" (Akers, 1997, p. 201). This difficulty, however, is not a problem for most feminist theorists, who do not want to develop accounts such Hagan et al.'s (1987) that make "global or grand theoretical statements" and generate hypotheses that are tested using "high-tech statistical analyses" (Daly & Chesney-Lind, 1988, p. 518). Nevertheless, some feminist scholars have tested hypotheses derived from feminist theories of woman abuse. For example, the late Michael D. Smith (1990), a Canadian sociologist, gathered victimization survey data from 604 women in Toronto and tested the feminist hypothesis that wife beating results from abusive husbands' adherence to the ideology of familial patriarchy. Similarly, together with some colleagues in Canada and in the United States, I have tested several feminist hypotheses using data generated by surveys of several different populations.[14]

Like all research methods (surveys, participant observation, and the like, for example), all theories have their limitations. Feminist perspectives are no exception, and attempts to address the criticisms raised here are already under way. Further, feminist theories of crime now play a key role in mapping the future of criminology. Keep in mind, too, that Sage Publications now publishes the scientific journal *Feminist Criminology*, the official journal of the American Society of Criminology's Division on Women and Crime. We can only hope that many more criminologists will answer Daly and Chesney-Lind's (1988) call to apply these perspectives to all aspects of crime and criminal justice.

Summary

This chapter reviewed several widely read and cited theories of women's and girls' involvement in crime. You can now appreciate the variety of ways in which people answer the question, "Why did she commit that crime?" Indeed, a social scientific understanding of crime and its control "contains not one vision but many" (Downes & Rock, 2003). Again, some theories are better than others, but all theories "have consequences" (Szasz, 1987). As Lilly, Cullen, and Ball (2002) remind us:

> The search for the sources of crime, then, is not done within a vacuum. Even if a theorist wishes only to ruminate about the causes of theft or violence, others will be ready to use these insights to direct efforts to do something about the crime problem. Understanding why crime occurs, then, is a prelude to developing strategies to control the behavior. (p. 5)

Unfortunately, most Canadian crime control policies are not based on sound sociological perspectives that focus on the major factors propelling women and girls into crime. Certainly, ample evidence shows that the "get tough" approaches advanced by Prime Minister Stephen Harper and other conservatives do little, if anything, to prevent many females from coming into conflict with the law. As Susan Miller (1998) puts it, "reducing crime is about getting smart, not about getting tough" (p. xxiii). She makes a valid point. As noted by Walker (1998), "One of the major obstacles in the search for sensible crime policies is the fact that there are many bad ideas" (p. 5). A prime example is a simplistic solution such as increasing the cost of committing crime. Perhaps, then, it is only fitting to end this chapter with a 10-year-old statement by Elliott Currie (1998) that is still relevant today: "In a civilized society what matters is not just *whether* we reduce crime, but *how*. And how seriously and honestly we confront that question in the coming years will be a test of our character as a nation" (p. 193, emphasis in original).

Notes

1. Many readers are likely familiar with December 6, 1989, the day that Marc Lépine killed 14 female engineering students at the École Polytechnique, an engineering school affiliated with the Université de Montréal. This terrifying event prompted the creation of the White Ribbon Campaign, a movement initiated in October 1991 by the Men's Network for Change (MNC) in Toronto, Ottawa, London, Kingston, and Montreal (DeKeseredy, Schwartz, & Alvi, 2000; Luxton, 1993). MNC drafted a document stating that violence against women is a major social problem, male silence about violence against women is complicity, and men can be part of the solution (Sluser & Kaufman, 1992).

2. From a legal standpoint, Karla Homolka does not meet the criteria of a serial killer because she was not officially found guilty in the deaths of three or more people.

3. See Chesney-Lind and Eliason (2006) and Chesney-Lind and Irwin (2008) for detailed critiques of media and popular constructions of girls, women, and violence.

4. This section includes revised sections of work published previously by DeKeseredy (2000) and DeKeseredy, Ellis, and Alvi (2005).

5. I was affiliated with Ohio University's Department of Sociology and Anthropology from 2000 to 2004.

6. This section includes modified sections of work published previously by DeKeseredy (2000).

7. Sadly, too, in death penalty cases in the United States, the more "manly" lesbians appear to juries, the more likely they are to be convicted and seen as unworthy of compassion (Streib, 1994).

8. See Chesney-Lind and Pasko (2004) and DeKeseredy (2000) for more in-depth critiques of these perspectives.

9. This section includes revised sections of work published previously by DeKeseredy and Schwartz (1996).

10. See DeKeseredy (2007) for a biographical account of how I became a feminist man.

11. Corporate crime is a type of white-collar crime (Friedrichs, 2007; Simpson, 2002). Following Clinard and Quinney (1973), corporate crime is defined here as "offenses committed by corporate officials for their corporation and offenses of the corporation itself" (p. 188).

12. Belknap (2007) refers to these scholars as feminist pathways theorists.

13. In Canada, it was not until 1983 that a man could be charged with sexually assaulting his wife.

14. For example, see Alvi, Schwartz, DeKeseredy, and Maume (2001); DeKeseredy et al. (2003); DeKeseredy and Schwartz (1998); and Schwartz, DeKeseredy, Tait, and Alvi (2001).

Discussion Questions

1. What is a theory and what is the practical value of a theory?
2. Why do most theories of crime ignore women and girls in conflict with the law?
3. What are the limitations of early theories of female crime?

4. What are the similarities and differences between women's liberation/emancipation theories and power-control theory?
5. What are the key strengths and limitations of feminist theories reviewed in this chapter?

Suggested Readings

Adler, F. (1975). *Sisters in crime: The rise of the new female criminal*. New York: McGraw-Hill.

> In this book, Adler describes her liberation/emancipation theory.

Belknap, J. (2007). *The invisible woman* (3rd ed.). Belmont, CA: Wadsworth.

> This widely read and cited US text provides a highly intelligible overview of early and contemporary theories of female crime.

Daly, K., & Chesney-Lind, M. (1988). Feminism and criminology. *Justice Quarterly, 5*, 497–538.

> This journal article is essential reading for students and faculty alike interested in learning about the main elements of four variants of feminist thought and their relevance to criminology and criminal justice studies.

DeKeseredy, W.S. (2000). *Women, crime and the Canadian criminal justice system*. Cincinnati: Anderson.

> This book is one of the few Canadian texts that provide an in-depth overview of theoretical perspectives on female crime.

Hagan, J. (1989). *Structural criminology*. New Brunswick, NJ: Rutgers University Press.

> This award-winning book is useful for people interested in acquiring a more sophisticated understanding of power-control theory.

Online Resources

1. Division on Women and Crime of the American Society of Criminology: www.asc41.com/dir4

   The official site of the American Society of Criminology's Division on Women and Crime is an excellent resource for students and faculty interested in learning more about theoretical and empirical contributions to an interdisciplinary understanding of female offenders and how the criminal justice system deals with them.

2. Division on Critical Criminology of the American Society of Criminology: http://critcrim.org

   This web source includes materials related to a feminist understanding of female crime and its control.

3. Texas Youth Commission: http://austin.tyc.state.tx.us/cfinternet/prevention/search.cfm

   This website focuses on social, economic, and individual factors that motivate young people to join gangs.

References

Adler, F. (1975). *Sisters in crime: The rise of the new female criminal.* New York: McGraw-Hill.

Akers, R.L. (1997). *Criminological theories: Introduction and evaluation* (2nd ed.). Los Angeles: Roxbury.

Alvi, S., DeKeseredy, W.S., & Ellis, D. (2000). *Contemporary social problems in North American society.* Toronto: Addison Wesley Longman.

Alvi, S., Schwartz, M.D., DeKeseredy, W.S., & Maume, M.O. (2001). Women's fear of crime in Canadian public housing. *Violence Against Women, 7,* 638–661.

Barak, G., Leighton, P., & Flavin, J. (2007). *Class, race, gender, and crime: The social realities of justice in America* (2nd ed.). New York: Roman & Littlefield.

Baskin, D., Sommers, I., & Fagan, J. (1993). The political economy of female violent street crime. *Fordham Urban Law Journal, 20,* 401–417.

Becker, H.S. (1967). Whose side are we on? *Social Problems, 14,* 239–247.

Beirne, P., & Messerschmidt, J.W. (1991). *Criminology.* New York: Harcourt Brace.

Beirne, P., & Messerschmidt, J.W. (1995). *Criminology* (2nd ed.). New York: Harcourt Brace.

Belknap, J. (2007). *The invisible woman: Gender, crime, and justice* (3rd ed.). Belmont, CA: Wadsworth.

Boritch, H. (1997). *Fallen women: Female crime and criminal justice in Canada.* Toronto: Nelson.

Chesney-Lind, M. (1999). [Review of the book *When she was bad: Violent women and the myth of innocence.*] *Women & Criminal Justice, 10*(4), 114–118.

Chesney-Lind, M. (2004, August). Girls and violence: Is the gender gap closing? *VAWnet Applied Research Forum,* 1–9.

Chesney-Lind, M., & Belknap, J. (2002, May). *Gender, delinquency, and juvenile justice: What about the girls?* Paper presented at Aggression, Antisocial Behavior and Violence Among Girls: A Development Perspective: A Conference, Duke University, Durham, North Carolina.

Chesney-Lind, M., & Eliason, M. (2006). From invisible to incorrigible: The demonization of marginalized women and girls. *Crime, Media, and Culture, 2,* 29–47.

Chesney-Lind, M., & Irwin, K. (2008). *Beyond bad girls: Gender, violence and hype.* New York: Routledge.

Chesney-Lind, M., & Pasko, L. (2004). *The female offender: Girls, women, and crime* (2nd ed.). Thousand Oaks, CA: Sage.

Chesney-Lind, M., & Shelden, R. (1992). *Girls: Delinquency and juvenile justice.* Pacific Grove, CA: Brooks/Cole.

Chesney-Lind, M., & Shelden, R. (2003). *Girls: Delinquency and juvenile justice* (3rd ed.). Pacific Grove, CA: Brooks/Cole.

Chisholm, P. (1997). Bad girls: A brutal B.C. murder sounds an alarm about teenage violence. *Maclean's, 110*(49), 12–16.

Clinard, M.B., & Quinney, R. (1973). *Criminal behavior systems.* New York: Holt, Rinehart and Winston.

Cohen, A. (1955). *Delinquent boys: The culture of the gang.* New York: Free Press.

Coren, M. (2007, July 28). End the blather. *Toronto Sun.* Retrieved from www.torontosun.com.

Cote, S. (2002). Introduction. In S. Cote (Ed.), *Criminological theories: Bridging the past to the future* (pp. xiii–xxiv). Thousand Oaks, CA: Sage.

Curran, D.J., & Renzetti, C.M. (2001). *Theories of crime* (2nd ed.). Boston: Allyn & Bacon.

Currie, E. (1998). *Crime and punishment in America.* New York: Metropolitan Books.

Daly, K., & Chesney-Lind, M. (1988). Feminism and criminology. *Justice Quarterly, 5,* 497–538.

Davis, A. (2003). *Are prisons obsolete?* New York: Seven Stories Press.

DeKeseredy, W.S. (2000). *Women, crime and the Canadian criminal justice system.* Cincinnati: Anderson.

DeKeseredy, W.S. (2007). Changing my life, among others: Reflections on the life and work of a feminist man. In S.L. Miller (Ed.), *Criminal justice and diversity: Voices from the field* (pp. 127–145). Boston: Northeastern University Press.

DeKeseredy, W.S., Alvi, S., Schwartz, M.D., & Perry, B. (1999). Violence against and the harassment of women in Canadian public housing. *Canadian Review of Sociology and Anthropology, 36,* 499–516.

DeKeseredy, W.S., Alvi, S., Schwartz, M.D., & Tomaszewski, E.A. (2003). *Under siege: Poverty and crime in a public housing community.* Lanham, MD: Lexington Books.

DeKeseredy, W.S., & Dragiewicz, M. (2007). Understanding the complexities of feminist perspectives on woman abuse: A commentary on Donald G. Dutton's *Rethinking domestic violence. Violence Against Women, 13,* 874–884.

DeKeseredy, W.S., Ellis, D., & Alvi, S. (2005). *Deviance and crime: Theory, research and policy.* Cincinnati: Anderson.

DeKeseredy, W.S., & MacLeod, L. (1997). *Woman abuse: A sociological story.* Toronto: Harcourt Brace.

DeKeseredy, W.S., & Schwartz, M.D. (1996). *Contemporary criminology.* Belmont, CA: Wadsworth.

DeKeseredy, W.S., & Schwartz, M.D. (1998). *Woman abuse on campus: Results from the Canadian national survey.* Thousand Oaks, CA: Sage.

DeKeseredy, W.S., & Schwartz, M.D. (2005). Masculinities and interpersonal violence. In M.S. Kimmel, J. Hearn, & R.W. Connell (Eds.), *Handbook of studies on men & masculinities* (pp. 353–366). Thousand Oaks, CA: Sage.

DeKeseredy, W.S., Schwartz, M.D., & Alvi, S. (2000). The role of profeminist men in dealing with woman abuse on the Canadian college campus. *Violence Against Women, 6,* 918–935.

Delacourt, S. (2007, August 15). Half of Canada lacks clout in cabinet: Female representation stuck at 22 percent. *Toronto Star,* p. A15.

Downes, D., & Rock, P. (2003). *Understanding deviance* (4th ed.). New York: Oxford University Press.

Dutton, D.G. (2006). *Rethinking domestic violence.* Vancouver: University of British Columbia Press.

Ehrenreich, B., & English, B. (1978). *For her own good.* Garden City, NY: Anchor.

Ellis, D., & DeKeseredy, W.S. (1996). *The wrong stuff: An introduction to the sociological study of deviance* (2nd ed.). Toronto: Allyn & Bacon.

Faith, K. (1993). *Unruly women: The politics of confinement and resistance.* Vancouver: Press Gang.

Faludi, S. (1991). *Backlash: The undeclared war against American women.* New York: Crown.

Fekete, J. (1994). *Moral panic: Biopolitics rising.* Montreal: Robert Davies.

Finkelhor, D., & Yllo, K. (1985). *License to rape: Sexual abuse of wives.* New York: Holt, Rinehart and Winston.

Flavin, J. (2004). Feminism for the mainstream criminologist: An invitation. In B. Raffeal Price & N.J. Sokoloff (Eds.), *The criminal justice system and women: Offenders, prisoners, victims, & workers* (pp. 31–50). New York: McGraw Hill.

Ford, R. (1998, May 24). The razor's edge. *Boston Globe Magazine,* pp. 13, 22–28.

Friedrichs, D.O. (2007). *Trusted criminals: White collar crime in contemporary society* (3rd ed.). Belmont, CA: Wadsworth.

Garbarino, J. (2006). *See Jane hit: Why girls are growing more violent and what we can do about it.* New York: Penguin Press.

Gavigan, S. (1983). Women's crime and feminist critiques. *Canadian Criminology Forum, 6,* 75–90.

Gelsthorpe, L., & Morris, A. (1988). Feminism and criminology in Britain. *British Journal of Criminology, 28,* 93–110.

Gora, J. (1982). *The new female criminal: Empirical reality or social myth.* New York: Praeger.

Griffiths, C.T. (2007). *Canadian criminal justice: A primer* (3rd ed.). Toronto: Thomson Nelson.

Hackler, J. (1994). *Crime and Canadian public policy.* Scarborough, ON: Prentice-Hall.

Hagan, J. (1985). The assumption of natural science methods: Criminological positivism. In R.F. Meier (Ed.), *Theoretical methods in criminology* (pp. 75–92). Beverly Hills, CA: Sage.

Hagan, J. (1989). *Structural criminology.* New Brunswick, NJ: Rutgers University Press.

Hagan, J., Gillis, A., & Simpson, J. (1987). Class in the household: A power-control theory of gender and delinquency. *American Journal of Sociology, 92,* 788–816.

Hahn Rafter, N., & Gibson, M. (Trans.). (2004). *Criminal woman, the prostitute, and the normal woman* by Cesare Lombroso with Guglielmo Ferrero (1893). Durham, NC: Duke University Press.

Hall, N. (1999, May 8). Reena Virk: A disposable kid to cruel attackers. *Vancouver Sun,* p. A10.

Hickey, E. (2005). *Serial murderers and their victims* (3rd ed.). Belmont, CA: Wadsworth.

Holmlund, C. (1994). A decade of deadly dolls: Hollywood and the woman killer. In H. Birch (Ed.), *Moving targets: Women, murder and representation* (pp. 127–151). Berkeley, CA: University of California Press.

Jaggar, A. (1983). *Feminist politics and human nature.* Totowa, NJ: Rowman & Littlefield.

Jiwani, Y. (2006). *Discourses of denial: Mediations of race, gender, and violence.* Vancouver: University of British Columbia Press.

Johnson, H. (1987). Getting the facts straight: A statistical overview. In E. Adelberg & C. Currie (Eds.), *Too few to count: Canadian women in conflict with the law* (pp. 23–46). Vancouver: Press Gang Publishers.

Kimmel, M.S. (2000). *The gendered society.* New York: Oxford University Press.

Lewis, N. (1992, December 23). Delinquent girls achieving a violent equity in DC. *Washington Post,* p. 1.

Lilly, J.R., Cullen, F.T., & Ball, R.A. (2002). *Criminological theory: Context and consequences* (3rd ed.). Thousand Oaks, CA: Sage.

Lilly, J.R., Cullen, F.T., & Ball, R.A. (2006). *Criminological theory: Context and consequences* (4th ed.). Thousand Oaks, CA: Sage.

Lombroso, C. (1958). *The female offender.* New York: The Wisdom Library.

Lombroso, C., & Ferrero, W. (1895). *The female offender.* New York: Philosophical Library.

Luxton, M. (1993). Dreams and dilemmas: Feminist musings on "the man question." In T. Haddad (Ed.), *Men and masculinities* (pp. 347–374). Toronto: Canadian Scholars' Press.

Maidment, M.R. (2006). Transgressing boundaries: Feminist perspectives in criminology. In W.S. DeKeseredy & B. Perry (Eds.), *Advancing critical criminology: Theory and application* (pp. 43–62). Lanham, MD: Lexington Books.

McCarthy, B., Hagan, J., & Woodward, T.S. (1999). In the company of women: Structure and agency in a revised power-control theory of gender and delinquency. *Criminology, 37,* 761–788.

Merton, R.K. (1938). Social structure and anomie. *American Sociological Review, 3,* 672–682.

Messerschmidt, J.W. (1986). *Capitalism, patriarchy, and crime: Toward a socialist feminist criminology.* Totowa, NJ: Roman & Littlefield.

Messerschmidt, J.W. (1993). *Masculinities and crime: Critique and reconceptualization.* Lanham, MD: Roman & Littlefield.

Messerschmidt, J.W. (1997). *Crime as structured action: Gender, race, class, and crime in the making.* Thousand Oaks, CA: Sage.

Miller, J. (2003). Feminist criminology. In M.D. Schwartz & S.E. Hatty (Eds.), *Controversies in critical criminology* (pp. 15–28). Cincinnati: Anderson.

Miller, J.M., Schreck, C.J., & Tewksbury, R. (2006). *Criminological theory: A brief introduction.* Boston: Allyn & Bacon.

Miller, S.L. (1998). Introduction. In S.L. Miller (Ed.), *Crime control and women: Feminist implications of criminal justice policy* (pp. x–xxiv). Thousand Oaks, CA: Sage.

Montreal gunman called himself "angel of death." (2006, September 14). CBC News. Retrieved from www.cbc.ca.

Mooney, L., Knox, D., & Schacht, C. (2005). *Understanding social problems* (4th ed.). Belmont, CA: Thomson Wadsworth.

Morris, A. (1987). *Women, crime, and criminal justice.* Oxford: Basil Blackwell.

Morrissey, B. (2003). *When women kill: Questions about agency and subjectivity.* London: Routledge.

Pearce, F. (1976). *Crimes of the powerful: Marxism, crime and deviance.* London: Pluto Press.

Pearson, P. (1997). *When she was bad: Violent women and the myth of innocence.* Toronto: Random House.

Pollak, O. (1950). *The criminality of women.* New York: Barnes.

Pollak, O., & Friedman, A.S. (Eds.). (1969). *Family dynamics and female delinquency.* Palo Alto, CA: Science and Behavior Books.

Renzetti, C.M. (1993). On the margins of the malestream (or, they *still* don't get it, do they?): Feminist analyses in criminal justice education. *Journal of Criminal Justice Education, 4,* 219–234.

Sartre, J.P. (1964). *The words.* London: Penguin.

Schur, E.M. (1984). *Labeling women deviant: Gender, stigma, and social control.* Philadelphia: Temple University Press.

Schwartz, M.D., DeKeseredy, W.S., Tait, D., & Alvi, S. (2001). Male peer support and routine activities theory: Understanding sexual assault on the college campus. *Justice Quarterly, 18,* 701–727.

Schwartz, M.D., & Milovanovic, D. (Eds.). (1996). *Race, gender and class in criminology.* New York: Garland.

Schwartz, M.D., & Slatin, G. (1984). The law on marital rape: How do Marxism and feminism explain its presence? *ALSA Forum, 8,* 244–264.

Simon, R.J. (1975). *Women and crime.* Lexington, MA: Lexington Books.

Simpson, S.S. (2002). *Corporate crime, law and social control.* New York: Cambridge University Press.

Sluser, R., & Kaufman, M. (1992, July). *The white ribbon campaign: Mobilizing men to take action.* Paper presented at the 17th National Conference on Men and Masculinity, Chicago, IL.

Smart, C. (1976). *Women, crime and criminology: A feminist critique.* London: Routledge & Kegan Paul.

Smart, C. (1987). [Review of the book *Capitalism, patriarchy and crime*]. *Contemporary Crises, 11,* 327–329.

Smith, M.D. (1990). Patriarchal ideology and wife beating: A test of a feminist hypothesis. *Violence and Victims, 5,* 257–273.

Steffensmeier, D.J., & Broidy, L. (2001). Explaining female offending. In C.M. Renzetti & L. Goodstein (Eds.), *Women, crime, and criminal justice: Original feminist readings* (pp. 111–134). Los Angeles: Roxbury.

Steffensmeier, D.J., & Steffensmeier, R.H. (1980). Trends in female delinquency: An examination of arrest, juvenile court, self-report, and field data. *Criminology, 18,* 62–85.

Streib, V. (1994). Death penalty for lesbians. *National Journal of Sexual Orientation Law, 1,* 40–52.

Sudbury, J. (2005). *Global lockdown: Race, gender and the prison-industrial complex.* London: Routledge.

Szasz, T. (1987). *Insanity: The idea and its consequences.* New York: John Wiley.

Toronto homicides in 2007. (2008). CBC News. Retrieved from www.cbc.ca.

Walker, S. (1998). *Sense and nonsense about crime and drugs: A policy guide* (4th ed.). Belmont, CA: Wadsworth.

You've come a long way, baby: Prodded by feminism, today's teenaged girls embrace antisocial male behaviour. (1995, July 31). *Alberta Report,* p. 1.

PART II

*Canadian Women
Offenders*

CHAPTER **3**

A *"Typical" Female Offender*

Jane Barker*

Introduction

I want to share a conversation that I had not so long ago with my sister. For the record, she has given her consent for me to relate it now and in this form. My sister is in her early forties, is married, and lives with her partner (and two cats and a dog) in a fashionable neighbourhood in Toronto. She has two university degrees and makes her living as a freelance journalist. She fits quite nicely into society—she is hardworking, responsible, and, if pressed to be categorized as such, she would likely describe herself as middle-class. Now that you have a mental picture of her, you may be surprised that she recently asked me how she could get a pardon.

Nearly 20 years ago, my sister was arrested, charged, and convicted of public mischief for participating in a demonstration in which a road was blocked (an act of civil disobedience) in Kingston.

The Oka crisis (a showdown between the Canadian Army and a group of Mohawks) captured the attention of the world and highlighted the issue of Native land rights in Canada (Canadian Broadcasting Corporation, 2006). As a result of actively participating in a demonstration to stop traffic on a bridge, my sister spent the day in jail.

Nearly 20 years later, my sister decided to see whether she could get a pardon. Although she was proud that she had been a part of the protest and didn't personally care about the record, it was problematic because it kept cropping up whenever she needed a security check. This background is a prelude to the conversation we had.

My sister called to tell me that she was having trouble getting information. She had left messages for a specific police officer (who, she had been told, could help her), but the officer

---

* The author thanks Jean Folsom for her constructive comments on the content of this chapter. Thanks also to Kate Barker for agreeing to share her experience with the justice system.

had not returned her calls. My sister expressed her surprise that the officer had not called. As a journalist, she is savvy when locating information and people, and her affable social skills afford her a rapport with the people she interviews, both in person and by phone. Her difficulty in making contact with this officer was particularly puzzling to her.

Without missing a beat, I said something to the effect of "Are you *really* surprised that he won't call you back? To him, you're a criminal." My sister was completely shocked. In that one sentence, I had reduced her to one very powerful label—a criminal. Although this was clearly not my intention, she was able to see why the officer had not called her: to him she was not worthy of the return call; she was one of "them," not one of "us."

This example is a powerful one, especially because my sister is not a "typical" offender (if such a thing really exists). The criminal justice system, like other aspects of society, operates on the basis of categories. At the broadest level are the dichotomous extremes of law breaker and law abider. As an accused person moves through the system, more categories appear. Categories are attached to crimes: offences are against the person or against property. In sentencing, there is federal and provincial (or territorial) time, defined by whether a sentence is more or less than two years. In prisons, offenders are classified according to security level (minimum, medium, or maximum). Everywhere in the criminal justice system are categorizations of some sort. Although categories may serve to impose order to a social world, some problematic and worrying consequences are associated with operating in this manner.

As Comack (1996) has noted, "women in prison are in very many ways no different from the rest of us: they are daughters, sisters, girlfriends, wives and mothers, and they share many of the experiences of women collectively" (p. 20). A similar comment was also made by Hatch and Faith (1989), who observed that "women in conflict with the law have more in common with other women than they do with male prison inmates, in terms of their socio-economic situation, program, and treatment needs" (p. 454). Comack (1996) asserts that very little utility is gained by categorizing female offenders according to their crime. She points to a number of problems with taking this approach as a starting point to understanding why women offend. Firstly, if only the most recent offence is used to categorize a woman, any information related to her history of offending is summarily discarded. According to Comack, we need to recognize that crime categories are simply legal constructions that represent the official version of the woman's behaviour. In an attempt to impose order on an event, the official version is given credence by the law, and any competing version is silenced (Comack, 1996). Crime categories serve to create a binary opposition between those who break the law and those who abide by it—thus emphasizing the criminal woman as "the other" (Comack, 1996). The setting up of this kind of an "us" versus "them" dichotomy may then lead to a positivist approach in which criminologists, in an attempt to understand why women break the law, look for the presence of variables, either intrinsic or extrinsic (Comack, 1996).

Although relying solely on crime categorizations to reduce women's crimes to some sort of categorization is clearly problematic, we need to understand and appreciate the kinds of crimes that women are committing and being accused of committing and then compare this information with the case for men. For this reason the nature and frequency of female offending in Canada is explored.

Types of Data Available

Each summer, the Canadian Centre for Justice Statistics publishes Canadian crime statistics for the previous year. In 2006, the national crime rate decreased by 3 percent from the previous year, dropping to its lowest rate in more than 25 years (Silver, 2007). Although the crime rate has been in decline since the early 1990s, the Canadian criminal justice system continues to grow: in 2002, federal expenditures for the protection of persons and property topped $20 billion (Statistics Canada, 2007e). Federal expenditures for the courts totalled nearly $0.5 billion, whereas corrections cost just less than $2 billion, and policing expenditures were $2.78 billion. Total justice-related (related to the protection of persons and property) expenditures at the provincial and territorial levels were just over $10 billion. Clearly, the criminal justice system holds considerable economic importance to Canadian society, as evidenced by its annual expenditures.

To study the nature and frequency of female offences, data are available from both the courts and the correctional system. We will examine court data from the Adult Criminal Court Survey (ACCS). These data are collected by the Canadian Centre for Justice Statistics, which works in collaboration with government departments (provincial and territorial) that are responsible for the criminal courts (Statistics Canada, 2007d). In the ACCS, the primary unit of measurement is the case, which comprises one or more charges against a person when the charges are disposed of in court on the same day (Statistics Canada, 2007d). The "most serious offence" refers to the piece of information that essentially defines each case. For example, if a person were charged and convicted (on the same day in court) on the two charges of uttering threats and attempted murder, then the more serious of the two charges—attempted murder—would define the case for statistical purposes. The ACCS collects data on all persons who, at the time of the offence, are 18 years of age or older and all youth whose cases are transferred to adult criminal court (Statistics Canada, 2007d).

The data concerning corrections (provincial, territorial, and federal) comes from the Adult Correctional Service Survey and the Integrated Correctional Services Survey (Statistics Canada, 2007a). A cursory examination of the table on annual admissions to federal programs for the adult correctional services illustrates that little attention is paid regarding women as a separate category. Only one statistic (the **warrant of committal** admissions of females as a percentage) addresses women separately from men. Although the raw data on other types of information specific to admission to federal programs (revocation of conditional release and aggregate sentence lengths by years) and information on women by region are collected, they are not included in tables provided to the public. Anyone who wants to access these data can request this custom work (for a fee) from Statistics Canada.

Warrant of Committal Admissions of Women to Federal Programs

As noted in chapter 1, women make up a very small percentage of those who come into conflict with the law. When considering the population of federal offenders in Canada (those sentenced to two years or more), recent estimates from 1997 to 2004 indicate that between 5 and 6 percent of all warrant of committal admissions to federal programs are female (Statistics Canada, 2007c). In this sense, federal warrant of committal admissions refers to all offenders who are "serving a 'determinate' sentence of two years or more" and excludes those who have been admitted into custody for revocation of parole (Boe, Motiuk, & Muirhead, 1998, p. 2). The most recent statistics available, from 2005, indicate that 4 percent of offenders in federal custody were female (Kong & AuCoin, 2008). Prior to 1997, estimates ranged between 2 and 3 percent (Statistics Canada, 2007c). Interestingly, the jump in the percentage of women's admissions seems to have coincided with the opening of the regional facilities for women. Some may speculate that the increase in federal sentences for women (as a proportion of all those sentenced to federal time) may be reflective of judges' perceptions that the new regional facilities for women offered improved rehabilitative services from what had been available at the Prison for Women. Thus, when judges had the option for either a federal or a provincial (or territorial) sentence, they may have leaned toward a federal sentence.

As noted previously, only one statistic (the warrant of committal admissions of females as a percentage) is provided separately for women in the statistical tables on annual admissions to federal programs for the adult correctional services. From this one statistic, we can calculate the number of women admitted to federal programs annually (Statistics Canada, 2007a). In 2004, 5 percent of 4,540 warrant of committal admissions were females, which amounts to 227 women. Data are available as far back as 1982, when 2 percent of all admissions (81 women) were admitted to federal programs. Over the past 20 years or so, the percentage of women being admitted to federal programs has been increasing gradually (Statistics Canada, 2007a). In absolute terms, from 1997 to 2004, more than 200 women were admitted to federal programs each year (between 5 and 6 percent of all federal admissions). The average number of women admitted over this time period was 223 women annually. This figure is in stark contrast to the previous 10-year period (1987 to 1996) when between 2 and 3 percent of all federal admissions were women—an average of 136 women each year (Statistics Canada, 2007a).

Sentenced Admissions of Women to Provincial and Territorial Programs

Similar to the statistics for federally sentenced women, relatively few women have been sentenced provincially or territorially compared with their male counterparts. Recent estimates suggest that about 10 percent of those sentenced to provincial and territorial facilities are women (Beattie, 2006). Since 1978 (when data were first available), the percentage of women being sentenced provincially has been increasing. In 1978, approximately 5 percent of all provincial and territorial admissions were women, which increased to about 7 percent in the early 1980s, to 9 percent in the 1990s, and more recently to 10 percent in 2000 (Statistics Canada, 2007b). Although the data have not always shown linear growth year to year, the overall trend shows a steady increase in the percentage of women incarcerated provincially and territorially. The most recent statistics for 2004–5 indicate that 6 percent of those in provincial and territorial custody were women, and 6 percent of those on remand[1] were women (Kong & AuCoin, 2008).

In 2004, there were 79,193 provincial and territorial sentenced admissions (Statistics Canada, 2007c). Based on the previously mentioned percentages for women (women represented 10 percent of provincial and territorial admissions in 2000), this figure translates to roughly 7,919 female provincial and territorial sentenced admissions, almost 35 times as many women sentenced to provincial and territorial custody as to federal custody (Statistics Canada, 2007b).

What Kinds of Crimes Are Women Committing?

Uniform Crime Reporting Survey

As noted in the previous chapter by Walter DeKeseredy, crime is predominantly a male endeavour. According to the Uniform Crime Reporting (UCR) survey in 2002, just over 71,000 women were charged with *Criminal Code* offences, representing a rate of 572 per 100,000 people (Statistics Canada, 2006). That same year, men were charged at a rate of 2,736 per 100,000, nearly fives times the women's rate. The most recent estimates for 2005 suggest that about 28 percent of women's crimes are considered **crimes against the person**, 44 percent are **property crimes**, 19 percent are violations against the administration of justice, and 8 percent consist of other *Criminal Code* violations (Kong & AuCoin, 2008). Compared with crimes charged against men, a smaller proportion of women's crimes are against the person (28 percent vs. 35 percent), and a larger percentage (44 percent vs. 36 percent) consist of crimes against property (Kong & AuCoin, 2008). But relying on only official police statistics as a measure of crime can be problematic. The most obvious criticism is that not all crimes are reported to police. Hence, the "dark figure of crime" prevents the true rates of criminal acts from being fully exposed through such statistics (Linden, 2004).

Adult Court Data

The statistics on those who attend Canada's adult courts can yield information regarding the kinds of offences that women are accused of committing. Below, data are presented according to the types of crimes committed, broadly categorized as crimes against the person, crimes against property, and administration of justice offences.

CRIMES AGAINST THE PERSON

From the most recent 10-year period available (1994–2003), of the total number of people appearing in court for crimes against the person, the percentage of women is increasing (Statistics Canada, 2007d). As shown in figure 3.1, just over 11 percent of those appearing in court in 1994 for crimes against the person were female, compared with 13.44 percent 10 years later. The largest increases occurred in cases of major assault, attempted murder, and common assault, where the relative percentage of women in each category has increased by about 3 percent over 10 years. The data in figure 3.1 show that women are in the minority of those accused and appearing in court for crimes against the person. Overall, males are clearly represented at a disproportionately higher rate than women.

Figure 3.1   Crimes Against the Person: Percentage of Accused Who Are Female, by Category of Crime

Year	Total crimes against the person	Homicide	Attempted murder	Robbery	Sexual assault	Major assault	Common assault
1994	11.18	10.33	8.15	8.27	1.32	12.76	13.37
1995	11.44	12.86	9.68	7.20	1.09	13.08	13.72
1996	11.67	10.42	10.45	8.07	1.08	13.41	14.01
1997	11.82	12.37	9.07	6.94	1.05	13.20	14.64
1998	12.40	13.26	13.12	7.46	1.04	14.37	15.17
1999	13.07	9.44	7.74	8.87	1.28	15.26	15.76
2000	13.36	10.03	9.63	8.47	1.24	15.33	16.24
2001	13.17	10.56	9.25	7.96	1.12	15.85	15.95
2002	13.40	10.74	9.26	8.64	0.88	16.40	16.16
2003	13.44	10.59	11.27	8.27	0.96	16.49	16.26

Source: Adapted from Statistics Canada. (2007d). *Adult criminal court survey, number of cases by sex of accused, annual* [CANSIM table 252-0023]. Available from http://estat.statcan.ca.

CRIMES AGAINST PROPERTY

As figure 3.2 illustrates, in the same 10-year period, of the total number of people appearing in court for crimes against property, the percentage of women remained fairly stable, at approximately 21 percent.

Of all crimes charged, the category of crimes against property shows the highest percentage of charges against women. The largest percentage increases from 1994 to 2003 were in the offence categories of possession of stolen property, break and enter, and other property offences. The categories of fraud and theft both approach the 30 percent level and have remained relatively stable over the 10-year period. Not surprisingly, a fairly small percentage of women appeared in court on break and enter charges (although the percentage of women in this category has increased over time). Break and enter is considered one of the more violent of the crimes against property, because it involves a physical violation of a dwelling or place of work. Women are more likely to engage in the writing of bad cheques or credit card fraud (which results in a fraud charge) or shoplifting (which results in a theft charge) than breaking into a home or office.

ADMINISTRATION OF JUSTICE OFFENCES

This category of offences refers to crimes related to the justice system and its administration. For example, a charge of failure to appear can be laid when an accused person does not

Figure 3.2   Crimes Against Property: Percentage of Accused Who Are Female, by Category of Crime

Year	Total crimes against property	Theft	Break and enter	Fraud	Mischief	Possession of stolen property	Other property offences
1994	21.35	29.01	4.76	28.96	11.27	13.94	12.93
1995	21.16	28.84	4.69	28.72	11.27	13.85	12.60
1996	20.90	28.72	4.78	28.14	11.25	13.74	14.27
1997	20.92	28.80	5.21	28.70	11.64	13.95	14.08
1998	21.03	28.53	5.47	28.39	12.24	15.00	13.50
1999	20.94	27.96	5.58	28.91	12.09	14.90	13.15
2000	20.95	27.64	6.04	28.91	12.15	15.12	14.94
2001	21.11	27.06	6.39	29.58	11.75	15.23	17.76
2002	21.62	28.06	6.51	29.58	11.76	16.67	11.55
2003	21.15	27.23	6.95	28.74	11.71	16.27	14.26

Source: Adapted from Statistics Canada. (2007d). *Adult criminal court survey, number of cases by sex of accused, annual* [CANSIM table 252-0023]. Available from http://estat.statcan.ca.

show up for a court date, or a breach of probation charge can be laid for failure to abide by the conditions of probation.

As shown in figure 3.3, of all persons appearing in court charged with administration of justice offences, approximately one in seven is a female. Relatively speaking, very few women appear in court for failing to comply with an order, for being unlawfully at large, or for breaching probation. About one in five cases of failure to appear is charged against a female, the highest rate of women charged with an administration of justice offence.

"Typical" Women's Offences

You now have an idea about the broad categories of offences (crimes against the person, property crimes, and violations against the administration of justice) that paint an overall picture of women's involvement in crime in Canada. However, this textbook would be remiss not to specifically mention those crimes that women are frequently associated with. By including this kind of a focus, we risk reinforcing the already negative stereotypes about women who come into conflict with the law. As will be noted later in this chapter, the public has a fascination with sensationalized media portrayals of female offenders. The media's distorted images of women in conflict with the law may then feed into these stereotypes. I do not want to perpetuate any caricatures of the female offender by including mention of specific sensationalized cases; instead, I hope to impart the need to acknowledge that women

Figure 3.3 Administration of Justice Offences: Percentage of Accused Who Are Female, by Category of Crime

Year	Total administration of justice offences	Fail to appear	Breach of probation	Unlawfully at large	Fail to comply with order	Other
1994	13.96	20.01	12.03	9.03	12.45	23.19
1995	14.30	20.09	12.58	9.14	12.70	24.17
1996	14.26	18.18	13.03	8.20	12.99	26.59
1997	14.25	19.20	13.21	8.97	12.44	24.94
1998	14.44	18.78	13.17	8.41	13.24	25.81
1999	14.71	19.49	12.98	8.54	14.03	25.36
2000	14.93	19.69	13.51	8.63	14.20	25.33
2001	13.92	17.92	12.70	7.69	13.33	25.52
2002	14.86	18.55	13.80	8.34	14.26	27.27
2003	14.68	18.19	13.30	9.60	14.32	25.80

Source: Adapted from Statistics Canada. (2007d). *Adult criminal court survey, number of cases by sex of accused, annual* [CANSIM table 252-0023]. Available from http://estat.statcan.ca.

commit some types of crimes more often than others. Although considerable debate has focused on whether some of these acts (prostitution and drug use, for example) should be criminalized, the fact remains that women in Canada are charged and convicted every day of engaging in drug- and prostitution-related activities. To ignore this reality would overlook an important facet of women's involvement with the criminal justice system in Canada.

When reading about so-called typical crimes that women have been convicted of committing, readers may find it worthwhile to consider how these crimes relate to issues of economic disempowerment. That is, what is the impact of having a low level of education, few marketable skills, being underemployed or unemployed, and relying on inadequate social assistance? How might these factors affect the probability that a woman could commit one of these crimes?

Crimes Related to the Sex Trade

The sex trade has been called the oldest profession—and it can be found in most (some might assert all) communities across the country. The legislation in Canada related to prostitution reveals that the act of prostitution was historically treated as a **status offence** associated with vagrancy (Duchesne, 1997). A prostitute could be arrested if she was in a public place and could not give a reasonable explanation for being there. This offence was replaced in 1972 by what was referred to as the soliciting law, which made it illegal to solicit other people in public for prostitution. The soliciting law faced a number of criticisms: the

Box 3.1   Selected Sections of the Criminal Code Related to Prostitution

Keeping common bawdy-house

210. (1) Every one who keeps a common bawdy-house is guilty of an indictable offence and liable to imprisonment for a term not exceeding two years.

Landlord, inmate, etc.

(2) Every one who

(a) is an inmate of a common bawdy-house,

(b) is found, without lawful consent, in a common bawdy-house, or

(c) as owner, landlord, lessor, tenant, occupier, agent or otherwise having charge or control of any place, knowingly permits the place or any part thereof to be let or used for the purposes of a common bawdy-house,

is guilty of an offence punishable on summary conviction.

Notice of conviction to be served on owner

(3) Where a person is convicted of an offence under subsection (1), the court shall cause a notice of the conviction to be served on the owner, landlord or lessor of the place in respect of which the person is convicted or his agent, and the notice shall contain a statement to the effect that it is being served pursuant to this section.

Duty of landlord on notice

(4) Where a person on whom a notice is served under subsection (3) fails forthwith to exercise any right he may have to determine the tenancy or right of occupation of the person so convicted, and thereafter any person is convicted of an offence under subsection (1) in respect of the same premises, the person on whom the notice was served shall be deemed to have committed an offence under subsection (1) unless he proves that he has taken all reasonable steps to prevent the recurrence of the offence.

Offence in relation to prostitution

213. (1) Every person who in a public place or in any place open to public view

(a) stops or attempts to stop any motor vehicle,

(b) impedes the free flow of pedestrian or vehicular traffic or ingress to or egress from premises adjacent to that place, or

(c) stops or attempts to stop any person or in any manner communicates or attempts to communicate with any person

for the purpose of engaging in prostitution or of obtaining the sexual services of a prostitute is guilty of an offence punishable on summary conviction.

Definition of "public place"

(2) In this section, "public place" includes any place to which the public have access as of right or by invitation, express or implied, and any motor vehicle located in a public place or in any place open to public view.

Source: *Criminal Code*, RSC 1985, c. C-46, as amended.

definition of "public place" was inadequate, a number of sexual acts were not included, and whether the law applied to men, either as prostitutes or clients, was unclear (Duchesne, 1997). In 1985, the so-called communicating law replaced the old soliciting law. Shortly thereafter, legislation was added to address living off the avails of youth and the purchasing of their services (Duchesne, 1997).

Although the act of prostitution is itself not illegal, the *Criminal Code* of Canada specifies a host of charges that can be laid in relation to prostitution (see box 3.1). According to Duchesne (1997), "the purpose of the communicating law ... is to maintain public order by making prostitution less visible, and therefore less of a nuisance, to the general public" (p. 2). Thus, the communicating law seeks to address the appearance of a behaviour that has been judged as immoral by some, and in so doing, the means of carrying out the act of prostitution has become the focus of the legislation, not the "immoral" act itself.

Sections 210 and 211 of the *Criminal Code* relate to keeping a common bawdy house and transportation to a bawdy house, while section 212 is concerned with procuring a person into prostitution or living off their avails. Section 213 (likely the most familiar to readers) is concerned with communicating for the purpose of prostitution. Nowhere in the *Criminal Code* does it state that the act of prostitution is illegal. Instead, it is illegal to be in, or to own, a place where prostitution occurs (a common bawdy house); it is illegal to talk to (to communicate with) another person about sex for sale; and it is illegal to support yourself (to live off the avails) using the profits obtained by another person's work in the sex trade. As shown in box 3.1, prostitution, as a behaviour, is not illegal, but the behaviours related to arranging for it are. If you are wondering exactly *how* a person can engage in street prostitution, which is legal, without breaking the law by engaging in a prostitution-related offence, then we share this query, as I am puzzled by this predicament, too.

The vast majority of prostitution-related charges laid are communicating charges (Duchesne, 1997). In a study of street prostitution in Canada in the late 1990s, 92 percent of charges were for communicating, whereas a mere 3 percent were bawdy-house offences, and 5 percent were procuring charges (Duchesne, 1997). Note that fluctuations in prostitution-related charges do not reflect changes in the level of prostitution in a community, but changes in the level of enforcement of the communicating law (Duchesne, 1997). This change in enforcement may be the result of community pressure and may reflect a NIMBY (not in my back yard) mentality. The majority of people charged for prostitution are adults.

Prior to the legislative changes made in the mid-1980s, most people charged with prostitution-related offences faced bawdy house charges. With the advent of the communicating charge in 1985, the pattern changed abruptly, and the majority of people were charged with communicating offences (Duchesne, 1997).

An examination of the pattern of charges and dispositions of those found guilty for communicating in 1995 reveals some interesting data. Of the more than 6,000 people charged that year, the charges laid were close to an even split between adult men (45 percent) and women (52 percent), with youth accounting for the balance (3 percent) (Duchesne, 1997). The data on dispositions, on the other hand, were disturbing. The most serious sanction for women was prison (39 percent), followed by a fine (32 percent) and probation (22 percent), whereas the most common disposition for men was a fine (56 percent) (Duchesne, 1997). Further, of the only 3 percent of men who faced a prison sentence, 13 percent were granted probation (Duchesne, 1997). In the data on the length of probation, the median length of time for women was twice that for men (one year vs. six months, respectively).

The picture that emerges is a justice system in which approximately equal numbers of men and women are charged with communicating for the purpose of prostitution, but the dispositions handed out to women, as a group, are more punitive than for men. Recent data from 2003–4 have shown a similar pattern: although very close in terms of the absolute number of charges laid (1,058 women charged and 1,271 men charged), more women were found guilty (59 percent vs. 31 percent for men). Approximately one-third of those women found guilty of prostitution were sentenced to custody, compared with only 9 percent of men (Kong & AuCoin, 2008). Although factors other than the actual charge may be influencing the seriousness of the disposition (for example, a history of previous offences), such differential patterns in the disposition of those found guilty of the same offence is troubling, particularly when the differential appears to be linked to the sex of the accused.

Crimes Related to Illicit Drugs

Drug-related crimes in Canada include such offences as driving under the influence of illicit drugs and the possession, trafficking, and importing of such drugs. Most drug crimes (three out of every four) are related to cannabis possession. Rates of drug offences (as reported by police statistics) appear to have increased substantially (42 percent) between 1992 and 2002 (Desjardins & Hotten, 2004). Reportedly, this increase was due primarily to a greater number of charges for cannabis possession. Trafficking offences in Canada seemed to peak in 1992 and have since declined (Desjardins & Hotten, 2004). Relatively few people are charged with importation or cultivation; however, these rates have been increasing and have doubled since the early 1990s (Desjardins & Hotten, 2004).

As is the case with other crimes, men significantly outnumber women in drug-related charges. In 2003, almost 88 percent of those charged with drug possession were male, as were 80 percent of those charged with drug trafficking (Statistics Canada, 2007d). A similar picture emerges with respect to production, importation, and exportation of illegal drugs in 2002, when 80 percent of those charged were men (Desjardins & Hotten, 2004). Although men clearly outnumber women in drug-related crimes, these offences represent some of the more common charges for which women are convicted, and for which they are sentenced to periods of incarceration (Finn, Trevethan, Carrière, & Kowalski, 1999). Interestingly, similar to the pattern for prostitution, more women than men (26 percent vs. 20 percent) who were found guilty of drug possession were sentenced to custody in 2003–4 (Kong & AuCoin, 2008). According to a recent analysis of data collected by Statistics Canada, in the last 25 years "the proportion of female drug offenders has not substantially increased" (Desjardins & Hotten, 2004, p. 5).

Theft and Fraud

The final category of so-called typical women's offences to be discussed are crimes of theft and fraud. As is the case with drug-related crimes, men again outnumber women with respect to these offences. However, from a relative perspective, both theft and fraud are particularly favoured by women (Kong & AuCoin, 2008). About 23 percent of thefts and 28 percent of frauds were committed by women in 2003–4 (Kong & AuCoin, 2008). These percentages are fairly high considering that women are charged with only 18 percent of all property crimes (Kong & AuCoin, 2008). When specific types of property crimes are considered, historically few women have been known to commit so-called masculine property crimes, such as break and enter or auto theft (Steffensmeier as cited in Hatch & Faith, 1989). This pattern has changed very little in the last 20 years. Recent statistics indicate that women represented approximately 5 percent of all people charged with break and enter offences in 2003–4 (Kong & AuCoin, 2008).

What kinds of thefts and frauds are women committing? Their crimes tend to centre on meeting the economic needs of themselves or their families. Historically, this crime has usually been committed through the passing of bad cheques, credit card fraud, and shoplifting. Hatch and Faith (1989) noted that, in 1987, women made up 44 percent of those

---

Box 3.2   Two Fraud Cases: Conrad Black and Kimberly Rogers

A $102-million corporate theft vs. $13,500 in unauthorized welfare benefits—which one will pay the greater penalty?

It will be interesting to see how Conrad Black fares compared to Kimberly Rogers.[2] Black and his long-time business partner, David Radler, were charged Monday with civil fraud by the U.S. Securities and Exchange Commission.

The commission alleges that the pair looted $85 million US ($102 million Canadian) from the shareholders of Hollinger International Inc.

"Black and Radler abused their control of a public company and treated it as their personal piggy bank," SEC Enforcement Director Stephen Cutler said in announcing the charges.

Just what, if anything, happens to Black (and Radler) is anybody's guess at this point. American authorities are at least attempting to bring them to justice. But given the abilities of the rich and powerful to wiggle off the hook, don't hold your breath.

Sudbury Welfare Case

By contrast, consider the case of Kimberly Rogers. The 40-year-old woman was found dead in her overheated Sudbury apartment in August 2001 after being convicted of welfare abuse.

Rogers was sentenced to house arrest for collecting $13,500 ($11,200 US) in social assistance benefits while attending school on a student loan.

She was caught by the tough-on-welfare former Conservative government, which slashed subsistence benefits to unlivable levels (for philosophical and budgetary reasons) and left it to the tender mercies of computers to work out the details.

Rogers was one of those details. Pregnant at the time she was caught, she was confined to her stifling apartment for all but three hours a week. She took her own life.

An inquest into her death revealed a glaring discrepancy between the government's view of "welfare bums" and the reality of life on welfare in Ontario.

"Rogers lived in desperate poverty," the *Toronto Star* reported. "(She) had been prescribed medication for a range of health issues that prevented her from working. She died trying to fight her way out of poverty ... The (inquest) jury saw through the stereotypes about poor people and made 14 thoughtful recommendations aimed at preventing future deaths in similar circumstances."

Silence and Inaction

Sadly, the Liberal government of Dalton McGuinty, which replaced the mean-spirited Conservatives in 2003, has been slow to act on the recommendations. Things are almost as bad today as they were when the Conservatives held power.

Meanwhile, Tory politicians, like former premiers Mike Harris and Ernie Eves (who are now out of power but in many cases are enjoying public pensions that make welfare benefits pale by comparison) have been conspicuous in their silence about the sins of Conrad Black.

To date, it has been left pretty much to American authorities (such as the SEC) to try to bring Black to justice. The toothless Ontario Securities Commission is still trying to decide whether shareholders were hurt.

As always in Canadian politics, the sins of welfare recipients are treated far more seriously than those of the rich and powerful.

Source: National Union of Public and General Employees. (n.d.). *Two fraud cases: Conrad Black and Kimberly Rogers*. Retrieved from www.nupge.ca. Reprinted by permission of NUPGE.

charged with shoplifting items with a value of less than $1,000 and nearly one-third of those charged with theft greater than $1,000. In that same year, women made up approximately 27 percent of those charged with cheque and credit card fraud (Hatch & Faith, 1989). Again, not much has changed since Hatch and Faith published their overview of female crime in 1989. As noted earlier, according to a recent publication from Statistics Canada, women account for about 23 percent of those charged with theft and 28 percent of frauds in 2003–4 (Kong & AuCoin, 2008).

Not all women who commit fraud are passing bad cheques or using credit cards fraudulently. As described in box 3.2, some women are charged with defrauding government agencies (such as welfare), a crime that can result in severe sanctioning.

Research on women and fraud in Canada has been fairly scant. Atkinson (1998), in her study on neutralizations in male and female offenders, noted that female fraud offenders, as a group, were the most likely to accept neutralizations about fraudulent activities, suggesting that any interventions that sought to reduce neutralizations in offenders would likely be best suited to female (and not male) fraud offenders. For a more detailed account of Atkinson's (1998) study, the reader is referred to chapter 6.

The Media Image of Female Offenders in Canada

The media is a powerful tool that can shape our perceptions. If you were to ask average Canadians to name a female offender in Canada, most people would say "Karla Homolka." If you were to ask the same people to name another Canadian female offender, they would probably be hard pressed to do so. They might be able to come up with some Americans, such as Aileen Wuornos or Andrea Yates—infamous women whose cases have been highly publicized in newspapers, magazines, television, and even the movies (Grosch, Hall, Lee,

Riley-Grant, & Schmid, 2004). Some might even include Martha Stewart in their response (although her case was considerably different from the kinds of women offenders usually in the media's focus).

Common to all the above-named women is that their lives have been sensationalized in the media, and as a result, their images have shaped our collective perception of what a typical female offender looks like. The reality is that most Canadian female offenders have not committed a heinous crime. They don't fit with the sensationalized images portrayed in the media. Canadian criminalized women are unlikely to become repeat offenders, and those that do reoffend tend not to escalate in terms of the severity of their crimes (Kong & AuCoin, 2008). A woman like Kimberly Rogers exemplifies, more often than not, the real picture of the female offender in Canada (see box 3.2). When Kimberly Rogers died, she was receiving $520 a month from welfare, from which $52 was clawed back (a collection for an overpayment), leaving her with a total of $468 a month. After she paid her rent of $450, only $18 remained ("Activists Push for Welfare Changes," 2003). How anyone could survive on this paltry amount of money is difficult to fathom.

Compare the case of Kimberly Rogers, and the general public's awareness of it, with the case of Karla Homolka. Many of you have probably heard of Karla Homolka, but perhaps not so many of you are familiar with the case of Kimberly Rogers. The case of Karla Homolka, perhaps "one of the most hated female killers in the world" (Morrissey, 2001, p. 83), was covered extensively on television, in the print media, and recently in film (Burton et al., 2006). In addition to these traditional media outlets, the Internet has spawned a new realm in which she can be vilified. If you Google the name "Karla Homolka," you will find 171,000 hits.[3] According to Morrissey (2001), around the time of Homolka's release from prison, the Internet site "Karla Homolka Death Pool: When the Game Is Over, We All Win" was launched to take bets on the date of her death (p. 83). This particular site was removed from the Internet, but as Morrissey pointed out, other websites focused on when and how Homolka would die (although the websites claimed they neither condoned nor promoted any sort of violence toward Homolka).

Most Canadians would agree that Karla Homolka has the dubious distinction of being Canada's most infamous female offender of the latter half of the 20th century and someone to whom the media have afforded considerable attention (see box 3.3). It remains to be seen, however, the extent to which her case and the media attention given to it have shaped the perceptions of Canadians regarding women offenders in general.

Box 3.3   Are You as Fed up with Karla as I Am?

How much Karla Homolka is too much?

As the release from prison of the notorious felon draws near,[4] those of us in the news business struggle with that question, not always with pretty results. The truth is, Ms. Homolka is an old story.

Her crimes date back 15 years to Christmas Eve of 1990, when she and then-husband Paul Bernardo cheerfully fed doctored drinks to Ms. Homolka's baby sister, Tammy, drugged her, and then took turns sexually assaulting and filming the other sexually assaulting her, all of which culminated in the 15-year-old girl choking to death on her own vomit.

Ms. Homolka's infamous plea bargain of 1993 (10 years each for her role in the deaths of Leslie Mahaffy and Kristen French, to be served concurrently—oh yeah, and two more thrown in for Tammy's death) has been explored, derided and defended every which way and back again ever since: Nothing much new there, despite the impression that may have been left these past weeks.

All the same people, and I include myself in this group, who, 12 years ago, believed the plea deal could have and should have been undone—when it was revealed that Ms. Homolka arguably had lied, and thus breached her side of the agreement, about two assaults on another young woman named Jane Doe—continue to believe that. All those who thought the deal defensible, and this group includes the architects of the plea bargain and most, if not all, of the psychiatrists who hurled themselves aboard the battered-spouse train that saw Ms. Homolka painted as a victim, still think it is …

With Mr. Bernardo and Ms. Homolka, as with the rest of us, deeds speak louder than words. We know all too well what they did. Must we now have to listen to their rationalizations for why they did it or how sorry they say they are?

The media has been full of the wisdom born of hindsight and from those with axes to grind …

Canadians themselves seem as torn about all this as reporters and editors, in that they, like us, have had too much and yet cannot quite pull themselves away. For every e-mail I receive from a reader complaining that we in the media are paying too much attention to the story, I get one from someone young who has just discovered what all the fuss is about, or someone angry enough to want the press to foist ourselves on Ms. Homolka from the minute she is set free.

I used to think I'd want to do that and, for a time, dreamed of winning the lottery and spending the spoils on a fleet of private detectives who would tail her everywhere, feeding me the information I would put in a little Karla Watch box in the pages of whichever paper then employed me: what she ate; where she went; what she wore; with whom she slept.

I have lost my taste for it, though, even if I had the resources—not, I regret to say, out of some charitable view that she has done her time and deserves a crack at making a life, but rather out of bone weariness.

I'm tired of her. I have Karla fatigue. She's reportedly a bright woman, on paper, but I've never seen a hint of intelligence, only cunning, will and self-preservation. She has the emotional range of the fictional Stepford Wives. She is as vapid as she is without a moral centre. I don't care, any more, what she eats, wears, says, does or, God forbid, believes—unless and until she breaks the law.

The voices that could tell us something important about her—those of her victims—have been stilled. Those who barely survived her—Jane Doe, and the parents and siblings of Ms. Mahaffy and Ms. French—remain so wounded they don't, or can't, bring themselves to speak.

We are left with Karla, stuck with her. We can't ignore her, not when her release will provide one of the few genuine news events of this whole mess. We can't hound her, either. We're stumbling around in the dark on this one.

Source: Blatchford, C. (2005, June 25). Are you as fed up with Karla as I am? *Globe and Mail*, p. A15. Reprinted with permission from The Globe and Mail.

A Snapshot of Female Inmates

In 1999, Finn et al. (1999) reported on data obtained through a survey they referred to as a "one-day snapshot" of inmates in Canadian adult correctional institutions. Women inmates were one of the groups the researchers focused on in this report.[5] For the one-day snapshot, data were collected for all inmates on register (that is, in facilities) in federal, provincial, and territorial institutions on Saturday, October 5, 1996. The researchers were allowed access to demographic information, personal history variables (such as marital status, education, employment history, citizenship, and language), and various case characteristics (such as legal status, security classification, and risk and need levels). The type of information available to the researchers was constrained by the data the institutions gathered, a limitation acknowledged by the authors and a problem common to most archival research. That is, the focus of the information collected and stored on the various institutions' computer databases would be limited in scope to just that information that had been entered regarding any one particular offender.

Although this study is constrained because the women studied were all on register with a federal, provincial, or territorial facility, it nonetheless provides useful information on this particular sample of women offenders. Because the data pertained only to those in a facility on that one day, "generalizations should be made with caution" (Finn et al., 1999, p. 2).

It should be no surprise that on snapshot day, women made up about 5 percent of all inmates on register: less than 2 percent of the federal inmates and 7 percent of the provincial or territorial inmates. As shown in figure 3.4, nearly half (46 percent) of the provincially and territorially incarcerated women were in maximum security institutions, compared with 39 percent of men. Most federally incarcerated women were housed in multi-level facilities, whereas only 2 percent of incarcerated men were in such facilities. These figures are not surprising because the Prison for Women and the new regional facilities were designed as multi-level institutions, reflecting the fact that women, as a group, number far fewer than men in the correctional system. Men, because of their sheer number, are more easily accommodated in single-level correctional facilities.[6]

Other interesting differences between men and women emerged from the data collected on October 5, 1996 (Finn et al., 1999). Relatively speaking, fewer women (3 percent) were in segregation compared with men (6 percent), and fewer women were serving time for crimes against the person compared with men. In provincial and territorial facilities, 28 percent of women (compared with 34 percent of men) were incarcerated for crimes against the person, whereas in federal facilities the percentage of women serving time for these types of crimes was higher. At the federal level, 64 percent of women (compared with 74 percent of men) were on register for crimes against the person.

For most of the women who were incarcerated provincially and territorially, the most serious offence listed was property crime (36 percent) or "other" *Criminal Code* or federal statute offences (36 percent) (Finn et al., 1999). The most serious offences listed for men included property crimes (35 percent), crimes against the person (34 percent), and "other" *Criminal Code* or federal statute offences (31 percent) (Finn et al., 1999). When examining the categories of crimes for which provincially and territorially sentenced people were most often convicted, theft (12 percent) and drug-related offences (13 percent) were the highest categories for women, whereas break and enter (19 percent) was the highest for men. Of the women on register in federal facilities, "the largest proportion of females were convicted

Figure 3.4   Distribution of Female and Male Inmates by Security Level

Security level	Provincial/Territorial		Correctional Service Canada	
	Males	Females	Males	Females
	%		%	
Minimum	8	13	14	6
Medium.	13	7	64	8
Maximum	39	46	20	—[a]
Multi-level.	41	35	2	86
Total[b]	100	100	100	100

[a] Nil or zero. Although there were 0% of women in maximum security facilities, this does not mean that there were no women in maximum security facilities.

[b] Totals may not add to 100% due to rounding.

Source: Finn, A., Trevethan, S., Carrière, G., & Kowalski, M. (1999). Female inmates, Aboriginal inmates, and inmates serving life sentences: A one day snapshot. *Juristat*, *19*(5), 4. Adapted from Statistics Canada publication *JURISTAT*, Catalogue 85-002, 19(5), Released April 22, 1999, Page 4, http://www.statcan.ca/bsolc/english/bsolc?catno=85-002-X.

for homicide/attempted murder (37 percent) and drug-related offences (27 percent) as their most serious offence" (Finn et al., 1999, p. 5). For federally incarcerated males, the two largest groups (at 24 percent each) were convicted for homicide or attempted murder and robbery.

Women, on provincial, territorial, and federal registers were serving time for fewer offences than men. Women also had much less extensive criminal histories than their male counterparts. When sentence length was examined, women's aggregate sentences were shorter than men's (Finn et al., 1999).

Similar patterns have been reported more recently. In 2004, men were more likely to face multiple charges, whereas women were not (Kong & AuCoin, 2008). Fifteen percent of women offenders in 2006 were classified as repeat offenders, up from only 10 percent who were classified as such in 1997, and women were more likely to be one-time offenders (Kong & AuCoin, 2008). In comparison with 30 percent of incarcerated men who had a previous federal sentence, incarcerated women were less likely to have one such sentence. Similarly, provincially and territorially sentenced women were less likely than provincially and territorially sentenced men to have had a previous provincial or territorial sentence.

Finn et al. (1999) examined employment levels (at the time of admission) and found that women were more likely to have been unemployed (80 percent of federally sentenced women and 64 percent of provincially and territorially sentenced women) compared with men (54 percent and 43 percent respectively). Women's and men's educational levels were equally low, with about one-third of all provincial and territorial inmates (and nearly half of federal inmates) having completed grade 9 or less. The authors noted that in 1996 approximately 19 percent of Canadian adults had a similar level of education (Finn et al., 1999).

Most inmates were between the ages of 25 and 34, with the median age for women being just older than males in provincial and territorial facilities (32 years compared with 31 years) and just younger than males at the federal level (32 years compared with 33 years) (Finn

Figure 3.5   Distribution of Risk by Gender: Provincial/Territorial and Federal Facilities

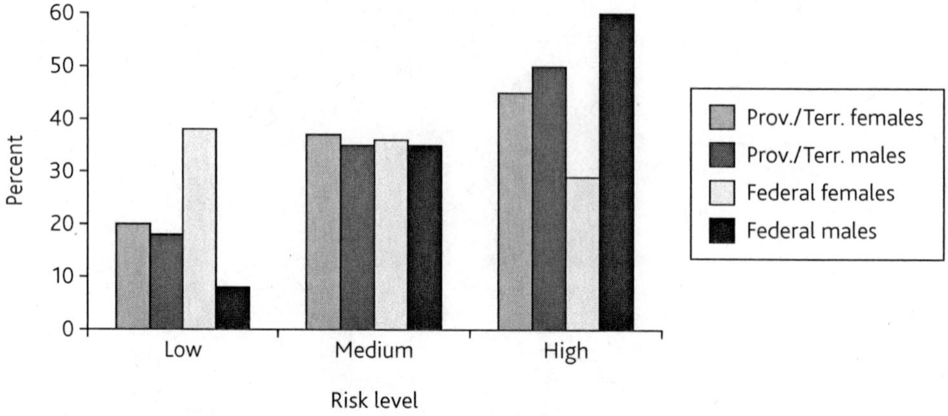

Source: Finn, A., Trevethan, S., Carrière, G., & Kowalski, M. (1999). Female inmates, Aboriginal inmates, and inmates serving life sentences: A one day snapshot. *Juristat, 19*(5), 8. Adapted from Statistics Canada publication *JURISTAT*, Catalogue 85-002, 19(5), Released April 22, 1999, Page 8, http://www.statcan.ca/bsolc/english/bsolc?catno=85-002-X.

et al., 1999). A more recent examination of female adult offenders in Canada found that those women sentenced federally were older (a mean age of 37.7 years) than women in the provincial and territorial system (a mean age of 32 years) (Kong & AuCoin, 2008). As will be highlighted in chapter 10, Aboriginal women were overrepresented across provincial, territorial, and federal facilities (Finn et al., 1999; Kong & AuCoin, 2008). Approximately 25 percent of the federally incarcerated women and almost 30 percent of the provincially and territorially sentenced women were Aboriginal (Kong & AuCoin, 2008). In most cases, the percentage of Aboriginal women inmates was higher than for Aboriginal males, although Aboriginal males were also clearly overrepresented in this sample (Finn et al., 1999).

Interestingly, women were classified as being a lower risk to recidivate than were men (see figure 3.5).

The needs of provincially and territorially sentenced women were reported to be higher (slightly) than provincially and territorially sentenced men on all dimensions except one (social interaction). Federally sentenced women did not follow the same pattern. In fact, according to the data presented by Finn et al. (1999), the federally sentenced women showed lower needs on all dimensions, in comparison with men (see figure 3.6). This pattern no longer is seen. A more recent examination of the risk and needs levels of federally sentenced women suggests a significant increase in women who are deemed to be both high risk and high needs (Kong & AuCoin, 2008). Since 1997, the percentage of federally sentenced women classified as high needs has doubled, from 26 percent to 50 percent in 2006. Federally sentenced women were found to have significantly greater needs than federally sentenced men in the domains of employment/education and marital/family. In other domains (associates/social interaction, attitudes, substance abuse, and personal/emotional orientation) men continued to show significantly more needs than the women (Kong & AuCoin, 2008). In

Figure 3.6   Distribution of Assessed High Needs by Gender

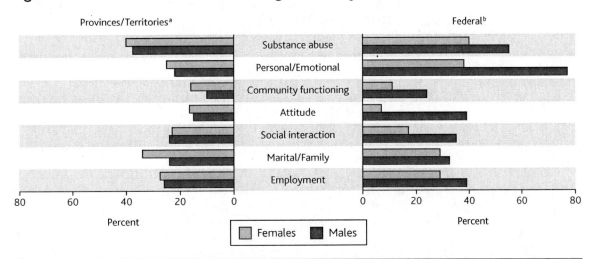

ᵃ Data were available for Newfoundland, Nova Scotia, New Brunswick, Prince Edward Island, Manitoba, Yukon, and Northwest Territories. Data were available for Ontario but were excluded because the rating method used to assess need levels was distinct from the other jurisdictions.

ᵇ Data were missing for 1,738 inmates in Correctional Service of Canada (13%).

Source: Finn, A., Trevethan, S., Carrière, G., & Kowalski, M. (1999). Female inmates, Aboriginal inmates, and inmates serving life sentences: A one day snapshot. *Juristat, 19*(5), 8. Adapted from Statistics Canada publication *JURISTAT*, Catalogue 85-002, 19(5), Released April 22, 1999, Page 8, http://www.statcan.ca/bsolc/english/bsolc?catno=85-002-X.

terms of risk, approximately 33 percent of federally sentenced women were considered to be high risk in 2006, compared with 10 years earlier when only 19 percent were classified as such (Kong & AuCoin, 2008). Given the reported increases in needs and risk levels among federally sentenced women in the past 10 years, one wonders whether federally sentenced women, as a group, have changed that dramatically, or whether another factor is responsible for this increase.

Overall, the report by Finn et al. (1999) must be commended as one of the few attempts in the literature to compare male and female Canadian federal, provincial, and territorial inmates. Although issues surround the reliance on this one-day snapshot as a means of providing information to describe the average or "typical" Canadian female offender, the work of Finn and colleagues is one of the few published accounts that sought to gather such a breadth of information. As such, it is worthy of note. In a timely coincidence, the Centre for Justice Statistics published an issue of *Juristat* in January 2008, just as the final touches were being put on this chapter (Kong & AuCoin, 2008). It is interesting to compare the recent statistics with those collected 10 years ago by Finn et al. (1999).

Not all women fit with the image of a woman offender as portrayed in the *Creating Choices* report (Canada, Task Force on Federally Sentenced Women [TFFSW], 1990). As noted in chapter 1, the mandate of the Task Force on Federally Sentenced Women (TFFSW) was to assess the correctional management of women sentenced to federal prison in Canada, from the beginning of their sentences to their date of warrant expiry. Included in the mandate was the need to develop a strategic plan to guide and direct this process in a way that was respectful of the needs specific to these women (Canada, TFFSW, 1990). The Correctional Service of Canada (CSC) faced some clear difficulties when it came to the operation of the new regional facilities for women. The TFFSW's report, *Creating Choices*, and the implementation of its recommendations were met with a number of criticisms (Hannah-Moffat, 2000). As Hannah-Moffat noted in 1995:

> Perhaps one of the most profound difficulties is that feminists have failed to adequately define the meaning and criteria of woman centeredness. The implementation of the task force's recommendations and the definition of *woman centered* have been left to Corrections Canada with little external (feminist) input. (p. 141)

When the new regional facilities were opened, they were not able to accommodate the needs of maximum security women. A chasm had developed between the ideal as illustrated in *Creating Choices* and the real as experienced by the Correctional Service of Canada in its attempt to operationalize the principles (that is, empowerment, meaningful and responsible choices, respect and dignity, supportive environment, responsibility) in the report. This failure to consider the pragmatics involved in implementing a woman-centred philosophy while balancing the systemic demands inherent in managing violent offenders was glaring. As Shaw (1999) pointed out:

> It is unfortunate that the model of the women-centred prison developed in *Creating Choices* failed to take account of the fact that women can be perpetrators of violence as well as victims. The failure to confront the issue of women's use of violence other than as a response to continued partner violence is not restricted to the Task Force alone, but has been characteristic of feminist accounts of women and violence within criminology more generally. (p. 258)

Other aspects of *Creating Choices* have also met with criticism (Pollack, 2000). In the section of *Creating Choices* entitled "Principle 2: Meaningful and Responsible Choices," the TFFSW, in explaining why this principle is important, notes that for many women their dependence on the state, on men, and on drugs and alcohol has meant that they have not had the kinds of opportunities or, in some cases, the ability to make sound choices in their lives. Pollack (2000) takes issue with this conceptualization of criminalized women as being dependent. She has eloquently challenged the "discourse of dependency" that permeates the *Creating Choices* document, asserting that the authors of the *Creating Choices* report adopted "liberal notions of dependency which, through the use of a psychological discourse, constructs women's lawbreaking as a result of individual personality characteristics that render them 'dependent'" (2000, p. 72). Dependency is then **pathologized** for the women. Pollack goes on to point out the classed, gendered, and racialized nature of dependency. In particular, her observations gleaned from interviews with Caribbean-Canadian women in prison were in stark contrast to the notions of dependency as described in *Creating Choices*.

According to Pollack, the "liberal notions of dependency in understanding these women's experiences" were totally inadequate (2000, p. 75). She noted that very few of the women she interviewed resembled the dependent women described by the TFFSW. The women interviewed by Pollack emphasized their wish to be self-sufficient, educated, and able to provide for their families. An undercurrent of "independence" was noted; however, it was ultimately undermined by societal factors (poor wages, difficulties with social services and other government agencies, systemic racism, and gender inequality, for example) that culminated in situations in which the women found it exceedingly difficult to attain or retain their independence (Pollack, 2000).

One of the main thrusts of Pollack's (2000) article was the need to challenge the TFFSW report's conceptualization of dependency as an issue that needed to be "worked through." She maintained that if dependency could be viewed "as a social relation of subordination" as opposed to some sort of personality disorder, then this perspective would "expose the state's role in enforcing and perpetuating marginalization based on gender, race and class" (Pollack, 2000, p. 80). She further postulated that some law-breaking behaviour could then be seen as "a conscious act of resisting enforced dependency" (Pollack, 2000, p. 80).

Although the voices of Aboriginal women were certainly one focus of the TFFSW, a similar statement cannot be made regarding Caribbean-Canadian women. The voices of these women remained conspicuously silent in that document, but Pollack (2000) has provided a vehicle through which those absent voices could be heard. You might wonder how criminalized women who believe they have issues with dependency might react to Pollack's (2000) views. As has been noted previously, the majority of women who eventually come into conflict with the law share some common ground (financial stress, lack of education, unemployment, few marketable skills) that may be directly or indirectly related to a dependency—on the state, on a man, or on crime—to make ends meet. For women who have identified their dependency issues as having affected their lives, denying them their belief can be problematic. This area clearly warrants further inquiry. To my knowledge, however, no published responses (by members of the TFFSW) have addressed Pollack's (2000) criticisms of the *Creating Choices* document and the "discourse of dependency" she identified.

Recent research examined the Level of Service Inventory-Revised: Self Report (LSI-R:SR), an estimate of risk of a person's likelihood of reoffending. Within samples of federally sentenced women, black women's scores on the LSI-R:SR were lower than those of white and Aboriginal women, indicative of a lower risk for **recidivism** (Folsom & Atkinson, 2007). The majority of the black women in this study were serving their first federal sentence for drug-related crimes, in particular, importing and trafficking (Folsom & Atkinson, 2007). Perhaps what Pollack (2000) identifies as "independency" is a factor that also differentiates this particular sample of federally incarcerated women from the larger population of women serving federal time. Clearly, more research is needed to examine these issues in more depth.

Summary

Recall Comack's (1996) point made at the beginning of this chapter: that women who find themselves in conflict with the law are often no different from any other women; they all share the collective experience of being female in our society. However, these wives, partners, mothers, daughters, sisters, aunts, and cousins are different from non-criminalized women in one respect: they have shared the experience of being in conflict with the law and of facing the justice system up close and in person from "the other side." This distinction of "us" and "them" is fashioned from our desire (conscious or not) to categorize our world into neat packages of what is good and what is bad. The danger inherent in this categorization is obvious: to reduce a person to one label, to the label of criminal, serves the interest of no one.

Perhaps it is more helpful to think in terms of who, in our society, tends to be criminalized. The research to date suggests that the majority of women who come into conflict with the law tend to be young (between the ages of 25 and 34), uneducated, and underemployed or unemployed (Finn et al., 1999). In comparison with their male counterparts, incarcerated women tend to have fewer convictions on their current sentence and fewer past convictions (Finn et al., 1999; Kong & AuCoin, 2008). As a group, these women are likely to be viewed as being at a lower risk than men to reoffend. Aboriginal women (and men) are greatly overrepresented among those incarcerated at both federal and provincial or territorial levels (Finn et al., 1999; Kong & AuCoin, 2008). Women's offences are varied, but without a doubt they have historically been clustered around crimes related to prostitution, theft, and drug use.

Although it may be said that a "typical" female offender does not exist, few would argue that societal issues, such as classism, sexism, and racism, have not had an impact on who becomes criminalized in Canada. Generally, it is a subset of women who are the most negatively affected by these "isms" in our society who come to know the inside of a jail cell.

Notes

1. Being on remand refers to being held in detention while awaiting an appearance in court.
2. Conrad Black was found guilty in the United States of three counts of mail fraud and one count of obstruction of justice. He was sentenced to six-and-a-half years' imprisonment, fined US$125,000, and ordered to forfeit US$6.1 million.
3. The term *Karla Homolka* was entered into the Google search engine by the author at approximately 1 p.m. on September 28, 2007; approximately 171,000 hits were obtained.
4. Karla Homolka was released from prison on July 4, 2005.
5. Other groups identified in this snapshot were Aboriginal inmates and inmates serving a life sentence.
6. The Isabel McNeil House is Canada's only federal facility that houses solely low-risk (minimum security) offenders. According to the Canadian Broadcasting Corporation (2007), it was scheduled to be closed in March 2007 because it was not deemed to be financially viable to continue in its operation.

Discussion Questions

1. Describe the data available from courts and correctional institutions in Canada. How are these data useful in identifying patterns of women's criminal behaviour?
2. Discuss the crimes that women are most often convicted of. What factors explain why women commit these crimes?
3. Do amendments need to be made to the *Criminal Code* with respect to prostitution-related offences? Explain.
4. According to Hatch and Faith (1989), "women in conflict with the law have more in common with other women than they do with male prison inmates." Does this statement ring true today? Discuss.

Suggested Readings

Canada, Task Force on Federally Sentenced Women. (1990). *Creating choices: Report of the Task Force on Federally Sentenced Women.* Ottawa: Department of the Solicitor General.

Comack, E. (1996). *Women in trouble.* Winnipeg: Fernwood Publishing.

Finn, A., Trevethan, S., Carrière, G., & Kowalski, M. (1999). Female inmates, Aboriginal inmates, and inmates serving life sentences: A one day snapshot. *Juristat, 19*(5), 1–14. Ottawa: Canadian Centre for Justice Statistics.

Pollack, S. (2000). Dependency discourse as social control. In K. Hannah-Moffat & M. Shaw (Eds.), *An ideal prison? Critical essays of women's imprisonment in Canada* (pp. 72–81). Halifax: Fernwood Publishing.

Shaw, M. (1999). "Knowledge without acknowledgement": Violent women, the prison and the cottage. *The Howard Journal, 38*(3), 252–266.

Online Resources

1. Correctional Service of Canada: www.csc-scc.gc.ca
2. Statistics Canada: www.statcan.ca

References

Activists push for welfare changes. (2003, December 18). *North Bay Nugget*, p. A6.

Atkinson, J. (1998). *Neutralizations among male and female fraud offenders.* Unpublished doctoral dissertation, Queen's University, Kingston. Theses Canada Portal, AMICUS No. 20673725.

Beattie, K. (2006). Adult correctional services in Canada, 2004/2005. *Juristat, 26*(5), 1–33.

Blatchford, C. (2005, June 25). Are you as fed up with Karla as I am? *Globe and Mail*, p. A15.

Boe, R., Motiuk, L., & Muirhead, M. (1998). Recent statistical trends shaping the corrections population in Canada. *Forum on Corrections Research, 10*(1), 1–7.

Burton, D., Goulding, R., Keskemety, R., McIntire, P., Miller, S., Perry, M., et al. (Producers), & Bender, J., Rosen, M., Rosen, B., & Sellers, M. (Writers). (2006). *Karla* [Motion picture]. United States: Quantum Entertainment & True Crime Investments LLC.

Canada, Task Force on Federally Sentenced Women. (1990). *Creating choices: Report of the Task Force on Federally Sentenced Women.* Ottawa: Department of the Solicitor General.

Canadian Broadcasting Corporation. (2006). The Oka crisis. Retrieved from http://archives.cbc.ca.

Canadian Broadcasting Corporation. (2007). Canada's only minimum-security women's prison to close. Retrieved from www.cbc.ca.

Comack, E. (1996). *Women in trouble.* Winnipeg: Fernwood Publishing.

Correctional Service of Canada. (2003). *Women offender statistical overview 2003*. Ottawa: CSC, Women Offender Sector.

Desjardins, N., & Hotten, T. (2004). Trends in drug offences and the role of alcohol and drugs in crime. *Juristat, 24*(1), 1–23.

Duchesne, D. (1997). Street prostitution in Canada. *Juristat, 17*(2), 1.

Finn, A., Trevethan, S., Carrière, G., & Kowalski, M. (1999). Female inmates, Aboriginal inmates, and inmates serving life sentences: A one day snapshot. *Juristat, 19*(5), 1–14.

Folsom, J., & Atkinson, J. (2007). The generalizability of the LSI-R and the CAT to the prediction of recidivism in female offenders. *Criminal Justice & Behavior, 34*(8), 1044–1056.

Gold, A. (2007). *The practitioner's Criminal Code: 2007 student edition*. Markham: LexisNexis Butterworths.

Grosch, A., Hall, S., Lee, S., Riley-Grant, M., Schmid, A. (Producers), & Jenkins, P. (Writer/Director). (2004). *Monster* [Motion picture]. United States: Newmarket Films.

Hannah-Moffat, K. (1995). Feminine fortresses: Woman-centered prisons? *The Prison Journal, 75*(2), 135–164.

Hannah-Moffat, K. (2000). Re-forming the prison: Rethinking our ideals. In K. Hannah-Moffat & M. Shaw (Eds.), *An ideal prison? Critical essays of women's imprisonment in Canada* (pp. 30–40). Halifax: Fernwood Publishing.

Hatch, A., & Faith, K. (1989). The female offender in Canada: A statistical profile. *Canadian Journal of Women and the Law, 3*, 432–456.

Kong, R., & AuCoin, K. (2008). Female offenders in Canada. *Juristat, 28*(1), 1–23.

Linden, R. (2004). *Criminology: A Canadian perspective* (5th ed.). Toronto: Thomson Nelson.

Morrissey, B. (2001). "Dealing with the devil": Karla Homolka and the absence of feminist criticism. In A. Burfoot & S. Lord (Eds.), *Killing women: The visual culture of gender and violence*. Waterloo: Wilfrid Laurier University Press.

National Union of Public and General Employees. (n.d.). *Two fraud cases: Conrad Black and Kimberly Rogers*. Retrieved from www.nupge.ca.

Pollack, S. (2000). Dependency discourse as social control. In K. Hannah-Moffat & M. Shaw (Eds.), *An ideal prison? Critical essays of women's imprisonment in Canada* (pp. 72–81). Halifax: Fernwood Publishing.

Shaw, M. (1999). "Knowledge without acknowledgement": Violent women, the prison and the cottage. *Howard Journal, 38*(3), 252–266.

Silver, W. (2007). Crime statistics in Canada. *Juristat, 27*(5), 1–14.

Statistics Canada. (2006). *Adults and youths charged, by sex and offence category, Canada, provinces and territories, annual* [CANSIM table 109-5009]. Available from http://estat.statcan.ca.

Statistics Canada. (2007a). *Adult correctional services, admissions to federal programs, annual* [CANSIM table 251-00031,16]. Available from http://estat.statcan.ca.

Statistics Canada. (2007b). *Adult correctional services, admissions to provincial and territorial programs, annual* [CANSIM table 251-0002]. Available from http://estat.statcan.ca.

Statistics Canada. (2007c). *Adult correctional services, admissions to provincial, territorial and federal programs, annual* [CANSIM table 251-0001]. Available from http://estat.statcan.ca.

Statistics Canada. (2007d). *Adult criminal court survey, number of cases by sex of accused, annual* [CANSIM table 252-0023]. Available from http://estat.statcan.ca.

Statistics Canada. (2007e). *Federal, provincial and territorial general government revenue and expenditures for fiscal year ending March 31, annual (dollars x 1,000,000)* [CANSIM table 385-0002]. Available from http://estat.statcan.ca.

CHAPTER 4

Background Experiences of Women Offenders

Jane Barker

Introduction

It has been said that we all begin as a *tabula rasa*—a blank slate upon which the experiences of our lives are then written. This concept may be useful to keep in mind as we explore in this chapter the kinds of experiences shared by many women in conflict with the law. Various types of childhood abuse (physical, sexual, emotional) and trauma, and both childhood and adult experiences of poverty, classism, racism, sexism, and partner abuse, can be viewed as experiences that may leave an indelible imprint. How people cope with these experiences is individualistic and will be discussed further in chapter 5. I must emphasize that not *all* individuals who have had these experiences as children or adults go on to encounter conflicts with the law. Many individuals, for whatever reason, cope with such adversity in a way that does not involve being charged criminally. Similarly, it would be fallacious to assume that every woman who has been in conflict with the law has been abused as a child, sexually assaulted by a part-

ner, or lived in poverty. Although these experiences are shared by many women in prison, they are not shared by *all*.

A few years before I met an incarcerated woman (or at least, before I was aware of having met an incarcerated woman), I read the book *Rock-A-Bye Baby*, by Anne Kershaw and Mary Lasovich (1991). This book chronicles the life and death of Marlene Moore, who, at age 28, was the first woman to be declared a dangerous offender in Canada.[1] Those who knew her best often commented that she was really more of a danger to herself (because of her extreme self-injurious behaviours) than she was to anyone else.[2] In 1988, Marlene Moore committed suicide at the Prison for Women (P4W) (Kershaw & Lasovich, 1991). Reading this book was an eye-opening experience for me and was my introduction to the realities faced by some incarcerated women in Canada. In many ways, although I did not know it at the time, reading this book was the first step in my developing an interest in working with women in conflict with the law.

In their book, Kershaw and Lasovich (1991) powerfully recounted the kinds of adversities that Marlene Moore experienced, including childhood physical, sexual, and emotional abuse, sexual assault, extreme poverty, classism, and sexism. Like many other women who are currently incarcerated, Marlene Moore had a low level of education, a minimal employment history, and very few marketable employment skills. Add society's stigmatization of women with a criminal record, and it is not surprising that she found it very difficult to cope outside of prison (see box 4.1).

Box 4.1   Prisoner's Suicide Followed Brutal Life

Marlene Moore's death by her own hand was inevitable in a society that knows how to wreck people but not how to put them together again.

A Canadian Press report said Marlene, 31, who hanged herself in a hospital room seven months after beginning a five-year sentence in the [Prison] for Women in Kingston, Ont., "had difficulty controlling her emotions" and that she had slashed her arms at least 20 times in rage and frustration.

Marlene would be richly amused by the understatement. There were many weeks when she slashed herself—arms, belly, vagina, legs—more than 20 times. The total number of cuts on her emaciated body numbered well over a thousand.

Part of her was a funny, bright woman, sentimental and sweet. The wonder of Marlene Moore was the resilience of that good person within her. Though she spent more than 12 years of her brief life in prison, she was never coarsened to the suffering of others. She made friends effortlessly, as a puppy does ...

On the other hand, Marlene Moore was filled with terrors she couldn't name or control and when frightened or hurt she was capable of irrational, impulsive, explosive behavior. That came from a nightmare childhood. She was one of 13 children born in a small town north of Toronto to a brutal father, a policeman, who beat them all mercilessly. As a result, many of the Moores are unpredictable and have been in and out of prison all their lives.

Marlene, small, frail and a bed-wetter, was a particular target. She once said she had never known such pain as that man inflicted on her. She started running away when she was 11. Later, her brothers gang-raped her. At 16, she was hitchhiking and was raped at knifepoint.

By the age of 17, she had evolved into a whip of a woman frantic with fear and quick to anger. When asked to leave a restaurant because her behavior was disruptive, she took it as a rejection and smashed a window. Her life in prison began ...

In the spring of 1985, when she was released to the supervision of the Elizabeth Fry Society, she was overwhelmed by the difficulty of adjusting to a life outside prison.

While she eventually mastered such commonplace matters as using a pay phone, she remained too nervous to travel around Toronto by herself.

When the period of parole ended, she found the stress of freedom so great that she started slashing herself again. Eventually, she spent six months in a locked ward in the Queen Street Mental Health Centre ...

She made one wonderful friend, a woman named Sue who is possessed of radiance and common sense. A troubled woman herself, tattooed and poor, she loved Marlene with her whole generous heart, and never stopped loving her.

It wasn't enough. Pat Capponi, a writer who also befriended Marlene, comments: "Marlene died because she was too needy. No one could cope with so much need."

A psychiatrist who specializes in people who abuse themselves consented to assess Marlene but decided not to accept her as a patient. Counsellors and other doctors came and went as her behavior deteriorated last winter. No co-ordinated package was ever put together to help her.

Last spring, she pulled off, with consummate incompetence, a string of five armed robberies. She was arrested and quickly pleaded guilty. The common wisdom is that she was longing to be back in prison, where she knew the rules of the game.

In the [Prison] for Women, she was a source of exasperation, taking on every sad cause of every sad woman in the place. Surgery was recommended to deal with the humiliation of her continuing incontinence, but she was afraid of it.

Last week, she was in segregation under 24-hour watch because she was considered suicidal. Sue was allowed to speak to her by telephone. Marlene sounded calm. She said she would have the surgery done at once.

On Saturday night, she killed herself. She had had enough.

Source: Callwood, J. (1988, December 6). Prisoner's suicide followed brutal life. *Globe and Mail*, p. A21. Reprinted by permission.

Marlene Moore first became acquainted with the justice system as a 13-year-old when she was sent to the Grandview Training School for Girls (under section 8 of the *Training Schools Act*, a young person could essentially be incarcerated for status offences such as truancy, swearing, or staying out all night) (Kershaw & Lasovich, 1991). As an adult, she was incarcerated provincially at Vanier Centre for Women, where she committed an offence[3] that led to her first federal sentence to P4W. For most of her teen years and her adult life, Marlene Moore was institutionalized in one way or another.

History of Abuse

The fact that so many girls and women who find themselves in conflict with the law report histories of childhood abuse is well documented in academic texts (Adelberg & Currie, 1993; Alarid & Cromwell, 2006; Chesney-Lind & Pasko, 2004a, 2004b; Comack, 1996; DeKeseredy, 2000; Pollock, 2002; Sommers, 1995), in journal articles on women and crime (Browne, Miller, & Maguin, 1999; Chesney-Lind & Rodriguez, 1983; Heney & Kristiansen, 1997; Maeve, 2000; Radosh, 2002), and in the popular press (Pearson, 1997; Tadman, 2001).

Because most of this research is correlational in nature, a causative relationship should not be inferred.

One study that used a prospective-cohorts design found that childhood sexual abuse didn't "uniquely increase an individual's risk for later delinquent and adult criminal behavior" (Widom & Ames, 1994, p. 303). However, the researchers did note an increased risk among the sample for being arrested as a juvenile for running away and as an adult for prostitution-related crimes (Widom & Ames, 1994). In a more recent prospective-cohorts design, a researcher who was interested in the intersection of race and gender with abuse history and crime found support for abuse as a stronger predictor of violence for women than for men, but no difference was found for abuse as a predictor across a variety of races (Makarios, 2007). This work suggested that "although the effects of abuse may be specific between males and females, the effects of abuse within the female population [are] general" (Makarios, 2007, p. 111). Blanchette and Brown (2006), in their text looking at the assessment and treatment of women offenders, noted that "collectively, the research to date suggests that victimization, although very common among female offenders, is not a criminogenic need" (p. 109). The authors emphasize that although they do not see this statement as being in any way in opposition to the view that victimization may play a role in the onset of criminal behaviour, no support exists for the role of victimization as being associated with recidivism (Blanchette & Brown, 2006). Irrespective of the issue of the role (or lack thereof) of victimization in the prediction of recidivism, high rates of victimization are found among criminalized women and should be acknowledged; even if victimization has not been found to relate to reoffending, it is an observation worth exploring.

In comparison with the general population, the violence experienced in the lives of some incarcerated women has been described as both severe and pervasive (Browne et al., 1999). Some researchers have investigated the link between past abuse and specific crimes. As noted previously, a relationship between childhood sexual abuse and later arrests for prostitution-related crimes has been demonstrated (Widom & Ames, 1994). Others have postulated that a host of possible pathways to incarceration may stem from abusive experiences (Gilfus, 2002). These pathways, from victimization to incarceration, may include various processes that are seen to criminalize the efforts made to escape from violence, or they may involve processes that serve to influence women's involvement in crime through their entrapment in violent relationships (Gilfus, 2002).

Comack (1996) has been quick to point out that a danger in looking at connections between abuse (or any other variable for that matter) and female offending is the question of whether these connections can be made at all "without pathologizing women's experiences and, at the same time, without losing sight of the structural context in which they move" (p. 82). The structural approach—to contextualize women's offending as a consequence of the kind of society (racist, capitalist, patriarchal) in which we live—allows for the focus of inquiry to shift from that of individual pathology as an explanation of women's offending (Comack, 1996). This approach may be preferable to viewing women's law-breaking behaviour as some sort of pathology; however, it is unable to fully account for or explain how these various structures (racism, capitalism, patriarchy) are truly experienced by women in their day-to-day lives (Comack, 1996).

We are left to ponder how the experiences of the past cast light on the behaviour of the present. Examining these connections may yield an indication as to why some women come into conflict with the law. This process must be done carefully, so as to not merely yield some simplistic model that fails to capture the complexity that surely exists in determining who will, and who won't, break the laws of society, get caught, be found guilty, and then be punished.

Prevalence of Abuse History Among Criminalized Women in Canada

In a survey of women who were under community supervision or in institutions in Ontario, Shaw (1994) found that 72 percent of the women indicated a history of physical abuse. In this same sample, nearly half (48 percent) reported having experienced sexual abuse. In total, more than three-quarters of the women surveyed reported a history of either physical or sexual abuse, and 70 percent indicated that they had experienced emotional abuse. Physical abuse was reported to have occurred more often in adulthood, whereas sexual abuse was reported to have occurred more often when the women were children. The reported perpetrators of the sexual abuse included all manner of relatives, whereas the physical abuse in adulthood tended to be perpetrated by partners—husbands, boyfriends, and common-law husbands.

According to the Task Force on Federally Sentenced Women (Canada, Task Force on Federally Sentenced Women [TFFSW], 1990), a large percentage of federally incarcerated women reported histories of physical and sexual abuse. Among the sample of federally sentenced women who were interviewed, 80 percent indicated they had suffered from some form of abuse in their lives. Just over half (54 percent) reported histories of sexual abuse, and approximately two-thirds (68 percent) stated they had been victims of physical abuse. When the rates of reported abuse history were looked at for Aboriginal women, the reported percentages were even higher. Among the Aboriginal women interviewed, 90 percent reported a history of physical abuse and 61 percent indicated a history of sexual abuse. Comparatively, the non-Aboriginal sample of women reported rates of physical and sexual abuse that were lower (61 percent and 50 percent respectively). Clearly, in the large sample of women interviewed as part of the research for the task force report, many of the criminalized women were survivors of some form of abuse.

Incarcerated Women's Accounts of Their Experiences of Violence

A number of books and articles have documented the voices of incarcerated women relating their own accounts of their experiences of violence (Chesney-Lind & Rodriguez, 1983; Comack, 2005; Comack & Brickey, 2007; Gilfus, 1992; Maeve, 2000; Sommers, 1995). This emphasis on asking women to describe how they conceptualize violence in their own lives is a positive step to a better understanding of why they have become criminalized. As Heidensohn (1994) has remarked, a shift (which she attributes to the impact of modern feminism) has occurred in the way in which so-called deviant women perceive themselves and ultimately act on their perceptions in order to address the problems that they encounter.

In one of the first studies of its kind, Chesney-Lind and Rodriguez (1983) used an open-ended question approach in their interviews of 16 incarcerated women in Hawaii. The researchers questioned the women about their backgrounds, including family histories, their exposure to general violence, and their experiences of physical abuse, incest, and rape. The authors reported that, for the most part, the women's biographies were replete with examples of their prior exposure, at an early age, to sexual victimization and violence. They further speculated that the "backgrounds reveal an interface between victimization and involvement in the criminal justice system that may constitute a systematic process of criminalization unique to women" (Chesney-Lind & Rodriguez, 1983, p. 62).

In the participatory research conducted by Maeve (2000), women's voices, in the form of their poetry, were examined as a gauge of their own awareness regarding the impact that violence has had in their lives. Maeve noted that it was the "early childhood experiences of sexual and physical abuse that emerged as life-shaping events that continued to both create and sustain chaotic and ultimately self-harming and community-harming lives" (2000, p. 474). Through the process of reading and writing poetry, the women in her study were reported to experience a raised consciousness regarding their own victimization and the violence that they themselves had perpetrated toward others.

Gilfus (1992) used the narratives from life history interviews of women incarcerated in an American prison to illustrate the transition of some women "from victims to survivors to offenders" (p. 5). Two of the dominant themes that emerged in her analysis of the interviews were "sexual abuse and incest" and "multiple types of abuse and neglect" in terms of childhood memories. One of the conclusions that she drew from this research was that prior violence was a strong factor in women's criminalization. Moreover, Gilfus speculated that for some women, the strategies that they employed to survive such abuse represented the "beginning of a process of transition from victim to offender" (p. 12).

Comack and Brickey (2007) noted a tendency to interpret women's violent behaviour in terms of three constructs which, as they point out, are different "yet not disconnected": women as "bad," "mad," or "victims" (p. 1). Comack and Brickey were interested in identifying to what extent women who were criminalized identified with, or rejected, these constructs. They found that the women who were interviewed did, to varying extents, identify with these constructs. However, the authors stressed that this identification was not absolute, and although they noted "some resonance in the women's accounts," there was a general failure to completely capture their complex histories (Comack & Brickey, 2007, p. 1). However, that being said, Comack and Brickey (2007) did stress that "the women's experiences of violence—both their own and that which has been directed at them—have had a long-lasting impact on who they are" (p. 27). This sentiment echoes previous research with incarcerated women (Chesney-Lind & Rodriguez, 1983; Comack, 2005; Gilfus, 1992; Maeve, 2000; Sommers, 1995).

Too Much Focus on Victimization Is Problematic

Some discussion has emerged on the dangers inherent in putting such focus on the link between criminal behaviour and experiences of abuse or victimization (Comack, 1999). As Comack (1999) has pointed out, the conceptualization of "women as victims" has not remained a theoretical construct, but has led to implications in the way that women are treated by the criminal justice system. Specifically, the impact—aimed both indirectly and directly at women in conflict with the law—comes from the research that serves to support the policies and practices ascribed to by the criminal justice system (Comack, 1999; Maidment, 2006). The development and implementation of the new "women-centred" prisons have been supported by the kind of research that emphasized the victimization of women (Comack, 1999, p. 163). According to Comack (1999), this tendency to view "women as victims" has negatively affected feminist criminology because this approach has allowed for the continued marginalization of concerns of paramount importance to feminist criminologists.

Comack (1999) has pointed out that the emergence of women's visibility in criminology has typically centred on a comparison with male offending patterns, or as a special case that is in need of additional explanation (such as battered woman syndrome). As Comack (1999) has stated, and as can be illustrated in many introductory criminology texts, women are often mentioned in sections on victimization, or, when discussed as offenders, they are often relegated to a chapter on "special" populations. Despite a surge in the number of texts published in the last 15 years on criminalized women, the number of these published works still pales in comparison with the number of mainstream texts whose focus is, for all intents and purposes, solely on men.

In addition, the conceptualization of "women as victims" may be problematic because it has been thought to mirror the same kinds of "us" vs. "them" dimensions that have plagued the criminal justice system, such as those of law abider/law breaker and victim/offender (Comack, 1999). The following quote succinctly illustrates the major problem with supporting such dualistic thinking: "So long as women are recognized only as victims and not as active agents, there is little need to embrace or integrate feminist analyses into the criminological agenda" (Comack, 1999, p. 165). Although acknowledging how a history of victimization may affect the lives of criminalized women is necessary, "putting all of one's eggs in one basket" is dangerous when attempting to understand a complexly determined outcome, such as that of becoming criminalized.

Others have pointed to the systemic way in which the concept of victim has been twisted to fit the agenda of those who serve to benefit from pathologizing and individualizing crimes of women (Maidment, 2006). Maidment challenges the way in which women's crime is conceptualized by the Canadian criminal justice system, and more specifically, the prison system. In her analysis, Maidment clearly illustrates how the language that is seen to dominate "the system" serves to both pathologize women's involvement in crime and, at the same time, individualize it so that it can then be "treated" by those employed within that same system. She stresses that this practice occurs in the absence of any kind of meaningful contextual analysis, which is a serious flaw in the current system. Maidment (2006) clearly emphasizes a need for those involved in the academic study of criminalized women

> to reverse our preoccupation with privileged accounts of knowledge which guide our research and policy agendas and focus our attention to seeing the world from the perspective of those with first-person knowledge of the racist, classist, heterosexist, and gendered ways in which our societal institutions operate. It is the thinking of those with a vested interest in promulgating an individualistic and pathological approach to treating those on the margins which is most urgently in need of correction. (p. 53)

Although Maidment (2006) has very clearly identified issues related to what she has termed the *individualization* and *pathologization* of women by the current system, women in the criminal justice system remain in need of assistance to reduce the probability that they will come into conflict with the law again. As will be discussed by Jill Atkinson and Jean Folsom in chapter 6, the assessment and treatment of criminalized women in Canada is an area that has received some significant attention in recent years (Blanchette & Brown, 2006).

Poverty and Financial Stress

Prior to a discussion of the impact that financial stress may or may not have on the lives of criminalized women, the reader should be aware of some staggering statistics related to poverty in general. In March 2000, *The Dynamics of Women's Poverty in Canada* (Lochhead & Scott, 2000) was published. The authors of this report relied on longitudinal data collected at two points in time (1993 and 1994) and concluded that variables such as age, educational level, and gender were all important determinants of who was considered to be economically vulnerable (Lochhead & Scott, 2000). Approximately 2.5 million women in Canada were estimated to be poor during 1993 or 1994—almost 23 percent of all women in Canada over the age of 15 (Lochhead & Scott, 2000). Almost one in four women were considered to be living at or below the poverty line in Canada, as measured by the low income cut-offs (LICOs) used by Statistics Canada (Lochhead & Scott, 2000). Rates of poverty among men were much lower. Only 17.5 percent of men in Canada (about one in six) were considered poor in 1993 or 1994. When age was examined, the largest divergence between male and female poverty was seen among seniors, where 29 percent of women were considered poor in 1993 or 1994, compared with about 13 percent of men in that same age group (Lochhead & Scott, 2000).

Although being poor is not a prerequisite for criminal behaviour, and certainly not all people living below the LICOs are at risk of becoming criminalized, we cannot ignore the influence that poverty might have for some people in terms of their probability of engaging in criminal behaviour. Earlier in this chapter, we noted that many incarcerated women share a history of poverty and financial stress. To draw a link between conditions of economic strife and criminal behaviour makes intuitive sense, especially for certain types of crimes. When considering the kinds of crimes that a large proportion of criminalized women are charged with—offences related to the drug trade and the sex trade, theft, and fraud, for example—an economic thread may very well tie these offences together.

Gilfus (1992), in her interviews of incarcerated American women, noted that many of the women thought of their illegal activities as a type of work. The women indicated that they resorted to acts that involved breaking the law mainly because of financial necessity (supporting their families). Further, Gilfus stressed how her research was supportive of the work of Chesney-Lind and Rodriguez (1983), who concluded that multiple factors led to women's criminalization, including histories of victimization, lack of education, and the absence of marketable employment skills. Added to this list, many of the young women were the sole supporters of their children (Chesney-Lind & Rodriguez, 1983). In consideration of the above, the coalescence of these factors may be interpreted as a recipe for economic deprivation.

Canadian research has also illustrated the importance of economic realities in the lives of criminalized women. Pollack (2000) has emphasized the experiences of the incarcerated Caribbean-Canadian women she interviewed, and suggested that their "lawbreaking is often an attempt to avoid dependency and to provide for the various family members who are in fact *dependent upon them* [emphasis in original]" (p. 75). The majority of the women she interviewed were convicted of the kinds of crimes (shoplifting, drug importation, drug trafficking, frauds) that are, more often than not, economically motivated. Many of the women interviewed by Pollack were very clear in drawing a causal relationship between financial strain and their criminal behaviour. In these instances, their income did not come close to what was needed to support themselves and their families. The following quote from R.J., one of the women Pollack (2000) interviewed, speaks volumes:

> So all the Black women I know are in this institution, they're here for financial gain. None of us are suffering from the norm of being a drug addict or being sexually molested by our father … We're in here purely for financial gain. We don't fit the stereotype of the "normal" inmate that's in here. We're here for *financial gain* [emphasis in original]. (p. 76)

Shaw's (1994) research on provincially incarcerated women in Ontario suggested, indirectly, that many of the women she interviewed may have experienced considerable financial strain prior to their incarceration. Approximately two-thirds of the women weren't working when they committed their offence, and for the majority of the women, their main source of income had consisted of social assistance (mother's allowance or welfare), which suggests that these women experienced economic hardship. A similar picture of economic stress was painted for federally sentenced women in *Creating Choices* (Canada, TFFSW, 1990). Of those who were working prior to incarceration, most reported having low-paying jobs. Many noted they wanted access to courses or programs to assist them to be economically self-sufficient upon release, suggesting that this situation was not the case prior to their incarceration (Canada, TFFSW, 1990). Again, although not explicitly stated, this information suggests that a high level of economic hardship existed in many of these women's lives.

Educational Level, Employment History, and Marketable Skills

In Canada, women comprise 47 percent of all employed people (Statistics Canada, 2006b). More than half (58 percent) of all women in Canada over the age of 14 had a job in 2006. In terms of social trends, the influx of women into the workforce in the past 30 years has been increasing. For example, in 1976, women comprised approximately 37 percent of the workforce, and only 42 percent of women over the age of 14 were working (Statistics Canada, 2006b). The above statistics take into account paid work only, not volunteer or unpaid work that many women also do.

The link between education level and employment in women appears clear: the higher a woman's education, the higher the likelihood that she will be employed (Statistics Canada, 2006b). In 2006, three-quarters of women who had a university degree were employed in a paid position, compared with 59 percent employment for women with a high school diploma, and 38 percent employment for women with some high school education. The group with the lowest level of paid employment comprised women with grade 8 or less; only 15 percent of this group were in the paid workforce (Statistics Canada, 2006b).

In the study of women's poverty in Canada described earlier in this chapter, high educational attainment did not translate into a guarantee that a woman would not become poor, but certain protective factors were found to be associated with having an education, albeit of less influence today than in the past (Lochhead & Scott, 2000). The authors noted that a shift in the level of educational attainment in Canada's population over the past few years, and that "a more highly educated poor population simply reflects the trend toward a more highly educated population in general" (Lochhead & Scott, 2000, p. 18). What are the implications of this finding for criminalized women? It would not be a stretch to assert that, according to this trend, criminalized women are at even more of a disadvantage relative to the general population given their low levels of educational attainment.

Comparatively speaking, women in prison tend to have lower levels of education than women in the community. Recent estimates suggest that about 10 percent of women in Canada have less than a grade 9 education (Statistics Canada, 2003). A larger proportion of incarcerated women have a similarly low level of education. Shaw (1994) found that the majority of women who were incarcerated provincially in Ontario (including women being supervised in the community) had a very low level of education. Almost one-third did not complete grade 10, and two-thirds didn't have a high school diploma or the equivalent. Similar results were reported by the TFFSW with respect to the educational attainments of federally incarcerated women. Two-thirds of their sample of women had not completed high school or training that would give them additional marketable qualifications (Canada, TFFSW, 1990).

Similar results have been reported in forensic clinical samples. In a study that looked at the socio-demographic characteristics of a group of 222 women who were defendants in criminal cases and had been referred for a forensic psychiatric assessment, the authors noted that these women tended to be "young, poorly educated, occupationally disadvantaged, unmarried, and from a broken home" (Aderibigbe, Arboleda-Florez, & Crisante, 1996, p. 74). Although these women were not in the correctional system, their demographic data appeared similar to the profile of women who end up in provincial or federal prisons.

Not surprisingly, Gilfus (1992) noted that educational neglect was one of the common themes identified in the childhood memories of incarcerated American women. Being marginalized in school, feeling as though they did not fit in, and experiencing the neglect of teachers all contributed to this particular theme and likely helped to explain the low educational attainment of so many incarcerated women (Gilfus, 1992).

When employment history was evaluated, Shaw (1994) found that most of the provincially incarcerated women she surveyed had a very limited employment history. A similar pattern was seen in women being supervised in the community. Most women were unemployed prior to their offence and had been out of work for more than a year. Their main source of income tended to be social assistance (welfare or mother's allowance). About half of the women in institutions and more than a quarter of the women being supervised in the community were interested in some form of job training. Again, a similar pattern was noted among federally incarcerated women, who reported histories of working in low-paying jobs that did not require any particular skills training (Canada, TFFSW, 1990). These women had been employed in unskilled positions in the service industry (stores, restaurants, and bars), in childcare services, in health care (as nurses aides), and in offices, but expressed an interest in attending meaningful skills training, particularly in the areas of office skills, skilled trades, and human services. Of particular note is that the women interested in human services expressed a desire to study sociology, social work, and child development to better prepare them for jobs working with ex-offenders, youth and children, substance abusers, Aboriginal people, and the elderly.

Partner Abuse

Interest in domestic violence has grown since the 1970s, predominantly as a result of the feminist movement (DeKeseredy & Hinch, 1991). Some debate surrounds the aspects of violence to be included in an operational definition of the term *domestic violence*. Whereas some have proposed limiting the construct to cases of physical abuse only, others have suggested that psychological, emotional, sexual, and economic abuse components should also be considered (DeKeseredy & Hinch, 1991). Regardless of which operational definition is used in its academic study, domestic violence, as a concept, can no longer be ignored by society.

In 2005–6, approximately $317 million was needed to operate Canada's shelters for abused women and children (Taylor-Butts, 2007). That year, more than 100,000 women and children used a shelter, and although not all women were there because they had been victims of domestic violence, the majority (74 percent) were (Taylor-Butts, 2007). An indication of the seriousness with which domestic violence is now viewed is the emergence of zero-tolerance policies in policing, which require charges to be laid in all cases of domestic violence that are investigated. Also, the use of tools to predict recidivism among men who assault their female partners is a fairly new focus, illustrating how domestic violence is viewed as a serious issue that can no longer be easily swept under the proverbial carpet (Hilton et al., 2004). Spousal violence not only affects the psychological and physical health of an individual but also creates social and economic impacts that must be acknowledged (Statistics Canada, 2006a). Recent trends in violence against women suggest that spousal assault is on the decline, with about 7 percent of women in Canada reporting that, at least once in the past five years, they had been sexually or physically assaulted by their partner (Statistics Canada, 2006a).

In an examination of the prevalence of physical and sexual victimization in a group of incarcerated women in the United States, Browne et al. (1999) investigated experiences of severe physical violence, threats of harm, and medical outcomes of intimate partner violence. The results they reported were staggering: 75 percent of the women in the study indicated they had experienced severe physical violence. In terms of specific acts of violence, 40 percent reported that they had been "choked, strangled, or smothered," more than 33 percent had been "threatened with a knife or gun," and 25 percent indicated they had been "cut with a knife or shot at by an intimate partner" (p. 313). A history of verbal threats was also commonplace among the women. More than half of the women stated that "a partner had threatened to kill them," and one-third stated that a partner had threatened them with suicide (p. 313). Not surprisingly, questions pertaining to the medical outcomes of partner violence indicated that many of the women (62 percent) reported having suffered from some sort of injury, with bruising mentioned most frequently. More serious types of injury (concussions and broken bones) were reported less frequently, but almost half of the women indicated they had sought some form of medical treatment to deal with the violence inflicted on them.

Although the research in Canada is fairly limited in terms of looking at violent adult relationships and women who have been criminalized, some studies have attempted to differentiate between the women's various forms of abusive experiences with their partners (Bonta, Pang, & Wallace-Capretta, 1995; Shaw, 1994). However, not all studies reported child and adult victimization separately (Lightfoot & Lambert, 1992). In their investigation of recidivism in a federal sample of incarcerated women, Bonta et al. (1995) noted that the only type of abuse significantly statistically related to recidivism was physical abuse as an adult. In their sample, adult physical abuse was actually inversely related to recidivism. Blanchette (1996, cited in Blanchette & Brown, 2006) noted that nearly 60 percent of a sample of federally sentenced women reported abuse in adulthood. In another Canadian study summarized by Blanchette and Brown (2006), more than 80 percent of a sample of federally sentenced women indicated they had been the victim of some type of abuse in their current relationship (Tien, Lamb, Bond, Gillstrom, & Paris, 1993, cited in Blanchette & Brown, 2006). Information reported in *Creating Choices* on abuse history did not explicitly differentiate between experiences of childhood abuse and experiences of adult abuse among federally sentenced women, and thus any specific comment on partner abuse among this group cannot be made easily (Canada, TFFSW, 1990). However, overall the literature on federally sentenced women suggests that partner abuse is a fairly common occurrence among these women.

Similar results have been reported among provincial samples. In Shaw's (1994) study of provincially incarcerated women, she reported that of abuse experienced by adult women, the majority of the emotional and physical abuse was at the hands of the woman's partner (husband, common-law spouse, or boyfriend). Almost two-thirds of the women surveyed indicated they had been physically abused in adulthood (Shaw, 1994). Of these cases of abuse, about 40 percent described the frequency of abuse as "regular," whereas another 40 percent described it as "occasional." In two-thirds of the cases, the women indicated they considered the abuse to be serious. A similar pattern was seen for cases of emotional abuse as adults. About 60 percent of the women stated they had suffered from emotional abuse, and most of this abuse was perpetrated by their partner (Shaw, 1994). The women noted that the emotional abuse was often associated with physical abuse. A different picture emerged when sexual abuse as an adult was examined. About one-third of the women indicated that they had been victimized sexually, and in the majority of these cases, the abuser had been a stranger or an acquaintance, not a husband, common-law spouse, or boyfriend (Shaw, 1994).

Battered Woman Syndrome

One aspect of domestic violence that has caught the attention of the media, and of society as a whole, are those cases in which abused women have killed their partners in acts of self-defence. The recognition of battered woman syndrome (BWS) as a defence when women have killed their abusive partners has generated considerably controversy. The concept of the battered woman was first described by Lenore Walker (1979). She defined the battered woman in the following manner:

> A battered woman is a woman who is repeatedly subjected to any forceful physical or psychological behavior by a man in order to coerce her to do something he wants her to do without any concern for her rights. Battered women include wives or women in any form of intimate relationships with men. Furthermore, in order to be classified as a battered woman, the couple must go through the battering cycle at least twice. Any woman may find herself in an abusive relationship with a man once. If it occurs a second time, and she remains in the situation, she is defined as a battered woman. (Walker, 1979, p. xv)

According to Walker (1979), the cycle of violence experienced by battered women in their relationships with their abusers consists of three predictable phases. The cycle begins with a period of tension-building, during which time the woman senses that a battering incident is imminent. The specific incident of battering constitutes the second phase and is immediately followed by the final phase, which Walker refers to as the period of calm and loving respite. Walker drew on the work of Martin Seligman and his concept of "learned helplessness" in dogs: animals placed in a situation of an unavoidable shock (a punishment that was delivered randomly) would eventually give up trying to escape. In these situations, when the shock actually became avoidable, in that the dogs could perform an act to escape the shock, they didn't even try, instead displaying "learned helplessness." Walker (1979, 1995) proposed that a similar mechanism was at work in cases of battered women:

> I hypothesized that battered women may also have lost their ability to predict that what they did would protect themselves from further harm if they perceived the abuse as non-escapable, random and variable punishment. I liked this theory because it explained how women could function so well in one setting and be so ineffective at home in stopping the violence. It also helped explain why women didn't leave; they developed coping strategies that helped them minimize the pain and danger from the abuse at the cost of escape skills. (Walker, 1995, p. 524)

In the 30 years since Walker first conceived of BWS, our understanding of BWS has evolved. As Walker (1995) notes:

> Today we know much more about the Battered Woman Syndrome (BWS). The psychological research has placed it as a subcategory of Post Traumatic Stress Disorder (PTSD). We know that many battered women develop psychological symptoms as coping strategies that my earlier work measured as learned helplessness strategies. While the high arousal and high avoidance and numbing behaviors may be adaptive in surviving abusing relationships, they are not useful once the woman has escaped. (p. 524)

Since developing the concept of BWS, Lenore Walker has testified as an expert witness in about 350 cases in which battered women have claimed self-defence in the killing of their abusive partners (Walker, 1995). She has emphasized that she never intended that BWS be construed as some kind of mental illness that could then be applied to a diminished capacity or insanity defence. Instead, she has been clear to state that BWS can be used as a way to conceptualize women's self-defence in these sorts of situations. According to Walker (1995), when women kill in self-defence, it "looks" very different from the male image of self-defence. Women who have killed in self-defence have tended to kill their male partners "during a moment of quiet, when he was sleeping after a beating leaving her with threats and intrusive memories of more to come, or before he started, anticipating the danger that lay ahead from the memories of past beatings" (Walker, 1995, p. 526). These sorts of situations are quite different from the typical image of male self-defence—like that of a barroom brawl gone awry.

The case of *R. v. Lavallee* was the first Canadian case in which a woman successfully used BWS in her claim of self-defence in the killing of her abusive partner (see box 4.2). The use of BWS as the defence in this case, and similar cases, has not gone without criticism (Comack

& Balfour, 2004; Shaffer, 1997; Tang, 2003; White-Mair, 2000). For the most part, feminists were supportive of the decision made by the Supreme Court; however, as Shaffer (1997) noted, the decision was conceptualized by some as a double-edged sword. On the one hand, the decision emphasized the importance of expert testimony in cases of BWS so that decision-makers could understand why an abused woman might not leave an abusive relationship, and why she might not see any other way out (other than killing). On the other hand, criticisms abound regarding yet another syndrome that serves to pathologize and "medicalize" the experiences of women (Shaffer, 1997; White-Mair, 2000). Some have conceptualized the use of BWS as yet another example of the "psy-discourse" (Comack & Balfour, 2004, p. 67). According to the criticisms, by naming or labelling the experience of some battered women as a syndrome, such as BWS, a battered woman is then "subject to the same kinds of individualizing effects as other psychological constructs" (Comack & Balfour, 2004, p. 76). In other words, the implication is that something is wrong with the woman for which she needs treatment.

Shaffer (1997) noted that at the time of the Supreme Court's decision she raised concerns that the *Lavallee* decision could have negative repercussions for women. Specifically, the view that battered women had some sort of a syndrome and as a result were pathological could prove to be problematic. She also expressed a concern that a stereotype could develop of what a battered woman looks like, which could be to the detriment of abused women who do not fit within the confines of such a stereotype (Shaffer, 1997). This thought has been echoed by others in the literature, who noted that the use of BWS actually creates a paradox in which the abused woman is conceptualized as having a mental illness that makes rational decision-making difficult. Yet, does this view not fly in the face of the previous logic that allowed observers to conclude that given her situation, the rational decision to defend oneself made sense using BWS as the means of explaining her behaviour (Tang, 2003)?

Other criticisms concerning BWS address the fairly narrow definition of BWS and its applicability in cases in which the defendant is a woman of colour (Tang, 2003). More specifically, Tang (2003) asserts that women who don't fit the mould of a passive and helpless victim run the risk of not having their claims of self-defence heard fairly: because the definition of BWS narrowly defines what a battered woman looks like, if a woman doesn't fit the BWS mould, then she may be ill-advised to try to use it as a defence.

Following the *Lavallee* decision, the Canadian Association of Elizabeth Fry Societies lobbied for four years to convince the Minister of Justice to agree to have an *en bloc* review of cases in which women had been convicted of killing their partners, both before and after the *Lavallee* decision (Sheehy, 2000). Ninety-eight women applied to have their cases included in the self-defence review by Judge Ratushny (Sheehy, 2000). Because of the exclusion criteria used, only 14 women were actually interviewed for the review, and in the end only seven were given some sort of recommendation of relief (Sheehy, 2000). The end result was that, in actuality, "no women were released from prison as a result of the SDR [self-defence review]" (Sheehy, 2000, p. 198).[4]

Box 4.2   R. v. Lavallee and the Legal Recognition of the Battered Woman Syndrome

Angelique Lyn Lavallee was charged with the second degree murder of her common law husband, Kevin Rust. That she killed Rust was not disputed. Lavallee admitted to shooting Rust in the back of the head as he was leaving her bedroom to return to a party going on elsewhere in their house, although she said that she was aiming to shoot over his head to scare him. What was not clear was whether Lavallee could lead expert evidence of the battering Rust had inflicted upon her in order to support her claim that she acted in self-defence, or even whether self-defence could be made out in the circumstances. While the evidence at trial revealed that Rust had abused Lavallee throughout their relationship* and that immediately before the shooting Rust had beaten Lavallee and threatened to kill her after the party if she didn't kill him first, Lavallee's actions in shooting Rust as he was leaving the room arguably did not fall within the traditional doctrine of self-defence ...

At trial, defence counsel called a psychiatrist, Dr. Fred Shane, as an expert witness. The purpose of Dr. Shane's evidence was to overcome the problems with Lavallee's self-defence claim by providing the jury with information about the effects on women of prolonged battering. The essence of his testimony was that Lavallee demonstrated a pattern of behaviour that abused women frequently exhibit known as the "battered woman syndrome" ...

Lavallee was acquitted at trial, but the acquittal was overturned by the Manitoba Court of Appeal on the ground that Dr. Shane's testimony should not have been admitted ...

The Supreme Court of Canada restored Lavallee's acquittal, holding that the trial judge had correctly admitted Dr. Shane's evidence. Expert evidence could, in Wilson J.'s view, assist the jury in fairly assessing a battered woman's plea of self-defence in several ways. First, it could dispel myths and stereotypes about battered women that might adversely affect a woman's claim to have acted in self-defence ... Second, expert evidence could explain how a battered woman's perception that she faced a threat of death or grievous bodily harm might be reasonable, even where an outside observer might not perceive an attack to be imminent. Such evidence could also explain why women often remain in abusive relationships and thus why battered women might not perceive leaving as a reasonable alternative to striking out with deadly force against their abusers.

---

*   Wilson J. notes that Lavallee's relationship with Rust was "volatile and punctuated by frequent arguments and violence" which often occurred several times a week. She also notes that between 1983 and 1986, Lavallee made several trips to the hospital for the treatment of injuries resulting from the abuse.

Source: Shaffer, M. (1997). The battered woman syndrome revisited: Some complicating thoughts five years after *R. v. Lavallee*. *University of Toronto Law Journal, 47*, 1–33.

Racism and Sexism

Issues pertaining to racism experienced by Aboriginal and visible minority criminalized women are covered in depth by Brenda Restoule and Shahid Alvi, respectively, in chapters 10 and 11. Therefore, the coverage of racism will be cursory in this chapter. Gilfus (1992) reported that a common theme of racial violence emerged in her dialogues with incarcerated women. According to the TFFSW, Aboriginal women who were federally incarcerated in Canada felt they had been subjected to racism. As noted in *Creating Choices*, some of the Aboriginal women who were interviewed believed they had been targets of racism in the prison and had been discriminated against. Further, it was their perception that few staff were sensitive to their cultural practices and backgrounds (Canada, TFFSW, 1990).

Pollock (2002) has discussed how the construct of dependency has been used as a means of social control. In her analysis, she noted that many of the Caribbean-Canadian women with whom she spoke reported that their criminal behaviour had occurred in an attempt to avoid having to be dependent on anyone—including the state, an intimate partner, friend, or a relative. Pollock noted that approximately 10 percent of women incarcerated federally were Black and, as is the case with Aboriginal women, Black women were also disproportionately represented among those incarcerated provincially. Interestingly, in the TFFSW report, the section "Freedom from Racism" mentions Aboriginal women, but no specific reference is made to Black women—despite the authors of the report having acknowledged that they didn't doubt that women from "other minority groups" had suffered from racism but that this information was not collected in the research studies commissioned by the TFFSW (Canada, TFFSW, 1990).

In terms of sexism, criminalized women, just like any other women in our society, may be exposed to sexist comments from others and sexist policies and practices of their employers, and may be accosted by sexist advertising and media portrayals of women (see box 4.3). For a thorough discussion of the gendered way in which girls and women are victimized, the reader should take note of chapter 12, by Walter DeKeseredy.

In terms of criminalized women, Comack and Balfour (2004) have explored how violent women may be conceptualized as betraying their gender because their behaviour and their criminal acts do not easily fit into how society tends to think of violence. A woman who has committed a violent act may be seen to be an anomaly because members of society (including those who work in the criminal justice system) tend to equate aggression with masculinity, and in so doing, set up certain cognitive representations about how a case should, or will, proceed (Comack & Balfour, 2004). In other words, for many people, to be aggressive is to be male. In this sense, a violent, aggressive woman fits neither the mental picture of a person who is usually aggressive, nor the concept of an aggressive person that Crown attorneys and defence lawyers are prepared to deal with in the context of the justice system (Comack & Balfour, 2004). The other way in which a violent woman can be seen to be betraying her gender is through the ways in which she might "breach the scripts of femininity" (Comack & Balfour, 2004, p. 62). The authors note that both sides of the courtroom will play on certain societal stereotypes; for example, the defence might emphasize "the abuse excuse" (Pearson, 1997, cited in Comack & Balfour, 2004). The Crown might cast the woman as evil incarnate, or might emphasize her differentness—as a prostitute or drug addict (Comack & Balfour, 2004).

In addition, some have suggested that criminalized women have also been affected by gendered public policy (Bloom, Owen, & Covington, 2004). Although making reference to policies in the United States, the arguments put forth by Bloom et al. are also applicable to Canada. They note some significant gendered effects associated with the "war on drugs," welfare reform, and policies related to public housing. Other areas of policy they believe differentially affect women offenders include "welfare benefits, drug treatment, housing, education, employment, and reunification with children" (Bloom et al., 2004, p. 37). To begin to improve policy for criminalized women, the gender-based experiences of these women must be the target of interventions that address "drug abuse and trauma recovery, education and training in job and parenting skills, and affordable and safe housing" (Bloom et al., 2004, p. 36).

Drug and Alcohol Abuse

The fact that a large percentage of women involved in the criminal justice system have had some problems associated with drug or alcohol use is fairly well documented in the literature (Comack, 1996; Lightfoot & Lambert, 1992; Lo, 2004; Pernanen, Cousineau, Brochu, & Sun, 2002; Shaw, 1994). To fully appreciate the scope of drug and alcohol problems among

---

Box 4.3   Halifax Billboard Joke Offends Women's Groups

It was meant to be a clever play on words to drum up business. But instead, a billboard at a Halifax beer hall has only drummed up controversy. The sign outside the Halifax Alehouse reads: "Our waitress uniforms were designed back when 'harass' was two words."

Many people in town find the sign offensive, including Irene Smith, with the city's Avalon Sexual Assault Centre, who called the Alehouse to complain.

"It sort of says: 'What's wrong with the good old days?'" she says.

"The ad promotes the notion that it's okay to go sexually harass women," Smith told ATV News. "And quite frankly, the Human Rights Act says sexual harassment is against the law. You are actually breaking the legislation to do that."

Although the manager of Alehouse refused to comment when contacted for an interview, an executive with the company that produced the billboard agreed to talk.

"Clearly, it's the Alehouse's intent to attract the young adult audience," CCL senior vice president Chris Keevill told ATV News. "And we would hope that customers recognize this billboard in the manner that it was intended to be: tongue-in-cheek."

Don Shiner, a marketing professor at Mount Saint Vincent University, says these days, advertisers and their clients are constantly pushing the envelope.

"It's always questionable when we use sex to sell," he says. But Shiner says sex and alcohol is a more sensitive combination.

Shiner says it's also interesting that because of the reaction, the Alehouse will probably receive more publicity than it would have if the billboard had been less controversial.

Source: Halifax billboard joke offends women's groups. (2004, November 6). *CTV.ca News*. Retrieved from www.ctv.ca. Reprinted by permission of CTVglobemedia.

criminalized women, it may be helpful to understand the role these substances play in the lives of women in Canada as a whole. In a national survey that looked at drug and alcohol use among Canadian women, a small percentage (10 percent) of women indicated having some problems associated with alcohol use (Hewitt, Vinje, & MacNeil, 1995). When the types of problems were examined more closely, about 6 percent of respondents indicated they had experienced physical health problems. Problems with "friends or social life" and problems with "outlook on life" were mentioned by 4 and 3 percent of women respectively. About 9 percent of women surveyed indicated that they had engaged in drinking and driving, reported most often (16 percent) among younger women aged 20 to 24 (Hewitt et al., 1995).

In terms of drinking patterns, Hewitt et al. (1995) noted that women who tended to drink more frequently than most women tended to be single or divorced, older, with a higher level of educational attainment, a higher income, and employed in either a managerial position or in a blue-collar job. A different set of characteristics emerged for those who tended to drink more than the average number of drinks in one drinking episode: these women also tended to be single or divorced, but they were younger, had a lower level of education, a lower income, and tended to be either a student, unemployed, or employed in a blue-collar job (Hewitt et al., 1995).

Interestingly, these two groups of women are likely to differ in their likelihood of coming into conflict with the law if just drinking behaviour is considered, that is, in the absence of other factors. Those who drink more frequently (but not more in terms of quantity) are more likely to be drinking socially in moderation, circumstances that are unlikely to bring them into conflict with the law (except for driving while under the influence of alcohol). Those who drink more in terms of quantity at each drinking occasion increase their likelihood of an interaction with police because of the kinds of behaviours most often associated with a higher than average intake of alcohol (a decrease in inhibitions, for example), especially if their drinking occurs in a public place.

With respect to drug use among Canadian women, results from a national survey indicated that about 18 percent of women in Canada had tried marijuana or hashish at some point in their life. About 3 percent reported having used cocaine or crack, and 3 percent indicated that they had used LSD, speed, or heroine (Hewitt et al., 1995). The authors of the report cautioned that these prevalence rates may have underestimated drug use among Canadian women: their sample may have been biased because the experiences of women who live on the streets (and who, the authors noted, would be more likely to use illicit drugs) would likely not have been captured using a general population survey methodology (Hewitt et al., 1995).

Many readers would likely not take issue with the statement that the abuse of alcohol and/or drugs can have devastating effects on the individuals involved, on their friends, families, peers, and communities, and on society as a whole. Drug-related charges are only one way in which illegal substances are directly related to criminal behaviour. Because being in possession of a small amount of a controlled substance is, in and of itself, a crime known as possession, a link exists between illicit substances and crime. That being said, women, as is the case with many other crimes, are a minority of all those who are charged with drug-related crimes. Only 14 percent of drug-related charges are laid against women (Department of Justice Canada, 2003). As is the case with men, the majority (44 percent) of those charges are for possession. However, in cases of importation/production and trafficking, a higher percentage of those charged are women (Department of Justice Canada, 2003). In addition to drug-related charges, drinking and driving can also result in criminal charges. Interestingly, although men continue to make up the majority of those charged with these offences, women's relative proportion of impaired driving charges has increased consistently from 1986, when 8 percent of those charged were women, to 2002, when women comprised 13 percent of those charged with impaired driving (Janhevich, Gannon, & Morisset, 2003).

In Canada, a recent study of the link between alcohol/substance use and crime found fairly strong support for the existence of a relationship between these variables among male and female offenders (Pernanen et al., 2002). The authors of the report concluded that for those serving either a federal or a provincial sentence in Canada, about 40 to 50 percent of the crimes could be attributed to drug and/or alcohol use. More specifically, about 10 to 15 percent of crimes were thought to be attributed solely to drugs, 15 to 20 percent to alcohol alone, and 10 to 20 percent to a combination of the two (Pernanen et al., 2002). The researchers were also interested in any patterns that might emerge for specific crimes and substance/alcohol use. They found that for violent crimes (such as homicide, attempted murder, and assault) about half could be attributed to alcohol and/or drugs. Similarly, for those crimes the researchers classified as gainful crimes (such as theft, break and enter, and robbery), an estimated 50 percent could be attributed to alcohol or drug use (Pernanen et al., 2002).

Some have pointed out that, in the United States, the so-called war on drugs has really been a "war on women," and more specifically, a war on Black women (Bloom et al., 2004; Bush-Baskette, 2004; Chesney-Lind & Pasko, 2004a; Paltrow, 2004). Those who tended to be the focus of the war on drugs were the people involved at the lower end of the drug trade spectrum: users and low-level dealers of drugs (Bush-Baskett, 2004). The kinds of policies that have been initiated in this war on drugs (mandatory sentencing laws, increased penalties, stricter enforcement of laws) have been linked to the increased incarceration rates of women that were seen in the 1980s and 1990s in the United States (Bush-Baskette, 2004; Chesney-Lind & Pasko, 2004a). Similar observations have been made with respect to women and the criminal justice system in Canada in terms of the sentencing of those found guilty of certain drug-related offences (Lawrence & Williams, 2006). While articulating that the typical drug mule[5] in Canada is often a poor, Black mother, Lawrence and Williams (2006) point out that what needs to be asked is "Why are these women the ones being caught for these offences? And is there any connection between their identity and the harsh punishments meted out for the crime?" (p. 322).

Links between victimization and drug and alcohol abuse in criminalized groups of women have been noted in the literature (Browne et al., 1999; Gilfus, 2002). Specifically, some have suggested that increased rates of intimate partner victimization may be related to women's involvement in substance use and other illegal behaviours (Browne et al., 1999). Others have suggested that substance abuse may serve as a coping strategy for those who face struggles associated with the stressors that they face, whether related to street life or to an abusive relationship (Gilfus, 2002). More information on coping strategies is presented in chapter 5.

Comack (1996) noted that "most of the women I spoke with reported that they had problems with drugs and/or alcohol" and that for a number of women, they were able to make some direct links between their use and their conflicts with the law (p. 119). Similar sentiments were expressed by women incarcerated in the United States (Gilfus, 1992). Some women were able to draw a connection between their experiences of failure in school and the ready supply of drugs that were available to numb their pain (Gilfus, 1992). In a related observation, for some women, it was among that drug subculture at school that they "found their first feeling of acceptance and belonging" (Gilfus, 1992, p. 8).

In Shaw's (1994) survey of provincial female offenders, she reported that alcohol and drugs "played a significant part in the lives of the majority of women: 79% of those in institutions and 60% of those in the community" (p. iv). Direct links between drug/alcohol use and offending were reported by half of the community sample of women and two-thirds of the institutional sample of women (Shaw, 1994). Similar results have been reported among federal samples of women. In *Creating Choices*, the TFFSW noted that two-thirds (69 percent) of the women who were interviewed stated that their offence and their offence history had been affected by substance abuse. The women noted that they either committed their offence while under the influence of drugs and/or alcohol, or that the offence was committed in an attempt to support a drug or alcohol addiction. Another group of women was incarcerated for crimes related to the drug trade (possession, trafficking, or importing) (Canada, TFFSW, 1990).

With respect to federal female offenders, a survey of their drug and alcohol use was completed in the early 1990s (Lightfoot & Lambert, 1991, 1992). The researchers sought to describe, in detail, the sample of federal female offenders in terms of a number of variables, including substance use. A total of 80 women agreed to take part in this research at the Prison for Women. This sample of women was similar to other samples of federally incarcerated women: the women were young (mean age of 34 years), most were single, and few reported having obtained education beyond high school, the majority (62 percent) had children, and most of these women reported that their work prior to incarceration had consisted of unskilled labour (Lightfoot & Lambert, 1991, 1992). In terms of alcohol use, the results of their research suggested that, compared with male offenders, the women reported lower levels of alcohol dependence, as measured by the alcohol dependence scale (ADS). Most of the women (72.5 percent) were classified as having low levels of dependence on alcohol as measured by the ADS (Lightfoot & Lambert, 1992). In the interviews, the women were asked to define their own patterns of drinking. Approximately one-fifth of the women described themselves as teetotallers, whereas one-third stated that they were occasional drinkers. The remainder of the women identified themselves as alcoholics (12.5 percent), heavy drinkers (16.2 percent), or moderate drinkers (10 percent) (Lightfoot & Lambert, 1992). Just less than half of the women reported some sort of problem associated with their use of alcohol. For most of the women, family problems predominated, followed by legal, work, and health problems (Lightfoot & Lambert, 1992).

In addition to alcohol use, the researchers were also interested in gaining a better understanding of the role that substances played in the lives of incarcerated women. In total, about two-thirds of the women reported some kind of a problem that related to their use of drugs in the six months prior to the commission of their index offence (Lightfoot & Lambert, 1992). The kinds of areas in which the women reported problems were legal, family, work/school, and health. Examination of the kinds of drugs that the women used in the six months prior to the commission of their offence showed that the most popular substances were benzodiazepines (38.7 percent), narcotic analgesics (35 percent), and cocaine (31.3 percent), whereas cannabis use was reported among about one-quarter of the women (Lightfoot & Lambert, 1992). When drug problems were quantified (using the drug abuse screening test, or DAST) the results indicated that about one-third of the women reported no problems associated with drug use, whereas the remainder scored as having low levels (11.1 percent), moderate levels (18.7 percent), substantial levels (21.3 percent), or severe levels (13.6 percent) of problems associated with drug use. In comparison with male offenders, similar proportions of women were reporting substantial and severe levels of problems, but more women scored as having "no problems" with drug use than did men (Lightfoot & Lambert, 1992). Interestingly, nearly half of the sample of women stated that in order to quit using drugs, they would have needed some sort of professional intervention (Lightfoot & Lambert, 1992).

Summary

As Walter DeKeseredy made reference to in chapter 2, the feminist pathways theorists have looked to the ways in which men's and women's lives differ in terms of the patterns that develop with respect to criminal behaviour. By taking a whole life perspective (Belknap, 2001, p. 402, cited in Bloom et al., 2004), we can appreciate the impact that various experiences may have had on a woman's life trajectory, whether that path intersects with aspects of the criminal justice system or not. We must be cognizant that the uniqueness of individuals is not lost when we search for commonalities in our attempts to better understand why some women become criminalized and others do not. Although many criminalized women share certain life experiences, we must be mindful that a person's experiences do not define the individual. As individuals, our lives are shaped by a host of factors: our innate abilities, our experiences, our thoughts and feelings, our interactions with others, our self-reflection and awareness of ourselves as separate autonomous beings, our identification of ourselves as similar to or different from others.

If I were to ask the readers of this text why you decided to go to school and take this particular course, I am sure that the answers that I would receive would reflect some common themes: "I want to work in a criminal justice field," "I am interested in why women are in prison," "I needed a half credit," but each answer would be varied and reflective of you as an individual. In a similar vein, if I were to ask 1,000 women in prison why they were there, undoubtedly some common themes would emerge; however, I would still get 1,000 different answers, each more or less similar to the next, but each an individual's account of their life circumstances. It would be simplistic to assume there is one answer to the question of why women are criminalized, but that doesn't mean that it isn't worth asking the question.

Notes

1. Marlene Moore was declared a dangerous offender in 1985. Justice Eugene Ewashuck, who made the declaration, did so reluctantly and did not impose an indeterminate sentence (which was not required in 1985). He sentenced her to six months in jail, with an additional three months of probation (Kershaw & Lasovich, 1991).

2. At the time of her death, it was reported that Marlene Moore had slashed herself more than 1,000 times. She had scars on virtually every reachable part of her body (Kershaw & Lasovich, 1991).

3. Marlene Moore and fellow inmate Isabella Fay Ogima took grounds supervisor, Harriet Ironside, hostage. Marlene pleaded guilty to seven abduction-related charges and was sentenced to six years (Kershaw & Lasovich, 1991).

4. For an in-depth analysis of the self-defence review, see Sheehy (2000).

5. The term *mule* is a colloquialism that refers to individuals who act as couriers to smuggle drugs into a country.

Discussion Questions

1. The focus on some criminalized women's histories of abuse is sometimes referred to as "the abuse excuse." In your opinion, is it a valid description?
2. Why is it important to consider a woman's own narrative in terms of her life experiences of violence?
3. Battered woman syndrome (BWS) as a defence has been applauded by some and criticized by others. What are the strengths and weaknesses associated with the use of BWS as a defence?
4. What kinds of socio-economic factors may be linked to the criminalization of some women? Discuss.
5. In the federal correctional system, women with a low level of education are encouraged to improve their educational level during their incarceration. Why would the correctional service place such an emphasis on educational attainment?
6. How is drug and/or alcohol use related to the criminalization of women?

Suggested Readings

Blanchette, K., & Brown, S. (2006). *The assessment and treatment of women offenders: An integrative perspective.* Chichester, UK: John Wiley & Sons.

Chesney-Lind, M., & Pasko, L. (2004). *The female offender: Girls, women, and crime* (2nd ed.). Thousand Oaks, CA: Sage.

Chesney-Lind, M., & Pasko, L. (2004). *Girls, women, and crime: Selected readings.* Thousand Oaks, CA: Sage.

DeKeseredy, W. (2000). *Women, crime and the Canadian criminal justice system.* Cincinnati: Anderson.

Kershaw, A., & Lasovich, M. (1991). *Rock-a-bye baby: A death behind bars.* Toronto: McClelland & Stewart.

Online Resources

1. VAWnet National Online Resource Center on Violence Against Women: http://new.vawnet.org
2. Canadian Centre on Substance Abuse: www.ccsa.ca
3. Statistics Canada: www.statcan.ca

References

Adelberg, E., & Currie, C. (1993). *In conflict with the law: Women and the Canadian justice system.* Vancouver: Press Gang.

Aderibigbe, Y., Arboleda-Florez, J., & Crisante, A. (1996). Reflections on the sociodemographic and medicolegal profiles of female criminal defendants. *International Journal of Offender Therapy and Comparative Criminology, 40,* 74–84.

Alarid, L., & Cromwell, P. (2006). *In her own words: Women offenders' views on crime and victimization.* Los Angeles: Roxbury.

Blanchette, K., & Brown, S. (2006). *The assessment and treatment of women offenders: An integrative perspective.* Chichester, UK: John Wiley & Sons.

Bloom, B., Owen, B., & Covington, S. (2004). Women offenders and the gendered effects of public policy. *Review of Policy Research, 21,* 31–48.

Bonta, J., Pang, B., & Wallace-Capretta, S. (1995). Predictors of recidivism among incarcerated female offenders. *The Prison Journal, 75,* 277–295.

Browne, A., Miller, B., & Maguin, E. (1999). Prevalence and severity of lifetime physical and sexual victimization among incarcerated women. *International Journal of Law and Psychiatry, 22,* 301–322.

Bush-Baskette, S. (2004). The war on drugs as a war against Black women. In M. Chesney-Lind & L. Pasko (Eds.), *Girls, women, and crime: Selected readings* (pp. 185–194). Thousand Oaks, CA: Sage.

Callwood, J. (1988, December 6). Prisoner's suicide followed brutal life. *Globe and Mail,* p. A21.

Canada, Task Force on Federally Sentenced Women. (1990). *Creating choices: Report of the Task Force on Federally Sentenced Women.* Ottawa: Department of the Solicitor General.

Chesney-Lind, M., & Pasko, L. (2004a). *The female offender: Girls, women, and crime* (2nd ed.). Thousand Oaks, CA: Sage.

Chesney-Lind, M., & Pasko, L. (2004b). *Girls, women, and crime: Selected readings.* Thousand Oaks, CA: Sage.

Chesney-Lind, M., & Rodriguez, N. (1983). Women under lock and key: A view from the inside. *The Prison Journal, 63,* 47–65.

Comack, E. (1996). *Women in trouble.* Black Point, NS: Fernwood.

Comack, E. (1999). New possibilities for a feminism "in" criminology? From dualism to diversity. *Canadian Journal of Criminology, 41,* 161–170.

Comack, E. (2005). Coping, resisting, and surviving: Connecting women's law violations to the histories of abuse. In L.F. Alarid & P. Cromwell (Eds.), *In her own words: Women offenders' views on crime and victimization* (pp. 33–43). Los Angeles, CA: Roxbury.

Comack, E., & Balfour, G. (2004). *The power to criminalize.* Halifax: Fernwood.

Comack, E., & Brickey, S. (2007). Constituting the violence of criminalized women. *Canadian Journal of Criminology and Criminal Justice, 49,* 1–36.

DeKeseredy, W. (2000). *Women, crime and the Canadian criminal justice system.* Cincinnati: Anderson.

DeKeseredy, W., & Hinch, R. (1991). *Woman abuse: Sociological perspectives.* Toronto: Thompson Educational Publishing.

Department of Justice Canada. (2003). *Drug use and offending.* Ottawa: Department of Justice Canada.

Gilfus, M. (1992). From victims to survivors to offenders: Women's routes of entry and immersion into street crime. In L.F. Alarid & P. Cromwell (Eds.), *In her own words: Women offenders' views on crime and victimization* (pp. 5–14). Los Angeles, CA: Roxbury.

Gilfus, M. (2002). Women's experiences of abuse as a risk factor for incarceration. Retrieved from http://new.vawnet.org.

Halifax billboard joke offends women's groups. (2004, November 6). *CTV.ca News.* Retrieved from www.ctv.ca.

Heidensohn, F. (1994). From being to knowing: Some issues in the study of gender in contemporary society. *Women and Criminal Justice, 6,* 13–37.

Heney, J., & Kristiansen, C. (1997). An analysis of the impact of prison on women survivors of childhood sexual abuse. *Women & Therapy, 20,* 29–44.

Hewitt, D., Vinje, G., & MacNeil, P. (1995). *Horizons two: Canadian women's alcohol and other drug use—Increasing our understanding.* Ottawa: Health Canada.

Hilton, N., Harris, G., Rice, M., Lang, C., Cormier, C., & Lines, K. (2004). A brief actuarial assessment for the prediction of wife assault recidivism: The Ontario Domestic Assault Risk Assessment. *Psychological Assessment, 16,* 267–275.

Janhevich, D., Gannon, M., & Morisset, N. (2003). Impaired driving and other traffic offences: 2002. *Juristat, 23*(9), 1–20.

Kershaw, A., & Lasovich, M. (1991). *Rock-a-bye baby: A death behind bars.* Toronto: McClelland & Stewart.

Lawrence, S., & Williams, T. (2006). Swallowed up: Drug couriers at the borders of Canadian sentencing. *University of Toronto Law Journal, 56,* 295–331.

Lightfoot, L., & Lambert, L. (1991). *Substance abuse treatment needs of federally sentenced women* (Technical Report #1). Ottawa: Correctional Service of Canada.

Lightfoot, L., & Lambert, L. (1992). *Substance abuse treatment needs of federally sentenced women* (Technical Report #2). Ottawa: Correctional Service of Canada.

Lo, C. (2004). Sociodemographic factors, drug abuse, and other crimes: How they vary among male and female arrestees. *Journal of Criminal Justice, 32,* 399–409.

Lochhead, C., & Scott, K. (2000). *The dynamics of women's poverty in Canada.* Ottawa: Status of Women Canada.

Maeve, M. (2000). Speaking unavoidable truths: Understanding early childhood sexual and physical violence among women in prison. *Issues in Mental Health Nursing, 21,* 473–498.

Maidment, M. (2006). "We're not all that criminal": Getting beyond the pathologizing and individualizing of women's crime. *Women and Therapy, 29*(3/4), 35–56.

Makarios, M. (2007). Race, abuse and female criminal violence. *Feminist Criminology, 2,* 100–116.

Paltrow, L. (2004). The war on drugs and the war on abortion. In B. Raffel-Price & N. Sokoloff (Eds.), *The criminal justice system and women: Offenders, prisoners, victims and workers* (pp. 165–184). New York: McGraw-Hill.

Pearson, P. (1997). *When she was bad: How and why women get away with murder.* Toronto: Random House Canada.

Pernanen, K., Cousineau, M., Brochu, S., & Sun, F. (2002). *Proportions of crimes associated with alcohol and other drugs in Canada.* Ottawa: Canadian Centre on Substance Abuse. Retrieved from www.ccsa.ca/NR/rdonlyres/2322ADF8-AF1E-4298-B05D-E5247D465F11/0/ccsa0091052002.pdf.

Pollack, S. (2000). Dependency discourse as social control. In K. Hannah-Moffat & M. Shaw (Eds.), *An ideal prison? Critical essays on women's imprisonment in Canada* (pp. 72–81). Halifax: Fernwood Publishing.

Pollock, J. (2002). *Women, prison and crime.* Belmont, CA: Wadsworth.

Radosh, P. (2002). Reflections of women's crime and mothers in prison: A peacemaking approach. *Crime and Delinquency, 48,* 300–315.

Shaffer, M. (1997). The battered woman syndrome revisited: Some complicating thoughts five years after R. v. Lavallee. *University of Toronto Law Journal, 47,* 1–33.

Shaw, M. (1994). *Ontario women in conflict with the law: A survey of women in institutions and under community supervision in Ontario.* Ottawa: Research Services, Strategic Policy and Planning Division, Ministry of the Solicitor General and Correctional Services.

Sheehy, E. (2000). Review of the self-defence review. *Canadian Journal of Women and the Law, 12,* 198–234.

Sommers, E. (1995). *Voices from within: Women who have broken the law.* Toronto: University of Toronto Press.

Statistics Canada. (2003). *Women and men in Canada: A statistical glance, 2003 edition.* Ottawa: Status of Women Canada.

Statistics Canada. (2006a). *Measuring violence against women: Statistical trends, 2006.* Ottawa: Federal/Provincial/Territorial Ministries Responsible for the Status of Women.

Statistics Canada. (2006b). *Women in Canada: Work chapter updates.* Ottawa: Minister of Industry.

Tadman, P. (2001). *Fallen angels: Inside Canada's toughest women's prison.* Calgary: Detselig Enterprises.

Tang, K. (2003). Battered woman syndrome testimony in Canada: Its development and lingering issues. *International Journal of Offender Therapy and Comparative Criminology, 47,* 618–629.

Taylor-Butts, A. (2007). Canada's shelters for abused women, 2005/2006. *Juristat, 27*(4), 1–19.

Walker, L. (1979). *The battered woman.* New York: Harper & Row.

Walker, L. (1995). The transmogrification of a feminist foremother. *Women & Therapy, 17,* 517–529.

White-Mair, K. (2000). Experts and ordinary men: Locating R. v. Lavallee, battered woman syndrome, and the "new" psychiatric expertise on women within Canadian legal history. *Canadian Journal of Women and the Law, 12,* 406–438.

Widom, C., & Ames, A. (1994). Criminal consequences of childhood sexual victimization. *Child Abuse and Neglect, 18,* 303–318.

CHAPTER 5

Coping Strategies of Women Offenders

Jane Barker*

Introduction

We all face challenges and situations in our life that we must cope with every day. Think back to that last time you were faced with a difficult situation. Perhaps you had a number of assignments all due on the same day, and you had to cope with the workload. You might have recently experienced a significant loss in your life when a friend or relative died. You and your partner may have had an argument last night, and you are still dealing with your emotional reaction. Life stresses can be acute, that is, they can happen all of a sudden and are fairly short-lived, or they can be of a more chronic or long-lasting nature. Events in our life don't have to be negative to be stressful. Anyone who has planned a wedding, prepared for the birth of a child, or started

a new job can attest that events we tend to categorize as positive can also be the source of a great deal of stress. The point I am trying to make is that we all have to cope with life—it is a part of being human. But the ways we cope might differ, and some of the coping strategies we choose are not always healthy for us.

People cope in many ways—some people exercise, while others meditate or immerse themselves in a hobby or sport that relieves their stress. Some coping strategies we use can become problematic. Drinking alcohol may serve the initial purpose of making one feel relaxed, but taken to extremes, either in one drinking episode or over time, it can create more problems than it solves. Other types of coping may be illegal in and of themselves,

---

* The author thanks Jean Folsom for her constructive comments on the content of this chapter and for her assistance in the wording of some sections of the text.

such as shoplifting, smoking marijuana, or taking prescription medication that has not been prescribed for you. These sorts of coping strategies may bring a person into conflict with the law, which may present as an additional stressor.

By definition, any behaviour that a person employs to deal with a difficult situation, or a stressor, can be deemed to be a coping strategy. Just the nature of its purpose—to assist a person in coping with a stressor—makes it a coping strategy. Whether the strategy is functional (or dysfunctional) in the long run may remain to be seen. Note that the determination of whether an act is considered functional or dysfunctional can be considered to be a value judgment. A coping strategy used by one person in one situation could be deemed dysfunctional by an onlooker, and that same strategy used by another person could be considered functional.

For example, consider the following situation and decide whether it is a functional strategy. A man has just found out that he has lost his job. After working at the same company in downtown Toronto for 20 years, he went to work one Friday and was told that he had been downsized. His desk had been packed up and security was waiting to escort him out of the building. Upon leaving work, he walked to a coffee shop, bought a cappuccino and a brownie, and then went to a table in the back of the establishment. He sipped his coffee, ate his brownie, then lit up a joint (marijuana) and began to smoke it. Just as he was exhaling, a police officer walked into the shop to get a coffee. So, is smoking marijuana in such a public place a functional or dysfunctional coping strategy?

This man is probably smoking the marijuana to relax, to feel more at ease, and to cope with the emotional turmoil associated with a significant loss in his life. His behaviour has a functional aspect in that it may reduce his negative emotional state. However, because he is breaking the law and because a police officer happened upon him doing so lends a significant dysfunctional element to the situation—his behaviour has now brought this man into contact with the criminal justice system.

Most people reading this scenario would likely say that this behaviour is dysfunctional. Although the inhalation of the drug might help in terms of numbing him to his painful emotions, this functional aspect would be nullified by the significant negative consequences of using illicit drugs, in public, and being caught red-handed by an officer of the law. Now, consider this very same example in Amsterdam, where some coffee shops cater to those who want to use marijuana or hashish, and where people do not get arrested for doing so. Is this same behaviour still dysfunctional? Or is it possible, in a country where the use of such drugs is not routinely criminalized, that in this situation, smoking marijuana would be a functional way to cope with a significant loss? Perhaps you would agree, perhaps not. Your view will likely depend on your values and beliefs regarding the use of drugs. Again, this scenario illustrates the value-laden aspects of judging a particular behaviour as being functional or not.

For the purpose of exploring these concepts of coping as they relate to criminalized women, we can broadly categorize the strategies into those that are functional and those that are not. Some coping strategies may start out as functional (by definition, most begin this way) and become dysfunctional over time. The point is not to cast aspersions on any individual or group of people for their choices of coping strategies but to illustrate that some strategies may create additional problems in a person's life, which may then require additional coping. For example, whether a person uses heroin will not be debated with regard to whether its use is ethical or not, nor will it be the subject of a moralizing rant.

That kind of opinion doesn't belong in a criminal justice text; however, this kind of drug use may be related to a criminal act that results in a conflict with the law, which *is* of import here, and as such, these types of coping strategies will be discussed.

Coping with Being Incarcerated

Imagine that you have just been sentenced to a period of incarceration and you are on your way to a correctional facility. What is running through your mind? Chances are you are worried about your family—your partner, kids, siblings, parents. You might be thinking about your job or school, and how you are going to handle being away for a period of time. You could be concerned about your living arrangements. Will you be able to keep your place? If not, how will you arrange to have your home packed up, or taken care of, and whom can you trust with these responsibilities? You might start to imagine the difficulties that you could face in prison. Will you be safe? Will anyone try to hurt you? Will you be treated fairly by the staff? What will it be like? All of these unknowns can lead to a feeling of anxiety and can be stressful. Even after a woman has arrived at a correctional facility, there is a lot to learn, a lot to get used to, and a lot to cope with. Although providing significant detail on the types of stressors facing incarcerated women is beyond the scope of this chapter, a cursory examination will illustrate the kinds of issues that contribute to the stress experienced by women in the correctional system.

Many women in prison are mothers, and they are often the primary caregivers for their children (Canada, Task Force on Federally Sentenced Women [TFFSW], 1990; Ferraro & Moe, 2003; Lightfoot & Lambert, 1992; Radosh, 2002; Reed & Reed, 1995; Shaw, 1994; Sugar & Fox, 1990). One of their biggest issues is the care of their children. Although some mothers are permitted to have their children with them in prison, the majority are not.[1] Issues arise pertaining to child custody and access. In some cases, the children of incarcerated women have been made wards of the court, effectively eliminating any future contact with their mothers. In other instances, mothers may worry about the safety of their children (Canada, TFFSW, 1990; Ferraro & Moe, 2003). Their children may be living with extended family, which might cause concern; however, the mothers may be loath to mention their concerns for fear that their kids would be taken away from their family, which could in turn limit the mothers' access even more.

Some mothers face real concerns about parenting their children while in prison, and they wonder how proper parenting can be accomplished when they are so physically removed from their kids (Canada, TFFSW, 1990). Some women choose to tell their children where they are, whereas others inform them that they are at school or at work and can't come home for a while. Regardless of what these mothers have told their children, they may have to deal with questions from their kids asking where they are and when they are coming home. When children themselves come into conflict with the law, mothers in prison may face a double dose of guilt for "not being there" for their child and for "setting a bad example." These day-to-day worries and stressors face mothers who are incarcerated.

Although some might argue that incarcerated fathers face the same kinds of issues, in reality for many of those incarcerated fathers, their partners in the community are and always have been the primary caregivers for the children (Ferraro & Moe, 2003). Because incarcerated fathers have this support in the community, for the most part, they do not face these same issues with the level of intensity experienced by incarcerated mothers.

Many women who are incarcerated face stressors related to the nature of the institution where they reside (Hayman, 2006). The policies and practices of any correctional facility may seem foreign to many, constituting stress on its own. For example, prisons offer very little privacy. Some might argue prisons have *no* privacy. Although this lack of privacy is expected, given the nature of an environment where the residents are constantly under the scrutiny of staff or other residents, it doesn't mean it is particularly easy to deal with. Try to imagine always being watched, or having your movements tracked. How do you think you would cope?

A related issue is the violation of personal space experienced by many women. Part of the prison protocol may involve searches and pat-downs—having your possessions examined or having your body physically searched by correctional staff who have the authority to do so (Hayman, 2006). You may be asked to give a urine sample or be strip-searched upon returning to the institution after being out on a pass. How would you cope with this violation of personal space, day in and day out?

Freedom is limited in prison. Not only is an inmate restricted to prison property, but movement within the institution is constrained by rules and regulations regarding where an inmate can go and when an inmate can leave the living unit. In the federal system, the regional facilities are structurally set up like small communities, with cottages surrounding a common green area; however, unlike in the community, a woman cannot decide to go out for some air in the middle of the night. Restrictions limit when a woman can leave the living unit; for example, having a smoke out on the porch at 2 a.m. is not allowed. During the day, women are also restricted to where they can go.

A woman who wants to speak to the warden would face a difficult time accessing her because the administration area of the prison is usually off limits to most inmates. A request to speak to the warden might take time to be processed. Comparatively, if you or I wanted to speak to the boss at work or the dean at the university, we could simply drop in to the appropriate office and make an appointment. The same cannot be said to be true in most prisons. Interestingly, in one prison where I worked a number of years ago, the deputy warden smoked, and many women would approach her while she was having a cigarette in the yard. This kind of informal access was appreciated by the women; however, this level of contact is likely not available to the women in most facilities in Canada.

Lastly, consider the stressors associated with being forced to live with people you may not even choose to be friends with. First and foremost, many women have concerns about their safety in prison. The new regional facilities do not have security personnel in most of the living units 24 hours a day. Instead, the primary workers complete rounds, entering each living unit on a regular basis and at specified times to check that everyone is there, and that all is as it should be. However, plenty of opportunities exist for women to be bullied or muscled by other offenders when the security staff is not present.

Although the people responsible for living unit placements try to take into account incompatible relationships (that is, they don't tend to house people together who really can't get along because of some prior relationship issue), the women who are placed in a living unit are expected to overcome any difficulties and get along as best they can. Such arrangements may not seem like a big deal, but imagine serving a life sentence in a prison, while living with people who really get on your nerves. Anyone who has ever had roommate problems can relate to how difficult this kind of situation can be. Unlike you and me, most incarcerated women can't choose the people they live with, and so they must cope with this lack of control and do the best they can to tolerate what is sometimes a very difficult living situation.

The daily stressors associated with prison life are varied, be they concerns about children, dealing with the lack of privacy, feeling physically constrained, worrying about personal safety, or tolerating the idiosyncrasies of those with whom you live. These concerns all lead to increased stress in the lives of incarcerated women, and women might benefit from addressing these stressors with various kinds of coping strategies.

Coping with a History of Abuse

Comack (1996) noted that by identifying the ways in which criminalized women who had been abused in childhood resisted and coped with their experiences, it might be possible to uncover the strategies they used to take some kind of control over their current situations. Comack hypothesized that by taking control, the women were "developing particular survival skills" (p. 62) that helped the women cope with the consequences of being abused. The coping skills they developed included behaviours such as becoming sexually active, engaging in prostitution, and using drugs and/or alcohol. Comack also discussed some of the strategies women used to cope with abuse as an adult. Women's aggression was seen as being one such coping strategy. In addition, women who experienced domestic violence may have coped by contacting the police in hopes that some sort of intervention would occur or by attempting to obtain support from a shelter. Comack has made links between women's experiences of abuse and their subsequent violations of the law, emphasizing that "women's law violations become part of coping with, resisting and surviving experiences of abuse" (p. 83).

Comack (1996, 2005) examined how the concepts of coping, resisting, and surviving, as originally conceptualized by Kelly (1988, cited in Comack, 1996, 2005), allow for the exploration of the interrelatedness that may exist between women's histories of abuse and their criminal behaviours. In her analysis, Comack (2005) differentiates between these terms in the following manner:

- *Coping* refers to interpreting a woman's criminal behaviour in the context of how it enables her to deal with the past abuse and its possible long-term effects.
- *Resisting* refers to the law-breaking behaviour of some women, which can be interpreted as an attempt to resist the abuse that they are experiencing in the present.
- *Surviving* captures the very real position that some criminalized women find themselves in as they try to actively survive the dangers of their existence and in so doing illustrates how their abuse (current, or past, or both) is linked to their law-breaking behaviour.

By recounting some of the experiences of the 24 women she interviewed who were serving provincial sentences, Comack (2005) was able to show how the effects of abuse had permeated their lives, and how these threads of coping, resisting, and surviving abuse were woven through the women's lives and illustrated in their experiences of law-breaking behaviour (see box 5.1).

Similar observations have been reported by Gilfus (1992, 2002). Gilfus (1992) proposed that for many of the 20 incarcerated women she interviewed, their use of criminal survival strategies was often the only viable option they could see to allow them to escape from the violence (physical and sexual) that permeated their lives. The women did not tend to characterize themselves as victims, but as survivors. In addition, they conceptualized their criminal actions—both their entry into criminal behaviour and their commitment to criminal behaviour—as being related to significant relationships in their lives. Gilfus (1992) noted that when it came to their criminal involvement, these women were not so much illustrating a "criminal career" as reflecting an "immersion in street crime" (p. 5). For them, the adoption of certain survival strategies that may involve criminal behaviour (which may seem like the only option available to some women) began the shift from being a victim to being an offender (Gilfus, 1992).

Some have suggested that for a woman who has been sexually abused as a child, certain aspects of a prison environment serve to constantly re-expose her to traumatic processes associated with prior abuse (Heney & Kristiansen, 1997). Using Finkelhor and Browne's (1985) conceptualization of these traumagenic dynamics, Heney and Kristiansen (1997) proposed that these dynamics of powerlessness, traumatic sexualization, stigmatization, and betrayal are all manifest, in one form or another, in the prison environment.

Traumatic sexualization refers to the way in which a child's sexuality is shaped (by the abuse) in a way that is developmentally inappropriate and dysfunctional in an interpersonal sense (Finkelhor & Browne, 1985). In prison, this dynamic is replicated in instances of institutionalized assaults, such as pat-downs, frisks, strip searches, and, in some cases, internal searches[2] (Heney & Kristiansen, 1997). Powerlessness, which was thought to be the most fundamental of the dynamics underlying child abuse, consists of the inherent power differential between the child victim of abuse and the abuser (Finkelhor & Browne, 1985). In prison, this dynamic of powerlessness is found in the structure of a correctional facility. The primary workers, warden, teachers, and case management officers—realistically, *everyone* who works or volunteers in a prison—are in a position of power over those who are incarcerated. Survivors of trauma may react to their sense of powerlessness by trying to control events in their environment, but this reaction is more of an illusion of control that ultimately contributes to their further feelings of powerlessness (Heney & Kristiansen, 1997).

The traumagenic dynamic of betrayal—that is, the experience of being betrayed by one's abuser or by those to whom disclosure of abuse has been made but who fail to do anything to intervene—is also re-experienced by women in prison. According to Heney and Kristiansen (1997), many incarcerated women feel betrayed by a society that didn't help them as children, which is the same society that later charged, convicted, sentenced, and imprisoned them, and is therefore seen to have become their persecutor.

Lastly, the dynamic of stigmatization refers to all of those negative messages conveyed to the victim of abuse by the abuser, and the experience of isolation that many face. These same messages are experienced by women in prison—that society views them as being different, abnormal, or in some way to be feared (Heney & Kristiansen, 1997). Women who are incarcerated must face many challenges while in prison, and for those women with an abuse history, the traumatic dynamics that might surface in the prison environment give them that much more to cope with.

Box 5.1   Brenda's Story

Brenda is in her midtwenties. Brenda's life to this point in time has been marked by being in and out of foster care, juvenile institutions, and prison, and being involved in a life on the streets that includes drugs and prostitution. Abuse and law violations have been part and parcel of her life ...

Brenda had difficulty getting anyone in authority to help her to deal with the abuse at home:

> I would even tell my schoolteacher that my dad's hurting me, and—I'd tell her what was going on at home. I tried to express, you know, how I was feeling and stuff, and then she got a worker involved and I would tell the worker what was going on at home and the worker didn't believe me! ... So she kept sending me back home, you know? ...

To get away from the abuse, Brenda decided to set a neighbor's house on fire:

> I was so angry and I was trying to figure out a way to get away from home. And I saw it on T.V., you know? I saw it on a, it was a western movie. Some guy was getting mad at another guy so he threw gasoline on the house. So I uh, I went and got my dad's gasoline tank out of the back—what he uses for his boat. And I poured gas in the house and lit it on fire ...

She also talked about what life on the street was like:

> Street life is a, it's a power game, you know? Street life? You have to show you're tough. You have to beat up this broad or you have to shank this person, or, you know, you're always carrying guns, you always have blow on you, you always have drugs on you, and you're always working the streets with the pimps and the bikers, you know? That, that alone, you know, it has so much fucking abuse, it has more abuse than what you were brought up with! You know? That crowd. You know, 'cause you have to deal with, "Oh, this person said that" and "Fight this person" and, you know. And it goes on—that cycle never stops. That's worse than, I find living on the street I went through more abuse than I did at home.

Brenda's story reveals how interconnected abuse and law violations have been in her ongoing struggle to survive. Unlike coping (where law violation becomes a way of dealing with the abuse) or resisting (where the woman takes action to oppose the abuse, which brings her into conflict with the law), surviving suggests that both the abuse and law violation are pervasive features of the woman's life. Trying to understand Brenda's life, then, involves understanding the conditions of her endangerment.

Source: Comack, E. (2005). Coping, resisting, and surviving: Connecting women's law violations to the histories of abuse. In L.F. Alarid & P. Cromwell (Eds.), *In her own words: Women offenders' views on crime and victimization* (pp. 39–41). Los Angeles, CA: Roxbury.

Different Types of Coping Strategies

As already noted, people use many different kinds of coping strategies to deal with stressful events in their lives. For the purpose of this chapter, we focus on those strategies that pertain most to women who have been criminalized in Canada. Although many criminalized women use positive ways in which to cope with stressors, the focus of this chapter is on those strategies that are dysfunctional in nature. Such strategies include self-injury, suicide, eating disorders, and alcohol and drug use and abuse. This list is not an exhaustive inventory of strategies, but consists of those behaviours that are most often discussed in the literature.

Self-Injury

Self-injurious behaviour is not a new phenomenon. It has been studied in both forensic (Adshead, 1994; Borrill et al., 2003; Heney, 1990; Roe-Sepowitz, 2007) and non-forensic samples of women (Abrams & Gordon, 2003; Brown, Comtois, & Linehan, 2002; Brumberg, 2006; Harned, Najavits, & Weiss, 2006; Marchetto, 2006; Schoppmann, Schröck, Schnepp, & Büscher, 2007). In a historical review of the scholarship on self-injurious behaviour in women, Shaw (2002) noted that published studies from the turn of the 19th century to the present tended to focus on middle-class, white women in England and North America. According to Shaw (2002), over this time period, self-injurious behaviour garnered four distinct shifts in attention: "1) varying degrees of clinical interest in and numbers of publications on self-injury, 2) changing conceptualizations of self-injury, 3) changing treatment approaches on self-injury, and 4) changing characterizations of women who self-injure" (p. 191).

In her feminist analysis, Shaw (2002) noted that women who self-injure do so to take control and to objectify their bodies, which helps them to alleviate symptoms of psychological distress they might be experiencing. Shaw points out the societal hypocrisy that exists because it is okay for society to objectify women's bodies, but if a woman objectifies her own body (through the act of self-injury), such an act is not "culturally sanctioned" (p. 206). Further, engaging in self-injury "is to make oneself ugly in this culture and to violate sacred beauty standards for women" (p. 206), an act not well tolerated by society.

Shaw (2002) summarized the major contemporary developments in terms of how self-injury has been conceptualized. She noted that the first development viewed self-injury as a "syndrome of impulse regulation" (p. 198) in which the self-injury itself was regarded as an addictive behaviour. In this approach, the contribution of environmental factors is minimized and emphasis is placed on the individual—the woman is unable to resist her own self-destructive impulses (Shaw, 2002). As a result of an increase in research that focused on childhood abuse, the second contemporary conceptualization emerged, that of self-injury as a coping strategy. Self-injury was seen as a way that "trauma survivors attempt to manage feelings of powerlessness, dissociation, intrusive memories, compulsions to re-enact the trauma and punish the body, and bodily alienation" (Shaw, 2002, p. 199). The most recent contemporary conceptualization involves neurological research that supports the view that the act of self-injury is accompanied by specific physiological antecedents and consequences that reinforce the act and contribute to the continuation of the behaviour, thus making the cessation of self-injury difficult to attain (Shaw, 2002). As Shaw points out, although the contemporary conceptualizations differ, some common threads run through each, and therefore more than one model is often considered. Most authors generally accept that "self-injury is a response to symptoms of psychological distress such as dissociation, feelings of helplessness and anxiety" and that "the act provides relief and a sense of control" (Shaw, 2002, p. 199).

An example of Shaw's (2002) second contemporary conceptualization can be seen in Jan Heney's (1990) *Report on Self-Injurious Behaviour in the Kingston Prison for Women* submitted to the Correctional Service of Canada (CSC). Heney worked from a model of self-injury that characterized the behaviour as "a coping strategy that manifests itself as a result of childhood abuse (usually sexual)" (p. 4). According to Heney, the abused child is able to reconcile the abuse through a mechanism of self-blame. If the child is able to blame herself, then she may believe that she actually has some control over the situation and thus will be able to stop the abuse from occurring. Over time, the self-blame and the continued abuse reinforce the notion that "bad things do and will happen" (Heney, 1990, p. 4). Thus, when faced with this sense of inevitability with respect to the occurrence of bad things in the future, anxiety may abound. Heney postulated that "self-injury is an attempt to control the extent and timing of the anticipated pain which is seen as inevitable" (p. 4). Following the pain (attained through self-injury), anxiety is immediately lessened. So, in this sense, the reduced anxiety can be viewed as an "adaptive and resourceful behaviour" (Heney, 1990, p. 4). Heney conceptualized this process in a schematic representation (see figure 5.1). Others have also conceptualized self-injury among prisoners as a coping strategy (Heney & Kristiansen, 1997; Pollack & Brezina, 2006).

For her study, Heney (1990) interviewed 45 inmates, 41 security staff, and members of the psychology department, the health care department, and the regional treatment centre. Heney (1990) was interested in gathering information related to injury response, injury reduction, and suicide identification. In her detailed report, she outlined the extent of the problem at the prison, described the current institutional response to self-injury, injury reduction, and suicide identification, and drew her conclusions, including recommending some directions for the future (Heney, 1990). Nearly 60 percent of the inmates interviewed by Heney reported they had engaged in self-injurious behaviour at some point in their lives. The majority (92 percent) of these women indicated that the method they had used was slashing.[3] Other types of self-injurious behaviour included "headbanging, starvation, burning and/or tattooing" (Heney, 1990, p. 8). Of those women who reported self-injurious behaviour, 73 percent also reported a history of childhood abuse (Heney, 1990). Lower rates of self-injurious behaviour were reported among samples of provincially sentenced women offenders (both incarcerated women and those serving time in the community) (Shaw, 1994). In her examination of provincially sentenced women in Ontario, Shaw (1994) noted that approximately 30 percent reported a history of slashing.

Heney (1990) also indicated that outbreaks of self-injury tended to coincide with periods of extreme tension in the prison. According to the inmates interviewed, the tension that existed in the prison was most often caused by changes in prison policy, the attitudes of certain staff members toward the women, and instances of mass punishment.[4] Situational factors were most often identified by inmates as triggers for self-injurious behaviour. Almost half of the women indicated that their urge to self-injure was strongest in situations where they experienced feelings of helplessness and powerlessness. Approximately 7 percent of women interviewed indicated that the urge to self-injure arose when they were experiencing isolation.

At the time the report was written, the institutional policy for self-injury advised taking the woman to health care (or the community hospital) and then to segregation until a psychologist could assess her. In addition, an appearance was required before the Segregation Review Board, which met twice a week. Heney (1990) pointed out that according to this policy, a woman who self-injured might be kept in segregation for a number of days. In some cases, women were transferred to the regional treatment centre as a result of extreme self-injury. In her recommendations, Heney (1990) asserted that it be recognized that "self-injurious behaviour is a mental health issue as opposed to a security issue" (p. 14). Heney was clear in her view that segregation was not an appropriate response to self-injury, because of the isolation experienced by the woman and the perception that she was being punished for her behaviour. According to Heney, the use of segregation in these instances was more likely to increase, not decrease, any suicide potential. She suggested that in cases of self-injury, an assessment should be made by a professional trained in these issues (psychiatrist, psychologist, nurse, or physician). In those cases where a woman was not deemed to be able to function in the prison population because of high suicide potential, Heney (1990) suggested that she be kept in the health care area of the prison. Alternatively, if this option was not viable, she recommended the woman be transferred to another health care facility until she could be stabilized and returned to the prison population.

Despite the closure of the Prison for Women (P4W) and the opening of the regional facilities, self-injury remains an issue of concern with respect to women who are incarcerated federally in Canada. Prison policy regarding self-injury has been criticized (Hannah-Moffat, 2006; Kilty, 2006), and the question has been raised about whether, with respect to self-injury, prisons can develop "gender-sensitive, or 'gender-responsive' prison policies at all" (Bosworth, 2006, p. 157). In a recent article, Kilty (2006) asserted that the Correctional Service of Canada policy, as it relates to self-injury, is problematic, in particular that "women who self-injure are still routinely disciplined for their behaviour in Federal Canadian prisons through admittance to administrative segregation" (p. 161). By placing a self-injurious woman in administrative segregation for monitoring, the CSC is effectively increasing the woman's risk to self-injure because of the punitive and isolating nature of segregation (Kilty, 2006). Further, Kilty maintained that "self-injuring prisoners are being inappropriately constructed as risks to the institution" by the CSC (p. 162).

This assertion was echoed by Hannah-Moffat (2006) in response to Kilty's (2006) article. In her reaction essay, Hannah-Moffat (2006) noted that although self-injurious behaviour is not scored as a risk factor in the third-generation risk assessment measures, it is included as a consideration. In addition, Hannah-Moffat (2006) asserts that self-injurious behaviour is now being viewed by the CSC as a behaviour that is difficult to manage and a symptom of a mental health issue, instead of being viewed primarily as a coping strategy. According to Hannah-Moffat (2006),[5] as an identified need, self-injurious behaviour will be targeted for treatment by programs such as dialectical behaviour therapy (DBT).[6] In her discussion of this issue, Hannah-Moffat (2006) raises the question of how the risk/need paradigm used in corrections is able to deal with those self-injurious women identified as having a need for treatment, but who do not embrace, for whatever reason, the treatment that is offered.

Thomas, Leaf, Kazmierczak,[7] and Stone (2006) have suggested that prison policy needs to recognize the role prison culture plays in self-injurious behaviour (SIB) because "viewing inmate difficulties in terms of a 'coping deficit' provides a policy guideline that, although recognizing the need to focus on the individual mental health of prisoners who self-injure,

Figure 5.1   Self-Injurious Behaviour as a Coping Strategy

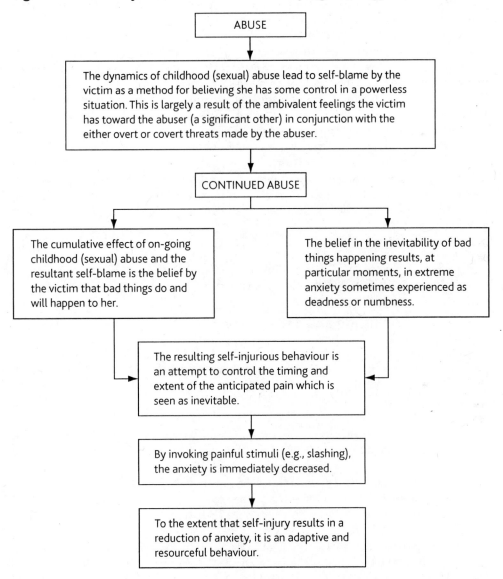

Source: Heney, J. (1990). *Report on self-injurious behaviour in the Kingston Prison for Women.* Ottawa: Correctional Service of Canada, p. 5. Reprinted with the permission of the Minister of Public Works and Government Services Canada, 2008.

shifts attention to the broader context in which SIB occurs" (p. 197). In this conceptualization, Thomas et al. view self-injury as a symptom both of the state of a person's mental health and "of the pathology of prisons" (p. 197). Thomas et al. also suggest that policy-makers need to ensure that punitive segregation is used "only as a last resort" (p. 197).

Every CSC institution must have procedures in place to ensure that any suicide attempts or self-injurious behaviours are appropriately handled and that staff are educated and aware of the official policy with respect to both self-injury and suicide attempts (Laishes, 2002). The CSC's official policy on suicide and self-injury may be found in Commissioner's Directive (CD) 843 (see box 5.2). As seen in the definitions of terms used in CD 843, the CSC differentiates between *self-injury* and *suicide*; however, the term *suicide watch* is used to denote the isolation of an inmate who is thought to be in imminent danger from either suicide or self-injurious behaviour (Correctional Service of Canada [CSC], 2002). CD 843 makes no distinction between monitoring for *suicidal* behaviour and monitoring for *self-injurious* behaviour. Although these two behaviours may be virtually indistinguishable from the point of view of an observer, the *intent* of each, from the perspective of the inmate, is very different.

Box 5.2   Commissioner's Directive 843: Prevention, Management and Response to Suicide and Self-Injuries[8]

Policy objective

1. To ensure the safety of and intervention for offenders who are suicidal or self-injurious.

Definitions

4. **Medical emergency:** an injury or condition that poses an immediate threat to a person's health or life which requires medical intervention.
5. **Suicide:** the intentional taking of one's own life.
6. **Suicide attempt:** an intentional self-inflicted injury or action that does not result in death although death was intended.
7. **Self-injury:** the deliberate harm of one's body without conscious suicidal intent.
8. **Suicide watch:** the isolation of an inmate in response to an assessment of imminent danger of self-injury or suicide.

Principles

9. Protection of life takes precedence over preservation of evidence.
10. Self-injurious or suicidal offenders shall not be subject to disciplinary measures for their self-injurious behaviour.
11. With the offender's consent, the input of support persons or groups shall be taken into consideration in the treatment plan to respond to the risk of self-injurious or suicidal behaviour.

Assessment

13. The sections of the Offender Intake Assessment pertaining to suicide and mental health shall be administered to all inmates:
    a) within 24 hours of the initial admission; and
    b) within 24 hours of a transfer from another institution.
14. Inmates who are potentially suicidal or self-injurious shall be referred to a psychologist on an emergency basis.
15. The psychologist or a designated member of the interdisciplinary mental health team shall closely manage the case.

Response to suicidal and self-injurious offenders

17. Staff shall take the necessary actions to ensure that suicidal and self-injurious offenders are referred on an emergency basis to a psychologist or a health service professional for appropriate intervention.
18. The psychologist or designated members of the interdisciplinary mental health team shall determine the degree of risk for suicide or self-injury and the appropriate level of intervention.
19. An inmate identified as being at a high risk for suicide or self-injury shall be placed on suicide watch, if the level of risk has not or cannot be reduced to an acceptably low level through other interventions.
20. When an inmate is identified as being at a high risk for suicide or self-injury, the psychiatrist or institutional physician shall review the inmate's medication profile and method of medication administration taking into account the inmate's suicide status.
21. If there will be a delay before an inmate is seen by a psychologist or health professional, the manager in charge may choose to place the inmate on suicide watch.
22. The psychologist or designated members of the interdisciplinary mental health team managing the case shall provide staff with directions on the specific conditions of the suicide watch, including the procedures to be used to monitor the inmate's activities.
23. Inmates placed on suicide watch shall be accommodated in a suicide watch cell designated by the institution, under continuous staff observation.
24. The psychologist or designated member of the interdisciplinary mental health team will recommend to the manager in charge when the suicide watch can be terminated.

Source: Correctional Service of Canada. (2002). *Commissioner's Directive 843: Prevention, management and response to suicide and self-injuries*. Ottawa: Author. Reprinted with the permission of the Minister of Public Works and Government Services Canada, 2008.

Suicide

Statistics indicate that offenders incarcerated in a federal prison are at more risk of killing themselves than they are of being murdered (Larivière, 1997). As noted in a review by Polvi (1997), those who are incarcerated have a higher suicide rate than do members of the general population in Canada. Over the period 1959 to 1975, the suicide rate was 95.9 per 100,000 for inmates in Canada, compared with an estimate of 14.2 per 100,000 for non-inmate males in Canada (Burtch & Ericson, cited in Green, Andre, Kendall, Looman, & Polvi, 1992). In their study of inmate suicides in Canada from 1977 to 1988, Green et al. (1992) noted that inmates who committed suicide tended to be male.[9] Their suicides most often occurred soon after sentencing and consisted mainly of hangings. In addition, suicide was found to be related to prior suicide attempts, marital status (single), prior abuse of alcohol or drugs, and history of prior psychiatric illness (Green et al., 1992).

Research has been completed in an effort to predict suicide attempts among Canadian male offenders (Wichmann, Serin, & Motiuk, 2000). Predictors of suicide attempts among male prisoners included age (younger), marital status (unattached), sentence type (more often serving life), and type of offence (more likely for offenders convicted of homicide, theft, and robbery). Psychiatric histories and problems with psychological adjustment were more likely to be found in those offenders who later attempted suicide than in those who did not (Wichmann et al., 2000). The researchers clearly suggest that a similar examination of suicidal behaviours in Canadian women offenders should be undertaken (Wichmann et al., 2000).

In 2002, a report on research on self-harm and women offenders appeared in a paper entitled "Women Offenders Who Engage in Self-Harm: A Comparative Investigation" (Wichmann, Serin, & Abracen, 2002). In this study, *suicide* and *self-injury* were noted as distinct concepts, but the researchers were unable to differentiate between the two using their chosen methodology, file review (Wichmann et al., 2002). Thus, the term *self-harm* was used to encapsulate suicide attempts and incidents of self-injury. Women who engaged in self-harm were reported to have substance abuse and psychiatric problems and adjustment difficulties that included dysfunctional families and social-cognitive problems (Wichmann et al., 2002). The researchers noted that the women who had a history of self-harm showed "considerable evidence of violence against other inmates and staff" (p. 14), suggesting that their violence was not entirely self-directed. Research has suggested that a link may exist between self-injury and suicide attempts. One American study found that women offenders who self-injured were 26 times more likely to attempt suicide than women offenders with no history of self-injury (Roe-Sepowitz, 2007). Although the Canadian study by Wichmann et al. (2002) has added to our understanding of self-harm among women offenders, further research is clearly needed to examine suicide attempts separately from incidents of self-injury in a Canadian sample of women offenders.

In 1992, the first retrospective report on inmate suicides in federal corrections was completed for the 1990–91 fiscal year (Larivière, 1997). Estimates for that year indicated the highest suicide rate for inmates since the mid-1980s, at 13.6 per 10,000 (CSC, 1992). The most recent retrospective report on inmate suicides available was for 1996–97 (Larivière, 1997).[10] In this publication, the rate of offender suicide was down from the early 1990s, at a reported 7.1 per 10,000. According to Larivière, from 1991–92 to 1996–97, 92 male suicides and 1 female suicide occurred in federal correctional facilities. Because of the low base rates for women, incidence rates of suicides for women offenders were difficult to calculate (Larivière, 1997).

Liebling (1994) has argued that the low numbers of women who kill themselves while incarcerated can be misleading when compared with the greater number of men who commit suicide while in prison. As readers are now well aware, far fewer women than men are incarcerated. Thus, a small absolute number of suicides in a year can actually represent a relatively large proportion of incarcerated women. In Liebling's (1994) research, she found that the rates of suicide for women incarcerated in England and Wales were as high as the rates for men incarcerated there. A study of deaths in an Australian cohort study of prisoners (from 1988 to 2002) suggested a lower rate of suicide for women prisoners compared with men prisoners: 79 per 100,000 for women, compared with 135 per 100,000 for men (Kariminia et al., 2007).

In 2003, a British study suggested that 46 percent of a sample of women offenders had reported a history of at least one suicide attempt (Borrill et al., 2003), whereas in an American study of 1,272 women offenders, more than half were deemed to have experienced suicidal ideation or suicidal behaviour in the past (Charles, Abram, McClelland, & Teplin, 2003). More than 33 percent reported they had thought about killing themselves at some point in their life, and more than 20 percent reported a history of at least one previous suicide attempt (Charles et al., 2003). Similar results have been reported in Canadian studies. In a sample of provincially incarcerated women, Shaw (1994) indicated that of the women she surveyed, more than 33 percent reported a history of a suicide attempt. In an article published that same year, Loucks and Zamble (1994) found that 40 percent of the women in a sample of 100 federally incarcerated women had a history of suicide attempt, compared with 13 percent of a sample of male offenders.

The authors of a study examining suicide among women incarcerated in Quebec (both provincially and federally) found that 53 percent of the women reported having tried to kill themselves at least once (Daigle, Alarie, & Lefebvre, 1999). Of the women surveyed, more provincially incarcerated women (60 percent) reported at least one prior suicide attempt than the group of federally incarcerated women (39 percent). A measure of suicide risk suggested that based on their elevated scores, 39 percent of the women should have been given a referral to a mental health clinician (Daigle et al., 1999). A more recent estimate of suicide risk and self-injurious behaviour among a subset of women offenders—that is, those with intensive mental health needs[11]—found that approximately two-thirds had attempted suicide in the past and approximately half were identified as being at risk for suicide (McDonagh, Noël, & Wichmann, 2002).

The question of *why* some incarcerated Canadian women attempt suicide remains to be fully addressed. Some research from Britain suggests that women in prison who attempt suicide but survive the attempt may have exhibited certain vulnerabilities before their incarceration, such as a history of self-harm, previous suicidal attempts, mental illness, sexual abuse, or sexual assault (Borrill, Snow, Medlicott, Teers, & Paton, 2005). According to this qualitative study, most of the women were able to identify specific triggers for their suicide attempt, many of which were situational[12] (Borrill et al., 2005). Similar vulnerabilities were identified in women who attempted suicide or self-injury in a quantitative study of nearly 3,000 incarcerated women in California and the United Kingdom (Kruttschnitt & Vuolo, 2007). The authors of this study reported an overlap in the predictors identified for self-injury and suicide attempt: prior self-injury, youthfulness, and current or prior mental health problems. The authors also report some evidence to suggest that "the prison regime in which particular prisons operate exerts a significant impact on mental health" (p. 138). Some would argue that sweeping correctional reforms are needed in Canada to prevent any more women from killing themselves in prison. Clearly, additional research is needed to more fully explore why some women attempt and commit suicide in Canadian jails and prisons, in the hopes that in the future, deaths, such as that of Ashley Smith (see box 5.3) can be prevented.

Box 5.3   Family Devastated by New Details in Teen's Death

A spokesperson for the family of a teen who died in custody says they are devastated by new revelations about their daughter's death, but hope something positive will come from the tragedy.

CTV News revealed new details on Monday about allegations against Corrections Canada officers charged with criminal negligence in connection to 19-year-old Ashley Smith's death.

Staff members at a Kitchener, Ont., prison monitored Smith's cell with a video camera, and allegedly saw the girl with a ligature around her neck on Oct. 19. But they chose not to intervene immediately, believing she wasn't seriously harming herself.

Smith, who suffered from a mental illness, died from self-asphyxiation.

"They're quite devastated," Kim Pate, spokesperson for the Elizabeth Fry Societies of Canada, told CTV's *Canada AM* on Tuesday, speaking on behalf of the parents.

"They agreed to have their daughter taken away from them believing the promises that she was going to get help, and she was sent back to them in a body bag, so they're quite devastated."

Four officers at Kitchener's Grand Valley Institution have been charged[13] in connection with the girl's death, under a section of the *Criminal Code* that relates to "omitting to do anything that it is his (or her) duty to do, shows wanton or reckless disregard for the lives or safety of other persons."

Travis McDonald, 36; Karen Eves, 52; Valentino Burnett, 47; and Blaine Phibbs, 31, will appear in court on Dec. 18.

Their union has protested the charges.

Pate said the officers should have acted quickly on any possible sign that Smith would kill herself.

"People should have been watching very closely and there should have been a great deal of concern, and certainly a much different intervention," she told CTV News on Monday.

Pate said her organization has requested video footage taken on the day Smith took her own life, and hopes to piece together a more complete picture of what happened during the last few hours of her life.

Pate said Smith's parents hope a valuable lesson will be learned from their daughter's tragic death, and more efforts will be undertaken to properly care for mentally ill prisoners.

"Those with the greatest amount of need often end up horribly in the most isolated conditions," Pate said on Tuesday.

Smith had spent more than two years in segregation at the jail, after being transferred from various institutions across the country. In 2003, she received a six-year prison sentence.

While in prison she received further charges, connected to unspecified incidents involving staff members.

There are four ongoing investigations into Smith's death, conducted by:

- The federal Office of the Correctional Investigator;
- Kitchener-Waterloo police;
- Correctional Service Canada; and,
- New Brunswick's youth advocate—Smith grew up in Moncton, N.B.

CTV News has learned that another corrections officer is facing charges in connection with a separate incident with Smith at a Saskatoon prison.

Correctional supervisor John Tarala was fired from his position last September for allegedly assaulting Smith. Last week, after Smith's death made headlines, he was formally charged.

He maintains his innocence.

Source: Family devastated by new details in teen's death. (2007, November 20). *CTV.ca News*. Retrieved from www.ctv.ca. Reprinted by permission of CTVglobemedia.

Eating Disorders

Bulimia nervosa and anorexia nervosa are eating disorders characterized by "severe disturbances in eating behavior" (American Psychiatric Association [APA], 2000, p. 583). Bulimics will binge eat, that is, they will eat a lot more than most people would eat in a similar circumstance. The binge occurs in a discrete time period, usually less than two hours long. The kinds of foods that bulimics binge on vary, but often include food that is sweet and high in calories (APA, 2000). Following the binge, the bulimic will purge, which involves getting rid of the food that has just been ingested. Bulimics use a variety of methods to purge, including vomiting and misusing laxatives and diuretics. Other compensatory behaviour, such as excessive exercise or fasting, may also be used in an attempt to counteract the effects of the binge (APA, 2000).

People with anorexia nervosa (commonly referred to as anorexia) refuse to maintain even a minimally normal weight. Their very low body weight is usually accomplished through dieting, fasting, or exercising excessively. Some anorexics also engage in binge eating and purging (APA, 2000). Prevalence for anorexia in the general population of females is about 0.5 percent and for bulimia is estimated to be between 1 and 3 percent (APA, 2000). Rates for the presence of eating disorders in Canadian samples of women in conflict with the law have ranged from 4 percent (Motiuk & Brown, 1994) to 20 percent (Shaw, 1994).[14]

Some interest has been expressed in examining the possible relationship between previous experiences of abuse or trauma and the later development of a pattern of disordered eating

(Connors & Morse, 1993; Schoemaker, Smit, Bijl, & Vollebergh, 2002; Tobin & Griffing, 1996). Root and Fallon (1989) suggested that nine aspects of the binge-purge cycle are related to dealing with memories, thoughts, and feelings of prior abusive experiences. One of the purposes of the binge-purge cycle was thought to involve a reduction in stress and a relief from tension; in other words, helping the individual to cope. In a review of the literature, Connors and Morse (1993) noted that approximately 30 percent of disordered eaters reported histories of childhood sexual abuse. They concluded that a history of abuse was likely best viewed as "a risk factor in a biopsychosocial etiological model of eating disorders" (p. 1), not as a direct link between sexual trauma and disordered eating. More recently, tentative support for the existence of a self-medication hypothesis has been suggested, in which bulimia serves as a way to cope with anxiety or mood disorders that result from prior abuse (Schoemaker et al., 2002).

Both of the eating disorders, anorexia nervosa and bulimia nervosa, can be seen to illustrate a component of control. The woman with anorexic tendencies may attempt to control her body by limiting her intake of food, exercising excessively, or abusing laxatives or diuretics. Similarly, in the case of bulimics, although they may report feeling out of control during a binge, their purging behaviour following the binge could be interpreted as an attempt to control for the effects of the binge. By vomiting, misusing laxatives or diuretics, or excessively exercising or fasting the following day, the woman is exhibiting control over her body.

Because of the control elements to these eating disorders, one can hypothesize that women who are in situations where they have very little control over their bodies, such as incarceration, might try to exert whatever control they have, which might take the form of disordered eating patterns. Whether prison serves to exacerbate an already existing condition or whether symptoms of an eating disorder first emerge in prison is not known. Clearly more research is needed to better examine the etiology of the patterns of disordered eating among criminalized women. Incarcerated women face some obvious limits to the kinds of behaviours they can engage in. For example, laxatives or diuretics may be difficult to obtain in prison. However, other elements characteristic of disordered eating, such as fasting and excessive exercise, are not as difficult to do in prison.

Although considerable attention has been paid to self-damaging behaviours, such as self-injury and suicide, a dearth of research has investigated disordered eating in forensic samples of women (Milligan, Waller, & Andrews, 2002). Women in prison have been shown to exhibit both binge eating and restrictive and bulimic eating patterns (Stewart, 1983, cited in Milligan et al., 2002). In a study of British prisoners, levels of disordered eating were evident in almost one-third of the women (Dolan & Mitchell, 1994). In another British study that looked at the role of anger and disordered eating in women offenders, Milligan et al. (2002) found that higher levels of disordered eating behaviours and attitudes were found in the sample of incarcerated women than would be expected in the general population. In addition, Milligan et al. found support for their hypothesis that problematic eating was related to **state anger**[15] and suppression of anger[16] in this group of women. The most likely explanation for the findings of this study was an anger–impulsivity relationship that was present for these women prior to their imprisonment. After incarceration, the prison environment and its constraints served to increase the chance that the impulsivity would be expressed in the form of a disturbed eating pattern (Milligan et al., 2002). Higher levels of state anger and anger suppression have also been seen in non-forensic samples of eating disordered women (Milligan & Waller, 2000; Waller et al., 2003).

Little research has examined disordered eating in criminalized women in Canada. For the most part, the research has not focused exclusively on disordered eating, but has included disordered eating as one of many variables studied. As a result, this issue has not been examined in detail as it pertains to incarcerated women. Shaw (1994) reported that in a sample of provincial women incarcerated in Ontario, approximately 20 percent mentioned eating disorders when asked about their mental health. In their examination of a small sample of women (n=31) who had been released from a federal institution into the community, Motiuk and Brown (1994) reported that less than 4 percent were identified as having an eating disorder. Interestingly, as the researchers pointed out, none of their sample had reported any history of self-injury or suicide attempt. Given what is known about the relatively high rates of prior suicide attempts and self-injury among federally sentenced women, this sample does not appear to be representative of federally sentenced women as a whole. Even in this sample of women who had reported no history of using self-injury or suicide attempts as a form of dysfunctional coping, one-third of the women were reported to cope poorly with stress or frustration (Motiuk & Brown, 1994).

Research has shown that women with disordered eating and a history of abuse were more likely to have attempted suicide and more likely to have engaged in self-injurious behaviour than eating disordered women who did not report a history of abuse (Tobin & Griffing, 1996). Given the possible associations between a history of abuse in childhood and later self-injurious behaviour (Borrill et al., 2003; Heney, 1990; Roe-Sepowitz, 2007), and between abuse history and disordered eating (Connors & Morse, 1993; Schoemaker et al., 2002; Tobin & Griffing, 1996), some researchers have investigated whether an association exists between self-injury and disordered eating in forensic samples. In a study that looked at self-injury in a group of incarcerated American women, Roe-Sepowitz (2007) found that bingeing and vomiting was one of a number of predictors of self-injury. Among women who self-injured, nearly 30 percent had engaged in bingeing/vomiting, compared with less than 4 percent of the comparison group of incarcerated women who had not self-injured (Roe-Sepowitz, 2007). Similar results have been reported among male inmates who self-injure, in that they too tend to show higher bulimic tendencies than male inmates who did not engage in self-cutting (Matsumoto et al., 2005).

Relatively few published studies have addressed issues related to disordered eating in criminalized women. Thus, although few firm conclusions can be made regarding the role of disordered eating in a prison environment, a variety of factors may be involved. For example, disordered eating possibly serves as a coping strategy related to issues of control, relief from tension and stress, as a form of self-medication, or as a means of anger suppression or expression. A more thorough examination of eating disorders among criminalized women might assist in answering some of these questions regarding the role of disordered eating in a prison environment.

Alcohol and Drug Abuse

As noted in chapter 4, the large percentage of women in the criminal justice system with problems associated with drug or alcohol use is well documented in the literature (Comack, 1996; Lightfoot & Lambert, 1992; Lo, 2004; Pernanen, Cousineau, Brochu, & Sun, 2002; Shaw, 1994). Although some crimes are directly related to illegal substances by definition (for example, importing and trafficking offences), other crimes are more indirectly linked in some way to drugs or alcohol. Approximately 40 to 50 percent of crimes committed by a Canadian sample of male and female offenders could be attributed to drug and/or alcohol use (Pernanen et al., 2002). We assume that most of these crimes were not offences specific to possession, cultivation, importing, or trafficking in drugs because these crimes make up a relatively small percentage of all admissions to custody in Canada (Beattie, 2006). Compared with non-substance-abusing women, federally sentenced women who had a substance abuse problem were younger, began committing crimes at an earlier age, had more adult court experience and more previous escape attempts or convictions for being unlawfully at large, and were more likely to have been sent to segregation for disciplinary reasons (Dowden & Blanchette, 1999). Substance abusers were also more likely to be classified as higher-need or higher-risk than the non-substance-abusing women.

In terms of needs domains, women with substance abuse problems exhibited (other than the obvious area of substance abuse) significantly more needs with respect to the domains of associates, attitudes, employment, and marital/family (Dowden & Blanchette, 1999). Because of the number of domains in which substance-abusing women were identified as having more needs, their substance use might have served as a coping mechanism for other areas of their life. Alternatively, the relationship could be multidirectional: substance abuse may serve as a coping strategy *and* be a source of stress for other domain areas. As the researchers noted, substance abuse has been suggested to have an exacerbating effect on other areas of a person's life (Lightfoot & Lambert, 1992, cited in Dowden & Blanchette, 1999).

Some criminalized women have themselves made a link between their criminal behaviour and their use/abuse of alcohol or drugs (Comack, 1996; Furlong & Grant, 2006; Gilfus, 1992). Associations between victimization and drug and alcohol abuse in criminalized groups of women have also been noted in the literature (Browne, Miller, & Maguin, 1999; Gilfus, 2002; McClellan, Farabee, & Crouch, 1997). In addition to linking childhood abuse with later criminal behaviour, some researchers have hypothesized that increased rates of intimate partner victimization may be related to women's involvement in substance use and other illegal behaviours (Browne et al., 1999). Substance abuse may serve as a coping strategy for everyday stressors, whether they are related to prior trauma, street life, or to an abusive relationship (Gilfus, 2002). In an attempt to dull the pain associated with prior victimization, people may choose to use substances as a way of self-medicating (Comack, 1996; McClellan et al., 1997). Having less emotional support and more negative coping behaviours was found to be associated with more regular use of a specific drug[17] (El-Bassel et al., 1996). Although the temporal nature of the relationship was not able to be examined, the association between heavier drug use, poor coping, and less social support was supported (El-Bassel et al., 1996). Criminalized women may be no different from many others in society who choose to self-medicate to deal with stress, a coping strategy that may be considered functional; however, when the consequences of a criminalized woman abusing drugs or alcohol are evaluated, their behaviour may be viewed as considerably more dysfunctional.

The CSC has recognized that a high level of substance abuse problems is found among women offenders incarcerated federally in Canada and that many incarcerated women are survivors of past trauma (Furlong & Grant, 2006). Reductions in recidivism have been observed in women offenders who have completed substance abuse programming, compared with those who did not partake in such treatment (Dowden & Blanchette, 1999, 2002). The CSC has implemented the Women Offender Substance Abuse Program (WOSAP), which was designed as an intervention to meet an offender's substance abuse needs for the duration of her sentence (Furlong & Grant, 2006). The WOSAP program is thought to assist women by teaching them "coping strategies to deal with negative emotions associated with their trauma" (Furlong & Grant, 2006, p. 47). In an evaluation of the program, the researchers noted that the majority of women who participated in the intensive therapeutic treatment indicated that they had used substances as a way to cope. After program completion, the women showed significant improvements in their ability to cope as measured by the coping behaviour inventory. In this same evaluation, the majority (91 percent) of the women reported they were under the influence of drugs or alcohol when they committed their offence. Of those who had used drugs, almost three-quarters of the women believed their crime to be directly related to their involvement with drugs, and nearly half of those who had used alcohol came to a similar conclusion.

Women who are incarcerated and those serving their sentence in the community may be subjected to certain sanctions regarding their use of alcohol. Although the use of illicit drugs or the use of prescription drugs for a purpose other than they were intended is not legal in Canada, the use of alcohol is.[18] If a criminalized woman decides to use alcohol as a means to cope with a stressor in her life (as many non-criminalized people do every day, without fear of repercussion), then she may face some dire consequences. If she drinks while incarcerated and is caught, she will be sanctioned in some manner: she may receive institutional charges, her security classification may be reviewed and increased, and she may be transferred to a more secure living unit or even another correctional facility. If her parole stipulations state that she must not drink, presumably because drinking has been identified as a criminogenic need,[19] and she drinks while out on parole, then she risks having her parole suspended or terminated. These consequences are very serious for a behaviour that many others in society engage in daily. Obviously, good reasons are behind the prohibition of alcohol in correctional facilities; the safety of other inmates and staff is paramount. Similarly, if alcohol and drug use have been identified as being associated with a woman's criminal behaviour, then her parole stipulations will take this relationship into account. To reduce her risk to recidivate, her parole conditions will likely stipulate that she refrain from drinking or using drugs.

Summary

We all must cope with life's stressors, and women who are criminalized are no different from anyone else in this regard. The coping strategies that we adopt lie on a continuum from being very functional and adaptive to being self-destructive and dysfunctional. Strategies that are functional in one situation may be dysfunctional in another, or may become dysfunctional over time. Clearly, some coping strategies are preferable to others. Criminalized women who are incarcerated face a host of stressors associated with their lives both outside and inside the prison walls. Although many cope adequately, some turn to strategies that have worked for them in the past, but that are ultimately problematic for them, both now and in the long term. Drinking and drug use, patterns of disordered eating, self-injury, and attempts at suicide have been identified as some of these negative coping strategies. Women who choose these kinds of coping strategies may inflict direct harm on themselves, such as serious injury or death, or their choices may lead to sanctions being placed on them by authorities (for example, being placed in segregation for the consumption of alcohol).

Positive or negative, functional or dysfunctional, good or bad, whichever coping strategy a woman chooses, she will select something that she has learned can offer her at least some short-term relief from the current stress that she is experiencing.

Although many women cope with the realities of prison each and every day, others struggle to deal with the stressors in their lives. Whether these women engage in self-injurious or suicidal behaviours, develop disordered eating patterns, or abuse alcohol or drugs, their method of coping may be considered dysfunctional, given the kinds of negative consequences that result. In recognition of the role that these strategies have played in the lives of some criminalized women, programs aimed at addressing deficits in coping have been undertaken by corrections, and are more fully described in the next chapter.

Notes

1. The Correctional Service of Canada has a mother-child program that allows for some women to keep their children, usually newborns, with them in their living unit. Women must be screened for this program, and very few women participate in this program at any one time. See the section "Parenting Skills and the Mother-Child Program" in chapter 6 for more details.

2. Internal searches are carried out when a woman is suspected of concealing contraband in a body orifice. This kind of search can only be conducted with the woman's consent, and by a medical doctor.

3. Slashing refers to the intentional cutting of one's own body as a way to self-injure.

4. Heney (1990) noted that one instance of mass punishment was the cancellation of a dance in December 1988, as a result of alcohol being found in a cell.

5. Hannah-Moffat noted that she came to this conclusion after examining the CSC's 2004 program strategy for women and the CSC's protocols in place for the secure prison units.

6. For a description of DBT, see the section "Dialectical Behaviour Therapy" in chapter 8.

7. On February 14, 2008, co-author Steve Kazmierczak went on a shooting rampage, killing himself and five other students at Northern Illinois University in DeKalb, Illinois (Davey, 2008).

8. Only portions of CD 843 have been reproduced in box 5.2. Sections that outline authority, cross-references, responsibilities, restraints, transfers, and medical emergency situations have not been included. To review the entirety of CD 843, readers are directed to www.csc-scc.gc.ca/text/plcy/cdshtm/843-cde-eng.shtml.

9. Of the 133 inmate suicides included in this study, 4 of the suicide cases were women.

10. A search of the CSC website for research publications listed the Larivière (1997) study as the most recent retrospective report on inmate suicide.

11. Women with intensive mental health needs included those in any (and sometimes more than one) of the following groups: women classified as maximum security, women with severe mental health issues, or women who experienced challenges with respect to daily living.

12. The triggering events included "bullying, bereavement, an upsetting visit or telephone call, missed medication, or hearing voices or flashbacks which urged them to kill themselves" (Borrill et al., 2005, p. 67).

13. On January 16, 2008, the Correctional Service of Canada announced that as a result of an investigation, three workers and one supervisor were fired, and four others were suspended for 60 days without pay (Dalton, 2008).

14. In the Shaw (1994) study, when offenders were asked to indicate any mental health concerns, 20 percent mentioned an eating disorder. The much smaller rate of 4 percent was identified in the Motiuk and Brown (1994) study by the question "Does the offender have an eating disorder (e.g., anorexia, bulimia, over-eating)?"

15. State anger refers to "feelings of anger at a particular time," as opposed to trait anger, which refers to "individual differences in the disposition to experience anger" (Milligan et al., 2002, p. 125).

16. Previously, Milligan and Waller (2000) had found that bulimic attitudes and behaviours correlated to state anger and anger suppression in a sample of undergraduate women.

17. The specific drug in this study was crack cocaine.

18. Legal ages for drinking alcohol vary from province to province. In Ontario, the legal age for drinking alcohol is 19 years of age.

19. See the section "The Needs Principle (Assessing Criminogenic Needs to Target in Treatment)" in chapter 6 for a discussion of criminogenic needs and how they relate to recidivism.

Discussion Questions

1. You have been asked to give a talk on self-injurious behaviour to a group of people being trained to work in a women's correctional facility. What are the key points to include in your talk?

2. Why might women with a history of childhood sexual abuse find it difficult to cope in prison? Which aspects of the prison environment might pose a particular difficulty for this group of women?

3. According to Anne Opinion, "Given that ingestion of alcohol by adults is not illegal in Canada, women who are incarcerated should be permitted to drink alcohol in prison." Discuss this statement. Do you agree or disagree?

4. It has been noted elsewhere that criminalized women in Canada are not that different from women in the community and likely have more in common with them than with male offenders. Discuss this statement in terms of coping strategies. Does this statement hold true in the context of coping strategies?

Suggested Readings

Alarid, L., & Cromwell, P. (2005). *In her own words: Women offenders' views on crime and victimization.* Los Angeles, CA: Roxbury.

Comack, E. (1996). *Women in trouble.* Black Point, NS: Fernwood.

Laishes, J. (2002). *Mental health strategy for women offenders.* Ottawa: Correctional Service of Canada.

Online Resources

1. Correctional Service of Canada's Commissioner's Directives: www.csc-scc.gc.ca/text/plcy/toccd-eng.shtml

References

Abrams, L., & Gordon, A. (2003). Self-harm narratives of urban and suburban young women. *Affilia, 18,* 429–444.

Adshead, G. (1994). Damage: Trauma and violence in a sample of women referred to a forensic service. *Behavioural Sciences and the Law, 12,* 235–249.

American Psychiatric Association. (2000). *Diagnostic and statistical manual of mental disorders* (4th ed.): *Text revision.* Washington, DC: Author.

Beattie, K. (2006). Adult correctional services in Canada 2004/05, *Juristat, 26*(5), 1–34.

Borrill, J., Burnett, R., Atkins, R., Miller, S., Briggs, D., Weaver, T., et al. (2003). Patterns of self-harm and attempted suicide among white and black/mixed race female prisoners. *Criminal Behaviour and Mental Health, 13,* 229–240.

Borrill, J., Snow, L., Medlicott, D., Teers, R., & Paton, J. (2005). Learning from "near misses": Interviews with women who survived an incident of severe self-harm in prison. *The Howard Journal, 44,* 57–69.

Bosworth, M. (2006). Self-harm in women's prisons [editorial introduction]. *Criminology and Public Policy, 5,* 157–160.

Brown, M., Comtois, K., & Linehan, M. (2002). Reasons for suicide attempts and nonsuicidal self-injury in women with borderline personality disorder. *Journal of Abnormal Psychology, 111,* 198–202.

Browne, A., Miller, B., & Maguin, E. (1999). Prevalence and severity of lifetime physical and sexual victimization among incarcerated women. *International Journal of Law and Psychiatry, 22,* 301–322.

Brumberg, J. (2006). Are we facing an epidemic of self-injury? *Chronicle of Higher Education, 53,* B6–B8.

Canada, Task Force on Federally Sentenced Women. (1990). *Creating choices: Report of the Task Force on Federally Sentenced Women.* Ottawa: Department of the Solicitor General.

Charles, D., Abram, K., McClelland, G., & Teplin, L. (2003). Suicidal ideation and behavior among women in jail. *Journal of Contemporary Criminal Justice, 19,* 65–81.

Comack, E. (1996). *Women in trouble.* Black Point, NS: Fernwood.

Comack, E. (2005). Coping, resisting, and surviving: Connecting women's law violations to the histories of abuse. In L.F. Alarid & P. Cromwell (Eds.), *In her own words: Women offenders' views on crime and victimization* (pp. 33–43). Los Angeles, CA: Roxbury.

Connors, M., & Morse, W. (1993). Sexual abuse and eating disorders: A review. *International Journal of Eating Disorders, 13,* 1–11.

Correctional Service of Canada. (1992). Violence and suicide in Canadian institutions: Some recent statistics. *Forum on Corrections Research, 4*(3), 3–5.

Correctional Service of Canada. (2002). *Commissioner's Directive 843: Prevention, management and response to suicide and self-injuries.* Ottawa: Author.

Daigle, M., Alarie, M., & Lefebvre, P. (1999). The problem of suicide among female prisoners. *Forum on Corrections Research, 11*(3), 41–45.

Dalton, M. (2008, January 18). Guards stage prison blockade: Latest "information picket" follows firing of 3 workers, supervisor. *Waterloo Record*. Retrieved from http://news .therecord.com.

Davey, M. (2008, February 16). Gunman showed few hints of trouble. *New York Times*, p. A1. Retrieved from www.nytimes.com.

Dolan, B., & Mitchell, E. (1994). Personality disorder and psychological disturbance of female prisoners: A comparison with women referred for NHS treatment of personality disorder. *Criminal Behaviour and Mental Health, 4,* 130–143.

Dowden, C., & Blanchette, K. (1999). *An investigation into the characteristics of substance-abusing women offenders: Risk, need and post-release outcome* (Research Report R-81). Ottawa: Correctional Service of Canada.

Dowden, C., & Blanchette, K. (2002). An evaluation of the effectiveness of substance abuse programming for female offenders. *International Journal of Offender Therapy and Comparative Criminology, 46,* 220–230.

El-Bassel, N., Gilbert, L., Schilling, R., Ivanoff, A., Borne, D., & Safyer, S. (1996). Correlates of crack abuse among drug abusing incarcerated women: Psychological trauma, social support, and coping behavior. *American Journal of Drug and Alcohol Abuse, 22,* 41–57.

Family devastated by new details in teen's death. (2007, November 20). *CTV.ca News*. Retrieved from www.ctv.ca.

Ferraro, K., & Moe, A. (2003). The impact of mothering on criminal offending. In L.F. Alarid & P. Cromwell (Eds.), *In her own words: Women offenders' views on crime and victimization* (pp. 79–92). Los Angeles, CA: Roxbury.

Finkelhor, D., & Browne, A. (1985). The traumatic impact of child sexual abuse: A conceptualization. *The American Journal of Orthopsychiatry, 55,* 530–541.

Furlong, A., & Grant, B. (2006). Women offender substance abuse programming: Interim results. *Forum on Corrections Research, 16*(1), 41–48.

Gilfus, M. (1992). From victims to survivors to offenders: Women's routes of entry and immersion into street crime. In L.F. Alarid & P. Cromwell (Eds.), *In her own words: Women offenders' views on crime and victimization* (pp. 5–14). Los Angeles, CA: Roxbury.

Gilfus, M. (2002). *Women's experiences of abuse as a risk factor for incarceration.* Harrisburg, PA: VAWnet, a project of the National Resource Center on Domestic Violence/ Pennsylvania Coalition Against Domestic Violence. Retrieved from www .vawnet.org.

Green, C., Andre, G., Kendall, K., Looman, T., & Polvi, N. (1992). A study of 133 suicides among Canadian federal prisoners. *Forum on Corrections Research, 4*(3), 22–28.

Hannah-Moffat, K. (2006). Pandora's box: Risk/need and gender-responsive corrections. *Criminology and Public Policy, 5,* 183–192.

Harned, M., Najavits, L., & Weiss, R. (2006). Self-harm and suicidal behavior in women with co-morbid PTSD and substance dependence. *American Journal on Addictions, 15,* 392–395.

Hayman, S. (2006). *Imprisoning our sisters: The new federal women's prisons in Canada.* Montreal & Kingston: McGill-Queen's University Press.

Heney, J. (1990). *Report on self-injurious behaviour in the Kingston Prison for Women.* Ottawa: Correctional Service of Canada.

Heney, J., & Kristiansen, C. (1997). An analysis of the impact of prison on women survivors of childhood sexual abuse. *Women and Therapy, 20*(4), 29–44.

Kariminia, A., Butler, T., Corben, S., Levy, M., Grant, L., Kaldor, J., et al. (2007). Extreme cause-specific mortality in a cohort of adult prisoners: 1988 to 2002—A data-linkage study. *International Journal of Epidemiology, 36,* 310–316.

Kilty, J. (2006). Under the barred umbrella: Is there room for a women-centered self-injury policy in Canadian corrections? *Criminology and Public Policy, 5,* 161–182.

Kruttschnitt, C., & Vuolo, M. (2007). The cultural context of women prisoners' mental health. *Punishment and Society, 9,* 115–150.

Laishes, J. (2002). *Mental health strategy for women offenders.* Ottawa: Correctional Service of Canada.

Larivière, M. (1997). *The Correctional Service of Canada 1996–1997 retrospective report on inmate suicides.* Ottawa: Correctional Service of Canada. Retrieved from www.csc-scc.gc.ca/text/pblct/health/96-9_suicide_report1.rtf.

Liebling, A. (1994). Suicide among women prisoners. *The Howard Journal, 33,* 1–9.

Lightfoot, L., & Lambert, L. (1992). *Substance abuse treatment needs of federally sentenced women* (Technical Report no. 2). Ottawa: Correctional Service of Canada.

Lo, C. (2004). Sociodemographic factors, drug abuse, and other crimes: How they vary among male and female arrestees. *Journal of Criminal Justice, 32,* 399–409.

Loucks, A., & Zamble, E. (1994). Some comparisons of female and male serious offenders. *Forum on Corrections Research, 6*(1), 22–24.

Marchetto, M. (2006). Repetitive skin-cutting: Parental bonding, personality and gender. *Psychology and Psychotherapy: Theory, Research and Practice, 79,* 445–459.

Matsumoto, T., Yamaguchi, A., Asami, T., Okada, T., Yoshikawa, K., & Hirayasu, Y. (2005). Characteristics of self-cutters among male inmates: Association with bulimia and dissociation. *Psychiatry and Clinical Neurosciences, 59,* 319–326.

McClellan, D., Farabee, D., & Crouch, B. (1997). Early victimization, drug use, and criminality: A comparison of male and female prisoners. *Criminal Justice and Behavior, 24,* 455–476.

McDonagh, D., Noël, C., & Wichmann, C. (2002). Mental health needs of women offenders: Needs analysis for the development of the intensive intervention strategy. *Forum on Corrections Research, 14*(2), 32–35.

Milligan, R., & Waller, G. (2000). Anger and bulimic psychopathology among nonclinical women. *International Journal of Eating Disorders, 28,* 446–450.

Milligan, R., Waller, G., & Andrews, B. (2002). Eating disturbance in female prisoners: The role of anger. *Eating Behaviors, 3,* 123–132.

Motiuk, L., & Brown, S. (1994). *The validity of offender needs identification and analysis in community corrections* (Research Report R-34). Ottawa: Correctional Service of Canada.

Pernanen, K., Cousineau, M., Brochu, S., & Sun, F. (2002). *Proportions of crimes associated with alcohol and other drugs in Canada.* Ottawa: Canadian Centre on Substance Abuse. Retrieved from www.ccsa.ca/NR/rdonlyres/2322ADF8-AF1E-4298-B05D -E5247D465F11/0/ccsa0091052002.pdf.

Pollack, S., & Brezina, K. (2006). Negotiating contradictions: Sexual abuse counseling with imprisoned women. *Women and Therapy, 29*(3–4), 117–133.

Polvi, M. (1997). *Prisoner suicide: Literature review.* Ottawa: Correctional Service of Canada. Retrieved from www.csc-scc.gc.ca/text/pblct/health/inmatesui08-eng.shtml.

Radosh, P. (2002). Reflections of women's crime and mothers in prison: A peacemaking approach. *Crime and Delinquency, 48,* 300–315.

Reed, D., & Reed, E. (1995). Mothers in prison and their children. In B. Raffel-Price & N. Sokoloff (Eds.), *The criminal justice system and women: Offenders, prisoners, victims and workers* (3rd ed., pp. 261–274). Boston: McGraw-Hill.

Roe-Sepowitz, D. (2007). Characteristics and predictors of self-mutilation: A study of incarcerated women. *Criminal Behaviour and Mental Health, 17,* 312–321.

Root, M., & Fallon, P. (1989). Treating the victimized bulimic. *Journal of Interpersonal Violence, 4,* 90–100.

Schoemaker, C., Smit, F., Bijl, R., & Vollebergh, W. (2002). Bulimia nervosa following psychological and multiple child abuse: Support for the self-medication hypothesis in a population-based cohort study. *International Journal of Eating Disorders, 32,* 381–388.

Schoppmann, S., Schröck, R., Schnepp, W., & Büscher, A. (2007). "Then I just showed her my arms...": Bodily sensations in moments of alienation related to self-injurious behaviour—A hermeneutic phenomenological study. *Journal of Psychiatric and Mental Health Nursing, 14,* 587–597.

Shaw, M. (1994). *Ontario women in conflict with the law: A survey of women in institutions and under community supervision in Ontario.* Toronto: Research Services, Strategic Policy and Planning Division, Ministry of the Solicitor General and Correctional Services.

Shaw, N. (2002). Shifting conversations on girls' and women's self-injury: An analysis of the clinical literature in historical context. *Feminism and Psychology, 12,* 191–219.

Sugar, F., & Fox, L. (1990). Survey of federally sentenced aboriginal women in the community. Retrieved from www.csc-scc.gc.ca/text/prgrm/fsw/nativesurvey/toce-eng.shtml.

Thomas, J., Leaf, M., Kazmierczak, S., & Stone, J. (2006). Self-injury in correctional settings: "Pathology" of prisons or of prisoners? *Criminology and Public Policy, 5,* 193–202.

Tobin, D., & Griffing, A. (1996). Coping, sexual abuse, and compensatory behavior. *International Journal of Eating Disorders, 20,* 143–148.

Waller, G., Babbs, M., Milligan, R., Meyer, C., Ohanian, V., & Leung, N. (2003). Anger and core beliefs in the eating disorders. *International Journal of Eating Disorders, 34,* 118–124.

Wichmann, C., Serin, R., & Abracen, J. (2002). *Women offenders who engage in self-harm: A comparative investigation.* Ottawa: Correctional Service of Canada.

Wichmann, C., Serin, R., & Motiuk, L. (2000). *Predicting suicide attempts among male offenders in federal penitentiaries* (Research Report R-91). Ottawa: Correctional Service of Canada.

CHAPTER 6

Correctional Assessment and Treatment: Toward Community Reintegration

Jill L. Atkinson and Jean Folsom

Introduction

In this chapter, we examine the theory and research that form the basis of effective correctional practice. Canada is a world leader in this area, having developed a model that emphasizes the importance of accurately assessing an offender's risk, identifying appropriate treatment needs, and providing effective treatment specifically suited to each offender.

Assessment is central to this model, and therefore it is important to understand how assessments are carried out: the type of information used, how it is collected, and how it is combined to help decision-makers. After an initial assessment has been completed, an offender is offered treatment services. To be effective, treatment must be responsive to an offender's needs and personal characteristics.

To promote successful community reintegration, preparatory programs are offered to women before they leave prison. These programs are followed by support and supervision when the woman is living in the community.

Throughout this chapter, we consider how assessment and treatment practices suit women in particular. Being "too few to count" (Adelburg & Currie, 1987) has meant that female offenders have less often been the focus of correctional research than male offenders. As a result, some of the assessment measures and treatment programs currently in use were developed for male offenders and then adapted to female offenders. Recently, however, there has been a move toward developing gender-specific assessment and treatment services.

Assessment

Psychological assessments are carried out to provide decision-makers and treatment providers with information at different points in the criminal justice system. In the court system, assessments are used to determine whether an accused is fit to stand trial and to help judges make sentencing decisions. In the correctional system, assessments are carried out to determine inmates' security levels, their treatment needs, and their risk of reoffending.

Assessment, therefore, is the foundation of effective correctional treatment as articulated by Andrews and his colleagues (Andrews & Bonta, 2003; Gendreau, French, & Gionet, 2004). These Canadian researchers outlined a model that guides the assessment and treatment of offenders. Made up of three principles—risk, needs, and responsivity—this model has informed correctional practice throughout the world and continues to play a central role in our understanding of effective correctional practice (Blanchette & Brown, 2006; Ward, Mesler, & Yates, 2007).

The Risk-Need-Responsivity Model

The Risk Principle (Matching Level of Service to Risk)

According to the risk principle, we should begin by estimating, as accurately as possible, an offender's likelihood to reoffend. After this risk is known, offenders should be provided with services according to their level of risk: higher-risk offenders should be given more intense services and lower-risk offenders, less intense, or no services (Andrews & Bonta, 1995).

To determine risk, and thus the level of service required, Andrews and his colleagues developed the **Level of Service Inventory** (LSI), a measure of offender needs across 10 domains: (1) criminal history, (2) employment/education, (3) financial, (4) family/marital, (5) accommodation, (6) leisure/recreation, (7) companions, (8) alcohol/drug problems, (9) emotional/personal, and (10) attitudes. The LSI was designed to assist with the decisions of how to implement the least restrictive amount of supervision and how to identify dynamic areas of risk and need that could be addressed by programming to reduce risk (Andrews & Bonta, 1995). This assessment tool has been used with women offenders and will be discussed in more detail later in the chapter.

The Needs Principle (Assessing Criminogenic Needs to Target in Treatment)

The needs principle focuses on assessing offenders' criminogenic needs. These needs are directly related to offenders' criminal behaviour and include antisocial attitudes, anger control, substance abuse, and, in men, deviant sexual interest. According to this principle, non-criminogenic needs, such as childhood sexual abuse, low self-esteem, eating disorders, and poor health, although potentially important areas for clinical treatment, should not be the focus and priority within the correctional setting if they are not related to offending.

As outlined in box 6.1, researchers have identified four major areas of **criminogenic need** that apply to male and female offenders. Although offenders of both sexes have been found to share similar criminogenic needs (Dowden & Andrews, 1999; Simourd & Andrews, 1994), some researchers have suggested that their level of importance and the way in which they

---

Box 6.1   Criminogenic Needs

The *needs principle* highlights the difference between offender needs that are related to recidivism and those that are not. Needs that are associated with recidivism are known as *criminogenic* needs, and these needs must be targeted in treatment to reduce recidivism. Four types of criminogenic needs apply to both male and female offenders:

1. Antisocial behaviour: having committed many crimes
2. Antisocial personality pattern: impulsive, daring, egocentric, lacking in empathy and remorse
3. Antisocial attitudes: holding values, beliefs, and rationalizations that support engaging in criminal activity
4. Antisocial associates: associating with people who approve of criminal behaviour and therefore provide social support for it

Source: Andrews, D.A., Bonta, J., & Wormith, S. (2006). The recent past and near future of risk and/or need assessment. *Crime & Delinquency, 52*, 7–27.

---

relate to offending may vary. Furthermore, additional criminogenic needs may be unique to female offenders (Atkinson, 1998; Blanchette, 2001).

The differentiation between criminogenic and non-criminogenic needs is especially relevant for women in the criminal justice system because women are generally more likely to seek help than men (Oliver, Pearson, Coe, & Gunnell, 2005). Therefore, establishing clearly which treatment targets relate to criminogenic needs and which to general well-being will help to ensure that offenders are not prevented from obtaining privileges, such as early release, due to either their willingness to seek help for their non-criminogenic needs or the severity of their mental health problems. Just as we should not deny parole to an offender with an unresolved heart condition, women should not be kept incarcerated due to their non-criminogenic problems. However, differentiating between criminogenic and non-criminogenic needs is not always easy in the area of mental health. For example, imagine that a woman is struggling with the effects of child sexual abuse. Is it fair to tie her level of risk to her progress in dealing with her anxiety or self-injury? Should a woman who admits to drinking four glasses of wine per day and who commits a large bank fraud over several years while maintaining an excellent work record as loans officer be required to deal with her problem drinking to gain release?

These questions need to be asked because women are more likely than men to be assessed as having high needs when they enter prison (Kong & AuCoin, 2008) and to seek treatment for a variety of issues while incarcerated; but they should not necessarily be required to resolve all of their issues to gain release or increased privileges. The challenge then is to identify those factors that are related to a specific woman's risk of reoffending (her criminogenic needs) and those related to her general well-being (her non-criminogenic needs).

Unfortunately, determining the cause of any individual's criminal behaviour can be difficult. Furthermore, as noted in chapter 2, theories of criminal behaviour are not well developed for women because they are much less frequently involved in criminal activity than men. This difference in criminal activity by sex increases with offence severity; thus, women who commit serious offences, or who offend chronically, are more atypical of their sex than male offenders are of theirs. As a result, in attempts to explain their atypical behaviour, mental health needs (depression, post-traumatic stress, and anxiety, for example) are likely to be identified as contributing factors. For male offenders, who are more typical of their sex and who are less likely to discuss emotional problems (Howerton et al., 2007), attitudes, substance abuse, and meaningful work are more frequently identified as relevant treatment goals.

Notwithstanding these observations, it is important to note that mental health needs can occasionally be criminogenic. For example, experiencing psychological distress, regardless of the circumstances of the original crime, may increase an offender's risk for relapse, which will be discussed further when we turn to dynamic risk assessment.

The Responsivity Principle (Matching Treatment to Clients' Characteristics)

This principle promotes the use of evidence-based treatments matched to an offender's personality, strengths, learning style, motivation, and abilities. Evidence-based treatments are those that have been found to be effective, at least in comparison with no treatment, in a number of scientific studies. *Cognitive behavioural* interventions are often recommended because they have shown the most promise to date across offender populations (Bonta & Andrews, 2007). The most effective treatment should be used, and it should be tailored to the offender, male or female, Aboriginal or white, well-educated or not. These responsivity issues will be discussed in detail later in the chapter.

Before we examine how the risk-need-responsivity model is applied to specific types of assessment, we will look at how decision-makers gather information about an offender and how they make their decisions.

Sources of Information Used in Decision-Making

Although correctional services and community programs vary considerably in the psychological measures (if any) they use in assessment, some assessment domains and sources of information are commonly used. Information about an offender can be gathered from the woman herself (self-report), from those who know her (collateral sources), from institutional records, and from psychological tests (Atkinson, 1995).

Self-Report Information

Information from the offender can be obtained from structured self-report questionnaires and interviews. Questionnaires are not psychological tests that assess underlying personality constructs or intelligence but are methods of systematically gathering self-report information about certain areas (such as assertiveness or depression) and providing norms for comparing groups of women. Some assessors prefer to collect this information in a face-to-face interview. Interviews allow the assessor to tailor questions to the individual offender and to probe further when comments are voiced that imply pro-criminal sentiments or cognitive distortions. Despite the number and type of assessment tools available, interviews are considered an important component of any offender assessment. Interviews should be structured and systematic to increase efficiency and to reduce the likelihood that significant information will be overlooked.

COLLATERAL SOURCES

In addition to gathering information directly from the offender herself, decision-makers need to corroborate the offender's account whenever possible. Corroboration is commonly achieved through internal file review, but when files are incomplete or inaccurate, corroboration can involve interviewing collateral sources, such as family and employers, and reviewing police reports, victim impact statements, and previous assessment and treatment reports. Although these tasks take time, especially when some reports are not readily available to the assessor, corroboration of the offender's self-report is essential prior to estimating an offender's risk of recidivism.

PSYCHOLOGICAL TESTS

The third source of information commonly used to assess risk comes from psychological testing. Psychological tests measure underlying constructs, such as intelligence or personality, and often include validity scales to identify purposeful faking or misunderstanding of the questions because of mental illness or lack of motivation. Psychological tests are less transparent than questionnaires or inventories and may therefore yield less-biased information. Unfortunately, in the absence of a commonly agreed upon theory of female offending, assessors may have difficulty determining which tests to use and the weights to assign to the scores.

Types of Decision-Making (Clinical Judgment vs. Actuarial Assessment)

Regardless of whether an assessor relies on an interview, a questionnaire, or a psychological test, the assessment is more accurate and therefore more useful when it is structured and based on *actuarial* information (Blanchette & Taylor, 2005; Quinsey, Harris, Rice, & Cormier, 2006). In the past few decades, much work has been carried out to improve the way in which we assess offenders, and risk assessment has improved the most.

Clinical judgment alone is no longer an acceptable basis for decision-making in most correctional services. Responsible correctional practice requires that psychologists use valid instruments designed for a specific purpose and shown to be reliable when applied properly. In correctional services, however, the lack of validated assessment tools for women has led to a heavy reliance on clinical judgment. Furthermore, even when actuarial, or statistical, methods have been shown to work with female offenders, the Canadian correctional service still advises those closest to the offender (that is, the correctional officers and case manager officers) to use their judgment (Correctional Service of Canada [CSC], 2006).

When it comes to predicting the likelihood that an offender will reoffend, correctional managers, lawyers, and the public have difficulty believing that expert opinion and clinical judgment are not as accurate as structured actuarial measures. Indeed, in a classic study, Quinsey and Ambtman demonstrated that experts such as forensic psychiatrists did not fare any better than high school teachers when it came to predicting reoffending based on file information (Quinsey & Ambtman, 1979). The experts' opinions were weakened by focusing on the current offence and institutional behaviours that reflect mental health problems, instead of focusing on risk-related characteristics.

What exactly *is* **actuarial prediction**, and how do we know that it is better than clinical judgment? We'll begin by describing the two types of decision-making.

CLINICAL JUDGMENT

Clinical judgments are opinions rendered by those working with offenders, such as parole officers, prison staff, and professionals (such as psychologists and psychiatrists), using informal, unstructured methods. Clinical judgment does not rely on pre-established guidelines regarding the information to consider, the sources to use, and how to combine different types of information. As such, the judgment varies from professional to professional and perhaps also within professionals over time. When asked, most professionals will provide a set of implicit guidelines that they use to make their decisions. Unfortunately, they do not always follow their own guidelines and can be biased by irrelevant factors, as demonstrated in the study of forensic psychiatrists and high school teachers described above.

ACTUARIAL ASSESSMENT

In contrast, actuarial decisions are based on the measurement and combination of clearly defined types of information. This statistical approach (Quinsey et al., 2006) is highly structured and objective and has proven to be more accurate than clinical judgment (Dawes, Faust, & Meehl, 1989; Grove & Meehl, 1996). Assessors collect information from files and/or from the offender herself and weigh this information according to a predetermined mathematical formula. The answer is then tallied, and the result is an estimate of the offender's probability of reoffending within a given period of time, usually 3, 7, or 10 years. The information used in actuarial instruments has been shown to best predict general and violent reoffending. Most instruments have converged on a similar set of items, which are related to the criminogenic factors discussed earlier (see box 6.1).

Many researchers have examined the accuracy of clinical judgment vs. actuarial assessment (Aegisdottir et al., 2006). The conclusion in the scientific literature is clear: actuarial prediction, although not perfect, is significantly more accurate than clinical judgment. Unfortunately, despite decades of research, some professionals continue to replace or override actuarial predictions with their own opinion (Garb & Boyle, 2003).

Assessment for Classification

Classification assessments are necessary for effective correctional treatment. Classification involves grouping people according to their similarities or differences. In corrections, offenders are grouped by security level (maximum, medium, or minimum), compatibility (ability to get along with other inmates), and treatment needs (substance abuse, emotion regulation, etc.). If carried out properly, classification aids in the effective and fair management of offenders. As Blanchette and Brown (2006) point out, classification guides the management of offender behaviour because it assists correctional staff in determining the kinds of privileges (often associated with security level) that may be safely made available to different groups of offenders as they progress through their sentences.

After an offender has been sentenced to serve time in either a prison or correctional centre, she is assessed by correctional staff to determine her security level and thus the most appropriate placement in her home region.

Placement decisions must take several factors into consideration:

- Public safety. Is the offender a high, medium, or low risk to escape? If she escapes, is she likely to reoffend violently?
- The smooth running of the institution. Will the offender integrate well into the general inmate population? Are there any offenders (such as a co-accused) or groups of offenders (such as a gang or racial group) with whom she is not compatible? If so, for her safety and the smooth running of the institution, she may be placed in a different institution or, in extreme cases, such as for those who have testified against others or committed certain sexual offences, in segregation.
- The least restrictive environment for the offender. Although public safety needs to be ensured and certain offenders need to be kept separated, women should not be housed in more restrictive environments than necessary. Prison itself is restrictive enough without having an inmate's liberty further curtailed by unnecessary placement in maximum security or segregation.

Classification assessments are usually carried out by correctional staff, such as case managers, who complete a thorough file review and then interview an offender soon after her arrival in a new institution. They collect information on known criminogenic factors such as criminal history, including age of first arrest and conviction, escape attempts, length of present sentence, nature of offence, substance abuse history, accomplices, and gang memberships. This information is then weighed and combined quantitatively in a predetermined manner to obtain a total score that indicates the offender's required minimum level of security. Classification assessments are carried out periodically throughout an offender's stay in an institution with the goal of reducing security levels as the offender demonstrates more prosocial attitudes and behaviours until she is ready for release to a halfway house or the community.

Unfortunately, the process of gradually reducing security, called **cascading**, despite being desirable, is not always possible prior to an offender's release. (For an illustration of cascading, see box 6.2.) Minimum security settings may have a shortage of beds or insufficient time may remain in a woman's sentence prior to release. As a result, women are sometimes released into the community from medium or, more rarely, maximum security. The practice of cascading is more common in male corrections. As has been commented on numerous times in this text, far fewer female offenders than male offenders are housed in the correctional system, and thus, far fewer correctional institutions exist for women. Male offenders have many more opportunities to be transferred to one of a number of medium or even minimum security facilities over the course of their incarceration. The same cannot be said for women.

The Correctional Service of Canada (CSC), which has committed to using gender-informed classification tools, has developed the Security Reclassification Scale for Women (SRSW) (Blanchette & Taylor, 2004). The SRSW was based on known risk factors for female offenders and risk factors identified through consultation both with researchers who have developed other classification measures and with those who work most closely with female offenders. The researchers began with 176 items and whittled these down to 9 items that

Box 6.2   An Example of Cascading

Admission to new institution	➜	Assessment for classification purposes

⬇

Placement in *maximum security* due to history of escape risk and substance abuse

3-month case management review	➜	Reclassification interview

⬇

Security level is dropped to *medium* due to pro-social behaviour within the institution, such as good job performance, lack of institutional charges, and active participation in treatment. The offender shows no evidence of substance use based on random urinalysis testing.

6-month case management review	➜	Reclassification interview

⬇

Security level dropped to *minimum* despite a recent institutional charge of disobeying a direct order. This act was considered a minor charge; job performance and treatment plan compliance (random urinalysis testing and substance abuse treatment) remained satisfactory.

⬇

Release to halfway house in the community for further supervision

best predicted institutional conduct using an actuarial approach (see box 6.3). The final version of the SRSW was carefully evaluated in a three-year field test and found to be reliable and valid for Aboriginal and non-Aboriginal female offenders alike (Blanchette & Taylor, 2005; CSC, 2006).

The SRSW is scored by a case manager who works closely with the offender, using information from institutional files and staff reports. The SRSW has a 30-point scoring range: higher scores represent a higher assessed risk and thus a higher security rating. Review periods are normally every six months.

When compared with the previous method of using structured clinical judgment to make classification decisions, this new scale resulted in fewer placements to maximum security and more placements to minimum security. The SRSW was also found to be significantly more predictive of institutional misconduct than its predecessor (Blanchette & Taylor, 2005; Gobeil & Blanchette, 2007). In sum, this new actuarial measure is more accurate and more liberal than the CSC's earlier measure, which relied more on clinical judgment.

Box 6.3   Security Reclassification Scale for Women (SRSW)

1. Correctional plan: program motivation
2. Maintains regular positive family contact
3. Number of convictions for serious disciplinary offences *during the review period*
4. Number of recorded incidents *during the review period*
5. History of escape or unlawfully at large from work release, temporary absences, or community supervision
6. Pay level *during the review period*
7. Number of times offender was placed in involuntary segregation for being a danger to others or the institution *during the review period*
8. Total number of successful escorted temporary absences *during the review period*
9. Custody rating scale incident history

Source: Blanchette, K., & Taylor, K. (2005). *Development and field test of a gender-informed security reclassification scale for women offenders* (Research Report R-167). Ottawa: Correctional Service of Canada.

Assessment for Release Decision-Making

Psychologists are frequently called on to make risk assessments for parole boards to use in release decision-making. Because these assessments often carry a lot of weight, psychologists working with female offenders need to choose appropriate instruments and methods for determining risk.

APPLYING ACTUARIAL RISK ASSESSMENT TO FEMALE OFFENDERS

The science of predicting criminal recidivism has improved dramatically in the past few decades. Few correctional services rely solely on unstructured clinical judgment. Several actuarial instruments are used to predict the risk of an offender committing a new offence of any kind, and of *his*[1] committing a new violent and/or sexual offence, in particular. These instruments tend to predict criminal recidivism quite well when applied to men of various ages and races, and even when used for men diagnosed with a personality or other mental disorder (for a comprehensive review of the actuarial prediction of antisocial behaviour, see Quinsey et al., 2006).

Unfortunately, we are only beginning to determine how such actuarial measures fare when applied to female offenders of various types (Bonta, Pang, & Wallace-Capretta, 1995; Folsom & Atkinson, 2007; Loza, Neo, Shahinfar, & Loza-Fanous, 2005). Women comprise a much smaller proportion of the inmate population, making up just 4 percent of federal offenders, 6 percent of provincial/territorial offenders in Canada (Kong & AuCoin, 2008), and approximately 5 percent of state and federal offenders in the United States (US Department of Justice, 2008). These small percentages likely explain why the validation of actuarial instruments for women lags behind that of men.

Therefore, correctional agencies need to work together to develop and test actuarial instruments. With such a small number of females incarcerated in any one jurisdiction in any given year, large-scale studies will need to be conducted across several years to gather enough data to determine which factors should be included and in what combination, for different types of women. These efforts can benefit from the large body of research on risk appraisal carried out with male offenders because the correlates of crime are, *in general*, similar across genders.

Sex Differences in the Correlates of Crime

Simourd and Andrews (1994) analyzed the results of 60 studies in which male and female youths were examined on the same risk variables. Risk factors included socio-economic status, family and parental problems (broken homes, for example), personal distress (such as anxiety and low self-esteem), "minor personality variables" (deficits in empathy and moral reasoning), poor parent–child relationships (lack of supervision, attachment issues), educational difficulties, temperament or misconduct (antisocial characteristics, impulsivity, and substance abuse, for example), and antisocial peers and associates. Although female delinquents committed fewer crimes than male delinquents, the correlates of offending were very similar for the two sexes. Anti-social peers, attitudes and temperament, and misconduct were the largest correlates of criminal offending, whereas socio-economic status, family and parental problems, and personal distress were less closely related.

Are the correlates of crime similar for adult male and female offenders? Females commit fewer crimes than males across the lifespan, making up only 21 percent of accused persons aged 12 and over (Kong & AuCoin, 2008). However, the peak of female offending occurs at age 15 and then drops significantly. By adulthood, women represent only 6 percent of the offender population (Kong & AuCoin, 2008). Adult women are far less likely to be incarcerated than men, and those who are may differ significantly from their male counterparts. Therefore, when examining the correlates of crime, we cannot yet use the sex differences in youth to generalize about sex differences between adults. One area in which sex differences have been found among adult offenders is in the use of **neutralizations**, or "rationalizations after the fact" among fraud offenders (see box 6.4).

Do risk assessment instruments developed for male offenders also work for female offenders? The General Statistical Information on Recidivism Scale (GSIR) (Nuffield, 1982) has been successfully used in Canada with male offenders for many years (Bonta, Harman, Hann, & Cormier, 1996). However, the GSIR does not fare as well in predicting recidivism for female offenders. Similarly, the Psychopathy Checklist-Revised (PCL-R) (Hare, 1991) predicts recidivism in male offenders (Hare, 1996) but has produced mixed results with female offenders (Loucks, 1995; Neary, 1990; Vitale, Smith, Brinkley, & Newman, 2002). In contrast, the Level of Service Inventory-Revised (LSI-R) (Andrews & Bonta, 1995) has successfully predicted recidivism in Canadian female offenders who were serving sentences of less than two years (Coulson, Ilacqua, Nutbrown, Giulekas, & Cudjoe, 1996; Rettinger, 1998) and those serving longer federal sentences (Folsom & Atkinson, 2007; McConnell, 1996).

Another scale developed for use with men, the Childhood and Adolescent Taxon Scale (CATS) measures the characteristics of early onset, persistent, male offenders and includes items related to school maladjustment and adolescent antisocial behaviour (Quinsey et al., 2006). The CATS has been useful in predicting recidivism in male offenders (Quinsey et al., 2006) and

Box 6.4   Neutralization Theory

Fraud offenders appear to endorse the dominant moral code of society (they agree that crime is wrong and also which crimes are the most serious), but seem to use neutralizations or rationalizations to excuse their illegal behaviour. For example, a fraud offender might tell herself that the money she is stealing from her bank is necessary for her to provide properly for her two young daughters, thereby neutralizing the "wrongness" of the act and allowing her to continue.

Atkinson (1998), who had observed female fraud offenders frequently using neutralizations in her clinical work, decided to test neutralization theory. Groups of male and female offenders, half of whom were convicted of fraud offences and half of whom had other types of convictions, were asked to rate the seriousness of a variety of crimes and immoral acts. Their ratings were compared with those of male and female community volunteers. As predicted by neutralization theory, participants in all six groups closely agreed with each other on the seriousness of various crimes and immoral acts. The dominant moral code was endorsed by offenders and non-offenders alike. The next step was to test whether offenders, especially fraud offenders, were more likely to accept neutralizations as explanations for crimes and whether there were sex differences.

All six groups were asked to complete a neutralization scale that described a number of crimes and asked participants to choose an appropriate disposition or sentence for the offender. Further information about the offence, the victim, or the offender was then provided, and participants were asked to reassess their original sentence. For example, a bank robber might be initially sentenced to five years in prison, but upon learning that the bank robber was crazed with grief due to the death of his child, some participants reduced the sentence by a few years. Likewise, if a man convicted of theft was assigned 18 months, but the thief was later described as a middle-aged school principal with no criminal record who was "a pillar of the community," some participants reduced his sentence to a $10,000 fine and community service. The degree to which participants reduced sentences as a result of different types of neutralizations was measured and compared.

The neutralization prediction was confirmed for women but not for men. Female fraud offenders neutralized more than male fraud offenders; that is, they believed more than their male counterparts that sentences should be reduced because of extenuating circumstances. Female fraud offenders also neutralized more often than female non-fraud offenders and female non-offenders. Among the men, all groups neutralized to the same degree. This finding suggests that correlates of crime are not always the same for men and women. In this case, neutralization is a criminogenic factor for female fraud offenders but not for their male counterparts. Thus, treatments targeting neutralizations may be uniquely suited to female fraud offenders.

Source: Atkinson, J.L. (1998). *Neutralizations among male and female fraud offenders*. Doctoral dissertation, Queen's University, Kingston, ON.

female offenders (McConnell, 1996), and in a recent validation study it proved especially useful in the prediction of violent recidivism among female offenders (Folsom & Atkinson, 2007). This scale is shown in box 6.5.

In summary, at least two measures are promising when applied to female offenders in Canada and the United States: the LSI (Coulson, 1993; Coulson et al., 1996; Folsom & Atkinson, 2007; McConnell, 1996; Rettinger, 1998) and the CATS (Folsom & Atkinson, 2007; McConnell, 1996). Thus, some evidence is emerging that risk assessment instruments developed for men may be valid for use with women, and some psychologists are therefore using these with caution. Others continue to rely on assessing factors that they believe are related to a woman's offence cycle and to general criminogenic needs.

Assessing Changes in Risk Level

Actuarial instruments combine known risk factors to produce an estimate of the likelihood that an individual offender will reoffend in general (commit any type of crime) or reoffend violently. The risk factors included are almost always static or unchangeable items, such as sex, criminal history, and childhood problems. The use of static or historical factors means that an offender's risk can never go down, only up. That is, if a woman accumulates further offences, her criminal history score will increase, but she can do nothing to improve the score based on her past.

In theory, intervention services are intended to reduce an offender's risk. To determine whether such services *do* reduce an offender's risk, and which types of services reduce risk the best, a measure of dynamic risk is needed. Dynamic risk predictors are changeable factors and can be divided into stable factors (personality disorders and deviant sexual preferences, for example) and acute factors (those that are rapidly changing, such as negative moods and intoxication) (Hanson & Harris, 2000).

If a measure were to be based on dynamic factors, especially those that could be changed through intervention, such as drug use or employment, then we could monitor an offender's changing risk status over time; when she took steps to lower her risk, by avoiding drugs and criminal peers, for example, her risk score would decrease. During periods of difficulty, (when unemployed, depressed, or using drugs), her dynamic risk score would increase, reflecting an increase in risk. If such dynamic risk assessments were possible, parole officers could monitor a woman's progress more accurately and provide appropriate services (including a possible return to incarceration) as needed.

Although an actuarial assessment tool based on dynamic factors alone would be ideal, and some have been developed for males (Hanson & Harris, 2000; Quinsey, Coleman, Jones, & Altrows, 1997), to date none has been shown to compare to the predictive accuracy of the more static measures. To test the predictive utility of a dynamic measure, research must show that changes in risk level (the total score) are associated with changes in recidivism. Unfortunately, this type of research is still in its infancy. As a result, psychologists usually employ a measure of static risk to determine an offender's long-term likelihood of reoffending and then note what steps, if any, she is taking to reduce that risk. In the end, therefore, a scientifically proven methodology with reasonably good accuracy (an actuarial assessment) is used to anchor an offender's risk level, and then clinical judgment is applied to determine how that risk can be modified.

Box 6.5   The Child and Adolescent Taxon Scale

1. Elementary school maladjustment (at least a minor discipline or attendance problem)
2. Teenage alcohol problem
3. Childhood aggression problem (at least occasional minor physical assaults before age 15)
4. Childhood behaviour problems before age 15 (at least three symptoms of antisocial personality disorder)
5. Suspension or expulsion from school
6. Arrest before age 16
7. Parental alcoholism
8. Living with both biological parents to age 16 (except for death of parent)

Source: Quinsey, V.L., Harris, G.T., Rice, M.E., & Cormier, C. (2006). *Violent offenders: Appraising and managing risk* (2nd ed.). Washington, DC: American Psychological Association.

Actuarial measures perform quite well, and much better than clinical judgment, at predicting the long-term recidivism risk for male offenders. These measures also appear promising when applied to female offenders. The drawback is that actuarial measures are unable to detect changes in risk levels. Thus, they cannot aid in the prediction of *when* an offender is at risk of reoffending; to accomplish this type of prediction, researchers are working on actuarial models based on dynamic, or changeable, factors.

Treatment

Why should prisons be concerned with treatment? Aren't offenders in prison as punishment for committing a crime? Isn't it enough that they are given a "time out" from society? Isn't being in prison enough of a deterrent not to offend again? If not, what else is needed? These issues have been debated throughout the history of imprisonment. This section examines these and other issues surrounding treatment for women offenders.

Why Treatment?

Criminal justice sanctions have many purposes, including punishment for the crime committed, protection of society from criminal activity, deterrence of the person from committing another crime, and rehabilitation of the offender. Rehabilitation requires some type of intervention to help offenders to avoid future criminal activity.

In recent years, much rhetoric has circulated on "getting tough" on crime. This sentiment has translated into harsher sentences and more intermediate sanctions, such as intensive supervision of offenders in the community, boot camps, and electronic monitoring. The effects of these types of punishments on recidivism were examined by Smith, Goggin, and Gendreau (2002) in a meta-analysis (that is, by combining the findings of a group of studies for statistical analysis). These researchers synthesized the results of 117 studies that had examined the effects of various criminal justice punishments on recidivism in male and female, youth and adult offenders. The results indicated that criminal justice punishments had no effect on recidivism. Offenders who received prison sentences were more likely to reoffend than those given community sanctions, and offenders with longer sentences were slightly more likely to reoffend than those with shorter sentences. The effects were the same for women as for men. The authors concluded that the "getting tough" approach to crime does not reduce recidivism. Instead, evidence-based rehabilitation programs are more effective at reducing crime.

Thus, imprisonment on its own is not enough to help offenders avoid further criminal activity. Treatment is required to assist offenders to make the changes in their lives that will support them remaining crime-free.

Types of Treatment

The correctional system uses two main types of treatment: interventions that focus on criminogenic needs and interventions that address non-criminogenic needs, such as self-esteem or past history of abuse. Female offenders have access to both types of treatments. Although a wide range of programs are available within the provincial correctional systems, most female offenders within these systems are serving very short sentences and therefore cannot take part in lengthy treatment programs. Thus, the focus of this section is on those programs that are available to federally incarcerated women because these programs tend to be lengthier and some have been subjected to systematic evaluation.

CORRECTIONAL TREATMENT PROGRAMS

Most correctional treatment programs are based on Andrews and Bonta's (2006) risk, needs, and responsivity principles. As described at the beginning of the chapter, according to the risk principle, treatment services need to match the offender's risk level. That is, offenders who are at a high risk to reoffend should receive the highest-intensity treatments (that is, longer programs, more hours per week of treatment, etc.), whereas offenders at low risk should receive little or no therapeutic services.

The needs principle highlights the difference between offender needs that are related to recidivism and those that are not. Those needs associated with recidivism, known as criminogenic needs, are the needs that are targeted in treatment to reduce recidivism.

The assessment process, as already discussed, identifies specific problems in the offender's life that led to her offending. These specific problems or criminogenic needs are the focus of correctional treatment programs.

The responsivity principle has two parts: (1) the *general responsivity principle*, which states that social learning and cognitive-behavioural strategies, which have been shown to be the most powerful interventions for change, should be used (see box 6.6 for more details on cognitive-behaviour therapy); and (2) the *specific responsivity principle*, which refers to delivering treatment in a way suited to the offender's learning style or ability. Treatment must be matched to the client, which may involve adapting materials to the appropriate literacy level, cultural background, or gender. In terms of gender, some of the responsivity factors for female offenders are the importance of relationships, including the therapeutic relationship in women's lives, and differences in communication style (Blanchette & Brown,

---

Box 6.6   Cognitive-Behaviour Therapy

Cognitive therapy focuses on the client's thoughts and teaches her to challenge or refute negative or self-defeating thoughts, such as "no one likes me" or "I will never be able to quit smoking." This therapy also helps clients to examine the origin of their thoughts and evaluate their reasonableness. For example, if a friend walks by Kristen in the hall at school and doesn't say hello, Kristen might think that her friend is angry with her and that she is not speaking to her. This situation could make Kristen feel angry with her friend, which in turn could interfere with their friendship. A cognitive therapist would challenge this conclusion and have Kristen seek other possible explanations, such as "maybe my friend was preoccupied and didn't see me, or perhaps she wasn't feeling well." In this way, Kristen would learn not to make assumptions without checking them out. If one of these alternative explanations turns out to be the case, instead of feeling angry, Kristen might feel empathy or concern for her friend.

2006). Women, for example, tend to communicate with more body language than men and to speak less and interrupt less in mixed groups.

In terms of the general responsivity principle, social learning refers to the acquisition of beliefs, attitudes, and behaviours from other people. Criminal behaviour, for example, may be learned from friends or associates whom we value. These people may teach the skills for committing crime and reinforce an involvement in crime.

Cognitive-behavioural treatments have been frequently used by psychologists to treat a variety of problems, including depression (Beck, Rush, Shaw, & Emery, 1979), anxiety (Burns, 1999), and personality problems (Linehan, 1993). The cognitive part of the treatment refers to how we think and, specifically, how we think about the problem, whether it is with low mood, anxiety, or some other problematic behaviour. The theory behind cognitive therapy is that by changing the way we think about a situation, we can change how we feel about it. In the example of this approach in box 6.6, the student attributed her friend's behaviour to anger, which made her feel angry. When she changed how she was thinking about the situation (perhaps her friend wasn't angry), her feelings about it also changed (from anger to concern).

In contrast to cognitive therapy, which focuses on thoughts, behaviour therapy focuses on concrete behavioural change. Clients keep records of their behaviour, set specific behavioural goals with their therapist, and evaluate their progress regularly. An example is a treatment for heavy drinking in which the goal may be to reduce the consumption of alcohol (Dimeff, Baer, Kivlahan, & Marlatt, 1999). The client records the number of drinks consumed per week, sets a goal of reducing her consumption, and monitors her drinking. Specific behavioural strategies to meet the goal include allowing more time between drinks, alternating alcoholic drinks with non-alcoholic drinks, or switching from stronger to weaker alcoholic drinks (from hard liquor to beer, for example).

Together, social learning and cognitive-behavioural techniques are the most effective interventions for criminal behaviour (Andrews & Bonta, 2006). With these techniques, people can gain better control over their thoughts and feelings and make behavioural change in their lives.

In addition to using evidence-based therapies, the responsivity principle directs us to adapt interventions to specific offenders' characteristics, including gender. All principles of effective correctional treatment have largely been developed on male offenders and later adapted for female offenders. How well do they apply to female offenders? Dowden and Andrews (1999) conducted a meta-analytic review of treatment outcome studies involving female offenders. They found that those programs that adhered to the basic tenets of effective correctional treatment were the most effective in reducing recidivism. That is, programs that targeted higher-risk offenders, focused predominantly on criminogenic needs, and used behavioural-social learning treatment strategies resulted in stronger treatment effects. Note that some of the most common needs that are targeted for female offenders (self-esteem and past victimization) were not included in any of the studies examined (Dowden & Andrews, 1999). Therefore, the authors concluded that "it remains unclear as to whether these are criminogenic or noncriminogenic needs for female offenders" (Dowden & Andrews, 1999, p. 449). It is also worth noting that most of the studies in the meta-analysis were based on young female offenders (Blanchette & Brown, 2006). As already noted, adult female offenders may vary in some important ways from young female offenders.

Blanchette and Brown (2006) have thoroughly reviewed evidence for treatment effectiveness with female offenders from a wide variety of sources. Included in their review were programs based on the risk-need-responsivity principle and those based on other principles, such as feminism and relational theory.

Feminist therapy focuses on the societal, cultural, and political causes of, and solutions to, issues presented by clients. This theory is sensitive to inequality in society, particularly gender inequality, and the role that it plays in women's psychological distress. Feminist therapy focuses on the client's strengths and on a collaborative relationship between the client and therapist.

According to relational theory, connecting with other human beings is necessary for healthy development. This theory defines healthy relationships as those based on empathy, empowerment, and mutuality.

Blanchette and Brown (2006) conclude that, to date, little solid evidence supports the effectiveness of treatments that are *not* based on the risk-need-responsivity principle. However, they also see other treatment approaches—such as feminist therapy and relational therapy—as being consistent with the risk-need-responsivity principle. Feminist therapy's focus on the client's strengths and a collaborative relationship is not contrary to the risk-need-responsivity principle. In terms of relational theory, a high-quality relationship is one of the conditions of effective correctional programs: "A high-quality relationship creates a setting in which modeling and reinforcement can more easily take place. Important to such a relationship is an open, flexible, and enthusiastic style wherein people feel free to express their opinions, feelings, and experiences" (Andrews & Bonta, 2006, p. 354). It is more likely that the high-quality relationship is a necessary condition for therapeutic change but never a sufficient condition on its own.

As a result of their review, Blanchette and Brown (2006) concluded that gender should be viewed as a general, not a specific, responsivity factor. A specific responsivity factor would deliver treatment in a way that is suited to an individual's learning style. However, because women have many commonalities, gender should be considered a general responsivity factor. Blanchette and Brown (2006) have reformulated the general responsivity principle for female offenders as follows:

A gender-informed responsivity principle states that in general, optimal treatment response will be achieved when treatment providers deliver structured behavioural interventions [grounded in feminist philosophies and social learning theory] in an empathic and empowering manner [a strength-based model] while simultaneously adopting a firm but fair approach. (p. 126)

Note that the reformulated general responsivity principle for female offenders incorporates feminist theory and assigns equal weight to women's strengths and risks in the rehabilitation process.

Principles for Treatment of Women Offenders

All programs for federal female offenders must be offered within a women-centred perspective to ensure recognition of women's social realities and the context of their lives. *Creating Choices*, a report by the Task Force on Federally Sentenced Women (Canada, Task Force on Federally Sentenced Women, 1990) outlined five principles for the treatment of female offenders:

1. Empowerment: The lack of power women feel to control their own lives and the low levels of self-esteem felt by them represent a primary need of female offenders. Empowerment is the process by which women gain insight into their situation, identify their strengths, and are supported and challenged to take positive action to gain control of their lives.
2. Meaningful and responsible choices: Female offenders need to be made aware of the resources available to them and the consequences of their decisions so they can make informed decisions. When women are able to make such decisions, they develop a sense of control over their lives, which ultimately leads to an improvement of self-esteem and self-worth.
3. Respect and dignity: Respect is essential between correctional staff and female offenders. A person treated with respect and dignity is likely to gain self-respect and to respond to others in a similar fashion.
4. Supportive environment: A positive environment can foster personal development and promote physical and psychological health. A supportive environment ensures equality of services in a respectful atmosphere while allowing for meaningful and responsible choices to be generated.
5. Shared responsibility: All levels of government, correctional services, businesses, voluntary and private sector organizations, and the community have a responsibility to help develop, implement, monitor, and evaluate programming services for federally sentenced women.

Core Correctional Programs

The principles outlined in *Creating Choices* have guided the development of the four core programs for female offenders: (1) substance abuse treatment; (2) reasoning and rehabilitation; (3) anger and emotions management; and (4) sex offender therapy for women (Correctional Service of Canada, 2008b). The following is a brief description of each.

SUBSTANCE ABUSE TREATMENT

The Centre for Addiction and Mental Health in Toronto was contracted to develop an extensive, state-of-the-art, women-specific substance abuse program rooted in gender-based principles for the federal correctional system. The result was the Women Offender Substance Abuse Program (WOSAP), which, in addition to dealing directly with the addiction, addresses issues important in women's lives, such as relationships, emotions, and sexuality (see box 6.7). The results of a preliminary evaluation of the program are promising (Hume, 2004). Participants in the program report high degrees of satisfaction, and program facilitators report that the content is challenging and effective. Program completion rates are also high. All these indices are suggestive of an effective program. Follow-up data is needed, however, to definitively indicate whether the program is making a difference in the lives of these women.

Box 6.7   Women Offender Substance Abuse Program

This program provides a continuum of care from first admission to release to the community. Shortly after admission, all female offenders receive eight sessions of treatment to initially engage them in the process and to educate them about substance abuse. All women are included in these sessions because so many of them are affected by substance abuse either through their own use or that of a partner or other family member. This process is largely educational and covers such issues as infectious diseases and fetal alcohol spectrum disorder.

Intensive Therapeutic Treatment. Women with a moderate to high substance abuse problem are offered this component of the continuum. Using a holistic approach, this treatment weaves issues related to substance abuse together with other concerns in women's lives, such as problems with emotions, issues with relationships, sexuality, and spirituality. Women are taught new skills to combat substance abuse, including problem-solving and how to prevent a relapse into abuse.

Relapse Prevention/Maintenance. Women can start this component in the institution and continue it in the community. This module reinforces the skills that she has already been taught by covering useful coping strategies and building on the woman's strengths. This component is designed to help women avoid relapsing after they are back in the community and the environment where they had abused substances in the past.

The relapse prevention process assists the woman in identifying high-risk situations, for example, the times and places she is likely to be tempted to use drugs or alcohol. She is taught strategies to avoid these situations and to find alternative ways of coping when these situations do occur. Also as part of relapse prevention training, she is taught that if she does use one of these substances, she should view the event as a lapse or a slip, not as a full-blown relapse. Thus, if a slip occurs, it does not mean she is a failure and she cannot stop using again. Lapses are frequent occurrences for people who are making any substantial change in their lives; understanding that lapses are a process of change, not an indication of failure, can have a large, positive effect on treatment.

Source: Hume, L. (2004). A gender-specific substance abuse program for federally-sentenced women. *Forum on Corrections Research, 16,* 40–41.

Reasoning and Rehabilitation

The purpose of this program is to develop interpersonal reasoning skills for effective life management. The program targets problem areas that are associated with criminal behaviour, such as impulsiveness, poor emotions management, egocentrism and social perspective taking, assertiveness and social interaction, criminal attitudes and attributions, critical reasoning, and rigid cognitive styles. Because faulty thinking or reasoning often lies behind these problems, by changing these thinking patterns, criminal behaviour may be reduced. Program participants are taught to think before they act and to anticipate problems and to plan their reactions in advance. The skills learned in this program are useful for avoiding further criminal activity.

Anger and Emotions Management

This program addresses the needs of female offenders who have used violence to resolve conflicts. It incorporates the past experiences of women, both as survivors of abuse and as aggressors. Based on a cognitive-behavioural approach to anger reduction, this program is intended to teach women offenders the skills required to handle negative emotions that are associated with aggression, such as anger. Participants learn to recognize triggers for their anger and to challenge the cognitions or thoughts that create and maintain negative emotions. Finally, they learn about relapse prevention to avoid returning to their pre-treatment patterns of responding to situations.

Sex Offender Therapy for Women

Sex offender therapy, typically provided on a one-to-one basis, is available for female offenders in institutions and in the community. The main goal of treatment is to identify and effectively deal with the factors that have contributed to the woman's offence. Chapter 7 provides in-depth coverage of this issue.

Aboriginal Offenders

Federally sentenced Aboriginal women offenders have access to a correctional institution that has been designed as a healing lodge. In recognition of the importance of nature in Aboriginal healing and culture, this institution is located in a rural area surrounded by woodland. The focus is on the safety of the women offenders, staff, and the public while encouraging healing, wellness, and a safe return to the community. Aboriginal culture and spirituality are an integral part of the life at the lodge. Elders are on-site all day, to lead prayers, healing ceremonies, and talking circles. All programs are presented in a manner that is cultural- and gender-sensitive, which addresses the responsivity factor for Aboriginal women offenders. The main programs offered at the healing lodge are the same as those offered at other women's facilities: the Woman Offender Substance Abuse Program, Circles of Change, Spirit of a Warrior, programs for survivors of abuse, and literacy and education programs.

CIRCLES OF CHANGE

This program treats criminogenic needs with three therapeutic approaches: relational theory, cognitive-behavioural therapy, and solution-focused therapy. In relational intervention, the goal is to increase women's capacity to engage in mutually empathic and empowering relationships. The goal of the cognitive-behavioural intervention is to help women identify, challenge, and replace their negative thinking patterns with more positive patterns. The solution-focused approach is aimed at helping women find solutions to the problems in their lives. Circles of Change recognizes the importance of cultural heritage for Aboriginal women offenders by teaching Aboriginal history and incorporating ceremonies in the program, which includes the following topics:

- The process of changes: Setting personal goals for change
- Knowledge of Canadian Aboriginal culture
- Communication styles: Boundaries, self-esteem, and self-care issues
- Problem-solving skills
- A woman's role in her family of origin
- Health and unhealthy relationships
- Social injustice (racism, sexism, and sexual exploitation)
- Developing and maintaining personal relationships

SPIRIT OF A WARRIOR

This program targets violent behaviour in Aboriginal women offenders. It is based on cognitive-behavioural strategies but incorporates Aboriginal ceremonies and cultural rituals to guide women to a non-violent way of life. The warrior is a symbol of inner strength and courage. Through experience, a woman can lose touch with her warrior but can reconnect with it and move toward wholeness through traditional teachings and reflection on the inner self. Some of the goals of this program are to analyze violence and its impact on the self and others, to guide participants through a self-awareness journey, to teach new skills, and to help participants improve their decision-making abilities.

Programs Addressing Non-Criminogenic Needs

Women offenders often have other needs that may not fit into the area defined as criminogenic. Some of these needs are mental health (including the effects of trauma from past abuse), education, employment, and social programs.

MENTAL HEALTH

Assessment and treatment for serious mental disorders is covered in chapter 8. One area of mental health treatment that may be provided for any woman offender is that of counselling for abuse and trauma.

Programs for Survivors of Abuse and Trauma

Because of the high rate of victimization in the lives of women offenders (Bonta, Pang, & Wallace-Capretta, 1995; Heney, 1990; Shaw, 1994), treatment programs have been developed to deal with past experiences of abuse (Correctional Service of Canada, 2008b). Such programs are available to all federal women offenders and are completely voluntary. These programs include an educational component that aims to increase awareness of trauma and abuse issues, such as the different forms of abuse and the context in which they occur. The programs also help women to build resources in the community and to know where to go for help. More intensive work is also provided on issues such as healthy relationships and coping strategies.

A history of past victimization, however, is not related to an increased risk for reoffending (Bonta et al., 1995), which is why it is not a criminogenic need. Past victimization may be viewed as a responsivity factor because emotional distress from the abuse may interfere with the woman's ability to benefit from treatment for her criminogenic needs. If she is very anxious, angry, or frequently injuring herself as a direct result of abuse, dealing with the abuse will allow her to reap more benefit from core treatment programs for her criminogenic needs.

In some situations, victimization may be directly related to a woman's offence, thereby making it a criminogenic need. For example, a woman might overreact to something a man says or does, by responding violently. The man's behaviour may have evoked memories of past abuse and led to her inappropriate response. Thus the issue of past abuse may blur the line between criminogenic and non-criminogenic needs for women offenders.

Some scholars, however, would take issue with this conceptualization of the effects of past victimization on criminal behaviour in women, arguing that such an approach ignores or minimizes the effects of the socio-economic background of female offenders (Hannah-Moffat, 2006; Pollack, 2005). Instead, the risk-need-responsivity approach places responsibility for problematic behaviours on the woman herself, not on a more global societal view to understanding her behaviour. Hannah-Moffat (2006) and Pollack (2005) emphasize the importance of socio-economic and gender issues, such as sexism, in shaping the behaviours of female offenders. For example, self-injurious behaviour may be seen as a rational response to an oppressive and abusive life situation because it provides emotional relief and a sense of control over a life that is controlled by others. These feminist-oriented authors have much to add to our understanding of women offenders. Yet a more individualistic approach is needed when one is faced with a woman in immediate need of assistance. Global societal change is not the mandate of a forensic or correctional service.

EDUCATION AND EMPLOYMENT PROGRAMS

Several other programs are available to women offenders based on the belief that they will be useful for successful reintegration into the community. Although education and employment needs may not be directly associated with offending, upgrading in these areas may have an influence on whether a woman will engage in either pro-social or criminal behaviour on release. For example, a lack of skills to earn a legitimate income may contribute to a woman's decision to seek illegal means to support herself, such as drug trafficking or prostitution. Improving her education or learning new job skills may provide a woman with the means of earning a legitimate income and avoiding crime.

PARENTING SKILLS AND THE MOTHER-CHILD PROGRAM

Two-thirds of incarcerated women are mothers of children under five years of age (Correctional Service of Canada, 2008a). These women are often single parents for whom living apart from their children is an ordeal for both themselves and their children. For these reasons, the Correctional Service of Canada created the Parenting Skills Program and the Mother-Child Program. Based on cognitive principles, the Parenting Skills Program is designed to help improve participants' thinking patterns and their understanding and skills in dealing with their family relationships, especially their children. By improving the family situations of offenders' children, the program gives these children a better chance of *not* growing up to follow in their parent's footsteps by becoming involved in criminal activity.

The aim of the Mother-Child Program is "to provide a supportive environment that fosters and promotes stability and continuity for the mother-child relationship" (Correctional Service of Canada, 2008a, ¶1). The pre-eminent consideration for participation in the program is the best interests of the child, including the child's safety, security, and physical, emotional, and spiritual well-being. The major components of the program are full-time on-site residency of children up to the age of four with their mother and part-time residency (weekends and holidays) of children up to the age of 12 with their mother. Both mother and child live in a house that is shared with several other women offenders who may or may not have children with them. Those offenders who do not have children are carefully screened prior to being placed in such a house to ensure that no one with a history of violence against children could reside there. All mothers must complete the parenting skills program and meet other criteria (such as being of minimum or medium security classification) prior to being allowed to live with their children.

SPIRITUALITY

All facilities have chaplains available, who can provide pastoral care directly to women offenders or arrange for care in a wide variety of faiths. Volunteers from various faith communities provide support to female offenders both while incarcerated and on their release into the community.

LEISURE, RECREATION, ARTS AND CRAFTS

Leisure and recreational facilities are widely available within the correctional system. Some sites offer specialized programs, such as a horticultural program, where women learn about growing and caring for plants, and a canine program, where women learn to care for and train dogs. A leisure skills program can help women to understand the role that leisure plays in society and the importance of leisure as part of a balanced lifestyle. Because leisure activities can contribute to personal development and to a sense of well-being, women are taught how to reach their leisure goals by effective planning for leisure, overcoming obstacles, and using creative ways to take part in low-cost activities.

THE COMMUNITY INTEGRATION PROGRAM

The object of this program is to teach women critical information to help them make the transition from the institution to the community. Several independent modules comprise the program, and women can attend the modules relevant to their situation. The content is based on areas that were found to be problematic for women offenders, such as money management and finding a job. To reduce the stress associated with community re-entry, stressful life situations, such as finding affordable housing, making new friends, and re-establishing family ties, are also addressed. At the end of the program, it is hoped that the women will be better equipped to re-enter society.

Community Reintegration

Because the transition from institutional life to community life is believed to be a key factor in the successful reintegration of offenders, correctional services strive to provide a continuum of care. Toward this end, the Correctional Service of Canada provides female offenders with services such as the community integration program, prior to their release. Other programs that may begin either in the institution or in the community include the Community Maintenance/Relapse Prevention module of the Women Offender Substance Abuse Program (Fortin, 2004).

To ensure the most successful reintegration possible, adequate planning is needed prior to release, supported by appropriate supervision and programming upon release. Ideally, planning should begin long before an offender is eligible for release and include an assessment of ongoing treatment needs and an audit of available resources (accommodation, family and friend support, job opportunities, for example) and potential obstacles (such as associates and type of work).

The challenge is determining which of these needs areas most closely relates to recidivism and therefore provides the most important target for ongoing intervention. A burgeoning body of research has examined the predictive validity of community functioning in general and specific factors, such as health, finances, and accommodation, which may relate to recidivism among female offenders. Although a generic rating of community functioning has not proven to be closely associated with recidivism among women (Brown & Motiuk, 2005; Gates, Dowden, & Brown, 1998), some specific areas, especially financial problems, hold promise. Several researchers have found a link between socio-economic disadvantage and risk for reoffending (Brown & Motiuk, 2005; Farrington & Painter, 2004; Holtfreter, Reisig, & Morash, 2004; Rettinger, 1998). Moreover, this association has been found to be stronger for female offenders (both youth and adult) than male offenders.

A Correctional Service of Canada questionnaire originally developed for male offenders on release in the community has recently been applied to help predict which changes in a released female offender's circumstances best predict non-violent and violent recidivism. The Community Integration Scale (CIS) has proven to be effective in predicting both non-violent and violent recidivism among female offenders in the community (Dowden, Serin, & Blanchette, 2001; Law, 2004). The CIS domains most predictive of recidivism among female offenders were employment and associates.

Programming

To reduce recidivism, offenders may be encouraged or required by law to participate in programming upon release. Such programming can include educational upgrading, vocational training, substance abuse treatment, cognitive skills training, or others types of programming as deemed necessary by the case management team and endorsed by the parole authorities. Programs available to offenders in the community vary across jurisdiction but include those provided by the CSC and the Canadian Association of Elizabeth Fry Societies (CAEFS) and those available to all community members (for example, Alcoholics Anonymous, Narcotics Anonymous, and community mental health programs).

About half of all women under federal jurisdiction in Canada are on conditional release in the community. Despite this high percentage, because so few women are serving federal sentences at any one time and because they are so widely dispersed geographically, services specific to female offenders in any single community are rarely available. Thus, programming for female offenders in the community must be flexible and creative, often making use of non-correctional programs (Fortin, 2004).

Supervision

Supervision is the second component of effective reintegration. Although the priority is to protect the public by monitoring the behaviour of offenders to anticipate when they may relapse and commit a new crime, offenders benefit by having a supportive supervisor close by to help them stay crime-free. Applying the risk-need-responsivity model, supervision services should be provided in relation to an offender's risk level. Thus, the highest-risk offenders receive the most intense supervision (placement in a halfway house and weekly check-ins with a parole officer, for example), and the lowest-risk offenders receive little or no supervision, perhaps monthly check-ins at the police station.

Supportive supervisors can help a woman identify when she is starting to slip and work with her to prevent a relapse. Risk factors might include a return to a dysfunctional relationship or an increasing association with drug users. By helping the woman to confront these behaviours, the parole officer can alert her to the need to apply what she has learned in treatment to avoid a return to anti-social behaviour and possibly to jail. In keeping with the risk-need-responsivity model, supervision should be responsive to the needs of offenders. Important considerations include the type and length of parole, gender, and Aboriginal status. For example, to address gender responsivity issues in supervision, specially selected and trained female parole officer teams have been organized in Montreal and Toronto (Gagnon, 2004).

As noted in chapter 1, the Canadian Association of Elizabeth Fry Societies (CAEFS) originated to support and advocate for women in conflict with the law. CAEFS plays a large role in supporting women upon release, operating halfway houses across the country, and providing supervision and programming to women on parole and probation.

Summary

After an offender has been classified according to her level of risk, her treatment needs, and her compatibility, she is placed in a living unit in a prison or correctional facility, usually in a region closest to her home. Following assessment of her criminogenic and non-criminogenic needs, she and her case manager will agree on a treatment plan.

Treatment may consist of individual or group programming for her criminogenic needs; that is, those needs that if treated will result in a reduction in the probability of her reoffending. Other non-criminogenic needs, such as self-esteem or the effects of victimization, may also be addressed. At times a blurring of these needs may occur; for example, the need to treat the effects of victimization may or may not be directly related to her pattern of offending. The importance of other areas of her life is not to be overlooked; for example, the need for employment, housing, parenting skills, and to be living with her young children. At all times, programs must be offered within a women-centred perspective that ensures women's social realities are recognized.

The offender will meet with her case manager at regular intervals to review her security level and treatment plan progress. If things are going well, she will be cascaded to a lower security level and granted passes to visit the community. When she is ready for parole, a psychologist will assess her risk using one of the actuarial instruments that have been validated for female offenders. Relying on her clinical judgment, the psychologist will then add her assessment of the dynamic factors by estimating the degree to which the static risk factors may have been reduced through correctional programming. The psychologist then offers her opinion about how to reduce this risk, often in consultation with the offender herself.

If the offender is deemed a manageable risk, she will be released on parole into a halfway house or to her home. She will be supervised by a parole officer and, if needed, attend programs offered by the CSC or those generally available in the community. Throughout this process, she will be supported by members of the Canadian Association of Elizabeth Fry Societies.

Note

1. The initial development of actuarial instruments to predict risk focused entirely on male offenders.

Discussion Questions

1. What is the purpose of offender classification?
2. What is meant by criminogenic and non-criminogenic risk factors?
3. What is the drawback of using static risk factors instead of dynamic risk factors in actuarial risk prediction?
4. Is the following statement true or false? Explain your answer. "There is no point in spending taxpayers' dollars on treating issues that are not related to a woman's offending."
5. What services are available to help women safely reintegrate into the community?

Suggested Readings

Andrews, D.A., & Bonta, J. (2006). *The psychology of criminal conduct* (4th ed.). Newark, NJ: LexisNexis.

Blanchette, K., & Brown, S. (2006). *The assessment and treatment of women offenders: An integrative perspective.* Chichester, UK: John Wiley & Sons.

Canada, Task Force on Federally Sentenced Women. (1990). *Creating choices: Report of the Task Force on Federally Sentenced Women.* Ottawa: Department of the Solicitor General.

Online Resources

1. Bonta, J. (2002). The effects of punishment on recidivism. *Public Safety Canada Research Summary,* 7(3): www.publicsafety.gc.ca
2. McMahon, M. (1998). *Assisting female offenders: Art or science? What works— Women and juvenile females in community corrections.* Chairperson's commentary on the 1998 annual conference of the International Community Corrections Association, Arlington, Virginia, September 27–30: www.maevemcmahon.com/femaleoffenders.htm
3. Correctional Service of Canada. (2007). Women offender programs and issues: www.csc-scc.gc.ca/text/prgrm/fsw/fsw-eng.shtml

References

Adelburg, E., & Currie, C. (Eds.). (1987). *Too few to count: Canadian women in conflict with the law.* Vancouver: Press Gang.

Aegisdottir, S., White, M.J., Spengler, P.M., Maugherman, A.S., Anderson, L.A., Cook, R.S., et al. (2006). The meta-analysis of clinical judgment project: Fifty-six years of accumulated research on clinical versus statistical prediction. *Counseling Psychologist, 34,* 341–382.

Andrews, D.A., & Bonta, J. (1995). *LSI-R: The Level of Service Inventory—Revised.* Toronto: Multi-Health Systems.

Andrews, D.A., & Bonta, J. (2003). *The psychology of criminal conduct* (3rd ed.). Cincinnati, OH: Anderson.

Andrews, D.A., & Bonta, J. (2006). *The psychology of criminal conduct* (4th ed.). Cincinnati, OH: Anderson.

Andrews, D.A., Bonta, J., & Wormith, S. (2006). The recent past and near future of risk and/or need assessment. *Crime & Delinquency, 52,* 7–27.

Atkinson, J.L. (1995). *The assessment of female sex offenders.* An unpublished, internal report prepared for the Correctional Service of Canada.

Atkinson, J.L. (1998). *Neutralizations among male and female fraud offenders.* Doctoral Dissertation, Queen's University, Kingston, Ontario.

Beck, A.T., Rush, A.J., Shaw, B., & Emery, G. (1979). *Cognitive therapy of depression.* New York: Wiley.

Blanchette, K. (2001). Classifying female offenders for effective intervention: Application of the case-based principles of risk and need. *Forum on Corrections Research, 14*(1). Retrieved from www.csc-scc.gc.ca/text/pblct/forum/e141/e141h-eng.shtml.

Blanchette, K., & Brown, S.L. (2006). *The assessment and treatment of women offenders.* West Sussex, UK: John Wiley & Sons.

Blanchette, K., & Taylor, K. (2004). Development and validation of a security reclassification scale for women. *Forum on Corrections Research, 16*(1). Retrieved from www.csc-scc.gc.ca/text/pblct/forum/Vol16No1/v16-a10-eng.shtml.

Blanchette, K., & Taylor, K. (2005). *Development and field test of a gender-informed security reclassification scale for women offenders* (Research Report R-167). Ottawa: Correctional Service of Canada.

Bonta, J., & Andrews, D.A. (2007). *Risk-need-responsivity model for offender assessment and rehabilitation* (User Report no. 2007-06). Ottawa: Public Safety Canada.

Bonta, J., Harman, W.G., Hann, R.G., & Cormier, R.B. (1996). The prediction of recidivism among federally sentenced offenders: A re-evaluation study of the SIR scale. *Canadian Journal of Criminology, 38*, 61–79.

Bonta, J., Pang, B., & Wallace-Capretta, S. (1995). Predictor of recidivism among incarcerated female offenders. *The Prison Journal, 75*(3), 277–294.

Brown, S.L., & Motiuk, L.L. (2005). *The Dynamic Factor Identification and Analysis (DFIA) component of the Offender Intake Assessment (OIA) process: A meta-analytic, psychometric and consultative review* (Research Report R-164). Ottawa: Research Branch, Correctional Service of Canada.

Burns, D.D. (1999). *The feeling good handbook* (rev. ed.). New York: Plume/Penguin Books.

Canada, Task Force on Federally Sentenced Women. (1990). *Creating choices: Report of the Task Force on Federally Sentenced Women*. Ottawa: Department of the Solicitor General.

Correctional Service of Canada. (2006). Response and action plan for inspection of Nova and Grand Valley Institution by Her Majesty's Inspectorate of Prisons. Retrieved from www.csc-scc.gc.ca/text/prgrm/fsw/wos27_response/CSC_Action_Plan-NOVA_GVIW_e.pdf.

Correctional Service of Canada. (2008a). Mother-Child Program. Retrieved from www.csc-scc.gc.ca/text/prgrm/fsw/pro02-5-eng.shtml.

Correctional Service of Canada. (2008b). Women offender programs and issues. Retrieved from www.csc-scc.gc.ca/text/prgrm/fsw/fsw-eng.shtml.

Coulson, G. (1993). Using the Level of Supervision Inventory in placing female offenders in rehabilitation programs or halfway houses. *IARCA Journal on Community Corrections, 5*, 12–13.

Coulson, G., Ilacqua, G., Nutbrown, V., Giulekas, D., & Cudjoe, F. (1996). Predictive utility of the LSI for incarcerated female offenders. *Criminal Justice and Behavior, 23*, 427–439.

Dawes, R.M., Faust, D., & Meehl, P.E. (1989). Clinical versus actuarial judgment. *Science, 243*, 1668–1674.

Dimeff, L.A., Baer, J.S., Kivlahan, D.R., & Marlatt, G.A. (1999). *Brief alcohol screening and intervention for college students: A harm reduction approach*. New York: Guilford Press.

Dowden, C., & Andrews, D.A. (1999). What works for female offenders: A meta-analytic review. *Crime and Delinquency, 45*, 438–452.

Dowden, C., Serin, R., & Blanchette, K. (2001). *The application of the Community Intervention Scale to women offenders: Preliminary findings* (Research Report R-97). Ottawa: Research Branch, Correctional Service of Canada.

Farrington, D.P., & Painter, K.A. (2004). *Gender differences in offending: Implications for risk-focused prevention* [online report]. Retrieved from www.homeoffice.gov.uk/rds/pdfs2/rdsolr0904.pdf.

Folsom, J., & Atkinson, J.L. (2007). The generalizability of the LSI-R and the CAT to the prediction of recidivism in female offenders. *Criminal Justice and Behaviour, 34,* 1044–1056.

Fortin, D. (2004). *Program strategy for women offenders.* Ottawa: Correctional Service of Canada.

Gagnon, R. (2004). Implementation of a supervision project for federally-sentenced women in Montreal. *Forum on Corrections Research, 16*(1), 13–14.

Garb, H.N., & Boyle, P.A. (2003). Understanding why some clinicians use pseudoscientific methods: Findings from research on clinical judgment. In S.O. Lillienfeld, S.J. Lynn, & J.M. Lohr (Eds.), *Science and pseudoscience in clinical psychology* (pp. 17–38). New York: Guilford.

Gates, M., Dowden, C., & Brown, S.L. (1998). Community functioning. *Forum on Corrections Research, 10*(3), 35–37.

Gendreau, P., French, S., & Gionet, A. (2004). What works (what doesn't work): The principles of effective correctional treatment. *Journal of Community Corrections, 13,* 4–30.

Gobeil, R., & Blanchette, K. (2007). Revalidation of a gender-informed security reclassification scale for women offenders. *Journal of Contemporary Criminal Justice, 23,* 296–309.

Grove, W.M.; & Meehl, P.E. (1996). Comparative efficiency of informal (subjective, impressionistic) and formal (mechanical, algorithmic) prediction procedures: The clinical–statistical controversy. *Psychology, Public Policy, and Law, 2,* 293–323.

Hannah-Moffat, K. (2006). Pandora's box: Risk/need and gender-responsive corrections. *Criminology and Public Policy, 5,* 183–192.

Hanson, R.K., & Harris, A.J.R. (2000). Where should we intervene? Dynamic predictors of sexual offense recidivism. *Criminal Justice and Behavior, 27,* 6–35.

Hare, R.D. (1991). *The Hare psychopathy checklist-revised (manual).* Toronto: Multi-Health Systems.

Hare, R.D. (1996). Psychopathy: A clinical construct whose time has come. *Criminal Justice and Behavior, 23,* 25–54.

Heney, J. (1990). *Report on self-injurious behaviour in the Kingston Prison for Women.* Ottawa: Correctional Service of Canada.

Holtfreter, K., Reisig, M.D., & Morash, M. (2004). Poverty, state capital and recidivism among women offenders. *Criminology and Public Policy, 3,* 185–209.

Howerton, A., Byng, R., Campbell, J., Hess, D., Owens, C., & Aitken, P. (2007). Understanding help seeking behaviour among male offenders: Qualitative interview study. *BMJ, 334,* 303–309.

Hume, L. (2004). A gender-specific substance abuse program for federally-sentenced women. *Forum on Corrections Research, 16,* 40–41.

Kong, R., & AuCoin, K. (2008). Female offenders in Canada. *Juristat, 28*(1), 1–22.

Law, M. (2004). *A longitudinal follow-up of federally sentenced women in the community: Assessing the predictive validity of the dynamic characteristics of the Community Intervention Scale.* Unpublished doctoral dissertation, Carleton University, Ottawa.

Linehan, M. (1993). *Cognitive-behavioral treatment of borderline personality disorder.* New York: Guilford Press.

Loucks, A. (1995). *Criminal behavior, violent behavior, and prison maladjustment in federal female offenders.* Unpublished doctoral dissertation, Queen's University, Kingston, Ontario.

Loza, W., Neo, L.H., Shahinfar, A., & Loza-Fanous, A. (2005). Cross-validation of the self-appraisal questionnaire: A tool for assessing violent and nonviolent recidivism with female offenders. *International Journal of Offender Therapy and Comparative Criminology, 49*(5), 547–560.

McConnell, B.A. (1996). *The prediction of female federal offender recidivism with the Level of Supervision Inventory.* Unpublished BA thesis, Queen's University, Kingston, Ontario.

Neary, A.M. (1990). DSM-III and Psychopathy Checklist assessment of antisocial personality disorder in Black and White female felons [Abstract]. *Dissertation Abstracts International, 51*(7-B), 3605.

Nuffield, J. (1982). *Parole decision-making in Canada: Research towards decision guidelines.* Ottawa: Supply and Services Canada.

Oliver, M.I., Pearson, N., Coe, N., & Gunnell, D. (2005). Help-seeking behaviour in men and women with common mental health problems: Cross-sectional study. *British Journal of Psychiatry, 186,* 297–301.

Pollack, S. (2005). Taming the shrew: Regulating prisoners through women-centered mental health programming. *Critical Criminology, 13,* 71–87.

Quinsey, V.L., & Ambtman, R. (1979). Variables affecting psychiatrists' and teachers' assessments of the dangerousness of mentally ill offenders. *Journal of Consulting and Clinical Psychology, 47,* 353–362.

Quinsey, V.L., Coleman, G., Jones, B., & Altrows, I. (1997). Proximal antecedents of eloping and reoffending among supervised mentally disordered offenders. *Journal of Interpersonal Violence, 12,* 794–813.

Quinsey, V.L., Harris, G.T., Rice, M.E., & Cormier, C. (2006). *Violent offenders: Appraising and managing risk* (2nd ed.). Washington, DC: American Psychological Association.

Rettinger, L.J. (1998). *A recidivism follow-up study investigating the risk and need within a sample of provincially sentenced women.* Unpublished doctoral dissertation, Carleton University, Ottawa, Ontario.

Shaw, M. (1994). *Ontario women in conflict with the law: A survey of women in institutions and under community supervision in Ontario.* Toronto: Research Services, Strategic Policy and Planning Division, Ministry of the Solicitor General and Correctional Services.

Simourd, L., & Andrews, D.A. (1994). Correlates of delinquency: A look at gender differences. *Forum on Corrections Research, 6*(1). Retrieved from www.csc-scc.gc.ca/text/pblct/forum/e061/e061g-eng.shtml.

Smith, P., Goggin, C., & Gendreau, P. (2002). *The effects of prison sentences and intermediate sanctions on recidivism: General effects and individual differences* (User Report 2002-01). Ottawa: Public Safety and Emergency Preparedness Canada.

US Department of Justice. (2008). *Bureau of Justice statistics: Prison statistics.* Retrieved from www.ojp.usdoj.gov/bjs/prisons.htm.

Vitale, J.E., Smith, S.S., Brinkley, C.A., & Newman, J.P. (2002). The reliability and validity of the Psychopathy Checklist-Revised in a sample of female offenders. *Criminal Justice and Behavior, 98,* 202–231.

Ward, T., Mesler, J., & Yates, P. (2007). Reconstructing the risk-need-responsivity model: A theoretical elaboration and evaluation. *Aggression and Violent Behavior, 12,* 208–228.

PART III

Topics of Special Interest

CHAPTER 7

Violence and Women Offenders

Franca Cortoni

Introduction

Theories that explain violence by women vary from biological to psychological approaches, but they largely fail to satisfactorily explain why women commit fewer violent crimes than men (Pollock & Davis, 2005). This is not surprising because women have long been an afterthought in research on criminal behaviour (Blanchette & Brown, 2006): the majority of research on violent behaviour has been conducted on male offenders. One reason for this lack of research is an assumption that the factors that lead to criminal behaviour are universal, regardless of gender. This assumption, however, has been proven inaccurate. Research has shown that although men and women share some of the same characteristics that lead to criminal behaviour, differences do exist. Consequently, a simple knowledge transfer from male to female offenders is not a viable option because these factors are not always identical (Blanchette & Brown, 2006). For example, one major concern of the criminal justice system is the assessment of risk of recidivism. Thus, extensive

research has been devoted to the development and validation of risk assessment tools. These tools predict, with a reasonable degree of accuracy, criminal recidivism *among male offenders*. When applied to female offenders, however, these tools consistently lose their predictive accuracy (Blanchette & Brown, 2006; Warren et al., 2005).

In recent years, research on women offenders has proliferated, and studies using both qualitative and quantitative methods have contributed to the understanding of violence perpetrated by women. In addition, theoretical postulations, supported by empirical veri-fication, are starting to provide a knowledge base from which have evolved assessment and treatment options for various types of violent female offenders. As we will see, however, much remains to be known, and accurate assessments and effective treatment of violent behaviour among women await empirical verification. The aims of this chapter are to review this knowledge base and outline current assessment and treatment practices for violent women offenders. Violent offending includes a wide range of offences, including assaults, homicides, and sexual offences. Because of the variety in violent crimes, this chapter exam-ines women who engage in non-sexual violence (assaults, domestic violence, and homicides) separately from those who engage in sexual violence (all crimes that have a sexual compon-ent, excluding prostitution and its related offences).

Women Who Offend Violently

One of the most consistent findings over the years is that women commit far fewer violent offences than men. Rates of violence by women, however, have increased tremendously (in comparison with earlier base rates) over the last two decades (Benda, 2005; Pollock & Davis, 2005). Why this situation has occurred is unclear. Some authors speculate this increase is due to changes in arrest decisions by the police (for example, changes in criminal justice system policy dictating that anyone who has engaged in domestic violence must be charged and the recognition that women engage in sexually assaultive behaviours), not to an actual increase in violence by women (Pollock & Davis, 2005). In Canada, the rate of women charged for a violent crime almost quadrupled between 1981 and 2001, then levelled off by 2005 to a rate of approximately 150 women charged for a violent offence[1] per 100,000 women in the popu-lation. In contrast, although the rate of men charged with violent offences peaked in 1993 at 930 males per 100,000 males in the population, it steadily decreased to reach approxi-mately 788 men per 100,000 by 2005 (Public Safety and Emergency Preparedness Canada [PSEPC], 2006). Despite this increase in violent offences by women, women clearly engage in aggressive behaviour less frequently than men.

In recent years, extreme acts of violence committed by women have attracted massive media attention. This situation has led to a general conclusion that women are becoming more violent, mostly as a result of the liberation of women (Pollock & Davis, 2005). The assumption is that women were not violent in the past because of their socialization and their traditional roles as nurturers. As women obtained more societal opportunities for equality, they also became "equal opportunists" in criminal behaviour. In essence, the prem-ise is that by becoming liberated, women were allowed to engage in previously unheard-of behaviour, such as violence. Pollock and Davis (2005) noted that this premise is a fallacy that has created more myths about women. These authors also state that although women are universally less violent than men, it is important to acknowledge that a small percentage of violent crimes have always been committed by women.

Assaults

Research on violence by women typically includes assaults and robberies, whereas domestic violence and homicides are treated as separate issues. Although robberies are considered violent offences by Canadian federal law (Department of Justice Canada, 1992), these crimes do not always involve interpersonal violence and will not be considered in this chapter. Violence by women is most often related to interpersonal conflicts (Pollock & Davis, 2005; Weizmann-Henelius, Viemerö, & Eronen, 2003). To examine the motives of women who engage in violent behaviour, Sommers and Baskin (1993) interviewed and examined the file information of 65 women who had been arrested for a violent street crime. Their study shows that the interaction between the victim and the offender, and sometimes the verbal interaction with a third party, were fundamental to the women's assaults. In most cases, the women were thrown into violence-prone situations in which the victim played a pivotal role. These findings do not blame the victim for the violence. The offender's behaviour was often found to be a direct response to some behaviour on the part of the victim, such as the victim becoming belligerent toward the offender. Typically, in such situations, the assaultive behaviour was not planned, and substance abuse was frequently involved. Sommers and Baskin found that in problematic situations, many of these women mistakenly attributed blame to others and perceived their violence as an appropriate response to the situation.

The finding that violent women's cognitive biases make them more likely to attribute blame to others and engage in violent behaviour in response to problematic situations is identical to the findings of cognitive biases found in violent men. These cognitive schemas prime the offender to interpret others' behaviour as hostile and to respond aggressively (Sestir & Bartholow, 2007). Although research is needed to better understand how these cognitive schemas develop in women, for at least some of the female offenders, hostile cognitions appear to be linked to life experiences. For example, Pollock, Mullings, and Crouch (2002) found that violent women offenders in Texas were more likely than non-violent women offenders to be younger and unemployed, to have criminal histories that started at a younger age, and to have experienced early physical abuse, resulting in anger and distrust of others.

Research supports the notion that at least a subset of female violent offenders has characteristics similar to those of male violent offenders. In their examination of hostility among female offenders, Verona and Carbonell (2000) found that repeat female violent offenders were more antisocial, had lower inhibitions against acting out violently, and made more use of instrumental violence during the commission of crimes than non-violent and homicidal female offenders. These characteristics are highly similar to those of male offenders who chronically under-regulate their emotions, suggesting that factors related to violence in some women may be *gender-neutral* as opposed to *gender-informed*. The term *gender-neutral* refers to characteristics that are linked to the criminal behaviour and are equally applicable to men and women. The term *gender-informed* refers to factors unique to women offenders. Although some authors argue that gender-neutral factors do not exist (Hannah-Moffat, 1999, for example), the research cited above suggests that some factors do relate to violent behaviour regardless of gender.

Individual characteristics alone, however, are not sufficient to explain assaults by women. An understanding of violence also needs to include a consideration of situational factors. Sommers and Baskin (1993) noted that as violent women became further enmeshed in criminal activities, they became increasingly both socially and psychologically alienated from conventional life. They found that high-crime neighbourhoods, associations with delinquent peers, and substance abuse contributed to the initiation of criminal, including assaultive, behaviour among these women. In addition, they found that weak school attachment, poor parental supervision, and social and economic difficulties all appear to contribute to violence by women, indicating the importance of considering the interaction between individual and situational characteristics to explain violence by women. It is noted that these factors are also important to understanding violence by men (Andrews & Bonta, 2003).

Domestic Violence

Although the use of violence by women toward their intimate partners has been recognized since the mid-1980s (Swan & Snow, 2003), domestic violence perpetrated by women is still not well understood. Consequently, the criminal justice system has tended to manage female perpetrators of domestic violence in the same way as male perpetrators, requiring them to undergo assessment and treatment services that are based on male models of domestic violence (Swan & Snow, 2003). These responses by the criminal justice system appear primarily based on research findings indicating that, contrary to all other types of violent behaviour, *gender symmetry* exists in domestic violence: women actually engage in as much domestic violence as men, and an equal number of women and men are victims of domestic violence (Archer, 2000; Kimmel, 2002). Despite this reported equivalency of rates of domestic violence, women continue to be much more injured than men in situations of domestic violence (Archer, 2000). Further, crime victimization studies consistently find that serious domestic violence that escalates over time is primarily perpetrated by males (Kimmel, 2002). These findings indicate the need to move beyond models of male violence to explain female domestic violence (Swan & Snow, 2003).

More than 100 studies have shown that men and women engage in domestic violence at equal rates (Kimmel, 2002). Despite these findings, a debate continues regarding the true nature of domestic violence perpetrated by women, focusing mostly on the way in which domestic violence is assessed. According to research examining rates of domestic violence among men and women, the overwhelming majority of studies used the Conflict Tactic Scale (CTS) (Kimmel, 2002) developed by Straus (1990) to assess how often violence occurred in domestic situations. The scale asks about the frequency with which a spouse engaged in a violent act against his or her partner during the past year, counting *each* reported act of violence to assess the overall amount of domestic violence in the relationship. Any act of violence is counted, including throwing an object, pushing, slapping, punching, or using an object to hit the other person. Research using the CTS has consistently shown that women engage in at least as many, if not more, violent acts as their male partners (Kimmel, 2002).

Although the CTS has proven helpful in research designed to understand domestic violence, it has been widely criticized for treating all acts of violence as equal, regardless of their severity. Perhaps more importantly, the CTS fails to take into account the context in which domestic violence is perpetrated (Kimmel, 2002). For example, according to Kimmel, if a woman pushes the man after being severely beaten by him, both persons would receive a score of 1, thereby being equated on rates of domestic violence. Similarly, if the woman pushes the man to stop him from hurting her children, she would receive a score of 1 and he would receive a score of 0, indicating that the woman engaged in domestic violence and her partner did not. In these examples, the violence by these women was reactive, committed in response to an act of violence by their partners. Kimmel (2002) argues that the failure to take this context into account supports the view that in domestic relationships, women are as violent as men. Kimmel agrees that violence by women toward their partners exists, but suggests that it tends to be very different from male domestic violence: far less severe and much less likely to be motivated by a need to dominate or control their partners.

Similarly, Dasgupta (2002) argues that the nature of domestic violence perpetrated by women looks very different depending on whether a narrow or a broader definition of domestic violence is adopted. In the narrow definition, in which the understanding of domestic violence is limited to physical assault, women are as likely as men to be violent. In a broader definition, in which patterns of intimidation, coercive control, and battering are considered, significant gender differences are revealed. Consequently, focusing only on the physical acts themselves, as opposed to the context in which these acts take place, and failing to consider coercive control and intimidation, obscures important information about the differences between male and female perpetrators of domestic violence.

The Nature of Domestic Violence by Women

Johnson (1995, 2000, cited in Swan & Snow, 2002) argued that domestic violence can be categorized into four different types. The first and most serious type, *intimate terrorism*, is typified by severe and frequent violence that escalates over time. According to Johnson, this type is the most commonly known and the most severe; it is associated with battered woman syndrome and is almost exclusively committed by males. The second type, *common couple violence*, considered the most frequent type of violence in domestic situations, is typically related to a need to control a specific situation as opposed to a generalized need for control of the other person. This type of domestic violence is most commonly initiated by either partner in response to a situational conflict and does not tend to escalate. The third type, *violent resistance*, is violence committed as a direct response, self-defence or otherwise, to violence (as opposed to the need to control the partner). This category primarily comprises women who engage in violence in response to male intimate terrorism. The final type, *mutual violent control*, the least common, describes relationships in which both partners engage in violence for generalized control of the other person and of the relationship.

Research shows that women typically tend to exhibit either common couple violence or a violent resistance pattern of domestic violence. For example, in her review of the literature, Dasgupta (2002) found that women list self-defence as a frequent motivation for their violent behaviour toward their partner. She also found that domestic violence by women is often triggered by actual abuse or perceived threats to her children or loved ones. Finally, Dasgupta found that women, through violence, are much more likely to secure short-term command over an immediate situation, whereas men strive to establish authority over a much longer period, typically striking fear in their partners. In a study of 95 women abusers, Swan and Snow (2003) found that self-defence was the most common motive for domestic violence by women, although retribution and the need to get their partner to do something were also frequent causes. Miller and Meloy (2006), also in a sample of 95 women undergoing treatment for domestic violence, found 65 percent of these women engaged in defensive violence, typically in response to their partner's abuse. An additional 30 percent identified frustration reactions at the root of their violence, engaging in violence when nothing else seemed to resolve their problems. Finally, Miller and Meloy identified 5 percent of the sample as violent women who engaged in violence in many circumstances, not only in domestic situations.

Swan and Snow (2002) proposed that the differences in male- and female-perpetrated domestic violence are the results of variations among two co-occurring dimensions of intimate partner violence. The first dimension is divided into two aspects perpetrated by each partner in the relationship: coercive control and physical abuse. Coercive control refers to non-physical tactics used to maintain control of a partner, including the use of intimidation, social and familial isolation, and economic control. Physical abuse refers to the amount of physical violence inflicted on a partner, such as shoving or hitting. The second dimension is both partners' history of abusive behaviour, which determines whether violence is occurring independently, in conjunction with, or as a reaction to the other partner's violence. Swan and Snow (2002, 2003) argue that to understand domestic violence, both dimensions must be concurrently examined to provide the context and the level of the domestic violence that took place.

In support of this proposition, in their research on female domestic abusers, Swan and Snow (2002) found that all but 6 of the 108 female perpetrators in their study had also been physically abused by their partners. Although these women used similar levels of emotional abuse as their partners, their partners used much more severe physical violence and coercive control. The women were, more often than the men, victims of coercive controls, such as intimidation and isolation, and of serious violence, including sexual violence leading to physical injury. These findings demonstrate the importance of considering the context in which domestic violence by women takes place. Failing to consider the context leads to an incomplete understanding of domestic violence by women, with the result that assessment and treatment services may not be appropriately targeted at the relevant contributing elements.

Women Who Kill

As with other violent crimes committed by women, research consistently shows that the victims of homicidal women tend to be people they know. Statistics show that approximately 93 percent of homicides by women in Canada are committed against people they know. Statistics from Australia and the United States are similar: only 7 percent of all homicides by women were committed against strangers. In contrast, approximately 25 percent of all homicides by men were against strangers (Greenfeld & Snell, 1999). Victims of women were principally acquaintances, intimate partners, or other family members, although they also included social and business relations and family members of the offender's spouse. In addition, similar to male offenders, women tend to kill men, not other women. In a pivotal study of 136 women convicted of homicides in Detroit, Michigan, Goetting (1988) found that 88 percent of the victims were males. These findings were also present in a Canadian study, where 74 percent of the victims of homicides committed by women were males (Hoffman, Lavigne, & Dickie, 1998). This difference suggests that, as with other types of violence, gender-specific factors are likely at play to explain why women kill.

The Nature of Homicides by Women

In 1996, to better understand the nature of homicides by women, Hoffman et al. (1998) studied 181 female offenders serving a Canadian federal sentence for homicide. The goal was to determine the factors in the women's lives that might relate to their offending behaviour. Half of these women were still incarcerated, and the other half were either on conditional release or had been deported. Of the 181 women, approximately 50 percent were serving a sentence for second-degree murder or its equivalent. Forty percent had been convicted of manslaughter, and the remaining 10 percent were serving a sentence for first-degree murder. Interestingly, 27 percent of all women had committed the homicides in the company of a co-offender, and 16 percent of the women in the study, although convicted for homicide, had not actually killed anyone: they had been convicted for their role as a conspirator or accomplice, typically during the commission of a robbery in which the co-offender killed the victim.

Approximately 50 percent of the women convicted of homicides had no prior criminal history, approximately 33 percent had other prior criminal convictions, and 7 percent had a prior conviction for homicide. Two-thirds of the women had a history of substance abuse. Although approximately 33 percent of the women presented with mental health concerns, only 8 percent had been diagnosed with schizophrenia. In Canada, women who kill while actively psychotic would typically be found "not criminally responsible for their crimes on account of mental disorder" (Greenspan & Rosenberg, 2007). These women would have therefore been diverted to the mental health system as opposed to the prison system and would not have been part of the study. Hoffman et al. found that depression was the most common mental health concern among the women in the study.

In their study, Hoffman and her colleagues (1998) provided a classification of the women based on the typology[2] of homicides in use by the Correctional Service of Canada (1995). The largest category of homicides by women (28 percent) consists of *theft/assault/robbery homicides*. This category includes situations in which the woman, either alone or with an accomplice, was attempting to obtain money or property from the victim, but homicide was the end result. When the offence started with an assault, the typical circumstances involved an argument between the offender and the victim, and escalated to the eventual death of the victim. The second category of homicide typology is *spousal homicides*, in which the victim was a current or former spouse. In the Hoffman et al. study (1998), 45 of the homicides (25 percent) fit this category. Of those 45 cases, 27 homicides had been committed in response to abuse by their spouse. The other 18 spousal homicides were committed by women who killed their partner because of emotional upset over such issues as infidelity or as the result of arguments fuelled by alcohol or drugs.

The third category was *child homicides*. Fourteen-and-a-half percent of the women in the study had killed their own child or a child in their care, such as a stepchild, a foster child, or a child she was babysitting. Although most of these homicides were the end result of a pattern of abuse against the child, in some cases the woman killed the child as an act of revenge against her partner, or to save the child from an abusive parent. The average age of the child was six years, although the majority of the children were younger than age five at the time of their death. The final category of homicides is *self-defence homicides*. In these cases, the woman used excessive force to defend herself against an assault by a man—for example, a sexual assault. Almost 6 percent of all homicides in Hoffman et al.'s (1998) study fit this category. The authors noted that drugs and alcohol were typically involved in these offences.

The Hoffman et al. (1988) study demonstrated that women kill for a variety of reasons, and relatively few women kill as a result of trauma or abuse. Their study, although comprehensive, did not shed much light on the factors that may have contributed to the homicides. More helpful in this regard is research by Kirkwood (2003), who conducted a review of all homicides committed by women in the state of Victoria, Australia, between 1985 and 1995.

Her research focused on the circumstances in which women killed and consisted primarily of in-depth case analyses. A total of 86 women were included in the study, and their homicides fell into one of three categories: women who killed partners, women who killed children, or women who killed non-intimate others.

Overall, Kirkwood (2003) found that 40 percent of the women in her study had killed a partner or ex-partner. She established that approximately one-third of those homicides occurred as a spontaneous response to an assault by the spouse. Another one-third of those women demonstrated a long history of victimization by their spouse. The data showed that these women had reached a point where they believed they had no escape from the violence and constantly feared they would be killed. These women were the most likely to plan and conceal their killing. This phenomenon, known as the battered woman syndrome, has been recognized in Canada as a legitimate defence for homicide (Greenspan & Rosenberg, 2007). Unfortunately, Kirkwood's research does not specify whether the women in her study were able to use a similar defence. The remaining one-third of women killed their partners for reasons other than violence, such as in response to the man's threat to take the children. In contrast to male spousal homicides, Kirkwood (2003) found no cases in which the woman had killed her spouse for such reasons as jealousy or as part of the woman's pattern of abuse and control of her partner.

Of the women in Kirkwood's (2003) study, 19 percent had killed a child. Central to these killings were problems and pressures associated with mothering; and some of these women had either attempted suicide or committed suicide after killing their children. Overall, this group comprised women who believed they could not fulfill their own and others' expectations of themselves as mothers. In all cases, these women struggled with poverty, difficulties with partners, social and cultural isolation, and/or mental illness. These findings are consistent with research showing that women who commit infanticide (the killing of an infant, usually one's own child) typically have social and economic stresses, a history of abuse, unsupportive partners, and difficulties caring for the child (Hatters-Friedman, McCue-Horwitz, & Resnick, 2005).

The final group in Kirkwood's study consisted of women who killed non-intimate individuals. Although some women killed other extended family members, the majority had killed friends, acquaintances, neighbours, or other known individuals. Only a few of these homicides involved strangers, and in those cases the women had acted with a co-offender. The majority of homicides of non-intimate individuals were the result of interpersonal conflicts that arose over such issues as sexual jealousy, arguments or insults, or previous assaults. Some offences took place during the commission of other criminal acts, such as prostitution or robbery. Most women in this category were younger than the women in the other two groups, had a history of substance abuse, and lived in a criminal subculture that condoned violence to resolve problems and to survive. Within this context, these women had been both victims and perpetrators of violence. These women were as likely to kill other women as they were to kill men.

Why Do Women Kill?

Historically, it was believed that most homicidal women killed because they were defective, mostly due to mental illness or other individual psychopathology (Goetting, 1988; Ogle, Maier-Katkin, & Bernard, 1995). As with beliefs about other violent women, this premise was based on traditional views of gender roles (Pollock & Davis, 2005). Research has indicated, however, that female offenders in general tend to be more traditional in their beliefs about sex roles than non-offending women (Ogle et al., 1995). These authors claim that theories of homicides by women based on traditional models of psychopathology have limited utility because they fail to take into account the social structural context in which these offences take place. Further, they argue that theories such as battered woman syndrome or postpartum blues psychosis blur the distinction between legal and scientific explanations.

Ogle et al. (1995) argued that a comprehensive theory of homicides by women needs to incorporate individual, situational, and structural variables. According to these authors, stress is generally higher for women than for men, leading to higher levels of anger. Despite these higher levels of stress and anger, women are not equipped to cope effectively with these stressors, due to traditional social roles in which women are taught to suppress their anger and to ignore their stressors, therefore developing an overcontrolled personality. The authors note that lower socio-economic status women are particularly vulnerable because they tend to experience higher levels of stress in their daily lives but are even less permitted by society to express their dissatisfactions than are women from the higher socio-economic strata. On those occasions when these overcontrolled women fail to control their anger, they erupt in extreme and violent expressions of aggression (Ogle et al., 1995). In support of this proposition, Verona and Carbonell (2000) found that women who had committed a homicide were significantly more likely to score high on a scale measuring overcontrolled hostility than repeat violent offenders and non-violent offenders.

The Assessment and Treatment of Violent Women

The goals of a specialized assessment of violent women offenders are to determine the likelihood of violent reoffending and to ascertain areas for therapeutic intervention to reduce that risk. Unfortunately, although research is focusing on developing risk assessments for female offenders, no valid risk assessment tools can currently assess the risk of violent recidivism among women (Blanchette & Brown, 2006). One factor agreed upon by most researchers, however, is the presence of a prior criminal history. Women (and men) who have prior criminal offences consistently have higher rates of reoffending. Research also suggests that although in general violent women have lower rates of recidivism than violent men, those women with personality disorders, particularly cluster B personality disorders (that is, antisocial, narcissistic, and borderline personality disorders), have similar recidivism rates as violent males (Putkonen, Komulainen, Virkkunen, Eronen, & Lönnqvist (2003).

The assessment of risk should therefore be based on a thorough analysis of the woman's criminal history, her current violent offending behaviour, the elements that contributed to the offence, the presence of personality disorders, her cognitive schemas about violence (for example, attitudes that justify violence), and her emotional regulation patterns (for example, impulsivity and anger problems). Consideration should also be given to whether the violent behaviour occurred within the context of a more generalized antisocial lifestyle, or whether it was limited to specific situations with unique considerations. For example, a battered woman who killed her partner because she feared for her life but who has an otherwise pro-social life would not be at the same risk of reoffending as a violent woman who has a varied criminal history and demonstrates antisocial traits. These differences would influence the assessment of risk of violent recidivism, with the latter woman being considered a higher risk. In the case of the battered woman, the likelihood of violent recidivism would likely be assessed as low provided she becomes able to recognize and avoid relationships with violent individuals. A woman with a varied criminal history, a history of antisocial peers, and demonstrated antisocial attitudes and beliefs would present at a higher risk.

A thorough understanding of the elements present in the woman's offending behaviour will help identify the areas to be targeted in treatment. The assessment of treatment needs of violent women should be guided by our current, albeit limited, empirical knowledge of the factors that appear related to female offenders. Factors related to general recidivism in women include antisocial attitudes and associates, problematic relationships, and emotional dyscontrol (Blanchette, 2001). Although these factors have not been necessarily linked to violent offending in all women, a subset of violent women would likely exhibit difficulties in these areas. Some evidence, although at times conflicting, suggests that substance abuse, particularly illicit drug use, is predictive of a return to custody and of both general and violent recidivism among women (Blanchette & Brown, 2006). Consequently, although risk of violent recidivism cannot be estimated with a reasonable degree of certainty, the continued presence of these factors would likely contribute to a greater likelihood of a return to criminal behaviour, including violent behaviour.

Although no assessment and treatment approaches have been formally established for generally violent women, some authors (for example, Blanchette & Brown, 2006; Ford & Cortoni, 2008) suggest that, similar to other women offenders, all areas of functioning of the woman offender be examined to determine her strengths and the areas that require therapeutic interventions. Given the consistent finding that most violence committed by women involves some type of interpersonal relationship, relationship issues and interpersonal problem-solving skills are likely central areas to target in treatment. Other areas that have likely contributed to a woman's offending behaviour and would likely benefit from intervention are attitudes and beliefs that supported her decision to engage in violence, emotional management (particularly anger management), and coping strategies (Ogle et al., 1995; Verona & Carbonell, 2000).

Based on the findings of the various types of violent behaviours committed by women, different approaches may be warranted according to individual crime differences. For example, the cognitive schemas of a battered woman who killed her partner because she feared for her life would likely be very different from those of an intoxicated woman who killed an acquaintance with whom she had a quarrel. Although cognitive interventions would be indicated in both cases, the focus of the interventions would be very different.

Similarly, based on current findings, the emotional self-regulation patterns of women who engage in violence with non-intimate individuals are likely to more closely resemble those patterns of generally antisocial women, including generalized problems with impulsivity and the acting out of anger and other negative emotions. In contrast, homicidal women may demonstrate a pattern of extreme control of a wide range of emotions, such as fear, despair, frustration, and depression, a pattern they have learned over the years in order to cope with stressors (Ogle et al., 1995). In both situations, these women would require help to more effectively regulate their emotions, but the treatment would focus on very different emotional self-regulation patterns. The impulsive woman would need to develop more self-control, whereas the homicidal woman would need to appropriately express her negative emotions instead of repressing them.

The assessment and treatment of domestic abusers would, by necessity, involve an examination of the context in which the violence took place. Although female perpetrators of domestic violence have typically been required to engage in therapeutic interventions based on male models of domestic violence, these models are inadequate for these women and are likely ineffective in addressing their treatment needs. An examination of the full context that led to the domestic violence would help to establish the pattern of domestic violence and the elements that contributed to the woman's behaviour. Tailored interventions could then be developed to address these elements.

Given the lack of clear empirical evidence about the factors that lead to violent behaviour among women, the literature is, not surprisingly, equally silent on validated treatment approaches for women who have committed homicide. Besides the treatment issues discussed above, homicidal women may need additional interventions to address some of the unique aspects of their crimes. In addition, the context of her relationship with her victim may be particularly significant (Kirkwood, 2003). For example, many of these women may present characteristics of battered woman syndrome, necessitating treatment for their victimization. Not all women who have killed their partner have been battered, however, demonstrating the importance of carrying out a comprehensive assessment of the elements that led to the homicide.

Women who have killed their children may present with characteristics of powerlessness, alienation from others, and an inability to effectively deal with life's pressures (Hatters-Friedman et al., 2005; Kirkwood, 2003). Treatment in these cases would include the development of self-esteem, effective coping strategies, and positive healthy relationships. These women may also need help to address the effects of living with the knowledge that they have taken a life. These reactions may actually be part of a trauma reaction, such as feelings of depression, worthlessness, guilt, and shame (Sullivan-Everstine & Everstine, 1993). These emotions may also be present in other female offenders. In fact, compared with male offenders, female offenders report more guilt and shame associated with their criminal behaviour (Blanchette & Brown, 2006). These negative emotions may, however, manifest themselves in more acute ways among homicidal women. If these emotional reactions are not addressed in the early stages of treatment, they may prevent therapeutic gains from interventions directly targeted either at changing attitudes and beliefs or at improving general coping strategies.

Finally, most violent women will need additional help to rebuild their lives in a manner that removes the need for violent offending. As with all female offenders, these women may require support to improve their general community functioning, with a particular focus on their ability to develop and maintain a more stable lifestyle with less dependence on others. Some women may have particular problems in the area of mental health, requiring additional specifically designed intensive intervention, such as dialectical behaviour therapy (Linehan, 1993). Areas such as education, employment, and recreational activities may also require additional services outside of treatment. Finally, in contrast to men, women tend to be in more need of extensive appropriate supportive social networks, which are an important part of their ability to deal with stress (Rumgay, 2004). Consequently, part of treatment will be to help these women develop and access appropriate networks and services.

Women Who Sexually Offend

The acknowledgment of females as sexual offenders has occurred only relatively recently. Thus, considerable gaps remain between the knowledge base for sexually deviant males and their female counterparts. Perhaps as a consequence, many current assessment and treatment approaches for females broadly follow those devised for males, although the appropriateness of this approach has been questioned (see, for example, Nathan & Ward, 2002; Saradjian, 1996). This section examines the phenomenon of sexual offending by women. As we will see, male and female sexual offenders have a few commonalities but a number of significant differences.

The Prevalence of Female Sexual Offending

The prevalence rate of female sexual offending is uncertain. Historically, some authors have doubted the existence of women who commit sexually motivated offences. For example, Freund, Heasman, Racansky, and Glancy (1984) declared that "pedophilia ... does not exist at all in women" (p. 193). Other authors, however, believe that sexual offending by females is common, but these offenders are unreported or diverted from the criminal justice system (Vandiver & Walker, 2002). Such assertions have typically been reported without reference to empirical evidence.

Because of this uncertainly, Cortoni and Hanson (2005) attempted to estimate the prevalence of female sexual offenders. In their study, the proportion of sexual offenders who are women was estimated based on two general sources of information: official records (police or court reports) that detail the gender of the offender and victimization surveys. Information from both sources was available for Canada, the United Kingdom, the United States, Australia, and New Zealand. On the basis of official records, Cortoni and Hanson found that the proportion of all sexual offenders who were female ranged from 0.6 percent in New Zealand to 8.3 percent for non-rape sexual offenders in the United States. When these numbers were averaged across all countries in the study, women constituted approximately 4 percent of all sexual offenders. When victimization studies were examined, Cortoni and Hanson (2005) found that the proportion of sexual offenders who were female, as reported by victims, ranged from 3.1 percent for New Zealand to 7.0 percent for Australia. Across the various victimization studies, women constituted an average 4.8 percent of all sexual offenders.

Overall, Cortoni and Hanson's review indicated that women, in comparison with males, commit sexual offences at a ratio of approximately 1 to 20, based on both official reports and victimization surveys. Interestingly, official reports and results from victimization surveys were remarkably consistent with each other and showed that women are responsible for between 4 and 5 percent of all sexual offences. Using data from the United States, the only country for which direct comparisons between official rates and victimization reports were possible, Cortoni and Hanson (2005) noted differential rates of police arrests according to the gender of the offender in relation to victimization survey results. Specifically, 34 percent of the sexual offences committed by men resulted in police arrest, whereas 57 percent of the sexual offences committed by women resulted in police arrest. These findings suggest that further research is needed to understand the personal and criminal justice responses to victimization by female offenders versus male sexual offenders.

The Nature of Sexual Violence by Women

Female sexual offenders, like their male counterparts, engage in a variety of sexually offending behaviours. Researchers have attempted to establish typologies of female sexual offenders to better understand the causes and processes of sexual offending among female offenders (Bickley & Beech, 2001).

TYPOLOGY BASED ON QUALITATIVE DATA

In one of the first attempts to establish a typology of these women, Mathews, Matthews, and Speltz (1989) carried out in-depth interviews over a one-year period with a sample of 16 female sexual offenders. From their research, Mathews et al. generated three types of female sexual offenders: the teacher/lover, the male-coerced/male-accompanied, and the predisposed. These types were based on the offenders' characteristics and their motivations for the sexual offences.

The *teacher/lover* sexual offender is an adult woman who acts as the initiator of the sexual abuse of an adolescent, usually a male. The offender tends to be in a position of power through her age and her role in the victim's life—for example, as a teacher. The offender views her sexual interactions with the victim not as a criminal act, but as an act of kindness and an overall expression of her love, thus minimizing and denying the harm inflicted on her victim. According to Mathews et al. (1989), the teacher/lover comes from a dysfunctional family, is usually a victim of severe emotional and verbal abuse as a child (particularly from an emotionally distant father), and may have a history of unsuccessful and abusive relationships as an adult.

The second type, the *male-coerced/male-accompanied* sexual offender, engages in sexual aggression in the company of a male. Male-coerced offenders are typically reluctant to participate in abuse but do so as a result of a fear of punishment. This type of offender tends to hold traditional views of gender roles, with the man in a dominant position. Male-coerced offenders tend to be dependent on men and fear abandonment. Overall, they are generally powerless in their relationships and fear their partner's abuse. Mathews et al. (1989) characterized these female offenders as passive, angry women with low self-esteem, problems with substance abuse, and low to average intellectual functioning.

The final type, the *predisposed* sexual offender, like the teacher/lover, acts alone. These women tend to have a long history of sexual abuse and are often involved in unhealthy and abusive intimate relationships as adults. According to Mathews et al. (1989), predisposed offenders are characterized by low self-esteem, passivity, extreme anger, and acting-out behaviour. They often display psychopathological traits, such as extreme distrust, anguish, nervousness, distorted thinking, feelings of persecution, and have a dependency on drugs, alcohol, food, or their relationships with men. For the most part, the victims of predisposed offenders tend to be family members, often their own children, and these offences tend to involve violence.

TYPOLOGY BASED ON QUANTITATIVE DATA

More recently, Vandiver and Kercher (2004) proposed a different typology of female sexual offenders based on their statistical analysis of 471 female sexual offenders registered in the state of Texas. The data in the analyses included the total number of arrests, the relationship between the offender and the victim, the type of sexual offence, the ages of the offender and the victim, the victim's gender, and whether the offender was rearrested after the sexual offence arrest. Using hierarchical loglinear modelling and cluster analyses, Vandiver and Kercher found six categories of female sexual offenders. The first category was the *hetero-sexual nurturers*. This group of offenders victimized only pubescent males (mean age was 12) and had very low rates of reoffending. This group of offenders is most similar to the teacher/lover type described in the previous section, who was typically in a mentorship or caretaking role over the victim. The second category was described as *non-criminal homo-sexual offenders*. The majority of their victims were females with an average age of 13. This group of offenders was least likely to commit new offences. On the basis of the type of vic-tims and the offenders' relative lack of other criminal history, Vandiver and Kercher specu-lated that these offenders were most likely to have committed their offences with a male accomplice. Due to lack of information on co-offenders, however, the researchers could not confirm this theory. The third group, female *sexual predators*, had the highest number of criminal offences (sexual or otherwise) and were the most likely of all groups to be rearrested. Their victims tended to be divided almost evenly between male (60 percent) and female (40 percent) and had an average age of 11. Because of the offenders' diversified criminal history, sexual offending appeared to be part of their broader criminal predisposition. The fourth group consisted of *young adult child exploiters*. This group was the youngest at arrest (mean age of 28) and had the youngest group of victims (mean age of 7).

The final two clusters differed from the others in that both groups comprised female sexual offenders who assaulted older female children or adult females. The *homosexual criminals* consisted mostly of offenders whose behaviour was based on economic reasons rather than sexual reasons. For example, no offenders in this group had a conviction for a sexual offence. Instead, they had been convicted of such offences as indecency or compelling the victim into prostitution. In Canada, forcing someone into prostitution, although a criminal offence, would not be considered a sexual offence. The final cluster was called *aggressive homosexual offenders* as they were most likely to be convicted of sexual assault (as opposed to other types of sexual offences) against adult females.

In a test of Vandiver and Kercher's (2004) typology, Sandler and Freeman (2007) used similar data points, but added drug use and violations of supervision history in their analy-ses. Sandler and Freeman also established six types of female sexual offenders, but only two categories completely overlapped those of Vandiver and Kercher (2004). The differences in the other four categories consisted essentially of variations in the difference between the offenders' and their victims' ages, and the gender of the victim. Similar to Vandiver and Kercher, Sandler and Freeman's typology did not consider the presence of a co-offender, an important variable among female sexual offenders, nor did it include information on the psychological functioning or abuse history of these offenders.

LIMITATIONS OF TYPOLOGIES OF FEMALE SEXUAL OFFENDERS

Typologies are meant to provide useful systems to permit a better understanding of the functioning and behaviours of female sexual offenders. As described above, current typolo-gies have clearly established that women, like men, engage in a variety of sexually offending behaviours against a variety of victims. These typologies help dispel myths about female sexual offenders (for example, that women are incapable of experiencing deviant sexual desires [Freund et al., 1984]; they only sexually offend as a result of coercion by a male) that have prevented the development of knowledge in this area.

To be helpful, however, typologies must be associated with a theory to explain sexual deviance in women (Bickley & Beech, 2001). On the one hand, Mathews et al.'s (1989) typology provides psychologically based information that may permit the development of such a theory. Their typology was developed, however, from a very small sample size that does not account for all types of female offenders and therefore limits theoretical developments. On the other hand, Vandiver and Kercher's (2004) and Sandler and Freeman's (2007) typologies were based on large sample sizes and provide a greater variety in types of female sexual offenders. The weakness of these typologies is that they are essentially a classification of the relationship, the gender, and the age differential between the offender and the victim. Further, they included cases that would not be considered sexual offences in Canada. Finally, the typologies have no theoretical background and do not provide descriptions or indices of the psychological or psychosocial functioning of these women, thereby shedding no light on the factors that led to sexual offending among these women. Therefore, although these typologies help to describe female sexual offenders, they cannot be used to draw conclusions about either the factors that led to the sexually offending behaviour or the risk for further sexual offending.

Female Offenders and Sexual Recidivism

Recidivism Rates

Although tremendous advances have been made in the understanding of the recidivism rates of adult male sexual offenders, until recently similar knowledge was non-existent for female sexual offenders. To examine this issue, Cortoni and Hanson (2005) undertook a review of the recidivism rates of female sexual offenders who were involved in the criminal justice system. The review was accomplished by a thorough search of published and unpublished literature. Included in the review were conference presentations, government reports, official recidivism data drawn from websites or through direct communication with government agencies, and reports of unpublished studies obtained directly from researchers. Information was obtained from the United States, England, Australia, and Canada.

A total sample of 380 female sexual offenders was included in the review. The researchers noted a substantial difference in recidivism rates between male and female sexual offenders. In meta-analyses of large samples of male sexual offenders, the five-year recidivism rates for male sexual offenders were 13 to 14 percent for sexual crimes, 25 percent for any violent crime, and 36 to 37 percent for any new crime (Hanson & Bussière, 1998; Hanson & Morton-Bourgon, 2004). In their study, Cortoni and Hanson (2005) calculated a weighted recidivism average across the studies and found that the sexual recidivism rate for female sexual offenders was 1.0 percent (3/306). In addition, they found the rate of any violent recidivism (including sexual) was 6.3 percent (12/191), and the rate of any recidivism (including violent and sexual) was 20.2 percent (68/337). The average followup period was five years. Not surprisingly, Cortoni and Hanson (2005) noted that the differences between the recidivism rates for the male and female sexual offenders were statistically significant for all types of recidivism, confirming that female sexual offenders have much lower rates of all types of recidivism than male sexual offenders.

Assessing Risk of Recidivism

Unfortunately, very little is known about the static and dynamic risk factors of women sexual offenders. The low rates of reported cases of sexual abuse by women and the low base rates[3] of sexual recidivism of these offenders make it difficult to research this area. A low base rate means that it is difficult to assess or predict who will engage in the given behaviour (Quinsey, Harris, Rice, & Cormier, 2006). For example, in a followup of 115 American female sexual offenders for an average of 5.5 years (ranging from 2 months to 10 years), Peterson, Cole-bank, and Motta (2001) found a zero rate of sexual recidivism. All the women in that study had been in or continued to be in treatment for their sexually offending behaviour. Given the lack of recidivism among these women, the researchers could not establish which characteristics are related to a return to sexually offending behaviour.

In a followup of 61 female sexual offenders incarcerated in Canada between 1972 and 1998, Williams and Nicholaichuk (2001) found a sexual recidivism rate of 3.3 percent (two cases). In their detailed analysis, these authors found one marker that differentiated these two women from the other female sexual offenders in their sample: these women had previously engaged exclusively in solo offending with no co-offender present during the sexual assaults. This particular finding is noteworthy and may serve as an important risk marker for sexual recidivism, but it requires validation through further research on women who have sexually recidivated.

Based on their research, Williams and Nicholaichuk (2001) suggested that a history of sexual reoffending, non-incest offending, and solo offending are static factors related to sexual recidivism in female offenders. As discussed earlier in this chapter, the dynamic risk factors related to general recidivism in women include antisocial attitudes and associates, substance abuse as a precursor to offending, problematic relationships, and emotional dyscontrol (Blanchette, 2001). These factors are likely to be equally present in female sexual offenders because many of these women also engage in other criminal activities.

Interestingly, based on the very low recidivism rates observed in Cortoni and Hanson's (2005) review, evaluators should perhaps be more concerned about the risk of non-sexual recidivism than sexual recidivism in female sexual offenders. Given that female sexual offenders had a much higher rate of general recidivism than sexual recidivism, Cortoni and Hanson (2005) recommended that evaluations of the risk of recidivism in women sexual offenders consider the dynamic risk factors related to general recidivism in women: antisocial attitudes and associates, substance abuse as a precursor to offending, problematic relationships, and emotional dyscontrol (Blanchette, 2001). Because these factors are commonly found in all female offenders, it seems reasonable to consider these factors when assessing the risk of recidivism among female sexual offenders.

Although some tools have been validated to assess the risk of sexual recidivism among men (see, for example, Hanson & Thornton, 1999), no instruments have been developed specifically to assess risk among female sexual offenders. Because tools for male sexual offenders have not been validated for women, using these tools to assess female sexual offenders would be inappropriate. Note that because of the low sexual recidivism rate of female sexual offenders, extremely large samples are required to establish empirically validated risk factors and tools to assess their risk for sexual recidivism. Only time and the accumulation of knowledge will permit such empirical validation. Until then, assessment of the risk of sexual recidivism among female sexual offenders remains tentative.

The Treatment of Female Sexual Offenders
Treatment Needs of Female Sexual Offenders

The goal of treating female sexual offenders is to address the factors related to their sexually offending behaviour. In contrast to the dearth of information about female violent offenders, much has been written about the treatment needs of female sexual offenders. Unfortunately, no empirically validated theory of female sexual deviance exists, and the paucity of research in this area precludes a solid understanding of the factors involved in female sexual aggression. Much of what is known about the psychological functioning of female sexual offenders and the factors that may be related to their offending is based on small sample sizes, consisting of clinical observations and file reviews. Based on this information, although the findings are still tentative, a number of common factors among these women are beginning to emerge.

According to Matthews (1993), female child molesters typically share the following traits: shame, low self-esteem, impaired empathy, and anger. Matthews further elaborated that this anger comprises underlying pain and fear, a typical reaction to victimization. Other authors have suggested that several factors may contribute to the development of sexual offending by women: troubled childhoods (McCarty, 1986; Mathews et al., 1989), sexual abuse as a child (Allen, 1991; Rowan, Rowan, & Langelier, 1990), severe psychological disturbance (McCarty, 1986; Rowan et al., 1990), and a history of compulsive sexual activity (Allen, 1991; Mathews et al., 1989).

Although most of these factors are frequently found among women offenders in general (Blanchette & Brown, 2006), female sexual offenders also share a few factors with male sexual offenders: denial and minimization of the offending behaviour, distorted cognitions about the sexual offences, attitudes that condone sexual abuse, intimacy deficits, and the use of sex to regulate emotional states or to fulfill dependence or intimacy needs (Eldridge & Saradjian, 2000; Grayston & De Luca, 1999; Nathan & Ward, 2002). For at least some of these offenders, a desire for sexual gratification is directly related to the abuse (Nathan & Ward, 2002).

The manifestation and the relative importance of these factors in women may be different from their relevance in men. For example, common to both male and female sexual offenders are denial and minimization of the offending behaviour. After female sexual offenders acknowledge their sexual offending behaviour, however, they tend to show much less minimization of their behaviour than males (Matthews, 1993). Further, when the sexually deviant behaviour occurred in the company of co-offenders, many of these women also wrongly took responsibility for the deviant behaviour of their offending partners (Mathews et al., 1989). Although both male and female sexual offenders have problematic relationships with significant others (Grayston & De Luca, 1999; Hanson & Morton-Bourgon, 2004; Matthews, 1993), women tend to demonstrate particularly excessive dependence or overreliance on the men in their lives (Eldridge & Saradjian, 2000). Finally, although some female sexual offenders engage in deviant sexual fantasies (Grayston & De Luca, 1999; Nathan & Ward, 2002), such fantasies do not appear to be as predominant as in male sexual offenders (Wiegel, Abel, & Jordan, 2003).

Note that, similar to other female offenders, a portion of female sexual offenders demonstrate mental health difficulties; high levels of substance abuse; personality disorders, including antisocial and borderline personality disorders; post-traumatic stress syndrome and depression; severe interpersonal difficulties, particularly in the area of romantic relationships; and general psychosocial deficits (Grayston & De Luca, 1999). The treatment of women who have engaged in sexually offending behaviour therefore has two intertwined goals: assessing and treating the central elements that are directly related to the sexual deviance and treating the broader additional problematic psychological and psychosocial factors that set the stage for the sexual deviance.

An element unique to female sexual offenders, in comparison with male sexual offenders, is the frequent presence of a co-offender (Grayston & De Luca, 1999). Between one-third and two-thirds of female sexual offenders are estimated to offend in the company of an accomplice. The co-offender of female sexual offenders is typically male, although female co-offending has occurred (Vandiver, 2006). Of the women who co-offend, one subgroup has clearly been identified as having been coerced into the offending behaviour, whereas another subgroup co-offends willingly, sometimes initiating the offending behaviour (Vandiver, 2006). In addition, among the coerced women, some will subsequently engage in solo sexual offending.

The presence of a co-offender is frequent enough among female sexual offenders to merit special attention during treatment. Treatment needs are likely to differ if the woman was coerced into the abuse, as opposed to being a willing participant or an initiator. For example, a coerced offender may demonstrate significant deficits in relationship skills, including an excessive dependence on her co-offender, necessitating interventions to help develop more autonomy in her life. Particular attention should focus on her views of gender roles and her ability to function without excessive reliance on others. On the other hand, initiators or willing participants in the sexual abuse may demonstrate more deviant arousal and fantasizing and may hold attitudes that condone sexual abuse, in which case, these issues should be the focus of treatment.

Treatment Approaches

Treatment models for female sexual offenders are based on a cognitive-behavioural approach and follow a relapse-prevention, self-management model. Treatment priorities and the preferred treatment delivery are determined through an assessment of both the factors related to the sexually deviant behaviour and the problematic areas of the client's life, including mental health, personality disorders, and substance abuse. The assessment should also identify the woman's strengths and resiliency factors, and her treatment plan should capitalize on these traits. Too often, the focus is on deficits, while ignoring the presence of positive attributes (Ford & Cortoni, 2008).

Generally, the treatment focuses on five broad areas: (1) cognitive processes; (2) emotional processes; (3) intimacy and relationship issues; (4) sexual dynamics; and (5) social functioning. The treatment addresses the interrelationships among these factors and develops a self-management plan to include goals for a healthier life. This approach recognizes that sexual offending behaviour is not treated in isolation from the rest of the woman's life, ensures that all areas of functioning are targeted, and allows for flexibility to tailor the treatment according to each woman's individual treatment needs (Ford & Cortoni, 2008).

Eldridge and Saradjian's (2000) model of sexual deviance in women posited that for these women, unmet needs result in aversive emotional states that are alleviated by their sexually deviant behaviours. These behaviours in turn become rewarding in themselves, leading to the development or reinforcement of knowledge, beliefs, and attitudes that facilitate further sexually deviant behaviour.

Treatment with female sexual offenders therefore specifically includes

- identifying sexually deviant patterns, including thoughts, emotions, and behaviours involved in these patterns;
- identifying the needs met by the sexually deviant behaviour and generating non-deviant alternative strategies to meet those needs;
- addressing the factors that gave rise to those otherwise unmet needs, including victimization histories and relationship issues;
- challenging distorted abuse-related cognitions and broader dysfunctional thinking patterns that contribute to a negative life cycle;
- managing negative emotional states and improving emotional self-management;
- managing sexual fantasies; and
- developing both coping strategies to deal directly with the factors that immediately place the woman at risk of sexually acting out and effective coping patterns that will generalize in all types of problematic situations (Denov & Cortoni, 2006).

Although a history of victimization is common in women who engage in antisocial behaviours, evidence suggests that the victimization histories of women who engage in sexual deviance may be particularly severe (Grayston & De Luca, 1999). For a large number of sexually deviant women, their histories of victimization, including their patterns of sexu-ally deviant behaviours, patterns of relating with others, and patterns of coping, are likely related to their current functioning (Eldridge & Saradjian, 2000) and therefore must be taken into account during treatment. The treatment based on the victimization histories of these women should not, however, take precedence over their sexually deviant behaviours. Failing to differentiate between past victimization and current sexual offending may prevent a woman in treatment from developing the necessary understanding of the issues that led to her decision to engage in sexually deviant behaviour. Such a failure may obscure the responsibilities these women have for their own behaviour and their responsibility for mak-ing necessary changes (Denov & Cortoni, 2006).

Additional Treatment Considerations

As previously discussed, sexually deviant women may present with mental health difficulties. When severe mental health issues are present, these issues must be addressed and the client sufficiently stabilized before dealing with the factors related to the sexual deviance. In more pronounced cases, psychiatric treatment, including medication, may be required. Failure to address these issues may eliminate any possibility that the woman will benefit from treat-ment for her sexual deviance (Ford & Cortoni, 2008). For some female sexual offenders, their mental health problems are such that treatment for the sexual offending behaviour is impossible. In these cases, the treatment focus should be on stabilizing the woman and providing her with psychiatric care and intensive support both while incarcerated and while in the community to help her manage her mental health problems.

Women account for the majority of diagnoses of borderline personality disorders (American Psychiatric Association, 2000), and borderline personality features are not uncommon among sexually deviant women (Grayston & De Luca, 1999). For such women, emotional management is a central treatment need. Although Eldridge and Saradjian (2000) incorporated treatment techniques to deal with this issue, some clients and some women offenders may require intensive interventions specifically designed for this problem.

Many women need additional help to rebuild their lives in a manner that removes the need for sexual offending. Similar to all other types of violent female offenders, these women may also require support to improve their general community functioning, with a particular focus on their ability to develop and maintain a more stable lifestyle with less dependence on others. Other aspects often neglected in women sexual offenders are their borderline, egocentric, or antisocial features (Grayston & De Luca, 1999; Nathan & Ward, 2002). Matthews (1998) noted that women with such features were particularly difficult in the context of group treatment, and were often discharged from treatment due to their attempts to sabotage the treatment process. Similarly, if the woman has a substance abuse problem, it should be brought under control before other treatment begins. Although substance abuse exacerbates problems in a woman's life, it may simultaneously have become a dysfunctional strategy to help the woman cope with either life difficulties (Blanchette & Brown, 2006) or her offending behaviour. Additional interventions may be required before starting treatment for their sexually deviant behaviour.

Mothers who have sexually abused children (her own or those in her care) also tend to have engaged in other types of child maltreatment (Grayston & De Luca, 1999); a thorough understanding is needed of the woman's attitudes and behaviours that are likely to lead to significant harm to a child, particularly if reunification is contemplated and regardless of whether she sexually abused her own child (Saradjian, 1996). Any reunification effort should occur only when children clearly wish to reunite with their mother and should include the involvement of child protection services and family therapists skilled in dealing with abused children. The continued involvement of agencies is also crucial to monitor progress and to detect warning signs that the woman is deteriorating (Matthews, 1993).

Summary

This chapter reviewed the prevalence of violent offending by females, the theories to explain their behaviour, and the assessment and treatment of these women. Female violent offenders can be divided into two general categories: women who engage in general violence and women who engage in sexual violence. General violence includes assaults, domestic violence, and homicides. Sexual violence includes all crimes with a sexual component, excluding crimes related to prostitution. Generally, female offenders have much lower rates of any types of offending than males and tend to recidivate at much lower rates than males. These lower rates are particularly true of female sexual offenders. Ongoing research is focused on understanding why women engage in violence; much remains to be known.

Although some women share some of the same characteristics as male offenders, some important differences must be taken into account when assessing and treating women offenders. Specifically, the context in which the offences took place in interaction with the factors contributing to women's criminal behaviour must be addressed. Women's lives and their societal experiences differ from those of men. Women's experiences will influence both their criminal behaviour and their rehabilitation. Although some women present prototypical antisocial features related to their violence, others commit their offences in response to stressors they have failed to effectively manage. The violent female offender's cognitive and emotional issues and her general community functioning must therefore be taken into account when assessing her needs and planning her treatment program.

Notes

1. In these statistics, violent offences include homicide, attempted murder, assault, robbery, abduction, and sexual offences (Public Safety and Emergency Preparedness Canada [PSEPC], 2006).
2. A typology is a system of groupings based on types or categories. Each type has specific attributes not found in the other types within the typology.
3. A base rate is the proportion of the population that exhibits the phenomenon of interest—in this case, sexual recidivism by women.

Discussion Questions

1. Although women commit fewer violent offences than men, their rate of violence is increasing. Given that the context of female offending differs from that of male offending, what might be appropriate societal responses to address this increase?
2. Some authors argue that determining a woman's risk of recidivism based on a male view of offending is inappropriate (Hannah-Moffat, 1999, for example). Considering that women have lower base rates of violence, including sexual violence, should we be concerned about assessing the risk of reoffending among female violent offenders?
3. Current assessment and treatment approaches for female violent offenders are based on limited theoretical and empirical knowledge of the factors that lead to violent offending behaviour. Some authors (for example, Blanchette & Brown, 2006) argue that to fully understand female offending behaviour, theories need to incorporate gender-neutral and gender-informed factors. How do gender-neutral and gender-informed factors differ? How would such factors manifest themselves among female violent offenders?

Suggested Readings

Bonta, J., Pang, B., & Wallace-Capretta, S. (1995). Predictors of recidivism among incarcerated female offenders. *The Prison Journal, 75*(3), 227–294.

Ford, H. (2006). *Women who sexually abuse children.* Chichester, UK: John Wiley & Sons.

Pollock, J. (1999). *Criminal women.* Cincinnati, OH: Anderson Press.

Online Resources

1. Public Safety Canada: www.ps-sp.gc.ca
2. Correctional Service of Canada: www.csc-scc.gc.ca

References

Allen, C.M. (1991). *Women and men who sexually abuse children: A comparative analysis.* Orwell, VT: Safer Society Press.

American Psychiatric Association. (2000). *Diagnostic and statistical manual of mental disorders* (4th ed.). Washington, DC: Author.

Andrews, D.A., & Bonta, J. (2003). *The psychology of criminal conduct* (3rd ed.). Cincinnati, OH: Anderson.

Archer, J. (2000). Sex differences in aggression between heterosexual partners: A meta-analytic review. *Psychological Bulletin, 126,* 651–680.

Benda, B.B. (2005). Gender differences in life-course theory of recidivism: A survival analysis. *International Journal of Offender Therapy and Comparative Criminology, 49,* 325–342.

Bickley, J., & Beech, A.R. (2001). Classifying child abusers: Its relevance to theory and clinical practice. *International Journal of Offender Therapy and Comparative Criminology, 45,* 51–69.

Blanchette, K. (2001). *Classifying female offenders for effective intervention: Application of the case-based principles of risk and need.* Unpublished manuscript, Carleton University, Ottawa.

Blanchette, K., & Brown, S.L. (2006). *The assessment and treatment of women offenders: An integrated perspective.* Chichester, UK: John Wiley & Sons.

Correctional Service of Canada. (1995). *A profile of homicide offenders in Canada.* Ottawa: Author.

Cortoni, F., & Hanson, R.K. (2005). *A review of the recidivism rates of adult female sexual offenders* (Research Report R-169). Ottawa: Correctional Service of Canada.

Dasgupta, S.D. (2002). A framework for understanding women's use of nonlethal violence in intimate heterosexual relationships. *Violence Against Women, 8,* 1364–1389.

Denov, M.S., & Cortoni, F. (2006). Adult female sexual offenders. In C. Hilarski & J. Wodarski (Eds.), *Comprehensive mental health practices with sex offenders and their families* (pp. 71–99). New York: Haworth Press.

Department of Justice Canada. (1992). *Corrections and Conditional Release Act.* Ottawa: Government of Canada.

Eldridge, H., & Saradjian, J. (2000). Replacing the function of abusive behaviors for the offender: Remaking relapse prevention in working with women who sexually abuse children. In D.R. Laws, S.M. Hudson, & T. Ward (Eds.), *Remaking relapse prevention with sex offenders: A sourcebook* (pp. 402–426). Thousand Oaks, CA: Sage.

Ford, H., & Cortoni, F. (2008). Sexual deviance in females: Assessment and treatment. In D.R. Laws & W. O'Donohue (Eds.), *Sexual deviance* (2nd ed., pp. 508–526). New York: Guilford Press.

Freund, K., Heasman, G., Racansky, I.G., & Glancy, G. (1984). Pedophilia and heterosexuality vs. homosexuality. *Journal of Sex and Marital Therapy, 10,* 193–200.

Goetting, A. (1988). Patterns of homicide among women. *Journal of Interpersonal Violence, 3*, 3–20.

Grayston, A.D., & De Luca, R.V. (1999). Female perpetrators of child sexual abuse: A review of the clinical and empirical literature. *Aggression and Violent Behavior, 4*, 93–106.

Greenfeld, L.A., & Snell, T.L. (1999). *Women offenders* (Special Report NCJ 175688). Washington, DC: Bureau of Justice Statistics, US Department of Justice. Retrieved from www.ojp.gov/bjs/pub/pdf/wo.pdf.

Greenspan, E.L., & Rosenberg, M. (2007). *Martin's annual Criminal Code.* Aurora, ON: Canada Law Book.

Hannah-Moffat, K. (1999). Moral agents or actuarial subject: Risk and Canadian women's imprisonment. *Theoretical Criminology, 3*, 71–94.

Hanson, R.K., & Bussière, M.T. (1998). Predicting relapse: A meta-analysis of sexual offender recidivism studies. *Journal of Consulting and Clinical Psychology, 66*, 348–362.

Hanson, R.K., & Morton-Bourgon, K.E. (2004). *Recidivism risk factors for sexual offenders: An updated meta-analysis* (User Report no. 2004-02). Ottawa: Corrections Research, Public Safety and Emergency Preparedness Canada.

Hanson, R.K., & Thornton, D. (1999). *Static 99: Improving actuarial risk assessment for sex offenders* (User Report 99-02). Ottawa: Department of the Solicitor General of Canada.

Hatters-Friedman, S., McCue-Horwitz, S., & Resnick, P.J. (2005). Child murders by mothers: A critical analysis of the current state of knowledge and a research agenda. *American Journal of Psychiatry, 162*, 1578–1587.

Hoffman, L.E., Lavigne, B., & Dickie, I. (1998). Women convicted of homicide serving a federal sentence: An exploratory study. Ottawa: Correctional Service of Canada.

Kimmel, M.S. (2002). "Gender symmetry" in domestic violence: A substantive and methodological research review. *Violence Against Women, 8*, 1332–1363.

Kirkwood, D. (2003). Female perpetrated homicide in Victoria between 1985 and 1995. *Australian and New Zealand Journal of Criminology, 36*, 152–172.

Linehan, M.M. (1993). *Cognitive behavioral therapy for borderline personality disorder.* New York: Guilford Press.

McCarty, L. (1986). Mother-child incest: Characteristics of the offender. *Child Welfare, 65*, 447–458.

Mathews, R., Matthews, J., and Speltz, K. (1989). *Female sexual offenders: An exploratory study.* Orwell, VT: Safer Society Press.

Matthews, J.K. (1993). Working with female sexual abusers. In M. Elliot (Ed.), *Female sexual abuse of children* (pp. 57–73). New York: Guilford Press.

Matthews, J.K. (1998). An 11-year perspective of working with female sexual offenders. In W.L. Marshall, Y.M. Fernandez, S.M. Hudson, & T. Ward (Eds.), *Sourcebook of treatment programs for sexual offenders* (pp. 259–272). New York: Plenum Press.

Miller, S.L., & Meloy, M.L. (2006). Women's use of force: Voices of women arrested for domestic violence. *Violence Against Women, 12*, 89–115.

Nathan, P., & Ward, T. (2002). Female sex offenders: Clinical and demographic features. *The Journal of Sexual Aggression, 8*, 5–21.

Ogle, R.S., Maier-Katkin, D., & Bernard, T.J. (1995). A theory of homicidal behavior among women. *Criminology, 33*, 174–193.

Peterson, K.D., Colebank, K.D., & Motta, L.L. (2001, November). *Female sexual offender recidivism.* Paper presented at the 20th Research and Treatment Conference, Association for the Treatment of Sexual Abusers, San Antonio, Texas.

Pollock, J.M., & Davis, S.M. (2005). The continuing myth of the violent female offender. *Criminal Justice Review, 30*, 5–29.

Pollock, J.M., Mullings, J., & Crouch, B. (2002). Drugs and criminality: Results from the Texas women inmates study. *Women and Criminal Justice, 13*, 69–97.

Public Safety and Emergency Preparedness Canada. (2006, December). *Corrections and conditional release statistical overview: Annual report 2006.* Ottawa: Author.

Putkonen, H., Komulainen, E.J., Virkkunen, M., Eronen, M., & Lönnqvist, J. (2003). Risk of repeat offending among violent female offenders with psychotic and personality disorders. *American Journal of Psychiatry, 160*, 947–951.

Quinsey, V.L., Harris, G.T., Rice, M.E., & Cormier, C.A. (2006). *Violent offenders: Appraising and managing risk* (2nd ed.). Washington, DC: American Psychological Association.

Rowan, E.L., Rowan, J.B., and Langelier, P. (1990). Women who molest children. *Bulletin of the American Academy of Psychiatry and the Law, 18*, 79–83.

Rumgay, J. (2004). Living with paradox: Community supervision of women offenders. In G. McIvor (Ed.), *Women who offend* (pp. 99–125). London: Jessica Kingsley.

Sandler, J.C., & Freeman, N.J. (2007). Typology of female sex offenders: A test of Vandiver and Kercher. *Sexual Abuse: A Journal of Research and Treatment, 19*, 73–89.

Saradjian, J. (1996). *Women who sexually abuse children: From research to clinical practice.* London: Wiley.

Sestir, M.A., & Bartholow, B.D. (2007). Theoretical explanations of aggression and violence. In T.A. Gannon, T. Ward, A.R. Beech, & D. Fisher (Eds.), *Aggressive offenders' cognition: Theory, research, and practice* (pp. 157–178). Chichester, UK: John Wiley & Sons.

Sommers, I., & Baskin, D.R. (1993). The situational context of violent female offending. *Journal of Research in Crime and Delinquency, 30*, 136–162.

Straus, M.A. (1990). Measuring intrafamily conflict and violence: The Conflict Tactic (CT) Scale. In M.A. Straus & R.J. Gelles (Eds.), *Physical violence in American families* (pp. 29–47). New Brunswick, NJ: Transaction Books.

Sullivan-Everstine, D., & Everstine, L. (1993). *The trauma response: Treatment for emotional injury.* New York: W.W. Norton & Company.

Swan, S.C., & Snow, D.L. (2002). A typology of women's use of violence in intimate relationships. *Violence Against Women, 8*, 286–319.

Swan, S.C., & Snow, D.L. (2003). Behavioral and psychological differences among abused women who use violence in intimate relationships. *Violence Against Women, 9*, 75–109.

Vandiver, D.M. (2006). Female sex offenders: A comparison of solo offenders and co-offenders. *Violence and Victims, 21*, 339–354.

Vandiver, D.M., & Kercher, G. (2004). Offender and victim characteristics of registered female sex offenders in Texas: A proposed typology of female sexual offenders. *Sexual Abuse: A Journal of Research and Treatment, 16*, 121–137.

Vandiver, D.M., & Walker, J.T. (2002). Female sex offenders: An overview and analyses of 40 cases. *Criminal Justice Review, 58*, 236–244.

Verona, E., & Carbonell, J.C. (2000). Female violence and personality. *Criminal Justice and Behavior, 27*, 176–195.

Warren, J.I., South, S.C., Burnette, M.L., Rogers, A., Friend, R., Bale, R., et al. (2005). Understanding the risk factors for violence and criminality in women: The concurrent validity of the PCL-R and HCR-20. *International Journal of Law and Psychiatry, 28*, 269–289.

Weizmann-Henelius, G., Viemerö, V., & Eronen, M. (2003). The violent female perpetrator and her victim. *Forensic Science International, 133*, 197–203.

Wiegel, M., Abel, G.G., & Jordan, A. (2003, October). *The self-reported behaviors of adult female child abusers.* Paper presented at the 22nd Annual Research and Treatment Conference, Association for the Treatment of Sexual Abusers, St. Louis, Missouri.

Williams, S.M., & Nicholaichuk, T. (2001, November). *Assessing static risk factors in adult female sex offenders under federal jurisdiction.* Paper presented at the 20th Research and Treatment Conference, Association for the Treatment of Sexual Abusers, San Antonio, Texas.

CHAPTER 8

Women Offenders and Mental Health

Jean Folsom

Introduction

The mental health status of women offenders presents significant issues for the people responsible for working with them. Mental health problems can complicate efforts to assist women offenders in dealing with issues in their lives and their reintegration into the community. Of course, the majority of women with mental health problems do not come into conflict with the law, and many women in prison do not suffer from mental illness. However, because a disproportionate number of women with mental health problems are in prison, relative to women in the community, the mental health of women offenders is worthy of attention.

Although the term *mental disorder* has no precise definition, the US Office of the Surgeon General (1999) provides the following descriptions:

Mental health: The successful performance of mental function, resulting in productive activities, fulfilling relationships with other people, and the ability to adapt to change and to cope with adversity.

Mental illness: A term that refers collectively to all mental disorders. Mental disorders are health conditions that are characterized by alterations in thinking, mood, or behaviour (or some combination thereof) associated with distress and/or impaired functioning.

Mental disorders are classified by the Diagnostic and Statistical Manual of Mental Disorders, referred to as the DSM-IV (American Psychiatric Association [APA], 2000), which defines *mental disorder* as:

a clinically significant behavioral or psychological syndrome or pattern that occurs in an individual that is associated with present distress (e.g., painful symptom) or disability (i.e., impairment in one or more important areas of functioning) or with a significant increased risk of suffering death, pain, disability, or an important loss of freedom. (p. xxxi)

Certain behaviours and thought processes are clustered into categories to simplify discussion about mental illnesses. For example, someone who is constantly preoccupied with recurring thoughts and the need to carry out rituals (such as constantly checking to see if the stove is turned off) may be diagnosed with an obsessive-compulsive disorder.

Mental disorders have two main types: Axis I and Axis II disorders. Axis I disorders are associated with major mental illnesses, such as schizophrenia, depression, and delusional disorders, and with anxiety disorders, such as obsessive-compulsive disorder. People with Axis I disorders may, depending on their disorder, hear voices, hold unusual views such as believing they are someone else, or repeat a behaviour such as washing their hands hundreds of times a day.

Axis II disorders comprise personality disorders and mental retardation. Personality disorders are most often seen among typical male and female criminals; that is, among those who are not considered to be mentally disordered because they have not lost contact with reality. For example, offenders with an antisocial personality disorder, which is more common in male than female offenders, are often irresponsible, tend to break the law and lack remorse for their actions, and generally have little regard for the needs of others. In women, the personality disorder most often seen is **borderline personality disorder**. People with this disorder lack stability in many areas of their lives, such as their interpersonal relationships, their self-image, and their mood; and they tend to be impulsive. See box 8.1 for further information on borderline personality disorder.

Box 8.1   Borderline Personality Disorder

The term *borderline personality disorder* was first coined in the early part of the 20th century when psychopathology was viewed as being on a continuum from "normal" to "neurotic" to "psychotic." People with severe emotional problems who did not fit into the neurotic or psychotic categories were labelled *borderline* to indicate that they fell between these two categories. The term has since come to refer to a particular personality structure with distinctive features.

According to the Diagnostic and Statistical Manual of Mental Disorders (DSM–IV), people with a diagnosis of borderline personality disorder go through life making frantic efforts to avoid real or imagined abandonment. They are overly sensitive to any possible indication of abandonment and react strongly with fear or anger, for example, when someone arrives unexpectedly late or leaves early. They often start intense relationships and idealize new friends or therapists. However, at the first sign that the new person is not there for them, they devalue the person and feel abandoned, leading to a drop in mood and a negative self-image. People with borderline personality disorder often have a history of childhood abuse, neglect, or early parental loss. These early traumatic experiences have likely contributed to the development of this disorder.

Another way of looking at the symptoms of this disorder is to categorize them into five areas:

1. Emotional dysregulation, characterized by emotional instability and problems with anger
2. Interpersonal dysregulation, characterized by unstable relationships and efforts to avoid loss
3. Behavioural dysregulation, characterized by suicide threats and self-damaging behaviours, including substance abuse
4. Cognitive dysregulation, characterized by disturbances in thinking
5. Self-dysfunction, characterized by unstable self-image and chronic feelings of emptiness.

Source: American Psychiatric Association. (2000). *Diagnostic and statistical manual of mental disorders* (4th ed.): *Text revision*. Arlington, VA: Author; Linehan, M.M. (1993). *Cognitive-behavioral treatment of borderline personality disorder*. New York: Guilford Press.

The prevalence of borderline personality disorder is estimated to be 1 percent of women in the community and from 3 to 30 percent of women in prison or forensic settings (APA, 2000). Therefore, borderline personality disorder is much more common among women offenders than among women in the community.

Women offenders with mental disorders are women who have some type of mental disorder and have also behaved in a manner that has brought them to the attention of the criminal justice system. See box 8.2 for a brief summary of the routes that may be taken by a woman with a mental disorder accused of breaking the law.

Box 8.2   Mental Health Facility or Prison?

How does a woman with a mental disorder end up in the prison system? When a woman with a mental disorder comes to the attention of the criminal justice system, she faces several decision points at which she may be directed to either the criminal justice system or the mental health system.

Police Contact

The first point of contact occurs when the police are involved. At this stage, a decision is made whether to charge the woman. The police also decide whether the woman's behaviour suggests that she is suffering from a mental disorder to the extent that she should be apprehended, taken to a judge, and ordered to a hospital for a psychiatric examination. This procedure is authorized by provincial and territorial mental health legislation. If the physician determines the woman meets the strict criteria that judge her as being dangerous to herself or others because of her mental disorder, she is deemed "certifiable" under the applicable mental health legislation and admitted for a longer period of examination or treatment.

Appearing Before Court

If the woman is charged with an offence under the *Criminal Code*, the judge may remand the woman to custody, place her on bail, or remand her to a psychiatric hospital for examination, usually for up to 30 days.

Fit or Unfit to Stand Trial

The outcome of the assessment will determine whether the woman is fit to stand trial. The woman will be found unfit to stand trial if, due to a mental disorder, she is unable to conduct a defence. This judgment is made when the accused cannot understand the nature and the object of the proceedings, cannot understand the consequences of the proceedings, or cannot communicate with counsel (is unable to discuss her case rationally with a lawyer).

Not Guilty, Guilty, or Not Criminally Responsible on Account of Mental Disorder (NCRMD)

A woman found not guilty is free to go without any conditions. If the woman is found guilty, the judge can exercise several sentencing options, ranging from fining the woman to sending her to prison. If the woman is found not criminally responsible on account of mental disorder (NCRMD), the judge again has several options from which to choose: an absolute discharge because the accused is judged not to be a threat to public safety; a discharge to the community with conditions, usually for some type of treatment; or sending the person to a forensic psychiatric hospital where a release decision is made by a review board of lawyers, psychiatrists, and lay people.

Therefore, to be diverted from the criminal justice system to the mental health system, a mentally disordered woman whose behaviour has attracted the attention of the law must meet strict criteria. A diagnosis of a mental illness is not sufficient: she must also meet specific criteria throughout the process. A woman with a mental disorder who has committed an offence could conceivably understand the proceedings of the court and instruct her lawyer that an NCRMD defence not be presented. Note that an NCRMD defence can only be brought forward in court by the defending lawyer. If the accused woman is charged with a relatively minor offence, the defence may not seek an NCRMD disposition fearing that more time may be served on an indefinite term in a psychiatric hospital than with a short prison sentence.

Source: Gray, J.E., Shone, M.A., & Liddle, P.F. (2000). *Canadian mental health law and policy*. Toronto: Butterworths.

The Prevalence and Nature of Mental Disorders Among Offenders

Offenders in Canada are managed by the federal, provincial, and territorial correctional systems. As noted in chapter 1, the provinces and territories are responsible for offenders who receive sentences of less than two years, whereas the federal government manages those with sentences of two or more years.

Prevalence refers to the number or proportion of cases of any disorder in a population at any given time. Precise numbers of offenders with mental disorders within the criminal justice system in Canada are difficult to obtain. No jurisdiction conducts thorough mental health assessments on offenders entering its correctional system. From the available information, the following questions will be addressed: What are the current rates of mental disorders among offenders? Are these rates different from those of the general population? Are the rates changing? What types of mental disorders are found among prisoners?

Scant information is available on the mental health status of women offenders in Canada. The only thorough attempt to document mental disorders among female federal offenders took place in 1989, at what was, at that time, the only federal institution for women in Canada—the Prison for Women (Blanchette & Motiuk, 1996). Male offenders had been surveyed in 1988, thereby providing an opportunity for comparison of various mental disorders between the groups (Motiuk & Porporino, 1992). All participants were administered a structured diagnostic interview aimed at determining whether they had ever had a psychiatric diagnosis during their lifetime.

Figure 8.1 displays the diagnoses for male and female offenders from these two studies. As compared with male offenders, the women had much higher rates of major mental disorders and depression. The category of major mental disorders includes schizophrenia and manic episodes. People with these disorders usually have irrational or disturbed thinking and may also experience delusions, hallucinations, and other severe thought disturbances. Female offenders, then, were found more often than male offenders to have serious mental illnesses.

On the other hand, female offenders had lower rates of anxiety and antisocial personality disorders. No comparisons were provided for borderline personality disorder, but it would likely have much higher rates among the women than the men. Women offenders also had high rates of alcohol and drug dependency, much higher than the men.

The Association of Elizabeth Fry Societies is an association of self-governing, community-based Elizabeth Fry societies that work with and for women and girls in the justice system. According to a survey of the mental disorders of the women offenders with whom these societies work, the most common diagnoses were bipolar disorder, personality disorders (including borderline personality disorder), depression, anxiety, post-traumatic stress disorder, and schizophrenia (Pollack, n.d.). These women's histories included childhood abuse (sexual and physical), experiences of violence as an adult, self-injurious and suicidal behaviours, grief, and drug and alcohol addictions. When considering the mental health disorders of women offenders, the people who work with these women need to be cognizant of the context of these women's lives.

Among federal offenders, women have experienced more mental health problems than men (Blanchette & Brown, 2006). Although the reasons are uncertain, evidence indicates

Figure 8.1   Lifetime Prevalence of Mental Disorders Among Several Samples

	Percentage of male federal offenders[a]	Percentage of female federal offenders[b]	Percentage of males in a Canadian community sample[c]	Percentage of females in a Canadian community sample[c]
Major mental disorder	7.7	17.1	0.5	0.7
Depression	21.5	32.9	7.1	13.2
Anxiety	44.1	19.7	8.7	13.8
Anti-social personality	56.9	36.8	6.5	0.8
Alcohol dependence	47.2	63.2	29.3	6.7
Drug dependence	40.9	50.0	10.6	3.2

[a] Source: Motiuk, L., & Porporino, F.J. (1992). *The prevalence, nature and severity of mental health problems among federal male inmates in Canadian penitentiaries.* Ottawa: Correctional Service of Canada.

[b] Source: Blanchette, K., & Motiuk, L. (1996). *Female offenders with and without major mental health problems: A comparative investigation* (Research Report no. R-6). Ottawa: Research Branch, Correctional Service of Canada.

[c] Source: Bland, R.C., Orn, H., & Newman, S.C. (1988). Lifetime prevalence of psychiatric disorders in Edmonton. *Acta Psychiatrica Scandinavica, 77*(Suppl. 338), 24–32.

that women offenders are more often abused physically and/or sexually in childhood and adulthood (Blanchette & Brown, 2006). In a Canadian study by Bonta, Pang, and Wallace-Capretta (1995), 61 percent of female offenders had been physically abused and 54 percent had been sexually abused. The authors of an American study of women offenders with substance abuse problems found that the women offenders had more extensive histories of victimization than male offenders with substance abuse problems (Messina, Grella, Burdon, & Prendergast, 2007). Not only did the women experience a higher rate of abuse than men but the abuse lasted over a longer period of their lives—from childhood into their teens and adulthood.

The high rate of abuse among women offenders may lead to coping strategies that result in their being diagnosed with a mental disorder (Heney, 1990; Pollack, 2005). Women who have been abused often continue to experience strong feelings of emotional distress and are motivated to seek relief. However, some of the methods that they choose—for example, substance abuse and self-injury—offer only short-term relief and create new problems in the long term. A thorough examination of coping strategies is addressed in chapter 5.

Childhood abuse may also lead to mental health problems in adulthood. For example, symptoms of borderline personality disorder, such as difficulties with trusting people and with regulating one's emotions, may have their roots in childhood abuse. Abused girls have had their trust violated, often repeatedly, and usually by adults they knew and trusted. Their ability to develop and maintain emotionally stable relationships is compromised by this experience.

In addition to the disorders described above, a disproportionate number of women offenders have below-average intellectual abilities, including some with intellectual disabilities. For our purposes, intellectual disability is defined as "a significant sub-average general intellectual functioning resulting in or associated with concurrent impairments in adaptive behaviour" ("A Health Care Needs Assessment," 2004, p. S37). Depending on their level of security, between 1.3 and 3.9 percent of males and 0.7 to 6.5 percent of females in federal prisons are estimated to meet the criteria for intellectual disability ("A health care needs assessment," 2004). More offenders with intellectual disabilities are housed in higher-security facilities, possibly because they are less capable of caring for themselves in the lower-security facilities where more independent functioning is required.

Less information is available on the mental health status of provincial and territorial offenders. Because these offenders are serving shorter sentences, they have usually committed offences less serious than those of federal offenders. The mental health of provincially sentenced women in Ontario was one of the issues examined by Shaw (1994) in her survey of female offenders living in institutions or in the community under supervision. Of the women interviewed, 80 percent of those in institutions and 67 percent of those in the community reported suffering from at least one mental health problem. Of all women surveyed, depression (51 percent) and anxiety (40 percent) were cited most often. Physical and sexual abuse were common among the sample with 72 percent reporting having been physically abused and 48 percent having been sexually abused at some point in their lives.

Finn, Trevethan, Carrière, and Kowalski (1999) conducted a profile of women offenders who were housed in Canadian federal, provincial, and territorial facilities in 1996. Data on the provincial and territorial offenders indicated that women offenders had more mental health needs than their male counterparts. Substance abuse and emotional problems were, once again, ranked higher for the women than the men. Thus, provincial and territorial female offenders have higher rates of mental illnesses than men, similar to their federal counterparts.

Co-occurring Disorders

Thus far, we have examined only individual diagnoses; however, in reality, most offenders with mental health problems are diagnosed with more than one disorder. In a study of the rate of mental disorders among male federal offenders, Brink, Doherty, and Boer (2001) found that 76 percent of the male offenders diagnosed with a psychotic disorder were also diagnosed with an additional disorder. For male offenders with a mood disorder, 80 percent were diagnosed with another disorder, and for those with a substance abuse disorder, 42 percent received a second diagnosis.

Women offenders with mental disorders who are diagnosed with one type of mental illness are also likely struggling with another mental health problem. For example, having both a schizophrenic disorder and a substance abuse problem is not uncommon. Some people who suffer from depressive disorders may abuse alcohol or drugs in an attempt to lift their mood. The assessment and treatment of women offenders with mental disorders are complicated by the multiple mental health problems faced by these women.

Women with mental health disorders have historically been treated differently from their male counterparts. Box 8.3 looks at the grim life that faced "criminal lunatic" women in the 19th century.

Box 8.3   Asylums for Women

Mentally disordered women offenders ("criminal lunatics") were the first offenders in Canada to be admitted into an early forensic mental health system, that is, an "asylum for criminal lunatics" as opposed to the penitentiary. Previously, criminals, "the insane," and debtors were all held in prison. In the late 1800s, criminals and those considered insane were separated into two new facilities: the Kingston Penitentiary in Kingston and the Provincial Lunatic Asylum in Toronto. However, "criminal lunatics" posed a problem. They did not fit into either facility. They also posed a philosophical problem: if they were insane, then they were not responsible for their behaviour but being convicted for an offence implied that they were responsible. This dilemma persists to some extent today.

In 1855, a temporary lunatic asylum was opened within the Kingston Penitentiary for male offenders. A decision was made not to house the women among these men and therefore they were kept at the Provincial Lunatic Asylum in Toronto. In 1857, the women were sent to what was to become the Rockwood Asylum in Kingston, a lunatic asylum that was still in the planning stages. Because the asylum had not yet been built when the women arrived, they were accommodated in the horse stables for the next 11 years—three years after the asylum had been opened to

accommodate male offenders from the penitentiary. The women lived in 3-metre by 1.5-metre cells that were illuminated only by the light that shone through the bars of their peepholes. The cells had thick wooden doors with slots where food was pushed through. As can be imagined, these women had very limited human contact.

Source: Kendall, K. (1999). Criminal lunatic women in 19th century Canada. *Forum on Corrections Research*, *11*(3), 46–49.

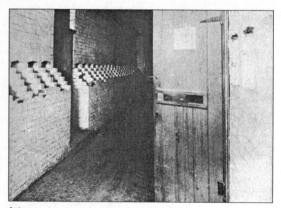

(Photo source: Kingston Psychiatric Hospital Archives/ Queen's University.)

Rates of Mental Disorders in the Community

Few thorough epidemiological studies report the rates of mental disorders in the Canadian community. One study, conducted in Edmonton, Alberta (Bland, Orn, & Newman, 1988), used the same method of assessment as was used in the studies on federal male offenders (Motiuk & Porporino, 1992) and on federal female offenders (Blanchette & Motiuk, 1996), allowing a ready comparison of the results of the prison and community samples.

As shown in figure 8.1, the rates of all forms of mental disorders are higher in both the male and female prison populations than in male and female populations in the community.

The discrepancies between the rates of mental disorders for the prison and community samples are higher for the women than for the men. The women offenders range from 1.4 times higher than the community for anxiety disorders and 46 times higher for antisocial personality disorder, whereas the men range from 1.6 times higher for alcohol dependency to 15 times higher for major mental disorders.

Note the large difference in the use of alcohol and drugs among the women offenders compared with the community sample of women. The women offenders were nine times more likely to be diagnosed with alcohol dependency and nearly 16 times more likely to be diagnosed with drug dependency than were women in the community. The differences were much smaller between male offenders and community samples of men. Male offenders were diagnosed with alcohol dependency only 1.6 times as often as the community men and with drug dependency less than four times as often. Therefore, in the area of substance abuse, the male offender population is more similar to men in the community than the women offenders are to women living in the community.

Changing Rates of Mental Disorders in Prison Populations

As early as the 1930s, a relationship was noted between the populations in the mental health system and in the criminal justice systems. Penrose's law states that the population size of prisons and psychiatric hospitals are inversely related: that is, as one goes up, the other goes down (Webster & Hucker, 2007). Although this description is probably an oversimplification, some association seems to exist between the populations of prisons and psychiatric hospitals, with some people moving between the two systems.

In Canada, the psychiatric hospital population has been reduced over the past two decades, which has led to an increase in the numbers of offenders with mental health problems entering the criminal justice system (Webster & Hucker, 2007). People who previously would likely have been hospitalized for behaviours inappropriate or unacceptable to society are now living in the community or on the street and are more likely to come into contact with police because of their behaviour. The Canadian Mental Health Association has stated that "Canadian prisons have replaced former psychiatric hospitals" (Canada, Senate Standing Committee on Social Affairs, Science and Technology, 2004, p. 98).

The proportion of people with mental health problems entering the criminal justice system appears to be on the rise. Within the federal correctional system, between 1997 and 2002, the proportion of male offenders who were assessed as having mental health problems on admission increased significantly (Boe & Vuong, 2002). The percentage of those who had been diagnosed at any time with a mental disorder rose from 8 percent of all admissions in 1997 to 13 percent in 2002 (a 63 percent gain). Offenders who entered the correctional system with a current diagnosis for a mental disorder rose from 6 percent of all admissions to 9 percent (a 50 percent gain). For women federal offenders, no significant change was noted in the proportion of those with mental disorders who entered the correctional system in 1997, as compared with those who entered in 2002 (Boe & Vuong, 2002). The percentage of offenders entering the criminal justice system who are women is still very small: 10 percent of provincial and territorial (Northwest Territories, Nunavut, and Yukon) offenders and just 5 percent of federal offenders (Statistics Canada, 2007).

Mentally Disordered Women Offenders

Women offenders with mental health problems are a varied group. The most common problems they experience are personality disorders and alcohol and drug abuse (see figure 8.1). Diane Charron has had problems in both areas (see box 8.4). She suffered a particularly difficult childhood that undoubtedly played a role in shaping the person she became. As an adult, she had tremendous difficulty managing her emotions and often felt sad or angry. At times, she felt hopeless. She frequently self-injured by cutting her arms, and she also attempted suicide. From prison, she speaks openly about her distress in a documentary film about her life (Ménard, Turgeon, & Cadieux, 2003).

Box 8.4   Diane Charron

Diane Charron was 19 years old when she participated in the stabbing death of a man. Her co-accused was a 43-year-old man who initiated an assault on the victim out of revenge, but it was Diane who dealt the fatal blows with a knife. Diane, who was under the influence of drugs at the time, agreed to participate because it seemed like an opportunity to get revenge for all of the bad things that had happened to her in her life. The two men were ex-criminals who she believed would get into a fight but she did not expect it to lead to death. As a result of this incident, her co-accused received a six-year sentence while she was sentenced to life.

Up to this point in her life, Diane had lived a very difficult life. As a child, she was placed in a foster home at the age of 18 months where she was neglected and frequently beaten. In her early teens, she was placed in a much better foster home where she was well treated but by this time she was quite damaged emotionally. As a result, she was often truant, started using drugs, and ran away from home. She was placed in a group home for a while but again she ran away. At the age of 15, she was raped.

In her late teens, she was living on her own, drinking heavily, and using drugs. She was also in and out of the local psychiatric hospital. She tended to hang around with older men, one of whom became her co-accused. Her situation was clearly unstable, if not chaotic.

Once in prison, Diane became very depressed and attempted suicide. She also frequently cut her arms for relief from her emotional torment. She would rather experience physical pain than emotional pain. She felt remorse for what she had done, writing to her second foster mother "I should be dead. I took someone's life. I shouldn't live." After a few years in prison, she was admitted to a psychiatric hospital where she was treated for several years. However, on her return to prison, her mental health problems worsened again. She was diagnosed with borderline personality disorder and frequently felt depressed and self-injurious. Eventually, she was again admitted to a psychiatric hospital where she once again showed much improvement.

In Diane's case, the severity of her mental health problems has resulted in her remaining in prison much longer than someone else with a similar sentence and probably much longer than was intended. At 10 years past her eligibility date for parole, she had never appeared before the Parole Board. The fragile state of her mental health made it more complicated for her to prepare for such an appearance. Also, she sabotaged any attempts for conditional release. When such opportunities were within reach, she became highly self-injurious or threatened staff, although she did not carry out these threats. For Diane, her lifelong struggle with mental health problems stemming from her abusive childhood has led to her offence and complicated her return to society.

Source: Ménard, J. (Producer), Turgeon. J. (Producer), & Cadieux, M. (Writer/Director). (2003). *Sentenced to life* [Motion picture]. Canada: National Film Board.

Another example of a personality disorder in a woman offender can be seen in box 8.5. In this case, the offender was older than a typical offender and did not have a criminal background. She was married and the mother of a young child at the time of her offence. Therefore, she had managed to live in society well into adulthood. At the time of her offence, however, she was experiencing a great deal of stress. Her emotional instability and impulsiveness affected the choices she made to deal with her stress.

Women offenders suffering from an Axis I disorder, such as schizophrenia, are less common than women offenders with other mental health problems, such as personality disorders.

Box 8.5 Lisa Samberg

Lisa Samberg was 40 years old when she fed her 16-month-old daughter 30 crushed sleeping pills mixed with apple sauce and then suffocated the baby with a plastic bag over her head while she slept. Then Lisa tried to take her own life by overdosing on pills, slashing her wrists and suffocating herself. However, she survived and was charged with the death of her child.

During the trial, it came to light that Lisa had mental health problems and severe stressors in her life. She was, however, able to understand the consequences of her actions and to understand the court proceedings so she was capable of facing her charge. She had been diagnosed with borderline personality disorder, her husband had threatened to serve her with divorce papers on her 40th birthday, and she was losing her apartment. She also felt betrayed by her parents who were helping her ex-husband.

Her lawyer argued that she should be found not criminally responsible on account of mental disorder. He suggested that the weight of so many stressors caused her to snap. Lisa honestly believed she was doing the right thing when she decided to kill her daughter. Lisa wrote in a suicide letter that she considered killing only herself but decided to kill the baby to save her from a dead mother and a bad father. She wanted the baby to have a chance of a stable family in the afterlife.

Lisa Samberg was convicted of manslaughter and sentenced to two years in a halfway house where she could receive treatment.

Source: McKenzie, C. (2003, December 4). Alice doesn't want to live here anymore. *Hour*. Retrieved from www.hour.ca/news/news.aspx?iIDArticle=336; Mom who smothered daughter convicted. (2003, November 17). *Brantford Expositor*, p. A7; Solyom, C. (2003, November 11). Jury to weigh child-killer's motives. *Montreal Gazette*. Retrieved from http://forthesakeofthechildren .blog-city.com.

Women who have schizophrenia hear voices that tell them to commit a crime. These voices can be very powerful and are referred to as "command hallucinations." When experiencing these hallucinations, the person feels compelled to obey the voices, which can order a person to steal, assault, or kill someone, leading to serious offences.

Depression and anxiety are often seen among women offenders and may have pre-existed the offence or developed in prison. The impact of dealing with one's crime and coping with a prison sentence can lead to low moods, anxieties, and feelings of worthlessness and hopelessness.

Because so many women offenders have been victims of physical and/or sexual abuse, post-traumatic stress disorder is not uncommon among prison populations. These women may have intrusive thoughts about the incidents or flashbacks to the incidents and are easily provoked to anger.

When assessing the mental health of women offenders, it is important to consider the background and environment in which these women have grown up and lived as adults. They may have experienced sexism and violence that have had a strong negative impact on their lives and have led to behaviours that have come to be labelled as criminal or patho-logical. The role that such labelling plays in the development and current status of their mental health should not be underestimated. Some authors would even argue against any such labelling of women offenders because it focuses the problem of women offenders onto the individual women whereas the root of the problem is the sexism, racism, classism, and violence that they have experienced (Kendall, 2000). In this analysis, solutions to the prob-lems of women offenders need to be targeted at a societal level not an individual level.

The Relation of Mental Health Status to Offending

In popular culture, people with mental illnesses are commonly depicted as being dangerous. They act in ways that are strange and unpredictable and provide fodder for sensational books and movies. But are they really more dangerous than others?

What we know about this area is unclear because there are many factors that complicate the interpretation of the research. In general, however, most studies that compare the rate of offending of people with mental illnesses with that of the general public find a higher rate of criminal activity among those with mental illnesses (Choe, Teplin, & Abram, 2008). Hodgins (1998), for example, found that both men and women who had been hospitalized with a diagnosis of a major mental disorder had more likely been convicted of a crime than people who had never been admitted to a psychiatric hospital. The difference in the propor-tion of offending between the hospitalized group and the non-hospitalized group was even larger for convictions of violent offences. Other authors have compared the amount of criminal or violent behaviour in discharged psychiatric patients with comparable commu-nity samples and found the rate among the patient groups to be higher (Choe et al., 2008; Erickson, Rosenheck, Trestman, Ford, & Desai, 2008; Steadman et al., 1998).

What role does mental illness play in offending? One factor that frequently appears in the literature is the abuse of alcohol or drugs in the criminal behaviour of people with mental illnesses (Erickson et al., 2008; Steadman et al., 1998; Wallace, Mullen, & Burgess, 2004). Steadman et al., for example, found that substance abuse was the main factor in predicting violent behaviour in discharged psychiatric patients. They stated that "there was no significant difference between the prevalence of violence by patients without symptoms of substance abuse and the prevalence of violence by others living in the same neighborhoods who were also without symptoms of substance abuse" (p. 393). Does this mean that people with mental illnesses are of no higher risk for violence than anyone else in the community? No. The patients in this study were twice as likely to abuse substances when they were first discharged from the hospital as the community sample (Torrey, Stanley, Monahan, & Steadman, 2008). These authors also noted that alcohol and drug abuse among the patients raised their risk of violence more than it did for the community sample. Substance abuse is thus an important factor in violent and criminal behaviour in people with mental illnesses.

A second factor that may have an impact on criminal behaviour in people with mental illnesses is whether they are compliant with their mental health treatment. Discharged patients who regularly attended their treatment sessions in the community were found to engage in less violent behaviour than those who did not (Steadman et al., 1998; Torrey et al. 2008).

What about women with mental illnesses? Hodgins (1998) noted that "mental disorders were associated with a greater increase in the risk of criminality and violence among women" (p. S31). Why?

It has been said that crime is a young man's activity. Relative to men, women are much less likely to become involved in crime. In Canada, criminal activity by women is a rare occurrence. Women represent only 5 percent of the adult incarcerated population (Blanchette & Brown, 2006) and an even smaller proportion (4 percent) of the more serious offenders who are incarcerated within the federal correctional system. As previously discussed, women with mental illnesses make up a larger proportion of the female offender population, relative to men with mental illnesses in the male offender population, which is a result of so many fewer women without mental disorders who commit crimes, compared with their male counterparts. Note in figure 8.1 the very high rate of alcohol and drug abuse among the women offenders as compared with women in the community. The rate of women offenders' substance abuse is even higher than that of male offenders, a trend contrary to the statistics on women and men in the community. Thus, substance abuse among women with mental health problems is likely contributing to their involvement in criminal activity.

Not all mental disorders have the same level of risk for criminal activity. Even within a certain diagnosis, the level of risk for offending can change. For example, schizophrenia is associated with an increased risk of offending (Bloom & Wilson, 2000; Wallace, Mullen, & Burgess, 2004). Not all people with schizophrenia are violent; only a minority are. But among this small minority, a relationship has been found between aggression and the appearance of psychotic symptoms; that is, when the psychotic symptoms were active, the person with schizophrenia was more likely to become violent (Bloom & Wilson, 2000). Also, people with schizophrenia who were not taking their medication and who were using alcohol or drugs were at increased risk of engaging in violent crime (Bloom & Wilson, 2000).

Mood disorders have a complex association with criminal activity. The main symptom of depression is a low mood. Other symptoms are a loss of concentration, a lowering of self-worth, a pessimistic view of the future, and thoughts of suicide or self-harm (American Psychiatric Association, 2000). When people are depressed, they often do not have the energy or inclination to become involved with crime. The exceptions are people who are depressed enough to not care about their life, because they can be dangerous to others. For example, in "suicide by cop," or victim-precipitated homicide, depressed people have been known to become aggressive toward police officers in the hope that the officers will kill them.

Manic episodes, on the other hand, involve a prolonged higher mood or irritable mood and include symptoms such as grandiosity, insomnia, and increased motor activity. People in a manic state are prone to taking risks that may bring them into conflict with the criminal justice system.

One could speculate that people with mental health problems may be targeted for arrest by police because of some sort of police bias toward the mentally ill, but this has not been borne out in recent research. One Canadian study examined the attitudes of police officers toward the mentally ill by surveying 150 officers in Ontario and British Columbia (Cotton, 2004). Police officers in the survey did not display high levels of authoritarianism or socially restrictive attitudes toward individuals with mental illnesses. Most officers were at least as benevolent as the general public in their attitude toward people with mental illnesses. Very few officers thought mentally ill people should be isolated from society. Rather, they believed that society needed to learn how to be more tolerant of those with mental illnesses.

The Cotton (2004) study, however, could not answer the question of whether the attitudes of the police officers translated into the officers' behaviours when faced with a decision to arrest an individual. This issue was looked at by Engel and Silver (2001), who examined the arrest patterns of five metropolitan police departments and found no evidence of such a bias. The police did not appear to be prone to arrest a disproportionate number of people with mental health problems.

Recidivism Rates of Mentally Disordered Offenders

How do the reoffence or recidivism rates of mentally disordered offenders in general, and women in particular, compare with the reoffence or recidivism rates of other offenders? As already noted, in comparison with low-risk populations (that is, the community), people with mental disorders have a higher rate of involvement with crime. When we compare mentally disordered offenders with other offenders, however, the story changes. Bonta, Law, and Hanson (1998) examined the predictors of reoffending for mentally disordered and non–mentally disordered offenders. In their study, they reviewed the research of many previous studies, which comprised both male and female offenders. Compared with other offenders, mentally disordered offenders were found to be less likely to reoffend in general or to reoffend violently. Severe mental disorders, such as schizophrenia, were inversely related to general and violent recidivism, whereas mood disorders, such as depression, showed no relationship with reoffending. Also, the researchers noted that the predictors of reoffending for mentally disordered offenders were the same as the predictors for other offenders (criminal history and early onset of criminality, for example); their clinical diagnosis was not shown to be a predictor of their reoffending.

One reason why no relationship was found between some severe mental disorders and offending is the transient nature of mental illness. Although hallucinations and delusions may trigger criminal behaviour in the short run, they have no predictive utility in the long run (Bonta et al., 1998). After the acute symptoms of the illness have abated, either on their own or with treatment, the psychopathology that was supportive of criminal behaviour may have disappeared.

Although mentally disordered offenders are at less risk to reoffend, people working in the criminal justice system and the general public view them as more dangerous than other offenders. Mentally disordered offenders are not released from prison as early as other offenders and tend to serve more of their sentences before release (Porporino & Motiuk, 1995; Villeneuve & Quinsey, 1995). After their release from prison, mentally disordered offenders are more often than other offenders returned to custody not for having committed a new offence but for having violated a condition of their supervision, such as drinking or using drugs (Porporino & Motiuk, 1995). Other offenders are most often returned only after committing a new crime. Porporino and Motiuk (1995) note that a bias appears to be working against mentally disordered offenders; they are handled so cautiously despite being less likely to reoffend than the non–mentally disordered offenders in the sample.

What about women offenders with mental disorders? One study compared the rate of recidivism for women offenders with mental disorders to that for women offenders without such disorders (Blanchette & Motiuk, 1996). These researchers found no difference in the recidivism rates between these two groups: both groups committed new offences at the same rate. The women with mental disorders were, however, more often returned to custody for violating the conditions of their release, just as in the mixed sample previously discussed. One important difference between this sample and the previous one is that the mentally disordered women offenders were not matched with the other women offenders for criminal history. The mentally disordered women offenders had more prior violent offences on their record, suggesting that they may have been at higher risk than the non–mentally disordered women. This finding may explain why their recidivism rate was not lower than that of the non–mentally disordered offenders as was found in the mixed sample previously discussed. If a less risky sample of mentally disordered women had been used, they may have recidivated at a lower rate than the non–mentally disordered women just as was found in the mixed sample.

In terms of determining predictors of recidivism, Blanchette and Motiuk (1996) found that, similar to the findings in the mixed sample, the same predictors that work for other populations are relevant for women with mental disorders (for example, criminal history and early onset of criminality).

The Assessment of Mentally Disordered Offenders

The assessment of mental disorders in prison is similar to assessments in other settings that deal with people with mental health problems. The main approaches to assessing mental disorders are interviews, structured interviews, paper and pencil tests, and behavioural observations. Each approach has strengths and weaknesses, and sometimes more than one method is used to maximize the collection of relevant information. A brief discussion of each approach follows.

Interviews

The most commonly used method of assessing mental disorders is for the clinician to interview the woman. Typically, a psychosocial interview is used to examine many facets of the woman's life. The clinician must first rule out the possibility that any current mental health problems are caused by a physical problem or by alcohol or drug use, so questions are asked pertaining to these two areas. Often an interview will begin with background information from childhood. Early childhood illnesses, injuries, and physical or emotional abuse may be relevant to current problems. For example, childhood sexual abuse may lead to low self-esteem and depression or to substance abuse, a behaviour used to try to deal with the emotional pain. Lingering symptoms of post-traumatic stress disorder may also persist into adulthood.

A thorough history will be taken of the present symptoms that brought the client to the clinician. The clinician needs to determine when these symptoms started, the nature of the woman's life at that time, and the seriousness of the symptoms in terms of their impact on her life. Is she able to do the things that she normally does? Are the symptoms keeping her from doing things that she typically enjoys?

A family history is usually included in a psychosocial interview. Such information typically includes the makeup of the family in which the woman was raised and some details of her childhood and adolescence. Another important area of family functioning is the extent of support that family members can provide, which can range from being extremely helpful to being non-existent to being just another stressor in the life of the woman. It is important for the clinician to know whether family members are available to provide assistance if needed.

Other areas that may be discussed in the interview are related to employment, finances, and social and recreational activities. These areas may be strengths or assets in the woman's life or further stressors that need to be dealt with. For example, if the woman is well educated, has a good job, and enjoys recreational activities, these assets will help to offset stressors in other areas of her life. If, however, the woman has little education, unstable employment, and few financial resources, then these areas incur additional stress, which she may need help with.

The outcome of all of this provides the clinician with a thorough history and detailed information about the present concerns and the resources already available to assist the woman. The clinician will then be able to determine whether significant mental health problems are present and to develop a plan to work on any identified problem areas.

One shortcoming of the interview process is the issue of the reliability of the information gathered. The woman, especially during times of acute episodes of a disorder, may be unwilling or unable to provide enough information to contribute to an accurate assessment. For this reason, information is typically also collected from external sources, such as official records from hospitals or schools or from interviews with other family members.

Structured Interviews

Another type of interview is the structured interview. Here, the questions have been set in advance and are geared toward a specific goal, such as making a diagnosis. One example is the Diagnostic Interview Schedule, which was used in the research on assessing the prevalence of mental disorders in male and female federal offenders discussed earlier in this chapter (Blanchette & Motiuk, 1996; Motiuk & Porporino, 1992). The answers provided by the participants determine whether a diagnosis is to be made and the nature of that diagnosis.

Another more commonly used structured interview is the Structured Clinical Interview for the DSM-IV, also referred to as the SCID (First, Spitzer, Gibbon, & Williams, 1997). The first author of the SCID was also the editor of the DSM-IV and therefore was thoroughly familiar with the diagnostic criteria for mental disorders. The SCID provides a systematic method of assessing the symptoms that make up the DSM-IV criteria for the various mental disorders. For example, a question that asks about hearing voices or sounds that others cannot hear addresses auditory hallucinations, one of the criteria for the diagnosis of schizophrenia. Other questions ask about moods, anxieties, and alcohol use. This structured interview then aids the clinician in making accurate psychiatric diagnoses.

Paper and Pencil Tests

Paper and pencil tests are widely used to assess all types of mental health problems. They have the advantages of being simple to administer, objective to score, and time-efficient, requiring little of the clinician's time. The results of the tests can be compared with other people's scores, thereby assisting the clinician with the diagnostic process. For example, if the woman's scores are similar to those of people who have been diagnosed with depression, then she is likely also depressed.

A variety of well-developed, standardized, comprehensive tests are available, such as the Minnesota Multiphasic Personality Inventory-2 (Butcher, Graham, Ben-Porath, Tellegen, & Dahlstrom, 1989), the Personality Assessment Inventory (Morey, 2003), and the Millon Clinical Multiaxial Inventory–III (Millon, 2006). These tests comprise questions related to symptoms associated with a wide range of mental disorders. The results from one of these tests will help determine whether a woman is experiencing symptoms severe enough to require treatment.

Other paper and pencil tests are much smaller in scale and aim to assess only one particular problem area. One example is the Beck Depression Inventory (Beck, Ward, Mendelson, Mock, & Erbaugh, 1961), a 21-item self-report scale that has been in use for decades. Extensive research has found this test to be a reliable measure of depression. The questions cover all symptoms of depression, such as feeling sad, feeling pessimistic, having suicidal thoughts, and problems with eating, sleeping, and lack of energy. This test takes only about 10 minutes to administer, so it is a quick and reliable screening tool for depression and possible suicide risk.

Because of the extent of abuse in the lives of women offenders, the traumatic effects of abuse are an area worthy of thorough assessment. One test designed for this purpose is the Trauma Symptom Inventory, developed by Briere, Elliot, Harris, and Cotman (1995). This test comprises 100 questions pertaining to trauma symptoms, such as depression, anger/irritability, anxiety, and intrusive experiences. People with histories of physical or sexual abuse score high on scales made up of these items. Therefore, women offenders who score high on this test would need further assessment and treatment.

Behavioural Observations

Another type of assessment is observing people and recording how they respond in various situations. Incarceration provides extensive opportunities for observing how a woman might interact with others, her communication style, and her activities. Such observations are a useful part of an assessment. Specific published scales of behavioural assessment may be used or the clinician may develop a scale tailored to the woman being assessed. For example, to determine whether a woman has difficulty controlling her emotions, such as anger, a checklist of her interactions with others could be devised. Staff who work closely with the woman could note any angry outbursts and the events that may have provoked her reaction. The clinician is then able to gather direct information relevant to the assessment and treatment of mental health problems.

One area in which direct observation is particularly important is the assessment of suicide potential. A woman may choose not to tell anyone that she is considering suicide. Observant staff, however, may notice changes in her behaviour, such as keeping to herself more than usual or not interacting with her usual friends or not engaging in her normal activities. Sudden changes in any areas of a woman's activities may alert staff to inquire further about her current mental state.

The object of assessment, then, is to identify and clarify problems that people are experiencing. The results of a thorough assessment will guide the direction that treatment will take. For example, if a woman is feeling low in mood, she could be clinically depressed or she might be feeling low as part of a pattern of unstable emotions that comprise borderline personality disorder. For each of these problems, a very different treatment approach would be used. Therefore the clinician needs to be able to fully understand the nature of the presenting problems, a process that is best achieved by a thorough assessment.

The Treatment of Mentally Disordered Offenders

The gold standard for treating offenders is the application of the risk-need-responsivity principles of Andrews and Bonta (2006). The *risk principle* states that criminal behaviour can be predicted and treatment services need to be matched to the risk level of the offender; that is, an offender of higher risk would need extensive treatment, whereas a low-risk offender would need little or no intervention. The *needs principle* states that, for treatment to be effective in lowering the risk of recidivism, it must target the needs of the offender that are directly related to reoffending (that is, the criminogenic needs—the needs related to the predictors of recidivism—such as criminal attitudes). The *responsivity principle* has two facets: (1) the *general responsivity principle* states that social learning and cognitive-behavioural strategies, which have been shown to be the most powerful interventions for change, should be used; and (2) the *specific responsivity principle* states that treatment should be delivered in a way that is suited to the offender's learning style or ability. For example, an offender who is of low intelligence would need services geared to her level of understanding.

Although most of the research on these principles has involved males or mixed samples of offenders, one study examined the effectiveness of the risk principle on women offenders in Ohio (Lovins, 2007). Women who had completed an intensive treatment program were compared with those who had not. The level of risk of these women was also examined. The researchers found that the high-risk women who completed treatment were half as likely to reoffend as those who had received no treatment. Low-risk women in intensive treatment were three times more likely to reoffend than those without treatment. The author did not speculate on why the low-risk women failed to benefit from treatment; however, because these women were already of low risk, determining any measurable improvement in their risk level might have been impossible. However, this supposition does not account for why their risk level increased, as opposed to staying the same.

In terms of the needs principle, research on effective correctional treatment has shown that treatment targets must relate to offending in order to be effective (Andrews & Bonta, 2006). Such needs are called "criminogenic needs" because these needs can lead directly to offending. Substance abuse is one of these needs, and treating this need can lead to a reduction in the risk of reoffending. A non-criminogenic need is a need that has been found in the research not to be associated with offending. That is, whether a person has such a need will have no bearing on whether the person will commit a crime. An example of a non-criminogenic need is personal distress. People who are more likely to be personally distressed are not more likely to commit a crime. Therefore, targeting personal distress will not be effective in reducing crime.

The subjects of most of this research, however, have been men. What about women? Hollin and Palmer (2006) conducted a review of the literature on the criminogenic needs of women offenders in a number of countries, including Canada. They found a large overlap between the needs of men and women. For example, male and female offenders both have problems with substance abuse, lack of education, lack of employment, and financial difficulties that directly relate to their patterns of offending. The researchers did not find any women-specific needs that related directly to offending. When they examined the issue of childhood abuse, which is a frequent occurrence among women offenders, they proposed a model of offending whereby such abuse is indirectly related to offending: abuse leads to personal problems, which leads to substance abuse and subsequently to offending. Therefore, for women offenders, a more complicated association may exist between childhood abuse and offending.

Women Offenders with Mental Health Problems

Mental illness is directly related to the criminal behaviour of a small proportion of women offenders. Targeting the symptoms of their illness is, therefore, targeting their criminogenic needs. For example, if a woman experienced delusions that a neighbour was the devil and believed her neighbour must be killed to protect the world, treating this delusion would reduce her risk of reoffending violently. If a woman is so depressed she believes the world is too awful a place for her child to live in and wants to free her child from this torment by killing the child, then her depression is a criminogenic need.

For most offenders with mental disorders, however, their disorder is not a criminogenic need. Instead, the disorder may be viewed as a specific responsivity factor. These offenders have criminogenic needs in addition to the symptoms of their illnesses; however, their mental health symptoms may need to be treated before they can productively engage in treatment programs for their criminogenic needs. For example, a woman may be depressed and unable to concentrate on any program material yet hold beliefs that are supportive of crime, such as that it is acceptable to steal from a bank because you are not hurting anyone. For this woman, treating the depression may be viewed as a responsivity issue: the depression needs to be dealt with before she will be able to respond to treatment for her criminal beliefs.

The high rate of childhood trauma among women offenders is another area that needs to be addressed before some women can fully benefit from programs aimed at addressing criminogenic needs. Many coping strategies that these women have adopted to deal with the pain are counterproductive to their living satisfying, pro-social lives in the community. For example, these women may abuse substances, self-injure, or have trouble forming trusting, supportive relationships. They may also still be suffering from symptoms of post-traumatic stress, such as recurring thoughts about the abuse, strong emotional reactions to situations that resemble the abusive situation, and difficulty controlling their emotions, including anger.

Therefore, although treatment of criminogenic needs is of primary importance in reducing reoffending, some women offenders would benefit from treatment for their mental health needs, which may be directly related to their pattern of offending, such as in the case of delusions or hallucinations. In other cases, the needs may be indirectly related to offending, such as childhood abuse. Other mental health needs that cause personal distress, such as depression or anxiety, may interfere with treatment of their criminogenic needs. This approach is in keeping with the specific responsivity principle of offending, which advocates dealing with mental health problems to allow the offender to be more responsive to treatment for the criminogenic needs.

Types of Treatment

In general, offenders with serious mental disorders, such as Axis I disorders, are treated similarly to psychiatric patients in the community. The main symptoms of their mental illnesses are addressed through appropriate treatment. For example, a depressed offender would have her low mood targeted for treatment, whereas the treatment for a schizophrenic offender would focus on her hallucinations or delusions. The main tools of psychiatry are employed: the wide range of psychotropic medications on the market.

In addition, psychological treatments, including cognitive-behavioural approaches, may be used. Cognitive-behaviour therapy can help change some thinking patterns, including such thoughts as "I am worthless," which sustain a depressed mood. By challenging the accuracy of this thought, for example, by examining the evidence for or against the statement, the patient is encouraged to change this thought to a more useful attitude, such as "I am a worthwhile person." Such a change in thinking can affect the woman's outlook and allow for positive changes in her life.

Within the Canadian federal correctional service, an overall mental health strategy has been developed for women offenders (Laishes, 2002). The goal of the strategy is "to develop and maintain a continuum of care that addresses the varied mental health needs of women offenders in order to maximize well-being and to promote effective reintegration" (Laishes, 2002, p. 10). The strategy notes that offenders are legally entitled to treatment for mental disorders regardless of its impact on recidivism.

Within the federal correctional system, specific units called structured living environments were built to address the needs of women experiencing mental health difficulties (Sly & Taylor, 2005). Women with minimum or medium security classifications are admitted voluntarily to these residential settings for more intensive treatment. Two therapeutic approaches are used in these units: psychosocial rehabilitation (PSR) and dialectical behaviour therapy (DBT) (Linehan, 1993).

PSYCHOSOCIAL REHABILITATION

Psychosocial rehabilitation (PSR) was developed to meet the needs of people with severe psychiatric disorders, such as Axis I disorders. This approach focuses on improving skills deficits. According to Sly and Taylor (2005), "the goal of PSR is to contribute to an improved quality of life while assisting individuals to assume responsibility and function as actively and independently as possible" (p. 2). Psychosocial rehabilitation is respectful of the client and emphasizes empowerment and client choice. Women in a PSR program are assisted with identifying their needs and developing a plan to meet those needs. Long-term goals include enhancing skills and learning to function more effectively.

The PSR program was evaluated at four federal women's facilities across Canada (Sly & Taylor, 2005). Staff and offenders were surveyed to determine whether they understood the goals of PSR and whether they thought it was an effective treatment approach. The researchers found that the staff understood the goals of PSR, and the participants believed that they were making progress toward accomplishing their goals. Women enjoyed living in the structured living environment and found the staff to be helpful. The staff, however, had mixed feelings about the effectiveness of the program. Many did not believe the program goals were being met. The staff also found that the manual was complicated and difficult to follow. However, although the majority of staff believed that PSR had the potential to assist the offenders in improving their lives, they were not convinced that, in its present form, it was doing so. The researchers made several recommendations that were aimed at improving the program, such as revising the manual and increasing communication among the facilities to share successful and unsuccessful experiences with the program.

DIALECTICAL BEHAVIOUR THERAPY

Dialectical behaviour therapy (DBT) is a variant of cognitive-behaviour therapy that was designed specifically to treat people diagnosed with borderline personality disorder (Linehan, 1993). People with borderline personality disorder have difficulty regulating their emotions and have very unstable relationships due to their tendency to initially idealize people and then to become angry and disappointed in them for minor or misperceived slights. They have negative feelings about themselves and often engage in self-damaging behaviours, such as self-injury, suicide attempts, and substance abuse.

The term *dialectic* refers to a logical examination of ideas, often through questions and answers, to determine their validity. Dialectics form the basis of the approach of this type of therapy; that is, the client's beliefs are examined logically and challenged appropriately. A hallmark of DBT is its "reconciliation of opposites in a continual process of synthesis" (Linehan, 1993, p. 19). One example is the acceptance of clients just as they are, while at the same time trying to teach them to change.

DBT has several main or core strategies, such as validating the woman's responses by acknowledging, for example, that her responses make sense in her current life. Other core strategies include skills training and problem-solving. Skills training is conducted in a group format, whereas individual psychotherapy sessions help women to integrate the new skills into their daily lives. The goals of the treatment, in the short run, are for the women to gain insight into their behaviours and to learn how to control their emotions and behaviours. In the long run, the goal is to move the women "toward more balanced and integrative responses to life situations" (Linehan, 1993, p. 124). Thus, through the acquisition of skills such as emotional control and problem-solving, the woman will be more effective in her responses and will have an increased quality of life. See box 8.6 for a description of how people learn to regulate their emotions.

A preliminary evaluation of the DBT program was conducted by Sly and Taylor (2003). Several of the staff and the women offenders in the program were interviewed to determine whether they understood the goals of DBT and whether they thought that the goals were being achieved. They found that the majority of the staff and offenders understood the goals of the program and believed it was effective. The staff thought DBT was a valuable treatment approach, and the participants reported learning positive behaviour changes in the skills

Box 8.6   Emotion Regulation Skills

People with borderline personality disorder experience strong and unstable emotions. They often feel angry, frustrated, depressed, and anxious. These strong emotions can lead to problematic behaviours, such as self-harm or substance abuse, which may be attempts to find relief from these emotions. Emotional regulation, then, is a very important component of treatment for borderline personality disorder.

The first step in learning to regulate emotions is identifying the emotion that is being experienced. Clients are taught how to pay attention and be mindful of what they are experiencing and to describe their emotional states. They learn how to increase their tolerance of distressing emotions and to use strategies to reduce negative emotions and to increase positive ones.

An example of this process is an exercise whereby the client learns to describe the feeling of sadness by many different terms, such as despair, grief, unhappiness, etc. Next, the client examines events that may have prompted the state of sadness. Perhaps not getting something that she wanted or being separated from a loved one precipitated the sadness. The client's beliefs behind the precipitating event are then interpreted; for example, perhaps she is sad after not getting something that she wanted because she believes she will not get what she wants or needs in life. Perhaps she is sad about being separated from someone she loves because she believes that the separation will last for a long time or forever. These beliefs can be examined and confronted in order to ascertain their validity. Lastly, positive experiences need to be built into the clients' lives. They learn how to focus on doing more pleasant things that bring them happiness. In this way, by learning how to manage negative emotional states and increasing the number of positive ones, they are better equipped to control their emotions and lead a more self-directed satisfying life.

Source: Linehan, M.M. (1993). *Cognitive-behavioral treatment of borderline personality disorder*. New York: Guilford Press.

training sessions. The researchers made several recommendations to improve the delivery of the program, such as simplifying the language used in the program so that the participants could more readily understand it. Currently, a quantitative evaluation of the program is under way. The preliminary findings are indicative of changes on the test scores from before and after the completion of the program (K. Blanchette, personal communication, November 7, 2007). Whether these changes are associated with changes in the offender's behaviour, such as being involved in institutional incidents, is yet to be determined.

Summary

Women offenders, as a group, have an increased incidence of mental disorders compared with male offenders and women in the community. Compared with male offenders, women offenders have higher rates of all mental disorders except for antisocial personality disorder. Compared with community women, women offenders have higher rates of all types of mental disorders. They particularly stand out in their abuse of alcohol and drugs as compared with community women.

One area of significance in the histories of women offenders is that of physical and sexual abuse. Compared with women in the community, women offenders have experienced both types of abuse at a much higher rate. Compared with male offenders, women offenders not only have a higher rate of abuse but also have experienced more severe abuse over a longer period of time.

The abuse that many women offenders have experienced as children and adults contributes to the emotional difficulties they face while incarcerated. They are dealing with issues of betrayal and abandonment and the emotional pain of past histories of physical and sexual abuse. These experiences are not easily overcome; they may lead to lasting difficulties with moods, self-image, and anger management. The mental health symptoms that women offenders subsequently exhibit, such as self-injury and substance abuse, may be coping strategies they engage in to find relief.

A smaller group of women suffer from problems such as schizophrenia and mental retardation, which are more likely due to their own physiological or biological makeup. For a number of reasons, these women have fallen into the criminal justice system instead of the mental health system.

Compared with other women, women with mental illnesses have a higher rate of involvement in criminal activity. Substance abuse, however, plays a key role in their violent or criminal behaviour. Compared with other women offenders, women offenders with mental illnesses are at no higher risk to reoffend.

Women offenders with mental health problems pose many challenges for the criminal justice system. One such challenge is the appropriate assessment and treatment of their problems. Much of this work is in its infancy and draws on the assessments and treatments that work for male offenders and for women in the community. Initial steps have been taken to evaluate the programs and services that are in place. Further work is needed to ensure that the needs of these women offenders are being best met to humanely address their mental health issues and to assist them to safely reintegrate and remain in the community.

Discussion Questions

1. Christina and Emily are discussing the issue of criminal behaviour and mental health. Christina says that people with mental health problems are more dangerous and more likely to engage in criminal activity than other people. Emily adamantly denies this. Where does the truth lie? Explain.

2. According to Penrose's law, what would you expect to happen if more resources were provided for mental health services in this country? Why?

3. Should women offenders with serious mental disorders be treated in the prison system or in the mental health system? Explain your answer.

4. You are asked for your opinion about a woman offender who is creating problems in the institution. She is often upset—for example, yelling at staff or crying and slashing herself. Several therapists have tried to help her to understand her problems with the hope that this understanding will lead to changes in her behaviour. However, she keeps "firing" them for not being there for her—that is, for not always being able to see her immediately and not always agreeing with her. What do you think may be going on with her? What possible approach within the prison system might be helpful for her?

Suggested Readings

Blanchette, K., & Brown, S.L. (2006). *The assessment and treatment of women offenders.* West Sussex, UK: John Wiley & Sons.

Bonta, J., Law, M., & Hanson, K. (1998). The prediction of criminal and violent recidivism among mentally disordered offenders: A meta-analysis. *Psychological Bulletin, 123*(2), 123–142.

Ménard, J. (Producer), Turgeon, J. (Producer), & Cadieux, M. (Writer/Director). (2003). *Sentenced to life* [Motion picture]. Canada: National Film Board.

Online Resources

1. *Out of the Shadows at Last: Transforming Mental Health, Mental Illness and Addiction Services in Canada* (the Kirby report): www.parl.gc.ca/39/1/parlbus/commbus/senate/com-e/soci-e/rep-e/rep02may06-e.htm
2. *The 2002 Mental Health Strategy for Women Offenders*: www.csc-scc.gc.ca/text/prgrm/fsw/mhealth/toc-eng.shtml

References

American Psychiatric Association. (2000). *Diagnostic and statistical manual of mental disorders* (4th ed.): *Text revision.* Arlington, VA: Author.

Andrews, D.A., & Bonta, J. (2006). *The psychology of criminal conduct* (4th ed.). Cincinnati: LexisNexis/Anderson.

Beck, A.T., Ward, C.H., Mendelson, M., Mock, J., & Erbaugh, J. (1961). An inventory for measuring depression. *Archives of General Psychiatry, 4,* 561–571.

Blanchette, K., & Brown, S.L. (2006). *The assessment and treatment of women offenders.* West Sussex, UK: John Wiley & Sons.

Blanchette, K., & Motiuk, L. (1996). *Female offenders with and without major mental health problems: A comparative investigation* (Research Report no. R-6). Ottawa: Research Branch, Correctional Service of Canada.

Bland, R.C., Orn, H., & Newman, S.C. (1988). Lifetime prevalence of psychiatric disorders in Edmonton. *Acta Psychiatrica Scandinavica, 77*(Suppl. 338), 24–32.

Bloom, J., & Wilson, W.H. (2000). Offenders with schizophrenia. In S. Hodgins & R. Müller-Isberner (Eds.), *Violence, crime and mentally disordered offenders: Concepts and methods for effective treatment and prevention* (pp. 113–130). West Sussex, UK: John Wiley & Sons.

Boe, R., & Vuong, B. (2002). Mental health trends among federal inmates. *Forum on Corrections Research, 14*(2), 6–9.

Bonta, J., Law, M., & Hanson, K. (1998). The prediction of criminal and violent recidivism among mentally disordered offenders: A meta-analysis. *Psychological Bulletin, 123*(2), 123–142.

Bonta, J., Pang, B., & Wallace-Capretta, S. (1995). Predictors of recidivism among incarcerated female offenders. *The Prison Journal, 75*, 277–294.

Briere, J., Elliot, D., Harris, K., & Cotman, A. (1995). Trauma symptom inventory: Psychometrics and association with childhood and adult victimization in clinical samples. *Journal of Interpersonal Violence, 104*, 387–401.

Brink, J.H., Doherty, D., & Boer, A. (2001). Mental disorder in federal offenders: A Canadian prevalence study. *International Journal of Law and Psychiatry, 24*, 339–356.

Butcher, J.N., Graham, J.R., Ben-Porath, Y.S., Tellegen, A., & Dahlstrom, W.G. (1989). *MMPI-2™ (Minnesota Multiphasic Personality Inventory-2™).* Minneapolis: University of Minnesota Press.

Canada, Standing Senate Committee on Social Affairs, Science and Technology. (2004). *Mental health, mental illness and addiction: Overview of policies and programs in Canada* (Interim report). Ottawa: The committee.

Choe, J.Y., Teplin, L.A., & Abram, K.M. (2008). Perpetration of violence, violent victimization, and severe mental illness: Balancing public health concerns. *Psychiatric Services, 59*, 153–164.

Cotton, D. (2004). The attitudes of Canadian police officers toward the mentally ill. *International Journal of Law and Psychiatry, 27*, 135–146.

Engel, R.S., & Silver, E. (2001). Policing mentally disordered suspects: A reexamination of the criminalization hypothesis. *Criminology, 39*, 225–252.

Erickson, S.K., Rosenheck, R.A., Trestman, R.L., Ford, J.D., & Desai, R.A. (2008). Risk of incarceration between cohorts of veterans with and without mental illness discharged from inpatient units. *Psychiatric Services, 59*, 178–183.

Finn, A., Trevethan, S., Carrière, G., & Kowalski, M. (1999). *Female inmates, Aboriginal inmates and inmates serving life sentences: A one day snapshot. Juristat, 19*(5), 1–14.

First, M.B., Spitzer, R.L, Gibbon, M., & Williams, J.B.W. (1997). *Structured clinical interview for DSM-IV personality disorders, (SCID-II).* Washington, DC: American Psychiatric Press.

Gray, J.E., Shone, M.A., & Liddle, P.F. (2000). *Canadian mental health law and policy.* Toronto: Butterworths.

A health care needs assessment of federal inmates in Canada. (2004). *Canadian Journal of Public Health, 95*(Suppl. 1), S1–S63.

Heney, J. (1990). *Report on self-injurious behaviour in the Kingston Prison for Women.* Ottawa: Correctional Service of Canada.

Hodgins, S. (1998). Epidemiological investigations of the associations between major mental disorders and crime: Methodological limitations and validity of conclusions. *Social Psychiatry & Psychiatric Epidemiology, 33*, S29–S37.

Hollin, C.R., & Palmer, E.J. (2006). Criminogenic need and women offenders: A critique of the literature. *Legal and Criminological Psychology, 11*, 179–195.

Kendall, K. (1999). Criminal lunatic women in 19th century Canada. *Forum on Corrections Research, 11*(3), 46–49.

Kendall, K. (2000). Psy-ence Fiction: Inventing the mentally-disordered female prisoner. In K. Hannah-Moffat & M. Shaw (Eds.), *An ideal prison? Critical essays of women's imprisonment in Canada* (pp. 83–93). Halifax: Fernwood.

Kendall, K., & Pollack, S. (2005). Taming the shrew: Regulating prisoners through women-centered mental health programming. *Critical Criminology, 13,* 71–87.

Laishes, J. (2002). *The 2002 mental health strategy for women offenders.* Ottawa: Correctional Service of Canada.

Linehan, M.M. (1993). *Cognitive-behavioral treatment of borderline personality disorder.* New York: Guilford Press.

Lovins, L. (2007, June). *Application of the risk principle to female offenders.* Poster presentation at the Canadian Psychological Association Conference, Ottawa.

McKenzie, C. (2003, December 4). Alice doesn't want to live here anymore. *Hour.* Retrieved from www.hour.ca/news/news.aspx?iIDArticle=336.

Ménard, J. (Producer), Turgeon, J. (Producer), & Cadieux, M. (Writer/Director). (2003). *Sentenced to life* [Motion picture]. Canada: National Film Board.

Messina, N., Grella, C., Burdon, W., & Prendergast, M. (2007). Childhood adverse events and current drug-dependent prisoners. *Criminal Justice and Behavior, 34,* 1385–1401.

Millon, T. (2006). *Millon Clinical Multiaxial Inventory–III (MCMI–III) manual* (3rd ed.). Minneapolis, MN: Pearson Assessments.

Mom who smothered daughter convicted. (2003, November 17). *Brantford Expositor,* p. A7.

Morey, L. (2003). Essentials of PAI assessment. Hoboken, NJ: John Wiley & Sons.

Motiuk, L., & Porporino, F.J. (1992). *The prevalence, nature and severity of mental health problems among federal male inmates in Canadian penitentiaries.* Ottawa: Correctional Service of Canada.

Pollack, S. (n.d.). *Results of CAEFS survey: Mental health service—Elizabeth Fry Societies.* Retrieved from www.elizabethfry.ca.

Porporino, F., & Motiuk, L.L. (1995). The prison careers of mentally disordered offenders. *International Journal of Law and Psychiatry, 18,* 29–44.

Shaw, M. (1994). *Ontario women in conflict with the law: A survey of women in institutions and under community supervision.* Ontario: Ministry of the Solicitor General and Correctional Service of Canada.

Sly, A., & Taylor, K. (2003). *Preliminary evaluation of dialectical behavior therapy within a women's structured living environment* (User Report no. 2003, R-145). Ottawa: Research Branch, Correctional Service of Canada.

Sly, A., & Taylor, K. (2005). *Evaluation of psychosocial rehabilitation within the women's structured living environments* (User Report no. 2005, R-163). Ottawa: Research Branch, Correctional Service of Canada.

Solyom, C. (2003, November 11). Jury to weigh child-killer's motives. *Montreal Gazette*. Retrieved from http://forthesakeofthechildren.blog-city.com/nov_11_2003_lisa _samberg_jury_to_weigh_childkillers_motives.htm.

Statistics Canada. (2007). *Adult correctional services, admissions to provincial, territorial and federal programs, annual 1978–2004* [CANSIM table 251-0001]. Available from http://estat.statcan.ca.

Steadman, H.J., Mulvey, E.P., Monahan, J., Robbins, P.C., Appelbaum, P.S., Grisso, T., et al. (1998). Violence by people discharged from acute psychiatric inpatient facilities and by others in the same neighborhoods. *Archives of General Psychiatry, 55*, 393–401.

Torrey, E.F., Stanley, J., Monahan, J., & Steadman, H.J. (2008). The MacArthur violence risk assessment: Two views ten years after its initial publication. *Psychiatric Services, 59*, 147–152.

US Office of the Surgeon General. (1999). *Mental health: A report of the Surgeon General*. Washington, DC: Department of Health and Human Services. Retrieved from www.surgeongeneral.gov.

Villeneuve, D.B., & Quinsey, V.L. (1995). Predictors of general and violent recidivism among mentally disordered inmates. *Criminal Justice and Behavior, 22*, 397–410.

Wallace, C., Mullen, P.E., & Burgess, P. (2004). Criminal offending in schizophrenia over a 25-year period marked by deinstitutionalization and increasing prevalence of comorbid substance use disorders. *American Journal of Psychiatry, 161*, 716–727.

Webster, C.D., & Hucker, S. (2007). *Violence risk: Assessment and management*. Toronto: John Wiley and Sons.

CHAPTER 9

Female Youth in Conflict with the Law

Shahid Alvi

Introduction

Youth offending in Canada is committed by both males and females. Nevertheless, according to the Canadian Centre for Justice Statistics, the overall rate of male youth offending is approximately three to four times that of young females, and the overall patterns and nature of female youth offending are consistently different from those of young males (Fitzgerald, 2003; Kong & AuCoin, 2008). Moreover, although females comprise approximately one-fifth of all young offenders charged by police, since the mid-1980s, more females have been charged with violent offences; however, as we will see, this trend has more to do with the perception that young women are becoming more violent, not the reality (DeKeseredy, 2000; Department of Justice Canada, 2005).

Because young males are more likely to offend than young females, more research and criminal justice attention has been paid to male youth offending. Deeply entrenched cultural expectations regarding girls' and boys' behaviours have played a significant role in limiting what we know about female youth offending (Corrado, Odgers, & Cohen, 2000). It is well known, for example, that social norms regarding normal behaviour for boys differ from those that girls are expected to conform to. Girls are expected to be less aggressive, and are socialized to be so, whereas aggressive or confrontational behaviours in young males are normalized as "boys being boys." Thus, when young females come into conflict with the law, they are often seen as more deviant than males because they are presumed to be acting out of the roles transmitted to them and reproduced by socialization processes (Chesney-Lind & Okamoto, 2001). Moreover, in criminology, female offending has historically been seen as a minor subset of male offending, not as a phenomenon that needs to be theorized in its own right as different from male crime (Belknap & Holsinger, 2006; Chesney-Lind, 2006).

My approach in this chapter is to provide a *contextualized* discussion of female youth offenders. In other words, my contention is that we cannot understand young female offenders (or offenders in general) unless we understand the contours and consequences of the many different ways in which people interact with their social, economic, and political environments. Furthermore, unless we take a serious interest in the ways that factors such as social class, ethnicity, and gender serve to condition and set limits on young people's behaviour, it is impossible to fully appreciate the nature of youth offending and to therefore provide appropriate criminal justice or other responses to offending.

In this chapter, we will briefly review the history of criminal justice responses to young offenders, examine the extent and contours of female youth offending in Canada, and consider the current criminal justice response to offending. We will begin by examining what we know historically about female youth in conflict with the law.

A Brief History of the Criminal Justice Response to Female and Male Offending[1]

Although very little is known about juvenile offending during the pioneer settlement era in Canada, much less is known about girl offending. Most historical commentaries in Canada in this time frame (and even later) focus on youth under the homogeneous category of *children*, comprising both males and females, with cursory attention paid to the differences between male and female offending. This focus is not surprising, given that scholarly efforts to render female delinquency visible have occurred only relatively recently (Chesney-Lind, 2001). We do know, however, that most transgressions committed by young males and females during the pioneer settlement era were relatively minor. According to Carrigan (1998), the bulk of wrongdoing consisted of "violations of local ordinances, nuisance offences, vandalism, petty theft, and breaches of the moral laws" (p. 25). Although boys were more likely to offend than girls, certain offences, such as prostitution, abortion, and infanticide, were more likely to be committed by girls.

At this point in Canada's history, young people were viewed as miniature adults. Working-class children toiled alongside adults and were expected to demonstrate the same sense of morality and duty as adults. Not surprisingly, when children were convicted of a crime, they were subject to the same set of laws and often the same dispositions, including incarceration alongside grown-ups.

Legislation focused specifically on youth in Canada began with the passing in 1857 of *An Act for the More Speedy Trial and Punishment of Juvenile Offenders*. This Act was designed to accelerate trial processes and to reduce the possibility of juvenile delinquents serving long jail sentences prior to trial. Juvenile delinquents were defined as offenders under the age of 16, and their sentencing consisted of imprisonment in a common jail or confinement in a correctional house, either with or without hard labour, for no longer than three months, or a fine not to exceed five pounds. The accused could also be ordered to restore stolen property or pay the equivalent compensation (Gagnon, 1984, pp. 21–22).

During the mid-1900s, a shift in the Canadian economy from an agricultural to an industrial base triggered new demands for industrial labourers, which in turn was fuelled by the arrival of immigrant children from Europe. Many of these poor and neglected children were labelled as tramps and drifters with emotional and moral problems, and they were often singled out as those responsible for the bulk of what was considered youth crime (Alvi, 2000; Carrigan, 1998). Furthermore, the so-called failures were seen by authorities as emanating from the failure of parents and families to adequately socialize and control their children. Gradually, the alleged malfunctioning of families stimulated a trend toward the use of other social institutions to control and discipline young people. Compulsory schooling began to be seen as the mechanism by which children could be trained for the new demands of the industrial economy and could be controlled and socialized to behave appropriately (Barrett & McIntosh, 1982).

In the justice system, a new doctrine of *parens patriae* emerged, encouraging the idea that children in conflict with the law required the state to act as a "kindly parent" that would take on the responsibilities of the "failed family" (Bala, 1997). Continuing assumptions were that lower-class families and their children were primarily to blame for youth deviance, and that youth who had failed to comply with the law were to be held to a set of middle-class standards emphasizing proper care and nurturance, love, discipline, and education so that they could rise above their station in life. Coupled with this development was the sense that modern societies needed to soften their response to youth crime, a view championed notably by the child-saving movement (Platt, 1977). A new legal approach to youth offending was thought to be necessary; in 1908, Parliament passed the *Juvenile Delinquents Act* (JDA).

Briefly, section 38 of the JDA instructed judges to treat the child offender as a "misdirected and misguided" individual (not a criminal) who required appropriate "aid, encouragement, help and assistance." In addition to focusing on proper judicial process, the Act represented a social welfare approach to youth in conflict with the law, emphasizing the best interests of the child. Despite this new philosophy, however, children over the age of 14 could still be transferred to adult court at the discretion of the juvenile court judge if they had been accused of serious crimes such as murder or treason.

Sentencing under the JDA consisted of a range of dispositions, including a fine not to exceed $25, probation, placement in a foster home or in Children's Aid, or commitment to an industrial school (see, Alvi, 2000, for a detailed discussion).

Although the JDA was a positive development because it focused on children's needs, not on bad children, problems with the legislation persisted. The idea of "the best interests of the child" could be interpreted in very different ways by judges and police, and a great deal of arbitrariness was evident across provinces with respect to age limits, legal representation, and sentencing. Due process was inconsistently applied across jurisdictions, and considerable class and gender bias had been built into the Act. For instance, immigrant and working-class children tended to receive harsher sentences compared with their middle-class counterparts, who were often released to their parents. In addition, girls, but not boys, could be arrested for the nebulous offence of "sexual immorality," a status offence usually applied to socially disadvantaged girls (Bala, 1997). Indeed, in this era, most criminal justice practitioners equated young female criminality with sexual delinquency and with women's increasing emancipation through access to work, wider contact with men, and wider opportunities for personal expression (Tanner, 1996, p. 191). Convicted female youth were more likely to be in custody, were subject to longer stays than males for similar offences, and were provided with little education other than training for domestic duties (Reitsma-Street, 1993; West,

1984). Despite these and other problems with the Act, for 75 years the JDA continued to provide the legal framework within which young offenders would be tried and sentenced.

In the 1950s and 60s, in the context of tremendous social and cultural changes in Canada and elsewhere, shifting perceptions about the role of youth in society stimulated debate over the utility of the JDA. The passing, in 1982, of the *Canadian Charter of Rights and Freedoms* guaranteed Canadians a range of legal rights, such as equal treatment before the law, the right to legal counsel, and the right not to be subjected to cruel or unusual punishment. Many policy-makers then realized that the JDA would probably not withstand legal challenges under the Charter (Hylton, 1994). In 1965, a federal committee tasked with studying the problem of the legal response to juvenile crime concluded that the legislation needed to be changed, and in 1984, the *Young Offenders Act* (YOA) was passed into law (see box 9.1).

Box 9.1   The Central Principles of the Young Offenders Act as Outlined in Section 3

3. (1) It is hereby recognized and declared that

(a) crime prevention is essential to the long-term protection of society and requires addressing the underlying causes of crime by young persons and developing multi-disciplinary approaches to identifying and effectively responding to children and young persons at risk of committing offending behaviour in the future;

(a.1) while young persons should not in all instances be held accountable in the same manner or suffer the same consequences for their behaviour as adults, young persons who commit offences should nonetheless bear responsibility for their contraventions;

(b) society must, although it has the responsibility to take reasonable measures to prevent criminal conduct by young persons, be afforded the necessary protection from illegal behaviour;

(c) young persons who commit offences require supervision, discipline and control, but, because of their state of dependency and level of development and maturity, they also have special needs and require guidance and assistance;

(c.1) the protection of society, which is a primary objective of the criminal law applicable to youth, is best served by rehabilitation, wherever possible, of young persons who commit offences, and rehabilitation is best achieved by addressing the needs and circumstances of a young person that are relevant to the young person's offending behaviour;

(d) where it is not inconsistent with the protection of society, taking no measures or taking measures other than judicial proceedings under this Act should be considered for dealing with young persons who have committed offences;

(e) young persons have rights and freedoms in their own right, including those stated in the *Canadian Charter of Rights and Freedoms* or in the *Canadian Bill of Rights*, and in particular a right to be heard in the course of, and to participate in, the processes that lead to decisions that affect them, and young persons should have special guarantees of their rights and freedoms;

(f) in the application of this Act, the rights and freedoms of young persons include a right to the least possible interference with freedom that is consistent with the protection of society, having regard to the needs of young persons and the interests of their families;

(g) young persons have the right, in every instance where they have rights or freedoms that may be affected by this Act, to be informed as to what those rights and freedoms are; and

(h) parents have responsibility for the care and supervision of their children, and, for that reason, young persons should be removed from parental supervision either partly or entirely only when measures that provide for continuing parental supervision are inappropriate.

Source: *Young Offenders Act*, RSC 1985, c. Y-1.

For the first time in Canadian history, federal legislation (that is, the YOA) reflected the idea that juvenile justice should embody a balance between the rights of society (to protection from crime) and the rights of the individual (to fair, equitable, and consistent justice). The Act emphasized personal responsibility, but did not abrogate parents of their responsibilities for proper supervision, control, and socialization of children. Importantly, the YOA also stepped away from the notion of young offenders as misguided children and toward the idea that young offenders are, indeed, special kinds of criminals.

A special section of the Act (section 4) addressed "Alternative Measures," a set of principles maintaining that, whenever possible, youth should be diverted from the criminal justice system because of its stigmatizing effects. Those deemed eligible to participate in Alternative Measures might be encouraged to reconcile with their victims or to provide restitution, an apology, or service to the community. Wardell (1986) argues that although Alternative Measures looked like a good idea on paper, more likely the government saw them as a way to reduce the cost of youth justice because the responsibility for the transgressing youth would fall to his or her community not the criminal justice system. Moreover, only about 20 percent of cases were dealt with via alternative methods, and some evidence suggests that Aboriginal and minority youth tended to be excluded from participation (Canadian Centre for Justice Statistics, 1994; Church Council on Justice and Corrections, 1996; Pleasant-Jette, 1993).

The federal government (Department of Justice Canada, 2005) pointed to three main concerns with the YOA:

First, not enough was being done to prevent troubled youth from entering a life of crime. Second, the system needed to improve the way it dealt with the most serious, violent youth: not just in terms of sentencing but also in ensuring that these youth were provided with the intensive, long-term rehabilitation that is in their and society's interest. Third, the system relied too heavily on custody as a response to the vast majority of non-violent youth when alternative, community-based approaches could do a better job of instilling social values such as responsibility and accountability, helping to right wrongs and ensuring that valuable resources are targeted where they are most needed. (p. 1)

Although the YOA was optimistically seen as a way of fixing the problems inherent in the JDA, its existence was relatively short-lived. By the late 1990s, dissatisfaction with the YOA had already resulted in numerous calls for reform. Essentially, those emphasizing the role of social issues (such as poverty, abuse, gender and class discrimination, to name a few) in the etiology of youth crime saw the YOA as a prime example of the gradual slide in Canadian society toward a law and order mentality, coupled with the decontextualization of criminal behaviour.

Although the term *law and order* has a *prima facie* inherent appeal, the content of the modern law and order efforts warrants scrutiny. In this respect, and as I have emphasized elsewhere, the modern approach to law and order essentially involves placing the emphasis for youth crime on young people's individual failings, thereby removing from analysis the role of social risks and protective factors. Moreover, modern law and order ideology assumes that we can do very little to prevent youth crime (or adult crime for that matter), and the focus, therefore, must be on managing the problem *post hoc*.

Thus, the *Young Offenders Act* was essentially a tool and administrative framework for managing young offenders, not a tool for addressing crime prevention (McGuire, 1997). Moreover, in a social environment in which the media (despite stable crime rates) happily constructed fake waves of youth crime (Sprott, 1996) and concomitant public fear about being victimized by youth superpredators, many stakeholders felt that the YOA was too soft on young offenders and that renewed calls for more stringent law and order would soon follow.

In 2003, the new and current Act governing youth crime—the *Youth Criminal Justice Act* (YCJA)—became law. The new Act, instead of being a completely different approach to the adjudication and treatment of youth offending is, I would argue, merely a continuation and indeed an intensification of the ideology of managing risky children and does not deal meaningfully with the social conditions that foster criminal behaviour. The YCJA represents the political desire to be all things to all people because it attempts to protect the public, while stating that rehabilitation, reintegration, and alternatives to incarceration of offenders should also be of paramount concern (Barber & Doob, 2004; Doob & Cesaroni, 2004; Hartnagel, 2004; Varma & Marinos, 2000). And, although alternatives to incarceration as codified in the "Extrajudicial Measures" section of the YCJA (formerly "Alternative Measures" under the YOA) may seem progressive, it is still too early to tell whether these alternatives have been implemented equitably across ethnic, class, and gender lines and whether they will have their intended effect. Indeed, as some writers have argued, it may be more accurate to see the so-called progressive elements of the YCJA as part of a "responsibilization" strategy, in which young people in conflict with the law must choose to cooperate and partner with communities to successfully reintegrate themselves into society (Garland, 2000; Mann, Senn, Girard, & Ackbar, 2007). Such a strategy, then, tends to place the onus for change squarely on the shoulders of individual youth, while glossing over or completely overlooking the social forces and conditions that generate crime.

The YCJA explicitly declares that the objectives of the youth justice system are to *prevent* crime, rehabilitate and reintegrate offenders, and hold young offenders accountable for their actions by enforcing meaningful consequences, while simultaneously understanding that young people lack the maturity of adults and that a youth's rights should be respected (Department of Justice Canada, 2007). Thus, the underlying principle of the YCJA can be captured in the phrase (used first in the United Kingdom) "tough on crime, tough on the causes of crime."

The extent to which real efforts are being made to deal meaningfully with the social causes of youth criminality remains to be seen. Recent political statements seem to indicate that in the near future more emphasis will be on strengthening the criminal justice system's response to youth crime, than on fortifying families, children, and the social conditions in which they live (see box 9.2), despite the difficulties associated with neighbourhood disorganization and government recognition that the most serious young offenders come from disrupted homes characterized by violence, physical and sexual abuse, poverty, substance abuse, attachment disorders, and poor housing. Furthermore, despite political promises nearly 20 years ago to eliminate child poverty by the year 2000, today nearly one in six Canadian children lives in poverty (Campaign 2000, 2005), youth suicide rates have risen (BC Partners for Mental Health and Addictions Information, 2006), and good evidence suggests that a large majority of incarcerated youth suffer from mental health problems (Odgers, Burnette, Chauhan, Moretti, & Reppucci, 2005).

Box 9.2   Tory Bill Proposes Violent Youth Be Tried as Adults

If the Conservative government has its way, more young offenders would be tried as adults ...

The government introduced their Crime Bill by starting off with proposed changes to the Youth Criminal Justice Act.

These are the key proponents of their proposal:

- Tougher sentences
- Allowing for pre-trial detention
- Allow courts to consider deterrence and denunciation as objectives of youth sentences

Justice Minister Rob Nicholson said young offenders need to be held accountable when they commit violent crimes.

"These amendments to the Youth Criminal Justice Act are intended to help hold young lawbreakers accountable to their victims and their community, and instill within them a sense of responsibility for their delinquent or criminal behaviour," he said.

The minister also said the new legislation would be tougher on bail conditions for repeat offenders or youth accused of committing violent crimes.

Nicholson also said there will be a more comprehensive review of the Youth Criminal Justice Act next year.

Critics were hesitant to applaud the move.

Yvon Godin, the NDP whip, called the move "smoke and mirrors" on CTV's *Mike Duffy Live*.

"If a youth is dangerous to the people, the judge already has that power. This bill won't change anything," he told the show's host Mike Duffy Monday.

However, Jay Hill, the Conservative Party whip, said a recent commission in Nova Scotia found that law officials feel like they do not have enough power when it comes to young offenders.

"In the opinion of the inquiry, judges do not have sufficient power to ensure proper detention of a violent youth if he does pose a threat to others," he told Duffy.

Liberal whip Karen Redman said the party agrees the Act needs to be re-examined but that they would want to study the Conservative proposal further.

"We certainly do agree that repeat violent offenders need to be looked at," she said.

"A lot of these recommendations seem to be consistent with the report that came out of Nova Scotia," she continued. "We've said all along we're very supportive of that but we do want to make sure that the principles of the Youth Criminal Justice bill are not undermined."

Source: Tory bill proposes violent youth be tried as adults. (2007, November 19). *CTV.ca News*. Retrieved from www.ctv.ca. Reprinted by permission of CTVglobemedia.

This brief history of youth crime legislation points to a gradual shift from welfare models of youth criminal justice, in which young people's social and economic needs are rightly seen as the primary focus in dealing with youth criminality, toward a law and order approach that focuses on individual traits, behaviours, and responsibilities, not on social factors. This shift has been conditioned by changing perceptions of what it means to be a young person in Canadian society, and only very recently by what it means to be a young *female* in our society.

Readers may have noticed that no attempts were made within the first two legislative frameworks to acknowledge and address how gender (or ethnicity and class) shapes both the level and content of youth crime. In contrast, as Mann and her colleagues (2007) point out, the YCJA *does* mandate that criminal justice practitioners respect gender and other differences. In light of this apparent acknowledgment of the gendered nature of youth offending, let us now turn to data on the extent and nature of young women's and girls' offending in Canada compared with their male counterparts.

The Extent and Nature of Female Offending

When confronted with statistical data on particular phenomena, a good tenet of social science methodology is to ask the question "compared with what or whom?" This section provides data on the extent and nature of young female offending, but will also compare these data with data on their male counterparts. The central reason for this approach is to first highlight similarities and differences between male and female young offenders and then to point to social and policy implications for the youth criminal justice system.

The problems associated with understanding crime by using official sources of data are legion and well known. Briefly, official statistics of crime, which emanate primarily from the police and the courts, represent police or court activity, not an accurate measure of criminal acts and do not provide much detailed information on the nature of the criminal acts themselves (Alvi, 2000). Also, official crime statistics will vary greatly depending on the willingness of the public to actually report criminal victimization, on the ways in which law enforcement is practised, and on changes in legislation (Canadian Centre for Justice Statistics, 1997; Carrington & Moyer, 1994).

Consider, for example, what has happened with respect to bullying in Canadian schools, which in previous eras was considered to be a fight or disagreement but is now often interpreted as an incident of assault warranting police intervention (DeKeseredy, 2000). Similarly, problems occur with the accuracy and quality of official statistics because police apprehend individuals but do not always charge them with crimes. Indeed, according to Statistics Canada (Silver, 2007), police laid fewer formal charges against youth in 2006 compared with the years prior to implementation of the YCJA, with the exception of violent crimes, for which almost 75 percent of youth who were apprehended were formally charged.

Another problem, particularly important in relation to offending by young women, is the critical role played by the media in inflating and sensationalizing female crime. For example, although it has been well established that males are primarily responsible for the vast majority of violent crime, the media sometimes misrepresent the nature and extent of female violence, for example, by making claims that such violence has "increased by 200 percent from last year," despite the raw counts of (for example) one female who committed homicide last year, compared with three this year. Although the reported percentage increase of 200 percent in this example is mathematically correct, the misleading impression is that of a massive increase in female youth homicides, a reaction that can and often does fuel fear and hysteria among the general public, policy-makers, and others, which is simply unwarranted (Artz, Nicholson, & Rodriguez, 2005; Schissel, 1997). Feminist criminologists have now developed a large body of work locating the motives for such hysteria in women's historical and contemporary inequality with men, gender stereotyping, and racism, thereby placing female youth and adult crime in its proper context and drawing attention to the ways in which media routinely sensationalize and misrepresent female youth crime despite the vast disparity in numbers compared with their male counterparts. Thus, the fact remains that data on female youth crime should be scrutinized and interpreted carefully.

For an understanding of the nature and extent of most crimes, victimization and self-report studies of crime are widely acknowledged to be more accurate than data from official sources (Macdonald, 2002). Although few in number, and for the most part confined to studies of particular jurisdictions, victimization and self-report surveys of youth criminality across Canada show clearly that females commit different kinds of crimes than males, less frequently than males, and for different motives.

The International Youth Survey is the Canadian portion of the International Self-Reported Delinquency Study, which collected data from Europe, the United States, and Canada. The 2006 Canadian study, conducted with 3,200 young people in grades 7 to 9, found that of the boys surveyed, twice as many had committed violent acts (30 percent) compared with girls (15 percent), and boys were marginally more likely (30 percent) to report committing property offences than girls (26 percent) (Savoie, 2007). This general pattern of findings has been replicated numerous times.

Figure 9.1 presents some results of a national sample survey of Canadian youth aged 12 to 15 years, focusing on self-reported delinquency and victimization. Drawing on a sample of youth from the National Longitudinal Survey of Children and Youth (NLSCY), young people were asked to report how often they had engaged in a range of property-related offences in the past year, such as stealing something from school, damaging property, fencing stolen goods, breaking into a vehicle to steal, stealing a vehicle, or setting fire to something on purpose. They were also asked to state how many times they had participated in violent delinquency, which included fighting causing physical injuries, carrying a stick or club as a

Figure 9.1   Self-Reported Delinquent Acts Committed by Males and Females Aged Between 12 and 15 Years, 1998–99

	Males	Females	Male-to-female ratio
	Percent		
Total property-related delinquency	29.3	19.1	1.6:1
Total violent delinquency	29.2	10.1	2.9:1

Source: Adapted from Fitzgerald, R. (2003). *An examination of sex differences in delinquency* (Report no. 85-561-MIE). Ottawa: Minister of Industry, p. 11.

weapon, carrying a knife as a weapon, fighting with a weapon, threatening someone for money or property, or carrying a gun for defence.

As can be seen from figure 9.1, nearly one-third of male youth reported committing both property-related and violent delinquency, whereas far fewer females (one in five, and one in ten, respectively) reported committing the same acts. Further, and as criminological research findings have shown for a very long time, males were only about one-and-a-half times more likely than females to engage in property offences, but nearly three times more likely to commit violent acts.

Other victimization studies corroborate the patterns shown in figure 9.1. For example, a study of Alberta school youth between grades 7 and 12 found that more than one-third (36.4 percent) of males reported engaging in a moderate number (three to seven) to a high number of (more than eight) incidents of delinquency in the past year, compared with less than one-third (29.8 percent) of females (Gomes, Bertrand, Paetsch, & Hornick, 2003). When these figures were further examined for differences between males and females in relation to the *types* of crime they reported committing, the authors found that 13.2 percent of males reported engaging in property-related delinquency more than four times in the past year, compared with 7.8 percent of females. As expected, twice as many males (12 percent) as females reported engaging in violence-related delinquency over the past year.

Both of these studies also tapped into male and female youths' experiences of victimization at the hands of other youth. Here, females in the NLSCY study reported a mean victimization score of 0.57, on a scale in which 0 indicated no victimization and 12 indicated frequent victimization. Conversely, the males in the study reported a mean score of 1.18 on the same scale. As the authors of this study note, however, the NLSCY questions on victimization were non-specific, meaning the questions did not distinguish between types of victimization. Thus, although young women are much more likely than young men to be the victims of crimes such as rape or sexual assault, young men are more likely to report being injured in the context of assaults or robbery (Loeber, Kalb, & Huizinga, 2001).

Authors of a more recent victimization and self-report study of high school and street youth in Toronto found important gender differences in deviant activities (Tanner & Wortley, 2002). Figure 9.2 presents self-report data from this study on lifetime offending for male and female high school students and street youth.

Figure 9.2   Percentages of High School Students and Street Youth Reporting Selected Non-Violent and Violent Offences at Some Time in Their Life, by Sex

	High school students		Street youth	
Non-violent offences				
	Females	Males	Females	Males
Break and enter	4.4	14.4	44	57.3
Auto theft	1.9	8.2	27.6	44.2
Bike theft	3.8	21.0	26.7	56.9
Selling of illegal drugs	8.1	19.0	62.9	66.4
Vandalism/property damage	31.0	51.9	61.2	58.4
Major theft (over $50)	10.9	23.6	55.2	68.2
Violent offences				
Carrying a weapon in public	3.3	13.7	37.6	48.4
Robbery/extortion	0.6	5.5	20.7	31.1
Assault with intent to cause serious harm	1.2	6.0	23.5	27.8
Sexual assault	0.0	1.2	0.9	3.3

Source: Adapted from Tanner, J., & Wortley, S. (2002). *The Toronto youth crime and victimization survey.* Toronto: Centre of Criminology, University of Toronto, pp. 116, 127.

As shown in figure 9.2, the differences in rates of offending between males and females are again entirely expected, given the results of prior studies. Notably, however, significant differences are shown in the rates reported by street youth (male and female) compared with high school students. The gender differences within street youth persist (with the exception of vandalism or property damage), and street youth reported engaging in criminal offences to a greater extent than high school students. This finding suggests that the *social context* and conditions within which young males and females live play a significant role in the nature and level of their offending. Indeed, as Tanner and Wortley (2002) point out:

> The traditional gender gap in offending is, however, significantly diminished among street youth ... This finding suggests that the conditions of the street may have a much greater impact on overall deviance than the social conditions imposed by one's gender. (p. 110)

Thus, these data and data from numerous other studies provide ample evidence pointing both to girls' lower likelihood of committing violent and non-violent offences and to how

Figure 9.3   Male and Female Youth Aged 12 to 17 Accused of Homicide in Canada, 1974–2005

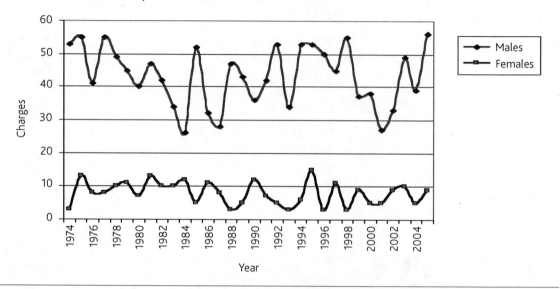

Source: Statistics Canada. (2007). *Homicide survey, victims and persons accused of homicide, by age group and sex, Canada* [CANSIM table 253-0003]. Available from http://estat.statcan.ca.

this likelihood changes when males and females encounter different social circumstances. However, although these data provide useful insights into the nature of female offending, another important question needs to be posed regarding *trends* in male and female offending in Canada. Put differently, is female youth crime on the rise, as many people seem to believe? Before answering this question, let us consider the problem of confidence in the reliability of data on youth crime. Doob and Cesaroni (2004) address the matter this way:

> We do not have definitive information about how much crime there is in a community, let alone how much youth crime. It follows that we do not have any definitive evidence as to whether youth crime has increased, decreased, or stayed the same in the past few years. (p. 118)

Despite the problem of less than perfect data, some conclusions about the nature of youth crime can be determined from official statistics on court appearances, which provide one measure of young people's involvement with the criminal justice system. By focusing on homicide statistics, we reduce the possibility of underestimating because homicide is a crime that is almost always reported. As Meloff and Silverman (1992) note, the vast majority of homicides committed by young people between 1961 and 1983 were perpetrated by boys (89 percent) as compared with girls (11 percent).

Data from the 1980s until the most recent period for which statistics are available paint a similar picture. As figure 9.3 shows, overall, the trends for both males and females who were accused of homicide over the past 30 years have essentially remained stable. Despite variations from year to year (particularly for males), these data do not support the claim of an "overall pattern in the number of young offenders charged with homicide offences"

Figure 9.4   Male and Female Youth Aged 12 to 17 Charged with Violent Crimes and Property Crimes, in Canada, 1996–2002

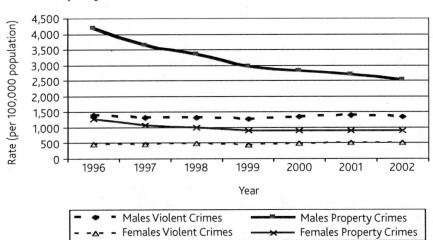

Source: Adapted from Statistics Canada. (2007). *Adults and youths charged, by sex and offence category, Canada, provinces and territories, annual* [CANSIM table 109-5009]. Available from http://estat.statcan.ca.

(Doob & Cesaroni, 2004, p. 126). One pattern we are already familiar with is obvious; namely, young males are far more likely to be accused of homicide than young females. Moreover, as noted earlier, the small *number* of females charged with homicide means that when a difference exists in the rate of homicides from one year to the next, reporting the *percentage* increase will overdramatize the reality of homicide perpetrated by females.

Figure 9.3 presents only raw counts of charges, not rates. Because rates account for changes in population, they are important if we are to gain accurate understandings of any real increase in crime rates for young offenders. Accordingly, figure 9.4 presents data on charge rates for young female and male offenders (from official data) between 1996 and 2002. From these data we can see that charges on both violent and property offences for female young offenders have essentially remained stable, whereas for young males, charges for property offences have decreased and charges for violent offences have remained stable. Some controversy surrounds the proper interpretation of these data.

Although the data suggest that rates of violent crime committed by young females have not increased (see, for example, Dell & Boe, 1998), others argue that girls (and boys) are committing more serious offences than in the past (see box 9.3). As noted earlier, this perception derives in part from the great deal of media attention accorded to the alleged increase in girls' use of violence and aggression, buttressed by sensational (but nevertheless tragic) cases such as that of Reena Virk (see box 9.4). The issue is further complicated because, in Canada, *charges* for violent offences filed against female youth have increased, although many scholars have argued that this increase in charge rates reflects bias in the justice system in which girls are increasingly being charged for minor offences at higher rates than boys (Chesney-Lind & Shelden, 1992; DeKeseredy, 2000; Sprott & Doob, 2003). Doob and Cesaroni (2004) support this theory:

Boys ... are being brought to court at a lower rate now than they had been and, as a result, can be seen as making girls look relatively worse ... Girls are not involved in as much violence as are boys, and when they are, they are disproportionately likely to be involved in *less serious* forms of violence. (p. 135, my emphasis)

In the International Youth Survey mentioned earlier, about half of the delinquent girls and boys reported that they started committing delinquent acts before the age of 12 (Savoie, 2007, p. 5). Thus, regarding the onset of delinquent behaviour, little difference separates girls from boys. However, males and females have distinct differences in terms of the pathways they take toward criminal behaviour. For example, the few young females who engage in violent behaviour tend to have been the victims themselves of sexual discrimination and physical, psychological, or emotional victimization, and these experiences are often related to the kinds of offences they commit (Belknap & Holsinger, 2006; Katz, 2000; Mallicoat, 2007).

Put differently, young females' social and emotional experiences are different in many ways from those of young males, and understanding these differences is essential in helping us to comprehend the clear gender gap in offending (Holsinger, 2000; Sharp, Brewster, &

Box 9.3   Viciousness of Youth Attacks Increases While Numbers Remain Static

The memories came rushing back for Len Libin with the news of a fatal attack on a Grade 11 student walking home from a game of pickup basketball last week.

Three years ago, Libin's son, then a 17-year-old athlete and bright student, was beaten into a coma in a random attack by two teenagers and an adult.

The victims of such attacks, says the senior Libin, "so often seem to be just good kids that you hear about that haven't really created problems and just for some reason, I don't know why, are picked."

Joel Libin survived and, despite having to go through extensive rehabilitation, has done "remarkably well," says his father.

The 17-year-old killed last week was not so fortunate.

He was buried Friday, a week after he and three Filipino friends walked past a group of Indo-Canadian teenagers who allegedly called out racial slurs.

There was a chase and the victim, apparently the slowest in the group, was caught and beaten with a blunt object. He died hours later in hospital.

The sheer viciousness of seemingly random attacks by teenagers seems to be increasing, say youth crime experts, although they maintain the actual number of youth murders has remained static.

"What strikes me as a researcher is what I say is an apparent increase in the brutality," says Ray Corrado, a criminologist at Simon Fraser University.

Sibylle Artz, an expert in youth violence at the University of Victoria, agrees.

"That seems to be a consensus among many people who deal with the youth directly," she says.

"They all tell the same story, that they have this experience of this being more brutal, more extreme," says Artz.

"When an attack is perpetrated, it doesn't stop when somebody's down."

The Vancouver teen's death comes on the heels of a Toronto 12-year-old's slaying, allegedly by three teenagers, who were charged with first-degree murder. The victim's brother is one of the accused.

In another high-profile case, three Alberta teenagers were sentenced last month to spend 60 days in custody for spiking a slushie with a toxic chemical and serving it to a fellow student.

The motive appears to have been a dislike for the victim, whom the girls suspected of hacking into one of their computers and erasing the hard drive.

Stranger killings are far more rare, says Corrado. Police aren't aware of any prior relationship between the Vancouver victim and his alleged attackers.

One of the more controversial aspects of the Filipino youth's killing is the suggestion that race was a contributing factor.

Police have hesitated to say the attack was racially motivated, although they acknowledge racial taunts were called out by members of the Indo-Canadian group before [the] Filipino teenager and his friends were chased.

The principal of the victim's school said last week she didn't view the attack as a racial incident.

"I think it was a violent incident," said Jennifer Palmer of Charles Tupper secondary school. "I think the people who perpetrated it may have behaved that way to any group of kids walking down the street."

In a narrow sense, the killing may have been racially motivated, says Corrado.

"The larger question is, would it have happened with another group of young people there that were even (Indo-Canadian)," he says, suggesting the answer would be "yes."

"The violence is what they are looking for; the particular target, they are not."

Regardless of motivation, Corrado and Artz said the number of youth killings in Canada has stayed at roughly the same level—40 to 50 a year—for the last few decades.

"While the acts are horrific, there is very little indication that youth murder has gone up," says Corrado.

"Canada's youth are still quantitatively relatively non-violent, definitely compared to the United States," he says. "We're not a society where we need to be in constant fear of young people."

The criminologist could only speculate when asked for an explanation as to why [the] brutality of random acts seems to be increasing.

"I've argued it might reflect the cultural norms of the last 15, 20 years, where video games and movies and music, even television, portray a level of violence that is really extraordinary," says Corrado.

Artz agrees. "I believe that having the imagery constantly in front of them, (communicating) that it's fine to use weapons, clubs, action-hero type behaviours.

"We are normalizing the use of violence in our efforts to sell goods."

Source: Yearwood-Lee, E. (2003, December 7). Viciousness of youth attacks increases while numbers remain static. *Canadian Press*. Available at www.thefreeradical.ca/Violent_crime _statistics_Canada.htm. Reprinted by permission of The Canadian Press.

Box 9.4   Accused in Virk Case Goes on Trial for Third Time

More than seven years after a burning cigarette was extinguished on her 14-year-old daughter's face, her beaten body tossed in a river to drown, Reena Virk's mother testified again Monday at the trial of the young woman accused of killing her.

Kelly Ellard, 22, has been tried twice previously for second-degree murder in Virk's death.

Suman Virk spat the words out again as she was asked to describe the last few hours she spent with her daughter.

The girl was troubled, in and out of foster homes, but that night she was just like a regular kid. Running to the store with her younger brother and sister to get candy. Watching TV with the family.

Virk said her daughter's name is forever associated with murder.

"I don't think anybody will ever forget the horrific details of this murder," she said outside the courthouse. "I think the name Reena Virk will always bring back the horrors of Nov. 14th, (1997), no matter when and where it's mentioned."

That was the night, Virk said, that Reena, an awkward girl with few friends, got a phone call from a girl she met at a group home. A bunch of kids were hanging out at a local school and after much hesitation, Reena decided to go meet them. She didn't know many of them.

The crowd of 14-, 15- and 16-year-olds were getting rowdy, drinking, smoking pot in a field and shattering a window at the school.

Crown prosecutor Catherine Murray said witnesses will testify that a group of eight girls went under the Craigflower Bridge with Reena and began beating her.

"You will hear that Reena was punched and kicked repeatedly. You'll hear she was then left sitting in the mud at the bottom of the stairs, slumped over, injured, crying and bleeding from the face."

Murray alleged that Reena pulled herself up the stairs and managed to make it across the bridge and that Kelly Ellard, and the key witness against her, Warren Glowatski, followed.

"Three people crossed the Craigflower Bridge that night, only two came back," Murray said.

Glowatski is serving time for his role in Virk's death.

Murray said Glowatski will testify that Ellard forced Virk to take off her jacket and her shoes. Glowatski will say that the two began to punch and kick the injured girl, Murray said, and that each grabbed one of Reena's legs.

Glowatski stopped as Ellard pulled Reena into the water, Murray said.

Reena Virk's body was pulled out of the Gorge waterway a week later.

During that week, Murray said, witnesses will testify that Ellard bragged at school about what she had done to Reena.

"Kelly Ellard told them she killed Reena. We say that the things Kelly Ellard told people reveal a knowledge only a murderer, the murderer, would have."

Ellard's lawyer, Peter Wilson, asked the jurors if they had ever been the subject of a nasty rumour, and how awful it felt.

"Have you ever noticed how rumours almost seem to fuel themselves? They build up such steam that they can't be stopped," he said.

"Most of the people involved were young. That means they were impressionable, as we all were. As the witnesses testify, take note of the difference between real evidence and recollection."

The trial is expected to last three weeks.

Source: Accused in Virk case goes on trial for 3rd time. (2005, February 22). *CTV.ca News*. Retrieved from www.ctv.ca. Reprinted by permission of The Canadian Press.

Love, 2005). Although male young offenders suffer what Belknap and Holsinger (2006) refer to as "alarmingly high" levels of physical, emotional, and verbal abuse (p. 65) and in many cases have suffered traumatic experiences with parents or guardians, most studies demonstrate that female young offenders have experienced much higher levels of such abuse, and the effects of such abuses in childhood are stronger predictors of future delinquency for girls than for boys (American Bar Association & National Bar Association, 2001; English, Widom, & Brandford, 2001; Makarios, 2007). Moreover, these experiences are also more commonly found in the lives of young males and females who come from economically and socially disadvantaged backgrounds (Jacob, 2006; Steffensmeier & Haynie, 2000).

Thus, as we have seen from data presented in this section, girls are less likely to commit offences for the vast majority of criminal offence categories, and they are more likely to have experienced a range of problems in their lives that are well known to be associated with crime and delinquency. In the following section, we examine the nature of Canadian criminal justice responses to girls in trouble with the law and relate these responses to the realities of girls' life experiences.

The Criminal Justice Response to Female Youth Crime

Despite overwhelming evidence of the different developmental needs and social experiences of girls and boys, the criminal justice system response to youth female offending in Canada has, for the most part, been less than adequate. One of the primary reasons for the gap between the realities of girls' lives and criminal justice responses to their offending likely lies once again in our society's deeply ingrained attitudes toward the proper roles and behaviours of women.

To illustrate this claim, consider that researchers have long known that girls tend to be punished more often than boys for minor crimes and for breaching court orders, thereby prompting these scholars to argue that girls are kept in custody "for their own protection"—in other words, so they will not get into further trouble associated with the pull of drugs, boyfriends, peers, and street life (Corrado et al., 2000). But another way of looking at this phenomenon is in terms of the deep paternalism that it reflects. As Artz and her colleagues (2005) note, some good evidence corroborates the notion that girls are still being handed sentences that reflect the ethos to "protect them as much as possible." However, because the YCJA prohibits incarceration of young people for child protection, social welfare, or mental health needs, future research is needed to determine the extent to which this provision has been successful in decreasing youth custody for females (Mann et al., 2007).

Derived from youth court data, figure 9.5 provides an overview of the types of sentences handed down to young female and male offenders in the year 2000 (the last year such data were available). The data suggest that females are slightly less likely to receive a custodial sentence (open or secure custody, for example) than males. Females are also correspondingly more likely to receive probation, community service sentences, or alternative sentences. For the most part, these slight differences probably reflect the relatively more minor nature of offences committed by girls (Bell, 2002). Further, according to Statistics Canada, the top three offences committed by female and male youth who reoffend are the same crimes—

Figure 9.5   Types of Dispositions in Canadian Youth Courts, as a Percentage of Total Dispositions, by Sex, 2000

	Males		Females	
	Number	Percent	Number	Percent
Total dispositions	48,144		11,897	
Secure custody	8,914	18.52%	1,544	12.98%
Detention for treatment	—	0.00%	—	0.00%
Open custody	8,620	17.90%	1,731	14.55%
Probation	22,600	46.94%	6,453	54.24%
Fine	2,940	6.11%	562	4.72%
Compensation	160	0.33%	20	0.17%
Pay purchaser	15	0.03%	2	0.02%
Compensation in kind	189	0.39%	22	0.18%
Community service	2,946	6.12%	960	8.07%
Restitution	30	0.06%	5	0.04%
Prohibition, seizure, forfeiture	120	0.25%	28	0.24%
Conditional discharge	98	0.20%	42	0.35%
Absolute discharge	782	1.62%	262	2.20%
Other dispositions (includes other sentences, such as essays, apologies, and counselling programs)	730	1.52%	266	2.24%

Source: Adapted from Statistics Canada. (2007). *Number of cases heard in youth courts, by most significant disposition, age and sex of the accused, annual data based on the fiscal year* [CANSIM table 252-0009]. Available from http://estat.statcan.ca.

theft, common assault, and offences against the administration of justice (Thomas, Hurley, & Grimes, 2002). However, female youth are less likely than male youth to be recidivists or to have prior convictions (Sanders, 2000).

In addition, responses to criminality differ *within* the category of young female offenders. For example, race plays a role in the sentencing response to young females. In 2004–5, although Aboriginal youth made up 5 percent of the Canadian population, they comprised more than one-third of the young females sentenced to secure custody and nearly one-third of the females admitted to open custody (Calverley, 2007). Although evidence suggests racism plays a role in the clearly disproportional representation of Aboriginal girls in some forms of custody, readers should note that Aboriginal families (and the children of recent immigrant and "racialized" families) are some of the poorest in Canada (Campaign 2000, 2006). Thus, some inherent quality of the individual associated with the concept of race is not at issue here. Instead, racism creates barriers to adequate education and employment, which lead to poverty and forms of discrimination, which in turn are strongly associated with youth crime (Alvi, 2002; Pearcy, 1991).

The Canadian justice system does not track the ethno-racial background of offenders (except for Aboriginals) for fear that such reporting may fuel discriminatory attitudes among the general public, create moral panics, or reproduce the false perception that race is a valid concept.[2] Consequently, we do not know with any certainty whether other visible minority girls are treated in discriminatory ways within the criminal justice system.

As we can see from figure 9.6, between 1997 and 2005, the likelihood (for both males and females) of being released from closed or open custody has been in steady decline. In

Figure 9.6   Number of Youth Custody and Community Services (YCCS) Releases from Canadian Correctional Services, by Sex, 1997–2005

	Males			Females		
Year	Total secure custody	Total open custody	Total community sentences	Total secure custody	Total open custody	Total community sentences
1997–98	6,005	5,743	—	1,073	1,295	—
1998–99	5,027	5,550	—	1,043	1,273	—
1999–2000	4,392	5,234	—	900	1,128	—
2000–1	4,319	5,362	—	887	1,183	—
2001–2	4,790	5,196	—	995	1,328	—
2002–3	2,664	2,732	—	508	557	—
2003–4	2,059	2,667	19,929	354	558	5,588
2004–5	1,765	2,221	22,383	280	505	6,752

Source: Adapted from Statistics Canada. (2007). *Youth custody and community services (YCCS), releases from correctional services, by sex and length of time served, annual* [CANSIM table 251-0015]. Available from http://estat.statcan.ca.

addition, as we might expect with the introduction of the YCJA, the number of youth sentenced to community services (including all services in which youth would be supervised in the community, such as probation, the community portion of a custody and supervision order, deferred custody, and restitution and community service orders) has seen a corresponding increase since 2003. It is too early to tell whether this trend toward decarceration will continue and whether sufficient resources are in place to service the increased community supervision orders within communities in some jurisdictions (Carrington & Shulenberg, 2005).

Female youth who are sentenced to closed or open custody face numerous challenges because few programs are specifically geared to the needs of young female offenders (Pate, 2008). Moreover, as seen in the quotation below, the experiences of some young female incarcerated offenders can be both extremely traumatic and dangerous. As the Canadian Association of Elizabeth Fry Societies (2008) points out:

> To make matters worse, young women usually end up being jailed in mixed youth centres. This results in many incidents of sexual harassment and rape, most of which go unreported. When we conducted research on young women in custody we found two rather shocking results. First, we discovered that many young women do not define what they experience as sexual harassment or rape. Instead, they talk about it as being flirting or fooling around, or their "turn in the closet." Secondly, for those who do identify what they experience as sexual harassment or rape, most claim that they would not report such assaults. (Institutional Abuse Issues, ¶ 5)

As a prelude to assessing the effectiveness of current strategies designed to deal with female young offenders, let us examine the data, presented in figure 9.7, from a study conducted with 500 incarcerated serious or violent young offenders in British Columbia.

These data point clearly not only to the importance of the roles played by a range of social problems in contributing to youth crime in general but also to the critical roles of race, class, and gender relations. Although both Aboriginal and non-Aboriginal offenders in this sample reported experiencing high levels of family dysfunction prior to being incarcerated, the experiences of Aboriginal youth differ in many respects from those of their non-Aboriginal counterparts. Indeed, alcoholism, drug abuse, physical and sexual assault, and being placed in foster care are all reported with greater frequency by Aboriginal youth than non-Aboriginal youth. Especially important given the focus of this chapter, however, is the comparison between non-Aboriginal and Aboriginal females. According to these data, Aboriginal females are far more likely to report having lived with foster care families or in families where alcoholism, drug abuse, and sexual and physical abuse were widely prevalent.

Once again, an important conclusion is that a recognition and understanding of gender differences are undoubtedly important in creating effective treatment responses for juvenile offenders because in many respects female youth needs are clearly different from male youth needs. And, in many ways, being an Aboriginal youth is a further complication. Thus, the *interrelationship* between race and gender (and other factors) should be considered when dealing with female young offenders. What then, are the implications of these realities, for policy, research, and programming?

The core intention of the YCJA is to deal with the causes of crime (such as poverty, racism, and social exclusion) while simultaneously imposing meaningful consequences on young offenders (Department of Justice Canada, 2005). Currently, however, the balance of the Can-

Figure 9.7 Percentages of Family Dysfunction Reported in a Sample of 500 Aboriginal and Non-Aboriginal Male and Female Youth Incarcerated for Serious or Violent Offences

	Aboriginal males	Aboriginal females	Non-Aboriginal males	Non-Aboriginal females
Alcoholism	85.9%	88.2%	70.6%	45.3%
Drug abuse	73.8%	73.5%	57.1%	55.3%
Victim of physical abuse	53.3%	75.0%	44.5%	55.4%
Victim of sexual abuse	19.3%	57.6%	17.3%	33.8%
Mental disorder	16.1%	29.4%	21.8%	32.0%
Criminal record	78.1%	70.6%	66.9%	69.3%
Foster care	68.9%	81.8%	30.8%	32.9%

Source: Corrado, R.R., & Cohen, I.M. (2002). A needs profile of serious and/or violent Aboriginal youth in prison. *Forum on Corrections Research, 14*. Retrieved from www.csc-scc.gc.ca/text/pblct/forum/e143/e143g-eng.shtml. Reproduced by permission of *The Canadian Journal of Criminology*. Copyright by the Canadian Criminal Justice Association.

adian criminal justice system's response to youth in conflict with the law seems to be tilted in favour of a risk management strategy, not the social correlates of criminal offending.

Briefly, the risk management approach assumes that the central task of criminal justice agencies is to efficiently manage away the risk these offenders pose to the general public, increasingly through the use of risk assessment tools, of which some scholars have been quite critical (see, for example, Pate, 2006). Thus, by focusing attention on the attributes of the offender and emphasizing an actuarial approach, risk management strategies are prone to diverting attention from the social, economic, and political forces that shape and condition young people's lives.

It is easy and important to legislate that gender differences should be taken into account in the youth criminal justice process. It is also straightforward to write into law a concern for understanding the ways in which the socio-economic milieu conditions the lives of young people. It is quite another thing, however, to use that legislation to drive real change at the social level. Poverty, for example, is associated with housing problems, parental stress, the inability to learn, and street crime, all of which are still a reality in Canada, as are sexism, violence against women and girls, bullying, and mental illness. Young people's use of anti-depressant drugs rose significantly in the 1990s, their use of illegal drugs has not decreased, and suicide is still the second-leading cause of death for young people in Canada (BC Partners for Mental Health and Addictions Information, 2006; Boyce, 2004). These and other *precursors* of youth crime must be the target of any real effort to reduce the problem. And in tackling these precursors, it is critical that policy-makers, criminal justice practitioners, and other stakeholders understand and take gender seriously.

Summary

This chapter has examined the history of youth criminal justice law in Canada, from its early incarnation as gender-blind legislation to its recognition, on paper at least, of the importance of recognizing gender differences in offending. The chapter has also provided data and commentary on persistent and important differences in the nature and extent of offending patterns between young females and males.

Key points for the reader are that young females offend at a far lower rate than males, and the kinds of offences they commit are less serious on the whole than those committed by males. Moreover, although many aspects of the social backgrounds that condition these young people's lives are similar, females have unique experiences, particularly in relation to physical and sexual abuse. The chapter concludes by suggesting that these unique experiences and the ways in which race, class, and gender intersect and play out in young women's lives deserve attention at the levels of both policy and practice.

Notes

1. Portions of this section contain revised material that was previously published by Alvi (2000).

2. For more on the issue of collecting data on race and ethnicity in the criminal justice system, see the debate in the *Canadian Journal of Criminology*, 1994, volume 36, number 2.

Discussion Questions

1. Given the theories of female crime proposed in this book, and based on your reading of this chapter, which theory or theories best explain female youth crime?
2. If you were in charge of reducing female offending among Canadian youth, what kinds of social programs would you emphasize or create?
3. Over the past decade, visible minorities' immigration to Canada has increased substantially. Focusing specifically on young females, what are the implications of this trend for the Canadian justice system?

Suggested Readings

Bell, S. (2002). *Young offenders and juvenile justice: A century after the fact* (2nd ed.). Toronto: ITP Nelson.

> This book is one of the most comprehensive analyses of youth crime in Canada.

Doob, A.N., & Cesaroni, C. (2004). *Responding to youth crime in Canada*. Toronto: University of Toronto Press.

> This book provides an excellent overview of the Canadian criminal justice response to youth in conflict with the law.

Chesney-Lind, M., & Shelden, M. (1992). *Girls, delinquency and juvenile justice*. Belmont, CA: Brooks/Cole.

> This classic American book offers a critical perspective on female youth crime and the criminal justice system's response to it.

Online Resources

1. Canadian Association of Elizabeth Fry Societies: www.elizabethfry.ca
2. Youth and Violence Fact Sheet, Public Health Agency of Canada: www.phac-aspc .gc.ca/ncfv-cnivf/familyviolence/html/nfntsyjviolence_e.html

References

Accused in Virk case goes on trial for 3rd time. (2005, February 22). *CTV.ca News.* Retrieved from www.ctv.ca.

Alvi, S. (2000). *Youth and the Canadian criminal justice system.* Cincinnati: Anderson Press.

Alvi, S. (2002). A criminal justice history of children and youth in Canada. In B. Schissel & C. Brooks (Eds.), *Marginality and condemnation: An introduction to critical criminology in Canada* (pp. 193–209). Toronto: Fernwood.

American Bar Association, & National Bar Association. (2001). *Justice by gender: The lack of appropriate prevention, diversion and treatment alternatives for girls in the justice system.* Washington, DC: Author.

Artz, S., Nicholson, D., & Rodriguez, C. (2005). Understanding girls' delinquency: Looking beyond their behaviour. In K. Campbell (Ed.), *Understanding youth justice in Canada* (pp. 289–312). Toronto: Pearson.

Bala, N. (1997). *Young offenders law.* Concord, ON: Irwin Law.

Barber, J., & Doob, A.N. (2004). An analysis of public support for severity and proportionality in the sentencing of youthful offenders. *Canadian Journal of Criminology and Criminal Justice, 46,* 327–328.

Barrett, M., & McIntosh, M. (1982). *The anti-social family.* London: Verso.

BC Partners for Mental Health and Addictions Information. (2006). *Suicide: Follow the warning signs.* Vancouver: Author.

Belknap, J., & Holsinger, K. (2006). The gendered nature of risk factors for delinquency. *Feminist Criminology, 1,* 48–71.

Bell, S. (2002). *Young offenders and juvenile justice: A century after the fact* (2nd ed.). Toronto: ITP Nelson.

Boyce, W. (2004). *Young people in Canada: Their health and well-being.* Ottawa: Health Canada.

Calverley, D. (2007). *Youth custody and community services in Canada, 2004/2005* (Report no. 85-002-XIE2007002). Ottawa: Canadian Centre for Justice Statistics.

Campaign 2000. (2005). *Decision time for Canada: Let's make poverty history—2005 report card on child poverty in Canada.* Toronto: Author.

Campaign 2000. (2006). *Oh Canada! Too many children in poverty for too long.* Toronto: Author.

Canadian Association of Elizabeth Fry Societies. (2008). *Labelling young women as violent: Vilification of the most vulnerable.* Retrieved from www.elizabethfry.ca/vilifica/ Contents.htm.

Canadian Centre for Justice Statistics. (1994). *A review of the alternative measures survey, 1991–92.* Ottawa: Statistics Canada.

Canadian Centre for Justice Statistics. (1997). Justice data fact finder [Monograph]. *Juristat, 16*(9).

Carrigan, D.O. (1998). *Juvenile delinquency in Canada: A history.* Concord, ON: Irwin.

Carrington, P., & Moyer, S. (1994). Trends in youth crime and police response, pre- and post-YOA. *Canadian Journal of Criminology, 36,* 1–28.

Carrington, P.J., & Shulenberg, J. (2005). *The impact of the Youth Criminal Justice Act on police charging practices with young persons: A preliminary statistical assessment.* Ottawa: Department of Justice Canada.

Chesney-Lind, M. (2006). Patriarchy, crime and justice: Feminist criminology in an era of backlash. *Feminist Criminology, 1,* 6–26.

Chesney-Lind, M., & Okamoto, S.K. (2001). Gender matters: Patterns in girls' delinquency and gender responsive programming. *Journal of Forensic Psychology Practice, 1,* 1–28.

Chesney-Lind, M., & Shelden, M. (1992). *Girls, delinquency and juvenile justice.* Belmont, CA: Brooks/Cole.

Chesney-Lind, M. (2001). "Out of sight, out of mind": Girls in the juvenile justice system. In C. Renzetti & L. Goodstein (Eds.), *Women, crime and criminal justice: Original feminist readings* (pp. 27–43). Los Angeles: Roxbury Publishing.

Church Council on Justice and Corrections. (1996). *Satisfying justice: A compendium of initiatives, programs and legislative measures.* Ottawa: Author.

Corrado, R., Odgers, C., & Cohen, I. (2000). The incarceration of female young offenders: Protection for whom? *Canadian Journal of Criminology, 42,* 189–207.

Corrado, R.R., & Cohen, I.M. (2002). A needs profile of serious and/or violent Aboriginal youth in prison. *Forum on Corrections Research, 14.* Retrieved from www.csc-scc.gc.ca/text/pblct/forum/e143/e143g-eng.shtml.

DeKeseredy, W.S. (2000). *Women, crime and the Canadian criminal justice system.* Cincinnati, OH: Anderson.

Dell, C., & Boe, R. (1998). *Female young offenders in Canada* (rev. ed.). Ottawa: Correctional Services of Canada, Research Branch.

Department of Justice Canada. (2005). *A strategy for the renewal of youth justice.* Ottawa: Author.

Department of Justice Canada. (2007). Youth Criminal Justice Act: Key elements of the proposed law. Retrieved from http://canada.justice.gc.ca/eng/news-nouv/nr-cp/2001/doc_25948.html.

Doob, A.N., & Cesaroni, C. (2004). *Responding to youth crime in Canada.* Toronto: University of Toronto Press.

English, D., Widom, C.S., & Brandford, C. (2001). *Childhood victimization and delinquency, adult criminality, and violent criminal behavior: A replication and extension* (Report no. NCJ 192291). Washington, DC: National Institute of Justice.

Fitzgerald, R. (2003). *An examination of sex differences in delinquency* (Rep. no. 85-561-MIE). Ottawa: Minister of Industry.

Gagnon, D. (1984). *History of the law for juvenile delinquents* (Government working paper no. 1984-56.) Ottawa: Ministry of the Solicitor General of Canada.

Garland, D. (2000). The culture of high crime societies: Some preconditions of recent "law and order" policies. *British Journal of Criminology, 40,* 347–375.

Gomes, J.T., Bertrand, L.E., Paetsch, J.J., & Hornick, J.P. (2003). Self-reported delinquency among Alberta's youth: Findings from a survey of 2,001 junior and senior high school students. *Adolescence, 38,* 75–91.

Hartnagel, T. (2004). The rhetoric of youth justice in Canada. *Criminal Justice, 4,* 355–374.

Holsinger, K. (2000). Feminist perspectives on female offending: Examining real girls' lives. *Women and Criminal Justice, 12,* 23–51.

Hylton, J.H. (1994). Get tough or get smart? Options for Canada's youth justice system in the twenty-first century. *Canadian Journal of Criminology, 36,* 229–246.

Jacob, J.C. (2006). Male and female youth crime in Canadian communities: Assessing the applicability of social disorganization theory. *Canadian Journal of Criminology and Criminal Justice, 48*(1), 31–60.

Katz, R.S. (2000). Explaining girls' and women's crime and desistance in the context of their victimization experiences: A developmental test of revised strain theory and the life course perspective. *Violence Against Women, 6,* 633–660.

Kong, R., & AuCoin, K. (2008). Female offenders in Canada. *Juristat, 28*(1), 1–22.

Loeber, R., Kalb, L., & Huizinga, D. (2001). *Juvenile delinquency and serious victimization.* Washington, DC: Department of Justice, Office of Justice Programs, Office of Juvenile Justice and Delinquency Prevention.

Macdonald, Z. (2002). Official crime statistics: Their use and interpretation. *Economic Journal, 112,* F85–F106.

Makarios, M.D. (2007). Race, abuse and female criminal violence. *Feminist Criminology, 2,* 100–116.

Mallicoat, S. (2007). Gendered justice: Attributional differences between males and females in the juvenile courts. *Feminist Criminology, 2,* 4–30.

Mann, R.M., Senn, C.Y., Girard, A., & Ackbar, S. (2007). Community-based interventions for at-risk youth in Ontario under Canada's Youth Criminal Justice Act: A case study of a "runaway" girl. *Canadian Journal of Criminology and Criminal Justice, 49,* 37.

McGuire, M. (1997). C.19: An Act to Amend the Young Offenders Act and the Criminal Code—"Getting tougher?"(Canada). *Canadian Journal of Criminology, 39,* 185–214.

Meloff, W., & Silverman, R.A. (1992). Canadian kids who kill. *Canadian Journal of Criminology, 34,* 15–34.

Odgers, C., Burnette, M., Chauhan, P., Moretti, M., & Reppucci, N.D. (2005). Misdiagnosing the problem: Mental health profiles of incarcerated juveniles. *Canadian Child and Adolescent Psychiatry Review, 14,* 26–29.

Pate, K. (2006). *The risky business of risk assessment.* Ottawa: Canadian Association of Elizabeth Fry Societies.

Pate, K. (2008). Why do we think young women are committing more violent offences? Retrieved from www.elizabethfry.ca/violent/page1.htm.

Pearcy, P. (1991). *Youth/criminal gangs in British Columbia.* Victoria, BC: Ministry of the Solicitor General.

Platt, A. (1977). *The child savers: The invention of delinquency.* Chicago: University of Chicago Press.

Pleasant-Jette, C.M. (1993). Creating a climate of confidence: Providing services within Aboriginal communities. In *National Round Table on Economic Issues and Resources (Royal Commission on Aboriginal Issues).* Ottawa: The commission.

Reitsma-Street, M. (1993). Canadian youth court charges and dispositions for females before and after implementation of the Young Offenders Act. *Canadian Journal of Criminology, 35,* 437–458.

Sanders, T. (2000). *Sentencing of young offenders in Canada, 1998/99.* Ottawa: Canadian Centre for Justice Statistics.

Savoie, J. (2007). *Youth self-reported delinquency, Toronto, 2006.* Ottawa: Statistics Canada.

Schissel, B. (1997). *Blaming children: Youth crime, moral panics and the politics of hate.* Halifax: Fernwood Publishing.

Sharp, S., Brewster, D.R., & Love, S.R. (2005). Disentangling strain, personal attributes, affective response and deviance: A gendered analysis. *Deviant Behavior, 26,* 122–157.

Silver, W. (2007). *Crime statistics in Canada, 2006* (Rep. no. 85-002-XIE). Ottawa: Ministry of Industry.

Sprott, J. (1996). Understanding public views of youth crime and the youth justice system. *Canadian Journal of Criminology, 38,* 271–290.

Sprott, J.B., & Doob, A.N. (2003). It's all in the denominator: Trends in the processing of girls in Canada's youth courts. *Canadian Journal of Criminology and Criminal Justice, 45,* 73–80.

Statistics Canada. (2007a). *Adults and youths charged, by sex and offence category, Canada, provinces and territories, annual* [CANSIM table 109-5009]. Available from http://estat.statcan.ca.

Statistics Canada. (2007b). *Homicide survey, victims and persons accused of homicide, by age group and sex, Canada* [CANSIM table 253-0003]. Available from http://estat.statcan.ca.

Statistics Canada. (2007c). *Number of cases heard in youth courts, by most significant disposition, age and sex of the accused, annual data based on the fiscal year* [CANSIM table 252-0009]. Available from http://estat.statcan.ca.

Statistics Canada. (2007d). *Youth custody and community services (YCCS), releases from correctional services, by sex and length of time served, annual* [CANSIM table 251-0015]. Available from http://estat.statcan.ca.

Steffensmeier, D., & Haynie, D.L. (2000). Gender, structural disadvantage, and urban crime: Do macrosocial variables also explain female offending rates? *Criminology, 38*, 403–439.

Tanner, J. (1996). *Teenage troubles: Youth and deviance in Canada.* Scarborough, ON: Nelson.

Tanner, J., & Wortley, S. (2002). *The Toronto youth crime and victimization survey* Toronto: Centre of Criminology, University of Toronto.

Thomas, M., Hurley, H., & Grimes, C. (2002). Pilot analysis of recidivism among convicted youth and young adults, 1999/00. *Juristat, 22*(9), 1–19.

Tory bill proposes violent youth be tried as adults. (2007, November 19). *CTV.ca News.* Retrieved from www.ctv.ca.

Varma, K.N., & Marinos, V. (2000). How do we best respond to the problem of youth crime? In J. Roberts (Ed.), *Criminal justice in Canada: A reader* (pp. 221–232). Toronto: Harcourt Brace.

Wardell, B. (1986). The Young Offenders Act: A report card 1984–1986. In D. Currie (Ed.), *The administration of justice* (pp. 128–158). Saskatoon: Social Research Unit, University of Saskatchewan.

West, W.G. (1984). *Young offenders and the state: A Canadian perspective on delinquency.* Toronto: Butterworths.

Yearwood-Lee, E. (2003, December 7). Viciousness of youth attacks increases while numbers remain static. *Canadian Press.* Available from www.thefreeradical.ca/Violent_crime_statistics_Canada.htm.

CHAPTER 10

Aboriginal Women and the Criminal Justice System

Brenda M. Restoule
(Waub-Zhe-Kwens; Eagle Clan)

Introduction

The criminal justice system in Canada has primarily focused on men, who make up the majority of offenders in the correctional system. The result is assessments, services, and programs that address male-specific needs and risk factors. In an attempt to address the needs of the relatively small number of women in the correctional system, these male-influenced assessments, services, and programs have been applied to female offenders. Defining the criminal justice system according to these standards has resulted in an ill-equipped system that is unable to adequately meet the unique needs and risk factors of women offenders.

In the last 25 to 30 years, community groups, national women's organizations, and female inmates have demanded that the correctional system develop assessments, services, and programs based on the unique needs and risk factors of women. The lack of gender-appropriate services within the correctional system was addressed through such documents as *Creating Choices* (Canada, Task Force on Federally Sentenced Women [TFFSW], 1990) and the report by the Arbour inquiry (Canada, Commission of Inquiry into Certain Events, 1996), which identified the priority for the correctional system in Canada to develop a gender-specific and -appropriate system of criminal justice that would adequately meet the unique needs of women. To date, the correctional system continues to strive to meet the many recommendations of these two documents.

If women in the criminal justice system have faced significant difficulties in having their needs and issues adequately recognized and addressed, then Aboriginal women are the hidden group who continue to be ignored within the Canadian criminal justice system. As a group, Aboriginal people[1] are marginalized from the Canadian population, and they experience significant social and health problems that exacerbate their marginalized status in society. Aboriginal communities are faced with numerous social and economic disadvantages, including poverty, high rates of unemployment, poor educational attainment, inadequate drinking water, poor sewage systems, poor housing conditions, high rates of both suicide and accidental deaths, high incidence of poor health conditions (diabetes and heart disease, for example), high rates of addictions (to alcohol, drugs, and other substances), disproportionate numbers of children in the child welfare system, and all forms of violence.

According to the 2001 census, 3.3 percent of the population identified themselves as an Aboriginal person yet they account for 16.3 percent of the federal offender population in Canada (National Parole Board, 2004). Aboriginal women comprise 29 percent of all federally sentenced women, with similarly high proportions found within the provincial correctional system (Canadian Human Rights Commission, 2003). Yet the correctional system in Canada fails to recognize Aboriginal women as a distinct group with unique needs and risk factors. Documents and policies that guide corrections in Canada, both federally and provincially, have grouped Aboriginal women either under the general category of women or under the general category of Aboriginal (grouping them with men), thereby ignoring the need to develop programs, services, and assessment tools that adequately meet both gender- and culture-specific needs of Aboriginal women. Consequently, Aboriginal women offenders and national organizations, such as the Native Women's Association of Canada, claim that Canada's correctional system is discriminatory and racist toward Aboriginal women. To date, the correctional system in Canada continues to struggle to meet the cultural needs of all Aboriginal people and the gender-specific needs of women. Because of the ongoing failure to rigorously consider how the criminal justice system's structure uniquely affects the lives of these women, Aboriginal women in conflict with the law continue to experience disenfranchisement, marginalization, and discrimination.

Aboriginal People in Canada

To comprehend the impact of the criminal justice system's failure to adequately address the culture- and gender-specific needs of Aboriginal women, a familiarity with the statistics, needs, and challenges of Canada's Aboriginal people will be helpful. Aboriginal people, and Aboriginal women specifically, face a myriad of issues prior to their involvement with the criminal justice system, which may be related to the disproportionate number of Aboriginal women in the correctional system.

The 2001 census identified 3.3 percent of the Canadian population as Aboriginal. The largest group of Aboriginal people are identified as North American Indian or First Nation (62 percent), followed by Métis (30 percent), and Inuit (5 percent). The remaining 3 percent identified with more than one Aboriginal group. The Aboriginal population is much younger (median age of 24.7 years) than the Canadian population (median age of 37.7 years), and seniors comprise only 4 percent of the Aboriginal population compared with 13 percent of the Canadian population. Many posit that the greatest reason for the significant disproportion in ages between the Aboriginal and non-Aboriginal population is the relatively poor health and social conditions of Aboriginal people, resulting in a shorter lifespan. The statistics are skewed because of the significantly higher number of births that occur each year for Aboriginal people.

Aboriginal people are the largest and fastest-growing population both in Canadian society and in the prison system, and their disproportionate growth could have serious implications for Aboriginal people and the criminal justice system for many years to come. Because 33 percent of Aboriginal people are under the age of 15, forecasters predict a significant increase in the youth and young adult population within the next decade. This growth is especially salient considering that those under the age of 35 are seen as being most at risk for criminal activity, according to the National Parole Board (2004). A variety of social and economic disadvantages are prevalent in Aboriginal communities, such as poverty, poor education, unemployment, marginalization, substance abuse, sexual abuse, a variety of forms of violence, and dysfunctional families. Most of these disadvantages have been identified as risk factors that contribute to the likelihood of becoming involved in the criminal justice system (National Parole Board, 2004) and may be exacerbated by the growing numbers of Aboriginal people who now reside in urban centres, where exposure to criminal activity is higher. Much like a revolving door, the social factors for Aboriginal people rarely change over time. Along with these disadvantages, the inability of Aboriginal people to navigate the criminal justice system (due to language barriers, for example) creates further problems. The conflicts Aboriginal people face with the police and the court system usually result in their being sentenced to a period of time in the correctional system. Box 10.1 summarizes the difficulties Aboriginal people face in the Canadian criminal justice system.

Often, many of the problems experienced by Aboriginal people in the criminal justice system are exacerbated by language barriers. The criminal justice system has failed to provide

Box 10.1   Aboriginal People and the Criminal Justice System

According to a report by the Canadian Criminal Justice Association, Aboriginal people experience the following problems with respect to the criminal justice system:

- Aboriginal people accused of a crime are more likely to be denied bail.
- Aboriginal people spend more time in pretrial detention.
- Aboriginal people accused of a crime are more likely to be charged with multiple offences, and often for crimes against the system.
- Aboriginal people are more likely not to have legal representation at court proceedings.
- Aboriginal clients, especially in northern communities, where the court party flies in the day of the hearing, spend less time with their lawyers.
- Because court schedules in remote areas are poorly planned, judges may have a limited time to spend in the community.
- Aboriginal offenders are more than twice as likely to be incarcerated than non-Aboriginal offenders.
- Aboriginal Elders, who are spiritual leaders, are not given the same status as prison priests or chaplains, in all institutions.

- Aboriginal people often plead guilty because they are intimidated by the court and simply want to get the proceedings over with.
- Aboriginal people often commit offences related to violence (usually against another Aboriginal person and/or a family member), social disorder, crimes against the system, or petty crimes.
- At least half of all offences are alcohol-related.

Source: Canadian Criminal Justice Association. (2000). Aboriginal peoples and the criminal justice system: Part IV—Aboriginal people and the justice system [Special issue]. *Bulletin*. Retrieved from www.ccja-acjp.ca/en/abori4.html.

information in the form of brochures, pamphlets, or videos in Aboriginal languages to assist individuals who must navigate through the court process (Canadian Criminal Justice Association [CCJA], 2000). Translation services are often less than adequate to meet legal standards, and Aboriginal-speaking persons are disallowed from sitting as jurors. According to the Royal Commission on Aboriginal Peoples (Canada, Royal Commission on Aboriginal Peoples [RCAP], 1996):

> It appears that they have little understanding of their legal rights, of court procedures, or of resources such as legal aid and most Indian people enter guilty pleas because they do not really understand the concept of legal guilt and innocence, or because they are fearful of exercising their rights. In remote areas the Aboriginal people appear confused about the functions of the court, particularly where the Royal Canadian Mounted Police officers also act as Crown Prosecutors, or where the magistrates travel about in police aircrafts. (p. 167)

Unsurprisingly, compared with non-Aboriginal offenders, Aboriginal offenders are younger, poorer, are more likely to be incarcerated for a violent offence, have higher needs related to employment and education, have more extensive involvement with the youth criminal justice system, have higher incidence of health problems, are more likely to have abused drugs and alcohol at an earlier age, are more likely to have been physically abused, report parental absence or neglect more frequently, and are more likely to have been involved in the child welfare system. Many were also sent to residential schools during their childhood, an experience without parallel for non-Aboriginal offenders.

Once again, this information supports the notion that the negative social factors experienced by Aboriginal people place this group at higher risk of becoming and remaining involved in the criminal justice system. Based on the 2005–6 correctional investigator's report (Correctional Investigator of Canada, 2006), Aboriginal people account for 18 percent of the overall federal inmate population: 69 percent identify themselves as First Nation or North American Indian, 27 percent as Métis, and 4 percent as Inuit. The disproportionate numbers are even more startling on a regional level. The Prairie region (Saskatchewan, Manitoba, Alberta, and Northwest Territories) has the highest proportion of Aboriginal offenders: 64 percent of all federally incarcerated inmates. According to a recent report, "the best estimate of the overall incarceration rate for Aboriginal people in Canada is 1,024 per 100,000 adults" (Correctional Investigator of Canada, 2006), compared with 117 per 100,000 incarcerated adults in the non-Aboriginal population.

The divergence between Aboriginal and Euro-Canadian values has also added to the disproportionate number of Aboriginal people in the criminal justice system. Core Aboriginal values, such as a desire for community harmony, avoidance of confrontational and adversarial positions, preservation of relationships, and reluctance to show emotions, often create a dissonance with the goals of the criminal justice system. Oftentimes, Aboriginal people choose to plead guilty to a crime to restore harmony to the community and preserve relationships; they are much less concerned with the issue of guilt and punishment. Ross (1992) also reports that many of these traditional Aboriginal values lead those involved in the court process (such as lawyers, judges, and psychiatrists) to falsely label Aboriginal people as unresponsive, uncommunicative, uncooperative, and lacking remorse. Figure 10.1 highlights the conflict that exists between Aboriginal and Western-based justice values (CCJA, 2000).

In an attempt to alleviate the conflict that exists between the Aboriginal understanding of justice and the Western-based meaning of justice, in 1994, the Canadian government introduced the *Corrections and Conditional Release Act* (CCRA). Section 4(h) of the Act states that correctional policies, programs, and practices shall "respect gender, ethnic, cultural and linguistic differences and be responsive to the special needs of women and aboriginal peoples," and sections 79 to 84 explicitly discuss the needs of Aboriginal offenders (Morin, 1999). Whether the CCRA has been successful at ameliorating the conflicting value systems and thereby reducing the disproportionate number of Aboriginal people in the criminal justice system will be discussed later in this chapter.

Aboriginal Women in the Correctional System: A Snapshot

> *If my little brother had died in a big city in Ontario rather than on a reserve in Saskatchewan I know I would have been allowed to go to his funeral.*
>
> Aboriginal prisoner at Prison for Women, cited in *Creating Choices*
> (Canada, Task Force on Federally Sentenced Women, 1990, p. 6)

Aboriginal women are disproportionately represented in the correctional system in Canada, provincially and federally: in 2003, they represented 29 percent of the federal women's population with similar representation (23 percent) in women's provincial and territorial institutions. Statistics from the Correctional Service of Canada (2000) indicate that the greatest overrepresentation for Aboriginal women occurs in the Prairie region, where they account for 48 percent of the female correctional population. In fact, 75 percent of all Aboriginal women who are federally sentenced are in the Prairie region. According to the Correctional Service of Canada (2000), the federally sentenced women's population has increased overall. The National Parole Board (2004) has also observed increases in Aboriginal overrepresentation every year since 1998–99. According to a number of reports investigating Aboriginal males and females in the correctional system, the greatest increase has occurred with Aboriginal women (Canadian Human Rights Commission, 2003; Correctional Service of Canada [CSC], 2000). Despite agreement that the number of federally sentenced Aboriginal women has increased, some discrepancy surrounds the extent of the

Figure 10.1   Comparison Between Western and Traditional Aboriginal Justice Values

	Western justice	Traditional Aboriginal justice
Justice system	• Adversarial	• Non-confrontational
Guilt	• European concept of guilty/not guilty	• No concept of guilty/not guilty
Pleading guilty	• The accused has the right against self-incrimination. Thus, it is not seen as dishonest to plead not guilty when one has actually committed the offence.	• It is dishonest to plead not guilty if one has committed the crime. (Aboriginal values of honesty and non-interference)
Testifying	• As part of the process, witnesses testify in front of the accused.	• Reluctance to testify. (Aboriginal values of being non-confrontational and preserving relationships)
Truth	• Expectation to tell the "whole truth."	• It is impossible to know the "whole truth" in any situation.
Witnesses	• Only certain people are called to testify in relation to specific subjects.	• Everyone is free to give their say. • Witnesses do not want to appear adversarial and often make every attempt to give answers that please counsel, thus often changing their testimony.
Eye contact	• Maintaining eye contact conveys that one is being truthful.	• In some Aboriginal cultures, maintaining eye contact with a person of authority is a sign of disrespect.
Verdict	• Accused is expected to show, during proceedings and upon a verdict of guilt, remorse and a desire for rehabilitation.	• Accused must accept what comes to him/her without a show of emotion.
Incarceration/probation	• Means of punishing/rehabilitating offender.	• Completely absolves Aboriginal offender of responsibility of restitution to victim.
Function of justice	• Ensure conformity, punish deviant behaviour and protect society.	• Heal the offender. • Restore peace and harmony to the community. • Reconcile the offender with victim/family that has been wronged. • Punishment is not the objective.

increase. According to the CSC (2000), rates for federally sentenced Aboriginal women have risen from 16 percent of all federally sentenced women in 1995 to 23 percent in 1999, representing a 144 percent increase over the five-year span from 1995 to 1999, whereas the Canadian Human Rights Commission (2003) reported increases of 117 percent between 1996 and 2000. The Public Inquiry into the Administration of Justice and Aboriginal People (Manitoba, Public Inquiry, 1991) attempted to address the high proportion of Aboriginal offenders:

> Why in a society where justice is supposed to be blind, are the inmates of our prisons selected so overwhelmingly from a single ethnic group? Two answers suggest themselves immediately; either Aboriginal people commit a disproportionate number of crimes, or they are the victims of a discriminatory justice system. We believe that both answers are correct, but not in the simplistic sense that some people might interpret them. We do not believe, for instance, that there is anything about Aboriginal people or culture that predisposes them to criminal behaviour. Instead, we believe that the causes of Aboriginal criminal behaviour are rooted in a long history of discrimination and social inequality that has impoverished Aboriginal people and consigned them to the margins of ... society. (p. 85)

Because for statistical purposes Aboriginal women are often grouped within the general category of women offenders or with Aboriginal men offenders, statistics that speak specifically about Aboriginal women offenders are difficult to locate. Next, we turn to some statistics (and a number of presuppositions) regarding the realities of Aboriginal women prior to and during their involvement in the criminal justice system.

Statistics indicate that women who are federally sentenced are likely to be of Aboriginal descent, first-time offenders, under the age of 35 years, survivors of physical and sexual abuse, single mothers with one or more children, substance abusers, serving shorter sentences than men (due to the nature of women's crimes), reporting symptoms of depression, and engaging in self-injurious behaviours at a higher rate than men (Dell & Boe, 2000; Trevethan, 1999). Not only do these statistics stand true for Aboriginal women offenders but the rates at which these traits occur are often greater than for their non-Aboriginal counterparts. For example, 66 percent of Aboriginal women offenders are under the age of 35, compared with 56 percent of non-Aboriginal women offenders; 90 percent of Aboriginal women offenders report physical abuse, compared with 68 percent of non-Aboriginal women offenders; and 61 percent of Aboriginal women offenders report sexual abuse, compared with 53 percent of non-Aboriginal women offenders.

Dell and Boe (2000) examined risk and need factors between Aboriginal and Caucasian women offenders and found that Aboriginal women had considerably higher employment needs than their Caucasian counterparts (80 percent of Aboriginal women reported being unemployed at the time of admission). Employment need is defined by a woman's employment skills and general employability, which is likely affected by educational attainment. In fact, federally sentenced Aboriginal women offenders' educational attainment is poorer (mean educational level of grade 8) than federally sentenced women as a whole (50 percent of whom have grade 9 or less).

Because Aboriginal women report greater levels of physical and sexual abuse, they likely exhibit a greater number of trauma-related symptoms, such as depression and self-injurious behaviours, which is supported by interviews conducted by the Task Force on Federally Sentenced Women, in its research for the *Creating Choices* report (Canada, TFFSW, 1990).

Aboriginal women shared their stories of exposure to all types of violence and racism, and they reported dealing with the traumatic memories of abuse by attempting suicide, abusing substances and prescription drugs, and using self-injurious behaviours in attempts to reduce the tension and anger they felt. These first-hand accounts support the information gathered by Dell and Boe (2000), who noted that Aboriginal women offenders reported significantly greater difficulties with substances than their Caucasian counterparts. According to the *Creating Choices* report (Canada, TFFSW, 1990) Aboriginal drug-abusing women offenders were addicted to substances for longer periods than their non-Aboriginal counterparts, usually for 10 to 25 years. The percentage of Aboriginal people who head up single-parent families is twice as high as the percentage of single-parent families in the general Canadian population; therefore, Aboriginal women are twice as likely to be single parents when entering the correctional system (CCJA, 2000).

Dell and Boe (2000) found that, overall, the needs of Aboriginal women offenders were much higher in the areas of employment, marital and family relationships, association and socialization, substance abuse, and community than their non-Aboriginal counterparts, based on factors collected at the time of admission.

Statistics on Aboriginal women while incarcerated also reveal disproportionately high levels across a number of domains. In a position paper written on behalf of the Native Women's Association of Canada, McIvor and Johnson (2003) reported that federally sentenced Aboriginal women commit disproportionately more violent crimes prior to and during their federal incarceration, thereby leading to longer federal sentences. They also reported that federally sentenced Aboriginal women were found to have completed suicide at a disproportionately high rate while in prison, particularly at the former women's penitentiary, the Prison for Women in Kingston, Ontario. The hopelessness experienced by Aboriginal women during incarceration can be felt in the words of an Aboriginal parolee: "When I went to prison I lost everything I ever had, not just the material things, but all the relationships I ever had in my life" (Canada, TFFSW, 1990, p. 7).

The National Parole Board's (2000) study on female offenders revealed that Aboriginal women were more likely to serve longer sentences for violent offences than non-Aboriginal women. The Canadian Human Rights Commission (2003) cites information from interviews with correctional staff and female inmates suggesting that Aboriginal women tend to be admitted to involuntary segregation more frequently (accounting for 35.5 percent of all involuntary admissions) and for longer durations than non-Aboriginal women. Federally sentenced Aboriginal women were less successful on conditional release than any other group of female offenders (see figure 10.2) and were found to have the lowest rate for being granted either day parole or full parole (see figure 10.3). Not surprisingly, federally sentenced Aboriginal women were more likely to be incarcerated than to be on conditional release.

Figure 10.3 notes release rates for federally sentenced women based on race and reveals that federally sentenced Aboriginal women are not granted conditional release at the same rates as non-Aboriginal women. The only area in which Aboriginal women exceed their non-Aboriginal counterparts is for grants for unescorted temporary absences.

Figures 10.4, 10.5, and 10.6 reveal the percentages for all federally sentenced women on conditional release. The statistics indicate that Aboriginal women are less successful in completing their conditional release, which results in their return to prison. Thus, they remain incarcerated for longer periods of time than non-Aboriginal women. Information

Figure 10.2   Percentage of Federal Female Offender Population by Race from 1995–96 to 1999–2000

	All	Aboriginal	Black	Visible minorities	Caucasian	Other[a]
Incarcerated	43.5	59.1	31.1	34.3	42.2	47.1
Conditional release	56.5	40.9	68.4	65.7	57.8	52.8
Day parole	15.6	23.9	12.8	15.5	14.1	21.5
Full parole	74.3	51.3	83.5	82.2	75.9	71.8
Statutory release	10.0	24.8	3.7	2.2	10.0	6.7

[a] Other includes other, unknown, and blank.

Source: National Parole Board. (2000). *Special study on federal female offenders from 1995/96 to 1999/00.* Ottawa: Performance Measurement Division, National Parole Board, p. 2. Reprinted by permission.

Figure 10.3   Percentages of Conditional Release Grants for Female Offenders from 1995–96 to 1999–2000

	All	Aboriginal	Black	Visible minorities	Caucasian	Other[a]
Day parole granted	83.6	76.6	88.4	82.8	84.3	88.5
Full parole granted	66.9	48.7	85.1	87.0	65.7	78.2
Unescorted temporary absences authorized	76.1	82.5	35.7	58.3	79.6	80.0

[a] Other includes other, unknown, and blank.

Source: National Parole Board. (2000). *Special study on federal female offenders from 1995/96 to 1999/00.* Ottawa: Performance Measurement Division, National Parole Board, p. 5. Reprinted by permission.

provided by the CSC (2000) suggests that efforts are being made to increase the number of Aboriginal women in the community through conditional release programs (of the total Aboriginal women offender population, the percentage of women in the community has increased by 9 percent, whereas the percentage of women who are incarcerated has decreased by 9 percent). Unfortunately, little information is provided on the strategies to increase the numbers of women on conditional release or whether the initiatives have been successful, resulting in fewer women having their releases revoked and being returned to prison.

Figure 10.4   Percentages of Female Offenders on Day Parole by Race

Results	All	Aboriginal	Black	Visible minorities	Caucasian	Other[a]
Successful completions	85.9	77.4	93.3	100.0	84.8	98.5
Revocation for breach of condition	9.1	14.3	4.5	0.0	10.0	0.0
Total recidivism	5.0	8.3	2.2	0.0	5.2	1.5
Non-violent offences	3.8	6.8	1.1	0.0	4.0	0.0
Violent offences	1.2	1.5	1.1	0.0	1.2	1.5

[a] Other includes other, unknown, and blank.

Source: National Parole Board (2000). *Special study on federal female offenders from 1995/96 to 1999/00.* Ottawa: Performance Measurement Division, National Parole Board, p. 6. Reprinted by permission.

Figure 10.5   Percentages of Female Offenders on Full Parole by Race

Results	All	Aboriginal	Black	Visible minorities	Caucasian	Other[a]
Successful completions	77.0	56.4	85.7	92.3	76.9	83.0
Revocation for breach of condition	15.7	25.8	10.2	0.0	16.8	10.6
Total recidivism	7.2	17.7	4.1	7.7	6.4	6.4
Non-violent offences	6.5	14.5	4.1	7.7	6.1	4.3
Violent offences	0.7	3.2	0.0	0.0	0.3	2.1

[a] Other includes other, unknown, and blank.

Source: National Parole Board. (2000). *Special study on federal female offenders from 1995/96 to 1999/00.* Ottawa: Performance Measurement Division, National Parole Board, p. 6. Reprinted by permission.

Figure 10.6   Percentages of Female Offenders on Statutory Release by Race

Results	All	Aboriginal	Black	Visible minorities	Caucasian	Other[a]
Successful completions	63.7	54.0	65.8	100.0	67.0	68.4
Revocation for breach of condition	26.0	34.7	24.4	0.0	22.7	26.3
Total recidivism	10.3	11.3	9.8	0.0	10.3	5.3
Non-violent offences	8.0	11.3	9.8	0.0	6.9	0.0
Violent offences	2.3	0.0	0.0	0.0	3.4	5.3

[a] Other includes other, unknown, and blank.

Source: National Parole Board. (2000). *Special study on federal female offenders from 1995/96 to 1999/00.* Ottawa: Performance Measurement Division, National Parole Board, p. 7. Reprinted by permission.

Needs and Risks for Aboriginal Women Offenders

> *Women offenders have some things in common with men offenders from their respective regions. But they have a lot more in common with each other as women than they do with their regional male counterparts. Their crimes are different, their criminogenic factors are different, and their correctional needs for programs and services are different. Most importantly, the risks that they pose to the public, as a group, are minimal and considerably different from the security risks posed by men.*
>
> The Arbour inquiry (Canada, Commission of Inquiry into Certain Events at the Prison for Women in Kingston, 1996, p. 228)

Upon admission to prison, all women undergo an offender intake assessment (OIA) to determine the woman's security classification and to identify recommended correctional programming that will reduce her criminogenic factors and assist her eligibility for conditional release. The OIA, introduced in 1994, is also used to "predict how well she … will integrate into the community upon release if identified needs are not adequately addressed" (Dell & Boe, 2000, p. 3). The tool, which is intended for both male and female offenders, uses dynamic and static risk factors to determine risk and identify programming needs. Regardless of gender, the same information is collected and analyzed; however, women and Aboriginal people are not assessed using the statistical information on recidivism (SIR) scale, a tool that combines measures of demographic characteristics and criminal history in a scoring system to derive a recidivism statistic. The risk component of the assessment focuses on the risk of recidivism by examining a number of static variables: the current offence, the criminal history record, the offence severity record, the sex offence history, the assessment of serious harm (to others), and statistical information on recidivism.[2]

The needs component of the assessment measures a variety of interpersonal and personal skills to determine criminogenic factors. This portion of the assessment investigates dynamic factors (that is, those factors that can change over time) to determine changes in the level of need and the significance of the offender's skill deficit. Information is collected from a variety of sources, including official documents, official versions of the offence, criminal history, post-sentence community assessment, intake assessment interviews, and supplementary assessments (which include psychological assessments, substance abuse assessments, educational and vocational assessments, family violence assessments, and sex offender assessments). The needs component of the assessment identifies seven primary domains: (1) employment, (2) marital/family, (3) associates/social interaction, (4) substance abuse, (5) community functioning, (6) personal/emotional orientation, and (7) attitude.

Dell and Boe (2000) examined the information collected as part of OIAs for federally sentenced female offenders and identified that Aboriginal women had a higher risk for reoffending (42 percent) than Caucasian women (29 percent). Aboriginal women were less likely than Caucasian women to be identified as having either a moderate risk for reoffending (37 percent vs. 44 percent) or a low risk for reoffending (21 percent vs. 27 percent). This information is consistent with information reported by the Canadian Human Rights Commission (2003), which indicated Aboriginal women accounted for 46 percent of all women in the maximum security population, 35 percent of all women classified as medium security, and 23 percent of all women classified as minimum security.

Considering the high reliance on criminal history in the risk assessment component, Aboriginal women are unsurprisingly overrepresented in the high-risk category, consistent with previous information identifying that Aboriginal people (women included) generally have more criminal offences and longer sentences than non-Aboriginal people particularly for violent offences. Dell and Boe (2000) note that 85 percent of Aboriginal women offenders had previous involvement in the adult court system, compared with 58 percent of the population of Caucasian women offenders. Further, federally sentenced Aboriginal women offenders were almost four times more likely to have had a previous admission to the federal correctional system. Similar youth statistics reveal that 65 percent of Aboriginal women offenders and only 19 percent of Caucasian women offenders had previous involvement in youth court.

As shown in figure 10.7, Aboriginal women offenders also have higher needs than Caucasian women offenders on all seven domains identified in the needs assessment component of the OIA. The most significant differences identified between Aboriginal and Caucasian women offenders were in two domains: substance abuse and employment. Substance abuse needs refer to a woman's use/abuse of alcohol and its impediment to community adjustment. Employment needs are defined as a woman's employment skills and general employability. Significant needs were also identified in three domains: marital/family, association/socialization, and community. Marital/family need is determined by the stability and support, or negative attributes, in a woman's interpersonal relationships. Association/socialization need refers to an offender's pro- and/or antisocial personal contacts, primarily determined by whether associates are involved in criminal activity. Community need refers to a woman's ability to function independently in the community, including her social skills, life skills, and money management skills. In the remaining two domains, personal/emotional and attitude, Aboriginal women's responses were not significantly different from their Caucasian counterparts. Personal and emotional needs are defined as a woman's psychological needs, whereas atti-

Figure 10.7   Percentage of Aboriginal and Caucasian Women Offenders Concentrated in Seven Needs Domains

	Aboriginal (%)	Caucasian (%)
Employment[a]	53%	25%
Marital/family[b]	55%	29%
Association/socialization[b]	37%	15%
Substance abuse[a]	82%	37%
Community[b]	18%	7%
Personal/emotional	57%	42%
Attitude	12%	8%

[a] $p < 0.001$
[b] $p < 0.01$

Source: Dell, A., & Boe, R. (2000). *An examination of Aboriginal and Caucasian women offender risk and needs factors* (Research Report R-94). Ottawa: Correctional Service of Canada, p. 11. Reproduced with the permission of the Minister of Public Works and Government Services Canada, 2008.

tude refers to a woman's orientation toward a pro-social lifestyle, her ability to recognize problem areas, and her receptiveness to assistance, including her attempts to further her own position through self-help measures and by demonstrating a pro-social attitude.

Once again, the overall high level of need for Aboriginal women is not surprising in light of the number of social disadvantages that Aboriginal people (including women) face in Canadian society. Madam Justice Arbour noted that the cumulative effect of a longer offence history, more violent offences, and a greater number of previous incarcerations among Aboriginal women results in higher security classifications and higher risk assessments (Canada, Commission of Inquiry into Certain Events, 1996).

Perhaps a more glaring reason why Aboriginal women are classified as both more likely to reoffend and requiring more extensive programming than non-Aboriginal women relates to the CSC's acknowledgment that more research is needed on the effectiveness of the OIA tool for predicting risk and assessing needs for women and Aboriginal offenders (Dell & Boe, 2000). The Canadian Human Rights Commission (2003) has stated that the tool has no validity for women or Aboriginal offenders; however, it asserts that the CSC continues to ignore research suggesting differences in men's and women's needs and in their criminogenic risk factors through its ongoing use of the OIA tool. Based on this information, the OIA tool is likely not capable of adequately measuring the unique factors that lead to Aboriginal people becoming involved in the criminal justice system; therefore, this tool is also unlikely to adequately identify programming needs to prevent reoffending, particularly for Aboriginal women. The information collected is possibly not gender-appropriate or culturally appropriate, which would lead to a mislabelling of the risk and needs for Aboriginal women both as a group and as individuals.

Challenges for Aboriginal Women Offenders

> *I am particularly concerned with silencing along the lines of race (more appropriately culture) ... It merely reflects that my voice is the voice of a Mohawk woman ... It is only through my culture that my women's identity is shaped. It is the teachings of my people that demand we speak from our own personal experiences.*
>
> Montour-Angus, 1996, cited in *The Lived Experience of Discrimination: Aboriginal Women Who Are Federally Sentenced* (Montour-Angus, 2002, p. 33)

The lack of a culture- and gender-specific needs and risk assessment at the time of incarceration creates further challenges for Aboriginal women in accessing culturally appropriate programming. Presently, the CSC offers culturally appropriate programming at Okimaw Ohci Healing Lodge (OOHL), a regional facility designed specifically for Aboriginal women and premised on Aboriginal values and healing. OOHL accepts only women who are classified as medium or minimum security, excluding the large proportion of Aboriginal women with high security classifications. The Correctional Investigator of Canada (2006) has recommended the CSC either reassess Aboriginal women offenders in a more gender- and culturally appropriate way or assess maximum security Aboriginal women offenders on an individual basis to support increasing their eligibility to OOHL.

The Correctional Service of Canada has refused to act on either recommendation, responding that the OIA tool is appropriate and follows protocols as outlined in the *Corrections and Conditional Release Act* (CSC, 2000). Similar recommendations have been made by the Native Women's Association of Canada (McIvor & Johnson, 2003) and the Canadian Human Rights Commission (2003) but the CSC has not taken any action. The CSC's response has been to cite the lack of empirical evidence to indicate the OIA tool overclassifies Aboriginal offenders (CSC, 2000). Instead, the CSC has attempted to deal with the overclassification by implementing "reclassification methods," which are conducted every six months for Aboriginal people, who are defined as a priority group. Throughout the CSC's response, it has asserted that it will continue to use evidence-based tools and conduct needs analyses to ensure the efficacy and cultural appropriateness of their tools and methods. They do not, however, acknowledge that the evidence-based tools they use have failed to create any changes in the disproportionate numbers of Aboriginal people in the correctional system or those who are classified as high risk. In fact, the CSC has violated its own guidelines, as defined by the CCRA (section 84) that states, "Where a person is, or is to be, confined in a penitentiary, the Service shall take all reasonable steps to ensure that the penitentiary in which the person is confined is one *that provides the least restrictive environment* for that person" (emphasis added). Although Okimaw Ohci Healing Lodge offers "the least restrictive environment" for Aboriginal women, a number of systemic factors create barriers for the majority of federally sentenced Aboriginal women to attend this facility, which was designed specifically to meet their unique needs and address their criminogenic factors in a culturally safe and appropriate way.

Aboriginal women who are assessed with an inadequate assessment tool may face longer prison stays due to overclassification, negative perceptions by guards and administration, difficulty accessing recommended programming, long-term reoffending, and social costs related to the negative impact on the Aboriginal woman's family (particularly her children). These implications affect not only an Aboriginal woman's daily life while incarcerated but also any future chances she may have when released into the community. As many Aboriginal women who are federally sentenced have stated time and time again, the correctional system is very similar to the kinds of institutions many of them have already been exposed to, from residential schools to the child welfare system to the youth and adult correctional system. As noted by LEAF (Women's Legal Education and Action Fund):

> Predictably the situation is more acute for Native women. They often receive more restrictive security classifications despite the fact that their offence or past institutional behaviour is comparable to that of a non-Native who is classified as low security risk. The Native woman is punished further when her participation in Native Sisterhood meetings is not recognized as serving a rehabilitative function by those assessing her eligibility for early release. Security classification is, therefore, an incident of racial discrimination. (LEAF, 1989, p. 3)

When exploring why a disproportionate number of Aboriginal women end up in the correctional system, we must resist the temptation to place the onus of responsibility on the CSC. Other factors play a significant role in Aboriginal women being overrepresented in the correctional system, including a lack of adequate gender- and culture-specific programming and the use of culturally and gender-inadequate assessment tools that result in mislabelling. However, overrepresentation of Aboriginal women in the criminal justice system occurs at both ends: when a woman first enters the court process and when she is incarcerated. Just as significant in comprehending the disproportionate number of Aboriginal women in the correctional system are factors that increase the likelihood that an Aboriginal woman will become involved in the court system, including overpolicing, overcharging, insensitive and uninformed legal professionals, and sentencing and structural barriers in the courts (Montour-Angus, 2002).

Overpolicing refers to certain geographical areas being conceptualized as crime-ridden and to racial groups that are viewed as engaging more often in criminal behaviour, resulting in a greater police presence. Overpolicing typically results in overcharging and can include situations in which the individual receives charges that are more punitive than charges made against other non-identified racial groups who commit the same offence.

In his book *Dancing with a Ghost*, Rupert Ross (1992), a Crown attorney in northwestern Ontario, discusses the lack of cultural awareness training the legal profession receives to equip them to comprehend Aboriginal values and worldview. According to Ross, without a sound knowledge and an understanding of an Aboriginal person's worldview, adequately representing the individual and making appropriate recommendations on sentencing of an Aboriginal person are nearly impossible. Ross espouses that learning about Aboriginal worldview must be embedded in a true understanding of the historical oppression and discrimination faced by Aboriginal people, which continues to this day for many Aboriginal communities and their members. As mentioned previously, a number of structural barriers exist in the court process, including language barriers, poor or inadequate legal representation, lack of adequate information, and an ill-equipped system that does not allot the time necessary to learn about the Aboriginal accused person, that person's community, and the impact of the offence on the accused, the victim, their families, and their communities.

The inappropriateness of the criminal justice system in meeting the unique culture- and gender-specific needs of Aboriginal women indicates that a combination of factors have played a significant role in the disproportionate number of Aboriginal women found in the correctional system. Unsurprisingly, Aboriginal female offenders, community groups, and national native women's organizations all point to systemic issues as a primary cause to the overrepresentation of Aboriginal women in the criminal justice system. These systemic issues are continually scrutinized as being racial and discriminatory in nature. Until major changes are made to the way the criminal justice system works, Aboriginal people, and Aboriginal women in particular, will remain overrepresented in the court and correctional systems.

Colonialism and Aboriginal Women

> *It is racism, past in our memories and present in our surroundings that negates non-native attempts to reconstruct our lives. Existing programs cannot reach us, cannot surmount the barriers of mistrust that racism has built. Physicians, psychiatrists and psychologists are typically White and male. How can we be healed by those who symbolize the worst experiences of our past?*
>
> Aboriginal parolee, cited in *Creating Choices* (Canada, Task Force on Federally Sentenced Women, 1990, p. 9)

Colonialism can be defined as the systematic oppression of a people through a variety of assimilationist measures that are intended to eradicate the peoples and/or their sense of individual and cultural identity.[3] In Canada, colonialism began with the arrival of the European settlers whose need to gain control and ownership of the land was in direct opposition with Aboriginal people, who believed that the land could not be owned and that, as stewards, they were meant to ensure its continuance and existence for future generations. Over the years, colonialism has taken many forms, from the establishment of treaties relegating Aboriginal people to reserves, to defining who an Aboriginal person was (and is), to emotional, psychological, and physical warfare against Aboriginal people, to controlling the movements and livelihoods of Aboriginal people, to the banning of their cultural practices and the banning of their traditional languages, to the institution of residential schools, to name a few.

Colonialist practices as they pertain to Aboriginal people continue today in Canada with the continued existence of policies and governmental laws that define Aboriginal people and how they conduct their lives. Many of these policies and laws are carried out by government departments and organizations that fail to comprehend the colonialist nature of their practices. These practices are far more subtle today but can also be found in such arenas as a separate (and ill-funded and ill-equipped) health care system, inadequate funding for programs to improve the livelihood of Aboriginal people, inadequate governmental response to the effects of the residential school system on Aboriginal people and their communities, lack of well-informed education on Aboriginal people's history and their contributions in Canada, negative media attention to Aboriginal rights and issues, lack of equal representation at political forums or in the government structure, and the continued marginalization of Aboriginal people in Canada.

Colonialism continues to affect Aboriginal people in their daily lives through both overt and subtle racism they may experience (due usually to a lack of understanding by non-Aboriginal people) and the lack of culturally safe and appropriate programming and services that they access and use in their daily lives. Many would argue that the negative social factors that affect Aboriginal people are a result of long-standing colonialism in Canada. The commissioners of Manitoba's Public Inquiry into the Administration of Justice and Aboriginal People discussed the complexities and impact of the colonial relationship that exists between Aboriginal people and the government:

> Cultural oppression, social inequality, the loss of self-government and systemic discrimination, which are the legacy of the Canadian government's treatment of Aboriginal people, are intertwined and interdependent factors, and in very few cases is it possible to draw a simple and direct correlation between any of them and the events which lead an individual Aboriginal person to commit a crime or to become incarcerated. We believe that the overall weight of the evidence makes it clear that these factors are crucial in explaining the reasons why Aboriginal people are over-represented in … jails. (Manitoba, Public Inquiry, 1991, p. 86)

The impact of colonialism on Aboriginal women has resulted in serious and long-standing consequences that continue to beleaguer contemporary Aboriginal women to this day. Traditional roles have been lost, such as that whereby Aboriginal women were seen as keepers of the community, language, and culture because they were the caretakers of the children. Now, negative stereotypes encourage the view of Aboriginal women as unequal, worthless, and unintelligent, thereby not requiring respect from those around them, both in their community and in society at large. Many argue that the high rates of violence against women and children in Aboriginal communities are a direct result of colonialism, which forever changed the way women and children were viewed by men. A great deal of literature has been written on the impact of colonial relations on Aboriginal women by such scholars as Anderson (2000), Gibson (1990), Razack (1998), and Solomon (1994), to name a few. All of the literature points to past systematic attempts at assimilating Aboriginal people and replacing their culture and worldview with a Euro-Canadian view that had a far different perception of women. Understanding colonialism as the foundation for the many social ills and the discrimination experienced by Aboriginal women (and people) must be the cornerstone to comprehending what is needed for Aboriginal women (and people) to reclaim their role in the community and society. As noted by an Aboriginal parolee:

> The critical difference is racism. We are born to it and spend our lives facing it. Racism lies at the root of our life experiences. The effect is violence, violence against us, and in turn our own violence. The solution is healing; healing through traditional ceremonies, support, understanding and the compassion that will empower Aboriginal women to the betterment of ourselves, our families and our communities. (Aboriginal parolee, cited in Canada, TFFSW, 1990, p. 9)

Montour-Angus (2002) and others have argued that the CSC has continually failed to meaningfully take into consideration how colonialism affects service delivery for federally sentenced Aboriginal women. This failure has been witnessed in the CSC's refusal to reconsider the use of ill-adapted assessment tools that mislabel Aboriginal women as high risk and high needs. Further examples include the lack of legitimacy extended to traditional healing practices as part of the rehabilitative component in the correctional plan and the absence of understanding about the protocols with regard to Aboriginal programming and cultural services offered in the correctional system. Federally sentenced Aboriginal women have had to deal with the erosion of their culture through various assimilationist acts, including separation from their families and removal from their homes at a young age. Because these women did not have a chance to gain a sense of their individual and cultural identity, such assimilationist acts have led to their marginalization not only from society but also from their families, their communities, and their people.

Federally sentenced Aboriginal women report that the Canadian criminal justice system has been unsympathetic to their needs and suffering. In fact, many have provided examples of having been the target of racism and discrimination throughout the court process and in the correctional system because no one understood the Aboriginal cultural values, traditions, or ceremonies, all important facets in regaining an Aboriginal woman's sense of empowerment to support her healing. Montour-Angus (2002) also argues that referring to Aboriginal correctional programming as "Aboriginal issues" inappropriately denotes Aboriginal people's realities as a problem that is akin to a form of victim blaming, another form of perpetuating discrimination against Aboriginal people. The *Creating Choices* report (Canada, TFFSW, 1990) also acknowledged the impact of colonialism on Aboriginal women in the criminal justice system, pointing out that colonialism has created a climate of distrust in which Aboriginal people do not view the criminal justice system as an equal system that adequately represents them but instead see it as another system that sets out rules to govern them without acknowledging the unique Aboriginal needs and realities. As described by Patricia Montour-Angus (2002):

> Not only can we not separate the Aboriginal and the woman, it is important to understand we also share a common Aboriginal history. That common history is the history of racism, oppression, genocide, and ethnocide. It is one further way in which we are distinct. This shared history impacts on Aboriginal federally sentenced women in two ways. First, as the racism of prisons or the criminal justice system has largely been ignored or vanished, the situation of Aboriginal women as participants in Canadian society cannot be understood by prison administrators or correctional bureaucrats. It is these individuals who have historically controlled the administration of criminal justice. This has left Aboriginal federally sentenced women in an impossible situation. The people who hold the key to their release, they cannot trust. This lack of trust is not the sole responsibility or failure of individuals (prisoners or correctional employees) but a systemic failure to address racism. (p. 7)

The temptation to perceive the multiple layers of discrimination perpetuated by colonialism and experienced by Aboriginal women in the criminal justice system as either additive or cumulative should be resisted. Taking either stance would suggest that the multiple layers of discrimination are separate from each other; however, these layers of discrimination should be considered interdependent, overlapping, and intersectional. **Intersectional discrimination**, a relatively new legal term, is defined as "intersectional oppression that arises out of the combination of various oppressions which, together, produce something unique and distinct from any one form of discrimination standing alone" and is a distinct experience for Aboriginal women (Montour-Angus, 2002, p. 34). Therefore, intersectional discrimination is experienced distinctly *only if* one is an Aboriginal woman.

An excellent example of intersectional discrimination is the labelling of Aboriginal women as violent. Compared with male violence, Aboriginal women's crimes do not stand out as excessive. However, when compared with non–Aboriginal women's crimes, they do stand out, which has resulted in Aboriginal women's overrepresentation in the maximum security classification. However, a further argument suggests that the discrimination experienced by Aboriginal women in the criminal justice system may be more likely referred to as compound discrimination. Compound discrimination is a form of "double-whammy" discrimination that an Aboriginal woman experiences because she is *both* Aboriginal and a woman. Using these definitions, one can decipher that Aboriginal women have experienced colonialism (due to being Aboriginal) and paternalism (due to being female)—a double whammy in the criminal justice system. Therefore, when Aboriginal women's needs are embedded in women's needs or Aboriginal needs, no true comprehension is possible of the distinct challenges that are faced by Aboriginal women in the correctional system. In the words of an Aboriginal woman parolee:

> To be a woman and to be *seen* as violent is to be especially marked in the eyes of the administration of the prisons where women do time, and in the eyes of the staff who guard them. In a prison with a male population, our crimes would stand out much less. Among women we [Aboriginal women] do not fit the stereotypes, and we are automatically feared, and labelled as in need of special handling. The label violent begets a self-perpetuating and destructive cycle for Aboriginal women within prisons. (Aboriginal parolee, cited in Canada, TFFSW, 1990, p. 12)

The Supreme Court of Canada has, in fact, recognized the colonialist nature of the law in dealing with Aboriginal women. In 1995, Jamie Tanis Gladue was found guilty of murdering her common-law husband while intoxicated and was sentenced to federal incarceration. She appealed the sentencing decision, stating that the court had not considered distinct issues that affect Aboriginal people. In a landmark decision in 1999, the Supreme Court of Canada stated that when determining sentencing, the court system must take into consideration the colonialist actions against Aboriginal people in comprehending why they engage in criminal behaviour. This landmark decision, known as the *Gladue* decision, has demanded that the court system examine culture- and gender-specific issues to learn who the offender is as a person and not base a determination solely on the nature of her offence.

Based on this writer's personal experience, the court system is still ill-equipped to enforce the principles of *Gladue* because many of the front-line workers responsible for determining sentencing do not comprehend the *Gladue* principles (some may not even know about *Gladue*) or the unique culture- and gender-specific issues for Aboriginal women. Without this information, justice workers are ill-equipped and lack the knowledge of the kinds of information that must be examined and explored in the work they prepare for sentencing and release planning. Ten years have passed since the landmark decision of *Gladue* yet only now are some provinces, including Ontario, considering specific training on the *Gladue* principles to increase their knowledge of colonialism in Canada and its historical and present-day impacts on Aboriginal people. As noted by Sugar and Fox (1990):

> Our understanding of law, of courts, of police, of the judicial system, and of prisons are all set by lifetimes defined by racism. Racism is not simply set by the overt experiences of racism, though most of us have known this direct hatred, have been called "dirty Indians" in school,

or in foster homes, or by police or guards, or have seen the differences in the way we are treated and have known this was no accident. Racism is much more extensive than this. Culturally, economically, and as Peoples we have been oppressed and pushed aside by Whites. We were sent to live on reserves which denied us a livelihood, controlled us with rules that we did not set, and made us dependent on services we could not provide for ourselves. (pp. 9–10)

Colonialism has created a two-tiered society, which includes the dominant people or the controllers, who are the mechanics of society on one tier, and the marginalized people, who are affected by the decisions of the dominant group on another tier. The marginalized people are the vulnerable population, who are often at the mercy of the decisions made by others (the dominant group) who have given little thought to the consequence or effect their decisions have on other members of society. Colonialism has rendered Aboriginal people marginalized and vulnerable and, for Aboriginal women, the marginalization continues with their experiences in all parts of the criminal justice system.

The Ever-Changing Face of Aboriginal Corrections

We have often said that the women inside have the understanding to help themselves, that all that is required is the right kind of resources, support, and help. The money spent on studies would be much better spent on family visits, on culturally appropriate help, on reducing our powerlessness to heal ourselves. But the reality is that prison conditions grow worse. We cry out for a meaningful healing process that will have real impact on our lives, but the objectives and implementation of this healing process must be premised on our need to heal and walk in balance.

Fox & Sugar, cited in *The Lived Experience of Discrimination: Aboriginal Women Who Are Federally Sentenced* (Montour-Angus, 2002, p. 1)

Two major documents in the correctional system formed the major impetus that led to redefining how women offenders were treated in the correctional system: *Creating Choices* (Canada, TFFSW, 1990) and the Arbour inquiry (Canada, Commission of Inquiry into Certain Events, 1996). Both documents acknowledged that the current correctional system was developed by males, for males, and with male needs in mind and had experienced limited to no success in dealing with federally sentenced women. The two documents agreed that women have unique needs and criminogenic factors and require specialized programming to support their reintegration into society. These documents also highlighted that within federally sentenced women, Aboriginal women are a distinct group whose needs are multi-layered due to gender and cultural needs. These two documents were supported by the 1994 release of the *Corrections and Conditional Release Act*, which specifically addressed the unique needs of Aboriginal people and women. The CCRA states that correctional policies, programs, and practices shall "respect gender, ethnic, cultural and linguistic differences and be responsive to the special needs of women and aboriginal peoples." Sections 79 to 84 address the needs of Aboriginal offenders, including programs, spiritual leaders and Elders, parole plans, and any other aspect that would address Aboriginal offenders' distinct needs.

These documents resulted in some significant changes to the correctional system's approach to women and Aboriginal people. *Creating Choices* (Canada, TFFSW, 1990) identified five principles of change that are the basis of programming for women offenders:

Principle 1: Empowerment
Principle 2: Meaningful and responsible choices
Principle 3: Respect and dignity
Principle 4: Supportive environment
Principle 5: Shared responsibility (among levels of government and services)

The following is a review of some of the major changes that were implemented and a critical analysis of the success of these changes for Aboriginal women in the correctional system.

Okimaw Ohci Healing Lodge

Healing for Aboriginal women means the opportunity, through Aboriginal teachings, programs, spirituality and culture, to recover from histories of abuse, regain a sense of self-worth, gain skills and rebuild families. Through healing, Aboriginal women are able to change or release negative behaviours such as addictions and criminal behaviour. Delving deep into issues allows for an intensive healing experience, which improves their ability to re-establish themselves in their community.

*Okimaw Ohci Healing Lodge Operational Plan, 2004, cited in The Ten-Year
Status Report on Women's Corrections, 1996–2006 (CSC, 2006, p. 22)*

One of the most significant recommendations from *Creating Choices* (Canada, TFFSW, 1990) was to abolish the old Prison for Women (P4W) at Kingston, Ontario in favour of regional facilities that would bring women closer to their homes and their families. This recommendation included the specific mention of the need for a regional facility that was premised on Aboriginal values and philosophies to support Aboriginal women's healing. The intent of the regional facilities was also based on a feminist perspective that recognized federally sentenced women had lower risk factors than men and did not require the same level of security.

Five regional facilities were opened across the country, including the Okimaw Ohci Healing Lodge (OOHL) in 1995. This 30-bed facility with single and family residential units (to accommodate children) was developed with, by, and for Aboriginal women, with significant contributions made by the Nekaneet First Nation, Saskatchewan, which is home to OOHL.

The operational plan and facility design focused on the importance of nature in Aboriginal culture, the need for privacy in healing, community interactions, and Aboriginal-specific intervention strategies (CSC, 2006). As envisioned in *Creating Choices*, the planning of OOHL included CSC representatives, Aboriginal community partners, and Elders who together identified a plan for staffing, training, and program development. The opening of OOHL (and other regional facilities) ameliorated past concerns of geographical and cultural isolation for all federally sentenced women. OOHL's Aboriginal-specific programming addressed past concerns identified by Aboriginal women, including their need for more female staff of Aboriginal descent who understood Aboriginal healing practices and for greater access to Elders and to cultural ceremonies and practices.

Perhaps the biggest criticism of OOHL remains the issue of security classification. Aboriginal women are required to be classified as medium or minimum security to be accepted to OOHL. As mentioned throughout this chapter, Aboriginal women continue to remain over-represented in the maximum security classification. Despite the calls made by the Arbour inquiry (Canada, Commission of Inquiry into Certain Events, 1996), the Canadian Human Rights Commission (2003), and the Correctional Investigator of Canada (2006) to reconsider the classification of Aboriginal women and/or to permit all Aboriginal women, regardless of their classification, to attend OOHL, such change has been staunchly refused by the CSC. The denial is based on the CSC's assertion that the existing method of classification is not biased and that Aboriginal women who are classified as maximum security present too great a risk and need to be able to meet the demands and expectations of OOHL. Many authors (for example, Montour-Angus, 2002; McIvor & Johnson, 2003) discount the CSC's reasons as discriminatory and colonialist with the result that not all Aboriginal women are able to take advantage of the unique programming offered at OOHL. To counter criticisms, the CSC has implemented such measures as a healing lodge readiness assessment, a healing readiness commitment form, and a "champion" for the lodge in each regional facility. These measures are an attempt to support Aboriginal women's desires both to attend OOHL and to reduce their security classification so they can be considered for a transfer. Limited information is available to adequately assess whether these measures are having promising results.

Box 10.2   Federally Sentenced Aboriginal Women's Perspective

- 100% identified the need for more contact with Elders. Elder counselling should be made available on a full-time basis. Elder interventions should also be available when disagreements arise, which should be recognized in the correctional plan.
- 76% indicated security levels are not explained to them. In order for the Aboriginal women to work on lowering their security level, reason for changes in security levels must be explained, and the correctional plan's relation to increases or decreases in security level must be deciphered.
- 100% stated Aboriginal ceremonies need to be recognized as part of the correctional plan for their healing effects.
- 100% stated programs facilitated by staff do not work but create animosity and anger among female inmates.
- 58% stated Aboriginal culture needs to be treated with respect. Some women reported that time limits have been placed on the ceremonies and that protocols for ceremonies were not followed by staff.
- 100% reported a lack of communication between management, the primary worker, and the woman. When problems occur, the Aboriginal women are often blamed for being manipulative. This displacement of authority is viewed as oppressive.

- 76% stated that CSC needs to ensure that core programs are available in all institutions. Completion of core programs is mandatory in the correctional plan to lower security levels but these programs are not available in some institutions.
- 76% stated that their application to the Okimaw Ohci Healing Lodge was not even considered or processed.
- 88% stated they had taken steps to reduce their security levels but were not supported by staff for various reasons.
- 76% stated that CSC needs to hire more Aboriginal staff who practise their culture and are not judgmental.
- 76% indicated they had controlled their behaviour and had requested programs but staff did not respond to their needs to provide the programs.

Source: Morin, S. (1999). *Federally sentenced Aboriginal women in maximum security: What happened to the promises of "Creating Choices"?* Ottawa: Correctional Service of Canada.

Although OOHL offers Aboriginal-specific programming, its status as the only facility of its kind in Canada creates barriers and challenges for Aboriginal women. Its placement was a wise decision, based on the overrepresentation of Aboriginal women from the Prairie region; however, women from other parts of the country who are interested in accessing Aboriginal-specific programming are often urged to transfer to OOHL, which would take them outside of their home region and away from their families. The programming offered at OOHL is based on the teachings and philosophy of the tribes located on the Prairies. This approach has implications for Aboriginal women from non-Prairie areas because such programming does not adequately meet the philosophy, worldview, and cultural practices of tribes from eastern Canada, the Pacific region (the People of the Longhouse), Inuit, or Métis people. A recommendation by the Correctional Investigator of Canada (2006) to consider a similar facility in eastern Canada has been denied by the CSC, which stated that the numbers of Aboriginal women in that region did not warrant such a facility. That being said, OOHL does not meet all of the cultural needs of Aboriginal women from different Aboriginal groups, which means that some Aboriginal women continue to experience cultural isolation while incarcerated.

Questions have been raised about how well the new regional facilities have ameliorated geographical isolation for federally sentenced women (Montour-Angus, 2002). During the operation of P4W, all women offenders and their families received financial compensation for family visits and phone calls home because of the significant geographical distances that many of them faced. After the establishment of the regional facilities, this compensation was abolished under the premise that women would now be closer to home. However, some federally sentenced women remain hundreds of miles from their homes, and if their families are poor (as is often the case for Aboriginal women), the likelihood of regular contact with them is low. This isolation from families is particularly relevant if an Aboriginal woman chooses to transfer to OOHL from outside of the Prairie region. Because Aboriginal women in this situation may be hundreds (or even thousands) of miles away from home, and their families do not have the financial means to attend the facility, these women continue to experience geographical isolation from their families.

Another unforeseen consequence of the new facilities has been the reduced profile of the Native Sisterhood, an active group of Aboriginal women at P4W who supported each other in their healing and their experiences of incarceration, while ensuring that the rights, needs, and challenges of federally sentenced Aboriginal women remained visible. The unity demonstrated through Native Sisterhood no longer is present because of the low numbers of Aboriginal women in some institutions (for example, Morin, 1999 noted only one Aboriginal woman incarcerated in Quebec). The deterioration of the Native Sisterhood has likely resulted in less sharing, less support, and less activism to highlight federally sentenced Aboriginal women's continued needs (which could be seen as a mechanism to increase feelings of empowerment for Aboriginal women). As stated by one former prisoner:

> Because of the Native Sisterhood I finally knew the meaning of spirituality. I learned how to pray in a sweat and with sweetgrass. I learned the meaning of the Eagle feather and colours. With that I was even more proud of who I was in my identity. (Aboriginal ex-prisoner, cited in Canada, TFFSW, 1990, p. 10)

Cultural Needs and Challenges Faced in the Correctional System

> *Native women believed that their behaviour was misinterpreted by white staff, and that this led to the prescribing of drugs. Several Native women talked about what an alien environment prison was compared to the familiarity of life in Native communities. The way Native women chose to respond to this was to become quiet and observe how things were conducted. These women said that their behavioural reaction, one of quietness, was misinterpreted by the prison psychologist as a type of suppression of their anger and bitterness ... believed that because the prison did not know how to relate to Native Americans they then wanted to control them.*
>
> The Lived Experience of Discrimination: Aboriginal Women Who
> Are Federally Sentenced (Montour-Angus, 2002, p. 25)

Since the release of *Creating Choices* in 1990, a major shift has occurred in the recognition of Aboriginal spirituality and ceremonies and in Aboriginal people's rights to have access to Aboriginal spirituality and ceremonies on a regular basis. The commissioner's directives, as outlined in Morin (1999), highlight the policy objectives related to ceremonies, spiritual practices, healing initiatives, recognition of spiritual Elders, and the Native liaison program. Although the most intensive Aboriginal programming is located at OOHL, the CSC asserts that Aboriginal women in the other regional facilities have access to spiritual Elders, Aboriginal ceremonies and practices, and Aboriginal-specific programming (such as Aboriginal Pathways, Spirit of a Warrior, and Circles of Change). During interviews with Aboriginal women at the Edmonton Institute for Women, where a large Aboriginal population is incarcerated, the following comment was made:

> A lot of women I find use the Elder as a resource, meet with her quite regularly. As far as programming goes, I was really, really shocked to see that there was nothing here, absolutely nothing Aboriginal based in the lines of programming. (Montour-Angus, 2002, p. 19)

Unfortunately, these programs are not always available in all regional facilities, possibly because of the low numbers of Aboriginal women in these facilities who would access these programs. This situation creates a barrier for Aboriginal women to receive culturally appropriate programming in their home region, particularly if it requires they seek a transfer to OOHL. Although Aboriginal women are given the opportunity to participate in Aboriginal-specific programming, they are also required to complete core programming (even at OOHL), which the CSC asserts is relevant for all federally sentenced individuals, regardless of gender or race. Because core programming is based on the needs identified in the OIA tool (which has been brought into question for its lack of gender- and culture-specific relevance), the core programming may also be irrelevant across genders and cultures.

This frustration is often exacerbated by concerns expressed by federally sentenced Aboriginal women that the staff delivering these programs, particularly within the regional facilities, are often non-Aboriginal. Aboriginal women report that having correctional officers deliver core programs creates a conflict of interest: Aboriginal women have reported that programs have been withheld from them as a form of punishment and to force conformity to the rules of the facilities. These disciplinary measures, as reported by Morin (1999), lead to tension between staff and inmate, uncooperative behaviour on the part of the woman, and negative perceptions held by the staff member. Such measures have further detrimental long-term effects on the Aboriginal woman because of the delay in accessing and completing programming required for their correctional plan. These delays then result in some Aboriginal women being incarcerated until their statutory release date, creating greater likelihood of reoffending because of fewer identified supports available further into a conditional release program. Another general concern of Aboriginal women is that the staff do not have the personal or practical experience to be teaching the skills the women require as part of their healing (Montour-Angus, 2002). A continuing issue for Aboriginal women is that non-Aboriginal staff have a limited understanding of Aboriginal realities, which may render them ignorant or unsympathetic to the suffering experienced by federally sentenced Aboriginal women.

For many Aboriginal women, their maximum security classification creates a barrier to being housed in a regional facility. Until recently, all women classified as maximum security were housed in special units in men's institutions, akin to segregation in a men's prison. This arrangement had implications for Aboriginal women because it resulted in less availability of both core and Aboriginal-specific programming, making it difficult for these women to reduce their security level, which was needed to transfer to a regional facility. Morin (1999) has also revealed that Aboriginal women housed in these institutions (such as the Regional Psychiatric Centre) have reported poor access to Native liaison services, cultural ceremonies, and Elder involvement. They also reported that the staff and institution afforded less respect for these initiatives or their positive impact on Aboriginal women. The staff in a male-dominated institution would likely have less gender-specific training and therefore have a poorer comprehension of the unique needs of women. Aboriginal women have noted that these facilities lack reintegration options, including contact with their families, which would have increased the support they received upon release (Montour-Angus, 2002).

Efforts are being made to house maximum security women in regional facilities but this effort has required the construction of a separate unit for women. Although maximum security women will be housed in a female-dominated institution, their units will not be constructed in the same manner as the rest of the regional facilities, that is, in a community-like setting. Thus, Aboriginal women will still be denied the ability to learn the skills they require to be successful on conditional release into the community, particularly if their security classification does not change.

Montour-Angus (2002) asserts that changes have been made within the regional facilities that were unintended by the recommendations of *Creating Choices* in 1990. She reports that security has been intensified to include fences, razor wire, repeated strip searching, and the use of security cameras—measures that are commonly found in a maximum security institution. The new challenges posed by the CSC's attempt to provide feminist perspectives to the correctional system while maintaining many of the existing (male-dominated) facets of the correctional system continues to result in a system that is less than adequate in its responsiveness to the needs of Aboriginal women. Cultural needs are an important part of programming and are sometimes seen as a secondary component for Aboriginal women. Therefore, the security classification of a woman appears to shape her experience while incarcerated because it determines the kind of facility she will be housed in. The quality of an Aboriginal woman's classification and the experience she has are marked more by her security classification than a man's because Aboriginal women are denied the benefits (that is, the cottage-like accommodations in a medium security facility) intended for incarcerated women. Once again, investigation reveals that Aboriginal women continue to experience cultural isolation during their period of incarceration regardless of the CSC's attempts to ameliorate these concerns.

Has Change Really Happened?

Morin (1999) conducted a study with Aboriginal women to learn whether *Creating Choices* had positively affected their lives since its introduction in 1990. Her work identified that maximum security Aboriginal women continued to experience discrimination despite government policies and programs to combat discrimination. See box 10.2 for a list of concerns identified by these women. From this list, it is obvious that the changes recommended by *Creating Choices* (1990) and the Arbour inquiry (Canada, Commission of Inquiry into Certain Events, 1996) are not being made adequately, timely, or in a gender- and cultural-appropriate manner.

Can the CCRA Create Meaningful Change?

Sections 81to 84 of the *Corrections and Conditional Release Act* grants authority for the CSC to facilitate and fund capacity-building initiatives in Aboriginal communities that would result in successful integration of Aboriginal people back into their communities. In order for these initiatives to work, federally sentenced Aboriginal women need to know their rights and privileges under the CCRA. The Native Women's Association of Canada (McIvor & Johnson, 2003) report that the CSC has failed to adequately educate federally sentenced Aboriginal women about their options for decarceration, including the possibility of serving their sentence in a community-based setting. The CSC also needs to identify, develop, and refine community initiatives that are willing and able to accept custodial care for an Aboriginal woman serving a prison sentence.

At the time of the release of the correctional investigator's report (Correctional Investigator Canada, 2006) and the simultaneous release of the CSC's *Ten-Year Status Report on Women's Corrections* (CSC, 2006), very few (if any) community initiatives were in place to support an Aboriginal woman serving her time in an Aboriginal community setting (Montour-Angus, 2002). Both reports highlighted that the CSC's Aboriginal Initiatives branch was in the process of developing regional and national action plans to address these shortcomings. One such action plan has resulted in a conditional release planning kit that is disbursed throughout the CSC, to all the regional facilities and to Aboriginal communities to provide a comprehensive guide to release options.

The Native Women's Association of Canada report (McIvor & Johnson, 2003) expressed a concern with the feasibility of the CSC implementing section 84 of the CCRA. In the report, the association identifies current budget constraints within the CSC that led to the denial of transfers under this section of the Act. The association also reported that the CSC determines the viability of an Aboriginal community to provide the necessary care and support for an Aboriginal woman during incarceration or parole supervision. This authority creates concerns because the CSC has not demonstrated its own internal viability in recognizing, acknowledging, developing, or offering cultural programs that are adequate and sufficient to meet the needs of federally sentenced Aboriginal women. Therefore, the Native Women's Association of Canada provides a valid concern about the implication of the CSC making such determinations because the CSC may not positively support innovative and culturally valid Aboriginal community initiatives that are willing to support Aboriginal women in their reintegration plans.

The CSC has also developed nine full-time positions across the country to create links between Aboriginal offenders (male and female) and Aboriginal communities. These positions, Aboriginal community development officers (ACDOs), are expected to increase Aboriginal "community interest in participating in the correctional process and to initiate section 84 release planning" (CSC, 2006, p. 24). Although these measures are a step in the right direction, they are more than 10 years overdue for Aboriginal people involved in the correctional system.

The criminal justice system has been remiss by not providing a timely response to the many government policies and accompanying documents from other sources, which could have reduced the number of Aboriginal offenders in Canada's correctional system, as outlined in both the *Gladue* decision and the *Corrections and Conditional Release Act*. The responses offered by all parts of the criminal justice system continue to describe the ongoing discrimination faced by Aboriginal people, evidence of a perpetuation of colonial behaviours. These types of colonialist acts contribute to keeping Aboriginal women separated from their families and isolated from the communities that would support their healing and improve their lifestyle.

Other measures within the criminal justice system have been implemented to assist in reducing the disproportionate number of Aboriginal people in the correctional system. The National Parole Board has implemented a panel review with an Aboriginal cultural advisor as an alternative hearing approach that is more sensitive to the unique needs of Aboriginal offenders. The hearing is based on Aboriginal values, including holding the hearing in a circle, using cultural ceremonies (prayers and smudges, for example), and inviting the participation of the affected parties. The board members are also briefed on Aboriginal culture, traditions, and experiences, including information specific to the tribe or culture of the offender. Statistics from the National Parole Board (2004) indicate both an increased use in alternative hearings and higher rates of Aboriginal offenders being granted all forms of conditional release over a five-year period (60 percent increase in day parole and 25 percent for full parole). Finally, in 1991, the federal government introduced the First Nations policing policy to allow for "access to police services that were professional, effective, culturally appropriate and accountable to the communities they serve" (CCJA, 2000, p. 31). This policy is an important step in making the criminal justice system more responsive to the cultural needs of Aboriginal people. Benefits that have been identified include the following:

- A decrease in the number of arrests
- Less tension when an Aboriginal police officer is involved
- The combination of police training and an officer's knowledge of and commitment to the community

However, problems also plague this initiative—mainly issues related to poor or inadequate funding that leads to high attrition rates because of low salaries and the pressures afforded to Aboriginal police officers who carry a dual role of policing (generally a profession with much distrust in the community) and being a family member and community member (CCJA, 2000).

Summary

Aboriginal women are disproportionately represented in the criminal justice system in Canada, and population statistics suggest this trend may continue into the next decade. Their over-representation is multi-causal: social and economic disadvantages, opposing values of justice, discrimination and racism, lack of gender- and culture-relevant assessment tools, lack of culture-relevant programming, and colonialism. In the last 10 years, significant documents, government policies, and court decisions have addressed ways to combat the negative implications of colonialism that incarcerated Aboriginal women continue to deal with on a daily basis.

Although the intent of these documents, policies, and decisions is valuable and significant, only a limited impact has been realized on reducing the number of Aboriginal women in the criminal justice system. Some promising initiatives can be expanded to improve the status of incarcerated Aboriginal women; for example, the measures used to develop and implement the opening of Okimaw Ohci Healing Lodge. However, careful consideration must be given to the need for Aboriginal involvement, participation, and ownership if such initiatives are to succeed. Until the criminal justice system is prepared to recognize, acknowledge, and address the imbedded colonialism within the system, only limited gains can be expected in improving the status of Aboriginal women in the criminal justice system.

Notes

1. The term *Aboriginal people* refers to First Nations, Inuit, and Métis.
2. The last variable, statistical information on recidivism, is not collected for women and Aboriginal people.
3. For a more complete discussion of the definition and impact of colonialism, see Montour-Angus (1999) and Stevenson (1999).

Discussion Questions

1. Discuss how the needs of Aboriginal women are unfairly recognized by the criminal justice system.
2. Colonialism plays a significant role in the reality of Aboriginal women's lives prior to, during, and after incarceration. Identify historical and present-day colonialist acts and describe their impact on Aboriginal women.
3. Examine how the Gladue decision, the *Corrections and Conditional Release Act, Creating Choices*, and the Arbour inquiry attempt to ameliorate colonial consequences that result in discriminatory treatment of Aboriginal women in the criminal justice system.
4. *Creating Choices* made a number of recommendations regarding federally sentenced women. Discuss the advantages and disadvantages of these recommendations for federally sentenced Aboriginal women.

Suggested Readings

Canadian Criminal Justice Association. (2000). Aboriginal peoples and the criminal justice system [Special issue]. *Bulletin*. Retrieved from www.ccja-acjp.ca/en/aborit.html.

Morin, S. (1999). *Federally sentenced Aboriginal women in maximum security: What happened to the promises of "Creating Choices"?* Ottawa: Correctional Service of Canada.

Montour-Angus, P. (1999). Considering colonialism and oppression: Aboriginal women, justice and the "theory" of decolonization. *Native Studies Review, 12*, 63–94

Montour-Angus, P. (2002). *The lived experience of discrimination: Aboriginal women who are federally sentenced*. Ottawa: Canadian Association of Elizabeth Fry Societies.

Ross, R. (1992). *Dancing with a ghost: Exploring Indian reality*. Markham: Reed Books Canada.

Ross, R. (1996). *Returning to the teachings: Exploring Aboriginal justice*. Toronto: Penguin Books.

Online Resources

1. *Creating choices: Report of the Task Force on Federally Sentenced Women*: www.csc-scc.gc.ca/text/prgrm/fsw/choices/toce-eng.shtml
2. *Report of the Royal Commission on Aboriginal People: Vol. 3. Gathering strength*: www.ainc-inac.gc.ca/ch/rcap/sg/si1_e.html#Volume%203

References

Anderson K. (2000). *A recognition of being: Reconstructing Native womanhood.* Toronto: Second Story Press.

Canada, Commission of Inquiry into Certain Events at the Prison for Women in Kingston. (1996). *Commission of inquiry into certain events at the Prison for Women in Kingston* (the Arbour inquiry). Ottawa: Public Works and Government Services of Canada.

Canada, Royal Commission on Aboriginal Peoples. (1996). *Report of the Royal Commission on Aboriginal Peoples: Vol. 3. Gathering strength.* Ottawa: Indian and Northern Affairs Canada.

Canada, Task Force on Federally Sentenced Women. (1990). *Creating choices: Report of the Task Force on Federally Sentenced Women.* Ottawa: Department of the Solicitor General.

Canadian Criminal Justice Association. (2000). Aboriginal peoples and the criminal justice system [Special issue]. *Bulletin.* Retrieved from www.ccja-acjp.ca/en/aborit.html.

Canadian Human Rights Commission. (2003). *Protecting their rights: A systemic review of human rights in correctional services for federally sentenced women.* Retrieved from www.chrc-ccdp.ca/legislation_policies/consultation_report-en.asp.

Correctional Investigator of Canada. (2006). *Annual Report of the Office of the Correctional Investigator 2005–2006.* Ottawa: Ministry of Public Works and Government Services Canada.

Correctional Service of Canada. (2000). *Statistical overview: Women offenders sector.* Ottawa: Correctional Service of Canada.

Correctional Service of Canada. (2006). *The ten-year status report on women's corrections, 1996–2006.* Ottawa: Correctional Service of Canada.

Corrections and Conditional Release Act. (1992). SC 1992, c. 20.

Dell, A., & Boe, R. (2000). *An examination of Aboriginal and Caucasian women offender risk and needs Factors* (Research Report R-94). Ottawa: Correctional Service of Canada.

Gibson, D. (1990). *The law of the charter.* Toronto: Carswell.

Manitoba, Public Inquiry into the Administration of Justice and Aboriginal People. (1991). *Report of the Aboriginal Justice Inquiry of Manitoba: The justice system and Aboriginal people* (vol. 1). Winnipeg: Queen's Printer.

McIvor, E., & Johnson, E. (2003). *Detailed position of the Native Women's Association of Canada on the complaint regarding the discriminatory treatment of federally sentenced women by the Government of Canada: Filed by the Canadian Association of Elizabeth Fry Societies.* Retrieved from www.elizabethfry.ca/submissn/nwac/1.htm.

Montour-Angus, P. (1999). Considering colonialism and oppression: Aboriginal women, justice and the "theory" of decolonization. *Native Studies Review, 12,* 63–94

Montour-Angus, P. (2002). *The lived experience of discrimination: Aboriginal women who are federally sentenced.* Ottawa: Canadian Association of Elizabeth Fry Societies.

Morin, S. (1999). *Federally sentenced Aboriginal women in maximum security: What happened to the promises of "Creating Choices"?* Ottawa: Correctional Service of Canada.

National Parole Board. (2000). *Special study on federal female offenders from 1995/96 to 1999/00.* Ottawa: Performance Measurement Division, National Parole Board.

National Parole Board. (2004). *Performance monitoring report, 2003–2004.* Ottawa: Performance Measurement Division, National Parole Board.

Razack, S.H. (1998). *Looking white people in the eye: Gender, race and culture in courtrooms and classrooms.* Toronto: University of Toronto Press.

Ross, R. (1992). *Dancing with a ghost: Exploring Indian reality.* Markham: Reed Books Canada.

Solomon, A. (1994). *Eating bitterness: A vision beyond prison walls.* Toronto: NC Press.

Stevenson, W. (1999). Colonialism and First Nations women in Canada. In E. Dua & A. Robertson (Eds.), *Scratching the surface: Canada and anti-racist feminist thought* (pp. 49–80). Toronto: Women's Press.

Sugar, F., & Fox, L. (1990). *Survey of federally sentenced women in the community.* Ottawa: Task Force on Federally Sentenced Women.

Trevethan, S. (1999). Women in federal and provincial-territorial correctional facilities. *Forum on Corrections Research, 11*(3), 9–12.

Women's Legal Education and Action Fund (LEAF). (1989). *Report to the court challenges program on case development regarding unequal treatment of federally imprisoned women.* Toronto: Author.

CHAPTER 11

Visible Minority Women as Offenders and Victims

Shahid Alvi

Introduction

The difficulty of writing about visible minority women offenders in Canada is almost impossible to overstate, and writing about them as victims of crime is only marginally easier. In this chapter, we begin by examining some of the reasons for these difficulties. The rest of the chapter is divided into two major sections. The first section covers, to the best of my knowledge, as much as is known in Canada about the nature and extent of offences committed by visible minority female offenders. In the second section, we examine a growing body of literature on the extent and nature of victimization of immigrant and visible minority women in Canada. We also draw on information from the United States, where much

richer data address the nature and contours of visible minority female offending and victimization. Of course, such information should be interpreted with caution; we cannot automatically assume that the experiences of such women in the United States are the same for women in Canada. Nevertheless, such evidence provides a sense of the kinds of issues we ought to be studying in the Canadian context.

This chapter will not discuss Aboriginal women's encounters with the criminal justice system, which are covered in chapter 10. Instead, we will examine the relationship between the Canadian criminal justice system and other categories of visible minorities. This focus entails that we must first define the term *visible minority*. At first glance, the definition seems easy. Visible minority women (or ethnocultural minority women) are those women who are statistically fewer in number than women belonging to the dominant culture and who are "visible" because of the colour of their skin. An official definition offered by Canada's *Employment Equity Act* (Statistics Canada, 2006) defines visible minorities as:

persons, other than Aboriginal peoples, who are non-Caucasian in race or non-white in colour. The visible minority population includes the following groups: Chinese, South Asian, Black, Arab/West Asian, Filipino, Southeast Asian, Latin American, Japanese, Korean and Pacific Islander. (p. 230)

However, as we shall see, this definition presents many problems for social scientists, criminal justice practitioners, the general public, and the impartial administration of justice for women of colour. For example, what is meant by "non-white in colour"? And how would someone like a police officer distinguish between a South Asian and a Southeast Asian (Roberts, 2002)? Before we address the central topics of this chapter, some understanding is needed of the changing nature of Canada's population over the past few decades and the significance of these changes.

A Brief Note on the Changing Face of Canada

Canada has long been known as a nation of immigrants. Indeed, Canadians long ago recognized and, in theory, welcomed multiculturalism as a distinctly Canadian approach to changing migration patterns around the world. Canada saw itself as a mosaic of cultures, a country at peace with its linguistic, ethnic, religious, and regional diversity. In 1965, the award-winning sociologist John Porter (1965) would remind us that although this notion held some ideological appeal, we should never forget that Canada was still first and foremost a class-based society—a "**vertical mosaic**," ruled by elites of British origin. Moreover, this vision of Canada stood in sharp relief to the approach taken by the United States, which had embraced the idea of a great cultural melting pot in which immigrants were encouraged to assimilate the American way of life.

Not much has changed since Porter's book. Despite shifting patterns of immigration to Canada, the bulk of power and wealth still resides disproportionately in the hands of white elites. This enduring fact has some important consequences in a Canadian mosaic that is changing dramatically.

Let us examine a few facts around the changing nature of immigration. The vast majority of the original settlers to Canada came from Europe, a pattern that persisted well into the 1900s. In 1961, nearly two-thirds of immigrants to Canada originated from European countries, such as the United Kingdom, Italy, Germany, the Netherlands, and Portugal. Today, people from these countries constitute about one-tenth of those who emigrate from other countries to settle in Canada. Since the 1970s, shifts in Canada's immigration policies, coupled with efforts to address the problem of growing numbers of refugees and migrants throughout the world, underpinned an unprecedented influx of immigration from non-European countries. And despite an increase in the number of individuals and families emigrating from Eastern Europe, the majority of immigrants to Canada are men, women, and children from the People's Republic of China, India, the Philippines, and Pakistan (Chui, Tran, & Maheux, 2007). Statistics Canada (2005) estimates that visible minorities will comprise nearly one-quarter of Canada's population by 2017. Visible minorities are a fast-growing population, and can generally be characterized as follows:

- Most are immigrants.
- The majority live in highly populated urban areas, and most live in either Ontario or British Columbia.

- They are a relatively young population; nearly one-quarter of visible minorities are under the age of 15.
- They are well-educated. Approximately one in five visible minorities holds a university degree, yet, compared with other Canadians, their employment levels are lower (and their unemployment levels higher).
- The vast majority (88 percent) of young visible minorities are in school.
- One in three has an income below the low income cut-offs, Statistics Canada's unofficial set of guidelines for determining poverty lines. (Statistics Canada, 2001, pp. 3–5)

According to Statistics Canada (2006), between 1996 and 2001, compared with only 1 percent growth for non–visible minority women, the female visible minority population grew 25 percent and now comprises approximately 14 percent of the total female population. These shifts in immigration patterns, coupled with the characteristics of visible minorities in Canada, lead to a number of significant consequences in relation to women's encounters with the criminal justice system:

- Canadian institutions, including the criminal justice system, need to develop competence in dealing with newcomers whose language, customs, and beliefs are likely to be very different from mainstream Canadian culture. Many immigrants lack knowledge of their rights under Canadian law and do not know where to turn when those rights are violated.
- As the population of visible minorities grows in Canada, greater potential exists for victimization of this group via hate crimes and discrimination.
- Many immigrant women in Canada are sponsored by their husbands, thereby making them dependent on their male partners, which, in combination with other factors, is a risk marker for abuse.
- A growing unease is developing over the sometimes conflicting relationship between Canadian law and other religious or cultural world views.

We cannot here discuss the many and varied social, political, and economic issues raised by these changes in immigration and the resulting new face of Canada. As noted earlier, although not all women of colour are immigrants, most are; and therefore we need to keep in mind the potential ways that these demographic changes might condition and shape the experiences of women of colour in relation to the criminal justice system. Before we turn to an examination of these issues, we will consider another critical aspect of the social context that criminalized and victimized women of colour must often contend with: the distinction between race and racialization.

Clarifying What We Mean

One of the most important scientific lessons of the past century has been learning that there is no such thing as *race*. Many years ago, biologists abandoned the concept of race as essentially meaningless, and despite a handful of individuals who claim that the notion of race is worth deeper examination, the vast majority of scientists agree that human beings have so few genetic differences that the concept of race as a biological construct must be abandoned

(Zack, 2001). Why, then, do we continue to see so much attention devoted to the concept of race in criminological and criminal justice research? *Race* is significant because it highlights the problem of racism and racialization. Put differently, although race does not exist biologically, racism and racialization are evident in Canadian society (Jiwani, 2005). Dozens of scholars have documented the ways that racism is experienced by women and men of colour, pointing to distinctions among systemic racism, institutionalized racism, colonialism, state racism, white privilege, and many other ways that race is given particular kinds of meaning to both create and sustain relations of power and control (Satzewich & Liodakis, 2007).

Furthermore, as many scholars are now pointing out, although acknowledging the power of racism in everyday life is important, equally important is that our understanding of social relationships not be reduced to racism and racialization alone, despite the tendency of the media to sensationalize and reduce victimization and offending by framing them in terms of race (see box 11.1). This realization is the basis of intersectional analyses of women's experiences in the social world, which examine how and why inequalities in race, sexuality, class, and gender work in concert to create and shape women's lives (Burgess-Proctor, 2006; Sokoloff & Dupont, 2005). As Josephson (2005) points out, intersectionality tries to analyze the many categories of identities in terms of their complex and often conflicting interactions (p. 85). We will follow this approach to understanding visible minority women's lives in relation to their experiences as both perpetrators and victims of crime in Canada.

Box 11.1   Media, Race, and Hirji Murder

Each province in Canada has its own "out group," says Vancouver-trained academic Yasmin Jiwani.

"In B.C., the South Asians are the out group, the group that is targeted quite frequently," Montreal-based Jiwani told the *Georgia Straight*. "In Toronto, it would be like the African Canadians or Afro-Caribbean Canadians. In Quebec, there's the Haitian community and there are the Arabs."

The associate professor at Concordia University's department of communication studies made this observation when sought for her opinion on why cases of violence involving South Asian families readily grab media headlines.

One such incident is the slaying of Surrey school principal Shemina Hirji inside her Burnaby home on July 5. She was killed just five days after marrying Narinder Cheema. The tragedy comes on the heels of recent high-profile killings of female spouses in the community.

Jiwani asserts that each group "gets a certain kind of attention, all of which fits into a dominant archetype." In the case of South Asians, she says, it's one of a culture that is oppressive of women.

"Cultural explanations keep coming up because they're easy," she said. "If you already have a stereotype in the background, the moment you see something you say, 'Ah this is an oppressive culture.'"

But it isn't always the case that the "dominant media," according to Jiwani, uses "definitions of culture" in explaining violence perpetrated against members of the South Asian community.

In Jiwani's 2006 book *Discourses of Denial: Mediations of Race, Gender, and Violence* (UBC Press), she juxtaposed the Reena Virk murder in Victoria in 1997 with the 1996 Vernon massacre. Two people instrumental in Virk's fatal swarming were white. The Vernon case involved the shooting death of Rajwar Gakhal and eight of her relatives by her estranged husband, Mark Chahal.

"In the case of the Vernon tragedy, the cultural signifiers used throughout the reportage clearly position the murders as arising from a cultural practice of arranged marriages and women's supposedly subordinate status within the Sikh religious tradition," Jiwani wrote. "The analysis of the murder of Reena Virk, however, points out how a cultural explanation is explicitly avoided in order to divert attention from issues of racism and the consequences of racialized difference, and to privilege a definition of the situation as emerging from girl violence and bullying."

In her book, Jiwani noted that these two cases "show how race is conveniently erased when it suits the public imagination and the media's agenda, and conversely, invoked in a culturalized form (to the exclusion of almost all else) when deemed necessary."

"Hence, the killing of Reena Virk is framed as a generic girl gang violence phenomenon, while the Vernon murders are attributed to a culturally specific ethnic phenomenon," she wrote.

When Hirji's killing became public, the community paper *Indo-Canadian Voice* reported that it's "just the kind of news that Indo-Canadians dread." In a follow-up report, outspoken editor Rattan Mall wrote that with the subsequent discovery of court documents detailing the violent past of Hirji's husband, "there was shock and anger in the community as the case only seemed to reinforce the stereotyping of Indo-Canadian males."

Indira Prahst, a sociology instructor at Langara College and a friend of the Cheema family, told the *Straight* that although media reportage of domestic violence is warranted, "sensationalized angles" aren't. "If we have a predator that is brown, the word South Asian or Indo-Canadian becomes very highlighted," she explained. "Framing violence against women as being inherent in the South Asian culture hinders us from understanding that the underlying cause of such violence is the culture of patriarchy."

Source: Pablo, C. (2007, July 19). *Straight.com*. Retrieved from www.straight.com. Reprinted by permission.

As stated at the outset of this chapter, the biggest challenge confronting a discussion of visible minority female offenders and victims is the lack of detailed statistical data. In Canada, we do not collect systematic data on the race of offenders with the exception of Aboriginal peoples (Roberts, 2002). Nevertheless, we will draw on the Canadian data that are available, supplemented where appropriate with findings from studies from the United States, where much more nuanced data are gathered on race and ethnicity.

What Do We Know About Visible Minority Female Offenders in Canada?

In the previous chapter, we learned that Aboriginal women are greatly overrepresented in Canada's correctional system, relative to the total population of Aboriginal people in Canada. But what about other minorities? In this section, we will glean as much as we can from the limited number of studies that address the ethnocultural background of female offenders. Much of the information on visible minority status comes from federal correctional data, which, with the exception of Aboriginal people, reflects some ambiguity regarding the ways in which *minorities* are defined. Note also that federal prisons house offenders who have been sentenced to two or more years in prison, representing only a small proportion of those serving time in Canada (Correctional Service of Canada, 2006).

The author of a study of a sample of federally sentenced women who had been released to the community found that the bulk (57 percent) of female offenders were white, whereas Aboriginal women accounted for nearly one in five offenders (19 percent), and the category of "other minority groups" together represented about 8 percent (Law, 2004). The most recent data available also indicate that the overall correctional population of women is more diverse than the composition of the male correctional population. As of 2007, "57% of the federal female offender population were White, 25% Aboriginal, 8% Black and 3% Asian compared to the male population which was 69% White, 17% Aboriginal, 6% Black and 3% Asian" (National Parole Board, 2007, ¶ 6). Data compiled by the Correctional Service of Canada (2003) on the patterns of incarceration in federal prisons by ethnic origin show the percentage of incarcerated Aboriginal women increased from 23.5 percent in 2001 to 29.2 percent in 2003. Similarly, the percentage of incarcerated Black women increased in the same time period from 6.7 percent to 7.3 percent. Offenders in both categories of "Asiatic" and Caucasian women decreased during this time period (Correctional Service of Canada, 2003).

Similarly, data reported in the landmark *Report of the Commission on Systemic Racism in the Ontario Criminal Justice System* also suggest that, with the exception of Black women, minority women represent quite a small portion of the total number of women who go to prison (Ontario, Commission on Systemic Racism in the Ontario Criminal Justice System, 1995). Figure 11.1 shows that Black and Aboriginal women combined comprise just more than one-quarter of the female adults incarcerated in 1992–93, but that other visible minority groups constituted a very small remaining proportion of such offenders.

Another significant finding from the commission's report is that certain visible minority women are far more likely to be admitted to prison than their Caucasian counterparts. In figure 11.2, we can see the admission rates to prison per 100,000 females in Ontario in 1992–93 were almost seven times higher for Black women compared with white women, whereas for all other categories (excepting Aboriginal women), the admission rates were half or less than those of white women. Thus, some evidence suggests the criminal justice system does indeed discriminate against some women on the basis of their racial background, a finding that coincides with the claim that racialized women across North America are the "fastest growing segment of the correctional population" (Wortley, 2003, p. 108).

These statistics lend support to the argument that racism is both pervasive and persistent in the Canadian criminal justice system (Roberts, 2002). One Canadian scholar rightly

Figure 11.1   Percentages of Adult Female Admissions to Ontario Prisons, by Race, 1992–93

Racial category	Percent
White	67.4
Black	17.1
Aboriginal	9.2
Asian	2.0
East Indian	1.0
Arab	0.3
Other/Unknown	3.1

Source: Adapted from Ontario, Commission on Systemic Racism in the Ontario Criminal Justice System. (1995). *Report of the commission on systemic racism in the Ontario criminal justice system.* Toronto: Queen's Printer, p. 24.

Figure 11.2   Adult Prison Admission Rates (per 100,000) for Females in Ontario, by Race, 1992–93

Racial category	Rate (per 100,000)
White	107.3
Black	730.7
Aboriginal	502.7
Asian	55.5
East Indian	48.3
Arab	39.5
Total	136.4

Source: Adapted from Ontario, Commission on Systemic Racism in the Ontario Criminal Justice System. (1995). *Report of the commission on systemic racism in the Ontario criminal justice system.* Toronto: Queen's Printer, p. 90.

claimed in 1999 that "there is, and there has been since Confederation, a disproportionate number of First Nations girls and females of colour in the justice system" (Reitsma-Street, 1999, p. 353). And, in an inquiry conducted by the federal government into the management of Kingston's Prison for Women, the commission found that with respect to minority women in prison:

Current research in this area is sparse and unable to adequately provide an understanding of the problems faced by minority women, and the implications for programming. Given these concerns, Corrections Canada, under the auspices of the Federally Sentenced Women Program, has begun to examine the needs of minority women, including foreign nationals. (Canada, Commission of Inquiry, 1996, p. 248)

Despite academic and government recognition of the existence of racism within the criminal justice system and the potentially unique needs of minority women, to the best of my knowledge, little has been done in the way of systematic research on this issue since that time, nor has much progress been made to reduce racism within the criminal justice system; most efforts have been tokenistic or fruitless (Denney, Ellis, & Barn, 2006).

Very little information is available pertaining to the specific offences committed by non-Aboriginal visible minority women in Canada, and whether these offences differ in any way from offences committed by women who are not visible minorities. Women account for a much smaller proportion of crime compared with men, and they are responsible for far less violent crimes. Indeed, more than half of the offences that land women in prison are (in order of frequency) accounted for by:

1. Theft under $5,000
2. Level 1 assault
3. Fraud
4. Drug-related offences (Addario, 2002, p. 17)

We need to pay close attention to the ways in which intersecting social factors help to explain these offending patterns. For example, most women charged with theft have shop-lifted items for themselves or their children, a finding that is not surprising, given that most of these women are poor (Chesney-Lind, 1999). Recall, too, that one in three persons of colour lives below the unofficial poverty line, and although we have no data on the number of visible minority women who have been charged with shoplifting, we can reasonably assume that their situation is no different from that of their white counterparts. Similarly, welfare fraud is a direct outcome of both decreases in real income from welfare for many women and the increasing enthusiasm in some jurisdictions for charging and prosecuting women who commit welfare fraud (Addario, 2002).

For many women charged with assault, their charges relate directly to their use of self-defence in cases of domestic violence, and the police practice of charging both men and women in these situations (DeKeseredy, 1992; Saunders, 1986). As we shall see in the next section of this chapter, like many other women, visible minority women are not immune to being victimized by domestic violence, although the contours of their victimization differ in important ways from those of non-minority women.

According to Lawrence and Williams (2006), some evidence indicates that Black women in the United Kingdom, the United States, and Canada "receive prison sentences for importing drugs at rates greatly disproportionate to their populations ... and that drug-importation offences contribute significantly to the over-representation of black women in prisons" (p. 286).

Women as a whole are more likely than men to be charged with trafficking, importation, and production of illicit drugs. However, female drug offenders do not usually play a large role in drug trafficking, but are more likely to be involved with drug use or, as mentioned above, as illegal drug couriers (Hannah-Moffat & Shaw, 2001). Moreover, according to the case histories of women imprisoned for selling drugs, these women had made many trans-actions, but for quite small amounts, averaging $10 (Addario, 2002). On the whole, although women tend to commit crimes for economic reasons, as do men, women's *modi operandi* differ because women are far less violent (Young & Adams-Fuller, 2006).

Although the foregoing discussion tells us a little about the kinds of offences committed by women in general, we have virtually no details on the kinds of offences committed by visible minority—but non-Aboriginal—female offenders in Canada. One study conducted by the National Parole Board offers some insight into the *broad* categories of offences com-mitted by visible minority female offenders. As illustrated in figure 11.3, the vast majority of federally incarcerated visible minority and Black female offenders had been imprisoned for Schedule II offences, which, for the most part, are serious drug offences. Considerably fewer visible minority women than Caucasian women were in prison for non-scheduled (less serious) crimes, although, interestingly, visible minority women had almost as high a rate for murder convictions as Aboriginal and Caucasian women.

Finally, our knowledge of the kinds of sentences received by visible minority women is also limited. The last available data from 1999–2000 (see figure 11.4) show that although Aboriginal females had the highest incarceration rates, Black female offenders were slightly

Figure 11.3   Offence Profile of Federal Female Offenders by Race from 1995/96 to 1999/2000 (percentages)

Offence type	All	Aboriginal	Black	Visible minorities	Caucasian	Other
Murder	15.4	14.7	2.1	13.9	19.2	11.1
Schedule I[a] (including sexual assault and sexual exploitation)	2.1	2.5	1.1	1.5	2.5	0.8
Schedule I (not involving sexual assault or sexual exploitation)	34.6	60.7	10.9	19.0	34.8	30.3
Schedule II[b]	35.6	17.2	81.3	62.8	27.9	42.5
Non-scheduled[c]	12.2	4.9	4.5	2.9	15.6	15.2
Totals[d]	100.0	100.0	100.0	100.0	100.0	100.0

[a] Schedule I offences are serious violent crimes and include but are not limited to manslaughter, attempted murder, sexual assault, assault, arson, robbery, use of a firearm, criminal harassment, and kidnapping. Here they are divided into offences involving sexual assault or other forms of sexual exploitation, and those that did not involve such acts.
[b] Schedule II offences include serious drug offences, such as trafficking, cultivation, and importing or exporting controlled substances.
[c] Non-scheduled offences are offences not contained within Schedule I or II offences and are therefore less serious crimes.
[d] Percentages may not add to 100, due to rounding.

Source: Adapted from National Parole Board. (2000). *Special study on federal female offenders from 1995–96 to 1999–00*, p. 4, table 3. Retrieved from www.npb-cnlc.gc.ca/reports/femaleoffenders_e.htm.

Figure 11.4   Federal Female Population by Race from 1995–96 to 1999–2000 (percentages)

	Aboriginal	Black	Visible minorities	Caucasian	Other (includes other, unknown, and blank)
Incarcerated	59.1	31.1	34.3	42.2	47.1
Conditional release	40.9	68.4	65.7	57.8	52.8
% of total population	14.6	12.3	3.6	59.7	9.7

Source: Adapted from National Parole Board. (2000). *Special study on federal female offenders from 1995–96 to 1999–00,* table 1. Retrieved from www.npb-cnlc.gc.ca/reports/femaleoffenders_e.htm.

less likely to be incarcerated than other visible minority women and Caucasian women. In addition, Black and visible minority offenders were more likely than Caucasian and Aboriginal offenders to receive conditional releases or to be serving community sentences (Trevethan & Rastin, 2004).

In light of the preceding discussion, what can we conclude about visible minority female offenders? First, a key issue is the clear lack of detailed official and non-official data from which stronger and more in-depth conclusions could be drawn about this population. Part of the reason for the paucity of good data is likely that these women represent a relatively small proportion of female offenders, just as female offenders are a much smaller proportion of all offenders generally. Also, the study of women and crime has until quite recently been ignored or trivialized as less important than male crime, or has been seen in the same terms conceptually and theoretically as men's offending. As the population of visible minorities increases in Canada, the possibility that more visible minorities will encounter the criminal justice system also increases; accordingly, understanding visible minority offenders' trajectories into crime and their experiences with and needs within the criminal justice system becomes more important.

Second, regardless of the limitations of available data, Aboriginal and Black women are clearly overrepresented in the criminal justice system. However, because of differences in the way visible minorities have been defined in other data collection procedures, whether (and which) other minorities are overrepresented in the system is difficult to assess. Again, gathering in-depth data on these women's immersion in criminal activities, including their motivations, from their point of view is crucial (Daly & Chesney-Lind, 1988).

Third, the types of offences that women commit are less violent than offences committed by men, and for visible minority females (like other women), their offences are related to women's subordinate economic and social status in Canadian society. Indeed, as one scholar points out, women's offending can be conceptualized as a form of economic survival tied to diminished opportunities and histories of personal victimization that reflect "the difficulty women have in extracting themselves from the relationships, addictions, and economic necessities which arise once they are immersed in 'street work'" (Gilfus, 2006, p. 13). Clearly, this link between criminalized behaviour and economic need has implications not only for prevention strategies that relate to the decriminalization and legalization of drugs such as marijuana and hashish (which would greatly reduce the criminalization of women and men) but also for the provision of adequate training, jobs, and social assistance for poor families and the ongoing struggle to eliminate violence against women.

Women's pathways to crime have long been recognized as differing from men's. Many women in prison have experienced poverty, abuse, substance abuse, and economic marginalization; and the majority are mothers, two-thirds of whom are single mothers (Boritch, 1997; Boritch, in press). The visible minority women who are the subject of this chapter, however, also must live with the day-to-day experiences and consequences of the many facets of racism. Thus, a fourth issue is that these women's pathways to and out of crime cannot be understood without first understanding the ways in which race, class, and gender intersect to shape their experiences. As Currie (1994) points out:

> It must be recognized that race or ethnicity, gender and class are not distinct categories in reality. They produce a compound effect which is the product of the three aspects being inseparably fused. The whole is different from the sum of its parts. (section 13.4, ¶ 2)

Visible Minority Women as Victims

In the previous section, we noted an important connection between the experiences of women as offenders and as victims. That is, many women in conflict with the law have histories of physical, psychological, and other forms of abuse; suffer from addictions (which are often tied to abuse); and endure social and economic marginalization. Thus, women who experience such injustices are at greater risk of themselves becoming offenders as a means of surviving their marginalized economic status and coping with their long-standing victimization.

In this section, we focus on what is known regarding the victimization experiences of minority women in Canada. According to the General Social Survey (GSS), in 1999, about one-quarter of visible minorities in Canada were victimized by personal crime (individual victimization) or household crime (all members of a household were victimized). The victimization rates for visible minority women and men were virtually identical (25 percent and 27 percent, respectively) (Statistics Canada, 2001, p. 6). These data should, however, be interpreted with caution. Because the GSS was a telephone survey conducted in English and French, aside from the problem presented by people who do not own telephones and those who have unlisted numbers, others who were not canvassed regarding their victimization experiences included individuals whose first language was neither English nor French and those who could not speak either language well enough to complete the survey (see box 11.2). Indeed, according to the 2001 census, 2.6 million women in Canada are not fluent in either language (Johnson, 2006).

The most recent profile of the victimization of visible minorities in Canada comes from the 2004 GSS, but only briefly distinguishes between the experiences of men and women. Similar to the findings reported above, the data in this survey indicate that victimization rates for violent crime against the visible minority population (Chinese, Asians, and Blacks) are about the same as those experienced by non–visible minorities for both sexes (Perreault, 2008). Compared with non–visible minority people, visible minority females and males were more likely to report being fearful of being victimized; Chinese women in particular were the most fearful.

Box 11.2   Limitations of the General Social Survey Methodology

Although the GSS provides information on women who have experienced partner abuse, several limitations in the survey must be noted when analyzing the data in relation to immigrant and visible minority women. These include the language of the interview, the data collection methods and the sensitive nature of the subject itself.

The GSS survey was conducted in Canada's two official languages: English and French. Women who were not proficient in either of these languages were therefore eliminated from the survey. As a result, a significant proportion of immigrant and visible minority women would not be represented in the survey sample.

The GSS relied on self-reports by respondents over the telephone as the sole data collection method. Women who were, or had been, in abusive relationships might not have wished to discuss their experiences with a stranger over the phone. For some—or perhaps, most women—their feelings about abusive relationships can be very delicate and require special sensitivity when discussing the subject. Some women may need the assurance of safety and privacy or counselling support before they are able to talk about their experiences. A survey with close-ended questions could be seen as marginalizing a woman's experience of the abuse and could oversimplify its complex nature.

As well, there can be feelings of shame associated with the subject of abuse by an intimate partner, and for some women, their responses to survey questions can be influenced by feelings of guilt, powerlessness, embarrassment, personal failure, and a general mistrust of authority. The sensitive nature of this subject puts further limitations on the findings of the GSS.

Source: Smith, E. (2004). *Nowhere to turn? Responding to partner violence against immigrant and visible minority women*. Ottawa: Canadian Council on Social Development, pp. 3–4.

According to another report from Statistics Canada (2001):

In total, visible minorities in Canada were victimized in approximately 483,000 incidents of personal crime. This translates into a rate of 195 per 1,000 persons in a visible minority. Of these incidents, 237,000 were violent crimes (which includes sexual assault, assault and robbery), and 246,000 involved theft. These rates do not differ remarkably from the general population. However, Canadians in a visible minority were more likely to report being victims of personal theft than a violent crime, whereas the reverse was true for the non-visible minority population. (p. 6)

Unfortunately, these data represent about as much as we know about victimization from non-violent crimes for visible minority women. However, we do have a bit more knowledge regarding their victimization by violent crime. In the remainder of this section, we will examine some of the patterns and contours of violence against minority women in Canada.

As we learned in other chapters, violence against women has existed throughout history, but only relatively recently has such violence been considered a serious social problem warranting academic, community, and public policy attention (Richie & Kanuha, 2000).

Compared with scholars in the United States, however, Canadian researchers are only now beginning to scratch the surface of the nature and extent of violence against immigrant and visible minority women (Krane, Oxman-Martinez, & Ducey, 2000).

Conducting research on violence against women with this population poses a number of challenges, which may, in part, explain the relatively embryonic state of Canadian research on this population. For cultural and religious reasons, visible minority women are a difficult population to reach for research purposes. Many of these women are reluctant to talk to researchers (or criminal justice or social welfare personnel) for fear of bringing shame to their family, because domestic violence in their culture is often viewed as a private matter, and the communities they live in are often characterized by high levels of secretiveness (Bui, 2003; Erez & Copps Hartley, 2003). Many of these women also face language barriers that preclude them from telling their stories, and some are entirely dependent upon the male partners who are also often their batterers (Abraham, 2000). Also, some women may not be willing to report on their encounters with violence because they feel that dealing with violence in their lives is a matter of endurance and of perseverance in the face of adversity, sentiments that are often deeply embedded in some cultures and are also regularly coupled with beliefs in the legitimacy of patriarchal norms and behaviour and in the unacceptability of divorce or separation from a male partner (Ahmad, Riaz, Barata, & Stewart, 2004; Alvi, Schwartz, DeKeseredy, & Bachaus, 2005; Bhuyan, Mell, Senturia, Sullivan, & Shiu-Thornton, 2005; Lee, 2005). Immigrant women are also often isolated and lack extended family members or friendship networks that might serve as social supports to mitigate abuse.

Official data on violence against visible minority and immigrant women in Canada exist, but should be interpreted with caution. The General Social Survey found that "visible minority women report lower five-year rates of spousal violence than other women: 4% compared with 8%" (Johnson, 2006, p. 41), while admitting that this rate may be an underrepresentation of the actual numbers due to the problems with the English and French language methodology mentioned earlier. The same data set also indicates that rates of spousal violence against *immigrant* women declined between 1999 and 2004, a finding that is explained in terms of the lower likelihood of the presence of risk factors, such as emotional and psychological abuse, rates of heavy drinking, and prevalence of common-law unions within visible minority communities (see figure 11.5).

In a study conducted for the Canadian Council on Social Development using GSS data from 1999, Smith (2004) found that:

> about 13% of immigrant and visible minority women who experienced partner violence reported that they were physically injured as a result of the abuse; among other women, 17% reported injuries from partner abuse. Some immigrant and visible minority women also reported being hospitalized (3%) and receiving medical attention (6%) as a result of abuse. (p. 18)

In another study, also conducted with 1999 GSS data, researchers found that rates of interpersonal violence (IPV) were similar for recent immigrant women (having lived in Canada 0–9 years) and non-recent immigrant women (having lived in Canada more than 10 years). The authors of the study also determined that the risk for experiencing current or ex-partner violence was significantly higher for non-recent immigrant women, a finding that might be explained in a number of ways (Hyman, Forte, Du Mont, Romans, & Cohen, 2006):

Figure 11.5   Five-Year Rates of Physical and Psychological Abuse Against Women by Spousal Partners, by Immigrant and Visible Minority Status, 2004

	Immigrant women	Non-immigrant women
Physical violence	5	8
	Visible minority women	Non–visible minority women
Physical violence	4	8
Damaging property	2[a]	5
Harming/threatening to harm someone close	2[a]	4
Put-downs and name calling	5	14
Checking her whereabouts	7	8
Limiting contact with others	5[a]	7
Jealousy	7	10
Preventing access to income	4[a]	4

[a] Use with caution because coefficient of variation is high.

Source: Adapted from Johnson, H. (2006). *Measuring violence against women: Statistical trends, 2006* (85-570-XIE). Ottawa: Minister of Industry, Statistics Canada, p. 41, figure 28; p. 42, figure 30.

Risk behaviors associated with IPV, such as alcohol and drug use, increase with length of stay in the adopted country because of alienation from traditional support systems, perceived discrimination, and acculturative stress. Other studies have suggested that post-migration stresses, such as poverty, underemployment, loss of status, and discrimination, affect the power dynamics between men and women and thus, increase women's risk for IPV. Alternate explanations do not relate to behavioral or social determinants but rather reflect changing perceptions and interpretations of IPV as newcomers learn what acts constitute abuse in the context of the adopted country and develop the language skills necessary for identifying and speaking about their experiences. If so, then previous cultural norms of what is considered abusive behavior change over time to accommodate new constructs, which may result in higher reported rates of IPV. (p. 657)

Brownridge and Halli (2002), who also conducted research with the GSS, found that immigrant women from developing countries were at higher risk for being victimized by violence and explained these results in terms of the women's male partners' high levels of sexual jealousy and lower educational levels.

One of the difficulties with the findings of some of the studies cited above is the conflated notions of *visible minority* and *immigrant*. That is, the two categories are used together, implying that they are the same thing, which despite being statistically correct in the sense that most recent immigrants are visible minorities, masks potentially significant differences within ethnic and religious-cultural groups. Further, categorizing people into groups that supposedly represent a particular ethnocultural grouping is tantamount to stereotyping such groups (for example, Asians are passive, Blacks are resilient, etc.). This homogenizing effect has consequences for community responses to violence because it tends to create one-size-fits-all models of policy and programming, when in fact these groups have a great diversity of needs (Dumbrill & Maiter, 1996).

As you have probably noted by now, the vast majority of studies that attempt to shed light on violence against immigrant and visible minority women in Canada are based on General Social Survey data. A handful of descriptive and non-representative sample studies are available, however, to provide additional useful information. A path-breaking qualitative study of 64 Italian, Chinese, Polish, and Indo-Canadian women conducted by MacLeod and Shin (1993) found that 44 (69 percent) of these women had been abused by their husbands. More than half of those reporting abuse stated that the abuse started when they came to Canada, and those stating that they had been victimized before coming to Canada said that the abuse became worse after their arrival in Canada. In addition, most of these women came to Canada under family sponsorship (more than one-third sponsored by their husbands), through arranged marriages, or as refugees. In addition to their experiences of racism and prejudice, most of them also detailed the problems they faced because they did not speak English or French, including finding work or being stuck in menial jobs; feeling that they had been taken advantage of or dismissed; being frustrated because they could not adequately communicate with doctors, lawyers, teachers, and other professionals; and feeling isolated and depressed (see box 11.3). Not surprisingly, these kinds of experiences contributed both to their lack of knowledge about available services and to their lack of access to those services. Consequently many of these women were more likely to turn to family and their immediate community for help, which presented further problems:

> The women generally received a double message from their families and friends. For the most part, they received no real help from the people in whom they confided. In some cases, there was disbelief and accusations were made against the women themselves ... The women explained that community involvement can be a trap for them, trapping them in gossip and fear of gossip, rather than freeing them by providing a support network. (MacLeod & Shin, 1993, p. 37)

Box 11.3   Two Cases of Domestic Abuse of Racial Minority Women: The Asian Community

Case #1

Many women immigrating to Canada hope that its laws will protect them from domestic abuse. Speakers presented participants with a case in which a woman came to Canada from her native Korea, with her abusive husband and her children, because she had been told that there would be social justice for women and children here. She soon found that Canadian laws are not protective enough to deter abusers. Her husband continued to beat her and to sexually abuse her oldest daughter from a previous marriage. On one occasion, police were called in and the husband was arrested. However, the woman spoke very little English and was unable to explain to the police officer what had happened. Instead of finding a qualified interpreter, he drove her to a Korean restaurant and asked a patron to act as interpreter. What may have seemed to the officer to be quick-thinking turned out to be a grave error. As it happened, the patron was a loyal friend to the woman's husband and he deliberately misinterpreted her story to the officer.

This case highlights some of the problems which result from the police's inept handling of domestic abuse cases—the police are often insensitive to the concerns of the abused woman, and they have little knowledge of the few culturally and linguistically-appropriate services which may address these concerns. This woman should have been taken, first to a safe haven or to a women's shelter, then provided with a qualified interpreter. As in many other cultures, Korean culture is very male-dominated, reminded the speaker; the men are highly likely to support each other in cases of domestic abuse; also, the Korean community in Toronto is very tightly-knit. A Korean woman who is brave enough to file a complaint may be ostracized by her entire community. Without access to appropriate ancillary services like safe havens and appropriately-qualified interpreters, racial minority women who suffer domestic abuse are unable to avail themselves of the legal protection which exists in the criminal code.

This Korean victim, said a speaker who is familiar with her case, did not appear as a witness at her husband's trial. She was afraid of deportation. She was also not legally permitted to seek employment in Canada. So she has been forced to spend the past two years in a shelter with her three younger children, while the eldest daughter remains in the care of Children's Aid.

Case #2

According to one speaker, Asian women are widely admired by men because of their perceived submissiveness. The "Madame Butterfly" stereotype endures. The mail-order-bride business capitalizes on these perceptions, and disadvantaged Asian women, seeking a better life, may use it to gain entry into Canada.

Case #2 described an Asian mail-order-bride who was repeatedly abused by her Caucasian husband. On one such occasion, the woman scolded her child, to the husband's displeasure. He beat his wife. In self-defense, she struck him. He continued to beat her, and then he offered her wine in order to calm her down. He then called the police and filed a complaint that she had been drinking and had abused him and the child. The officer, smelling alcohol on her breath, arrested her. Despite the fact that there was visible evidence that *she* was beaten, the officer did not charge the husband. This incident seems to suggest that, since the husband was a Caucasian "Canadian" and spoke English, the officer felt that his complaint was more credible than hers.

Source: Urban Alliance on Race Relations. (1993, March). Legal protection for Aboriginal and racial minority women. In Urban Alliance on Race Relations Justice Conference Planning Committee (Eds.), *The justice system: Is it serving or failing minorities?* [Workshop proceedings from the Urban Alliance on Race Relations Justice Conference, Osgoode Hall, York University, Toronto] (pp. 33–36). Retrieved from www.urbanalliance.ca/justice/jusconf.htm.

MacLeod and Shin's work is singular because it provides a great deal of rich information on the contours, consequences, and barriers to dealing with violence in immigrant women's lives. Other scholars are also beginning to examine the intricacies of the problem in this population. For example, the authors of a recent study of Portuguese-Canadian women found that second-generation women were less likely to be tolerant of abuse, whereas first-generation women were more likely to approve of it while holding positive views of patriarchy (Barata, McNally, Sales, & Stewart, 2005). Another analysis of Indian women in Canada points to their major impediments to escaping abusive relationships: lack of financial resources coupled with language and cultural barriers (Shirwadkar, 2004). Also, a range of US studies on violence against minority and immigrant women are beginning to reveal more about the similarities and differences between these women's experiences and needs versus those of mainstream women (Bui, 2003; El-Bassel et al., 2003; Grossman & Lundy, 2007; Hilbert & Krishnan, 2000; Rasche, 2001; Thomas, 2000; Yick, Shibusawa, & Agbayani-Siewert, 2003; Yoshihama, 2000).

Overall, however, the study of visible minority women's victimization in Canada is still in its infancy. What we do know is that, like the situation faced by all women, violence in the lives of visible minority women is both pervasive and complex. But for visible minority women, their victimization is often complicated by racism, poverty, and cultural and religious beliefs that intersect in significant but as yet not fully understood ways. As the demographic makeup of Canada continues to reflect greater and richer diversity, the continuation of research into the nuances of these women's lives is critical, as is the use of this research to inform policy and response strategies. Indeed, as the recent experience in Ontario around the legitimacy of **sharia** (Islamic) law to handle domestic disputes illustrates (see box 11.4), responding to violence against visible minority and immigrant women in Canada will continue to generate controversy and challenges, requiring all Canadians to open their eyes to the complexities of difference.

Box 11.4 McGuinty Rules Out Use of Sharia Law in Ontario

Ontario Premier Dalton McGuinty says there will be no sharia law in his province and that he will move to ban all faith-based arbitrations.

Seeking to end months of debate, McGuinty said he would not let his province become the first Western government to allow the use of Islamic law to settle family disputes and that the boundaries between church and state would become clearer by banning religious arbitration completely.

"There will be no Shariah law in Ontario. There will be no religious arbitration in Ontario. There will be one law for all Ontarians," McGuinty told *The Canadian Press*.

The proposal to let Ontario residents use Islamic law for settling family disputes drew protests Thursday in Canada and at some of its diplomatic sites across Europe.

Ontario, the most populous province in Canada, has allowed Catholic and Jewish faith-based tribunals to settle family law matters such as divorce on a voluntary basis since 1991.

The practice got little attention until Muslim leaders demanded the same rights.

Officials had to decide whether to exclude one religion, or whether to scrap the religious family courts altogether.

McGuinty said such courts "threaten our common ground," and promised his Liberal government would introduce legislation as soon as possible to outlaw them in Ontario.

"Ontarians will always have the right to seek advice from anyone in matters of family law, including religious advice," he said. "But no longer will religious arbitration be deciding matters of family law."

Just hours before McGuinty's announcement, a group including prominent Canadian author Margaret Atwood and actress Shirley Douglas issued an open letter to the premier on behalf of the No Religious Arbitration Coalition.

Homa Arjomand, a women's rights activist, was elated after hearing the announcement.

"I think our voice got heard loud and clear, and I thank the government for coming out with no faith-based arbitrations," Arjomand told CP.

"Oh, I am so happy. That was the best news I have ever heard for the past five years."

However a representative from Ontario's Jewish community expressed disappointment and shock over McGuinty's decision.

"We're stunned," Joel Richler, Ontario region chairman of the Canadian Jewish Congress, told CP.

"At the very least, we would have thought the government would have consulted with us before taking away what we've had for so many years."

Some observers said McGuinty's means of pulling the plug on sharia, by talking to one news agency on a Sunday afternoon, was a strange way to end a debate that has raged for months.

"By letting it go on, and suddenly ending it mysteriously on a Sunday afternoon, is not probably the best kind of leadership that one could show," Progressive Conservative Leader John Tory told CP.

Last year, former NDP attorney-general Marion Boyd recommended the province handle Islamic arbitrations as it long has other religious arbitrations. She said participants must go into the process voluntarily, and that all decisions could be appealed in court.

Shariah comes from several sources including the Quran, the Muslim holy book, and it governs every aspect of life.

Under most interpretations, Islamic law gives men more rights than women in matters of inheritance, divorce and child custody.

Source: McGuinty rules out use of sharia law in Ontario. (2005, September 12). *CTV.ca News*. Retrieved from www.ctv.ca. Reprinted by permission of CTVglobemedia.

Summary

This chapter has considered visible minority women as both offenders and victims of crime in Canada. Two of the most salient points here are that very little is known about such women and that much more research needs to be done if criminal justice practitioners, policy-makers, and other stakeholders are to both prevent offending and reduce (and ideally eventually eliminate) victimization. Moreover, some urgency underpins the need for more detailed information, given the changing nature of immigration in Canada and future projections that almost guarantee a large proportion of Canada's future population will consist of people of colour who may not necessarily subscribe to Western values or Western cultural and legal norms. A further implication of these changes is that Canadian institutions also need to seriously consider how to become more culturally competent. The problems of definition further complicate the research agenda that must emerge, especially in relation to the operationalization of terms such as *visible minority*.

Visible minority female offenders are more diverse than their male counterparts and, like Aboriginal women, Black female offenders are overrepresented in the criminal justice system. For the most part, visible minority female offenders commit property and drug-related offences, and most have been victimized at some point in their lives, which, in turn, highlights their subordinate economic status in Canadian society.

Like other women around the world, visible minority female victims experience violence and other forms of abuse at the hands of male partners or ex-partners. This chapter has tried to point out the additional and multiple other kinds of difficulties that women of colour must contend with, often on a daily basis, including issues relating to culture, religious beliefs, isolation, dependence, and different forms of racism. Finally, the chapter has emphasized the importance of understanding the role of these multiple and intersecting factors in conditioning the lives and experiences of visible minority female victims and offenders.

Discussion Questions

1. A long-standing debate continues on whether Canada should collect official statistics on the race or ethnocultural background of offenders (see the debate in the *Canadian Journal of Criminology*, 1994, vol. 36, no. 2). What are the arguments, pro and con, for collecting such data? What is your position on this issue, and how would you defend it?
2. How would you define the concept of *visible minority*? Why would you define it this way?
3. How would you use the concept of intersectionality to explain the victimization or offending of a hypothetical Black woman arrested for welfare fraud? What different factors might have combined to create this hypothetical woman's life circumstances? Describe how these factors might intersect.

Suggested Readings

Alarid, L.F., & Cromwell, P. (2006). *In her own words: Women offenders' views on crime and victimization.* Los Angeles: Roxbury.

> One of the few books that examine female offending from the perspectives of female offenders.

MacLeod, L., & Shin, M. (1993). *Like a wingless bird: A tribute to the survival and courage of women who are abused and who speak neither English nor French.* Ottawa: Department of Canadian Heritage.

> A classic, and one of the first Canadian statements on the victimization experiences of female minorities.

Sokoloff, N.J., & Pratt, C. (2005). *Domestic violence at the margins: Readings on race, class, gender, and culture.* New Brunswick, NJ: Rutgers University Press.

> This excellent anthology presents the work of scholars trying to understand women's victimization through the lens of intersectionality.

Online Resources

1. Bibliographic References for Multicultural Perspectives on Domestic Violence in the US: www.lib.jjay.cuny.edu/research/DomesticViolence

   > This website, compiled by Natalie Sokoloff, provides a large bibliography on multicultural perspectives on domestic violence.

2. Incite! Women of Color Against Violence: www.incite-national.org

   > Incite! is an organization of activist women of colour dedicated to eradicating violence against women of colour.

3. Correctional Service of Canada's Women Offender Programs and Issues: www.csc-scc.gc.ca/text/prgrms-eng.shtml

   > This Government of Canada website presents statistical data on women offender programs and issues.

References

Abraham, M. (2000). *Speaking the unspeakable: Marital violence among South Asian immigrants in the United States.* New Brunswick, NJ: Rutgers University Press.

Addario, L. (2002). *Six degrees from liberation: Legal needs of women in criminal and other matters.* Ottawa: Research and Statistics Division, Department of Justice Canada.

Ahmad, F., Riaz, S., Barata, P., & Stewart, D. (2004). Patriarchal beliefs and perceptions of abuse among South Asian immigrant women. *Violence Against Women, 10,* 262–282.

Alvi, S., Schwartz, M.D., Dekeseredy, W.S., & Bachaus, J. (2005). Victimization and attitudes towards woman abuse of impoverished minority women. *Western Criminology Review, 6,* 1–11.

Barata, P.C., McNally, M.J., Sales, I.M., & Stewart, D.E. (2005). Portuguese immigrant women's perspectives on wife abuse: A cross-generational comparison. *Journal of Interpersonal Violence, 20,* 1132–1150.

Bhuyan, R., Mell, M., Senturia, K., Sullivan, M., & Shiu-Thornton, S. (2005). "Women must endure according to their karma": Cambodian immigrant women talk about domestic violence. *Journal of Interpersonal Violence, 20,* 902–921.

Boritch, H. (1997). *Fallen women: Female crime and criminal justice in Canada.* Cambridge, UK: Cambridge University Press.

Boritch, H. (in press). Women in prison in Canada. In C. Brooks & B. Schissel (Eds.), *Marginality and condemnation.* Black Point, NS: Fernwood.

Brownridge, D.A., & Halli, S.S. (2002). Double jeopardy?: Violence against immigrant women in Canada. *Violence and Victims, 17,* 455–471.

Bui, H.N. (2003). Help-seeking behavior among abused immigrant women. *Violence Against Women, 9,* 207–239.

Burgess-Proctor, A. (2006). Intersections of race, class, gender, and crime: Future directions for feminist criminology. *Feminist Criminology, 1,* 27–47.

Canada, Commission of Inquiry into Certain Events at the Prison for Women in Kingston. (1996). *Commission of Inquiry into Certain Events at the Prison for Women in Kingston* (the Arbour inquiry). Ottawa: Public Works and Government Services Canada.

Correctional Service of Canada. (2003). *Women offender statistical overview: 2003.* Ottawa: Author.

Correctional Service of Canada. (2006). *Ten-year status report on women's corrections: 1996–2006.* Retrieved from www.csc-scc.gc.ca/text/prgrm/fsw/wos24/index-eng.shtml.

Chesney-Lind, M. (1999). Trends in women's crime. In J. Winterdyk & D. King (Eds.), *Diversity and justice in Canada* (pp. 132–150). Toronto: Canadian Scholars' Press.

Chui, T., Tran, K., & Maheux, H. (2007). *Immigration in Canada: A portrait of the foreign-born population, 2006 Census.* Ottawa: Statistics Canada.

Currie, A. (1994). *Ethnocultural groups and the justice system in Canada: A review of the issues.* Retrieved from www.nizkor.org/hweb/orgs/canadian/canada/justice/ethnocultural-groups.

Daly, K., & Chesney-Lind, M. (1988). Feminism and criminology. *Justice Quarterly, 5,* 497–538.

DeKeseredy, W.S. (1992). In defence of self-defence: Demystifying female violence against male intimates. In R. Hinch (Ed.), *Crosscurrents: Debates in Canadian society* (pp. 245–252). Scarborough, ON: Nelson.

Denney, D., Ellis, T., & Barn, R. (2006). Race, diversity and criminal justice in Canada: A view from the UK. *Internet Journal of Criminology.* Available from www.internetjournalofcriminology.com/ijcprimaryresearch.html.

Dumbrill, G.C., & Maiter, S. (1996). Developing racial and cultural equity in social work practice. *The Social Worker, 64,* 89–95.

El-Bassel, N., Gilbert, L., Witte, S., Wu, E., Gaeta, T., Schilling, R., et al. (2003). Intimate partner violence and substance abuse among minority women receiving care from an inner-city emergency department. *Women's Health Issues, 13,* 16–22.

Erez, E., & Copps Hartley, C. (2003). Battered immigrant women and the legal system: A therapeutic jurisprudence perspective. *Western Criminology Review, 4,* 155–169.

Gilfus, M. (2006). From victims to survivors to offenders. In L. Alrarid & P. Cromwell (Eds.), *In her own words: Women offenders' views on crime and victimization* (pp. 5–14). Los Angeles: Roxbury.

Grossman, S.F., & Lundy, M. (2007). Domestic violence across race and ethnicity: Implications for social work practice and policy. *Violence Against Women, 13,* 1029–1052.

Hannah-Moffat, K., & Shaw, M. (2001). *Taking risks: Incorporating gender and culture into the classification and assessment of federally sentenced women in Canada.* Ottawa: Status of Women Canada.

Hilbert, J.C., & Krishnan, S.P. (2000). Addressing barriers to community care of battered women in rural environments: Creating a policy of social inclusion. *Journal of Health and Social Policy, 12,* 41–52.

Hyman, I., Forte, T., Du Mont, J., Romans, S., & Cohen, M.M. (2006). The association between length of stay in Canada and intimate partner violence among immigrant women. *American Journal of Public Health, 9,* 654–659.

Jiwani, Y. (2005). Walking a tightrope: The many faces of violence in the lives of racialized immigrant girls and young women. *Violence Against Women, 11,* 846–875.

Johnson, H. (2006). *Measuring violence against women: Statistical trends, 2006* (85-570-XIE). Ottawa: Minister of Industry, Statistics Canada.

Josephson, J. (2005). The intersectionality of domestic violence and welfare in the lives of poor women. In N. Sokoloff (Ed.), *Domestic violence at the margins: Readings on race, class, gender and culture* (pp. 83–101). New Brunswick, NJ: Rutgers University Press.

Krane, J., Oxman-Martinez, J., & Ducey, K. (2000). Violence against women and ethno-racial minority women: Examining some assumptions about ethnicity and race. *Canadian Ethnic Studies, 32*(3), 1–18.

Law, M. (2004). Federally sentenced women in the community: Dynamic risk predictors. *Forum on Corrections Research, 16*(1), 18–20.

Lawrence, S., & Williams, T. (2006). Swallowed up: Drug couriers at the borders of Canadian sentencing. *University of Toronto Law Journal, 56,* 285–332.

Lee, M.-Y. (2002). Asian battered women. In A.R. Roberts (Ed.), *Handbook of domestic violence intervention strategies: Policies, programs and legal remedies* (pp. 472–482). New York: Oxford University Press.

MacLeod, L., & Shin, M. (1993). *Like a wingless bird: A tribute to the survival and courage of women who are abused and who speak neither English nor French.* Ottawa: Department of Canadian Heritage.

McGuinty rules out use of sharia law in Ontario. (2005, September 12). *CTV.ca News.* Retrieved from www.ctv.ca.

National Parole Board. (2000). *Special study on federal female offenders from 1995/96 to 1999/00.* Retrieved from www.npb-cnlc.gc.ca/reports/femaleoffenders_e.htm.

National Parole Board. (2007). *Performance monitoring report 2006–2007.* Retrieved from www.npb-cnlc.gc.ca/reports/report_e.htm.

Ontario, Commission on Systemic Racism in the Ontario Criminal Justice System. (1995). *Report of the commission on systemic racism in the Ontario criminal justice system.* Toronto: Queen's Printer.

Perreault, S. (2008). *Visible minorities and victimization.* Ottawa: Statistics Canada, Minister of Industry.

Porter, J.A. (1965). *The vertical mosaic: An analysis of social class and power in Canada* (Studies in the structure of power: Decision-making in Canada series, no. 2). Toronto: University of Toronto Press.

Rasche, C.E. (2001). Minority women and domestic violence: The unique dilemmas of battered women of color. In H.M. Eigenberg (Ed.), *Woman battering in the United States: Till death do us part* (pp. 86–102). Prospect Heights, IL: Waveland.

Reitsma-Street, M. (1999). Justice for Canadian girls: A 1990's update. *Canadian Journal of Criminology, 31,* 335–364.

Richie, B.E., & Kanuha, V. (2000). Battered women of color in public health care systems. In M. Baca-Zinn, P. Hondagneu-Sotelo, & M. Messner (Eds.), *Gender through the prism of difference* (pp. 129–137). Boston: Allyn and Bacon.

Roberts, J. (2002). Racism and the collection of statistics relating to race and ethnicity. In W. Chan & K. Mirchandani (Eds.), *Crimes of colour: Racialization and the criminal justice system in Canada* (pp. 101–112). Peterborough, ON: Broadview Press.

Satzewich, V., & Liodakis, N. (2007). *Race and ethnicity in Canada: A critical introduction.* Toronto: Oxford University Press.

Saunders, D.G. (1986). When battered women use violence: Husband-abuse or self-defense? *Violence and Victims, 1,* 47–60.

Shirwadkar, S. (2004). Canadian domestic violence policy and Indian immigrant women. *Violence Against Women, 10,* 860–879.

Smith, E. (2004). *Nowhere to turn? Responding to partner violence against immigrant and visible minority women.* Ottawa: Canadian Council on Social Development.

Sokoloff, N.J., & Dupont, I. (2005). Domestic violence at the intersections of race, class, and gender: Challenges and contributions to understanding violence against marginalized women in diverse communities. *Violence Against Women, 11,* 38–64.

Statistics Canada. (2001). *Visible minorities in Canada* (85F0033MIE). Ottawa: Author.

Statistics Canada. (2005). *Population projection of visible minority groups, Canada, provinces and regions: 2001–2017* (91-541-XIE). Ottawa: Author.

Statistics Canada. (2006). *Women in Canada: A gender-based statistical report.* Ottawa: Author.

Thomas, E.K. (2000). Domestic violence in the African-American and Asian-American communities: A comparative analysis of two racial/ethnic minority cultures and implications for mental health service provision for women of color. *Psychology, 37*(3–4), 32–43.

Trevethan, S., & Rastin, C. (2004). *A profile of visible minority offenders in the federal Canadian correctional system* (R-144). Ottawa: Research Branch, Correctional Service of Canada.

Urban Alliance on Race Relations. (1993, March). Legal protection for Aboriginal and racial minority women. In Urban Alliance on Race Relations Justice Conference Planning Committee (Ed.), *The justice system: Is it serving or failing minorities?* [Workshop proceedings from the Urban Alliance on Race Relations Justice Conference, Osgoode Hall, York University, Toronto] (pp. 33–36). Retrieved from www.urbanalliance.ca/justice/jusconf.htm.

Wortley, S. (2003). Hidden intersections: Research on race, crime, and criminal justice in Canada. *Canadian Ethnic Studies, 35*(3), 99–117.

Yick, A.G., Shibusawa, T., & Agbayani-Siewert, P. (2003). Partner violence, depression, and practice implications with families of Chinese descent. *Journal of Cultural Diversity, 10,* 96–104.

Yoshihama, M. (2000). Reinterpreting strength and safety in a socio-cultural context: Dynamics of domestic violence and experiences of women of Japanese descent. *Children and Youth Services Review, 22,* 207–229.

Young, V.D., & Adams-Fuller, T. (2006). Women, race/ethnicity, and criminal justice processing. In C. Renzetti, L. Goodstein, & S. Miller (Eds.), *Rethinking gender, crime and justice* (pp. 185–199). Los Angeles: Roxbury.

Zack, N. (2001). Philosophical aspects of the "AAA Statement on 'Race.'" *Anthropological Theory, 1,* 445–465.

CHAPTER 12

Girls and Women as
Victims of Crime

Walter DeKeseredy*

Introduction

If the term *crime victim* comes up in the course of our daily conversations with friends, relatives, acquaintances, or even with university peers and professors, it generally is in reference to a person harmed by a sexual assault, burglary, act of vandalism, or another form of interpersonal violence, such as homicide. However, knowingly or unknowingly, all of us have been, or will be, victimized by one or more highly injurious behaviours that commonly escape the purview of criminal law. As University of San Francisco criminologist Robert Elias (1986) put it more than 20 years ago:

> We may have a limited social reality of crime and victimization that excludes harms such as consumer fraud, pollution, unnecessary drugs and surgery, food additives, workplace hazards and diseases, police violence, censorship, discrimination, poverty, exploitation and war. We suffer victimization not only by other individuals, but also by governments and other social institutions, not to mention the psychological victimization bred by our own insecurities. (p. 4)

Box 12.1 provides one recent, controversial example of what Elias was talking about. In early September 2007, the Canadian government led by Prime Minister Stephen Harper added more fuel to an ongoing fire by eliminating funding to a non-profit women's group that struggles to help end violence against women and other forms of female victimization. Thus, we will likely see more and more cases where many women are "twice victimized"—

---

* The author thanks Jane Barker, Carla Cesaroni, and Mike Thompson for their advice and guidance.

first by violence and the men who abused them and then by the lack of social support provided by the Canadian federal government (Elias, 1993).

Shortly after I read the article in box 12.1, a flyer sent from federal Finance Minister Jim Flaherty's office arrived at my house[1] and included this statement: "Canada's New Government is standing up for safe communities by tackling violent crime and keeping criminals off the streets." The flyer also announced, "Serious Crime = Serious Time." Given that most violence against women occurs behind closed doors and not on the streets, leading experts

---

Box 12.1   "Turning Back the Clock" on Funding for Women's Groups

Women's rights advocates accused the Harper government of ignoring their struggle for equality after a leading women's group closed its doors because of a lack of federal funding.

Supported by opposition MPs, the National Association of Women and the Law (NAWL) vowed yesterday to use volunteers to keep up its efforts to combat violence against women, improve living conditions for those on low incomes, achieve pay equity, obtain funding for universal childcare and other causes.

NAWL lost its funding of $300,000 a year after government spending cuts announced last fall. Despite a $13 billion budget surplus, the government slashed outlays for women's advocacy projects and eliminated the Court Challenges Program, which funded legal actions by rights advocates. The Tories said Status of Women Canada would no longer fund organizations pressing policymakers to improve conditions for women.

"The Harper government is trying to silence women's groups who speak out against its right-wing agenda," NAWL board member Pamela Cross said. "These are ideologically driven cuts that demonstrate a defective concept of women's equality and democracy."

Opposition MPs denounced the moves by the Harper government.

"Women are being silenced in Canada," Liberal MP Maria Minna (Beaches–East York) told the NAWL press conference. "How can we ... say we are promoting rights for women in Afghanistan when our government is forcing women's organizations to close?"

New Democrat MP Irene Mathyssen said "the closure of NAWL will turn back the clock on women's equality in Canada."

NAWL, a non-profit legal reform organization set up in 1974, has, among other things, worked to strengthen laws dealing with rape, improve family law and ensure women's equality was specifically included in the Charter of Rights. Cross said the group will continue by using volunteers, but that its effectiveness as a resource will be undercut by the closing of its office.

Heritage Minister José Verner told a news conference that NAWL might have some projects eligible for funding but that research and advocacy work would not qualify.

Source: Whittington, L. (2007, September 9). Women's group closes after losing its funding: Opposition MPs say Harper government "turning back clock." *Toronto Star*, p. AA12. Reprinted with permission—Toronto Syndication Services.

in the field could easily assume that Mr. Flaherty's government does not view date or acquaintance rape or woman battering as "serious crimes," which may also explain why the National Association of Women and the Law lost its annual funding of $300,000.

Related to what Elias stated above, entire categories of people sometimes (often if they are women) are not "allowed" to be crime victims. For example, one California police department stamped all reports of violent crimes against prostitutes as NHI—"No Human Involved"—and did not follow up on them (DeKeseredy & Schwartz, 1996; Fairstein, 1993). Certainly, prostitutes and street people in many North American cities feel that the police refuse to take their victimization seriously, despite having been brutally victimized in ways similar to that described in box 12.2 by a sex worker interviewed by Jody Miller and Martin D. Schwartz (1995).[2] This woman had, to say the least, a "bad date."

Scores of other women and girls suffer in silence and receive little, if any attention, from the media, politicians, and even criminologists. Consider female victims of corporate violence. As Rynbrandt and Kramer (2001) remind us, "Women as employees and consumers have long been special targets of corporate indifference, greed and arrogance" (p. 167). Corporate violence is defined as:

> any behaviour undertaken in the name of the corporation by decision makers, or other persons in authority within the corporation, that endangers the health and safety of employees or other persons who are affected by that behaviour. Even acts of omission, in which decision makers, etc., refuse to take action to reduce or eliminate known health and safety risks must be considered corporate violence. It is the impact the action has on the victim, not the intent of the act, which determines whether or not it is violence. (DeKeseredy & Hinch, 1991, p. 100)

Research reviewed elsewhere[3] reveals that many workers are safer on the streets than they are on the job. Some scholars estimate the corporate death rate at more than six times greater than the street crime death rate and the rate of non-lethal assault in the workplace

---

Box 12.2   A "Bad Date"

Well, a girlfriend brought a date over to a friend's house where we was staying. And, uh, she was gonna go out with him but instead he saw me and he wanted to date me. Ok, so I said yeah. And, uh, we went back and got in his car, and as we was leavin' he pulled a knife out and stuck it to my throat with one hand and drove with the other on ... And he drove me all the way to ***, and on the way here, he stopped on the side of the freeway and he tied my hands behind my back, and tied my feet together, and put a thing around my mouth so I couldn't scream or nothin' no more. And, uh, after that, we got to *** in this field and he put a rope around my neck and tied it to the steering wheel. He blacked both of my eyes, he busted two ribs, and busted up my back real bad. He beat me for like four hours. And he was gonna kill me, if it weren't for my friend having' his—the color of his car and stuff was and all that, he would've killed me I think. And then he gave me twenty dollars put me out in the field. Told me to find my own way back.

Source: Miller, J., & Schwartz, M.D. (1995). Rape myths and violence against prostitutes. *Deviant Behavior, 16,* 1–23.

at more than 30 times greater than the rate of predatory street crime (DeKeseredy, Ellis, & Alvi, 2005). Although close to 73 percent of Canadian women in the paid workforce are in so-called pink ghettos (that is, clerical jobs, nursing, and retail sales), they are not immune to safety hazards. Indeed, these workers are at great risk of experiencing the ill effects of exposure to toxic substances, stress, repetitive strain injury, and other work-related dangers. As pointed out in box 12.3, a back injury suffered by a nurse is just as debilitating as the same injury suffered by a man at a heavy construction site.

Reading this chapter is a task I would define as work, and I assume that because you are reading these words, you are now working—at home, at school, or at another place that is not riddled with toxic fumes and other industrial health hazards. So, is it logical to assume that you and all of the contributors to this book are at very low risk of being victimized by corporate violence? No, this is not the case, because we are all consumers, and shopping can be very hazardous to your health (DeKeseredy et al., 2005). Sykes and Cullen (1992) are

---

Box 12.3   Back Injuries Plaguing Nursing Profession

I must admit to being shocked when Health Minister Dave Hancock said last week that 1,000 nurses around the province are off at any given time with back problems.

Like many people, I don't necessarily think about heavy lifting when I think about the lives of nurses, even though I have seen this when visiting aging relatives in hospitals or nursing homes.

But nurses rank right up there with steel workers for back injuries.

A National Survey of the Work and Health of Nurses found that 25.2 per cent of nurses have chronic back problems.

In Alberta, the amount of money that back injuries cost our health service is staggering—a 2006 report from Alberta Human Resources and Employment says lost time claims cost the Alberta health system more than $13 million per year, and more than half the injuries were to the back and trunk of health care workers.

Capital Health loses about 75,000 hours of employee time to all injuries a year, and again more than half are related to patient handling.

Elly Gelasco, a licensed practical nurse at the Glenrose, wasn't expecting this kind of occupational hazard when she went into nursing about nine years ago relatively late in life at the age of 46.

"When I started at the Alex, the nurses looked at me and said I was crazy," Gelasco says.

"I never took it (heavy lifting) into consideration—I just wanted to do bedside care."

She optimistically predicts she has a long nursing career ahead of her, but she has suffered two serious injuries that have affected both her health and her career.

She was off for three months with a torn tendon in her shoulder after catching a falling patient.

She was off for a month with a strained lower back after a patient who was holding onto her collapsed and brought her down with him.

These injuries never totally disappear and as a result, she has gone into rehab nursing because it is less stressful, but her heart is still in acute-care nursing.

Gelasco described taking many shortcuts during her days as an acute-care nurse, simply because there wasn't time to get help wheeling or lifting a patient during the past decade of staff shortages.

Health officials recognize the back problems suffered by nurses and they are doing something about it.

One of the ways is by investing $27 million across the province in high-tech ceiling lifts, which are a great aid to nurses in moving immobile patients.

Capital Health is increasing the number of these lifts from 40 to 1,300.

I watched three nurses skillfully shift a 240-pound stroke patient around in his bed so he could be lifted from his bed to his wheelchair.

Even with a lift, it doesn't look like a piece of cake, but Gelasco says it's much less dangerous than other methods, including portable lifts, which must be manipulated around furniture and which still require nurses to do a lot of pushing and lifting.

Capital Health spokesman Steve Buick says the lifts aren't going to replace all patient lifting, and he notes that patients getting back on their feet after surgery, for instance, still have to be helped by nurses.

"We can't take human contact out of health care," he says.

The lifts will likely result in cost savings in terms of reduction of lost time, but Buick says that's not the reason for putting them in.

"I don't know if the lifts will bring in pots of money, but I know they are an important instrument for staff safety—they are worth it, period."

Nurses and other health-care professionals are hearing a lot about their backs these days.

Capital Health aims to have every worker take a refresher course in safer lifting and safe patient handling.

Dave Dyer, director of nursing for the Glenrose, where a course has been developed for the whole health region, says part of the education process is knowing where the risk is in a patient lift.

The hospital contracted a consulting group of kinesiologists to spend entire shifts with nurses, filming them during patient transfers and breaking down the movements to figure out which are risky. A DVD that shows the breakdown of patient transfers is part of the training.

Dyer says it will become more important over coming years to ensure that nurses are better trained to avoid back injuries. Every year they are dealing with heavier patients, he says. At the Glenrose, the number of people admitted weighing more than 200 pounds rose by 50 per cent from 200 to 300 in the last two years.

And, partly as a legacy of the cutbacks in the early '90s, over half the nurses on some of the biggest units are over 50, and hospitals can't afford to lose them because of the general staff shortage, he says.

"We're doing a lot of work to make it a safer environment so they can stay for as long as we need them," Dyer says.

Source: Sadava, M. (2007, September 22). Back injuries plague nursing profession: Province investing in hundreds of patient lifts. *Edmonton Journal*, p. B3. Material reprinted with the express permission of Edmonton Journal Group Inc., a CanWest Partnership.

right to claim that the old adage "let the buyer beware" has special meaning in light of the corporate violence against the US woman described in box 12.4.

Box 12.4   One Woman's Experiences with Silicone Breast Implants

Joan received the bad news in 1977: Her breasts must be removed because of precancerous tumors. The good news, however, was that reconstructive surgery was possible. She received silicone implants and again looked forward to life as a busy young woman with a family and a career. Soon, however, she suffered from extreme fatigue and arthritis. Often she was so ill that she could not leave her bed. Joan was forced to quit her job, and her family had to learn to function without her. This caused the entire family great emotional distress. Joan eventually suspected that her ill health was linked to her silicone implants and had them replaced with saline implants in 1993. Although her health has improved somewhat, she is still unable to work. Because of concerns about saline implants, Joan is seriously considering removing them as well, in what she calls her "third mastectomy" in less than two decades.

Source: Rynbrandt, L., & Kramer, R.C. (2001). Corporate violence against women. In C.M. Renzetti & L. Goodstein (Eds.), *Women, crime, and criminal justice: Original feminist readings* (pp. 165–175). Los Angeles: Roxbury.

The case presented in box 12.4 is, as Rynbrandt and Kramer (2001) accurately observe, "not unusual" (p. 165). For example, a study published in the highly prestigious *New England Journal of Medicine* uncovered that 25 percent of all women with breast implants required a second surgery, especially women who received implants after cancer surgery (Gabriel et al., 1997). Some readers may be saying to themselves that I have presented an extreme example of a product that can be very dangerous in the first place because of the risks posed by "going under the knife." Still, scores of products most people view as being intrinsically safe are also major threats to your physical health, such as some food additives and chemicals added to drinking water and hygienic products (Friedrichs, 2007; Simon, 2005).

Let us briefly examine the risks posed by tampons, products that many thousands of Canadian women frequently use and trust. Tampons can cause toxic shock syndrome, a deadly illness caused by staphylococcus bacteria from the vagina or cervix entering first the uterus and then the bloodstream. Some scientists assert that tampons provide an environment for the proliferation of these bacteria and their resultant toxins. Symptoms of toxic shock include a skin rash and the peeling of thin layers of skin from the affected person's body. Toxic shock also affects the kidneys, liver, intestines, and stomach. In many cases, toxic shock is first detected as flu-like symptoms followed by a rash. Women who have had vaginal, cervical, or uterine surgery and women who have given birth are advised not to use tampons until they are completely healed (DeKeseredy et al., 2005; DeKeseredy & Hinch, 1991). Another problem for some women is that they develop allergic reactions to deodorant or scented pads and tampons, which are marketed as being essential in helping women to feel "clean and fresh," even though such products have no noticeable advantages over washing with soap and water.

I could provide a much longer list of injurious acts committed against girls and women that many people do not regard as crimes in the strict sense of the word. One of the most important points to consider here is that, like many other social problems, crime is often "not a quality of the act the person commits, but rather a consequence of the application by others of rules and sanctions to an offender" (Becker, 1973, p. 9). Nevertheless, Canadians share considerable agreement about the seriousness of the behaviours discussed in subsequent sections of this chapter (Alvi, DeKeseredy, & Ellis, 2000). The acts to be examined are what John Hagan (1994) refers to as consensus crimes. In other words, members of all or most Canadian groups share norms and values that legally prohibit these forms of conduct and impose the most severe penalties on those who violate laws relating to them. Homicide is a prime example of a consensus crime, and it is this problem I turn to first.

Homicide[4]

Homicide, also commonly referred to as murder, is the intentional killing of one person, directly or indirectly, by another (Gartner, 1995). According to the Canadian *Criminal Code*, there are four types of homicide: first-degree murder, second-degree murder, manslaughter, and infanticide (see box 12.5). Homicide, which is viewed by the majority of Canadians as the most serious crime, is a relatively rare offence for both males and females (DeKeseredy, 2000b). For example, homicides account for a very small proportion (0.02 percent) of all crimes known to police in Canada on an annual basis (Li, 2007).

Consistent with previous years, 2006 homicide data collected by Canadian police and compiled by the Canadian Centre for Justice Statistics show that most victims were young

---

Box 12.5   Four Types of Homicide in Canada

First-degree murder occurs when:

a. the murder is planned and deliberate; or
b. the victim is a person employed and acting in the course of employment for the preservation and maintenance of the public peace (for example, a police worker or a correctional worker); or
c. the death is caused by a person committing or attempting to commit serious offences (for example, sexual assault, kidnapping, or hijacking).

Second-degree murder is all murder that is not first-degree murder.

Manslaughter is generally considered a homicide committed in the heat of passion by sudden provocation. It also includes other culpable homicides that are not murder or infanticide.

Infanticide occurs when a female causes the death of her newborn child, and her state of mind is disordered because of her having given birth.

Source: Adapted from DeKeseredy, W.S. (2000b). *Women, crime and the Canadian criminal justice system*, Cincinnati: Anderson; Dauvergne, M., & Li, G. (2006). Homicide in Canada, 2005. *Juristat*, 26(6), 1–25; Siegel, L.J., & McCormick, C. (2003). *Criminology in Canada: Theories, patterns, and typologies* (2nd ed.). Toronto: Thomson Nelson.

males: 442 male victims, compared with 162 female victims. The female victimization rates were highest between the ages of 18 and 24. Moreover, most victims were killed by someone they knew (Li, 2007).

Like our neighbours south of the border, when we are not worried about the economy, terrorist attacks, or deadly viruses (SARS and the Avian flu, for example), we worry about violent crimes committed by strangers on the streets or in other public places (DeKeseredy, 2005; Glassner, 1999). Canadians' intense fear of "stranger danger," however, is not well founded. Of course, small percentages of Canadians are robbed, mugged, or murdered by unknown predatory offenders; and their pain and suffering should not be trivialized. Nevertheless, what US sociologists Richard Gelles and Murray Straus (1988) stated 20 years ago still holds true for Canadian women and girls today: "You are more likely to be physically assaulted, beaten, and killed in your own home at the hands of a loved one than anyplace else, or by anyone else in society" (p. 18). Many people find this statement and the recent case described in box 12.6 hard to believe because they were socialized to view the family primarily as a source of love and as a safe refuge from the pains inflicted by the outside world (Duffy & Momirov, 1997). Others do not see violence in the family as a social problem because they have never directly or indirectly experienced it. Unfortunately, few families are conflict-free, and many are plagued by harms that few of us could imagine, such as those discussed in box 12.6.

Box 12.6   Double Tragedy Turns Joy to Grief

With homicide detectives waiting outside, a team of 30 doctors and nurses fought frantically early yesterday morning to save an unborn child and her mother.

When Aysun Sesen was brought to St. Michael's Hospital, with multiple stab wounds to her abdomen, her fetus still had a faint heartbeat. But when they performed a Caesarean, the girl was stillborn.

Doctors also could not save Sesen, whose husband, Turan Cocelli, 29, was charged with her slaying.

Family and friends of the 25-year-old victim congregated at an Etobicoke house last evening, some sitting despondently, others embracing, praying and sobbing.

Instead of anticipation over Sesen's first child, expected in December, a group of relatives and members of the local Kurdish community searched for answers into this woman's death.

"We are shocked," Nirman Cocelli, a cousin, said. "We don't know what happened, we don't know what to do. Everybody is sitting around discussing it. We just try to figure out what happened."

Toronto's 64th homicide victim had been taken to hospital about 1 a.m. after emergency personnel were called to a red-brick bungalow on Whitburn Cres., near Keele St. and Sheppard Ave.

Neighbours said that while the family was quiet and kept to themselves, they could often be heard arguing.

Source: Henry, M., & Powell, B. (2007, October 3). Double tragedy turns joy to grief: Husband charged as woman expecting first child in December is slain—Efforts to save fetus fail. *Toronto Star*, pp. A1, A10.

Included in box 12.6 are the phrases "We don't know what happened" and "We are shocked." The media's use of phrases or quotations like these "makes the cause of death appear inexplicable or the result of a man's suddenly having 'snapped'" (Myers, 1997, p. 110). The tragic death of Aysun Sesen is hardly an exceptional incident. Consider these statistics:

- In Ontario, between 1995 and 2005, 231 women were murdered by their partners or former partners.
- Ontario's Domestic Violence Death Review Committee noted in its 2004 report that 100 percent of the victims in the cases it reviewed were women, concluding that domestic violence is not gender-neutral (Ontario, Domestic Violence Death Review Committee, 2004). The most common risk factor was actual or pending separation, followed closely by a prior history of violence. In its 2005 report (Ontario, Domestic Violence Death Review Committee, 2005), the committee noted, "In eight out of nine cases, the homicide appeared both predictable and preventable" (p. 6).
- In 2005, in Canada, spousal homicides accounted for close to 16 percent of all solved homicides and about half (47 percent) of all family homicides. Women were five times more likely than men to be killed by their spouse (Cross, 2007; Dauvergne & Li, 2006).

Newspaper stories like the one in box 12.6 generally do not portray the killing of intimate female partners as a major social problem (Bullock & Cubert, 2002). The truth, however, is that in Canada systemic violence against women does exist, and it has little to do with mental illness (Cross, 2007). Another point to consider is that most Canadian pregnant homicide victims were killed by their male intimate partners (Dauvergne & Li, 2006).

At parties and other social gatherings, I am sometimes asked about my line of work. When I tell non-academics about the nature of my job and research, they often ask this question, which is the title of David Adams's (2007) new book, "Why do they kill?" It is beyond the scope of this chapter to provide an in-depth review of the theoretical literature on *intimate femicide*, which is the "killing of females with whom they [men] have, have had, or want to have, a sexual and/or emotional relationship" (Ellis & DeKeseredy, 1997, p. 592). However, it is necessary to emphasize that a combination of risk factors increase the likelihood of a man killing a current or former female partner (Campbell et al., 2003; Gosselin, 2005). Below are the major correlates of this crime as identified by leading experts in the field (Campbell, 1995, p. 111; DeKeseredy & Schwartz, in press; Gosselin, 2005; Seymour et al., 2002):

- Access to or ownership of guns
- Use of a weapon in prior abusive incidents
- Threats with a weapon
- Threats to kill
- Serious injury in prior abusive incidents
- Threats of suicide
- Drug or alcohol abuse
- Forced sex of female partner
- Obsessiveness, extreme jealousy, or extreme dominance

Perhaps nothing hurts more than the loss of a loved one; and the death of a child is especially painful. Many parents frequently worry about their children being abducted and possibly killed by strangers. In fact, such concern is so common that the absence of precautions is sometimes viewed as unusual behaviour. In the summer of 2006, a friend and colleague from Sweden joined the Faculty of Criminology, Justice and Policy Studies at the University of Ontario Institute of Technology. He and his family moved into a quiet middle-class neighbourhood close to where I live, and his young daughter would often answer the door alone when visitors arrived. Another of my colleagues and his wife worried about the young girl's behaviour and told my friend that his daughter was at risk of being kidnapped. True, in recent years, in Canada and elsewhere, we have witnessed a few widely publicized cases of child abduction and murder (Barnett, Miller-Perrin, & Perrin, 2005). Nevertheless, most child and youth homicide victims are not killed by strangers.

In 2004, 55 homicides (30 male and 25 female victims) were committed against children and youth (under the age of 18) in Canada. Of the perpetrators, 62 percent were family members and only 6 percent were strangers (Dauvergne, 2006). Statistics Canada does not provide much published information on the characteristics of female youth homicide victims. Still, we know from publications based on data generated by Statistics Canada's homicide survey that since 1994, 90 percent of all youth aged 0 to 17 years who were killed were murdered by a parent (Dauvergne, 2005). Note, too, that data presented here may underestimate the extent of child and youth homicide because some killings may have been misclassified on the official records as either accidental or due to "natural causes." Indeed, as Barnett et al. (2005) put it, "What we fear and what we *should* fear are not always the same things" (p. 23, emphasis in original).

Youth and child homicides are more likely to occur in poor communities and in families affected by separation or divorce. Substance abuse is another major risk factor (Finkelhor, 1997; Garbarino, 1977). Moreover, surprising to many people is that between 1995 and 2004, fathers were responsible for the majority (59 percent) of family-related homicides involving child and youth victims in Canada (Dauvergne, 2006). One possible explanation for this statistic is that men are less involved in childrearing than women, and thus have a much lower tolerance for crying, disobedience, and soiling (DeKeseredy, 2005; Duffy & Momirov, 1997; Finkelhor, 1997).

Physical Assault[5]

Canadians in general perceive family and household settings as "havens in a hostile world" (Lasch, 1977). Further, like our neighbours south of the border, many Canadians like to brag that we live in "the freest country on earth" (Katz, 2006, p. 1). Perhaps these folks would change their minds if they knew what really goes on behind closed doors in numerous homes across the country.

Physical Assault in Marriage and Cohabiting Relationships

Sadly, each year in Canada, at least 11 percent of women in marital and cohabiting relationships are physically assaulted by an intimate male partner (DeKeseredy, 2005). For these women, the home is a "house of horrors," and the people who share their lives and we would expect would love them are the people who restrict their ability to live in peace (Sev'er, 2002).

Ann Menard (2001) is one of many feminist scholars who assert that the physical abuse of adult women occurs "in all demographic and social groups, cutting across age, race, ethnicity, sexual orientation, and economic circumstances" (p. 708). Although her contention is factually true, assault is not spread equally among these groups (DeKeseredy, 2007a; Sokoloff & Dupont, 2005). Some women are at higher risk than are others. For example, Brownridge and Halli's (2001) review of 14 studies (eight in the United States, five in Canada, and one in New Zealand) reveals dramatic differences in violence rates obtained from married persons and cohabiters. They found that the rate of violence for the latter typically exceeds that of the former by two times, but the difference can be greater than four times. Cohabiting women are also more likely to experience more severe types of violence than their married counterparts.

However, the above data do not speak for themselves, and crude counts of violent behaviours must be interpreted or theorized. One interpretation offered is that marriage results in healthier relationships and is a panacea for intimate partner violence. Still, this argument is made without a careful assessment of other factors that predict violence against women, including depression, alcohol and drug abuse, living in public housing, unemployment, and men's associations with sexist or violent peers (DeKeseredy & Schwartz, 2002; DeKeseredy, Alvi, Schwartz, & Tomaszewski, 2006; Fox, Benson, DeMaris, & Van Wyk, 2002; Riger & Krieglstein, 2000).

These variables are more likely to be associated with the conditions of poverty than with marital status (DeKeseredy, Alvi, et al., 2006; Rennison & Welchans, 2000). For example, many low-income women believe that men should live up to the culturally defined role of breadwinner. The man's role as the economic provider is not only part of many women's expectations but is still fundamental to most men's self-identity (Adams & Coltrane, 2005; Conway, 2001; Edin, 2000). Specifically, we know that women whose male partners suffer from job instability are three times as likely to be victims of intimate violence, a situation that worsens when the couple lives in a financially disadvantaged neighbourhood (Benson & Fox, 2004; DeKeseredy, Alvi, Schwartz, & Tomaszewski, 2003). This information is tied to other studies showing that married men are more likely to meet the prescribed breadwinner objective than are cohabiting men, and therefore are at lower risk of experiencing the gender-status inconsistency (Ellis & DeKeseredy, 1989) that is related to abuse (Raphael, 2001a). Part of the entire picture is that more women are becoming the main wage earners for their family. In fact, one of the fastest-growing family formations has been the "wife-only working" family, which is predicted to increase by 6 or 7 percent this decade (Conway, 2001; DeKeseredy, 2007a). Using US national victimization survey data, Schwartz (1990) found that the pattern of wife-only working was more commonly tied to wife abuse. Thus, in terms of earning power, it is not only male job instability that contributes to violence. Consequently, it is reasonable to speculate that although violence in marital relationships might increase because of a growing disparity in income (Raj, Silverman, Wingood, & DiClemente, 1999), this trend will at least be matched in marriages created by state intrusion. This prediction is based on studies showing that "when the economic differential leans in favor of the women in the relationship, domestic violence is exacerbated" (Raphael, 2001a, p. 454).

More broadly, men who feel they are unable to live up to gender expectations are more likely to abuse their partners compared with men whose ability to conform affirms their masculinity and sense of control (Johnson, 1997). As more recent studies have found, the higher a woman's income, the lower the man's perception of the quality of the relationship

(Raphael, 2001a). We also know that the rapid disappearance of male-dominated manufacturing jobs coupled with women's increased labour force participation and earnings have exacerbated cohabiting relationship tensions (Adams & Coltrane, 2005; Conway, 2001). Such tensions also increase the likelihood of cohabiting men's eviction from households because their partners see them as irresponsible and/or they cannot afford to house and feed them (Edin, 2000). Thus, because married men are more likely to be employed than cohabiting men, it is not surprising that they are happier than cohabiting men because they do not face the same "dramatic assaults" on their "sense of masculine dignity" (Bourgois, 1995, p. 215; Conway, 2001). Further, married men are less likely to experience the same degree of emotional stress that plagues male cohabiters. This stress is a major correlate of various kinds of woman abuse found in impoverished relationships (DeKeseredy & Schwartz, 2002). However, stress alone cannot explain why cohabiters report higher rates of violence than married men.

Unemployed men drink more alcohol than those who work. Thus, it is not surprising that cohabiters have more problems with alcohol than married men (DeKeseredy, Alvi, et al., 2006; Ellis & DeKeseredy, 1989; Horwitz & White, 1998; Stets, 1991). Although the relationship between alcohol and woman abuse is "not one of direct cause and effect" (Brownridge & Halli, 2001, p. 19), chronic alcohol abuse is consistently found to be a strong predictor of male-to-female violence (Tolman & Bennett, 1990). In addition, the social context of alcohol consumption may play a stronger role than the drinking itself. For instance, Schwartz, DeKeseredy, Tait, and Alvi (2001) found that college men who drink two or three times a week and have male peers who support both emotional and physical violence are almost 10 times as likely to assault women than are men who do not drink or have this support.

In sum, then, the reality is that cohabitation alone cannot explain why more violence occurs in cohabitation relationships than in marriages. However, this lack of evidence does not seem to matter to those people intent on misconstruing and deliberately using crude counts of behaviour against vulnerable populations (Sokoloff & Dupont, 2005), such as poor people in cohabiting relationships.

Economically disadvantaged women are also at higher risk of being physically assaulted by their male spouses. For example, when DeKeseredy et al.'s (2003) Quality of Neighbourhood Life Survey was administered to poor residents of six public housing estates in the west end of a metropolitan centre in eastern Ontario, 19.3 percent of the female sample stated that they had been physically assaulted by intimate partners in the year before the study. This figure is much higher than the past year's rate (1.3 percent) uncovered by the US National Violence Against Women Survey (Tjaden & Thoennes, 2000). One could easily dismiss the discrepancy by arguing that these two surveys used different methods and thus obtained different results. Nevertheless, Renzetti and Maier's (2002) Camden, New Jersey study provides further support for the assertion that public housing women are at higher risk than their more affluent counterparts. Fifty percent of the women they interviewed reported victimization. As Holzman, Hyatt, and Dempster (2001) remind us, "demographic, economic, and geographic factors associated with high incidence of violent victimization of women appear to find a nexus in public housing" (p. 665).

Referred to by some scholars as "cities-within-cities" (Venkatesh, 2000), most public housing estates are purposely concentrated in high-poverty metropolitan areas. Clustering the poor in these places is a strategy that exacerbates their stigmatization and inability to find work; intensifies **spatial poverty**, crime, and other social pathologies (drug use, for example); facilitates the withdrawal of government and private sector capital from neighbourhoods

(Leavitt & Loukaitou-Sideris, 1995; Massey & Kanaiaupuni, 1993; Popkin, Gwiasda, Olson, Rosenbaum, & Baron, 2000); and perpetuates racial and ethnic segregation and isolation (Kazemipur & Halli, 2000; Massey & Denton, 1993; Santiago, Galster, & Tatian, 1999). Many, if not all, of these elements strongly affect the frequency and severity of violence against women (Raphael, 2001b).

Separated and divorced women are also at higher risk of being beaten than married women (DeKeseredy, 2007a). For example, Statistics Canada's national Violence Against Women Survey found that about one-fifth (19 percent) of the women who reported violence by a previous male partner stated that the violence increased in severity at the time of separation (Johnson & Sacco, 1995; Rodgers, 1994). The 2004 Canadian General Social Survey (GSS) data show that, among women with a former husband or male cohabiting partner who had been violent during the relationship, 49 percent were assaulted by their ex-partners after separation (Mihorean, 2005). Several other North American studies, most of which are Canadian, uncovered similar data with the risk of assault peaking in the first two months following separation and when women attempted permanent separation through legal or other means (Ellis, 1992; Ellis & Stuckless, 1996). Hence, it is no wonder that many of Evan Stark's female clients told him that "they were never more frightened than in the days, weeks, or months after they moved out" (2007, p. 116).

Separation and divorce assaults are not restricted to North America. For example, McMurray, Froyland, Bell, and Curnow (2000) found that 21 percent of the 146 separated Western Australian men in their sample were violent during separation. Thus, as Douglas Brownridge (2006) points out in his in-depth review of the international social scientific literature on violence against women post-separation:

> In short, studies that allow a comparison of violence among separated, divorced, and married women show a consistent pattern of separated and divorced women being at elevated risk for violence compared to married women, with separated women having by far the greatest risk for post-separation violence. It appears that separated women have as much as thirty times the likelihood, and divorced women have as much as nine times the likelihood, of reporting non-lethal violence compared to married women. (p. 517)

Racial and ethnic differences are also seen in violence against women. For example, Statistics Canada's 2004 GSS found that Aboriginal women are more than three times more likely to be victims of intimate violence than are their non-Aboriginal counterparts (24 percent versus 7 percent) (Mihorean, 2005). The 1999 GSS uncovered similar data (Trainor & Mihorean, 2001). Note, too, that most intimate violence studies show that young men between the ages of 16 and 24 use violence against women more often than older males (DeKeseredy, 2007a; Barnett et al., 2005).

More research demonstrating variations in male-to-female violence in marital and cohabiting relationships across different socio-economic categories could easily be presented here. However, a key point is that different groups of women may require different types of social support. For example, in addition to attending to their basic safety concerns, impoverished women require financial assistance, immigrant and refugee women who cannot speak English or French need interpreters to help them express their experiences, and abused women with physical disabilities require services tailored to meet their special needs. "One size fits all" models, albeit well intentioned, have many limitations and can be highly ineffective for many women.

Several widely read and cited representative sample surveys, such as those conducted by the late Michael D. Smith (1986, 1987), show that Canadian men are just as, if not more, likely to beat their spouses as American men. However, it is not only women in marital or cohabiting relationships who are in danger of being physically abused.

Physical Assault Among Dating Couples and Adolescents

The Canadian national survey of woman abuse in university and college dating (CNS) found the following:[6]

- · Of the male respondents, 13.7 percent indicated that they had physically assaulted their dating partners in the year before the survey. Of the female respondents, 22.3 percent indicated that they had been physically victimized by their dating partners during the same time period.
- Approximately 35 percent of the women reported having been physically assaulted since leaving high school, and 17.8 percent of the men reported having been physically abusive during the same time period (DeKeseredy & Kelly, 1993; DeKeseredy & Schwartz, 1998).

Why does woman abuse in Canadian postsecondary school[7] dating happen "with alarming regularity" (Lloyd, 1991, p. 14)? Demographic or behavioural characteristics (termed *risk factors*) are associated with the types of male-to-female victimization uncovered by the CNS and other dating violence studies. However, a growing body of qualitative and quantitative research shows that male peer support is one of the most powerful determinants. The term *male peer support* refers to "the attachments to male peers and the resources that these men provide which encourage and legitimate woman abuse" (DeKeseredy, 1990, p. 130). Male peer support is also strongly associated with separation and divorce assault in rural Ohio, wife abuse in Canada and the United States, and other variants of woman abuse (Bowker, 1983; DeKeseredy, Donnermeyer, Schwartz, Tunnell, & Hall, 2007; DeKeseredy & Schwartz, in press; Smith, 1991).

In Canada, physical violence is also common in many heterosexual adolescent dating relationships (Department of Justice Canada, 2007). Even at young ages, boys can develop strong masculinist and pro–woman abuse attitudes (Adams & Coltrane, 2005; Connell, 1995). They are heavily influenced by the ideology of familial patriarchy, which is a key determinant of various types of woman abuse in later dating contexts (DeKeseredy & Schwartz, 1998). According to Mercer (1998):

> Adolescence is clearly not a period when young people reject the traditional gender roles for which they have been groomed. It is characteristically a time when they act them out—sometimes to their worse extremes. The alarming revelations about this process testify to the grave personal implications that male power has for females long before they become adults. (p. 16)

For example, of the male CNS participants who answered questions about abusive behaviours in elementary school dating relationships (grades 1 to 8), 3.6 percent admitted to having intentionally physically hurt one or more female partners. As expected, women reported higher rates of victimization (7.2 percent). Given that high school students spend more time dating than those in elementary school, higher rates of disclosure were anticipated from both male and female CNS participants because they spend greater "time at risk" (Ellis & DeKeseredy, 1996). Of the women surveyed, 89 percent said they dated in high school, whereas 38.2 percent said they dated in elementary school. Of the men surveyed, 87.1 percent dated in high school and 48.3 percent dated in elementary school. However, men's increased rate in dating did not result in an increased rate of self-reported violence against women: only 1.4 percent of men reported intentionally hurting their female partners in high school dating relationships.

On the other hand, data gathered from female CNS participants support the hypothesis that the more time at risk, the more likely women were to have been the objects of violence during their high school (grades 9 to 13)[8] dating: 9.1 percent of women reported having been physically assaulted during a high school date (DeKeseredy & Schwartz, 1998). This figure is slightly lower than the Canadian female high school figure (11 percent) obtained by Mercer (1988). Other Canadian studies reviewed by Department of Justice Canada (2007) reveal even higher rates. For example, 22 percent of grades 7, 9, and 11 girls who participated in a New Brunswick survey (Price, Byers, Sears, Whelan, & Saint Pierre, 2000) had a psychologically or physically abusive dating experience that upset them.

Key risk factors for physical assaults against women in elementary and high school dating relationships include jealousy, possessiveness, male peer support, community violence, substance abuse, low self-esteem, and patriarchal attitudes and beliefs (Callahan, Tolman, & Saunders, 2003; DeKeseredy & Schwartz, 1998; Lavoie, Robitaille, & Herbert, 2000; Malik, Sorenson, & Aneshensel, 1997; Powers & Kerman, 2006; Silverman, Raj, Mucci, & Hathaway, 2001). These factors are also associated with sexual assault in dating relationships, the topic of the next main section. However, prior to addressing this topic, it is necessary to examine assaults against another vulnerable group—children.

Physical Assaults on Children

Statistics Canada data derived from 119 police services in 2004 strongly suggest that children are at greater risk of experiencing physical assault than adults (775 incidents per 100,000 children versus 631 incidents per 100,000 adults). However, the rate of physical assault among boys was 50 percent higher than that among girls. Not surprisingly, too, most of the physical assaults against girls were committed by someone they knew, most commonly a male relative (Kong, 2006).

Sexual Assault[9]

To this day, despite massive education efforts, many men are unaware of how the fear of male violence affects women on a daily basis. For example, similar to colleagues such as Jackson Katz (2006), to help sensitize university students to the male–female differences regarding the fear of sexual assault and other types of woman abuse, I first ask men in my undergraduate woman abuse class to describe the techniques they use to prevent themselves from being raped. At first, none of the men says anything; the classroom is filled with a deafening silence. Then, one or two men will eventually say something like, "Avoid going to prison." Under the heading "Men" written on the blackboard, I write this response. Next, I ask the women to describe their avoidance strategies. A completely different picture emerges. I am given a long list of responses to write under the heading "Women," including avoiding night classes, not walking alone at night, carrying whistles and alarms, calling the campus foot patrol for escorts to the bus or a car, and a host of other preventive measures.

As Katz (2006) observes, this exercise "can go on for almost an hour" and the "board fills up on the women's side" (p. 3). Moreover, this exercise serves two important functions. First, it shows male students that many women worry about their safety and that their routine activities are heavily governed by a well-founded fear of being sexually assaulted. Second, many women who thought they were the only ones who worried about being victimized discover that they are not alone or "deviant" (DeKeseredy, 1999).

Defining Sexual Assault

In addition to lacking awareness about women's ongoing fear of sexual assault, many people offer a narrow definition of this type of victimization, one that is restricted to forced penetration (DeKeseredy, 2000a). Consider the September 25, 2007 Ontario case described in box 12.7. Despite these boys having committed acts that were legally considered sexual assault and their having been dealt with accordingly by the police, many people, including some conservative university professors (Fekete, 1994; Gilbert, 1994, for example) regard labelling these perpetrators' behaviours sexual assault as "definitional stretching." However, just because some people do not define what happened to the victims as serious does not mean that their perspective coincides with the girls' real-life feelings and experiences. Indeed, what happened to these young women generated much pain and suffering.

Even much more violent sexual assaults are often dismissed or considered "overblown." Let's examine an event that occurred about 20 years ago in Glen Ridge, New Jersey, "an affluent, idyllic suburb, the kind of town that exemplifies the American Dream" (Random House, 2003, p. 2). If you were to visit Glen Ridge, your first impression might be similar to that described by journalist Bernard Lefkowitz (1997):

> My first mental snapshot: Glen Ridge was a squeaky-clean, manicured town that liked to display its affluence by dressing its high school graduates in dinner jackets and gowns. What impressed me most was the orderliness of the place. The streets, the lawns, the houses—everything seemed in proportion. There were no excesses of bad taste, no evidence of neglect or disrepair. (pp. 5–6)

As is often said, looks can be deceiving, and in March 1989, something went terribly wrong in "paradise" (Random House, 2003). Thirteen male athletic students who attended Glen Ridge High School (actor Tom Cruise's alma mater) lured a mentally disabled girl into a basement where four of them raped her with a baseball bat and a drumstick while the others looked on. To make matters worse, it was weeks before anyone reported this crime to the police and years before the boys went to trial. Four of them were eventually convicted of various crimes. Still, one was convicted only of a third-degree conspiracy charge and received a sentence of three years of probation and 200 hours of community service. The other three were granted bail and remained free until their appeals were decided, which at that time were estimated to take five or six years.

Box 12.7   Charges of Sexual Assault on School Grounds

Eight students at Smithfield Middle School in Rexdale have been charged with sexual assault after allegedly restraining and groping four girls on school property after class. The boys are all 12 and 13, and can't be identified under the Youth Criminal Justice Act. The girls are all 13.

All are students at the public school for grades 6, 7 and 8.

The alleged incidents occurred separately over 45 minutes on Sept. 25, during a basketball game on the court behind the school, which is on Mount Olive Dr., near Finch Ave. W. and Kipling Ave.

A surveillance camera in the area and videotape "did play a part of the investigation," said Supt. Ron Taverner of nearby 23 Division.

Taverner declined to discuss what the tape shows or what exactly police and the girls are alleging.

However, Trevor Ludski, superintendent of the Toronto District School Board, said the girls were allegedly restrained and "the boys then touched the girls over their clothing."

But some parents of the accused boys have expressed concern that the criminal charges are a result of actions that may have been blown out of proportion.

School officials have called a parents' meeting for 7 p.m. next Tuesday, which will include police and school social workers. The school has sent a letter home with students informing parents about the "serious occurrences."

Ludski said a vice-principal was watching a school basketball game in the field outside the school when she noticed a female student who appeared to be upset. Police were then called. The board has issued the eight charged students a letter denying them access to school pending the police investigation, said board officials.

They are being assigned lessons to do at home.

Several of the girls have returned to class.

By mid-afternoon yesterday, parents of some of the accused boys were at 23 Division, angry their sons had been held for hours and perplexed at the severity of the charges. A woman whose 13-year-old son was charged said she is keeping an open mind about what went on.

"I will not say he was right. I can't say he was wrong, but the video should tell the story."

Behind her sat her son quietly shuffling his feet, his wide eyes peering out from beneath the brim of his baseball cap.

His mother said he told her there was "contact" and "touching" but he doesn't believe he did anything wrong.

If evidence suggests the girls were subjected to unwanted, inappropriate touching, then she certainly wouldn't condone it, she said.

"If it's done, and the person doesn't want it done to them, that's bad."

Another woman, who brought her son in at 7:30 a.m. yesterday, said she's convinced what happened was not of a criminal nature.

"It's kids playing basketball. People touch people—it's not that they were groping the vagina or breasts or nothing, they were just playing around," she said.

"I think it is a little more than that," responded Taverner.

But he acknowledged sexual assault is broadly defined in the *Criminal Code.* "We're not in a position to put degrees of sexual assault," he said, noting the offence can run the gamut of a grope to a rape.

The boys are scheduled to appear in Court Nov. 8.

Source: Powell, B., & Brown, L. (2007, October 5). 8 boys charged with sex assault on school grounds: 12- and 13-year-old students accused of restraining and groping girls—Parents fear charges overblown. *Toronto Star*, A1, A27. Reprinted with permission—Torstar Syndication Services.

Such treatment would never be granted to a poor African-American or Canadian Aboriginal male arrested for allegedly committing similar crimes. On the contrary, as Lefkowitz (1997) concludes:

Most likely he wouldn't have been able to come up with the bail money when he was arrested. He would have to spend months, maybe years, locked up waiting to go to trial or to cop a plea. He wouldn't have been represented by the best legal talent that money could buy. He would have been represented by an underpaid public defender with a huge case-load. After he was convicted of first-degree sexual assault, he probably would have been jailed immediately. (p. 487)

As noted by Ron Scott, a reporter for New York's CBS television, by allowing the three white affluent boys out on bail, the judge essentially told the Glen Ridge community and the rest of the United States that "If you're white, it's all right" (cited in Lefkowitz, 1997, p. 487). Although the offenders clearly committed what Hagan (1994) labels consensus crimes, the community stood by the boys and attacked the media for covering the case. Further, a boy of colour who witnessed the rape and reported it to the authorities was ostracized by his peers. And, the judge made it explicit that he "didn't want to lock up all-American boys and throw away the key" (Lefkowitz, 1997, p. 486).

Many researchers define the offenders' acts in Glen Ridge as sexual assault and broadly define this harm. Sexual assault is not restricted to acts of forced penetration for several key reasons. First, many women experience a wide range of sexually abusive behaviours, such as assaults when they were drunk or high, or when they were unable to give consent (Bachar & Koss, 2001; DeKeseredy, 2007b; Schwartz & Leggett, 1999). Married and cohabiting women may also experience other threats that can result in painful, unwanted sex and "blackmail rapes." Consider the following incident that "Mrs. Brown"[10] described to Russell (1990). Just because there was no threat or actual use of force does not mean that her experience was not frightening or highly injurious, and she clearly labels what her first husband did as rape:

The worst raping occasion was in the morning I awoke in labour with my first child. The hospital I was booked into was a thirty-minute drive away, and this being the first time I had undergone childbirth. I had no idea of how close I was to giving birth, or what was to happen to me next. I laboured at home for a few hours until perhaps 11:00 a.m., and then said to my ex-husband that I thought we'd better go to the hospital. The pains were acute and I was panicking that I would not be able to bear them. He looked at me, and said, "Oh, all right. But we'd better have a screw first, because it'll be a week before you're home again." I couldn't believe it, even of him. "Please, W., take me to the hospital," I begged as another contraction stormed across my body. "Not until we have a screw," he insisted. I wept, I cried, I pleaded, but he wouldn't budge. The pleading went on until midday, by which time I was frantic to get nursing help. He stood adamant with his arms crossed, a smirk on his face, and jiggling the car keys as a bribe. In the end I submitted. It took two minutes, then we dressed and drove to the hospital. The baby was born five hours later. (p. 338)

Most definitions of rape do not include unwanted sex "out of a sense of obligation" (Bergen, 1996, p. 40), sexual relations stemming from ex-partners' threats of fighting for sole custody of children, and other acts that do not involve the use of or threat of force. Unfortunately, excluding the abusive behaviours identified here exacerbates the problem of under-reporting and ultimately underestimates the extent of sexual assault (DeKeseredy, Rogness, & Schwartz, 2004). Thus, Koss, Gidycz, and Wisniewski's (1987) conceptual and empirical work describes how I, and others, classify sexual assault:

- *Sexual contact* includes sex play (fondling, kissing, or petting) arising from menacing verbal pressure, misuse of authority, threats of harm, or actual physical force.
- *Sexual coercion* includes unwanted sexual intercourse arising from the use of menacing verbal pressure or the misuse of authority.
- *Attempted rape* includes attempted unwanted sexual intercourse arising from the use of or threat of force, or the use of drugs or alcohol.
- *Rape* includes unwanted sexual intercourse arising from the use of or threat of force and other unwanted sex acts (anal or oral intercourse or penetration by objects other than the penis) arising from the use of or threat of force, or the use of drugs or alcohol. (p. 166)

Woman abuse is multi-dimensional in nature (DeKeseredy & Hinch, 1991). Thus, it is not surprising that many women experience multiple forms of sexual assault. As shown in figure 12.1, only a few of the 43 women who participated in my collaborative study of separation/divorce sexual assault in rural Ohio had experienced just one of the above four forms of sexual assault, and virtually all experienced rape or attempted rape. Further, women victimized by sexual assault are rarely only victimized by variants of this harm. Instead, they typically suffer from a variety of male behaviours that may include physical violence; psychological abuse; economic blackmail; or other abuse, such as denying the woman money even if she earns a wage, harming animals or possessions to which she has an attachment, or engaging in stalking behaviour. Most (80 percent) of the rural Ohio women my colleagues and I interviewed were victimized by two or more of these forms of abuse. The rates at which they reported this abuse are listed in figure 12.2, where each different type of abuse is counted once, but a single person can be counted in more than one category (DeKeseredy, Schwartz, Fagen, & Hall, 2006).

Figure 12.1   Separation/Divorce Sexual Assault Prevalence Rates (n = 43)

Type of sexual assault	Number	%
Sexual contact	19	44
Sexual coercion	32	74
Attempted rape	8	18
Rape	35	81

Source: DeKeseredy, W.S., Schwartz, M.D., Fagen, D., & Hall, M. (2006). Separation/divorce sexual assault: The contribution of male peer support. *Feminist Criminology, 1*, 236.

Figure 12.2   Non-Sexual Abuse Prevalence Rates (n = 43)

Type of non-sexual abuse	Number	%
Physical violence	36	84
Psychological abuse	38	88
Economic abuse	30	70
Abuse of pets	5	12
Stalking	16	37
Destruction of prized possessions	22	51

Source: DeKeseredy, W.S., Schwartz, M.D., Fagen, D., & Hall, M. (2006). Separation/divorce sexual assault: The contribution of male peer support. *Feminist Criminology, 1*, 236.

Sexual Assault Among Dating Couples and Adolescents

Not everybody uses the same definition of sexual assault. For example, although the CNS questions on sexual assault in university and college dating were guided by the aforementioned four categories, the categories used in collecting data on sexual assaults in elementary school dating were more limited because gathering this data was not the main priority of the CNS. Men were asked to answer two questions, whereas women were asked to disclose victimization. Below are the female questions; respondents were asked to circle "yes" or "no":

In elementary school, did a male dating partner and/or boyfriend ever…

- threaten to use physical force to make you engage in sexual activities?
- use physical force in an attempt to make you engage in sexual activities, whether this attempt was successful or not?

The same questions were asked about sexual assault in secondary school courtship, except the words *high school* replaced *elementary school* in the preamble. Of the men who answered the elementary school questions (and reported having dated before the ninth grade):

- 1.7 percent stated that they had threatened to physically force their partners to engage in sexual activities
- 1.5 percent disclosed having physically forced women to engage in sexual activities.

Not surprisingly, women reported higher rates of victimization:

- 3 percent stated that their partners had threatened to physically force them to engage in sexual activities
- 4.3 percent stated that they had been physically forced to engage in sexual acts.

Turning, now, to CNS high school data:

- 1 percent of the men stated that they had threatened to use physical force to make their partners engage in sexual activities
- 2.3 percent of the men reported having used physical force to make a woman engage in sexual activities
- 8.3 percent of the women stated that their partners had threatened to physically force them to engage in sexual activities
- 14.5 percent of the women revealed that their dates had physically forced them to engage in sex acts (DeKeseredy & Schwartz, 1998).

Smaller-scale surveys conducted in Canada and the United States found that 11 to 19 percent of adolescent boys reported having sexually assaulted girls (for example, Davis, Peck, & Storment, 1993; Foshee, 1996; Hilton, Harris, & Rice, 1998, 2003; Poitras & Lavoie, 1995). The rates of aggression reported by boys are typically lower than the rates of victimization reported by girls. For example, a 1995 study of Quebec adolescents aged 15 to 19 years found that 54 percent of the female respondents reported experiencing sexual coercion in dating (Poitras & Lavoie, 1995).

Many women's lives do not become safer when they enter university or college. For example, the CNS found that:

- Of the female participants, 28 percent stated that they had been sexually abused in the past year, whereas 11 percent of the males reported having sexually victimized a female dating partner during the same time period.
- As was expected, the prevalence estimates are significantly higher: 45.1 percent of the women stated that they had been sexually assaulted since leaving high school, and 19.5 percent of the men reported at least one incident in the same time period (DeKeseredy & Schwartz, 1998).

Additional Canadian national representative sample survey data show that sexual assault is a major problem in dating and not only in university and college relationships. For example, Statistics Canada's 1993 Violence Against Women Survey found that approximately

12 percent of women had been sexually assaulted by a dating partner since the age of 16 (Johnson, 1996). Moreover, 16 percent of the women aged 15 or older who participated in Statistics Canada's 2004 GSS stated that they had been sexually assaulted by a spouse in the five years preceding the survey (Mihorean, 2005).

Family-Related Sexual Assault

No overview of sexual assault is complete without a discussion of family-related sexual assaults of girls. Police data analyzed by Statistics Canada show that girls are at much higher risk of experiencing a family-related sexual assault than are boys. In 2004, girls were sexually assaulted by a family member at a rate close to four times that of boys (110 incidents per 100,000 population versus 29 incidents per 100,000 population), and sexual assaults against children in families "overwhelmingly involved a male relative (97%)" (Kong, 2006, p. 32). Ironically, most people think that the "typical child sexual abuser" is either a priest, a minister, a childcare worker, or a stranger (Moyer, 1992). In reality, many child sexual abuse cases involve a girl who has been victimized by a father figure, who could be a biological · father, stepfather, or grandfather (Payne & Gainey, 2002; Russell, 1984).

Family-related child physical and sexual abuse data presented in this chapter are underestimates for the following reasons:

- Only the most extreme cases come to the attention of the professional community.
- Most people do not disclose incidents because of fear of reprisal, shame, or their failure to recognize that parent-to-child victimization is abuse.
- There are no Canadian national representative sample survey data (DeKeseredy, 2005).

Child abuse is criminal behaviour, and its impact extends into other areas of Canadian social life. For example, child abuse increases the risk of crime outside the family (Alvi et al., 2000). In fact, many North American adult and adolescent female offenders have a history of having been physically and sexually abused and neglected (Chesney-Lind & Pasko, 2004; DeKeseredy, 2000a). Furthermore, the background of many women in Canadian federal correctional facilities "underscores the important links between women's childhood victimization and their later criminal careers" (Chesney-Lind, 1997, p. 27). Consider Widom's (1989) US study, which shows that abused or neglected girls were twice as likely as other girls in the study to later have an adult criminal record. Similarly, in Canada, the National Longitudinal Survey of Children and Youth found that girls raised in punitive environments were more likely to score higher on a scale of aggressive behaviours (for example, bullying) than girls raised in less punitive families or household settings (Thomas, 2004).[11] Thus, it appears that if we could prevent assaults against children and neglect, we could reduce adolescent and adult crime (Currie, 1998; DeKeseredy, 2005).

Summary

Although women and girls are victimized by a broad range of harms, much of the pain and suffering they endure occurs behind closed doors. Contrary to popular belief, many households are not safe refuges from the hassles of day-to-day life. Instead, for an alarming number of Canadian females, their homes are "dangerous domains" (Johnson, 1996). Similarly, many girls and young women in dating relationships are victimized by glaring examples of "not the way to love" (Fitzpatrick & Halliday, 1992).

The good news, though, is that the types of victimization covered in this chapter are increasingly demanding the attention of Canadian journalists, law enforcement personnel, policy-makers, researchers, and many members of the general public. Nevertheless, much work is still needed to enhance Canadian women's safety and well-being. The violence described in this chapter is not restricted to Canada. For example, in advanced industrialized countries, rape and other types of violence are estimated to "take away one in every five healthy years of life of women aged 15 to 44" (United Nations, 1995, p. 4). Clearly, woman abuse is a major international health issue.

What DeKeseredy and MacLeod (1997, p. 194) stated 10 years ago still holds true today. Lethal and non-lethal forms of violence against women are part of *your* history, directly or indirectly. These crimes will also affect *your* future. What part will *you* play in the ever-changing and ongoing struggle to end one of Canada's most pressing social problems?

Notes

1. Jim Flaherty lives about one block away from my house in Whitby, Ontario.

2. For more rich information on violence against women and girls in prostitution, see a special issue of the journal *Violence Against Women*, volume 8, number 9, September 2002.

3. See DeKeseredy, Ellis, and Alvi (2005); Friedrichs (2007); and Reiman (2007) for in-depth reviews of the criminological literature on corporate violence.

4. This section includes revised sections of work published previously by DeKeseredy (2000b, 2005).

5. This section includes revised sections of work published previously by DeKeseredy (2007a); DeKeseredy, Alvi and Schwartz (2006); and DeKeseredy and Schwartz (1998).

6. See DeKeseredy and Schwartz (1998) for a more in-depth overview of the Canadian national survey data and methods.

7. Postsecondary schools refer to universities, community colleges, and technical schools.

8. Grade 13 courses were taught in Ontario at the time the CNS data were gathered in the fall of 1992.

9. This section includes modified sections of work published previously by DeKeseredy et al. (2005) and DeKeseredy, Schwartz, et al. (2006).

10. This is a pseudonym to protect this woman's identity.

11. Punitive parenting was determined in this study by asking parents how often they used physical punishment, yelled, or shouted at their child, and how often they calmly discussed a problem or provided examples of more appropriate behaviour to the child (Kong, 2006; Thomas, 2004).

Discussion Questions

1. Why do we need reliable statistics on the extent of the types of victimization covered in this chapter?

2. Why are so many women victimized by male violence in Canada?

3. What needs to be done to reduce male-to-female violence in Canada?

4. What are the key risk factors associated with the abuse of women in adolescent dating relationships?

5. Why do large numbers of Canadians worry more about "stranger danger" than they do about family violence?

Suggested Readings

DeKeseredy, W.S., & MacLeod, L. (1997). *Woman abuse: A sociological story.* Toronto: Harcourt Brace.

> Still relevant today, this is one of the first books to provide a comprehensive sociological overview of theoretical and empirical work on woman abuse in Canada. Societal and political responses to male-to-female victimization are also examined.

DeKeseredy, W.S., & Schwartz, M.D. (1998). *Woman abuse on campus: Results from the Canadian national survey.* Thousand Oaks, CA: Sage.

> This book presents the results of the very first Canadian national representative sample survey of woman abuse in university and college dating relationships. The authors examine the extent of this problem, the reaction against women's use of self-defence, risk factors associated with woman abuse in dating, and progressive prevention and awareness programs.

Johnson, H. (1996). *Dangerous domains: Violence against women in Canada.* Scarborough, ON: Nelson Canada.

> This book presents the results of Statistics Canada's 1993 national Violence Against Women Survey.

Renzetti, C.M., Edleson, J.L., & Bergen, R.K. (Eds.). (2001). *Sourcebook on violence against women.* Thousand Oaks, CA: Sage.

> This widely read and cited book is essential reading for anyone seeking an in-depth social scientific understanding of different types of violence against women, including rape, wife beating, and sexual harassment. Considerable attention is also given to prevention and intervention strategies.

Sev'er, A. (2002). *Fleeing the house of horrors: Women who have left abusive partners.* Toronto: University of Toronto Press.

> Written by one of Canada's leading experts on separation and divorce assault, this book presents the results of an important study of women who have left abusive partners.

Online Resources

1. Health Canada's National Clearinghouse on Family Violence: www.phac-aspc.gc.ca/ncfv-cnivf/familyviolence

    > This website offers a wide range of information on various types of family violence in Canada. This national resource is used by many people across the country, including researchers and practitioners.

2. Centre for Research and Education on Violence Against Women and Children: www.crvawc.ca

    This website is a collaborative venture of The University of Western Ontario, the London Coordinating Committee to End Woman Abuse, and Fanshawe College. The site is an excellent resource for information on violence against women and children.

3. Violence Against Women Online Resources: www.vaw.umn.edu

    This US website offers current information on interventions to stop violence against women. The site offers links to documents on related topics, including stalking and sexual assault.

References

Adams, D. (2007). *Why do they kill? Men who murder their intimate partners.* Nashville: Vanderbilt University Press.

Adams, M., & Coltrane, S. (2005). Boys and men in families: The domestic production of gender, power, and privilege. In M.S. Kimmel, J. Hearn, & R.W. Connell (Eds.), *Handbook of studies on men & masculinities* (pp. 230–248). Thousand Oaks, CA: Sage.

Alvi, S., DeKeseredy, W.S., & Ellis, D. (2000). *Contemporary social problems in North American society.* Toronto: Addison Wesley Longman.

Bachar, K., & Koss, M.P. (2001). From prevalence to prevention: Closing the gap between what we know about rape and what we do. In C.M. Renzetti, J.L. Edleson, & R.K. Bergen (Eds.), *Sourcebook on violence against women* (pp. 117–142). Thousand Oaks, CA: Sage.

Barnett, O.W., Miller-Perrin, C.L., & Perrin, R.D. (2005). *Family violence across the lifespan: An introduction* (2nd ed.). Thousand Oaks, CA: Sage.

Becker, H.S. (1973). *Outsiders: Studies in the sociology of deviance.* New York: Free Press.

Benson, M.L., & Fox, G.L. (2004). *When violence hits home: How economics and neighborhoods play a role.* Washington, DC: US Department of Justice.

Bergen, R.K. (1996). *Wife rape: Understanding the response of survivors and service providers.* Thousand Oaks, CA: Sage.

Bourgois, P. (1995). *In search of respect: Selling crack in El Barrio.* New York: Cambridge University Press.

Bowker, L.H. (1983). *Beating wife-beating.* Lexington, MA: Lexington Books.

Brownridge, D.A. (2006). Violence against women post-separation. *Aggression and Violent Behavior, 11,* 514–530.

Brownridge, D.A., & Halli, S.S. (2001). *Explaining violence against women in Canada.* Lanham, MD: Lexington Books.

Bullock, C.F., & Cubert, J. (2002). Coverage of domestic violence fatalities by newspapers in Washington state. *Journal of Interpersonal Violence, 17,* 475–499.

Callahan, M., Tolman, R., & Saunders, D. (2003). Adolescent dating violence victimization and psychological well-being. *Journal of Adolescent Research, 18*, 644–681.

Campbell, J.C. (1995). Prediction of homicide of and by battered women. In J.C. Campbell (Ed.), *Assessing dangerousness: Violence by sexual offenders, batterers, and child abusers* (pp. 96–113). Thousand Oaks, CA: Sage.

Campbell, J.C., Webster, D., Koziol-McLain, J., Block, C., Campbell, D., Curry, M.A., et al. (2003). Risk factors for femicide in abusive relationships: Results from a multisite case control study. *American Journal of Public Health, 93*, 1089–1097.

Chesney-Lind, M. (1997). *The female offender: Girls, women, and crime.* Thousand Oaks, CA: Sage.

Chesney-Lind, M., & Pasko, L. (2004). *The female offender: Girls, women, and crime* (2nd ed.). Thousand Oaks, CA: Sage.

Connell, R.W. (1995). *Masculinities.* Berkeley: University of California Press.

Conway, J.F. (2001). *The Canadian family in crisis* (4th ed.). Toronto: Lorimer.

Cross, P. (2007, July 6). Femicide: Violent partners create war zone for women. *Toronto Star*, p. AA8.

Currie, E. (1998). *Crime and punishment in America.* New York: Metropolitan Books.

Dauvergne, M. (2005). Family-related homicides against children and youth. In K. AuCoin (Ed.), *Family violence in Canada: A statistical profile 2005* (pp. 51–53). Ottawa: Statistics Canada.

Dauvergne, M. (2006). Family-related homicides against children and youth. In L. Ogrodnik (Ed.), *Family violence in Canada: A statistical profile 2006* (pp. 58–60). Ottawa: Statistics Canada.

Dauvergne, M., & Li, G. (2006). Homicide in Canada, 2005. *Juristat, 26*(6), 1–25.

Davis, T.C., Peck, G.Q., & Storment, J.M. (1993). Acquaintance rape and the high school student. *Journal of Adolescent Health, 14*, 220–224.

DeKeseredy, W.S. (1990). Male peer support and woman abuse: The current state of knowledge. *Sociological Focus, 23*, 129–139.

DeKeseredy, W.S. (1999). "I don't want to hear this stuff": Teaching woman abuse in sociology of deviance courses. In M.D. Schwartz (Ed.), *Teaching the sociology of deviance* (pp. 30–34). Washington, DC: American Sociological Association.

DeKeseredy, W.S. (2000a). Current controversies in defining nonlethal violence against women in intimate heterosexual relationships: Empirical implications. *Violence Against Women, 6*, 728–746.

DeKeseredy, W.S. (2000b). *Women, crime and the Canadian criminal justice system.* Cincinnati: Anderson.

DeKeseredy, W.S. (2005). Patterns of family violence. In M. Baker (Ed.), *Families: Changing trends in Canada* (5th ed., pp. 229–257). Toronto: McGraw-Hill Ryerson.

DeKeseredy, W.S. (2007a). Factoids that challenge efforts to curb violence against women. *Domestic Violence Report, 12*, 81–82, 93–95.

DeKeseredy, W.S. (2007b). *Sexual assault during and after separation/divorce: An exploratory study*. Report prepared for the US Department of Justice. Washington, DC: National Institute of Justice.

DeKeseredy, W.S., Alvi, S., & Schwartz, M.D. (2006). An economic exclusion/male peer support model looks at "wedfare" and woman abuse. *Critical Criminology, 14*, 23–41.

DeKeseredy, W.S., Alvi, S., Schwartz, M.D., & Tomaszewski, E.A. (2003). *Under siege: Poverty and crime in a public housing community*. Lanham, MD: Lexington Books.

DeKeseredy, W.S., Donnermeyer, J.F., Schwartz, M.D., Tunnell, K.D., & Hall, M. (2007). Thinking critically about rural gender relations: Toward a rural masculinity crisis/male peer support model of separation/divorce sexual assault. *Critical Criminology, 15*, 295–311.

DeKeseredy, W.S., Ellis, D., & Alvi, S. (2005). *Deviance and crime: Theory, research and policy*. Cincinnati: LexisNexis.

DeKeseredy, W.S., & Hinch, R. (1991). *Woman abuse: Sociological perspectives*. Toronto: Thompson Educational Publishing.

DeKeseredy, W.S., & Kelly, K. (1993). The incidence and prevalence of woman abuse in Canadian university and college dating relationships. *Canadian Journal of Sociology, 19*, 137–159.

DeKeseredy, W.S., & MacLeod, L. (1997). *Woman abuse: A sociological story*. Toronto: Harcourt Brace.

DeKeseredy, W.S., Rogness, M., & Schwartz, M.D. (2004). Separation/divorce sexual assault: The current state of social scientific knowledge. *Aggression and violent behavior: A review journal, 9*, 675–691.

DeKeseredy, W.S., & Schwartz, M.D. (1996). *Contemporary criminology*. Belmont, CA: Wadsworth.

DeKeseredy, W.S., & Schwartz, M.D. (1998). *Woman abuse on campus: Results from the Canadian national survey*. Thousand Oaks, CA: Sage.

DeKeseredy, W.S., & Schwartz, M.D. (2002). Theorizing public housing woman abuse as a function of economic exclusion and male peer support. *Women's Health and Urban Life, 1*, 26–45.

DeKeseredy, W.S., & Schwartz, M.D. (in press). *Dangerous exits: Escaping abusive relationships in rural America*. New Brunswick, NJ: Rutgers University Press.

DeKeseredy, W.S., Schwartz, M.D., Fagen, D., & Hall, M. (2006). Separation/divorce sexual assault: The contribution of male peer support. *Feminist Criminology, 1*, 228–250.

Department of Justice Canada. (2007). Dating violence: A fact sheet from the Department of Justice Canada. Retrieved from www.justice.gc.ca.

Duffy, A., & Momirov, J. (1997). *Family violence: A Canadian introduction*. Toronto: James Lorimer.

Edin, K. (2000). What do low-income single mothers say about marriage? *Social Problems, 47*, 112–133.

Elias, R. (1986). *The politics of victimization: Victimology and human rights.* New York: Oxford University Press.

Elias, R. (1993). *Victims still: The political manipulation of crime victims.* Newbury Park, CA: Sage.

Ellis, D. (1992). Woman abuse among separated and divorced women: The relevance of social support. In E.C. Viano (Ed.), *Intimate violence: Interdisciplinary perspectives* (pp. 177–188). Bristol, UK: Taylor & Francis.

Ellis, D., & DeKeseredy, W.S. (1989). Marital status and woman abuse: The DAD model. *International Journal of Sociology of the Family, 19,* 67–87.

Ellis, D., & DeKeseredy, W.S. (1996). *The wrong stuff: An introduction to the sociological study of deviance* (2nd ed.). Toronto: Allyn & Bacon.

Ellis, D., & DeKeseredy, W.S. (1997). Rethinking estrangement, interventions and intimate femicide. *Violence Against Women, 3,* 590–609.

Ellis, D., & Stuckless, N. (1996). *Mediating and negotiating marital conflicts.* Thousand Oaks, CA: Sage.

Fairstein, L. (1993). *Sexual violence: Our war against rape.* New York: Morrow.

Fekete, J. (1994). *Moral panic: Biopolitics rising.* Montreal: Robert Davies.

Finkelhor, D. (1997). The homicides of children and youth: A developmental perspective. In G.K. Kantor & J.L. Jasinski (Eds.), *Out of the darkness: Contemporary perspectives on family violence* (pp. 17–34). Thousand Oaks, CA: Sage.

Fitzpatrick, D., & Halliday, C. (1992). *Not the way to love.* Amherst, NS: Cumberland County Transition House Association.

Foshee, V.A. (1996) Gender differences in adolescent dating abuse prevalence, types and injuries. *Health Education and Research, 11,* 275–286.

Fox, G.L., Benson, M.L., DeMaris, A., & Van Wyk, J. (2002). Economic distress and intimate violence: Testing family stress and resources theories. *Journal of Marriage and the Family, 64,* 793–807.

Friedrichs, D.O. (2007). Trusted criminals: White collar crime in contemporary society (3rd ed.). Belmont, CA: Wadsworth.

Gabriel, S., O'Fallon, M., Karland, L., Beard, M., Woods, J., & Melton, L.J. (1997). Complications leading to surgery after breast implantation. *New England Journal of Medicine, 336,* 677–682.

Garbarino, J. (1977). The human ecology of child maltreatment: A conceptual model for research. *Journal of Marriage and the Family, 39,* 721–735.

Gartner, R. (1995). Homicide in Canada. In J. Ross (Ed.), *Violence in Canada: Sociopolitical perspectives* (pp. 186–222). Toronto: Oxford University Press.

Gelles, R.J., & Straus, M.A. (1988). *Intimate violence: The causes and consequences of abuse in the American family.* New York: Simon & Schuster.

Gilbert, N. (1994). Miscounting social ills. *Society, 31,* 18–26.

Glassner, B. (1999). *The culture of fear.* New York: Basic Books.

Gosselin, D.K. (2005). *Heavy hands: An introduction to the crimes of family violence* (3rd ed.). Upper Saddle River, NJ: Pearson/Prentice Hall.

Hagan, J. (1994). *Crime and disrepute.* Thousand Oaks, CA: Pine Forge Press.

Henry, M., & Powell, B. (2007, October 3). Double tragedy turns joy to grief: Husband charged as woman expecting first child in December is slain—Efforts to save fetus fail. *Toronto Star,* pp. A1, A10.

Hilton, N.Z., Harris, G.T., & Rice, M.E. (1998). On the validity of self-reported rates of interpersonal violence. *Journal of Interpersonal Violence, 13,* 58–72.

Hilton, N.Z., Harris, G.T., & Rice, M.E. (2003). Adolescents' perceptions of the seriousness of sexual aggression: Influence of gender, traditional attitudes, and self-reported experience. *Sexual Abuse, 15,* 201–214.

Holzman, H.R., Hyatt, R.A., & Dempster, J.M. (2001). Patterns of aggravated assault in public housing: Mapping the nexus of offense, place, gender, and race. *Violence Against Women, 6,* 662–684.

Horwitz, A.V., & White, H.R. (1998). The relationship of cohabitation and mental health: A study of a young adult cohort. *Journal of Marriage and the Family, 43,* 675–692.

Johnson, A.G. (1997). *The gender knot: Unraveling our patriarchal legacy.* Philadelphia: Temple University Press.

Johnson, H. (1996). *Dangerous domains: Violence against women in Canada.* Scarborough, ON: Nelson Canada.

Johnson, H., & Sacco, V.F. (1995). Researching violence against women: Statistics Canada's national survey. *Canadian Journal of Criminology, 37,* 281–304.

Katz, J. (2006). *The macho paradox: Why some men hurt women and how all men can help.* Naperville, IL: Sourcebooks.

Kazemipur, A., & Halli, S.S. (2000). *The new poverty in Canada: Ethnic groups and ghetto neighbourhoods.* Toronto: Thompson Educational Publishing.

Kong, R. (2006). Family violence against children and youth. In L. Ogrodnick (Ed.), *Family violence in Canada: A statistical profile 2006* (pp. 29–43). Ottawa: Statistics Canada.

Koss, M.P., Gidycz, C.A., & Wisniewski, W. (1987). The scope of rape: Incidence and prevalence of sexual aggression and victimization in a national sample of higher education students. *Journal of Consulting and Clinical Psychology, 50,* 455–457.

Lasch, C. (1977). *Haven in a heartless world: The family besieged.* New York: Basic Books.

Lavoie, F., Robitaille, L., & Herbert, M. (2000). Teen dating relationships and aggression: An exploratory study. *Violence Against Women, 6,* 6–36.

Leavitt, J., & Loukaitou-Sideris, A. (1995). A decent home and a suitable environment: Dilemmas of public housing residents in Los Angeles. *Journal of Architectural and Planning Research, 12,* 221–239.

Lefkowitz, B. (1997). *Our guys.* New York: Vintage.

Li, G. (2007). Homicide in Canada, 2006. *Juristat, 27*(8), 1–18.

Lloyd, S. (1991). The dark side of courtship: Violence and sexual exploitation. *Family Relations, 40,* 14–20.

Malik, S., Sorenson, S.B., & Aneshensel, C.S. (1997). Community and dating violence among adolescents: Perpetration and victimization. *Journal of Adolescent Health, 21,* 291–302.

Massey, D., & Denton, N. (1993). *American apartheid: Segregation and the making of the underclass.* Cambridge, MA: Harvard University Press.

Massey, D., & Kanaiaupuni, S. (1993). Public housing, the concentration of poverty, and the life chances of individuals. *Social Science Quarterly, 74,* 109–123.

McMurray, A.M., Froyland, I.D., Bell, D.G., & Curnow, D.J. (2000). Post-separation violence: The male perspective. *Journal of Family Studies, 6,* 89–105.

Menard, A. (2001). Domestic violence and housing: Key policy and program challenges. *Violence Against Women, 7,* 707–721.

Mercer, S. (1988). Not a pretty picture: An exploratory study of violence against women in high school dating relationships. *Resources for Feminist Research, 17,* 15–23.

Mihorean, K. (2005). Trends in self-reported spousal violence. In K. AuCoin (Ed.), *Family violence in Canada: A statistical profile 2005* (pp. 13–32). Ottawa: Statistics Canada.

Miller, J., & Schwartz, M.D. (1995). Rape myths and violence against prostitutes. *Deviant Behavior: An Interdisciplinary Journal, 16,* 1–23.

Moyer, I. (1992). Changing conceptualization of child sexual abuse. *The Justice Professional, 7,* 69–92.

Myers, M. (1997). *News coverage of violence against women: Engendering blame.* Thousand Oaks, CA: Sage.

Ontario, Domestic Violence Death Review Committee. (2004). *Annual report to the chief coroner: 2004.* Toronto: Office of the Chief of the Ontario Coroner.

Ontario, Domestic Violence Death Review Committee. (2005). *Annual report to the chief coroner: 2005.* Toronto: Office of the Chief of the Ontario Coroner.

Payne, B.K., & Gainey, R.R. (2002). *Family violence and criminal justice: A life-course approach.* Cincinnati: Anderson.

Poitras, M., & Lavoie, F. (1995). A study of the prevalence of sexual coercion in adolescent heterosexual dating relationships in a Quebec sample. *Violence and Victims, 10,* 299–313.

Popkin, S.J., Gwiasda, V.E., Olson, L.M., Rosenbaum, D.P., & Baron, L. (2000). *The hidden war: Crime and the tragedy of public housing in Chicago.* New Brunswick, NJ: Rutgers University Press.

Powell, B., & Brown, L. (2007, October 5). 8 boys charged with sex assault on school grounds: 12- and 13-year-old students accused of restraining and groping girls— Parents fear charges overblown. *Toronto Star,* pp. A1, A27.

Powers, J., & Kerman, E. (2006, February). Teen dating violence. *ACT for Youth Upstate Center of Excellence: Research Facts and Findings* [newsletter], 1–4. Retrieved from www.actforyouth.net/documents/Feb06.pdf.

Price, E.L., Byers, S.E., Sears, H.A., Whelan, J., & Saint Pierre, M. (2000). *Dating violence amongst New Brunswick adolescents: A summary of two studies.* Fredericton, NB:

Muriel McQueen Fergusson Centre for Family Violence Research, University of New Brunswick.

Raj, A., Silverman, J.G., Wingood, G.M., & DiClemente, R.J. (1999). Prevalence and correlates of relationship abuse among a community-based sample of low-income African-American women. *Violence Against Women, 5,* 279–291.

Random House. (2003). Our Guys reading group center. Retrieved from www.randomhouse.com/vintage/read/ourguys.

Raphael, J. (2001a). Domestic violence as a welfare-to-work barrier: Research and theoretical issues. In C.M. Renzetti, J.L. Edleson, & R. Kennedy Bergen (Eds.), *Sourcebook on violence against women* (pp. 443–456). Thousand Oaks, CA: Sage.

Raphael, J. (2001b). Public housing and domestic violence. *Violence Against Women, 7,* 699–706.

Reiman, J. (2007). *The rich get richer and the poor get prison: Ideology, class, and criminal justice* (8th ed.). Boston: Allyn & Bacon.

Rennison, C.M., & Welchans, S. (2000). *Intimate partner violence.* Washington, DC: US Department of Justice.

Renzetti, C.M., Edleson, J.L., & Bergen, R.K. (Eds.). (2001). *Sourcebook on violence against women.* Thousand Oaks, CA: Sage.

Renzetti, C.M., & Maier, S.L. (2002). Private crime in public housing: Fear of crime and violent victimization among women public housing residents. *Women's Health and Urban Life, 1,* 46–65.

Riger, S., & Krieglstein, M. (2000). The impact of welfare reform on men's violence against women. *American Journal of Community Psychology, 28,* 631–647.

Rodgers, K. (1994). *Wife assault: The findings of a national survey.* Ottawa: Canadian Centre for Justice Statistics.

Russell, D.E.H. (1984). *Sexual exploitation: Rape, child sexual abuse, and workplace harassment.* Beverly Hills, CA: Sage.

Russell, D.E.H. (1990). *Rape in marriage.* New York: Macmillan Press.

Rynbrandt, L., & Kramer, R.C. (2001). Corporate violence against women. In C.M. Renzetti & L. Goodstein (Eds.), *Women, crime, and criminal justice: Original feminist readings* (pp. 165–175). Los Angeles: Roxbury.

Sadava, M. (2007, September 22). Back injuries plague nursing profession: Province investing in hundreds of patient lifts. *Edmonton Journal,* p. B3.

Santiago, A.M., Galster, G.C., & Tatian, P. (1999, August). *Why not in my neighborhood?: The positive impacts of the dispersed housing subsidy program in Denver.* Paper presented at the annual meeting of the Society for the Study of Social Problems, Chicago, IL.

Schwartz, M.D. (1990). Work status, resource equality, injury and wife battery: The National Crime Survey data. *Free Inquiry in Creative Sociology, 18,* 57–61.

Schwartz, M.D., DeKeseredy, W.S., Tait, D., & Alvi, S. (2001). Male peer support and routine activities theory: Understanding sexual assault on the college campus. *Justice Quarterly, 18,* 701–727.

Schwartz, M.D., & Leggett, M.S. (1999). Bad dates or emotional trauma? The aftermath of campus sexual assault. *Violence Against Women, 5,* 251–271.

Sev'er, A. (2002). *Fleeing the house of horrors: Women who have left abusive partners.* Toronto: University of Toronto Press.

Seymour, A., Murray, M., Sigmon, J., Hook, M., Edmunds, C., Gaboury, M., & Coleman, G. (Eds.). (2002). *National victim assistance academy textbook.* Washington, DC: Office for Victims of Crime.

Siegel, L.J., & McCormick, C. (2003). *Criminology in Canada: Theories, patterns, and typologies* (2nd ed.). Toronto: Thomson Nelson.

Silverman, J., Raj, G., Mucci, A., & Hathaway, J.E. (2001). Dating violence against adolescent girls and associated substance use, unhealthy weight control, sexual risk behavior, pregnancy, and suicidality. *Journal of the American Medical Association, 286,* 372–379.

Simon, D. (2005). *Elite deviance* (8th ed.). Boston: Allyn & Bacon.

Smith, M.D. (1986). Effects of question format on the reporting of woman abuse: A telephone survey experiment. *Victimology, 11,* 430–438.

Smith, M.D. (1987). The incidence and prevalence of woman abuse in Toronto. *Violence and Victims, 2,* 173–187.

Smith, M.D. (1991). Male peer support for wife abuse: An exploratory study. *Journal of Interpersonal Violence, 6,* 512–519.

Sokoloff, N.J., & Dupont, I. (2005). Domestic violence at the intersections of race, class, and gender. *Violence Against Women, 11,* 38–64.

Stark, E. (2007). *Coercive control: How men entrap women in personal life.* New York: Oxford University Press.

Stets, J.E. (1991). Cohabiting and marital aggression: The role of social isolation. *Journal of Marriage and the Family, 53,* 669–680.

Sykes, G., & Cullen, F.T. (1992). *Criminology* (2nd ed.). New York: Harcourt Brace Jovanovich.

Thomas, E.M. (2004). *Aggressive behaviour outcomes for young children: Change in the parenting environment predicts changes in behaviour.* Ottawa: Statistics Canada.

Tjaden, P., & Thoennes, N. (2000). *Extent, nature, and consequences of intimate partner violence: Findings from the National Violence Against Women Survey.* Washington, DC: US Department of Justice.

Tolman, R.M., & Bennett, L.W. (1990). A review of quantitative research on men who batter. *Journal of Interpersonal Violence, 5,* 87–118.

Trainor, C., & Mihorean, K. (2001). *Family violence in Canada: A statistical profile 2001.* Ottawa: Statistics Canada.

United Nations. (1995). *Focus on women, violence against women.* Report prepared for the Fourth World Conference on Women, Action for Equality, Development and Peace. Beijing: Author.

Venkatesh, S.A. (2000). *American project: The rise and fall of a modern ghetto.* Cambridge, MA: Harvard University Press.

Whittington, L. (2007, September 9). Women's group closes after losing its funding: Opposition MPs say Harper government "turning back clock." *Toronto Star,* p. AA12.

Widom, C.S. (1989). Child abuse, neglect and violent criminal behavior. *Criminology, 27,* 252–271.

PART IV

Women Working in the Canadian Criminal Justice System

CHAPTER 13

Women's Work? Feminization and the Future of Police Work in Canada

Kellie Woodbury and Gregory P. Brown

Introduction

According to Statistics Canada (2006), Canada had more than 62,400 police officers in 2006. Females now account for 18 percent of all Canadian police officers (approximately 11,232 in total), up from only 10 percent in 1986, and from less than 1 percent in 1966 (Statistics Canada, 2006). Paralleling changes in female representation in other traditionally male-dominated occupations, Canadian policing is slowly inching toward equitable representation by women—though with much trepidation about what greater representation of women in policing will mean in terms of police organization and practice in Canada.

The Ontario Provincial Police is Canada's largest provincial police service, the third-largest police organization in Canada (Statistics Canada, 2006), and a current leader in the promotion of gender equity among Canadian police services. Consequently, it provides a unique vantage point from

which to assess the historical experience of female police officers and to reflect on the impact that the growing number of women in policing will have on police organization and police practice in Canada. Key among the gender issues currently confronting the Ontario Provincial Police, and Canadian policing in general, are the difficulties in recruiting and retaining female officers; the need for alternative work schedules, including job-sharing and part-time status; pregnancy, parental leave, and childcare requirements; and the addressing of gender discrimination and harassment, alternative career paths, and the promotion process.

The Early History of Policing in Canada

The early history of policing in Canada can be traced to 1651 and the appointment of the first police officers (actually night watchmen) in Quebec City, in what was then the French colony of New France (Barnes, 1991; Kelly & Kelly, 1976). For the most part, however, the early colonists relied on the military to enforce order in the towns and rural areas or, if needed, took matters into their own hands (Carrigan, 1991).

The fall of New France in 1759 ushered in a new era in the development of the colonies: English law and legal institutions were imposed,[1] and martial rule and order slowly gave way to civil law and order, at least in the towns. The American Revolution in 1776, and later the 1837 rebellions in both Upper and Lower Canada, coupled with growing levels of crime in the towns, further pressed home the need to establish law and order throughout the remaining English colonies in North America (Barnes, 1991). Although the *Parish and Town Officers Act* of 1793 had provided for the appointment of unpaid constables in each of the provincial districts in Upper Canada, the first paid, full-time police constables were not appointed until 1835, in Toronto, followed shortly thereafter by Kingston (in 1841), Hamilton (in 1846), Montreal (in 1853), and Halifax (in 1864), among others (Barnes, 1991; Schmalleger, MacAlister, & McKenna, 2004). The creation of Canada as a country in 1867 further stimulated the need for and establishment of police forces both in towns and cities (for example, in Victoria in 1873, in Winnipeg in 1874, and in Calgary in 1885) and nationally in the North and the West, in the form of the North West Mounted Police in 1873 (Barnes, 1991; Griffiths, Whitelaw, & Parent, 1999; McKenna, 1998; Schmalleger et al., 2004).

Early Canadian policing in towns and cities was based on the English model of policing originated in 1829 by Sir Robert Peel (Ericson, 1982; McKenna, 1998). The North West Mounted Police was modelled on the Royal Irish Constabulary (Seagrave, 1997), a para-military force designed (under Peel's influence) to maintain order in rural Ireland (Police Service of Northern Ireland, 2008).

Women in Early Policing in Canada

Canada's first policewomen were hired in Vancouver and Edmonton in 1912, followed by similar hirings in Toronto in 1913 and in Montreal in 1915 (LeBeuf & McLean, 2004). Gender stereotyping characterized the duties of these early female police officers, relegating them mainly to the roles of social workers and guardians of public morality (LeBeuf & McLean, 2004; Lewis-Horne, 2002), which was reinforced by not issuing these early policewomen with either uniforms or other police paraphernalia. In fact, police forces had been pushed by increasingly influential middle-class women's organizations (such as the Women's Christian Temperance Union) into hiring at least a few early women officers on moral grounds to shield vulnerable children and women from the too-often drunken, disorderly, and corrupting behaviour of men (LeBeuf & McLean, 2004; Lewis-Horne, 2002).

The use of policewomen fell into decline during the 1920s, '30s, and '40s, a consequence of declining interest and support from women's organizations, resistance and/or lack of acceptance from male-dominated police forces, and rising unemployment rates among males (LeBeuf & McLean, 2004). At the same time, the rise of the "professional" (Kelling & Moor, 1998) or crime-control model of policing further contributed to the decline in hiring of female officers. This model's emphasis on a paramilitary command structure, reactive response, and strict adherence to the definition of the law conflicted with the perceived roles that women could serve in policing (LeBeuf & McLean, 2004).

Although the post–World War II period (1945–1965) saw an increase in the representation of women among police officers (Lewis-Horne, 2002), by 1966, less than 1 percent of police officers in Canada were women. Not until the baby-boom generation (those born between 1946 and 1966) had matured into adulthood did traditionally male-dominated occupations, policing among them, take serious notice of the need to address the representation and role of women in policing (LeBeuf & McLean, 2004; Ranson, 2005). By the late 1960s, confronted by increasingly well-educated and career-oriented women, coupled with legal requirements to ensure equitable opportunities for employment of women in government agencies (Frost, 1997; Goff, 2001), police organizations began to creep toward equitable representation of women in policing (Statistics Canada, 2006).

The Ontario Provincial Police, 1909 to 1970

By the close of the 19th century, the old system of appointing provincial constables to enforce the law in the rural areas of Ontario had become clearly unworkable. In addition to municipal police forces operating in Toronto, Hamilton, Kingston, Niagara Falls, and a few other centres, some 70 provincial constables (legacies of the *Parish and Town Officers Act* of 1793), most with little or no training, operated in different rural districts throughout the province (Higley, 1984). In an attempt to bring a semblance of consistency and order to the operations of these constables, the Ontario government by order in council established the Ontario Provincial Police on October 13, 1909 (Higley, 1984). The 45-member force was led by Superintendent L.E. Rogers and, similar to the North West Mounted Police (in 1920 renamed the Royal Canadian Mounted Police), was based on the Royal Irish Constabulary model of policing (Higley, 1984; Seagrave, 1997).

The first Ontario Provincial Police constables received an annual salary of $400 (Barnes, 1991). Constables were required to be "generally intelligent," able to "read and write understandably," and of good moral character (Barnes, 1991, p. 16). Physical requirements for the job stated that constables must be between the ages of 21 and 40, stand at least 5 feet 9 inches tall (175 cm) and—presumably—be male (Barnes, 1991; Higley, 1984). Fully 80 percent of the first constables appointed to the new Ontario Provincial Police force were former military personnel (Barnes, 1991).

Following the initial appointment of Superintendent L.E. Rogers in 1909, the next two commissioners[2] of the Ontario Provincial Police were recently retired senior military officers (Higley, 1984). Both men made a profound impact by professionalizing the provincial force, introducing military-style uniforms and insignia, implementing a formal administrative structure, reorganizing and increasing the number of operational policing divisions in the province, and implementing a formal, hierarchical, rank-based structure (Higley, 1984). Cars and motorcycles were added to assist constables in patrolling the large rural areas policed by the provincial force (Barnes, 1991).

By the early 1930s, the Ontario Provincial Police force numbered more than 400 officers. In addition to general police duties, the provincial force was responsible for a wide range of other duties, including deterring so-called undesirables from entering the province, enforcing the *Liquor Licence Act* and other laws prohibiting liquor, enforcing game and fish laws and the *Military Service Act*, monitoring and maintaining public order in relation to strikes and other public demonstrations, and, increasingly, enforcing traffic rules and regulations (Barnes, 1991; Higley, 1984).

In the 1940s, marked police cars and a radio system were added to the tools used by the Ontario Provincial Police, enhancing the force's capacity to patrol in rural areas, at least where roads existed (Barnes, 1991). By 1949, the force had grown to more than 1,000 officers and nearly 400 vehicles, operating in 235 detachments across the province (Barnes, 1991). Specialized criminal investigation functions were increasingly incorporated into the force's mandate, along with contract policing arrangements with municipalities (Higley, 1984).

The 1950s and 1960s witnessed further growth and expansion of the Ontario Provincial Police force. A key figure in this growth and expansion was Eric Silk, a civil servant and lawyer who was appointed commissioner in 1963. Under Silk, the force grew to more than 4,000, and the Ontario Provincial Police underwent a massive administrative and operational reorganization that included a new recruiting system and a merit-based promotional system. Many new detachment buildings were constructed, and the headquarters and specialized divisions were expanded, as were the force's emergency response and public order capabilities. To support the growing force and its expanded responsibilities, new patrol vehicles, boats, and snow machines were added, and five new patrol aircraft were leased (Barnes, 1991; Higley, 1984). By 1970, the Ontario Provincial Police force had emerged as one of the largest, best-equipped, and best-trained police organizations in North America, fitting perfectly the stereotype of the professional, hierarchical, centralized, paramilitary police force (Griffiths et al., 1999; Kelling & Moore, 1988).

Women in the Ontario Provincial Police (OPP)[3]

Although women civilians had probably worked for the Ontario Provincial Police force in secretarial capacities since nearly the very beginning of the force, according to Higley (1984), the first recorded official appointment of a female civilian, as secretary to the commissioner, took place in May 1921. A full 65 years of OPP history had passed before the first female constables were appointed for duty (Higley, 1984).

In 1972, the Solicitor General of Ontario established the Task Force on Policing in Ontario to review police administration, organization, and efficiency. The 1974 report of the task force to the Solicitor General contained a whopping 170 recommendations. Significantly, an entire section was devoted to the role of female police officers. Specifically, recommendation 4.6 of the report recommended that:

> Ontario police forces be encouraged by the Ministry of the Solicitor General and the Ontario Police Commission to recruit female police officers for specialized and general duties, with the opportunity for advancement equal to their male counterparts, and that there be no discrimination according to sex in recruiting or promotional opportunities. (Task Force on Policing in Ontario, 1974, p. 35)

Anticipating the task force findings, in September 1973, OPP Commissioner Graham announced his intention to enlist women into the organization as constables, proclaiming "The present changing social climate clearly indicates that women have a definite role within the [OPP] service" ("After 65 Years," 1974, p. 1).

A total of 214 women applied for the first 15 spaces allotted to female recruits (Barnes, 1991). Female applicants were subject to the same qualifications as male recruits, with two exceptions: height and weight minimums were reduced to 5 feet 4 inches (163 cm) and 110 pounds (50 kg) ("After 65 Years," 1974).[4] The proposed course content of the basic constable training would be nearly the same for men and women with the addition of 20 hours of judo training mandatory for women and optional for men ("After 65 Years," 1974).[5]

In May 1974, 15 women joined the members of OPP recruit class #90 to begin training in Toronto, followed by completion of the basic constable training program at the Ontario Police College in Aylmer (Higley, 1984). Upon completion of training, the new female constables were posted to various detachments throughout Ontario and assumed the full range of constable duties ("After 65 Years," 1974). Female constables were prepared, equipped, and paid equally to their male counterparts and were held accountable to the same disciplinary and performance ratings ("After 65 Years," 1974; Higley, 1984). OPP Commissioner Graham proudly proclaimed that the Ontario Provincial Police would be the first provincial force in Canada to employ women as constables (Higley, 1984).[6]

As 15 women worked alongside more than 4,000 males in a male-dominated occupation steeped in paramilitary tradition, the reality of the role that female constables were to play was quickly made apparent. Female OPP constables wore a skirt, nylons, and heels and carried handcuffs and the standard-issue revolver in a handbag issued for that purpose (Ontario Provincial Police Association, 1999). These early female constables were relegated mostly to the traditional roles that women had played in policing—dealing with women and children and defending the public morality (LeBeuf & McLean, 2004). In reality, similar to most other police organizations, female police constables continued to be viewed as auxiliary to the real work in policing (LeBeuf & McLean, 2004), which continued to be performed by men.

By the early 1980s, profound changes were taking place in Canadian society, as in other Western countries, related to women's participation in the workplace. Between 1971 and 1981, the percentage of adult women in the Canadian labour force increased from 44 percent to more than 60 percent (Cooke-Reynolds & Zukewich, 2004). Significantly, much of the growth in women's participation occurred among married women and women with children (Cooke-Reynolds & Zukewich, 2004). At the same time as participation rates increased, pressure to give women access to non-traditional (that is, male-dominated) jobs mounted, prompting Western governments at all levels to implement a host of employment equity legislation and policies designed to address demands for equity in hiring (Busby, 2006; Fleming & Lafferty, 2003; LeBeuf & McLean, 2004; Potts, 1983). In Canadian policing, employment equity was translated mostly into fair recruitment and selection policies (Seagrave, 1997; Stansfield, 1996), followed later by efforts to promote women into senior ranks.

Women in the OPP broke through the so-called glass ceiling in 1984, 10 years after they were first allowed to join as constables. Dona Brown was the first female officer to attain the rank of corporal (Ferguson, 1984). Later the same year, two other female officers also attained the rank of corporal. The next rank achieved by a woman was that of sergeant, by

Box 13.1   Women in Policing: Chief Superintendent Kate Lines

Chief Superintendent Kate Lines began her career in policing in 1977, as a uniform officer in the Ontario Provincial Police. As a front-line officer, she worked in a wide variety of capacities, including undercover work.

In 1990, Kate Lines was one of seven candidates competing for a coveted opportunity to attend the FBI's year-long Police Fellowship Program. The Police Fellowship Program offers seven international and US law enforcement students the opportunity to attend the famed FBI Academy in Quantico, Virginia. The chosen students receive academic training and participate in actual case studies in criminal investigative analysis, what we have come to know as profiling. Kate Lines was successful in her bid to attend the FBI Academy and in September 1990 left for Quantico to undertake the rigorous year-long program. Upon graduation from the program, she became one of only two FBI-certified profilers in Canada, and the only female profiler in the country.

On her return to her duties at the Ontario Provincial Police in 1991, Kate Lines was made responsible for establishing the Ontario Provincial Police Criminal Profiling Unit, and until 1995 served as its only trained criminal profiler. In 1995, the Criminal Profiling Unit was merged with the ViCLAS (Violent Crime Linkage Analysis System) Unit to form the Behavioural Sciences Section (BSS). By bringing together the profiling and data-tracking capabilities of the Ontario Provincial Police, along with other investigative and criminal intelligence components, the BSS assumed an increasingly important role in threat assessment, investigative support, and research. Additional profilers were added to the BSS, under then OPP Inspector Kate Lines.

In 2005, Kate Lines was promoted to the rank of OPP detective superintendent and appointed director of the Intelligence Bureau, the first female in this position. The Intelligence Bureau encompasses a diverse range of criminal intelligence activities, including those related to anti-terrorism, hate crime/extremism, witness protection, and strategic and tactical analysis. Although no longer the director of the Behavioural Sciences Section at the OPP, Lines continues to be a strong presence in the criminal profiling area, as the president of the International Criminal Investigation Analysis Fellowship.

Chief Superintendent Kate Lines's groundbreaking work in criminal profiling is recognized worldwide; no less is she recognized for being a role model for women in policing. Her awards are numerous, including the Officer Order of Merit Medal, the International Association of Women Police Excellence in Performance award, the Ontario Women in Law Enforcement Excellence in Performance & Team Achievement award, and the 2003 Police Leadership Forum, Police Leader of the Year award.

Kate Lines graduated with a bachelor's degree in sociology and criminology and completed a diploma program at The University of Western Ontario in police management. OPP Chief Superintendent Kate Lines continues to serve as a model of dedication and achievement for all police officers.

Source: "D/Superintendent Kate Lines O.P.P. Director–Intelligence Bureau." (2004, December). Ontario Women in Law Enforcement. Retrieved from www.owle.org/archives.html; Klaasen, E.K. (2004). Award recipient known for innovation. *Blue Line, 16*(3), 8–9; K. Lines (personal communication, May 2007).

Figure 13.1   Ontario Provincial Police Sworn Officers, 2006

Rank	Females	Males	Total
Commissioned officer 3	2	11	13
Commissioned officer 2	2	32	34
Commissioned officer 1	12	115	127
Staff sergeant	11	167	178
Sergeant major	2	4	6
Sergeant	109	840	949
Constable	873	3,347	4,220
Grand total	1,011	4,516	5,527

Source: Inspector Sandy Thomas, manager, uniform recruit, OPP (personal communication, August 17, 2007).

Irena Lawrenson in 1988 (Stancu, 1988). In 1989, Gwen Boniface, a constable with 12 years' experience and a completed law degree, was promoted from constable to inspector, a first in the nearly 80-year history of the OPP (Donovan, 1989). Nine years later, in May 1998, Boniface was sworn in as the first female commissioner of the Ontario Provincial Police (Ontario Ministry of Community Safety and Correctional Services, 2006).

Currently, women represent 18.3 percent of sworn officers in the OPP and 9 percent of senior (commissioned) officers.[7] For statistics on male and female sworn officers in the OPP, see figure 13.1.

To promote the recruitment of women, the OPP uses a number of special recruitment strategies. OPP Bound is a unique five-day course that invites interested women to experience life as a recruit at the Provincial Police Academy, where they can meet and talk with current female and male officers about their careers, and learn about the requirements for being recruited into the OPP (Jones, 2004).[8] The OPP Women's Symposium, another specialized program designed to recruit females, selects 100 applicants to spend a day with an OPP officer and meet with female officers and civilians who share their experiences of policing and answer questions (Ontario Provincial Police, 2006).

Women in Non-Traditional Jobs

According to the traditional "gender model" explanation of job behaviour (Feldberg & Glenn, 1979), women who enter non-traditional, male-dominated occupations are governed by their prior socialization to identify primarily with their family role as opposed to their job role. Jurik and Halemba (1984) summarize the main features of the gender model by noting that, compared with males:

> Female workers are (1) less involved in their work and less committed to their careers than men (Brim, 1958; Psathas, 1968), (2) disinterested in the intrinsic aspects of their work (Kuhler,

1963), (3) more concerned with friendships than organizational influence or other working conditions (Rossi, 1965), and (4) more willing to submit to bureaucratic subordination and less concerned with autonomy than men (Simpson & Simpson, 1969). (p. 551)

Conversely, according to this explanation, males are job-driven (Jurik & Halemba, 1984). Gender and gender-socialization processes are therefore key variables in explaining the attitudes, expectations, experiences, and career choices of females and males at work. Alternatively, Kanter's (1976, 1977) job model of occupational behaviour argues that attitudes, expectations, experiences, and career choices are more a function of one's location in the organization than a consequence of one's gender (Jurik & Halemba, 1984). According to this model, the jobs available to women in organizations are often lower-level positions and/or are jobs that are not perceived to lead to advancement or promotion (Kanter, 1977; South, Bonjean, Corder, & Markham, 1982).

In fact, definitions of gender roles (gender models) and the way in which we have organized how work is done (job models) derive from long-standing social-structural arrangements and cultural ideas that lead us to accept without question that so-called important jobs can only be done in one way to be considered professional and to remain competitive (Mirchandi, 1999; Prokos & Padavic, 2002). Consequently, women are slotted into the jobs they have, especially in male-dominated areas of work, based on the assumption that because they have a greater commitment to their family and domestic roles, their commitment to the job will be much less than a man's (Armstrong & Armstrong, 1990). As evidence of women's lesser degree of job commitment, male co-workers and employers often point to women's higher rates of workplace absenteeism, their interest in part-time positions and job-sharing arrangements, their requests for pregnancy-related accommodations and parental leaves, coupled with their higher rates of attrition (Bagilhole, 2002; Hadfield, 1995; Lassalle & Spokane, 1987). As justifications for hiring and promoting males over females, some traditionally male-dominated workplaces point to their need for full-time work continuity, availability for overtime work, and overall 100 percent commitment to the work (Collander & Woos, 1997).

For women, then, the availability of jobs *per se* and the availability of specific jobs within a workplace are a function of both (1) the long-standing cultural stereotypes about which role will inevitably be *more* important to women (the family/domestic role or the work/ career role) and (2) the cultural belief that the employment of too many women in so-called important positions in the workplace organization will, consequently, negatively affect the professionalism and competitiveness of the organization (Ranson, 2005). Women entering non-traditional occupations can therefore expect to experience treatment based not on *who* they are, but rather on *what* they are believed to represent in terms of future job performance and commitment (Bagilhole, 2002).

Anker (1998) and Bolton and Muzio (2007) note that as female representation in male-dominated jobs increases, pressure to address *what* women are as workers in the workplace grows, such that the organization must, of necessity, address workplace issues that stem from the dual responsibility (the family/domestic role *and* the work/career role) that biologically and culturally has been defined for women. Significantly, research shows that women do not demonstrate lower levels of commitment to the workplace, nor are their career aspirations significantly different from those of men (Bagilhole, 2002; Jurik & Halemba, 1984; Phillips & Imhoff, 1997; Worden, 1993); instead, confronted by the dual role they must play in society, women are blocked from pursuing job and career goals in the same

Box 13.2   Women in Policing: Jane Bartlett,[9] Emergency Response Team (ERT)

What first inspired you to join the ERT unit?

I was first inspired to join the ERT during recruit training at the OPP Academy in Orillia. During the "hell week" portion, recruits were woken up at 3 a.m. for a variety of exercises, including running in boots and belts, mock search and rescue missions, evidence searches, and defensive tactics. Despite the sleep deprivation, humid weather, and mosquitoes, it felt rewarding to overcome the physical and psychological challenges while working towards a goal as a team.

My desire to get on the ERT continued after working in conjunction with ERT members at various calls, such as break and enters, stolen vehicles, and weapons-related occurrences. The increased responsibilities and roles of ERT members I observed were really appealing. I was also drawn to the team atmosphere and was impressed by the motivation and professionalism of the ERT members I knew. Also, I believed the additional training received from ERT would make me a more competent and safer officer.

I made a commitment to apply to ERT after having the opportunity to participate in "OPP Emergency Services Bound." This was a week-long program for female police officers to learn more about the duties and requirements of OPP emergency response teams. The program was extremely informative and encouraging.

How long did you work as a patrol officer before you applied to join the ERT?

I had 15 months as a cadet, and 2½ years of regular uniform experience prior to joining ERT. Although the team requires a three-year minimum of experience as a police officer, applicants were informed that the three-year minimum was not absolute and other experience may be taken into consideration.

What qualifications were you required to meet to be considered for the ERT?

During the application process, ERT candidates were advised to demonstrate the following criteria:

- Minimum three years' experience as a constable
- Good physical fitness
- Current firearms qualifications
- Sound judgment and decision-making skills
- High motivation
- Flexibility
- Dependability

10 ptThe selection process consisted of an ERT task-specific test (navigating an obstacle course in 35 minutes or less, while wearing a 40-lb [18-kg] vest, to experience the challenges encountered during ERT calls), a panel interview, and psychological/aptitude testing.

Successful applicants were required to successfully complete a nine-week basic training course that included physical training; the use of firearms; and practices related to containment, search and rescue, canine backup, and public order.

What challenges/barriers did you face in trying out for the team?

During the application process to ERT, I was competing against three other highly competent and qualified officers from my office. I had the least amount of road experience in the group and felt that would be a negative factor. To overcome this, I made a strong effort to prepare myself physically for the testing, while thoroughly studying the policies and procedures to prove my competence and eagerness to learn.

What was the feeling of other officers toward you during your ERT tryouts? Did it make a difference that you were female?

I was fortunate to have a supportive detachment and received a lot of encouragement during tryouts from fellow officers and from supervisors. The relationship between me and the competing officers was positive as we often compared notes and study material prior to testing.

Although I did encounter some officers that thought I would be successful because I would get special treatment due to gender bias, the majority of officers were supportive. I also received a lot of positive support and encouragement from other ERT members I knew. They assured me the team wouldn't accept someone based on gender status, and would look for the best overall suitable candidate.

How did the other ERT members respond to you as a new team member?

It is natural for new members to encounter a transition period when first coming to the team. As new members become acquainted and build trust with other members, their acceptance from the team grows. I felt this initial awkwardness that was perhaps slightly elevated by the fact that I was one of only 2 females in a team of 47 men. However, I felt I was accepted into the team as quickly as the other four males I had trained with from the course.

Did the responsibilities of ERT conflict with your home life?

ERT did not have a profound effect on my home life as I am currently single and have no children. When I made the commitment to apply I was in a relationship with a partner who had mixed feelings about ERT (mainly because I'd be working with a higher number of members of the opposite sex, the increased risk, and potential lifestyle changes from having to wear a pager and be on call). However ERT was not a factor in why that relationship ended.

Being free of dependants and other commitments were considerations in why I wanted to pursue ERT early in my career, before such conflicts or sacrifices arose. The only area really affected has been my social life due to the demands of working with a pager and being on call so much. The biggest adjustment has been getting woken by a pager and responding to calls with little rest.

What types of sacrifices have you had to make in order to accommodate the on-call lifestyle?

I have made limited lifestyle sacrifices but have had to cancel plans numerous times with friends and family in order to respond to calls. I usually ensure that I have equipment with me at all times for quicker response time when paged off-duty. Being flexible and able to adapt to situations is something ERT members need to possess not only to complete tasks but also to cope with the additional challenge of working on call.

Are there any other women on the team with you?

I currently work with one other female on the ERT team (which consists of 47 members in total).

There were two other females on the ERT basic training course when I took it, but one did not complete the course successfully.

What's in store for you career-wise now?

I have been on the Emergency Response Team for almost a year now and intend to remain an active member for a minimum four more years. After that time frame I may desire to remain on the team or pursue other avenues depending on factors that may arise from my personal life (desire to have a family, etc). I have always had an interest in criminal investigations but I have a stronger desire to explore opportunities within Emergency Response while I am still young and physically capable of doing so.

What is your overall opinion about women working in specialty teams in the OPP?

I recognize now that the lack of women in specialty teams once gave me an incorrect impression that women were not as physically capable of fulfilling the duties of specialty teams (such as ERT). My own insecurities and self-doubts were my biggest obstacles when making the decision to apply. After participating in OPP Emergency Services Bound, I was grateful for the experience because it gave me the necessary confidence to train and prepare myself for the application process.

Although I am personally opposed to recruitment initiatives that target specific groups based on gender, ethnicity, or other lifestyle considerations, I support programs such as Emergency Services Bound that focus not on recruitment but on dispelling myths and providing information to those who may consider a career path towards such services.

I don't think women should receive consideration based on gender when applying for specialty teams; however, I encourage all interested females to take the initiative to research such teams and decide for themselves if it is something they wish to pursue.

Women should never let their own self-doubt or anyone else's prejudices deter them from pursuing their goals.

Source: J. Bartlett (personal communication, July 17, 2007).

way that men are able to (McKinnon & Ahola-Sidaway, 1995; Metcalfe & Dick, 2002; Ranson, 2005). Consequently, as the proportion of women in non-traditional jobs grows, and as women's workplace needs and arrangements are addressed, changes in workplace organization and, eventually, workplace culture will occur, although these changes may be initially perceived as threatening to male co-workers and to the organization itself (Anker, 1998; Ranson, 2005).

Women's Work and the Future of Policing

The experience of women in policing in Canada generally conforms to the experience of women in other traditionally male-dominated jobs. Although women have been a part of Canadian policing for nearly 100 years, today only 21 percent of constables in Canada are women, and only 11 percent of non-commissioned officers and 6 percent of senior officers are female (Statistics Canada, 2006). Policing continues to have one of the lowest proportions of females of all the traditionally male-dominated occupations (Anker, 1998), despite considerable evidence that females perform equally as well as males in carrying out the range of policing duties (Brown, 1998; Janzen, Muhajarine, & Kelly, 2007; Linden & Minch, 1984; Seagrave, 1997).

Similar to other police organizations, the Ontario Provincial Police force has recognized the need to recruit and promote more female police officers. According to the National Center for Women in Policing (2002), increasing the numbers of women at all ranks of law enforcement is a strategy that will "reduce police excessive force, strengthen community policing reforms, and improve police response to violence against women" (p. 9). In particular, if police organizations are to truly reflect Sir Robert Peel's 1829 founding principle that "the police are the public and the public are the police" (Melville, 1901, cited in Schmalleger et al., 2004, p. 100), representation from women must increase markedly in the future.

If the OPP and other police organizations are to increase female representation, and if such efforts are to go beyond merely putting women into uniform and plunking them into what remains essentially a man's world, fundamental changes are required in the way police work is organized and undertaken (Walker, 1993). Among the issues that the OPP and other policing organizations must confront for the future are their policies regarding equipment, work schedules, parental leaves, gender harassment, job performance, and job retention.

Equipment

The OPP and other police services now accommodate individuals with smaller hands by determining the appropriate size of the pistol grip and issuing either a modified standard-issue firearm or a similar but smaller version to those who require it, typically women. The OPP also issues a smaller magazine pouch with the smaller-version firearm, which allows for more room around the waist of the officer. Women often have smaller waists than their male counterparts and thus have less room around the duty belt for the various tools of the trade. Women may choose to carry first-aid materials and gloves in the cargo pocket of their pants instead of on their belt to reduce the weight and to avoid having items in the small of their back.[10]

Work Schedules

Accepting the dual role that women must play requires that organizations recognize that many women continue to shoulder the burden of caring for home and children (Ranson, 2005). This responsibility requires consideration of work schedules to accommodate women's dual role while at the same time meeting the work-related goals of both the female worker and the organization. As the proportion of women in policing grows, police organizations will need to introduce shorter shift schedules, job-sharing, and part-time work, as have other male-dominated occupations (Anker, 1998).

The standard schedule of 12-hour shifts, with four days on, four days off, is not conducive to female officers managing both a career and a family. At the same time, part-time work is almost non-existent in Canadian policing; most police organizations and police associations maintain that policing has no room for part-timers. Nevertheless, the OPP and a few other Canadian police organizations have accommodated requests for part-time status on a limited basis and are developing policies to address broader requests for part-time work among constables.[11]

Currently, a procedure to request regular part-time work can be found in chapter 6 of the *Ontario Provincial Police Orders*.[12] For the OPP, the regular part-time policy allows an officer upon approval to "perform full policing duties on a part-time basis to address an immediate need for a specific duration and to assess each and every situation on its own merit."[13] The regular part-time policy is designed to accommodate the needs of officers to address personal issues on a temporary basis, with primary consideration being given to family issues, including child care and eldercare. When requesting consideration for regular part-time work, the officer must state the reason for the request, the proposed total weekly hours to be worked, the duration of the requirement for regular part-time work, anticipated scheduling limitations, any other factors to be addressed, and alternatives to be considered. Once approved, the part-time status is reviewed on a regular basis and is subject to cancellation on 30 days' notice. The OPP has no provision for ongoing part-time status.

Job-sharing is a work arrangement in which two employees agree with the employer to share the work hours of one position, each receiving half of the pay. The Calgary Police Service is one of the few Canadian police services that have developed a policy for job-sharing by officers, though on a restricted basis (Calgary Police Service, 2008). The OPP is currently drafting a job-sharing policy. Significantly, part-time and job-sharing policies are restricted by Canadian police services to current, generally long-standing employees; opportunities for part-time work and job-sharing are not advertised to potential recruits.

Parental Leaves

Although parental leave has become an accepted practice in almost all workplace settings, in male-dominated workplace environments, use of parental leave may be viewed negatively. Other officers may view use of parental leave as evidence of an individual's lack of commitment to the work organization (Liff & Ward, 2001) and as increasing the workload for others (Bagilhole, 2002). At the same time, management may point to adverse financial impacts of parental leave, in terms of hiring, transferring, or equipping other officers to assume the positions of those on parental leave (Metcalfe & Dick, 2002). Certainly, women's experience shows that leaving the workplace for child-rearing purposes has a negative impact on career aspirations and promotion (Ranson, 2005). Similarly, even short-term leaves and absenteeism related to child care are perceived negatively by traditionally male-dominated organizations (Collander & Woos, 1997).

Gender Harassment

Because females comprise only 18 percent of police officers overall, they too often find themselves isolated and vulnerable, as the only female on a platoon working alongside men, or the lone female in management supervising almost exclusively men. Consequently, like in other male-dominated work environments, female officers may be the subject of a variety of forms of gender harassment, including sexist locker-room talk (McKinnon & Ahola-Sidaway, 1995), questioning of their commitment and job competency, assertions of preferential treatment for females, assignment to menial duties, and exclusion from informal social activities at work and outside of work (Gruber, 1998; Heidensohn, 1992; Morash & Haarr, 1995; Seklecki & Paynich, 2007). Isolation, vulnerability, and exclusion from the so-called boys' club too often incur negative consequences for women's career advancement (Holdaway & Parker, 1998; Prokos & Padavic, 2002).

Job Performance

In three decades, researchers (Koenig, 1978; Sims, Scarborough, & Ahmad, 2003; Worden, 1993) have found no significant differences in the overall performance of male and female police officers, though the competency of female police officers continues to be called into question by male officers, and even the public (Prokos & Padavic, 2002). In fact, research shows that female officers are sometimes perceived to be more competent than their male counterparts (Ffrench & Waugh, 1998; Seagrave, 1997; Sichel, Friedman, Quint, & Smith, 1978) and are less likely to use force to resolve conflicts (Bazley, Lersch, & Mieczkowski, 2007).

Despite the research evidence, Prokos and Padavic (2002) found that policing continues to be perceived as a man's job, a perception reinforced through the hidden curriculum used to train new police recruits, which extols male values related to toughness, violence, weaponry, and action.

Job Retention

Research has demonstrated that women officers are more likely than men to leave the job early in their career (Boni, Adams, & Circelli, 2001; Doerner, 1995; Edwards & Robinson, 1999). The commonly cited reasons for the lower retention rates of women include harassment, negative attitudes of male co-workers and supervisors, family and childcare responsibilities, lack of support from management, blocked career opportunities, and inflexible work arrangements (Fleming & Lafferty, 2003; Metcalfe & Dick, 2002; Morash & Haarr, 1995).

In the OPP, a lone female officer among a complement of male officers is not uncommon, especially in northern detachments. Some women feel they do not fit in, and their lack of female role models to look up to and learn from further compounds their sense of isolation.

Summary

The Ontario Provincial Police, like other Canadian police organizations, recognizes the need to increase the number of women constables and senior officers, if it truly wishes to reflect the communities it serves and to address the issues relevant to those communities.

The National Center for Women and Policing (2003) outlines six performance and organizational-related advantages to employing greater numbers of women police officers:

1. Female officers have proven to be as competent as their male counterparts in meeting the requirements of policing.
2. Female officers are less likely to use excessive force.

3. Female officers are more likely to embrace the community policing model.
4. More female officers will improve law enforcement's response to violence against women.
5. Increasing the presence of female officers reduces problems of sex discrimination and harassment within a law enforcement agency.
6. The presence of women can bring about beneficial changes in policy for all officers. (pp. 3–10)

Although women police officers have been demonstrated to perform as competently as their male counterparts, the abilities, skills, and life experiences that women bring to the job add a different dimension to policing: an emphasis on negotiation instead of the use of force; a stronger focus on child protection and prevention of violence against women; greater awareness of the dynamics of inequality and diversity; and demands for creativity and flexibility in the organization of the workplace (Dantzker, 2005; Fleming & Lafferty, 2003; Jurik & Halemba, 1984).

At the same time, the growth in the number of women in policing has led to increased opportunities for other groups in society—First Nations people, visible minorities—even males who would not have met the formerly rigid height requirements.

Perhaps the most important of Sir Robert Peel's nine principles of policing is the seventh principle, which states:

> The police should at all times maintain a relationship with the public that gives reality to the historic tradition that the police are the public and the public are the police; the police are the only members of the public who are paid to give full-time attention to duties which are incumbent on every citizen in the interest of the community welfare. (Melville, 1901, cited in Schmalleger et al., 2004, p. 100)

As modern police services such as the OPP move toward truly reflecting the public they serve, and as more and more women, First Nations, and visible minority groups assume the various positions and ranks within the police services, the police will be the public and vice versa. And perhaps, as Peel hoped, law, order, and community will be one and the same for all. What will such a vision of policing look like?

Notes

1. The exception was matters of civil law in Quebec.
2. The office of Commissioner of the Ontario Provincial Police was established in 1921 (Higley, 1984).
3. Under Commissioner Eric Silk, the distinctive OPP shoulder flash insignia was added to the uniform (Higley, 1984); and for most Ontarians, the force has been known as the OPP since that time.
4. This reduction in physical qualifications was also advantageous to many future male applicants.
5. This requirement eventually became mandatory for all recruits, with the addition of "defensive tactics" to the standard recruit training curriculum.
6. As already noted, municipal police services across Canada have employed female constables since 1912. The Royal Canadian Mounted Police (RCMP) added female constables in 1975 (Royal Canadian Mounted Police, 2007).

7. This information was provided to the principal author, Kellie Woodbury, from internal documents of the Human Resources Bureau of the Ontario Provincial Police.

8. OPP Bound proved to be so successful that it has since been expanded to include males and females from visible minority groups.

9. For security reasons, a pseudonym is used in place of the officer's real name.

10. This observation was made by the principal author, Kellie Woodbury, based on her own use of equipment on the job.

11. This information was provided to the principal author, Kellie Woodbury, from internal documents of the Human Resources Bureau of the Ontario Provincial Police.

12. The *Ontario Provincial Police Orders* is an internal document that cannot be accessed by the public.

13. This quotation is from the *Ontario Provincial Police Orders*, section 4.15.

Discussion Questions

1. What factors were behind the first hirings of women police officers in Canada? How was the role of the first policewomen defined, and why?

2. What factors make it difficult for present-day police agencies to recruit and retain women as police officers? How are police agencies in Canada attempting to address these factors? Are these police agencies being successful? Why or why not?

3. If Canadian police agencies were to hire more women, to the point where men and women were equally represented (50/50) among police officers, what would the structure, organization, and operations of police agencies look like? Would the public be better served by equal representation of men and women in policing? Why or why not?

Suggested Readings

Jackson, L.A. (2006). *Women police: Gender, welfare and surveillance in the twentieth century.* Manchester, UK: Manchester University Press.

Schulz, D.M. (2004). *Breaking the brass ceiling: Women police chiefs and their paths to the top.* Westport, CT: Greenwood.

Wells, S.K., & Alt, B.L. (2005). *Police women: Life with the badge.* Westport, CT: Greenwood.

Film/Video Resources

Crouch, L. (Producer), & Pequenza, N. (Director). (2005). *Women behind the badge* [3-part television documentary series]. Canada: A Telefactory production in association with TVO. Available at www.newswire.ca/en/releases/mmnr/tvo/pov.html.

Kovanic, G.D. (Producer), Johnson, G. (Producer), & Simpson, M. (Director). (2000). *Flipping the world: Drugs through a blue lens* [Motion picture]. Canada: National Film Board.

MacDonald, J. (Producer), & Lank, B. (Director). (2004). *Women on patrol* [Motion picture]. Canada: National Film Board.

Online Resources

1. National Center for Women and Policing: www.womenandpolicing.org/aboutus.asp
2. International Association of Women Police: www.iawp.org
3. Ontario Provincial Police (OPP): www.opp.ca/recruitment/index.htm
4. Calgary Police Service: www.calgarypolice.ca/recruiting/html/women_in_policing.htm
5. Canadian Police College: www.cpc.gc.ca

References

After 65 years: Women. (1974). *The Review, 9*(2), 1–3.

Anker, R. (1998). *Gender and jobs: Sex segregation of occupations in the world.* Geneva: International Labour Office.

Armstrong, P., & Armstrong, H. (1990). *Theorizing women's work.* Toronto: Garamond Press.

Bagilhole, B. (2002). *Women in non-traditional occupations: Challenging men.* New York: Palgrave Macmillan.

Barnes, M. (1991). *Policing Ontario: The OPP today.* Erin, ON: Boston Mills Press.

Bazley, T.D., Lersch, K.M., & Mieczkowski, T. (2007). Officer force versus suspect resistance: A gendered analysis of patrol officers in an urban police department. *Journal of Criminal Justice, 35,* 183–192.

Bolton, S.C., & Muzio, D. (2007). Can't live with 'em; can't live without 'em: Gendered segmentation in the legal profession. *Sociology, 41,* 47–64.

Boni, N., Adams, K., & Circelli, M. (2001). *Educational and professional development experiences of female and male police employees.* Payneham, South Australia: Australasian Centre for Policing Research.

Brown, J.M. (1998). Aspects of discriminatory treatment of women police officers serving in forces in England and Wales. *British Journal of Criminology, 38,* 265–282.

Busby, N. (2006). Affirmative action in women's employment: Lessons from Canada. *Journal of Law and Society, 33,* 42–58.

Calgary Police Service. (2008). Women in policing. Retrieved from www.calgarypolice.ca/recruiting/html/women_in_policing.htm.

Carrigan, D.O. (1991). *Crime and punishment in Canada: A history.* Toronto: McClelland & Stewart.

Collander, D., & Woos, J.W. (1997). Institutional demand-side discrimination against women and the human capital model. *Feminist Economics, 3*(1), 53–64.

Cooke-Reynolds, M., & Zukewich, N. (2004, Spring). The feminization of work. *Canadian Social Trends,* 24–29.

Dantzker, M.L. (2005). *Understanding today's police.* Monsey, NY: Criminal Justice Press.

Doerner, W.G. (1995). Officer retention patterns: An affirmative action concern for police agencies? *American Journal of Police, 14*(3/4), 197–210.

Donovan, K. (1989, May). OPP names first woman as inspector. *Toronto Star,* p. A5.

"D/Superintendent Kate Lines O.P.P. Director–Intelligence Bureau." (2004, December). *Ontario Women in Law Enforcement.* Retrieved from www.owle.org/archives.html.

Edwards, C., & Robinson, O. (1999). Managing part-timers in the police service: A study of inflexibility. *Human Resource Management Journal, 9*(4), 5–18.

Ericson, R.V. (1982). *Reproducing order: A study of police patrol work.* Toronto: University of Toronto Press.

Feldberg, R.L., & Glenn, E.N. (1979). Male and female: Job versus gender models in the sociology of work. *Social Problems, 26*, 524–538.

Ferguson, M. (1984). It's a first for three women. *The Review, 19*(6), 10–11.

Ffrench, M., & Waugh, L. (1998). The weaker sex? Women and police work. *International Journal of Police Science and Management, 1*, 260–275.

Fleming, J., & Lafferty, G. (2003). Equity confounded? Women in Australian police organizations. *Labour and Industry, 37*(13), 37–49.

Frost, S. (1997). Gender equity analysis. In M.E. LeBeuf & J. McLean (Eds.), *Women in policing in Canada: The year 2000 and beyond—Its challenges* (Workshop proceedings, Canadian Police College, May 20–23, 1997, pp. 89–97). Ottawa: Canadian Police College.

Goff, C. (2001). *Criminal justice in Canada* (2nd ed.). Toronto: Nelson Thomson Learning.

Griffiths, K.T., Whitelaw, B., & Parent, R.B. (1999). *Canadian police work.* Toronto: ITP Nelson.

Gruber, J.E. (1998). The impact of male work environments and organizational policies on women's experiences of sexual harassment. *Gender and Society, 12*, 301–320.

Hadfield, G.K. (1995). Rational women: A test for sex-based harassment. *California Law Review, 83*, 1151–1189.

Heidenshohn, F. (1992). *Women in control: The role of women in law enforcement.* Oxford: Clarendon Press.

Higley, D.D. (1984). *OPP: The history of the Ontario Provincial Police Force.* Toronto: Queen's Printer.

Holdaway, S., & Parker, S.K. (1998). Policing women police. *British Journal of Criminology, 38*, 40–60.

Janzen B.L., Muhajarine, N., & Kelly, I.W. (2007). Work-family conflict, and psychological distress in men and women among Canadian police officers. *Psychological Reports, 100*, 556–557.

Jones, R. (2004, April). Recruiting women. *The Police Chief, 71*(4). Retrieved from www.policechiefmagazine.org/magazine/index.cfm?fuseaction=archives.

Jurik, N.C., & Halemba, G.J. (1984). Gender, working conditions and the job satisfaction of women in a non-traditional occupation: Female correctional officers in men's prisons. *Sociological Quarterly, 25*, 551–566.

Kanter, R.M. (1976). The impact of hierarchical structures on the work behaviour of women and men. *Social Problems, 23*, 415–430.

Kanter, R.M. (1977). *Men and women of the corporation.* New York: Harper and Row.

Kelling, G.L., & Moore, M.H. (1998). The evolving strategy of policing. *Perspectives on Policing, 4*, 1–15.

Kelly, W., & Kelly, N. (1976). *Policing in Canada*. Toronto: Macmillan.

Klaasen, E.K. (2004). Award recipient known for innovation. *Blue Line, 16*(3), 8–9.

Koenig, E.J. (1978). An overview of attitudes toward women in law enforcement. *Public Administration Review, 38*, 267–275.

Lassalle, A.D., & Spokane, A.R. (1987). Patterns of early labor force participation of American Women. *Career Development Quarterly, 36*, 55–65.

LeBeuf, M.E., & McLean, J. (2004). Women in policing in Canada. In S.E. Nancoo (Ed.), *Contemporary issues in Canadian policing* (pp. 318–335). Mississauga, ON: Canadian Educators' Press.

Lewis-Horne, N. (2002). Women in policing. In D.P. Forcese (Ed.), *Police: Selected issues in Canadian law enforcement* (pp. 98–109). Ottawa: Golden Dog Press.

Liff, S., & Ward, K. (2001). Distorted views through the glass ceiling: The construction of women's understandings of promotion and senior management positions. *Gender, Work and Organization, 8*, 19–36.

Linden, R., & Minch, C. (1984). *Women in policing: A review*. Ottawa: Ministry of the Solicitor General.

McKenna, P. (1998). *Foundations of policing in Canada*. Scarborough, ON: Prentice Hall Canada.

McKinnon, M., & Ahola-Sidaway, J. (1995). "Workin' with the boys": A North American perspective on non-traditional work initiatives for adolescent females in secondary schools. *Gender & Education, 7*, 327–340.

Melville, W.L. (1901). *A history of police in London*. London: Methuen.

Metcalfe, B., & Dick, G. (2002). Is the force still with her? Gender and commitment in the police. *Women in Management Review, 17*, 392–403.

Mirchandi, K. (1999). Feminist insight on gendered work: New directions in research on women and entrepreneurship. *Gender, Work and Organization, 6*, 224–235.

Morash, M., & Haarr, R.N. (1995). Gender, workplace problems and stress in policing. *Justice Quarterly, 12*, 113–140.

National Center for Women and Policing. (2002). *Recruiting and retaining women: A self-assessment guide for law enforcement*. Beverly Hills, CA: Author.

National Center for Women and Policing. (2003). *Hiring & retaining more women: The advantages to law enforcement agencies*. Beverly Hills, CA: Author.

Ontario, Ministry of Community Safety and Correctional Services. (2006, July 28). *OPP Commissioner Gwen Boniface takes on new role in Ireland* [News release]. Retrieved from http://ogov.newswire.ca/search_e.html.

Ontario Provincial Police. (2006). *OPP Women's Symposium 2007*. Retrieved from www.opp.ca/Recruitment/opp_001619.html.

Ontario Provincial Police Association. (1999). *Ontario Provincial Police Association Yearbook*. Orillia, ON: Author.

Phillips, S.D., & Imhoff, A.R. (1997). Women and career development: A decade of research. *Annual Review of Psychology, 48*, 31–59.

Police Service of Northern Ireland. (2008). Early policing in Ireland. Retrieved from www.psni.police.uk/index.htm.

Potts, L.W. (1983). Equal employment opportunity and female employment in police agencies. *Journal of Criminal Justice, 11*, 505–523.

Prokos, A., & Padavic, I. (2002). "There oughtta be a law against bitches": Masculinity lessons in police academy training. *Gender, Work and Organization, 9*, 439–459.

Ranson, G. (2005). No longer "one of the boys": Negotiations with motherhood, as prospect or reality, among women in engineering. *Canadian Review of Sociology and Anthropology, 42*, 145–166.

Royal Canadian Mounted Police. (2007). *Historical notes: Women in the RCMP.* Retrieved from www.rcmp.ca/index_e.htm.

Schmalleger, F., MacAlister, D., & McKenna, P.F. (2004). *Canadian criminal justice today* (2nd ed.). Toronto: Pearson Education Canada.

Seagrave, J. (1997). *Introduction to policing in Canada.* Scarborough, ON: Prentice Hall Canada.

Seklecki, R., & Paynich, R. (2007). A national survey of female police officers: An overview of findings. *Police Practice and Research, 8*, 17–30.

Sichel, J.K., Friedman, L.N., Quint, J.C., & Smith, M.E. (1978). *Women on patrol: A pilot study of police performance in New York City, NY.* New York: Vera Institute of Justice.

Sims, B., Scarborough, K.E., & Ahmad, J. (2003). The relationship between police officers' attitudes toward women and perceptions of police models. *Police Quarterly, 6*, 278–297.

South, S.J., Bonjean, C., Corder, J., & Markham, W.T. (1982). Sex and power in the federal bureaucracy: A comparative analysis of male and female supervisors. *Work and Occupations, 9*, 233–254.

Stancu, H. (1988, April 12). "Pioneer" becomes 1st woman appointed sergeant by OPP. *Toronto Star*, p. A6.

Stansfield, R.T. (1996). *Issues in policing: A Canadian perspective.* Toronto: Thompson Educational Publishing.

Statistics Canada. (2006). *Police resources in Canada 2006.* Ottawa: Canadian Centre for Justice Statistics.

Task Force on Policing in Ontario. (1974). *Task Force on Policing in Ontario: The police are the public and the public are the police.* Toronto: Queen's Printer.

Walker, G.S. (1993). *The status of women in Canadian policing.* Ottawa: Ministry of the Solicitor General.

Worden, A.P. (1993). The attitudes of women and men in policing: Testing conventional and contemporary wisdom. *Criminology, 31*, 203–241.

Women Working in the Courts

Shelley Lechlitner and Jane Barker

Introduction

As is the case with other areas of the Canadian criminal justice system, women's foray into the field of law has occurred relatively recently. Although some women broke ground early in the 20th century, the frequency with which women entered the legal profession did not reach parity with men until the mid-1980s. In the last 20 years, we have seen considerable progress made by women in various fields of law.

The jobs that women perform in the Canadian legal system are varied and interesting. Women are everywhere—women handle civil litigation and practise real estate law, criminal law, taxation law, family and divorce law, immigration law, and corporate and commercial law. In many of these areas, marked differences are still evident between men and women with respect to equality and work-related issues and challenges; however, readers should not infer that the issues to be discussed in this chapter are not experienced by women working in other fields in the criminal justice system. To the contrary, many similarities are shared by all women across the criminal justice system. By examining the challenges specific to women in the courts, the authors of this chapter hope to illustrate the issues faced by many women working in the field of law.

The first author, Shelley Lechlitner, would like to highlight the introduction to this chapter with a personal anecdote, one that both authors hope will shed some light on just how far women have come in the field of law and the room available for more progress in the years to come.[1]

This particularly memorable day occurred fairly early on in my law practice. The court day started as many before—a mad rush to provide the daily dose of infant care instructions and the household to-do list to the near stranger I had left in charge of my child, double-checking my clothes and my general appearance, mentally shifting gears from the job at home to the one that lay ahead—in other words, the start of an average day in the life of a female criminal lawyer. Although *average* might describe the aforementioned, the conclusion of the day was anything but.

Having finished with the matter before us, the Crown and I began to pack our briefcases. Court had run late, and we were both anxious to leave for the myriad of duties awaiting us at home. Realizing that the judge had not yet left the dais, we both looked up. The judge indicated he had not yet closed court because he wanted to take a moment to comment on something that he felt was necessary and had been overlooked that day. The following words from the Honourable Judge J.G. Lebel are forever etched in my mind:

> It is indeed a momentous day in the history of the Nipissing Law Association and I felt it neces-sary to publicly comment on a significant event. It is with great pleasure that I draw attention to the fact that to date, I have never had the pleasure of having both a female defence lawyer and a female Crown appear before me on a matter. Times have changed in North Bay and this certainly is a welcome one. I am honoured to have been part of this momentous day. (The Honourable Judge J.G. Lebel, personal communication, 1997)

Driving home, I realized that this was indeed a momentous day. Although it was interest-ing to have been part of a significant shift in the legal landscape of North Bay, this was 1997, not 1957. This was the modern era for women employed in the legal profession. That something so simple had taken so long to materialize seemed unfathomable.

At law school, I was in a class that seemed to be fairly evenly split between males and females, the result of a trend since the 1970s, in which increasing numbers of women gravi-tated to the practice of law. Since the mid-1980s, in both Canada and the United States, men and women have enrolled in law schools in a ratio of approximately 50:50 (Mossman, 2005; van Wormer & Bartollas, 2007). I had never turned my mind to the significant difference between the environment of equality that I perceived to be present in law school and the reality of life in the trenches, where some areas of the law did not seem to be as welcoming to women as to men.[2]

After considering the words of Judge Lebel, I was left wondering whether women were that much further ahead in the legal system in Canada. What percentage of lawyers working in the profession were women? And more importantly, what was the difference for those of us who had chosen to work in the criminal courts, compared with those working in other fields of the law, such as corporate law or property law? Interestingly, as I discovered years later, differences *did* exist, and these will be addressed later in this chapter (Kay, Masuch, & Curry, 2004a, 2004b).

A Brief Historical Overview of Women and the Practice of Law

On February 2, 1897, Clara Brett Martin became the first female to be called and admitted to the practice of law both in Ontario and in all of the British Commonwealth (Backhouse,

1985; Leiper, 2006). A year earlier, Family Compact[3] leader John Strachan stated that lawyers "will gradually engross all the colonial offices of profit and honour" (Backhouse & Backhouse, 2004, p. ix). Strachan was referring to the rise of "lawyering" in the colonial outposts, including Canada. He forecast a significant growth in the legal profession, envisioning the role of lawyers in society as occupying the upper echelons of business and commerce in all facets of the public and private sector. In some ways, Strachan's forecast has proven accurate. Regrettably, with respect to equality and integration of women in the profession, his prediction has yet to be fulfilled.

Although little information appears to exist with respect to the early history of Clara Brett Martin, much has been written about her from the pivotal point when she entered Trinity College in Toronto, as an arts student, in 1888, to the end of her career as a prominent lawyer in Ontario (Backhouse, 1985). In both her undergraduate and legal studies, she faced monumental hurdles in her quest for equality:

> In 1867, an article in the Toronto *Globe* on the topic of "Higher Female Education" noted that Canadians were "for the most part, of one mind … as to the rivalry of the boys' grammar school, and [were] still less likely to claim for them the right of mingling in the classes of University or Trinity College…" The prospect of admitting women to university provoked disastrous prophecies of "desexed, enfeebled, and arrogant female students." Critics expressed fears that the female co-ed would be "ill-suited" to take her "primary place" in the social order, and would threaten the "sanctity of the domestic circle."
>
> Male physicians also contributed to the furor by expressing concern over the debilitating effects of higher education on women, arguing that studying and working "weakened their developing wombs" which could cause infertility, the inhibition of lactation in nursing mothers, serious mental disturbance, and even pelvic distortion (presumably from sitting too much). (Backhouse, 1985, p. 3)

Clara Brett Martin's career was a distinguished one that blazed the way for women to take up the practice of law but it was short-lived. She died at age 49 of a heart attack after suffering ill health for a number of years as a result of a cold she caught during an important case (Backhouse, 1985).[4] Clara Brett Martin's accomplishments have not been given the recognition they deserve. As Backhouse (1985) has stated: "tragically, the women who were to follow in her footsteps often failed to recognize her importance and adopted an all too frequent attitude of belittling and diminishing Clara Brett Martin's accomplishments" (p. 40). Although she was clearly a woman who made significant headway in forging a path for other women to practise law in Canada, recent discoveries have cast a shadow on her personal attitudes and beliefs (Backhouse, 1992).[5]

In the 1920s, another woman had the courage to almost single-handedly challenge the leading members of Canada's legal establishment (Backhouse & Backhouse, 2004). In the pursuit of her family inheritance, Elizabeth Bethune Campbell became the first woman to argue a case in front of the Law Lords at the Privy Council.[6] In a case that stretched for more than a decade and touched on all facets of the male-dominated legal profession in Ontario, Campbell emerged victorious (Backhouse & Backhouse, 2004). Her pioneering spirit set the stage for women to slowly work their way into a profession that had, for the most part, been previously off limits. We could say that the spirit of Elizabeth Bethune Campbell is still carried forward in each female lawyer as she heads off to the various jobs, tasks, and duties that she performs in the Canadian justice system.

Figure 14.1   Women's Admission to the Bar and Amending Legislation

Province	Women's admission	Year and amending legislation
Ontario	1897 Clara Brett Martin	1892: *Act to Provide for the Admission of Women to the Study and Practice of Law,* SO 1892, c. 32 and SO 1895, c. 27.
New Brunswick	1907 Mabel Penery French	1901: *Act to Remove the Disability of Women so Far as Relates to the Study and Practice of Law,* SNB 1906, c. 5.
British Columbia	1912 Mabel Penery French	1912: *Act to Remove the Disability of Women so Far as Relates to the Study and Practice of Law,* SBC 1912, c. 18.
Alberta	1915 Lillian Ruby Clements	1930: *Sex Disqualification Removal Act, 1930,* SA 1930, c. 62.
Manitoba	1915 Melrose Sissons	1912: *Act to Amend "An Act to Amend the Law Society Act,"* SM 1912, c. 32, s. 2.
Saskatchewan	1917 Mary Cathcart	1912: *Act to Amend the Statute Law,* SS 1912–13, c. 46, s. 27.
Nova Scotia	1917 Frances Fish	1917: *Act to Amend the Barristers and Solicitors Act,* SNS 1917, c. 41, s. 2.
Prince Edward Island	1926 Roma Stewart	1918: *Act to Amend an Act to Incorporate a Law Society and Amending Acts,* SPEI 1918, c. 14, s. 6.
Newfoundland	1933 Louisa Maud Saunders	1910: *Act to Amend ... [an act] Entitled "Of the Law Society, Barristers and Solicitors,"* SN 1910, c. 16.
Quebec	1942 Elizabeth Monk	1941: *Act Respecting the Bar,* SQ 1941, c. 56, s. 1.

Source: Petersson, S. (1997). Ruby Clements and early women of the Alberta bar. *Canadian Journal of Women and the Law,* 9, appendix I, p. 393.

Ontario's Clara Brett Martin and Elizabeth Bethune Campbell paved the way for women across Canada to pursue a legal career in their respective provinces. For example, in 1911, Melrose Sissons, from Portage la Prairie, Manitoba, "made an application to the Law Society of Manitoba to be admitted as a student" (Kinnear, 1992, p. 412). Not surprisingly, given the tenor of the day, the Manitoba Law Society refused her application. After considerable persistence, Melrose Sissons won her battle in the Manitoba legislature, and an amendment was passed in 1912 to effectively open the doors for the women of Manitoba to enter the practice of law. As shown in figure 14.1, by the early 1940s, the first women were practising law throughout Canada. Interestingly, although some of the early pioneers in Ontario and Manitoba faced considerable resistance to their quest to become lawyers, this struggle was not the case in Alberta:

> Lillian Ruby Clements enrolled as a student-at-law in 1912. She would become the first woman admitted to the Alberta bar. The absence of formal opposition places her experience in sharp contrast to that of women in many other provinces, particularly to that of Clara Brett Martin. All other Canadian provinces found that, regardless of her level of legal training, a woman was not qualified to practise law because of her sex—a bar no amount of training could alter. Certainly Ruby Clements never questioned her qualifications on the grounds of sex, nor did the Law Society of Alberta. (Petersson, 1997, p. 368)

Three Waves of Women Lawyers in Canada

The first women to practise law in North America did so in the 1870s in the United States. The first women to be admitted to the bar in Canada followed shortly thereafter (see figure 14.1). In Mary Jane Mossman's (2005) analysis of women's entry into the law profession in Canada, she identified three distinct phases, or waves. The pioneering group of women represented the first wave of women to enter the field of law. Some of these first women were not able to officially practise law because they did not receive full accreditation and were not members of the bar. Not until various changes in legislation occurred were women able to fully participate in the practice of law in their respective provinces (Mossman, 2005).

According to Mossman (2005), the second wave of women's entry into the legal profession occurred over a long period of time, from the 1920s to the 1970s in Canada.[7] This period was characterized by a gradual and fairly steady increase in the number of women being admitted to the practice of law in Ontario. However, proportionally speaking, the ratio of women to men in the field of law was still considerably skewed, with males far outnumbering their female counterparts (Mossman, 2005). By 1970, a total of 313 women had been admitted to the bar in Ontario, and one-third of these admissions occurred from 1961 to 1970 (Mossman, 2005).

In the 1970s, a noticeable shift occurred both in the number of women applying to law school and in the number who continued on to practise law (Mossman, 2005). This rapid increase of women's entry into the profession was termed by Mossman (2005) as the third wave. In Ontario, by 1986, the ratio of women to men in law schools across the province was approaching parity. The University of Windsor law school has the distinction of being the first, in 1985, to reach this mark (Mossman, 2005).

A Brief Outline of the Court Process

To fully comprehend some of the challenges facing women lawyers in the courts, readers may find it helpful to review the roles of the Crown, the defence, and the judge, and the basic process in the handling of a file. Essentially, we are providing a very simple overview of the process. This approach is almost identical for both Crown attorneys or prosecutors and barristers or defence lawyers.

When individuals are charged with an offence, they are referred to as *accused persons* (also known as defendants) and are prosecuted by the State for their alleged crimes (Goff,

2008; Law Society of Upper Canada [LSUC], 1996; Roberts & Grossman, 2008). In Canada, the **Crown attorneys** prosecute matters on behalf of the State—Her Majesty the Queen. The complainant, or victim of a crime, works with the Crown prosecutor but is not the Crown prosecutor's client (Roberts & Grossman, 2008). The Crown prosecutor endeavours to obtain convictions on behalf of Her Majesty the Queen. Crown prosecutors receive their information pertaining to a crime from the police agency that arrested the accused, essentially taking over the file from the investigating officer for prosecutorial purposes (Goff, 2008). The investigating officer remains involved with the file; however, this involvement is minimal unless the matter proceeds to trial (Roberts & Grossman, 2008).

The Crown Attorney's Role

The offices of the Crown attorneys (the Crowns) are usually situated in the courthouse for their region. The location and size of their region determines the number of Crown counsel and the various duties they assume. For example, in a small town such as Parry Sound (population 5,818),[8] the office might operate with only two or three Crowns, whereas in a larger centre, such as North Bay (population 53,966), 8 to 12 Crowns will likely execute the duties of their office. Metropolitan areas, such as Ottawa (population 812,129), have many more Crowns. Recent estimates for the Ottawa office show a total of 50 Crown attorneys, 40 percent of whom are women (LexisNexis Canada, 2008). The duties of the Crown include, but are not limited to, the following:

- Prosecuting criminal and quasi-criminal offences
- Conducting bail hearings
- Liaising with witnesses, police, and support workers
- Preparing and arguing motions and cases
- Attending trials and appeals
- Performing intake and remand court duties, such as adjournments, plea negotiations, and sentencings.

The work is very demanding. The hours can be unpredictable because court time takes on a life of its own—the Crown attorneys have little to no control over how the day in court will progress. The nature of the charges before the court can also take an emotional toll on the Crowns and indeed on everyone involved. Crowns are made privy to all the available details associated with a case, and the evidence before the court can be very disturbing.

The above is clearly an oversimplification of the day-to-day work undertaken by Crown counsel. As government employees, Ontario Crowns receive a salary based on their experience and year of call.[9] Employees of the government who make more than $100,000 per year are included in the so-called sunshine list; thus, the salaries for most Crowns are known to the public. In 2006, the published salaries for Crowns in the District of Nipissing, where the authors of this chapter reside, ranged from $101,356.22 to $166,384.26 (Ontario, Ministry of Finance, 2007).

As expressed by Roberts and Grossman (2008):

the majority of prosecutors earn their living in the courtroom. Their role focuses on searching for the truth during the trial process. However, many issues that are integral to the administration of justice are dealt with far from the courtroom. (p. 37)

The Defence Lawyer's Role

Unlike the Crown, defence counsel represent clients, who are accused persons charged with offences (Goff, 2008). Contrary to what many people believe, the majority of cases result in some form of resolution; thus, most clients and lawyers do not experience an actual trial (Roberts & Grossman, 2008). To avoid trial and to facilitate negotiation, much of the work done by the defence lawyer occurs outside of the courtroom. Unlike the Crowns and judges, many defence counsel also perform duties associated with the operation of their business. Much like any other small private business, they must concern themselves with issues that relate to administrative and staffing functions in addition to activities associated with lawyering, including the receipt and review of the Crown disclosure,[10] supplementary interviews and investigation of witnesses, jail and hospital visits for client meetings, legal research, drafting of documents, and trial and court preparation.

Preparation and research are the keys to every successful case closure (LSUC, 1996). Success is not measured in terms of who wins and who loses for either the Crown or the defence counsel. Instead, the pursuit of truth and justice is the cornerstone of criminal justice, which is best illustrated as follows:

> Without a doubt, the best definition of the role of the Crown can be found in the often-quoted words of Mr. Justice Rand of the Supreme Court of Canada in the case of *Boucher v. R.* "It cannot be over-emphasized that the purpose of a criminal prosecution is not to obtain a conviction; it is to lay before a jury what the Crown considers to be credible evidence relevant to what is alleged to be a crime. Counsel have a duty to see that all available legal proof of the facts is presented: it should be done firmly and pressed to its legitimate strength, but it must also be done fairly. The role of the prosecutor excludes any notion of winning or losing; his function is a matter of public duty: in civil life there can be none charged with greater personal responsibility. It is to be efficiently performed with an ingrained sense of the dignity, the seriousness, and the justness of judicial proceedings (*Boucher v. R.* (1955), 110 CCC 263 at 270)." (Roberts & Grossman, 2008, p. 37)

As with their prosecutorial counterparts, defence counsel often work long hours, represent very demanding clients, and exert little control over their schedules. Despite the best efforts of all involved with the criminal court process, predicting exactly how long a case will take to resolve is almost impossible, because of the human factor—absent witnesses, conflicts of interest, unexpected illnesses, and the like. With respect to remuneration, the defence counsel must rely on client payment through either a private retainer or legal aid.

The Role of the Judge

The judge is the head of the courtroom who oversees and adjudicates all legal proceedings in the courtroom. In addition to their court duties, judges "also supervise pretrial conferences, meet with lawyers, see police officers about warrants, write judgments (quite lengthy at times), and need to stay current with a large number of areas of the law" (Roberts & Grossman, 2008, p. 59).

Judges of all levels of court must, as a minimum, have practised law as a lawyer (not necessarily in the criminal field) for at least 10 years before they can apply to the bench.[11] Judges are appointed either provincially or federally, depending on the level of court they preside over. Like Crown salaries, judges' salaries are paid by the government. In the District of Nipissing, three provincial judges each made $211,594.45 in 2006 (Ontario, Ministry of Finance, 2007).

General Statistics Regarding Women in the Legal Profession

According to an article published in April 1992, 20 percent of people practising law in Ontario were women (Federal/Provincial/Territorial Working Group of Attorneys General Officials on Gender Equality in the Canadian Justice System [FPTWG], 1992). The paper noted that, as a group, women lawyers tended to be younger than their male counterparts and tended to work in southern Ontario. In terms of the types of firms where women practise law, the report noted "a steady increase in the percentage of women lawyer-employees in private practice" (FPTWG, 1992, p. 7). That is, women were gravitating toward working in law firms, a pattern that has continued to be observed since that report. Ornstein (2004) noted that 45 percent of women lawyers in Ontario were law firm employees, whereas only 33 percent of male lawyers were similarly employed. The authors of the FPTWG report went on to comment that although more women were working in firms, fewer than the expected number of women were making partner, an observation that was also reported in more recent publications (FPTWG, 1992; Kay et al., 2004b). In addition to the increase in the number

---

Box 14.1   Worldwide Statistics on Women in the Legal Profession

In Canada, women represent 53 percent of new entrants to the bar (LSUC, 2003). In the United Kingdom, 30 percent of all **barristers** (those who argue cases in court) and 40 percent of all **solicitors** are women (UK Department for Constitutional Affairs, 2005). In 2007, about half of those called to the bar in the UK were women. Irish law professor Ivana Bacik (2003), who participated in the first-ever report on women lawyers in Ireland, remarked on the dramatic increase in the numbers of women entering the legal profession in recent years. In Ireland, two-thirds of law students are women, and 41 percent of solicitors are women while one-third of barristers (courtroom lawyers) are women and one-fifth of judges are women. The latter figure, as Bacik (2003) indicates, compares favorably with the ratio of judges in the United Kingdom, but not with France and Finland where the sex ratios for judges is about even. In Norway, over half of law students are female. Women are well represented in the legal profession in Russia, where the practice of law is highly bureaucratized, and in countries like China, where they are likely to work in public service (Menkel-Meadow, 1995). In Germany, women flock into civil service jobs because family and maternity leaves are substantial; approximately one-third of the judges are women. The proportion of women lawyers is smallest in Japan and India where traditional sex roles remain very strong.

Source: van Wormer, K., & Bartollas, C. (2007). *Women and the criminal justice system* (2nd ed.). Boston: Pearson, pp. 339–340.

of women working in firms, more and more women lawyers were working in government (FPTWG, 1992), which was also noted in later studies (Kay et al., 2004b; Ornstein, 2004).

Statistics Canada reported that in 1995 nearly half of all employed persons in Canada over the age of 25 were women;[12] however, in stark contrast, only 30 percent of our nation's 57,700 lawyers were female (Rashid, 2000). In a similar comparison, women represented 35.1 percent of all lawyers in Ontario in 2001, similar to the percentages of Ontario's women physicians (33.5 percent), university professors (35.8 percent), and middle-level managers (38.5 percent) (Ornstein, 2004). As a group, women lawyers were reported to be younger than male lawyers (see figure 14.2). Specifically, the median age for women lawyers was seven years younger than the median age for male lawyers: 36.1 years for women compared with 43.4 years for men (Rashid, 2000). A similar pattern was not observed for all employed persons over the age of 25 in Canada. In comparison with the number of hours worked by Canadians in general, lawyers worked longer hours (Rashid, 2000). On closer examination, male lawyers were working 28 percent more than the average for males employed in all other areas, and female lawyers were putting in 41 percent more hours than the average for all women earners in Canada (Rashid, 2000).

Unlike the general population of earners in Canada, where few individuals (14 percent) are self-employed, 54 percent of lawyers were considered self-employed in 1995 (Rashid, 2000). Male lawyers were more likely to be self-employed than their female counterparts. Approximately two-thirds of men were self-employed, compared with just more than one-third of women lawyers (Rashid, 2000). Of interest, for comparative purposes, van Wormer and Bartollas (2007) succinctly summarized the state of women's involvement in the legal profession worldwide (see box 14.1).

Women Lawyers in Ontario

More recently, a number of publications have been devoted to an analysis of the role of women in the legal profession in Canada (Kay et al., 2004a, 2004b; Ornstein, 2004). Across Canada, provincial law societies publish statistics about their members in their annual reports and in reports written by consultants hired by the law societies to address specific issues, such as diversity and equality (Kay et al., 2004a, 2004b; Ornstein, 2004). Reports are also published by various provincial county law associations, district law associations, and the Canadian Bar Association. An examination of the most recently published reports from the Law Society of Upper Canada (LSUC) provides a sense of women's current role in the legal profession in Canada, as illustrated using a sample of lawyers from Ontario. Although the LSUC studies are looking only at lawyers in Ontario (and thus are not representative of all lawyers in Canada), the kinds of issues faced by women lawyers in Ontario are likely to be shared by other women lawyers across the country. Ontario was of particular interest because of the many lawyers employed in the financial capital of Canada (Toronto) and in the largest centre of federal government (Ottawa).

Over the past two decades, the Law Society of Upper Canada has commissioned a series of reports focused on women in the law. The first report, published in 1989, *Women in the Legal Profession*, was commissioned by the LSUC's Subcommittee on Women in the Legal Profession (Kay et al., 2004b). This report initially identified some significant differences in Ontario in the way women and men were represented across the various fields of law, their work settings, and their positions held (Kay et al., 2004b).

Figure 14.2   Comparison of Lawyers with Other Earners in Canada

	All earners			Lawyers			Other university graduates			All others		
	Both sexes	Men	Women	Both sexes	Men	Women	Both sexes	Men	Women	Both sexes	Men	Women
	'000						'000			'000		
Total	12,148	6,588	5,560	57,680	40,175	17,505	2,285	1,237	1,048	9,805	5,311	4,494
25 to 29	1,650	865	785	6,550	2,990	3,555	383	174	209	1,260	688	572
30 to 34	2,005	1,072	933	10,020	5,690	4,330	397	198	198	1,599	868	731
35 to 39	2,080	1,109	971	9,975	6,150	3,830	370	194	176	1,700	908	791
40 to 44	1,914	1,005	909	10,920	7,950	2,965	360	192	167	1,544	805	739
45 to 49	1,709	909	800	9,535	7,730	1,805	342	194	148	1,358	708	650
50 to 54	1,231	678	553	4,900	4,310	590	219	134	85	1,007	540	467
55 to 59	813	472	341	2,400	2,170	230	115	77	39	695	393	302
60 to 64	471	290	181	1,645	1,550	90	57	40	17	412	248	164
65 and over	275	187	88	1,730	1,615	115	42	33	9	231	152	78
Median age in years	40.9	41.2	40.5	41.0	43.4	36.1	39.9	41.3	38.3	41.1	41.1	41.0
Average years of education	13	13	13	19	19	19	18	18	18	12	12	12
Class of worker	'000						'000			'000		
Employee	10,454	5,457	4,997	26,340	15,075	11,270	1,966	1,023	943	8,462	4,419	4,043
Self-employed	1,650	1,122	528	31,330	25,095	6,230	315	214	102	1,303	884	420

(The figure is concluded on the next page.)

Figure 14.2 Concluded

	All earners			Lawyers			Other university graduates			All others		
	Both sexes	Men	Women	Both sexes	Men	Women	Both sexes	Men	Women	Both sexes	Men	Women
Weeks worked												
1 to 13	635	287	349	810	430	385	93	42	51	542	245	297
14 to 26	1,082	537	544	2,465	1,160	1,305	164	71	93	915	465	450
27 to 39	898	472	426	2,225	1,115	1,110	150	62	87	746	408	337
40 to 52	9,533	5,293	4,241	52,175	34,470	14,705	1,878	1,062	816	7,603	4,193	3,410
Work intensity												
Mostly full-time	10,091	6,040	4,052	54,815	38,695	16,120	1,936	1,131	805	8,100	4,869	3,231
Mostly part-time	2,056	548	1,508	2,860	1,475	1,385	348	106	243	1,705	441	1,264
Average annual hours	1,609	1,805	1,377	2,198	2,308	1,945	1,736	1,934	1,502	1,576	1,771	1,346

Source: Adapted from Rashid, A. (2000). Earnings of lawyers. *Perspectives on Labour and Income*, 12(1), 17, Catalogue 75-001-XWE. Ottawa: Statistics Canada. http://www.statcan.ca/bsolc/english/bsolc?catno=75-001-X.

Following this first report, *Transitions in the Ontario Legal Profession* was commissioned. This study entailed a survey of the membership of the LSUC. The focus of this report was to look at "job changes, promotions, career switches, and departures from law practice" and to compare the career patterns of men and women (Kay et al., 2004b, p. 2). This survey was the first of three such surveys that, taken together, constitute a longitudinal approach to study a cohort of Ontario lawyers who were called to the bar between 1975 and 1990 (Kay et al., 2004b).

The second survey, published in 1996, *Barriers and Opportunities Within Law*, focused on women who had entered the practice of law in large numbers and who then faced significant barriers to advancement within the profession (Kay et al., 2004b). The study examined the relationships between gender and the various types of practice, earnings, partnership opportunities, fields of law, attitudes toward the profession, challenges to the profession, and job satisfaction (Kay et al., 2004b). The third survey, *Turning Points and Transitions: Women's Careers in the Legal Profession*, explored the most recent survey data from 2002, integrating these data with data from the previous two surveys (Kay et al., 2004b).

These studies provide a picture of the emerging careers of both men and women lawyers over the past 20 years in Ontario. Interestingly, the cohort of study corresponds to a time period during which women were entering the law profession in greater and greater numbers. Kay et al. (2004b) have reported on the most recent survey that was sent to this cohort of interest. Although all three surveys (administered in 1990, 1996, and 2002) have provided very detailed information on women lawyers in Ontario, only the most recent survey (from 2002) will be considered in any depth here.

Although we have seen "impressive advances in the status and mobility of women in the legal profession," these exist alongside "sizeable gaps that persist between men and women in remuneration, promotional opportunities, and levels of job satisfaction" (Kay et al., 2004b, p. 1). The authors noted the considerable challenges for both men and women in the field of law, including balancing career and family obligations, inflexibility of the workplace, discrimination, and blocked mobility (Kay et al., 2004b).

Men continue to be more likely to be partners than women in Ontario (Kay et al., 2004b). Only 65 percent of women working in law firms in Ontario are partners, compared with 78 percent of men. In addition, when the type of partner is explored, just more than half of the women are considered senior partners, whereas more than 70 percent of men are senior partners. Women (40 percent) are far more likely to be junior partners or to be considered salaried or part-time partners than are men (28 percent) (Kay et al., 2004b). No doubt related to these statistics is the observation that men tend to be more satisfied with the partnership policies at their firm than are the women.

Women are more likely to work as lawyers in government (16 percent) compared with men (12 percent). Women are also more likely to leave the profession altogether (21 percent of women compared with 11 percent of men). In terms of the various fields of law, women are more likely to work in "other" fields of law (23 percent), in family and divorce law (18 percent), and in corporate and commercial law (11 percent), whereas men are more often found working in civil litigation and real estate law (19 percent and 17 percent, respectively), and 14 percent of men work in corporate and commercial law (Kay et al., 2004b). For an illustration of the main fields of law practised by men and women in 2002, see figure 14.3.

Figure 14.3   Main Fields of Law Practised in 2002 in Ontario

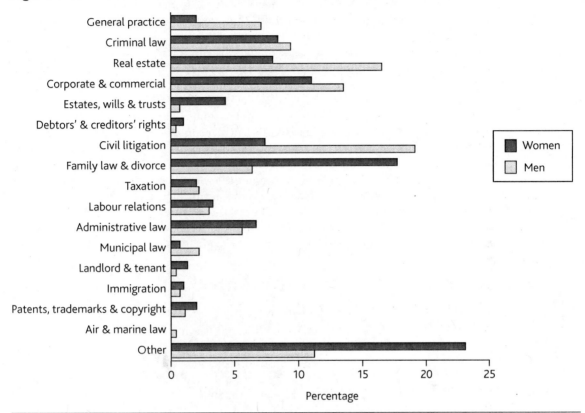

Source: Kay, F., Masuch, C., & Curry, P. (2004). *Turning points and transitions: Women's careers in the legal profession— A report to the Law Society of Upper Canada.* Toronto: Law Society of Upper Canada, p. 25.

In terms of earnings, women's remuneration continues to pale in comparison with that of their male counterparts (Kay et al., 2004b), even when such factors as practice setting and years of experience are taken into account. In government settings, "men earn on average $123,818, compared with $119,757 among women," whereas "among law firm partners, men earn $296,830 and women earn $263,549" (Kay et al., 2004b, p. 107). Women are also not rewarded at the same rate as men in terms of professional responsibilities. Kay et al. (2004b) reported that women are not as likely to own their own business, to be in management, or to be in positions where they supervise others.

When questioned about their job satisfaction, women lawyers appeared to be less satisfied than male lawyers in Ontario (Kay et al., 2004b). Although both men and women were equally likely to show the strongest agreement to statements asserting their jobs are intellectually challenging, they are able to use their talents and legal skills, and they have a feeling of accomplishment from their job, women were more likely to disagree that they had excellent opportunities for promotion or that promotions were granted on the basis of ability (Kay et al., 2004b). Male lawyers showed higher agreement with statements that suggest job satisfaction, such as "the pay is good," "I am rewarded for the amount of effort that I put in," and "I feel a real loyalty to this firm/organization" (Kay et al., 2004b, p. 108). Women were also more likely to perceive the existence of sexual discrimination in the workplace. Almost one-third of the women reported they believed they had been assigned a specific case because of their sex, whereas only 5 percent of men endorsed this statement (Kay et al., 2004b).

With respect to the main challenges confronting those working in the legal profession in Ontario, a number of issues tend to be of particular concern to women: balancing family and career, equality for women in the profession, alternative careers and part-time work arrangements, and expanding family responsibilities (Kay et al., 2004b). The most recent LSUC reports looking at the role of women in the legal profession in Ontario suggest that despite some headway in gaining a foothold in this historically male-dominated profession, challenges continue to face women lawyers in Ontario. A more up-to-date profile of women in the legal profession will soon be submitted to the Law Society of Upper Canada and is expected to be forthcoming in 2008 (Bonnie Warkentin, personal communication, 2007).

A Few More Firsts for Women in the Law in Canada

As noted in chapter 1, the Supreme Court of Canada has final authority over all private and public law in Canada. This court has jurisdiction over matters in all of the areas of the law, including criminal and civil law and constitutional and administrative law. The Supreme Court of Canada comprises a chief justice and eight additional judges (Supreme Court of Canada, n.d.). For the first time in the history of the Supreme Court, a woman was appointed chief justice in 2000 (Supreme Court of Canada, n.d.). The Right Honourable Beverley McLachlin has had, and continues to have, a very distinguished career in the law. She obtained her LLB in 1968 from the University of Alberta. Prior to being appointed to the Supreme Court of Canada in 1989, she was chief justice of the Supreme Court of British Columbia. She has no less than 20 honorary doctorate of law degrees from universities across Canada, the United States, and Ireland (Supreme Court of Canada, n.d.). Chief Justice McLachlin sits with three other women judges on the Supreme Court: the Honourable Madam Justice Marie Deschamps, the Honourable Madam Justice Rosalie Silberman Abella, and the Honourable Madam Justice Louise Charron (Supreme Court of Canada, n.d.).

Canadian history books will make note of the contributions of a famous Canadian female lawyer in politics: Kim Campbell, who was Canada's first (and, to date, only) female prime minister. Kim Campbell served as prime minister for about six months, from June 25 to December 14, 1993 (Library and Archives Canada, n.d.). Following her political defeat, she accepted a fellowship at Harvard University where she taught prior to appointment as Canada's consul general in Los Angeles, California. She accepted this position in September of 1996 and continues to hold this office today (Library and Archives Canada, n.d.).

Statistics Specific to Women Working as Lawyers in the Canadian Criminal Justice System

Unfortunately, a dearth of information is available on specific statistics for women working as defence lawyers in Canada. Part of the problem in obtaining these sorts of estimates relates to the nature of the work. In particular, women practising as defence counsel are predominantly working on their own. Although the various provincial law societies and legal associations all produce annual reports, and some have commissioned specific reports related to equity and diversity, the level of statistical detail regarding their memberships varies considerably. As a result, the number of women in Canada working as defence lawyers is impossible to easily identify, unlike the situation for judges and Crowns, who are government employees, and thus detailed statistics on their numbers are readily available. According to recent estimates for 2000–1, "female lawyers accounted for 43 percent of all permanent and contract lawyers (staff lawyers) employed by criminal prosecutions services," which represented an increase of 5 percent since 1998–99 (Snowball, 2002, p. 5). As can be seen in figure 14.4, a total of 114 women lawyers were employed by Justice Canada in 2000–1, 44 percent of all lawyers employed at the federal level.

Other Occupations in the Criminal Justice System

In addition to lawyers and judges, some of the traditional jobs associated with the court process include court translators, probation officers, special court constables, paralegals, and law clerks (Goff, 2008). In recent years, changes in the court system have resulted in a number of new occupations linked directly or indirectly to the courts and courthouses.

Specialty courts, such as domestic violence courts and drug courts, have created new positions for support workers (Goff, 2008; Roberts & Grossman, 2008). Intake workers, liaison officers, and on-site support workers have also emerged in the field. Many of these jobs appear to be performed by women, as can be seen in figure 14.4, in the columns pertaining to "other personnel" (Snowball, 2002). Women are particularly evident working in areas dealing with domestic violence and young offenders. The first author of this chapter has observed that in some areas of the province, intake workers are almost exclusively women, as are the staff in victim witness offices at courthouses and Victim Crisis Assistance & Referral Services (VCARS) at police stations.[13] The jobs outlined above do not comprise an exhaustive list, but are intended to give the reader a sampling of the variety of jobs currently in the criminal justice field.

Women Lawyers in the Criminal Courts

Shakespeare's character of Portia is frequently referred to in discussions on the role of women lawyers in the courtroom (Leiper, 2006; van Wormer & Bartollas, 2007). As noted by van Wormer and Bartollas (2007), "besides Shakespeare's Portia, who, disguised as a young man, brought a soft touch to the law in her famous 'the quality of mercy is not

Figure 14.4   Criminal Prosecutions Personnel (Full-Time Equivalents) by Category and by Sex, 1998–99 and 2000–1

Jurisdiction	Fiscal year	Staff lawyers			Prosecutorial support			Other personnel[a]			All personnel		
		Male	Female	Total	Male	Female	Total	Male	Female	Total	Male	Female	Total
Justice Canada	1998/99	124	83	207	2	20	22	3	95	98	129	198	327
	2000/01	143	114	257	1	29	30	16	133	149	160	276	436
Newfoundland and Labrador	1998/99	22	14	36	—	—	—	—	13	13	22	27	49
	2000/01	20	16	36	—	—	—	—	13	13	20	29	49
Prince Edward Island	1998/99	4	3	7	0	1	1	0	4	4	4	8	12
	2000/01	5	3	8	1	0	1	0	4	4	6	7	13
Nova Scotia	1998/99	56	17	73	0	0	0	2	46	48	58	63	121
	2000/01	59	17	76	0	2	2	1	50	51	60	69	129
New Brunswick[b]	1998/99	32	10	42	0	0	0	0	14	14	32	24	56
	2000/01	35	11	46	0	1	1	1	15	16	36	27	63
Quebec[b, c]	1998/99	186	128	313	4	7	11	14	157	172	204	292	496
	2000/01	186	159	346	3	9	12	12	179	192	201	347	548
Ontario	1998/99	311	234	545	39	52	91	19	268	287	369	554	923
	2000/01	343	368	711	54	42	96	24	326	350	421	736	1,157
Manitoba	1998/99	49	24	73	2	3	5	0	34	34	51	61	112
	2000/01	57	30	87	2	3	5	0	51	51	59	84	142

(The figure is concluded on the next page.)

Figure 14.4   Concluded

Jurisdiction	Fiscal year	Staff lawyers			Prosecutorial support			Other personnel[a]			All personnel		
		Male	Female	Total	Male	Female	Total	Male	Female	Total	Male	Female	Total
Saskatchewan	1998/99	55	22	77	2	1	3	0	53	53	57	76	133
	2000/01	55	24	79	2	—	2	1	52	53	58	76	134
Alberta	1998/99	111	47	158	8	7	15	5	103	108	124	157	281
	2000/01	119	46	165	9	7	16	3	112	115	131	165	296
British Columbia[b]	1998/99	210	127	337	0	0	0	11	275	286	221	401	622
	2000/01	212	139	351	1	1	2	14	274	288	227	414	641
Provincial total[d]	1998/99	1,036	625	1,661	55	71	127	51	966	1,017	1,142	1,662	2,804
	2000/01	1,091	813	1,904	72	65	136	56	1,077	1,133	1,219	1,955	3,173
Canada total	1998/99	1,160	708	1,868	57	91	149	54	1,061	1,115	1,271	1,860	3,131
	2000/01	1,234	927	2,161	73	94	166	72	1,210	1,282	1,379	2,231	3,609

[a] Other personnel includes ad hoc and per diem lawyers, except for Justice Canada.
[b] Province with prosecutor-based charging systems.
[c] Excludes criminal prosecution personnel in municipal courts.
[d] Totals may not add up due to rounding.

Source: Snowball, K. (2002). *Criminal prosecutions: Personnel and expenditures 2000–01*, Catalogue 85-402-XIE. Ottawa: Canadian Centre for Justice Statistics, p. 17. http://www.statcan.ca/bsolc/english/bsolc?catno=85-402-X.

strained' exhortation (Shakespeare, 1600/1970:4.1.182), few literary or historical examples of women advocates in court exist" (p. 341).

Take a moment to consider that statement. Whether you are a fan of Shakespeare or not, in films and literature, both fiction and non-fiction, few women lawyers exist as role models or heroines. Although Nancy Drew revolutionized the male-dominated detective world in fiction, no women appear to have been portrayed as ground-breakers in the legal field. Classic television programs, such as *Perry Mason* and *Matlock,* always showed women working alongside male lawyers in more traditional roles, as assistants or clerical support. This stereotype began to change in the late 1970s, with the introduction of secondary characters, such as Phyllide Erskin-Brown, QC, in *Rumpole at the Old Bailey.* Only in the last decade or so have television programs, such as *LA Law, Ally McBeal,* and *Law and Order,* and movies, such as *The Pelican Brief* and *The Client,* routinely depicted and more explicitly focused on women working in the court system as lawyers and judges. In the recent style of reality TV, Judge Judy has entertained all with her sarcastic and in-your-face style of adjudicating disputes. This shift to show more women in the legal profession on television and in movies is reflective of, and parallels, the reality of the growth of women in this field.

Not reflective of the Canadian criminal justice system, however, is the American-style lawyering depicted in the mass media, which has led many people to assume that lawyers in Canadian criminal courts argue cases in a similar manner. Thus, Canadian lawyers are often subjected to questions about their roles based on people's understanding of US court proceedings. In Canada, however, lawyers follow a more conservative, British-style approach to advocacy and litigation, which is a far cry from the drama seen daily on our televisions and in movie theatres.

Many interesting and rewarding jobs have been created as a result of the need for some lawyers to work on a part-time basis. More women lawyers are employed on a part-time basis than are men (Kay et al., 2004b). Of the following part-time positions, not all receive salaries or other forms of remuneration; as such, they do not appeal to all people:

- Benchers for the Law Society of Upper Canada[14]
- Commissioners for inquiries
- Ombudspersons
- Political positions and ministerial appointments
- Members of review boards and tribunals
- Small Claims Court judges
- Judicial advisory committee members
- Elected positions in the various associations that assist lawyers in provinces and the country, such as the County and District Law Presidents' Association (CDLPA) and the Canadian Bar Association (CBA, or in Ontario, the Ontario Bar Association, or OBA).

Challenges Faced by Women Working in the Courts

As noted at the beginning of this chapter, Clara Brett Martin was the first woman to be admitted to the bar in Ontario (Backhouse, 1985, 1992). Although she was clearly a pioneer in this field, her success did not come without a cost. Reportedly, Martin "had to put up with the curiosity and scrutiny of the profession and members of the public generally throughout her career" (Backhouse, 1985, p. 33). In one instance, a newspaper reporter for the *Toronto Star Weekly* made a point of emphasizing not her skills, but commented in a sexist manner that the arrangement of her office did not match that of a male lawyer (Backhouse, 1985).

Despite the rise in the number of women entering Canadian law schools, and their subsequent entry into the workforce, not all women continue to work in the legal profession. Proportionally more women leave the law profession than do men (Brockman, 1994; Kay, 1997; Kay et al., 2004a, 2004b; Sheehy & McIntyre, 2006). Some authors have hypothesized that significant retention issues might affect women differently from men (FPTWG, 1992; Hagan & Kay, 2007; Kay, 1997; Leiper, 2006; Mossman, 2005). Many challenges faced by women lawyers cut across the various fields of law; however, this chapter's focus is to explore these issues as they pertain to women working in the criminal courts.

Career Development and Career Path

In recent years, women in Canada have been entering law school at the same rate as men and in some cases at an even higher rate (Brockman, 2001, cited in Krakauer & Chen, 2003; Ornstein, 2004; Wilson, 1993, cited in Krakauer and Chen, 2003). However, when working in the field, women continue to encounter gender-based barriers, which are thought to contribute to the higher rate at which women leave the practice of law (Krakauer & Chen, 2003). These gender-based barriers faced by today's women lawyers are not the kinds of legal hurdles that confronted Clara Brett Martin, but are thought to be more informal and structural in their form and, in many ways, more insidious (Brockman, 2001, cited in Krakauer & Chen, 2003). The barriers that women lawyers face in achieving equality with their male peers include but are not limited to "the allocation of work, opportunities for advancement, income differentials, lack of accommodation for family responsibilities, and sexual harassment" (Krakauer & Chen, 2003, p. 66).

Women appear to enter law school for reasons similar to those of men, but because women frequently make different choices at graduation, their career paths become more divergent from men as time passes (Kay, 1997; Krakauer & Chen, 2003; Leiper, 1997). Most men, on leaving law school, will article, qualify to practise law, work as an associate for six or seven years, and then become a partner in a law firm (Krakauer & Chen, 2003). This kind of linear career path is typical for male lawyers (Krakauer & Chen, 2003; Leiper, 1997). However, some have noted that career paths appear to be more fluid now, compared with the past (Kay, 1997; Kay et al., 2004b).

Women lawyers do not tend to have linear careers. Research has shown that women's career paths within the profession tend to be more lateral: they have more career interruptions and are more likely to be unemployed at some point in their career (Kay et al., 2004b; Krakauer & Chen, 2003). Women who work in large firms are more likely to have linear careers (Krakauer & Chen, 2003; Leiper, 1997). Research has shown that "female lawyers are underrepresented in the partnership ranks, overrepresented in the public sector, and more likely to be working in marginal positions or leaving law altogether" (Krakauer & Chen, 2003, p. 68). Their integration into the field of law has been described as marginal at best (Kay, 1997). Male lawyers tend to make a career change to pursue a better opportunity, whereas women tend to make a career change for personal or family reasons (Krakauer & Chen, 2003).

Although the impact of gender on career choice has been studied, very little research has looked at the impact of gender and race on career choice. Early in their careers, minority women can be seen to be "heavily overrepresented in entry-level positions in government, legal clinics, and legal education" (Krakauer & Chen, 2003, p. 70). According to a report published by the Canadian Bar Association (1993, cited in Krakauer & Chen, 2003), minority women who decided to pursue public service work thought that their career choices were more limited, right from the start of their careers, as compared with their white peer group (Krakauer & Chen, 2003). Their decision to work in the public sector was heavily influenced by their belief they would face fewer barriers there than in the private sector (CBA, 1993, cited in Krakauer & Chen, 2003).

Some have questioned whether women lawyers might be treated as tokens within the law firms where they work (MacCorquodale & Jensen, 1993). Despite being a US study, MacCorquodale and Jensen's (1993) research is worth noting because the issues identified are likely salient for Canadian female lawyers. The researchers found evidence to support the existence of tokenism as illustrated by heightened visibility, polarization, and stereotyping. Because tokens are usually few in numbers and considered a novelty, they often have heightened visibility, which can put them under considerable performance pressure and can lead to either overachievement or underachievement (MacCorquodale & Jensen, 1993).

Polarization is seen as the differences that seem to be exaggerated between the dominant group and the tokens. An example of polarization can be seen in the loyalty tests that tokens may be subjected to and expected to tolerate: women lawyers may have to put up with sexist jokes, swearing, and sexual innuendoes (MacCorquodale & Jensen, 1993). Stereotyping may also occur, in that women lawyers may be expected to fill a certain role, such as that of pet, mother, or seductress. When this role is not fulfilled, she may be regarded as tough or bitchy (MacCorquodale & Jensen, 1993). In terms of heightened visibility, the women noted they were more likely to be complimented for characteristics not related to achievement (such as appearance and clothes) than for achievement-related characteristics (such as their legal reputation or the way they handled a case). Women were also more likely to be seen as "having less credibility in professional settings" (MacCorquodale & Jensen, 1993, p. 590). When it came to polarization, the women reported that they heard more sexist jokes and remarks than did the men. Evidence of stereotyping was found in the women's reports of being patronized, being called by their first names, and being questioned about whether they were lawyers (MacCorquodale & Jensen, 1993).

Earnings and Market Sector

On average, women lawyers earn less than male lawyers, which has been well documented in the literature (Hagan, 1990; Kay & Hagan, 1995; Kay et al., 2004a, 2004b; Robson & Wallace, 2001; Stager & Foot, 1988). Although similar wage discrepancies are also the case in other professions, this gender-based earnings differential seems more offensive in a profession that professes to seek "justice for all." Inspection of the mottos for a selection of law societies in Canada reveals their ideology of equality and justice: the Law Society of Upper Canada's "Let Right Prevail," the Law Society of British Columbia's "Law is the king of a free people," and the Law Society of Newfoundland and Labrador's "Pro lege rege grege"—For the law, the King, and the people.

Although women have made considerable strides in the law profession in Canada in the last 30 years, they still face many obstacles to equality, including their lower earnings. To the credit of the law societies in Canada, many have struck gender and equality committees and published reports in an attempt to address these disparities (Law Society of Alberta, 2006; LSUC, 2004, 2006). The purpose of these committees is to acknowledge the gender inequality and other issues related to diversity and to develop and implement policy and practice guidelines to address these inequities (LSUC, 1997, 2003).

As noted in the previous section, women who work in large firms tend to have a more linear career path (Krakauer & Chen, 2003; Leiper, 1997). The choice surrounding where a lawyer decides to work (large firm vs. small firm vs. sole proprietorship) is related to the expected remuneration. Many perceive that working in larger firms leads to more pres-tige—and more money (Kay & Hagan, 1995). According to recent estimates, an articling student in a large Toronto firm might expect to be paid $1,300 per week, whereas those in government articling positions might be paid between $700 and $900 per week, and those in legal clinics or small firms may earn only $400 or $500 a week (Navarrete, 2002, cited in Krakauer & Chen, 2003). These disparities in salaries continue throughout lawyers' careers, resulting in very large differences between the annual salaries of those who work in the large firms and those who choose a less prestigious career path, such as in government (Kay et al., 2004a, 2004b; Krakauer & Chen, 2003).

Robson and Wallace (2001) studied gender inequality in terms of lawyers' earnings in Canada. They proposed the **human capital theory**, in which the gender gap in earnings is likely due to "gender differences in education, training and experience and as the outcome of both efficiency and choice" (p. 76). Men's increased earnings are explained as reward because they put more investment toward developing their human capital and are rewarded for making the choice to put a greater priority on their careers (Becker, 1991, cited in Robson & Wallace, 2001; Kay & Hagan, 1995). On the other hand, women in the legal profession are seen to gravitate to jobs that, despite allowing for more of a balance in terms of work and family, "offer the lowest returns on their human capital investments" (Robson & Wal-lace, 2001, p. 76).

Research on lawyers in western Canada has shown that although the sex of a lawyer does not have a direct effect on earnings, women lawyers are perceived to be disadvantaged in a number of areas related to the amount of money they can make (Robson & Wallace, 2001). Generally, a lawyer's income is determined by firm-specific variables, such as hours worked, protegé status, and general law experience (Robson & Wallace, 2001). Lawyers in small firms tend to earn less than those in larger firms, and exposure to corporate clients is associated with a higher income (Robson & Wallace, 2001). Not surprisingly, those working in the larger firms are more likely to have corporate clients and to specialize in the more prestigious types of law. Robson and Wallace (2001) found that women lawyers earned only 62 percent of their male counterparts' income. The researchers noted that women lawyers differed from the men in a number of areas: the women worked shorter hours, had less experience practising law, were less likely to have preschool-aged kids, and had less autonomy (Robson & Wallace, 2001).

As Kay and Hagan (1995) summarized, a body of literature has documented the earnings differentials that have existed between male and female lawyers over the years. Although these studies highlighted the existence of pay inequity, they did not explore why such dis-parity existed:

An early study by White (1967) sampled men and women from the graduating classes of 1956 through 1965 of 134 American law schools and discovered that "the males make a lot more money than do the females" (p. 1057). A study of Harvard law school graduates (Glancy 1970: 25) found fewer than 12 per cent of the women as compared to 57 per cent of the men earned in excess of $20,000 annually. Furthermore, a study (Vogt 1987) conducted in 1985 of seven north-eastern US law schools reports that among graduates 11 years out and in the same size firms, men earn on average $75,000 and women $46,500. In Canada, a five-year follow-up study (Adam and Baer, 1984: 39) of the 1974 graduates of Ontario law schools reports that women graduates earn on average about $3,000 a year less than their male counterparts. (Kay & Hagan, 1995, p. 280)

In a Canadian study completed almost 20 years ago, Hagan (1990) found that male lawyers earned more than women lawyers; when this difference was examined, gender discrimination accounted for more than one-quarter of this difference. Hagan (1990) noted support for the notion of gender-specific mobility ladders in the legal profession. In a modification of a taxonomy of class relations developed by Wright et al. (1982, cited in Hagan, 1990), Hagan (1990) proposed a way to conceptualize positions within the field of law. Hagan's resultant taxonomy looked at such factors as "ownership relations, number of employees, authority, participation in decision making, work autonomy, and hierarchical position" and conceptualized the various positions as rungs on a hierarchical ladder (p. 837).

The mobility ladder was thought to "be conceived as having steps which form a power hierarchy that extends across private practice, government and corporate settings" (Kay & Hagan, 1995, p. 284). The highest rung on the ladder consisted of the managing partners in large and medium-sized firms, the "managerial bourgeoisie" (Hagan, 1990, p. 837), who had ownership of the firm, sanctioned others, exercised task authority, formed the decision-making group for the firm, and supervised at least two levels of subordinates (excluding secretaries) below them. The next rung down comprised the "supervisory bourgeoisie" (p. 837), the non-managing partners in large and medium-sized firms. These individuals had no firm-related decision-making role, did not sanction others, and did not have task authority over those below them. The lowest rungs on the mobility ladder were held for what Hagan referred to as "semiautonomous and nonautonomous lawyers" (p. 838), who were not responsible for any kind of supervision of others and had only secretaries below them in the hierarchy.

The existence of gender-specific mobility ladders is related not only to career path but also to earnings, because the mobility ladders are thought to lead to an income hierarchy stratified by gender (Hagan, 1990). In his study of Toronto lawyers, Hagan (1990) found that men made $40,000 more than women and noted a widening of the gender gap as it related to income; that is, as men made more and more money, women's earnings also increased, but not at the same rate as men's.

In a more recent publication, Kay and Hagan (1995) investigated the gendered inequality of earnings in terms of human capital theory, labour segmentation theory, and Marxist theories. Even after taking into account such factors as differences in specializations, positions within a firm, and different employment settings, a gendered gap in earnings was evident. As noted earlier, human capital theory postulates that the decisions that men and women make concerning their careers will influence their earnings: those who choose to invest more in their human capital will reap the rewards in an increased income, compared with those who choose to invest less in their human capital (Kay & Hagan, 1995).

A labour segmentation approach to earning differentials involves acknowledging the differences in types of employers. Dual labour market theories posit the existence of a core labour market, which offers greater pay, more job stability and security, good working conditions, and plenty of opportunity for advancement (Kay & Hagan, 1995). The secondary or less preferable peripheral labour market comprises more unstable work, where earnings are lower, benefits are fewer, working conditions are poorer, employee turnover is frequent, and staff have minimal opportunity for advancement (Kay & Hagan, 1995). In this conceptualization, women's lower earnings are reflective of their higher concentration in the peripheral labour market. On the other hand, a Marxist framework takes more of a relational approach to investigate the impact of power and authority.

Kay and Hagan (1995) noted their intention to "introduce an analysis of the role of authority and power dimensions to explanations of the gender differences in earnings" (p. 284). They proposed the existence of three market sectors for the law: private practice, corporate settings, and government. Within these sectors, the researchers found that women were less likely than men to work in private practice, equally as likely as men to work in corporate settings, and more likely than men to work in government (Kay & Hagan, 1995). In addition, they found women were more likely to work in large or mid-sized firms, but men were more likely than women to be found working as sole practitioners or in small firms (Kay & Hagan, 1995).

Kay and Hagan's results supported the human capital theory: men received more reward for their human capital acquisitions and were able to "reap greater income rewards from experience and from elite law school education than women" (Kay & Hagan, 1995, p. 304). They also found evidence of sex segregation both between and within the different market sectors of the profession, which, they noted, served to disadvantage women. So, although lawyers in the core labour market (private practice) were at an advantage over lawyers in the second tier (corporate settings), men in private practice showed economic gains over the women in this sector. Similarly, in the second-tier settings, both men and women showed economic gain over those in the peripheral sector (government). But again, men in the second tier showed economic gains over women in that same tier. Notably, the researchers observed an apparent "amplification of earning differentials with movements to higher positions of the mobility ladder" (Kay & Hagan, 1995, p. 304). That is, as women moved up the mobility ladder, the disparity between their earnings and those of men at the same level increased.

Job Satisfaction and Gender

The "paradox of the contented female worker" has been described as the observation that "although women have jobs with lower pay and less authority than men, they are equally satisfied with their jobs and employers" (Phelan, 1994, p. 95). This paradox has been investigated in samples of lawyers (Chiu, 1998; Hagan & Kay, 2007; Mueller & Wallace, 1996). Mueller and Wallace (1996) noted that such a paradox with respect to job satisfaction did not exist for female lawyers when the correct model specifications were made.[15] The researchers did, however, report a paradox with respect to pay satisfaction (Mueller & Wallace, 1996). Chiu (1998), in a sample of 326 American lawyers, found that the women lawyers (who had similar career expectations as the men) reported lower job satisfaction. Chiu concluded that the difference in job satisfaction was due to inequality in opportunity.

More recently, this notion of a paradox has been investigated by Hagan and Kay (2007), who pointed out the overall support in the literature for an apparent paradox with respect to job satisfaction among women lawyers (Chambers, 1989, cited in Hagan & Kay, 2007; Dinovitzer et al., 2004, cited in Hagan & Kay, 2007; Kay et al., 2004b). The researchers noted that although the literature is consistent in the findings that women lawyers tend to enter firms at the same rate as men, the similarities end there. Women are more likely than men to leave the job, leave earlier, be paid less, and are less likely to become partners (Brockman, 1994; Hagan, 1990; Hagan & Kay, 2007; Kay, 1997; Kay et al., 2004a, 2004b; Stager & Foot, 1988). In their research involving a sample of Toronto lawyers, Hagan and Kay (2007) found three indirect pathways that connected gender and job dissatisfaction and despondency. Using LISREL[16] analyses, the researchers made the following conclusions:

- Women lawyers have less occupational power, which relates to more despondency about their job.
- Women lawyers' perceived powerlessness serves to dampen their job satisfaction.
- Women are more likely to be concerned about the career consequences of having children, which results in despondency.

Hagan and Kay (2007) suggest that to fully explore the relationship between gender and job satisfaction among lawyers, studies of job satisfaction should include measures of despondency because gender appears to be indirectly connected to job satisfaction through feelings of despondency. As the authors note, "women are more likely to respond to their professional grievances with internalized feelings of despondency than with externalized expressions of job dissatisfaction" (Hagan & Kay, 2007, p. 51).

Role Overload and Role Strain

Gomme and Hall (1995) identified aspects of qualitative and quantitative role overload that have contributed to role strain among prosecutors. According to the researchers, "role overload occurs where insufficient time exists in which to properly execute all necessary work-related tasks" (Gomme & Hall, 1995, p. 192). Quantitative overload occurs when insufficient time is available to complete the work because of the large volume of work to be done. In contrast, qualitative overload refers to the experience of being unable to complete one's work because the material resources available are insufficient to meet the demands of a very complex task within a limited time period (Gomme & Hall, 1995). Both forms of overload have been found to be associated with role strain—the negative psychological and physical consequences of role overload, such as difficulty sleeping, exhaustion, heart palpitations, anxiety, irritability, frustration, and burnout (Kemery, Mossholder, & Bedeian, 1987, cited in Gomme & Hall, 1995). The researchers note that the job of a prosecutor is very demanding and difficult, involving high caseloads, difficult witnesses, disturbing case material, and various administrative challenges, complicated by a lack of control over one's schedule (Gomme & Hall, 1995). The deleterious effects of role strain are illustrated in the following quotation from a Crown attorney in the Maritimes:

It's really frustrating—exhausting. It's always stressful. You're always there [in court]. There's always someone mad at you ... We're all here, we're all under stress—tremendous amounts of stress ... There are days I didn't want to go to work—just felt so sick—physically sick from the anxiety and the stress of the work. But you push yourself.

There should be more to life than tolerating. That, you know what I mean, there should be time for family and happiness.

It does. It does. It affects your family life terribly. And it can affect you mentally too, especially over a period of time ... Your system breaks down. [There is] constant pressure from a job like this. (Gomme & Hall, 1995, p. 196)

Clearly, levels of stress associated with this kind of work can affect a prosecutor's performance. The issues raised by Gomme and Hall (1995) cut across gender lines and encompass more than just the experiences of prosecutors. Without a doubt, many defence lawyers and even judges have similar kinds of experiences.

Sexism, Harassment, and Discrimination

Although a great deal of what has already been discussed in this chapter would fall under the category of sexism, harassment, and discrimination (for example, women's earnings compared with men's and the longer time period for women to become a partner), some specific issues are worth mentioning explicitly. An American study published in the mid-1990s reported that sexist behaviours were found to be more frequent both in the private sector (as opposed to the public sector) and among those who were in token positions (Rosenberg, Perlstadt, & Phillips, 1993). Also, more sexist behaviours were reported to occur after women were on the job (with respect to salary, promotion, and types of jobs assigned to them) as opposed to during the recruitment and hiring process (Rosenberg et al., 1993). Interestingly, the authors noted that women with careerist orientations, those who "deny the importance of gender in stratifying the profession," reported more sexual harassment than did those with a feminist orientation (Rosenberg et al., 1993, p. 420).

In a study of Ontario lawyers, Kay et al. (2004a) noted significant differences between men and women lawyers with respect to incidents of discrimination based on gender. The researchers found that women more often identified witnessing examples of discriminatory practices than did men. For example, women reported with greater frequency than men that women had:

- been assigned tasks that were below their skill level;
- not been invited to work with a specific senior partner;
- been excluded from a social gathering;
- been denied work even when an interest had been expressed;
- been the recipient of comments about their appearance;
- heard derogatory comments about their family status;
- heard disrespectful remarks from judges or other lawyers; and
- experienced a lack of support from office staff.

In their longitudinal study of a cohort of Ontario lawyers, Kay et al. (2004b) found that over the course of three surveys, women were more likely to perceive sexual discrimination in the workplace than were men. Three times as many women (18 percent) as men (6 percent) believed they had been denied responsibility for a file because of their sex. Similarly, more women perceived they had been assigned a specific case because of their sex, and more women thought fewer opportunities were afforded to them because of their sex (Kay et al., 2004b).

Future Directions

From this chapter, readers should find it readily apparent that many challenges face women in the legal profession. If the profession is to see continued growth and equality, then some of these challenges will require creative solutions. Serious consideration will need to be given, both in private and public practices, to increased flexibility in the workplace to deal with expanding family responsibilities (child care and eldercare), to more flexibility with respect to the costs associated with practising law, and to a better use of technology. Great strides have been taken to accommodate the needs of accused persons and litigants, yet that same technology does not seem to have offered any assistance to the people working with them. If we can bring court to the jails in the interest of expediency and justice, can we not offer better assistance to the people working with the accused persons and litigants who find themselves in the system?

Additionally, a concern to be addressed in the very near future is the rising cost of obtaining a legal education. The dramatic rise in admissions to law schools in the third wave needs to continue to ensure a continuous flow of women into the practice of law (Mossman, 2005). Exorbitant tuition fees, lack of subsidies, and inflexibility in the law school curriculum will likely contribute to a decline in the number of women practising law in this country (LSUC, 2004).

The recent death of the Honourable Madam Justice Bertha Wilson, the first woman appointed to the Supreme Court of Canada, should help to remind those who enter the practice of law that the issues women face are similar regardless of when we start our journey. When Bertha Wilson enrolled in law at Dalhousie in 1955, Horace Read, the dean of the law school, was reported to have said to her, "Have you no appreciation of how tough a course the law is? This is not something you can do in your spare time. We have no room for dilettantes. Why don't you go home and take up crocheting?" (McPhee, 2007, p. 1). We are certainly glad that she did not. Clara Brett Martin and others paved the way for women to enter law school and the practice of law, and pioneers such as Justice Wilson ensured that we understand there are no limits to what women can achieve.

Summary

It is sobering to think that a little more than 100 years ago, Canada had no women lawyers. Times have changed, and women are now an integral part of the practice of law. Their presence in the field does not, however, mean that their representation is equal to that of men. We know that as many women enter law school as do men. We know that they attend law school for the same reasons as men. They graduate and pursue jobs in the field, as do men. However, somewhere along the way, their equality with male lawyers ends. More women can be found working in lower-paid and less prestigious government positions, whereas more men work in more lucrative private practices. Although some women decide to work in law firms, examination of those who make partner shows that fewer women than men in law firms are partners. Even among those who are partners, fewer women than men are considered senior partners. Women lawyers earn considerably less than their male counterparts, even when taking into account their years of practice, the type of law practised, and the positions held.

What is clear is that, over the years, varying types of barriers have impeded women's progress in the field of law. Initially, legislation prevented their entry into the profession. Although such structural barriers no longer exist, women continue to face some significant challenges that may be seen to affect their progress in their chosen career. Factors related to the inflexibility of the job (hours of work and lack of part-time alternatives, for example), lower earnings, sexual discrimination, and sexual harassment may be related to the observation that more women than men leave the practice of law altogether.

As is the case in many other areas of the Canadian criminal justice system, the study of women in the legal field has not taken centre stage until fairly recently. Only in the last couple of decades have we seen an intensive push to investigate issues related to women in the legal profession. Academics and a number of law societies in Canada have taken the lead in this area. The commission of various studies and the publication of reports on issues relating to women lawyers have furthered our understanding of women's role in the legal profession in Canada. Continued focus on issues of gender and discrimination may enable women to one day attain equality with men in all aspects of the legal profession.

Notes

1. In this chapter, all references to personal anecdotes are from Shelley Lechlitner.

2. This sentiment is a personal one, gleaned from conversations with colleagues over the past decade.

3. The Family Compact refers to an elite group of wealthy Anglican conservatives who, as a group, had major influence in Upper Canada following the War of 1812.

4. Clara Brett Martin is believed to have been left permanently weakened by a cold she caught while working on the John Doughty–Ambrose Small case in 1920 (Backhouse, 1985).

5. Examination of the life and times of Clara Brett Martin has revealed that she espoused anti-Semitic views both in her personal and professional life (Backhouse, 1992).

6. In Canada, the Queen's Privy Council, which includes Cabinet ministers and members appointed by the Queen on the advice of the prime minister, exercises formal functions of law.

7. This increase was steady, apart from a period during the 1930s (Mossman, 2005).

8. The populations for Parry Sound, North Bay, and Ottawa are from the 2006 census (Statistics Canada, 2007). Estimates of the number of Crown attorneys for Parry Sound and North Bay were provided by Shelley Lechlitner.

9. The term *year of call* refers to the year that a lawyer was called to the bar in the province of Ontario.

10. The term *disclosure* refers to the Crown's case and all materials pertaining to it. In Canada, the law requires the disclosure of all relevant materials, by the Crown, to the defence.

11. The term *bench* is the seat occupied by a judge in a court and also refers to a judge's general position in the legal field.

12. In 1995, 12,147,500 people in Canada over the age of 25 were employed.

13. These observations were made by Shelley Lechlitner in her Northern Ontario–based practice. Although not quantitative, these observations are worthy of note.

14. Successful candidates to these elected positions are involved in the many operations and functions surrounding the monitoring, educating, and disciplining of the lawyers in the province of Ontario.

15. For an in-depth discussion, see Mueller and Wallace (1996).

16. LISREL, a statistical program developed by Jöreskog and Sörbom, allows for the estimation of covariance structure models (Hagan & Kay, 2007).

Discussion Questions

1. Fewer women than men are partners in law firms. Why do you think women are under-represented among partners in these firms?

2. Being a lawyer is associated with many stressors. In what ways can stressors be gendered?

3. John and Jane Doe went to law school at the same time. They both were called to the bar at the same time and accepted positions in mid-sized law firms in the same town at the same time. Ten years into their respective careers, John makes $20,000 a year more than Jane. How would human capital theory explain this difference?

4. Women's representation in the legal profession has changed drastically over the last 100 years. Discuss Mossman's three waves of women lawyers in Canada. What would a fourth wave look like?

5. Briefly outline the role of the Crown, the defence, and the judge in a criminal court.

Suggested Readings

Leiper, J. (2006). *Bar codes: Women in the legal profession.* Vancouver: University of British Columbia Press.

Roberts, J., & Grossman, M. (2008). *Criminal justice in Canada: A reader* (3rd ed.). Toronto: Nelson Canada.

Sheehy, E., & McIntyre, S. (2006). *Calling for change: Women, law and the legal profession.* Ottawa: University of Ottawa Press.

Online Resources

1. Law Society of Upper Canada: www.lsuc.on.ca
2. National Association of Women and the Law: www.nawl.ca
3. Women's Law Association of Ontario: www.wlao.on.ca
4. The Canadian Bar Association: www.cba.org
5. The County and District Law Presidents' Association (CDLPA): www.cdlpa.org

References

Backhouse, C. (1985). "To open the way for others of my sex": Clara Brett Martin's career as Canada's first woman lawyer. *Canadian Journal of Women and the Law, 1,* 1–41.

Backhouse, C. (1992). Clara Brett Martin: Canadian heroine or not? *Canadian Journal of Women and the Law, 5,* 263–279.

Backhouse, C., & Backhouse, N. (2004). *The heiress vs. the establishment: Mrs. Campbell's campaign for legal justice.* Toronto: University of British Columbia Press.

Brockman, J. (1994). Leaving the practice of law: The wherefores and the whys. *Alberta Law Review, 32,* 116–180.

Chiu, C. (1998). Do professional women have lower job satisfaction than professional men? Lawyers as a case study. *Sex Roles, 38,* 521–536.

Federal/Provincial/Territorial Working Group of Attorneys General Officials on Gender Equality in the Canadian Justice System. (1992). *Gender equality in the Canadian justice system background papers: Women working in the justice system.* Ottawa: Department of Justice.

Goff, C. (2008). *Criminal justice in Canada* (4th ed.). Toronto: Nelson Canada.

Gomme, I., & Hall, M. (1995). Prosecutors at work: Role overload and strain. *Journal of Criminal Justice, 23,* 191–200.

Hagan, J. (1990). The gender stratification of income inequality among lawyers. *Social Forces, 68,* 835–855.

Hagan, J., & Kay, F. (2007). Even lawyers get the blues: Gender, depression and job satisfaction in legal practice. *Law and Society Review, 41,* 51–78.

Kay, F. (1997). Flight from law: A competing risks model of departures from law firms. *Law and Society Review, 31,* 301–335.

Kay, F., & Hagan, J. (1995). The persistent glass ceiling: Gendered inequalities in the earnings of lawyers. *British Journal of Sociology, 46,* 279–310.

Kay, F., Masuch, C., & Curry, P. (2004a). *Diversity and change: The contemporary legal profession in Ontario—A report to the Law Society of Upper Canada.* Toronto: Law Society of Upper Canada.

Kay, F., Masuch, C., & Curry, P. (2004b). *Turning points and transitions: Women's careers in the legal profession—A report to the Law Society of Upper Canada.* Toronto: Law Society of Upper Canada.

Kinnear, M. (1992). "That there woman lawyer": Women lawyers in Manitoba, 1915–1970. *Canadian Journal of Women and the Law, 5,* 411–441.

Krakauer, L., & Chen, C. (2003). Gender barriers in the legal profession: Implications for career development of female law students. *Journal of Employment Counseling, 40,* 65–79.

Law Society of Alberta. (2006). *Diversity and equality initiatives: 1991–2006.* Edmonton: Author.

Law Society of Upper Canada. (1996). *38th bar admission course materials: Criminal procedure.* Toronto: Author.

Law Society of Upper Canada. (1997). *Bicentennial report and recommendations on equity issues in the legal profession: Report to bicentennial convocation.* Toronto: Author.

Law Society of Upper Canada. (2003). *Guide to developing a policy regarding workplace equity in law firms.* Toronto: Author.

Law Society of Upper Canada. (2004). *Bicentennial implementation status report and strategy.* Toronto: Author.

Law Society of Upper Canada. (2006). *Equity and Aboriginal issues committee: Report to convocation.* Toronto: Author.

Leiper, J. (1997). It was like "wow!": The experience of women lawyers in a profession marked by linear careers. *Canadian Journal of Women and the Law, 9,* 115–137.

Leiper, J. (2006). *Bar codes: Women in the legal profession.* Vancouver: University of British Columbia Press.

LexisNexis Canada. (2008). Job detail: Articling/summer student. Available from www.totallegaljobs.ca.

Library and Archives Canada. (n.d.). *Canadian women in government: The Right Honourable A. Kim Campbell.* Retrieved from www.collectionscanada.gc.ca/femmes/002026-822-e.html.

MacCorquodale, P., & Jensen, G. (1993). Women in the law: Partners or tokens? *Gender and Society, 7,* 582–593.

McPhee, J. (2007). A powerful flame extinguished. *Law Times, 18*(16), 1.

Mossman, M. (2005). Defining moments for women as lawyers: Reflections on numerical gender equality. *Canadian Journal of Women and the Law, 17,* 15–25.

Mueller, C., & Wallace, J. (1996). Justice and the paradox of the contented female worker. *Social Psychology Quarterly, 59,* 338–349.

Ontario, Ministry of Finance. (2007). *Salary disclosure 2006.* Retrieved from www.fin.gov.on.ca/english/publications/salarydisclosure/2006/judiciary06.html.

Ornstein, M. (2004). *The changing face of the Ontario legal profession 1971–2001: A report to the Law Society of Upper Canada.* Toronto: Law Society of Upper Canada.

Petersson, S. (1997). Ruby Clements and early women of the Alberta bar. *Canadian Journal of Women and the Law, 9,* 365–393.

Phelan, J. (1994). The paradox of the contented female worker: An assessment of alternative explanations. *Social Psychology Quarterly, 57,* 95–107.

Rashid, A. (2000). Earnings of lawyers. *Perspectives on Labour and Income, 12*(1), 16–28.

Roberts, J., & Grossman, M. (2008). *Criminal justice in Canada: A reader* (3rd ed.). Toronto: Nelson Canada.

Robson, K., & Wallace, J. (2001). Gendered inequalities in earnings: A study of Canadian lawyers. *Canadian Review of Sociology and Anthropology, 38,* 76–95.

Rosenberg, J., Perlstadt, H., & Phillips, W. (1993). Now that we are here: Discrimination, disparagement, and harassment at work and the experience of women lawyers. *Gender and Society, 7,* 415–433.

Sheehy, E., & McIntyre, S. (2006). *Calling for change: Women, law and the legal profession.* Ottawa: University of Ottawa Press.

Snowball, K. (2002). *Criminal prosecutions, personnel and expenditures, 2000/01.* Ottawa: Canadian Centre for Justice Statistics.

Stager, D., & Foot, D. (1988). Changes in lawyers' earnings: The impact of differentiation and growth in the Canadian legal profession. *Law and Social Inquiry, 13,* 71–85.

Statistics Canada. (2007). *2006 community profiles.* Available from www12.statcan.ca/english/census06/data/profiles/community/Index.cfm?Lang=E.

Supreme Court of Canada. (n.d.). *About the court.* Retrieved from www.scc-csc.gc.ca/aboutcourt/index_e.asp.

van Wormer, K., & Bartollas, C. (2007). *Women and the criminal justice system* (2nd ed.). Boston: Pearson.

CHAPTER 15

Women Working in Corrections

Jane Barker

Introduction

Women work in many different capacities within Canada's correctional system. Their roles include but are not limited to correctional officers, clerks, wardens, deputy wardens, chaplains, parole officers, probation officers, primary workers, case management officers, psychologists, nurses, and doctors. Much of the day-to-day workload and the responsibilities of these staff remain a mystery to the general public because so much of what goes on is literally behind a fence or behind a stone wall. In comparison with other justice occupations (such as the police or lawyers), very few people have actually come into contact with correctional staff acting in their official capacity. For example, think of the last time you saw a police officer in uniform, spoke to a police officer on the phone, or saw a police cruiser in your neighbourhood. Now think of the last time you saw a correctional officer in uniform, spoke to a correc-

tional officer on the phone, or saw a corrections vehicle in your neighbourhood. If you are like most Canadians, you have likely encountered a police officer, but have rarely, if ever, encountered a correctional officer.

For the most part, the general public is unaware of what prisons are like on the inside, a collective ignorance that reflects the kind of institution a prison is—a closed institution. Unless you live, work, or volunteer in a prison, you are unlikely to know what it is like inside. Tours of prisons have sometimes been made available to the general public, but they occur rarely (Outhit, 1999). Many people's only contact with the interior of a prison is through the news and media. Their perceptions of prison are shaped by the images portrayed through television, films, and print media.

When I was doing some work at a federal prison in the early 1990s, I was asked by my young cousin (who was about ten at the time) what I did for a living. When I explained that I worked in a prison, without missing a beat, he asked in horror, "Does your mother know you work there?" His astonishment and the way he expressed his surprise were refreshing. I am sure that some of my friends and family (who were equally shocked that I worked in a prison) would have liked to have asked me a similar question, but they were far more constrained by social custom. The general public has a natural curiosity and some confusion toward those who spend their days working with offenders. These feelings are especially pronounced when sensationalized cases are highlighted in the news. People wonder why anyone would want to work in what is sometimes a dangerous and toxic environment (van Wormer & Bartollas, 2000).

Over the years, numerous studies have focused on the lives of offenders, yet we know very little about the attitudes, behaviours, and experiences of the people who supervise offenders and how they interact with offenders and with each other (Bensimon, 2005b). This chapter will introduce the reader to various components of the Canadian correctional system, the staff who work in corrections, and the challenges faced by women who choose to work in what has, for the most part, been a male-dominated regime.

The Correctional System

The correctional system in Canada comprises custodial services (both provincial or territorial and federal), community supervision services, and the national and provincial parole boards. In 2004–5, total expenditures for correctional services in Canada were $2.8 billion (Beattie, 2006). The federal system accounted for 54 percent of that total, and provincial and territorial correctional services accounted for the remaining 46 percent. Nearly three-quarters (71 percent) of total expenditures were for custodial services. Expenditures associated with parole boards were approximately 2 percent of total expenditures (Beattie, 2006).

On average, it cost $259.05 per day to incarcerate a federal offender, whereas incarcerating a provincial offender was much cheaper, at $141.78 per day (Beattie, 2006). When federal expenditures were examined in depth, the costs to incarcerate federally sentenced women far surpassed the costs to incarcerate similarly sentenced men (Public Safety and Emergency Preparedness Canada [PSEPC], 2006). Recent estimates for 2004–5 show that it cost $166,642 annually to incarcerate a woman at a federal women's facility, whereas the costs to incarcerate a man ranged from $83,643 a year for a minimum security institution to $113,591 for a maximum security facility (PSEPC, 2006).

We can speculate why it costs so much more to federally incarcerate a woman than a man. Fewer women are incarcerated, yet they still require facilities, security, and staff to work in the institutions, and specially designed programs need to be developed and delivered to address the unique needs of incarcerated women. Comparatively speaking, supervising an offender in the community costs less ($20,320 annually) than incarcerating that offender (on average, $87,919 annually) in a correctional facility (PSEPC, 2006). Expenditures for federally incarcerated inmates are expected to top $1.9 billion by 2009–10 (PSEPC, 2006).

Federal, provincial, and territorial governments share the workload for adult correctional institutions. Offenders sentenced to two years or more will find themselves under the control of the federal correctional system—the Correctional Service of Canada (CSC). Those who are sentenced to two years less a day, or shorter sentences, are destined for a provincial or territorial facility, which also houses individuals held on remand and temporary detainees, such as those who are held for reasons related to immigration (Statistics Canada, 2005a).

The Correctional System Workload

Historically, two key indicators have been used to assess the workload of corrections: the average daily count of offenders and the annual admissions to corrections (Statistics Canada, 2005a). Recent information from Statistics Canada (2005a) indicates that on a typical day in 2002–3, approximately 3,000 young offenders were in custody in Canada, a decrease of 28 percent since 1994–95.

Most of the youth in custody were in secure custody (36 percent) or open custody (36 percent), and the remaining 28 percent were in custody for the purposes of remand. Youth who are considered to be flight risks and those considered to be a danger to the public may be held in remand prior to their sentencing or their court hearing. Secure custody facilities are typically like jails, operating with secure containment. Open custody facilities consist of group homes or other residential settings where the security level is not as high. Those working with young offenders in custody perform a myriad of tasks, including the preparing reports, escorting the movement of offenders, providing treatment programs, and supervising offenders (Statistics Canada, 2005a).

According to recent statistics, the average daily count of adult inmates in Canadian correctional facilities has undergone an interesting shift. Beginning in the middle of the 1990s, the size of the adult inmate population serving a custodial sentence decreased in federal, provincial, and territorial facilities. However, the reduction in provincial and territorial divisions was not equal to the reduction in the federal division, nor did the decreases occur at the same time (Statistics Canada, 2005a). Because the decrease began earlier in the provincial and territorial divisions, and because their decreases were, on average, larger each year than the decrease in federal institutions, the reduction in the provincial and territorial facilities has been more dramatic. As of 2004–5, more inmates (12,301) were serving sentences in federal facilities in Canada than in provincial and territorial facilities (9,830) (Beattie, 2006). This pattern is a reversal of the situation prior to the mid-1990s when more adults were sentenced provincially and territorially than federally (Statistics Canada, 2005b). However, it is important to note that in 2004–5 there were nearly as many people being held on remand (9,640) in provincial and territorial facilities as there were being sentenced to them. Thus, the total number (19,816) of individuals (9,830 sentenced admissions, 9,640 remands, and 346 other temporary detainees) held in provincial and territorial facilities in 2004–5 surpassed the total (12,301) who were incarcerated federally (Beattie, 2006).

The relatively larger number of federally sentenced incarcerates, compared with provincially or territorially sentenced offenders, holds some interesting implications, especially because federal offenders have been shown to have higher needs levels than their provincial and territorial counterparts (Trevethan, MacKillop, Robinson, Porporino, & Millson, 1999). In their "one-day snapshot" of Canadian inmates, Trevethan et al. (1999) reported that federal offenders showed significantly higher needs than provincial and territorial inmates in the areas of personal/emotional issues, attitude, and substance abuse.

Recent counts of the inmate population in Canada indicated that in 2004–5, women comprised 5 percent of those admitted to federal institutions, and twice that percentage (10 percent) of those admitted to provincial and territorial custody (Beattie, 2006). That same year, women accounted for 17 percent of those admitted to probation and conditional sentences and 11 percent of those admitted on remand (Beattie, 2006). Almost one-third (30 percent) of all women inmates who were sent to custody in 2004–5 were Aboriginal (Beattie, 2006).

Correctional Personnel

Consistent with the past 10 years' pattern of declining sentenced populations of provincially and territorially incarcerated offenders, the levels of provincial correctional personnel have also decreased. In 2003, fewer people were employed in adult provincial and territorial corrections than in 1999 (Statistics Canada, 2005a). In 1992–93, more than 14,000 provincial and territorial personnel were employed, compared with fewer than 12,000 provincial and territorial personnel in 2002–3 (Statistics Canada, 2005a).

The opposite pattern has occurred in federal corrections, where the numbers of personnel increased over the same 10-year time period. In 1992–93, a little more than 8,000 federal personnel were employed, and that number climbed to more than 12,000 in 2002–3. Data from 2002–3 suggest that federal personnel outnumber those working in provincial and territorial correctional facilities (Statistics Canada, 2005a).

The *Correctional Service Canada: Report on Plans and Priorities* noted that the CSC employed approximately 14,500 staff in 2006, and staffing levels were estimated to increase to 15,802 by 2009–10 (Correctional Service of Canada [CSC], 2007). The majority of staff (87 percent) worked in institutions or in the community. The report further noted that the CSC was attempting to maintain a workforce reflective of the Canadian public as a whole, employing persons from visible minority groups (5 percent), persons with disabilities (4 percent), and Aboriginal people (7 percent). The CSC noted that these levels were "at or above the labour market availability of workers in these operational groups" (CSC, 2007, p. 9). In terms of the CSC's employment of women, recent estimates suggest that women comprised less than 45 percent of the CSC's workforce (CSC, 2007; Human Resources and Social Development Canada [HRSDC], 2006). Since women comprise slightly more than half (50.4 percent) of Canada's population, the CSC still has some headway to make in its hiring of women if it wants to be reflective of Canada's population (Statistics Canada, 2005b).

Estimates from the late 1990s indicated that correctional service workers in Canada tended to be between the ages of 25 and 44, with a mean age of 40 (Statistics Canada, 2002). Compared with other justice personnel in Canada, correctional service workers had less education, earned less income, and had lower entry-level incomes (Statistics Canada, 2002). In 1995, their average income from employment as correctional workers was $40,488, approximately 18 percent less than other justice personnel in Canada that year (Statistics Canada, 2002). This lower entry-level income likely reflects the lower average educational level among correctional service workers. In recent years, however, higher education has been encouraged among correctional officers based on a belief that increased education would lead to increased professionalism (Robinson, Porporino, & Simourd, 1997).

In a Canadian study of educational attainment, attitudes, and job performance of correctional officers, researchers found that those with a university degree were less punitive, showed less interest in custody, and were more supportive of rehabilitation (Robinson et al., 1997). However, the researchers did not find that these officers were any more willing to partake in rehabilitative activities, nor were they any more likely to want to work with people.

Education was unrelated to the belief that counselling offenders was an appropriate activity for correctional officers (Robinson et al., 1997).

FEMALE CORRECTIONAL SERVICE OFFICERS

According to the 2001 Census of Canada, just over 5,400 women were working as correctional service officers in Canada, representing 29 percent of the total number of correctional service officers that year (Statistics Canada, 2005b). Over a 10-year period (from 1991 to 2001), the number of female correctional officers in Canada increased by 1,455, an increase of 7 percent of the total number of Canadian correctional officers (Statistics Canada, 2005b). This increase was consistent with increases over the same time period in other justice-related occupations, such as judges, lawyers and notaries, paralegals, and probation and parole officers (Statistics Canada, 2005b).

The History of Women Working in Provincial Corrections

As noted in chapter 1, women have had a long history of working with incarcerated women. Because they could be paid less than their male counterparts, women were historically employed as matrons (Strange, 1985). Although they were mainly responsible for the female offenders, their jobs sometimes included such tasks as cooking and making beds (Ministry of Correctional Services, 1983, cited in McMahon, 1999). In some cases, a matron was employed by virtue of her husband's occupation (as a jail superintendent or governor). In these cases, women weren't always eager to assume the role of matron (Ministry of Correctional Services, 1983, cited in McMahon, 1999). In 1971, the Ministry of Correctional Services determined that husbands and wives would not be allowed to work together, effectively abolishing the practice of hiring the wives of correctional officials as matrons (Ministry of Correctional Services, 1983, cited in McMahon, 1999).

The history of women working strictly with male offenders is more limited and, as McMahon (1999) has pointed out, is not extensively documented. In her book, *Women on Guard: Discrimination and Harassment in Corrections*, McMahon (1999) extensively traced the history of women working in male provincial corrections. A shift appeared to occur in the 1970s. Prior to this time, most women employed in corrections filled stereotypically female roles (as nurses and in clerical positions). In more recent years, women have assumed roles traditionally reserved for men in correctional work. McMahon further pointed out that the paramilitary manner in which institutions were run prior to the 1970s encouraged an authoritarian structure that catered to males with a military background, effectively excluding women (who did not tend to have military experience) from the job pool. In a related finding, Jurik and Halemba (1984) noted that the majority of their male sample of correctional officers had previous law enforcement or military backgrounds, whereas none of the female sample of officers had any military background, and only one-third had a law enforcement background.

The first institution in Ontario to hire women as correctional officers was the Alex Brown Clinic/Ontario Correctional Institute (OCI) in Brampton, in the 1970s (Ministry of Correctional Services, 1983, cited in McMahon, 1999). By the end of that decade, women were working as correctional officers in no less than 24 facilities (Ministry of Correctional Services, 1983, cited in McMahon, 1999). According to figures presented by McMahon (1999), by 1998 more than 1,000 women were working as correctional officers in Ontario, 969 of them in male institutions. Women's rise to management positions in male institutions did not occur in Ontario until the mid- to late 1970s, and it wasn't until 1982 that the first woman was hired as the superintendent of a male adult prison (Ministry of Correctional Services, 1983, cited in McMahon, 1999). Although no specific piece of legislation encouraged the hiring of women into traditionally male roles in the prison system in Ontario, both the Ontario government and the Ontario Ministry of Correctional Services were reported to have been proactive in their response to a series of federal and provincial reports, including the 1970 *Report of the Royal Commission on the Status of Women* (McMahon, 1999).

The History of Women Working in Federal Corrections

According to its mission statement:

> The Correctional Service of Canada (CSC), as part of the criminal justice system and respecting the rule of law, contributes to public safety by actively encouraging and assisting offenders to become law-abiding citizens, while exercising reasonable, safe, secure and humane control. (CSC, n.d., ¶ 2)

Women have worked in the CSC for many years in traditionally female roles (Griffiths, 2004). However, in the early to mid-1980s, the CSC attracted a flurry of media attention when it first began integrating female correctional officers into male institutions ("Across Canada," 1983; Cleland, 1986; Kershaw, 1985a, 1985b; Large, 1986). The inclusion of women into this prior bastion of male domination could be traced to developments in the late 1960s and early 1970s.

In 1969, the *Public Service Employment Act* became applicable to the Canadian Penitentiary Service (Canada, Public Service Commission [PSC], 1977). According to the *Public Service Employment Act*, section 12, a federal public service was not to discriminate on the basis of sex (Canada, PSC, 1977). However, up until that time, the penitentiary service had hired only men as guards in male institutions. Exemptions were applied for and received in 1973 and again in 1975 (Canada, PSC, 1977). However, in the mid-1970s, the rationale for this exemption was questioned. Complaints were filed with the Anti-Discrimination Branch of the Human Rights Commission, which, in 1975, was tasked to perform an in-depth investigation to identify the justifications for maintaining only men in guard positions. By 1977, a report was issued, and no justification was determined for limiting the guard positions to men; the practice of excluding women from these jobs was set to change (Canada, PSC, 1977). In 1978, the first eight women were hired as correctional officers in male penitentiaries within the Correctional Service of Canada (Sakowski, 1986).

In the early 1980s, the results from the "Female CX Pilot Project"[1] were published, suggesting that as long as women were introduced into the institutions in a methodical manner and were actively supported by management, they would have no problems integrating into the male institutions (CSC, 1980). An account of the experiences of the first women employed in the CSC in male institutions suggested otherwise (Sakowski, 1986). Similarly, a report from the Canadian Human Rights Commission published in 1981 suggested the integration was not a smooth one. Whereas the senior managers at institutions where female correctional officers were deployed exhibited "a positive or at least a neutral position" toward the presence of women in these positions, the union representatives expressed a less enthusiastic view (Canadian Human Rights Commission [CHRC], 1981, p. 4). The union representatives were neutral or negative about having women correctional officers in male institutions (CHRC,

1981). Key concerns included issues of inmate privacy and the testing of authority with female officers, including whether they could handle violent incidents (CHRC, 1981).

In 1984, Kingston Penitentiary was the first maximum security federal male prison to hire women as guards (Cleland, 1986). Within a year, it was not uncommon to find women working as guards in maximum security institutions (Cleland, 1986). In 1985, Millhaven penitentiary was the last federal prison in Ontario to prepare to hire women as guards. At that time, 120 females were employed in male federal institutions in Ontario, as guards and living unit officers (Kershaw, 1985b). In the mid-1980s, the federal correctional service was attempting to increase women's representation among junior guards and living unit officers to 19 percent by 1988; to assess the "policies, guidelines and practices" that would allow for flexibility in attaining this target, an operational and resource management review was undertaken in 1985 (CSC, 1985, p. 1).

Not surprisingly, a backlash against this increased representation of women was played out in the media. Concerns were expressed that women were being given priority in terms of hiring for correctional officer positions. In addition, the emphasis on a university education had some individuals upset about the so-called whiz kids with degrees who were being promoted over more seasoned guards without degrees (Kershaw, 1985a). According to a report in the media, an Ontario region official and a Kingston lawyer carried out a secret report that alleged "widespread sexual harassment of female officers at the Collins Bay Institution that included name-calling, grabbing, vicious gossiping, refusal by male guards both to talk to their female colleagues on the job and to adequately train them for certain posts" (Kershaw, 1985a, p. 1). Such a claim was counter to the conclusions previously drawn regarding the relative ease with which women could be integrated in male institutions (CSC, 1980).

By 1990, although one-third of those working in the CSC were women, upon closer inspection, these women tended to be employed in stereotypical kinds of positions (Jamieson, Beals, Lalonde & Associates Inc., 1990). Specifically, the report noted that the women in the CSC tended to be clustered in positions of administrative support. In 1990, only 12 percent of the CSC's operations sector employees were female, and only 10 percent of those at the executive level in the CSC were women (Jamieson, Beals, Lalonde & Associates Inc., 1990). The surveyed women expressed disillusionment about their work and collectively felt "isolated from the positions of power within the organization" (Jamieson, Beals, Lalonde & Associates Inc., 1990, p. i). In its final report on the employment barriers for women in the CSC, Jamieson, Beals, Lalonde & Associates Inc. (1990) noted that the largest barriers for women tended to be the attitudes and behaviours shown mainly by men in the male-dominated organizational culture of the CSC:

> Many men and women believe discriminatory practices such as gender-biased selection boards, tokenism, sexual harassment, biased perceptions toward family life, and a persistent, underlying ethos that corrections work is men's business, are factors hampering the realization of equitable participation for women. (Jamieson, Beals, Lalonde & Associates Inc., 1990, p. ii)

In 1991, the Correctional Service of Canada organized a conference for 110 of its female middle managers. The conference participants represented all regions and various occupations within the CSC. As a result of the conference meetings, the group came up with 26 recommendations regarding areas of particular interest to women working in the CSC, including training, staffing development, anti-harassment programs, and support of female personnel (CSC, 1992). No similar kind of gathering appears to have been held in the past 15 years.

FEDERAL CORRECTIONAL OFFICER RECRUITS

Some researchers have investigated the attitudes and behaviours of correctional officers; however, very few have looked at the attitudes and behaviours of correctional officers as recruits and early in their careers (Bensimon, 2005b). A longitudinal study on recruits, the first of its kind in Canada, sought to examine recruits' experiences of training, their beliefs, and their attitudes as they embarked on a new career in the Correctional Service of Canada (Bensimon, 2004, 2005a, 2005b). In addition to providing interesting data on recruits as a whole, Bensimon's (2004, 2005a, 2005b) work also affords a glimpse at some of the ways in which female recruits are similar to and different from their male counterparts. For this reason and because a unique profile of female correctional officers is revealed, this study is reported here in depth.

In this Canadian longitudinal study of correctional officer recruits, Bensimon (2004, 2005a, 2005b) assessed both behavioural and attitudinal adjustments among recruits in the CSC. The study consisted of a series of questionnaires administered at various times over 15 months, spanning the three-month recruit-training period to the end of one year on the job. Examination of the data indicated no significant differences with respect to attrition rates between men and women who dropped out of the Correctional Training Program. The attrition rate for men was 37.4 percent and for women was 36.4 percent (Bensimon, 2005a). Clearly, more than one-third of those who passed the selection process decided that a career in corrections was not what they envisaged.

A total of 233 participants completed the first series of testing, and some interesting descriptive statistics emerged regarding the female recruits (Bensimon, 2005a). Just less than half the group was female (47.2 percent). Most of the women were single (59 percent), 34.5 percent were married or living in common-law relationships, and approximately 6 percent were separated or divorced. The men did not have as high an education level as the women. The majority of the women had a college education (42 percent) or a university education (38 percent), in both cases a higher percentage than the men (27 percent for college and 32 percent for university). The mean age for the women (30.6 years) was lower than that of the men (33.9 years). Similar to policing, correctional officer recruits tend to be in their late 20s or early 30s when they enter the profession. Their maturity is likely a benefit because of the significant life experiences that older recruits bring to their job.

The results of the study by Bensimon (2005a) highlighted some interesting gender differences among recruits. Women differed from men on a number of measures. On scales that tapped the sources of their motivation for correctional work, their support for rehabilitation, and their attitudes toward correctional work, female recruits had more positive responses than male recruits. Similarly, with questions concerning the importance of a human service orientation, women initially evidenced more positive responses than did the men, although the number of positive responses for this variable for both genders increased over time (Bensimon, 2005a).

In the final phase of the longitudinal study, recruits were evaluated over the course of their first 12 months on the job. Results indicated three areas where correctional officers (both male and female) showed very positive attitudes that did not change over time, from their first day of recruitment to the end of one year on the job. These three areas were empathy, desire to learn, and counselling or helping relationships (Bensimon, 2005b). These abilities were repeatedly endorsed by correctional officers as key skills that would enable them to do their job. Over the course of their first year, the officers continued to demonstrate high scores for positive attitudes in the following domains: (1) support for rehabilitation, (2) human service orientation, (3) attitudes toward correctional work, (4) sources of motivation for correctional work, (5) intrinsic job motivation, (6) correctional self-efficacy, (7) empathy, (8) deterrence, and (9) social desirability (Bensimon, 2005b). The researcher noted that despite decreases in some scores over the year, overall the scores for all of these nine areas were still high. In terms of significant differences between male and female officers, women tended to score higher on support for rehabilitation, empathy, and attitudes toward correctional work. Interestingly, similar results have been reported for female correctional officers in Canada who were found to have more positive attitudes than men toward the field of corrections and expressed more commitment than men to the correctional organization (Robinson et al., 1997).

Over the first 12 months of a correctional officer's service, mixed results were seen for the areas of organizational commitment (no differences between men and women), job satisfaction (no differences between men and women), attitudes toward inmates (significant decrease for both men and women over time, with more of a decrease for men), and some dimensions of empathy (Bensimon, 2005b). Within the empathy domain, three subscales were all in the average range: perspective taking, fantasy, and personal distress related to empathy. Of significance was the observation that men and women did not differ in their scores on these three subscales, except that women showed more positive scores on the scale that measured perspective taking. From these specific findings, the researcher hypothesized that these results were indicative of a lack of contact with the offender population during the first year on the job and speculated that most new recruits found themselves working in a fairly static role within an institution, counter to their expectations formed during training (Bensimon, 2005b).

The study also identified the major disadvantages to the job: shift work, stress related to the anticipation of violence, and environment and negative atmosphere (Bensimon, 2005b). Environment and negative atmosphere was further divided into three constituent parts: job insecurity (because their positions were not yet permanent), anxiety (due to a lack of recognition concerning their role and duties as correctional officers), and relations among colleagues (a perception that relations were strained, expressed as a lack of reciprocity and recognition in their relationships with co-workers).

A steady decrease in positive attitudes (from the 3-month to 12-month questionnaire) was seen in four areas: role conflict, role ambiguity, supervisory support, and job stress (Bensimon, 2005b). The decrease in positive attitudes toward role conflict reflected the monotony of a job that was routine and repetitive. The officers did not perceive themselves to be challenged, nor were they involved in a counselling role because of the static nature of their work (Bensimon, 2005b).

With respect to role ambiguity, the officers indicated they believed their skills were being underutilized. Related to this perceived underutilization was their degree of autonomy in decision-making situations, which also contributed to their sense of role ambiguity. In terms of supervisory support, the officers expressed concern that it was difficult to manage the requirements of the new environment. Job stress was expressed as a strain in trying to meet the needs of a unique client group: people who may be in crisis, who are likely being imprisoned against their will, and who are being exposed (sometimes daily) to very stressful situations (Bensimon, 2005b).

This longitudinal study of Canadian correctional officers as recruits and early career officers was the first of its kind (Bensimon, 2005b). This research sought to examine the recruits' experiences of training, their beliefs, and their attitudes as they embarked on a new career in the CSC. The objectives of the study included examination and analysis of their various attitudinal adjustments and behaviours over the course of training and into their first year of service as a correctional officer. Of paramount importance were the recommendations (based on the research) that could then be passed along to the CSC concerning recruitment strategies.

In his concluding remarks, Bensimon (2005b) stressed the importance of studying the attitudes and beliefs of correctional officers. In order for the CSC to be competitive in its retention of employees, correctional workers need to "feel supported, guided and fairly recognized at their full worth" (Bensimon, 2005b, p. 183). Without this sense of purpose in one's work, the tasks of a correctional officer can be described as routine, and even mundane. With respect to gender differences, interestingly, women tended to score more positively on dimensions of work motivation and attitudes, support for rehabilitation, and the importance of taking a human service orientation toward their work. That being said, issues of job stress and job satisfaction are of paramount concern to correctional personnel and administrators and will be discussed further in this chapter.

Community Supervision
Probation and Parole Officers

Probation officers are tasked with "monitoring the conduct and behaviour of criminal offenders serving probation terms" (HRSDC, n.d., ¶ 1). Parole officers are concerned with the reintegration of the offender into the community and supervise offenders who have been conditionally released into the community to serve the remainder of their sentence (HRSDC, n.d.). Because of the human service orientation of probation and parole officer work, this career is especially attractive for women who are interested in the social service side of criminal justice work.

According to the Probation Officers Association of Ontario (POAO), in 2000, the Ontario Ministry of Correctional Services employed more than 600 probation and parole officers, who were responsible for overseeing approximately 60,000 adult offenders residing in the community. The POAO maintained that the average caseload for a probation and parole (P&P) officer was 117 offenders, significantly higher than the national average estimate of 70 offenders per officer (POAO, 2000). In 2000, the Ministry of Community and Social Services also employed approximately 200 probation officers, who were responsible for between 9,000 and 10,000 young offenders (POAO, 2000). In 2004, responsibility for the supervision of youth in conflict with the law was shifted to the new Ontario Ministry of Children and Youth Services (National Union of Public and General Employees, 2004).

Unlike some other positions in the criminal justice system in Canada (such as correctional officer or police officer), P&P officers require a university degree, which may explain why, on the whole, P&P officers tend to be better educated than other justice-related personnel (Statistics Canada, 2002). The degree requirement stems from the role that P&P officers play in the protection of the public and the need to ensure that candidates for the job are of the "highest calibre" (Ontario, Ministry of Community Safety and Correctional

Services [MCSCS], 2006, ¶ 2). In addition, candidates need to have excellent written and verbal communication skills, counselling and assessment skills, and the ability to establish a rapport and maintain a relationship with their clients and stakeholders (Ontario, MCSCS, 2006). After new P&P officers are hired, they complete a basic training program that emphasizes the latest "research and principles of effective correctional intervention and programming" (Ontario, MCSCS, 2006, ¶ 3).

The job of a probation and parole officer requires their staying current with both research in the field and the most up-to-date intervention methods (POAO, 2000). In addition to supervising offenders and enforcing the different types of supervision orders, P&P officers may be required to provide some educational services and counselling to help victims make informed decisions (POAO, 2000). Public education is also stressed as a means of increasing awareness about issues such as crime prevention (POAO, 2000).

A P&P officer's duties include the supervision of offenders who are in the community on parole, on probation, on a conditional sentence, or on a conditional supervision order (POAO, 2000). P&P officers ensure that offenders comply with their restitution orders and complete their community service. Good written communication skills help in the preparation of pre-sentence, pre-disposition, and pre-parole reports. Because a large part of a P&P officer's job involves counselling offenders in areas such as life skills and employment skills, interpersonal communication skills are also needed (POAO, 2000). Case management skills are needed when acting as a link between institutions and the community and when assessing risk (POAO, 2000). In addition to liaising with victims for the purposes of education, referrals, and advocacy, P&P officers also need to act as liaisons with various community groups (POAO, 2000).

According to Statistics Canada, approximately 4,600 probation and parole officers were employed in Canada in 1996, a 26 percent increase over 1991 (Statistics Canada, 2002). Most (66 percent) were between 25 and 44 years of age in 1996. Their average age of 40 was similar to the average age of police, legal, and all justice personnel in Canada for that year (Statistics Canada, 2002). On average, a P&P officer earned $43,403, 12 percent less (on average) than other justice personnel employed in Canada in 1995. Their lower income may be explained by their lower entry-level wages, which were 23 percent less than the wages for entry-level police and 12 percent less than the wages for entry-level correctional officers (Statistics Canada, 2002). According to the most recent census information available, in 2001, 3,735 women accounted for just more than half (54 percent) of all probation and parole officers, an increase of 4 percent from 10 years earlier when half of the total of 3,770 P&P officers were women (Statistics Canada, 2005b). Interestingly, in this area of the justice system, women comprise the majority of employees, and the average worker has a higher level of education than the average criminal justice worker; however, the average salary for P&P officers is lower than the average salary of other criminal justice system personnel.

Parole Boards

Canada has the National Parole Board (NPB) and two provincial parole boards, in Ontario and Quebec (NPB, 2007b). The NPB is an administrative tribunal that operates as an independent body and is responsible for determining whether offenders are suitable for conditional release from federal penitentiaries and from facilities in provinces and territories where no parole board exists (NPB, 2005). The NPB is also responsible for granting pardons to people who have been convicted of committing an offence in the past and who are now able to show that they are law-abiding citizens (NPB, 2005). Candidates for a position on the NPB must have attained an adequate educational level (at minimum, a secondary school diploma, but a postsecondary degree is an asset), must have experience with decision-making, and must have some appreciation or understanding regarding issues related to the criminal justice system in Canada (NPB, 2005). They must also know the applicable acts (the *Corrections and Conditional Release Act* and the *Criminal Records Act*). A suitable candidate for the NPB will be capable of understanding and synthesizing information from the courts, able to work under considerable pressure and time constraints, and have proven skills as an effective communicator (NPB, 2005). Other ideal characteristics include being flexible and adaptive; being an independent thinker; being sensitive to gender, Aboriginal, and multicultural issues; and having the ability to be discreet when managing sensitive material (NPB, 2005). In some geographic locations, members of the NPB may be required to be proficient in both official languages.

According to the NPB website, in 2007, 86 people were employed as National Parole Board members across Canada: half employed part-time and half employed full-time (NPB, 2007a). From a cursory inspection of the names of the NPB members, approximately 40 percent of the NPB members were women. Just more than 44 percent of those employed full-time were women, and 35 percent of those employed part-time were women (NPB, 2007a). The percentage of women on the NPB as full-time members differs across the various regions. Representation was highest for women in the Prairies, where more than 75 percent of the full-time members were women. In contrast, women's representation as full-time members varied from a low of 25 percent (in the Atlantic region) to a high of 40 percent for the Quebec region. For Ontario and the Pacific region, women comprised 37.5 percent and 33 percent of the full-time NPB members, respectively.

Barriers to Employment in the Correctional System

Occupational Interests

Approximately 25 years ago, at about the same time that careers in criminal justice for women were beginning to open up in the United States, Golden (1982) surveyed a sample of 288 criminal justice students for their interest in various criminal justice–related jobs. Golden found that female students showed a higher interest in positions considered to be more traditionally female, such as juvenile probation officer and youth service worker. Less interest was expressed by the women (compared with the men) for occupations traditionally considered to be male, such as patrol officer.

This kind of gendered occupational interest could pose a barrier to women whose specific interests might limit the options available to them, both in the criminal justice field overall and in the correctional system in particular. It would be interesting to attempt to replicate Golden's (1982) study to see whether any significant change has occurred in the last 25 years regarding the occupational interests of female criminal justice students. One could hypothesize that a similar study would find less of a gendered influence on job preferences today, given the large influx of women into the criminal justice field over the last 25 years, in both the United States and Canada.

Role Traps and Stereotypes

Jurik (1988) noted that women who were employed as correctional officers needed to develop certain strategies to avoid both organizational and interactional barriers that might hinder their career advancement. Organizational barriers were defined as those "character-istics that shape worker attitudes and performance: the power structure, and the relative proportions of social types employed in the organization" (Jurik, 1988, p. 291). Interactional barriers, which are faced by women in non-traditional occupational roles, are caused by the sexist attitudes of the people they work with—subordinates, peers, supervisors, and clients (Jurik, 1988). These attitudes may result in women being harassed and denied information critical to their organizational survival (Jurik, 1988).

Zimmer's (1986) typology of female correctional officers' work styles classified these women as falling into one of three roles: the institutional role, the modified role, or the inventive role. Women who tried to do their job in the same manner as the male officers were thought to be in the institutional role. Female correctional officers in this role might express themselves in the following manner:

> When I put on this uniform and this badge, I'm a prison guard and that's all the inmate needs to know. If he does what he's supposed to do, we'll have no trouble. If he decides to break the rules, then I'm here to enforce them—just the same as any other officer. Once the inmate understands that, there's no problem. (Zimmer, 1986, p. 111)

Those women who expressed doubt that they could perform the job in the way the men did, who sought the protection of their male colleagues, and who settled for what would be traditionally seen as women's roles in the institution would be classified as being in the modified role. These women seemed to embrace the notion that they could not be equal to men on the job and believed that this inequality did not just apply to themselves but was extended to all women. In this sense, they could be seen to be in direct opposition (in terms of their beliefs about women's appropriate roles in the institution) to those in the institu-tional role. The following quotation encapsulates a woman in this modified role:

> Any woman who starts to believe that she can compete with the men here is in serious trouble. Women aren't built the same as men—we're not built to fight. If an inmate decides to make trouble, there's just no way he's going to be stopped by a woman. (Zimmer, 1986, p. 122)

Women in the inventive role sought to work in posts where face-to-face inmate contact was high—for example, on housing units or on work details. These women would then be able to get to know the inmates better and to learn more about their backgrounds, their lives, and their problems. These women stressed the importance of knowing the inmate as an individual person, which would, in turn, enable them to better perform their job. The following is an example of how this strategy could work:

> I know the guys on this unit so well that when I come on duty I can tell right away who is mad at whom, who is upset, who got a bad letter from home, etc. Instead of letting them go at each other, I can usually stop trouble before it begins by giving them a chance to talk these things out. (Zimmer, 1986, p. 130)

Zimmer (1986) noted that no female guard would ever be forced to adopt one of these three roles, but they might, at different points in their careers, find themselves making a conscious decision about the kind of role they wanted to play in the institution. According to Zimmer (1986), the choice an individual makes depends on a number of factors, including personality characteristics, situational circumstances, interactions with inmates, and subjective responses to on-the-job experiences. Most women would be predisposed to fill positions in which they would either be on an equal footing with men or have a more limited role than men, predispositions that Zimmer hypothesized to be linked to sex-role attitudes, especially those that concerned women's innate abilities and their appropriate role in society (Zimmer, 1986).

Interestingly, in a study by Belknap (2004) looking at women correctional officers in the United States, more of her sample (48.6 percent) self-identified as following the institutional style compared with Zimmer's sample (11 percent). More than half (51.4 percent) saw themselves as following the inventive style, similar to Zimmer's sample where 46 percent were assigned this style. None of Belknap's sample of women correctional officers self-identified as fitting the modified role, in contrast to Zimmer's (1986) study, in which 43 percent were assigned the modified role.

Zimmer's (1986) typology has been described as static because it does not address the day-to-day situations in which a worker handles a particular situation with inconsistencies or differences (Jurik, 1988). Although Zimmer's typology is an efficient way to conceptualize the various roles that a female correctional officer may favour, it does not fully capture why worker styles can change (Jurik, 1988). In comparison with Zimmer's views, Jurik (1986) favoured the conceptual reframing of the occupational styles to a more positive image, in which the worker projected a positive image on the workplace. Female correctional officers could then be seen as "replacing derogatory images with more positive presentations of self, that is, women as competent, collegial and promotable" (Jurik, 1988, p. 293).

Various role traps and stereotypes have been theorized to apply to female correctional workers (Kanter, 1977, cited in Jurik, 1988; Zimmer, 1986). About 20 years ago, some researchers applied the concept of tokenism to female correctional workers (Kanter, 1977, cited in Jurik, 1988). At that time, the number of women working in corrections was low compared with today. Token status was defined as being a member of a collection of people who represent less than 15 percent of a total group. Consequences of tokenism were thought to include high degrees of performance pressure and visibility within an organization, role encapsulation, and boundary heightening (that is, emphasizing the unique qualities about the members of a group, which can then be distorted to result in stereotyping) (Kanter, 1977, cited in Jurik, 1988). Although women now comprise more than 15 percent of the workforce in corrections, these consequences may still exist for some women working in non-traditional occupations.

When stereotypes exist, they form role traps that maintain the distance between the tokens and the dominant group (Jurik, 1988). A number of informal stereotypes have been said to exist for women who work in occupations not traditionally filled by females: the pet, the seductress, the iron maiden, and the mother. The pet is described as a woman who is weak, innocent, and incompetent, akin to a little sister who needs some sort of protection from a male. The seductress is "sexually desirable, potentially available, often manipulative, and as incompetent as the little sister" (Jurik, 1988, p. 292). The iron maiden is just that—a woman who is seen as being competent, but who is cold, harsh, and asexual. Lastly, the mother is "supportive, scolding, and incapable of independent action" (Jurik, 1988, p. 242). In all these stereotypes, the female correctional officer, as a woman working in a traditionally male role, is seen as having characteristics that make her an undesirable colleague.

The strategies that female officers have used to avoid role traps and stereotypes include casting a professional image, using humour, demonstrating unique skills, taking a team approach, and enhancing visibility through the use of sponsorship (Jurik, 1988). Each strategy has its pros and cons. Those who have a professional demeanour may effectively remove any problems related to the perception of female officer sexuality; however, they might be prone to "Queen Bee" syndrome, where very rule-minded behaviour may be seen in a negative light by co-workers and supervisors (Kanter, 1977, cited in Jurik, 1988, p. 297). Similarly, those who are able to use humour might find it an effective strategy, but it doesn't always work. For some, humour is not an option as a strategy to avoid role traps and stereotypes (Jurik, 1988).

By demonstrating a unique skill, a woman can establish competence in a way that allows others to appreciate her unique contributions to the workplace. As an example, a woman who has excellent communication and crisis management abilities might find that she is able to use these skills in an effective manner in the prison setting. The use of this unique skill may enable a female officer to enhance her profile in a manner that is less threatening to her male colleagues (Jurik, 1988).

Officers who are able to take a team approach may be seen to avoid role traps and stereotypes because the rapport among their colleagues is enhanced when, in tough situations, the team-oriented players are there to help the others. Lastly, making effective use of sponsorship involves "striking a balance between isolation and being too closely identified with a sponsor" (Jurik, 1988, p. 301). Informal mentoring can be an effective strategy; however, if an officer seeks too much sponsorship she may be viewed not as being competent but as being overly dependent on another officer. These kinds of strategies are individual-level adaptations, and even when such strategies are used, they are not always successful in avoiding negative stereotypes. In the absence of organized support to assist the integration of female correctional officers into men's facilities, women have often been left to make these kinds of individual-level adaptations on their own (Jurik, 1988).

Job Stress and Job Satisfaction

Job Stress

Stress needs to be considered from both an individual and an organizational perspective. Occupational or workplace stress has been described as any disturbance that affects individuals in terms of their social, psychological, or physiological functioning; arises in response to a condition that exists in the environment or at work; and poses a threat, perceived or real, to a person's safety or well-being (Armstrong & Griffin, 2004). Not only does stress negatively affect the individual but it can also have negative effects on the organization. When the staff of an organization is stressed, job satisfaction may be low, and the organization may experience high absentee rates, poor morale, internal conflicts, and difficulties retaining staff. Absenteeism has been associated with job stress, job satisfaction, organizational commitment, and personal characteristics (Lambert, Edwards, Camp, & Saylor, 2005).

When considering stress in the workplace, a pioneer in the field of stress must first be acknowledged. Hans Selye, a medical scientist from the University of Montreal, was the first person to define stress as "the nonspecific response of the body to any demand" (1976, p. 1). According to Selye, stress could result from both pleasant and unpleasant conditions. Further, Selye believed that the nature of stress depended on how a person received it. That is, stress was not necessarily something bad. The kind of stress brought on by pleasant conditions was referred to as *eustress*, from the Greek *eu*, which means *good*. Stress brought on by unpleasant conditions was termed *distress*, from the Latin *dis*, which means *bad* (Selye, 1976, p. 74).

Selye was interested in the physical effects of stress on the body. He noted that stress led to changes in various parts of the body (for example, enlarged adrenal glands, shrunken thymus and lymph nodes, ulcerated stomachs), which led him to conclude that the effects of stress caused a syndrome he termed the general adaptation syndrome (GAS) (Selye, 1976). Selye (1976) operationally defined stress as "the state manifested by a specific syndrome which consists of all the nonspecifically-induced changes within a biologic system" (p. 64). He was clear to point out that stress was not something that should be avoided, because the human body will always be under some sort of stress, even while sleeping. He eloquently noted that "stress can be avoided only by dying" (Selye, 1976, p. 63). Although Selye's concept of stress and his operational definition of stress focused on the physical nature of stress, more recent attention has been paid to the psychological nature of stress and its effects (Huckabee, 1992).

JOB STRESS AND CORRECTIONAL WORK

Although sources of stress for correctional officers in Canada are varied, the sparse research on Canadian correctional officers suggests that, for the most part, officers are able to adequately cope with the stressors they encounter (Griffiths, 2004). In his review of the stressors associated with correctional work, Griffiths identified some threats to personal safety that most correctional officers face daily, including violence and exposure to disease (HIV/AIDS, tuberculosis, and hepatitis). Compounding this stress is the fact that correctional officers do not know which inmates in their institution are potential disease threats (for example, they don't know who is HIV positive). Accordingly, they must operate as if every inmate is a potential disease threat and take universal precautions to manage their exposure to potentially dangerous bodily fluids (Griffiths, 2004).

In a large study of Canadian correctional officers, Millson (2002) found similar results: the largest predictor of stress was the perception of personal security. Variables related to the operation of the organization were also predictors of stress: staff empowerment, the impact of shift work, job security, and an understanding of work procedures (Millson, 2002). Others have found that a lack of respect or lack of support from senior management and the increased emphasis on inmate rights are sources of stress (Griffiths, 2004). Additionally, stressors related to the nature of the job itself (shift work, lack of training, the need to multi-task, negative effects on one's family) are common (Griffiths, 2004). Frequently, the institutional environment itself is viewed as a source of stress (Griffiths, 2004).

Most of the research on stress and correctional work has focused on the experiences of correctional officers (Cheek & Miller, 1983; Dollard & Winefield, 1994; Huckabee, 1992; Keinan & Malach-Pines, 2007; Pollak & Sigler, 1998). Research into stress levels among correctional supervisors found that stress levels were low for this group, and no differences were seen between the stress levels of male and female supervisors (Owen, 2006). In a Canadian study of stress levels among correctional officers in northern Ontario, similarly low levels of stress were reported (Pollak & Sigler, 1998). Contrary to this finding, most of the research on correctional officers has found that they experience considerable levels of stress on the job, as evidenced by their high rates of divorce and such serious health problems as hypertension and heart disease (Cheek & Miller, 1983; Huckabee, 1992; Lambert, Hogan, Camp, & Ventura, 2006). However, some have suggested that correctional officers tend not to acknowledge their stress because such an admission might imply weakness on their part (Cheek & Miller, 1983). Some recent evidence suggests that despite their high levels of stress and burnout, correctional officers appear satisfied with their work and do not plan on leaving their jobs in the future (Keinan & Malach-Pines, 2007).

In 1992, Robert Huckabee provided an overview of the research conducted to that date on stress in corrections. This work has been extensively referenced because it served as an effective summary of the research in the area and, more importantly, made some sage recommendations about the direction the field needed to move toward. Huckabee (1992) noted that research had, until that point, been very much "hit and miss"—that is, not well organized in terms of addressing specific patterns or themes (p. 479). He recommended the research become more systematic to address questions about how much stress was in correctional work, how it manifested itself, where it was located, what it correlated with, and how it could be reduced or eliminated (Huckabee, 1992). He concluded that "there seems to be no clear consensus as to which factors can be consistently correlated with stress in corrections" and that "much work is needed in this area" (Huckabee, 1992, p. 484).

Considerable research has been carried out looking at stress and correctional work in many countries, including the United States (Armstrong & Griffin, 2004; Auerbach, Quick, & Pegg, 2003; Cheek & Miller, 1983; Lambert et al., 2006; Owen, 2006; Tewksbury & Higgins, 2006), Canada (Pollak & Sigler, 1998), Israel (Keinan & Malach-Pines, 2007), South Korea (Moon & Maxwell, 2004), and Australia (Brough & Williams, 2007), to name a few. Early research in the area of stress and corrections tended not to focus on gender as a variable of interest; research that did focus on gender as a variable tended to be in the minority (Jurik, 1988), likely reflective of the low percentage of women employed in these predominantly male roles. Because increasing numbers of women are being employed in correctional work, more recent studies have been able to focus exclusively on women or to include enough women in their samples to allow for comparisons to be made with men in similar jobs (Armstrong & Griffin, 2004; Auerbach et al., 2003; Moon & Maxwell, 2004; Triplett, Mullings, & Scarborough, 1999).

Correctional workers face a unique set of stressors associated with their jobs, and some have asserted that correctional officers face multiple sources of strain (Dollard & Winefield, 1994). Researchers have proposed that among the environmental correlates of stress, an institution's culture can be seen as a stressor, as can the various administrative and organizational practices of the prison, the physical characteristics of the environment, and the social climate of the workplace (Armstrong & Griffin, 2004). These stressors, in combination with such factors as perceptions of safety, dangerousness, and powerlessness, can contribute to an individual's level of stress. Individuals who have more contact with offenders (such as custody personnel) are likely to have more job stress than non-custody personnel, who do not work directly with offenders (Lambert et al., 2006). Job stress has also been found to increase as the length of time working at a correctional facility increases (Lambert et al., 2006). The importance of supervisor support has also been identified as a key factor in addressing occupational stress in correctional officers (Brough & Williams, 2007). Furthermore, the level of work stress has been shown to be a determinant of employees' satisfaction with their supervisor in a correctional setting (Tewksbury & Higgins, 2006).

Stress also has personal correlates (Armstrong & Griffin, 2004). Various social structural factors, such as age, race, and gender, have been studied as stress correlates (Armstrong & Griffin, 2004), as have combinations of factors (such as poor diet, inactivity, overeating, smoking, lack of exercise, and drinking to excess), which may serve as one unique kind of stressor (Pollak & Sigler, 1998). In addition to higher levels of job stress, correctional officers have also reported much lower levels of job satisfaction than non-custody correctional personnel (Lambert et al., 2006). Their higher stress levels are not surprising considering the obvious link between experiencing stressors on the job and feeling a sense of satisfaction at work.

In a recent meta-analysis, Dowden and Tellier (2004) analyzed 20 studies for an examination of job stress in correctional workers. This statistical technique allowed the researchers to aggregate the results of a group of studies (that had been conducted independently) to come to a conclusion regarding the results (Dowden & Tellier, 2004). In the majority (more than 75 percent) of the effect sizes studied, the samples were composed of mainly male officers, and nearly three-quarters comprised almost entirely Caucasian samples.

Dowden and Tellier's results suggested demographic variables had an unimpressive effect on correctional stress, and when individual variables were examined, the researchers found that gender, education, marital status, and number of children were all very weak predictors. Much stronger predictors were found for work-related attitudes, such as participation in decision-making, commitment, and job satisfaction. These factors showed significant negative effects on stress. That is, those officers who were engaged in decision-making, who were committed to the organization, and who had higher job satisfaction were less likely to express work stress. They also found that intent to leave the job was a positive predictor of work stress: those employees who expressed a desire to leave their job were more likely to experience higher levels of job stress (Dowden & Tellier, 2004). Additionally, the researchers found that perceived dangerousness was also linked to significantly higher levels of work stress. In this meta-analysis, little support was found for the role of job characteristics.

JOB STRESS SPECIFIC TO WOMEN WORKING IN CORRECTIONS

Huckabee (1992) highlighted some important considerations regarding women's experiences of stress in the correctional context, including experiences of harassment and discrimination in which female correctional officers reported more problems with the behaviour of male co-workers than with the male inmates they were guarding (Pogrebin & Poole, 1998; Zimmer, 1986). To compound the issue, an additional stressor that served to increase the negative experiences was supervisory inaction (Zimmer, 1986). Higher stress levels experienced by women correctional officers (compared with their male counterparts) may be explained by women's experiences of sexism on the job (Jurik, 1988; Lovrish & Stohr, 1993). In these situations, sexism could be "manifested in the behaviors of coworkers and supervisors which may reflect either intentional or unwitting discrimination, sexual and/or gender harassment (either *quid pro quo* or a more subtle hostility), or a conflict between gender-based family roles and work roles" (Lovrich & Stohr, 1993, p. 78).

Some stressors specific to women have been identified in the more recent literature. Women employed as juvenile correctional officers reported higher levels of stress resulting from both lack of agency support and everyday activities of the job (Auerbach et al., 2003). Women have also been reported to experience greater stress levels at work when behaviour-based work–home conflict was evident (Triplett et al., 1999). The higher levels of work–home conflict seen for women were not surprising given the very different cultural expectations for women both at home and at work. As Triplett et al. (1999) noted, their findings suggested women are still struggling to find a way to deal with this work–home conflict. Women correctional officers (and younger officers) have been found to report significantly more health-related concerns than men and older officers (Armstrong & Griffin, 2004).

Job Satisfaction

Job satisfaction is a concept that has been studied frequently, and despite the lack of a single agreed-upon definition of this concept, the general agreement is that job satisfaction involves "a subjective, individual-level feeling reflecting whether a person's needs are or are not being met by a particular job" (Lambert, Hogan, & Barton, 2002, p. 116). Studies on job satisfaction among correctional workers tend to use global measures of job satisfaction, in which individuals are asked to form their own opinion about their overall level of job satisfaction (Lambert et al., 2002).

JOB SATISFACTION AND CORRECTIONAL WORK

In recent years, researchers have shown an increased interest in studying factors that affect job satisfaction in correctional workers (Griffin, 2001; Jurik & Halemba, 1984; Jurik, Halemba, Musheno, & Boyle, 1987; Lambert et al., 2002; Lovrich & Stohr, 1993; Tewksbury & Higgins, 2006). The reason for this interest is pragmatic. When people have high levels of job satisfaction, they tend to engage in positive behaviours (such as support for rehabilitation and performance) (Lambert et al., 2002). On the other hand, low levels of job satisfaction have been associated with more negative kinds of behaviours, such as absenteeism and job turnover (Lambert et al., 2002). Organizations that want to attract and retain quality staff need to maximize job satisfaction. Correctional services are no different from any other corporation when it comes to these kinds of human resources issues. Therefore, they need to increase job satisfaction among correctional workers. As with job stress, correlates of job satisfaction tend to fall into one of two groups: personal characteristics and work environment (Lambert et al., 2002). In correctional settings, factors related to work environment appear to have more of an effect on job satisfaction than personal factors (Griffin, 2001; Lambert et al., 2002).

Personal characteristics include background factors (educational level, specifics regarding a person's upbringing), demographic factors (gender, age, race, ethnicity), and other factors (family income, religion, distance from work), although the latter tend to be infrequently investigated (Lambert et al., 2002). These sorts of personal characteristics are the attributes that we take to our jobs, and they tend to shape the way we interpret the world around us.

Lambert et al. (2002), in their recent review of the correctional literature, noted the research that looked at job satisfaction and educational levels reported mixed results. However, they came to the tentative conclusion that a negative relationship existed between education level and job satisfaction among correctional officers. They reported no overall relationship between job satisfaction and race and no clear link between gender and job satisfaction. Although the reviewers reported that age and tenure related to job satisfaction, the results were mixed (Lambert et al., 2002).

Work environment is more than the workplace setting; it consists of "the factors or characteristics that comprise the overall work conditions and situations for an employee, both tangible and intangible" (Lambert et al., 2002, p. 125). The work environment can be divided into two areas: the organizational structure (how the organization operates and manages staff) and the characteristics of the job (what the job entails) (Lambert et al., 2002). Factors that are considered part of the work environment and have been studied for their possible links to job satisfaction include stressors and job stress, autonomy and participation, supervision and administration, managerial approaches, position factors, security level, and dangerousness (Lambert et al., 2002; Reisig & Lovrich, 1998).

Of these factors, job stress and stressors have been studied most frequently for their possible relationship to job satisfaction. For the most part, the research literature has shown a negative association between these two variables: the greater the job stress, the lower the job satisfaction among correctional staff, especially correctional officers (Lambert et al., 2002). In addition, job autonomy and participation in decision-making are positively linked to job satisfaction, as are positive attitudes toward supervisors and administration (Lambert et al., 2002). From their review of the literature, Lambert et al. (2002) concluded that no significant relationships existed between job satisfaction and security level, financial factors, or perceived dangerousness.

JOB SATISFACTION IN WOMEN WORKING IN CORRECTIONS

The literature specific to women's job satisfaction in correctional settings is fairly sparse. However, researchers found that female correctional employees reported lower levels of job satisfaction than male correctional staff, which, they pointed out, was counter to the findings in the majority of the literature (Lambert et al., 2006). Most other studies have not reported significant relationships between gender and job satisfaction (Jurik & Halemba, 1984; Moon & Maxwell, 2004). In Lambert et al.'s (2002) review of the recent literature, gender did not appear to have any relationship with job satisfaction.

In a recent study, Griffin (2001) found that although male and female correctional officers shared similar levels of job satisfaction, the factors that influenced their job satisfaction differed. Females tended to believe that the work environment was safer than did the men, yet the women viewed themselves as being more vulnerable in this setting. Perhaps because the male correctional officers had embraced the stereotypical image of a dominant, aggressive, and authoritarian guard, they viewed the setting as more dangerous (Griffin, 2001). As reported in earlier studies, the women also valued the human service aspect of the work (Griffin, 2001; Jurik & Halemba, 1984). According to this study, women and men differ very little in their level of job satisfaction, but they do differ in why they find the job satisfying (Griffin, 2001). In this sense, gender may be seen to play a "moderating role in the relationship between organizational climate and job satisfaction" (Griffin, 2001, p. 228).

THE CONSEQUENCES OF JOB SATISFACTION IN CORRECTIONAL STAFF

Research has looked at the consequences of low and high job satisfaction on variables such as productivity, staff turnover, and absenteeism. High levels of job satisfaction have been associated with a number of positive outcomes, such as motivated workers and good productivity, whereas low levels of job satisfaction have been linked with negative outcomes, such as high absenteeism and job turnover (Lambert et al., 2002). In the correctional literature, a number of studies have found support for a relationship between high levels of job satisfaction and positive work outcomes, such as better staff–inmate relations, safer environments, and better correctional standards and conditions (Lambert et al., 2002).

Absenteeism, turnover, tardiness, poor or hostile relations between staff and management, and psychological withdrawal from the job are all examples of negative behaviours associated with low levels of job satisfaction in the non-correctional literature (Lambert et al., 2002). In their review of the literature, Lambert et al. (2002) noted a relationship between low levels of job satisfaction and negative work behaviour. However, only turnover and, to a lesser extent, absenteeism were researched to any degree. A negative relationship between staff turnover (or turnover intent) and job satisfaction was reported in their literature review (Lambert et al., 2002). The reviewers noted that a negative relationship between job satisfaction and absenteeism also existed, but this relationship had only been researched in two studies (Lambert et al., 2002).

The conclusion from Lambert et al.'s (2002) thorough review of the job satisfaction literature among correctional staff is that correctional administrators should be paying attention to job satisfaction. To be accountable, administrators should be concerned with retaining their well-trained staff members, because each trained employee represents a considerable financial commitment. In addition, high job satisfaction is associated with a plethora of positive outcomes for the organization. Lambert et al. (2002) recommended that to improve job satisfaction among correctional staff, administrators should focus on the work variables that can be changed, not the staff's personal characteristics. Thus, ensuring that job stress is lowered should be a priority. Other ways that administration can work to improve job satisfaction in their staff are to increase autonomy and participation in the decision-making process, provide an open line of communication between staff and management, increase positive feedback to staff, and provide fair promotional opportunities (Lambert et al., 2002).

Salient Issues for Staff in the Canadian Correctional System

A number of different issues face those working in the correctional system in Canada, regardless of whether they are male or female. Despite few studies specific to Canada, the research from other countries is clearly applicable to those working in the Canadian correctional system. Cross-gender staffing is an issue for staff regardless of whether a worker is a male employed in a female prison or a female employed in a male prison. The research into this issue in the United States is relevant to workers in Canadian prisons. Similarly, the dangers of working in a prison exist for both men and women, and many of the issues identified in American studies are also pertinent in a Canadian context. Regardless of whether one works in a Canadian or American prison, in some situations women or men may be perceived to be more or less vulnerable than the opposite sex, and some issues will be more salient to one sex than the other. For these situations, the differences are highlighted and commented upon.

Cross-Gender Staffing Issues

The debate regarding cross-gender staffing is not a new one, but was highlighted as an issue following the release of the Arbour report in 1996. In her report, Madam Justice Louise Arbour made a number of recommendations specific to the issue of cross-gender staffing. She recommended, among other things, that at least one federal women's institution not be staffed with any men in the living units. She further suggested that explicit protocols be put into place regarding male access to the living units to ensure that men were always paired with a female staff member when on patrol, that men not patrol the living units at night, and that men be required to announce their presence on a living unit or at a woman's cell or room. Justice Arbour recommended that the CSC's sexual harassment policy be extended to apply to both inmates and staff. In addition, recommendations were made concerning the design of the new prisons, to ensure appropriate levels of privacy for inmates, especially when bathing, using the washroom, and dressing and undressing. For areas where inmates were being closely monitored, she recommended the installation of modesty barriers.

In terms of cross-gender monitoring, Justice Arbour recommended that

> a woman be appointed to monitor and report annually for the next three years following the opening of each new regional facility, to the Deputy Commissioner for Women on the implementation of the cross-gender staffing policy in the living units of the new institutions, and on related issues, including the effectiveness of the extension of the sexual harassment policy to the protection of inmates. (Canada, Commission of Inquiry, 1996, p. 253)

The recommendations specific to the cross-gender monitor included the suggestion that the monitor be independent from the CSC and have confidential access to both inmates and staff. The mandate of the monitor was to assess the system, not the individuals per se, and to recommend improvements to the system (Canada, Commission of Inquiry, 1996). Further, any reports generated should be made public, and the deputy commissioner for women should, after three years, make recommendations to the commissioner regarding the future of the cross-gender staffing policy, taking into account the findings of the monitor (Canada, Commission of Inquiry, 1996).

The first of three cross-gender monitoring reports was released in October 1998 (CSC, 1998). The purpose of the monitoring project was to "assess the systematic impact of cross-gender staffing in federally sentenced women's facilities, to identify operations and policy issues and to make appropriate recommendations" (CSC, 1998, ¶ 2). In this first report, the monitor recommended that inmate grievance data should be sorted according to the types of complaints and grievances, and sexual harassment complaints and grievances should be given their own code in the grievance system (CSC, 1998). The monitor also recommended a clear policy regarding the definition and prohibition of sexual harassment and the accompanying penalties regarding sexual harassment of offenders by staff members. The first annual report was to act as a blueprint for the subsequent monitoring of cross-gender staffing in the CSC.

The second report included an in-depth investigation into such issues as employment, staff training, sexual harassment, privacy, grievances, abuse of power, special needs offenders, and Aboriginal women (CSC, 2000). Contained in the second report were five interim recommendations, including the continuance of men in front-line staffing positions, as long as their numbers did not exceed 20 percent of all primary workers. Emphasis was also placed on the importance of recruitment, screening, and training of personnel. A second recommendation was that the screening and training apply not only to CSC employees but also to contract staff. According to the third interim recommendation, men's night-time contact with inmates should be restricted. A fourth recommendation related to the availability of adequate resources for the training and screening of staff. The last recommendation was that, to show respect and dignity to the women, staff should always knock and wait for a response prior to entering a woman's room, unless the staff have reason to suspect an emergency (CSC, 2000).

The third and final annual report of the cross-gender monitoring project was completed in 2001 (Lajeunesse, Jefferson, Nuffield, & Majury, 2000). This report recommended the screening of all personnel, women-centred training for all staff, and the availability of sufficient resources to accomplish both. The monitor also recommended that women never be left alone with men in unobserved areas and that the CSC complete a review to determine which (if any) positions should be designated female only. A series of recommendations was offered to better deal with allegations of sexual harassment and sexual misconduct. Recommendations were also made concerning the correctional investigator's role. The most striking recommendation in the final report was that there be "an end to the use of male staff members as front-line primary workers (PWs) in facilities for federally sentenced women inmates" (Lajeunesse et al., 2000, p. 1).

Around the same time that the monitor's report was being completed, the Canadian Human Rights Commission (CHRC) began a review of how women offenders were treated by the CSC (CHRC, 2003). This review was in response to a complaint laid by the Canadian Association of Elizabeth Fry Societies and the National Women's Association of Canada (CSC, 2005). In its report, the CHRC determined that the CSC should "vigorously pursue other alternatives before impairing the employment rights of men in such a fashion" (CHRC, 2003, p. 43). The CHRC noted that the CSC had undertaken a number of steps in an attempt to reduce the probability that staff would harass offenders, and the CHRC supported the continued use of a gender-neutral staffing policy by the CSC. The CSC implemented a special protocol for men in front-line positions, women-centred training was offered to staff, and the selection process for staff was improved. The CHRC reiterated in its recommendations the importance of the steps that had already been taken and made specific recommendations that "the *National Operational Protocol—Front Line Staffing* be made into a formal policy in the form of a Commissioner's Directive or Standard Operating Procedure" (CHRC, 2003, p. 44). In addition, the CHRC recommended that women-centred training (and a refresher course) be mandatory and that an independent external evaluator assess the national protocol after two years.

The CSC began both an internal and external consultation process on the recommendations contained in the report of the cross-gender monitoring project (CSC, 2005). In its response to the report, the CSC made reference to the CHRC report in which the employment of men as front-line workers was supported. The CSC also reported on the results of its consultations and indicated that the majority of those consulted disagreed with the monitor's assertion that men should not be allowed to be employed as front-line workers in women's facilities. Although in disagreement with the monitor's recommendation here, the CSC publicly acknowledged the importance of the monitor's report because it reflected

> a strong commitment to ensuring that women's corrections in Canada continues to evolve within a frame that respects the law, the right of women offenders to be protected from discrimination and contributes to public safety ... CSC wishes to assure the public, staff, women offenders and stakeholders that it is committed to strengthening its gender- and rights-based analysis required to meet the challenge of designing and delivering effective corrections for women offenders. (CSC, 2005, p. 3)

A number of initiatives were implemented to address cross-gender staffing concerns (CSC, 2005). The women-centred training program was updated to fit with the national operational protocol. A process was introduced to address issues related to the deployment of primary workers (to ensure that the staff was prepared to work in a women-centred environment). The CSC has also enhanced and standardized its selection process for primary workers and has developed a process to select assistant team leaders (CSC, 2005). Men continue to be employed as primary workers in federal women's prisons in Canada.

Sexual Relationships with Inmates

Although sexual relationships between correctional staff and inmates are isolated incidents, reports of this behaviour are publicized widely. The media has reported numerous stories of staff who have lost their jobs because of inappropriate relationships with inmates (Blackwell, 2004; Dawson, 2000; "Female Staff," 1994; "High Proportion," 1994; "Jail Love," 1993). Consider these headlines: "Boyfriends Behind Bars: It's Not Unusual for Female Guards to Have Relations with Prisoners" (Blackwell, 2004), "Jail Love Affairs 'Rare' Feds Say" ("Jail Love," 1993), and "High Proportion of Female Guards Cited by Probe of Guard-Inmate Sex" ("High Proportion," 1994). Even a cursory examination of these few Canadian newspaper headlines leaves the impression that sexual relationships between staff and offenders are a common occurrence, a view not shared by corrections officials (Blackwell, 2004). Neither the federal correctional system nor the provincial and territorial correctional systems condone any kind of a sexual relationship between staff and offenders. According to the Commissioner's Directive Code of Discipline, in the federal system a staff member is not to enter into any kind of a personal relationship with an offender. Engaging in this kind of behaviour is clearly a violation of professional standards.

Dangers of Working in the Correctional System

Through the media, we seem to be inundated with the message that prisons and jails are violent places to work. In reality, most people employed in corrections in Canada spend their lives working in prisons and are never harmed by offenders. However, that is not to say that injuries never occur or that dangers do not exist. Moreover, some evidence suggests that male and female correctional officers differ with respect to their fears and their perceptions of risk associated with their work (Gordon & Moriarty, 2005). In a study of youth correctional workers, female officers had higher levels of fear and their perception of risk was higher when surveyed about the potential occurrence of riots and being attacked by an inmate (Gordon & Moriarty, 2005). Their perception of risk was also higher for a variable related to personal threats from offenders (Gordon & Moriarty, 2005).

Working in a correctional setting has more potential for danger and violence than working in an office or other community setting. In 2005–6, 243 staff members in the federal correctional system were injured on the job as a result of 357 inmate assaults on staff and 557 assaults on other offenders (CSC, 2007). One of the five priorities identified by the CSC for 2007–8 was the safety and security of both staff and offenders in CSC institutions (CSC, 2007). A major concern for both men and women working in corrections is offenders' assaults on staff and on other offenders. From 2004–5 to 2005–6, the rate of offender assaults increased (on both staff and other offenders) (CSC, 2007). Possible reasons for the observed increase include the higher percentage of offenders who reported gang affiliation at intake, high rates of substance abuse in offender populations, and an increase in poor institutional adjustment and antisocial behaviour (CSC, 2007). In addition, according to the CSC (2007), front-line staff reported a change in the institutional climate evidenced by "assaultive behaviour becoming more pronounced" (p. 22). In addition, staff noted "more incidents of aggressive, intimidating behaviour that is problematic but short of reportable assaults" (CSC, 2007, p. 22). Increased incidents of verbal assault and the throwing of bodily fluids and waste were also noted. These behaviours could be seen as "precursors to physical violence and indicative of an ingrained lack of respect for others" on the part of offenders (CSC, 2007, p. 22).

To effectively address the identified priority of the safety and security of staff and offenders, the CSC (2007) proposed a number of measures, including specialized training for staff, enhanced security, self-defence awareness, and the improvement of communication techniques between staff and violent offenders. Because drug use and violent behaviour seem to be intertwined, especially in an institutional setting, the CSC proposed a targeted campaign to reduce drug use in its facilities. By increasing public awareness about the dangers of bringing drugs into an institution, the CSC hoped to reduce the temptation of visitors, staff, and volunteers to smuggle contraband into prisons. The CSC also stated its commitment to increasing the use of routine searches and urinalysis of offenders to address drug use and proposed more non-intrusive searches of the belongings of staff, contractors, and visitors when they enter an institution. In addition, the CSC hoped to stem the flow of illicit drugs into their institutions through the increased use of technology, drug dog teams, and security and intelligence (CSC, 2007).

Work–Family Conflict

Work–family conflict (WFC) has been described as "a multi-dimensional, bi-directional concept" (Lambert et al., p. 372). This conflict takes on two distinct forms: work on family conflict and family on work conflict. In work on family conflict, issues and problems related to the workplace have a negative effect on the person's family life. For family on work conflict, the opposite occurs: issues and problems related to family life spill over into the person's work life. In either case, conflict is created.

WFC can be further divided into time-based conflict, strain-based conflict, and behaviour-based conflict (Netemeyer, Boles, & McMurrian, 1996). In time-based conflict, the amount of time that employees spend at work (or home) interferes with their home (or work) responsibilities in some way. Those working in correctional settings may experience time-based conflict because the nature of the job requires 24-hour-a-day shift scheduling and mandatory overtime to accommodate staffing shortages or crisis response (Lambert et al., 2006). Strain-based conflict is an issue for those working in a correctional setting, when the effects of the job (fatigue, tension, irritability, shock, for example) spill over into family life (Lambert et al., 2006). Lastly, behaviour-based conflict can result when the requirements of the job (barking orders and taking physical control of inmates, for example) conflict with how one should respond to and treat family members (Lambert et al., 2006). Research has shown that job satisfaction among correctional staff can be significantly affected by both behaviour-based and strain-based conflicts. Time-based conflicts, behaviour-based conflicts, and family on work conflicts have been found to have significant effects on organizational commitment (Lambert et al., 2006).

Perceptions of Competency and Sexism

In the past, female correctional officers were viewed by their male co-workers as being innately inferior (Zimmer, 1986). They have also been tokenized and viewed as sex objects by their peers (Pogrebin & Poole, 1997). Some of the women who were among the first to break into this male-dominated occupation allege that they experienced so much abuse from their co-workers that they now suffer from post-traumatic stress disorders (Lu, 2001). In an Ontario case in which compensation was being sought for job harassment, the plaintiffs reported abuses that included criticism over their weight, being called derogatory names, being forced to ask for a washroom key, having their cars tampered with, being exposed to pornography on the job, and having sanitary napkins displayed in an attempt to mock the women (Lu, 2001). In a landmark case in Quebec, Claudine Lippe was awarded almost $143,000 for the sexual harassment that she experienced during the two years she worked as a jail guard. The Quebec Public Security Department was ordered to pay her this money as compensation and for moral damages resulting from the sexual harassment that she endured on the job (Cornacchia, 1998).

Negative experiences were documented among the pioneering women who first worked in federal male institutions in the late 1970s and into the early 1980s (Sakowski, 1986). These women suffered from both systemic and individual harassment. As an example of systemic harassment, because the majority of the women had not been issued uniforms when they began work, they had to wear civilian clothes to work. They did not have their own washroom; they had to use a washroom open to the public. There were no showers and no change room designated for them. They were constantly monitored by middle management (whereas their male counterparts were not).

The most disturbing cases of harassment by individuals were the abuses that women were subjected to by their co-workers. Comments were made about their "lack of 'appropriate' male genitalia ... degrading comments referring to tits and ass" and "the underlying motive behind the harassment appeared to be the resignation en masse of the women" (Sakowski, 1986, p. 53). After five years on the job, the three women who remained in the job (out of the original eight) noted that although the harassment was no longer as overt, it was far from over (Sakowski, 1986). Despite each of the women having applied for a transfer or a promotion on at least one occasion, none had been approved, yet male officers with far less experience had been routinely promoted (Sakowski, 1986). The women commented that the only equality they had truly achieved was economic, but it was at the expense of their self-esteem and their emotional health.

In an early text dedicated to the topic of women guarding men, Zimmer (1986) noted that female guards "will be harassed, shunned, ignored, teased, commented on, joked about, snickered at, and excluded from informal social interaction—on as well as off the job" (p. 78). This treatment has not, according to Zimmer, come from the inmates, but predominantly from the women's co-workers. Some evidence suggests that those working in predominantly female institutions may be at less of a risk to experience this kind of harassment from co-workers. Research has shown that levels of sexual harassment reported by female workers in jails tend to be lower in predominantly female institutions compared with institutions for males (Stohr, Mays, Beck, & Kelly, 1998).

Crouch (1985) noted that the major source of difficulties faced by women correctional officers working in male prisons stems from the "male guards and the traditional norms that define appropriate behavior for males and females rather than from an inability to handle task demands" (p. 543). Evidence also suggests that women continue to be underrepresented in occupations such as correctional officer because of barriers related to bias, stereotyping, and tokenism (Grube-Farrell, 2002). Sexism may appear in a variety of ways and can be either intentionally or unconsciously expressed (Jurik, 1988; Lovrich & Stohr, 1993; Pogrebin & Poole, 1997). Regardless of how sexism is expressed, systemic sexism is often identified as being at the root of women's difficulties when they work in what have been traditionally defined as male roles (Pogrebin & Poole, 1997). As Pogrebin and Poole (1997) have noted, the sex typing of different jobs tends to follow one basic tenet: men and women are different and so they should be doing different things.

This sort of stereotypical thinking leads to the stigmatization of those (usually women) who are seen to be in violation of the aforementioned occupational segregation. In turn, this attitude reinforces the sex-role stereotyping that occurs in the workplace (Pogrebin & Poole, 1997), which accomplishes a number of objectives: women are kept busy in supportive and ancillary roles and are kept at a distance from any real positions of authority, independence, or achievement (Pogrebin & Poole, 1997). The woman who chooses to challenge the sex-role stereotypes in the workplace risks having her abilities, skills, and overall competence evaluated negatively by her peers, subordinates, and supervisors (Pogrebin & Poole, 1997).

Discrimination and Harassment of Women in the Canadian Correctional System

No discussion of the issues that face women working in corrections would be complete without some reference to discrimination and harassment. Harassment of women working in corrections must be acknowledged because, as in other traditionally male occupations, it has been so systemic. A distinction that is not often made in the literature is between gender harassment and sexual harassment (Belknap, 2004); yet we need to acknowledge the differences between these two types of harassment. Gender harassment has been described as any non-sexual slur against either women or men based on their gender, whereas sexual harassment refers to offensive behaviours or comments that are sexual in nature (Belknap, 2004).

A key facet of Canada's conceptualization of human rights is the understanding of equality between men and women. However, despite the focus that the Status of Women Canada (SWC) has placed on this very issue in the 30 years since its inception, "women are still unequal" to men in this country (Status of Women Canada, 2007, p. 3). Although advances have been made for and by women in terms of their education and employment, some rather disturbing facts remain as reminders of just how far women have yet to come to be considered truly equal to men.

Women are less likely than men to have a university degree, they are far less likely than men to earn an advanced degree (only 27 percent of PhDs are held by women), and although more women are entering the workforce than in the past, they tend to be clustered in traditionally female occupations (Statistics Canada, 2005b). Of all working women, 67 percent are employed in nursing and related health occupations; teaching, clerical, or administration positions; and sales and service occupations (Statistics Canada, 2005b). Women earn less money than men in this country: in 2003, the average woman's income (pre-tax) was $24,400 (62 percent of men's average income). Among women who work, their average earnings in 2003 for full-time, full-year work was $36,500, a mere 71 percent of what men averaged (Statistics Canada, 2005b).

Unfortunately, women in Canada continue to experience discrimination and harassment despite attempts to address these issues by various governments and the private sector. Women are periodically assaulted en masse by advertising that sends out particularly disturbing messages. As noted in chapter 4 (see box 4.3), an example of this sort of communal assault occurred in 2004 when a Halifax drinking establishment erected a billboard that read, "Our waitress uniforms were designed back when 'harass' was two words." The billboard was described by some as tasteless, but it could be argued that its message went far beyond poor taste and ventured into the realm of gender harassment.

Sexual and gender harassment and discrimination are not unique to the correctional system in Canada. Harassment and discrimination are issues faced by many individuals across a variety of situations and circumstances. That this chapter deals with harassment and discrimination in corrections does not mean that harassment and discrimination do not exist elsewhere; in this chapter, the focus has been placed on these issues as they pertain to the correctional system. The level of sexual harassment that exists in correctional systems is difficult to estimate. According to Griffiths (2004), researchers who conducted internal surveys within the CSC "found a high incidence of sexual harassment, discrimination, and abuse of authority in many federal institutions" (p. 234). He indicated that at one federal institution in particular, a startling 62 percent of the female employees had been harassed by a co-worker (Griffiths, 2004). Rates of more than 50 percent were reported for the Ontario and Pacific regions (Griffiths, 2004). Some women even reported having threatening notes placed on their car windshields (Griffiths, 2004).

Maeve McMahon (1999) has written a thorough and detailed account of two Ontario case studies of women's experiences of sexual harassment and discrimination in corrections (one at a training facility for correctional officers and another at a provincial jail). In her summary of the events leading up to the temporary closure (in July 1992) of the Bell Cairn Staff Training Centre for correctional staff in Hamilton, Ontario, McMahon (1999) highlights the inadequacy of the responses by Ministry of Correctional Services officials to the complaints by officers who had been harassed at the training centre. Bell Cairn was opened on August 29, 1991, and formal training classes began in September of that year. Complaints began to be filed as early as September 26 (McMahon, 1999). By February 1992, the list of disturbing occurrences reported to the manager of Bell Cairn included obscene and unwelcome late-night telephone calls, high noise levels, feeling unsafe in the halls because others were drunk, sexist remarks about the anatomy of participants, solicitations for sex by a male knocking on doors, and unwanted physical touching (McMahon, 1999).

By March 1992, the Ministry of Correctional Services had drafted a new code of behaviour for Bell Cairn, which, for the first time, made reference to sexual and personal harassment (McMahon, 1999). However, as was pointed out by McMahon, the penalties associated with these egregious behaviours were disappointingly vague. Not surprisingly, the disruptive and disrespectful behaviour was not curtailed. Two females at Bell Cairn alleged they had been sexually assaulted by more than one male at the training centre, allegations that the deputy minister was made aware of in early June 1992 (McMahon, 1999). Senior officials of the ministry met July 2 to determine how to respond to the emerging situation. Neither woman was willing to officially come forward with a complaint. However, by the middle of July 1992, these allegations became public, and the Ministry of Correctional Services faced intense scrutiny regarding how it had dealt with and was going to continue to deal with the problems at Bell Cairn (McMahon, 1999).

In her post-mortem of the Ministry of Correctional Services' failings with regard to its response to the ever-worsening situation at Bell Cairn, McMahon (1999) pointed out that one of the earliest mistakes may have been a failure to acknowledge the gendered nature of the abuses. Those who were reporting incidents of harassment were most probably women; however, the Ministry of Correctional Services failed to acknowledge this detail in its responses. In addition, the Ministry of Correctional Services did not have sufficient policies and procedures in place to deal with harassment prior to the opening of the facility. The staff at Bell Cairn (including the contracted security staff) did not have sufficient authority over participants, and thus were not in a position to discipline those responsible for the harassing behaviour.

The situation was exacerbated by insufficient monitoring and followup in response to complaints. In consideration of the alleged sexual assaults, the requirements as outlined by the Ontario Public Service Workplace Discrimination and Harassment Prevention Policy that such reports be pursued were mistakenly superseded by the desire to honour the alleged victims' rights of confidentiality. McMahon (1999) also noted the absence of members from the Ministry of Correctional Services' Workplace Harassment and Discrimination Prevention unit at strategy meetings held to draft responses to the incidents at Bell Cairn. Lastly, the tendency to conceptualize the problems as operational (that is, managerial or administrative) instead of policy-related (that is, related to gender) meant that the Minister of Correctional Services was not apprised of some key pieces of information (McMahon, 1999). All these failings could be seen to culminate in a public perception of a "passive cover-up" (McMahon, 1999, p. 49).

Summary

Up until the 1970s, women were permitted to occupy predominantly stereotypically female kinds of jobs within the correctional system in Canada. With the emergence of women into more traditionally male jobs, that of correctional officer, for example, the last bastion of male domination in the correctional system was breached. Much progress has been made in the last 30 years, but equality with men has not been achieved in the correctional service.

Historically, women have faced some unique barriers to working in corrections. Included among these were their own occupational interests—that is, women's tendency to favour jobs that were more traditionally female within the justice system. Also, various role traps and stereotypes could hinder a woman's career advancement in corrections. Researchers studying job stress and job satisfaction in correctional work have suggested that correctional officers are, for the most part, able to effectively cope with the myriad of stressors they face daily (Griffiths, 2004). Men and women who work in a correctional setting are subjected to stressors that may be associated with the institutional environment and the nature of the job itself. Women, in particular, have reported higher stress levels that relate to the lack of agency support, the everyday activities of the job, and higher levels of work–home conflict (Auerbach et al., 2003; Triplett et al., 1999). In addition, women correctional officers have reported more health-related concerns than their male counterparts (Armstrong & Griffin, 2004).

A number of salient issues face those who work in Canada's correctional systems regardless of whether they are male or female, including cross-gender staffing, sexual relationships with inmates, and physical dangers. Other issues, such as those that relate to work–family conflict, perceptions of competency and sexism, and discrimination and harassment, may be experienced by both men and women, but are likely to be of greater concern to women than to men.

Women's involvement in correctional work is a comparatively recent phenomenon. The gains made to date will likely continue to be built upon as more and more women explore the career opportunities that exist in provincial, territorial, and federal correctional services in Canada.

Note

1. The abbreviation CX refers to a correctional officer.

Discussion Questions

1. It was not until the 1970s that women in Canada could be employed as correctional officers in male institutions. Why did it take so long?
2. What are the concerns that currently exist regarding cross-gender staffing in prisons?
3. How do female correctional recruits differ from male recruits in terms of their attitudes toward the job of correctional officer? What do these differences mean in terms of the day-to-day operation of a prison?
4. What are the role traps for female correctional officers that Zimmer (1986) outlined? Do you think that these traps still exist today?
5. "The job stress that is associated with being a correctional officer is the same for men as it is for women." Do you agree with this statement? Discuss.

Suggested Readings

Griffiths, C. (2004). *Canadian corrections*. Toronto: Thomson Nelson.

McMahon, M. (1999). *Women on guard: Discrimination and harassment in corrections*. Toronto: University of Toronto Press.

Online Resources

1. Correctional Service of Canada: www.csc-scc.gc.ca
2. Ministry of Community Safety and Correctional Services: www.mcscs.jus.gov.on.ca
3. Probation Officers Association of Ontario: www.poao.org
4. National Parole Board: www.npb-cnlc.gc.ca

References

Across Canada women have edge for prison guard jobs. (1983, October 5). *Globe and Mail*, p. 12.

Armstrong, G., & Griffin, M. (2004). Does the job matter? Comparing correlates of stress among treatment and correctional staff in prisons. *Journal of Criminal Justice, 32,* 577–592.

Auerbach, S., Quick, B., & Pegg, P. (2003). General job stress and job-specific stress in juvenile correctional officers. *Journal of Criminal Justice, 31,* 25–36.

Beattie, K. (2006). Adult correctional services in Canada, 2004/05. *Juristat, 26*(5), 1–3.

Belknap, J. (2004). Women in conflict: An analysis of women correctional officers. In B. Raffel Price & N. Sokoloff (Eds.), *The criminal justice system and women* (pp. 543–561). Boston, MA: McGraw-Hill.

Bensimon, P. (2004). *Correctional officer recruits and the prison environment: A research framework.* Ottawa: Research Branch, Correctional Service of Canada.

Bensimon, P. (2005a). *Correctional officer recruits during the college training period: An examination.* Ottawa: Research Branch, Correctional Service of Canada.

Bensimon, P. (2005b). *Correctional officers and their first year: An empirical investigation.* Ottawa: Research Branch, Correctional Service of Canada.

Blackwell, T. (2004, January 8). Boyfriends behind bars: It's not unusual for female guards to have relations with prisoners. *National Post*, p. A5.

Brough, P., & Williams, J. (2007). Managing occupational stress in a high-risk industry: Measuring the job demands of correctional officers. *Criminal Justice and Behavior, 34,* 555–567.

Canada, Commission of Inquiry into Certain Events at the Prison for Women in Kingston. (1996). *Commission of inquiry into certain events at the Prison for Women in Kingston* (the Arbour inquiry). Ottawa: Public Works and Government Services of Canada.

Canada, Public Service Commission. (1977). *A study of the existing sex restrictions in the correctional group CX: An emotional and controversial issue.* Ottawa: Public Service Commission.

Canadian Human Rights Commission. (1981). *Review of Correctional Service Canada's special employment program to integrate women into the correctional officer occupational group (CX-COF and CX-LUF) in male penitentiaries.* Ottawa: Author.

Canadian Human Rights Commission. (2003). *Protecting their rights: A systematic review of human rights in correctional services for federally sentenced women.* Ottawa: Author.

Cheek, F., & Miller, M. (1983). The experience of stress for correction officers: A double-bind theory of correctional stress. *Journal of Criminal Justice, 11*, 105–120.

Cleland, D. (1986, December 10). More female guards expected in Canadian prisons, hearing told. *Kingston Whig-Standard*, p. 1.

Cornacchia, C. (1998, November 16). A victory for Quebec women: Claudine Lippe wins landmark victory in sexual harassment case after complaining that fellow jail guards made her working life hell. *Montreal Gazette*, p. E1.

Correctional Service of Canada. (n.d.). *Our mission*. Retrieved from www.csc-scc.gc.ca/text/organi-eng.shtml.

Correctional Service of Canada. (1980). *Employment of female correctional officers in male institutions*. Ottawa: Correctional Service of Canada.

Correctional Service of Canada. (1985). Flexibility in attaining national targets for female correctional/living unit officers. *Operational and Resource Management Review* (Review #148). Ottawa: Affirmative Action Division, Personnel Branch, Correctional Service of Canada.

Correctional Service of Canada. (1992). *Towards equal partnership: Report on the conference for women in CSC*. Ottawa: Solicitor General of Canada.

Correctional Service of Canada. (1998, September 9). *The cross-gender monitoring project first annual report* [News release]. Ottawa: Author.

Correctional Service of Canada. (2000, February 2). *The cross-gender monitoring project second annual report* [News release]. Ottawa: Author.

Correctional Service of Canada. (2005). *The cross-gender monitoring project: CSC's response to the third and final annual report*. Retrieved from www.csc-scc.gc.ca/text/prgrm/fsw/gender4/CGM_response_e.pdf.

Correctional Service of Canada. (2007). *Correctional Service Canada: Report on plans and priorities*. Ottawa: Public Safety and Emergency Preparedness Canada.

Crouch, B. (1985). Pandora's box: Women guards in men's prisons. *Journal of Criminal Justice, 13*, 535–548.

Dawson, F. (2000, February 28). Female guard investigated for having sex with inmate: Lesbian love affair is said to have been going on for some time. *Vancouver Province*, p. A4.

Dollard, M., & Winefield, A. (1994). Organizational response to recommendations based on a study of stress among correctional officers. *International Journal of Stress Management, 1*, 81–101.

Dowden, C., & Tellier, C. (2004). Predicting work-related stress in correctional officers: A meta-analysis. *Journal of Criminal Justice, 32*, 31–47.

Female staff out of jobs after jail sex. (1994, February 20). *Vancouver Province*, p. A38.

Golden, K. (1982). Women in criminal justice: Occupational interests. *Journal of Criminal Justice, 10*, 147–152.

Gordon, J., & Moriarty, L. (2005). Who's afraid of Johnny Rotten?: Assessing female correctional staff's perceived fear and risk of victimization in a juvenile male institution. In R. Muraskin (Ed.), *It's a crime: Women and justice* (pp. 661–678). Upper Saddle River, NJ: Pearson Prentice-Hall.

Griffin, M. (2001). Job satisfaction among detention officers: Assessing the relative contribution of organizational climate variables. *Journal of Criminal Justice, 29,* 219–232.

Griffiths, C. (2004). *Canadian corrections.* Toronto: Thomson Nelson.

Grube-Farrell, B. (2002). Women, work, and occupational segregation in the uniformed services. *Affilia: Journal of Women and Social Work, 17,* 332–353.

High proportion of female guards cited by probe of guard-inmate sex. (1994, March 3). *Montreal Gazette,* p. A13.

Huckabee, R. (1992). Stress in corrections: An overview of the issues. *Journal of Criminal Justice, 20,* 479–486.

Human Resources and Social Development Canada. (n.d.). *Career handbook* (2nd ed.). Probation and parole officers. Retrieved from www23.hrdc-drhc.gc.ca/ch/e/docs /group_4155_1.asp.

Human Resources and Social Development Canada. (2006). *Employment Equity Act: Annual report 2006.* Ottawa: Author.

Jail love affairs "rare" feds say. (1993, September 3). *Windsor Star,* p. F7.

Jamieson, Beals, Lalonde & Associates Inc. (1990). *Employment barriers for women: Final report.* Ottawa: Correctional Service of Canada.

Jurik, N. (1988). Striking a balance: Female correctional officers, gender role stereotypes, and male prisons. *Sociological Inquiry, 58,* 291–305.

Jurik, N., & Halemba, G. (1984). Gender, working conditions and the job satisfaction of women in a non-traditional occupation: Female correctional officers in men's prisons. *The Sociological Quarterly, 25,* 551–566.

Jurik, N., Halemba, G., Musheno, M., & Boyle, B. (1987). Educational attainment, job satisfaction, and the professionalization of correctional officers. *Work and Occupations, 14,* 106–125.

Keinan, G., & Malach-Pines, A. (2007). Stress and burnout among prison personnel: Sources, outcomes, and intervention strategies. *Criminal Justice and Behavior, 34,* 380–398.

Kershaw, A. (1985a, August 10). The changing of the guard "whiz" kids with degrees lead to prison staff woes increasing danger, stress two recent reports. *Kingston Whig-Standard,* p. 1.

Kershaw, A. (1985b, December 13). Millhaven is ready to take applications from women for guard jobs. *Kingston Whig-Standard,* p. 1.

Lajeunesse, T., Jefferson, C., Nuffield, J., & Majury, D. (2000). *The cross gender monitoring project: Third and final annual report.* Winnipeg: Thérèse Lajeunessé and Associates Ltd.

Lambert, E., Edwards, C., Camp, S., & Saylor, W. (2005). Here today, gone tomorrow, back again the next day: Antecedents of correctional absenteeism. *Journal of Criminal Justice, 33,* 165–175.

Lambert, E., Hogan, N., & Barton, S. (2002). Satisfied correctional staff: A review of the literature on the correlates of correctional staff job satisfaction. *Criminal Justice and Behavior, 29*, 115–143.

Lambert, E., Hogan, N., Camp, S., & Ventura, L. (2006). The impact of work-family conflict on correctional staff: A preliminary study. *Criminology and Criminal Justice, 6*, 371–387.

Large, B. (1986, March 1). Women guarding men. *Kingston Whig-Standard*, p. 1.

Lovrich, N., & Stohr, M. (1993). Gender and jail work: Correctional policy implications of perceptual diversity in the work force. *Policy Studies Review, 12*, 66–84.

Lu, V. (2001, March 2). Women guards in male jails: "They were trying to humiliate us"— Compensation being sought for job harassment. *Toronto Star*, p. A1.

McMahon, M. (1999). *Women on guard: Discrimination and harassment in corrections.* Toronto: University of Toronto Press.

Millson, W. (2002). Predictors of work stress among correctional officers. *Forum on Corrections Research, 14*(1), 45–47.

Moon, B., & Maxwell, S. (2004). The sources and consequences of corrections officers' stress: A South Korean example. *Journal of Criminal Justice, 32*, 359–370.

National Parole Board. (2005). *Selection criteria for board members.* Retrieved from www.npb-cnlc.gc.ca/org/bmselcr_e.htm.

National Parole Board. (2007a). *Full and part-time board members by region.* Retrieved from www.npb-cnlc.gc.ca/org/bmlist_e.htm.

National Parole Board. (2007b). *Parole applications for provincial/territorial offenders.* Retrieved from www.npb-cnlc.gc.ca/infocntr/Parole_Applications/parole_app_e.htm.

National Union of Public and General Employees. (2004). *Probation and parole officers working group.* Retrieved from www.nupge.ca/publications/probation_parole_2004.pdf.

Netemeyer, R., Boles, J., & McMurrian, R. (1996). Development and validation of work-family conflict and family-work conflict scales. *Journal of Applied Psychology, 81*, 400–410.

Ontario, Ministry of Community Safety and Correctional Services. (2006). *Careers in corrections: Becoming a probation and parole officer.* Retrieved from www.gov.on.ca.

Ontario, Ministry of Correctional Services. (1983). *Historical perspective in corrections* [Unpublished manuscript].

Outhit, J. (1999, November 25). Neighbors warming to prison for women; Residents who once opposed the Grand Valley Institution give it a high rating during tour. *Kitchener Record*, p. B3.

Owen, S. (2006). Occupational stress among correctional supervisors. *Prison Journal, 86*, 164–181.

Pogrebin, M., & Poole, E. (1997). The sexualized work environment: A look at women jail officers. *Prison Journal, 77*, 41–47.

Pogrebin, M., & Poole, E. (1998). Women deputies and jail work. *Journal of Contemporary Criminal Justice, 14,* 117–134.

Pollak, C., & Sigler, R. (1998). Low levels of stress among Canadian correctional officers in the northern region of Ontario. *Journal of Criminal Justice, 26,* 117–128.

Public Safety and Emergency Preparedness Canada. (2006). *Corrections and conditional release statistical overview: Annual report 2006.* Ottawa: Public Works and Government Services Canada.

Probation Officers Association of Ontario. (2000). *Presentation to the Ministry of Finance.* Retrieved from www.poao.org/positionpapers.htm.

Reisig, M., & Lovrich, N. (1998). Job attitudes among higher-custody state prison management personnel: A cross-sectional comparative assessment. *Journal of Criminal Justice, 26,* 213–226.

Robinson, D., Porporino, F., & Simourd, L. (1997). The influence of educational attainment on the attitudes and job performance of correctional officers. *Crime & Delinquency, 43,* 60–77.

Sakowski, M. (1986). Women guards in Canada: A study of the first women to work in a federal penitentiary for male offenders. *Resources for Feminist Research, 13,* 52–53.

Selye, H. (1976). *The stress of life.* New York: McGraw-Hill.

Statistics Canada. (2002). *A statistical profile of persons working in justice-related professions in Canada, 1996.* Ottawa: Author.

Statistics Canada. (2005a). *Criminal justice indicators 2005.* Ottawa: Author.

Statistics Canada. (2005b). *Women in Canada: A gender-based statistical report* (5th ed.). Ottawa: Author.

Status of Women Canada. (2007). *Report on plans and priorities, 2006–2007.* Ottawa: Author.

Stohr, M., Mays, L., Beck, A., & Kelley, T. (1998). Sexual harassment in women's jails. *Journal of Contemporary Criminal Justice, 14,* 135–155.

Strange, C. (1985). The criminal and fallen of their sex: The establishment of Canada's first women's prison, 1874–1901. *Canadian Journal of Women and the Law, 1,* 79–92.

Tewksbury, R., & Higgins, G. (2006). Examining the effect of emotional dissonance on work stress and satisfaction with supervisors among correctional staff. *Criminal Justice Policy Review, 17,* 290–301.

Trevethan, S., MacKillop, B., Robinson, D., Porporino, F., & Millson, W. (1999). A one-day snapshot of inmates in Canada's adult correctional facilities. *Juristat, 18*(8), 1–14.

Triplett, R., Mullings, J., & Scarborough, K. (1999). Examining the effect of work-home conflict on work-related stress among correctional officers. *Journal of Criminal Justice, 27,* 371–385.

van Wormer, K., & Bartollas, C. (2000). *Women and the criminal justice system.* Boston: Allyn & Bacon.

Zimmer, L. (1986). *Women guarding men.* Chicago: University of Chicago Press.

Glossary

Actuarial prediction: A quantitative method of risk assessment based on the scoring of known causal factors.

Anomie theory: A term coined by Émile Durkheim and derived from Greek: the prefix *a*, signifying *without*, and *nomos*, a set of causal rules that structure our social relations and help to achieve our aims in society. Thus, anomie, the lack of *nomos*, is an individual's perception of the absence of legitimate means by which legitimate needs can be satisfied.

Barrister: In Anglo-Canadian tradition, a lawyer who pleads cases in court.

Borderline personality disorder (BPD): A serious mental disorder affecting 2 percent of adults, characterized by severe mood swings, unstable self-image, and extreme behaviour. A person with BPD may experience short episodes of anger, anxiety, or depression. BPD may result in sudden aggression or drug and alcohol abuse.

Cascading: The process of placing offenders in progressively lower-security facilities as they respond positively to rehabilitative programs and near their release date. Although cascading is frequently desirable, it is not always possible.

Clinical judgment: A predominantly qualitative decision made by a corrections professional regarding the recidivism risk posed by an offender.

Crimes against the person: Illegal acts that are the result of force being applied to an individual or physical harm being inflicted on an individual. These crimes include assault, sexual assault, manslaughter, and murder.

Criminogenic need: A factor or behaviour that is related to criminal behaviour or recidivism.

Crown attorney: In Canadian criminal courts, the lawyer representing the prosecution.

Decarceration: The opposite of incarceration. The decarceration movement strives to remove people from prisons. The Elizabeth Fry societies in Canada are proponents of decarceration.

Dynamic security: The use of interpersonal relationships between prison staff and inmates to enhance prison security. Typically, the use of a dynamic security regime relies on building a rapport between prison staff and inmates.

Exchange of service agreement: Within the Canadian penal system, an agreement between a province or territory and the federal government that allows for the incarceration of provincial or territorial inmates in federal institutions or vice versa.

Habeas corpus: An order by a judge instructing a detaining authority (usually the police) to produce the detainee in a court of law so that the judge can determine whether the individual is being lawfully detained or should be set free.

Healing lodge: A facility designed to meet the needs of Aboriginal offenders by offering services and programs that reflect Aboriginal culture, beliefs, and traditions.

Human capital theory: The view that income varies according to individuals' investment in their education and job skills. Thus, the holder of a PhD earns more than the receptionist because the PhD is the result of a 10-year investment in education. The higher wages represent the corresponding return on a greater investment in human capital.

Intersectional discrimination: A prejudice based, not on a single factor (as is the case in racial discrimination), but on two or more factors, such as race and gender. Thus, Aboriginal women may face discrimination based on both their race and their gender.

Level of Service Inventory: A theoretically based tool for measuring risk and criminogenic need, consisting of 54 risk and need items across 10 domains.

Mania: An extreme psychological condition exhibiting high energy, elevated mood, and unusual thought patterns. Mania is commonly associated with bipolar disorder wherein episodes of mania alternate with bouts of clinical depression.

Marxism: A 19th-century political theory advanced by Karl Marx and Friedrich Engels suggesting that society is divided into economic classes. In any given era, one class is dominant and another is ascendant. Marxists believe that all social forces are ultimately economic in character and that all racial, social, and gender problems are ultimately reducible to fundamental economic issues.

Matriarchy: By strict definition, the rule of the household (or society) by the mother or the female.

Melancholia: A mood disorder characterized a lack of enthusiasm and an overall depression.

Neutralization: An offender's rationalization that seeks to mitigate the effects of a crime. For example, a fraud offender passing bad cheques might tell herself that the money from the cheques was used to buy groceries to feed her children. In her mind, the damage from the fraud is mitigated by the good from the groceries.

Pathologize: To view a situation as medically or psychologically abnormal, thus rendering it an illness to be treated.

Patriarchy: By strict definition, the rule of a household (or society) by the father or the male. In more general use, it refers to the domination of men over women. The concept of patriarchy is founded on a belief in the natural differences between men and women, particularly regarding muscular strength. Sociologists and criminologists focus their attention on the gender role within a situation and its effect on the gender power differentials.

Positivist criminology: Claims that the causes of a criminal offence can be found in the physical, psychological, genetic, or moral composition of the individual who is predisposed to commit those acts. Italian criminologist Cesare Lombroso suggested that criminals exhibited certain identifiable physical characteristics that identified them as less evolved (atavistic) human beings. According to the positivists, because they believe certain individuals are innately criminal, the criminological emphasis should be on the criminal rather than the crime.

Property crimes: Illegal acts involving the taking of property or money with no threat of force against an individual. Property crimes include burglary, theft, shoplifting, and vandalism.

Recidivism: The repetition of a criminal behaviour by an individual who has already been convicted and punished for a previous offence. Because recidivism can be viewed as a measure of rehabilitative failure, it is also a measure of the effectiveness of rehabilitation programs and deterrents.

Segregation unit: An area of a prison where inmates are kept separate from the rest of the prison population.

Sharia: Law according to Islamic law and tradition.

Solicitor: In Anglo-Canadian tradition, a lawyer who represents and advises a client and instructs a barrister should a case go to court.

Spatial poverty: Poverty that arises from geographic remoteness or an individual's habitation in an economically depressed area where the poverty of one household serves to impoverish its neighbours.

State anger: The anger that is felt at a particular time due to a specific set of circumstances.

Static security: The reliance on physical security measures (cameras, fencing, and alarms, for example) to control the inmate population of a prison.

Status offence: A breach of the law that can only be committed by persons occupying a certain status in society. For example, children can be charged with truancy but adults cannot. A young person's status as a juvenile is a necessary condition to the occurrence of the offence.

Strain theory: A criminological view that an individual's social setting generates certain goals and expectations. The failure of individuals to achieve these goals, and thus the inability to achieve the social treatment they expect, results in strain and creates alienation and negative relationships with others. When others are seen as blocking the means to achieve their goals, some alienated individuals resort to criminal behaviour.

Vertical mosaic: The view presented by John Porter in 1965 that describes Canada as a mosaic of cultures existing in harmony with individuals of the British culture who are over-represented in the elites.

Warrant of committal: A judicial order requiring the imprisonment of an individual.

White Ribbon Campaign: A campaign founded in 1991 by a group of men seeking to end violence against women, in response to the 1989 massacre at École Polytechnique. The White Ribbon Campaign now operates in more than 55 countries.

Index